Lessons from the Financial Crisis

Lessons from the Financial Crisis
Insights from the Defining Economic Event of Our Lifetime

Edited by Arthur M. Berd

Published by Risk Books, a Division of Incisive Financial Publishing Ltd

Haymarket House
28–29 Haymarket
London SW1Y 4RX
Tel: + 44 (0)20 7484 9700
Fax: + 44 (0)20 7484 9797
E-mail: books@incisivemedia.com
Sites: www.riskbooks.com
       www.incisivemedia.com

© 2010 Incisive Media

ISBN 978-1-906348-47-2

British Library Cataloguing in Publication Data
A catalogue record for this book is available from the British Library

Publisher: Nick Carver
Commissioning Editors: Lucie Carter and Sarah Hastings
Managing Editor: Lewis O'Sullivan
Designer: Lisa Ling

Copy-edited and typeset by T&T Productions Ltd, London

Printed and bound in the UK by PrintonDemand-Worldwide

Conditions of sale

All rights reserved. No part of this publication may be reproduced in any material form whether by photocopying or storing in any medium by electronic means whether or not transiently or incidentally to some other use for this publication without the prior written consent of the copyright owner except in accordance with the provisions of the Copyright, Designs and Patents Act 1988 or under the terms of a licence issued by the Copyright Licensing Agency Limited of 90, Tottenham Court Road, London W1P 0LP.

Warning: the doing of any unauthorised act in relation to this work may result in both civil and criminal liability.

Every effort has been made to ensure the accuracy of the text at the time of publication, this includes efforts to contact each author to ensure the accuracy of their details at publication is correct. However, no responsibility for loss occasioned to any person acting or refraining from acting as a result of the material contained in this publication will be accepted by the copyright owner, the editor, the authors or Incisive Media.

Many of the product names contained in this publication are registered trade marks, and Risk Books has made every effort to print them with the capitalisation and punctuation used by the trademark owner. For reasons of textual clarity, it is not our house style to use symbols such as TM, ®, etc. However, the absence of such symbols should not be taken to indicate absence of trademark protection; anyone wishing to use product names in the public domain should first clear such use with the product owner.

While best efforts have been intended for the preparation of this book, neither the publisher, the editor nor any of the potentially implicitly affiliated organisations accept responsibility for any errors, mistakes and or omissions it may provide or for any losses howsoever arising from or in reliance upon its information, meanings and interpretations by any parties.

Contents

About the Editor		ix
About the Authors		xi
Introduction		xxiii

PART I THE ROOTS OF THE CRISIS — 1

1 The Credit Crunch of 2007: What Went Wrong? Why? What Lessons Can be Learned? — 3
John C. Hull
Rotman School of Management, University of Toronto

2 Underwriting versus Economy: A New Approach to Decomposing Mortgage Losses — 23
Ashish Das, Roger M. Stein
Moody's Research Labs

3 The Shadow Banking System and Hyman Minsky's Economic Journey — 49
Paul McCulley
PIMCO

4 The Collapse of the Icelandic Banking System — 65
René Kallestrup; David Lando
Danmarks Nationalbank, Copenhagen Business School; Copenhagen Business School

5 The Quant Crunch Experience and the Future of Quantitative Investing — 121
Bob Litterman
Goldman Sachs (Partner, retired), Commonfund (Trustee)

PART II THE IMPACT ON THE MARKETS — 127

6 No Margin for Error: The Impact of the Credit Crisis on Derivatives Markets — 129
Jeffrey Rosenberg
Bank of America Merrill Lynch

7 The Re-Emergence of Distressed Exchanges in Corporate Restructurings — 167
Edward I. Altman, Brenda Karlin
NYU Salomon Center

PART III RISK MANAGEMENT AND REGULATION 185

8 Modelling Systemic and Sovereign Risks 187
Dale F. Gray, Andreas A. Jobst
International Monetary Fund

9 Measuring and Managing Risk in Innovative Financial Instruments 231
Stuart M. Turnbull
C. T. Bauer College of Business

10 Forecasting Extreme Risk of Equity Portfolios with Fundamental Factors 265
Vladislav Dubikovsky, Michael Y. Hayes, Lisa R. Goldberg, Ming Liu
MSCI Risk Analytics

PART IV QUANTITATIVE MODELLING 281

11 Limits of Implied Credit Correlation Metrics Before and During the Crisis 283
Damiano Brigo; Andrea Pallavicini; Roberto Torresetti
King's College London; Banca Leonardo; Quaestio Capital Management

12 Another view on the pricing of MBSs, CMOs and CDOs of ABSs 319
Jean-David Fermanian
CREST–ENSAE

13 Pricing of Credit Derivatives with and without Counterparty and Collateral Adjustments 347
Alexander Lipton; David Shelton
Bank of America Merrill Lynch, Imperial College London; Bank of America Merrill Lynch

14 A Practical Guide to Monte Carlo CVA 379
Alexander Sokol
CompatibL

PART V MARKET EFFICIENCY AND (IN)STABILITY 407

15 The Endogenous Dynamics of Markets: Price Impact, Feedback Loops and Instabilities 409
Jean-Philippe Bouchaud
Capital Fund Management

16 Market Panics: Correlation Dynamics, Dispersion and Tails 439
Lisa Borland
Evnine and Associates Inc

17 Financial Complexity and Systemic Stability in Trading Markets 455
Matteo Marsili; Kartik Anand
Abdus Salam International Centre for Theoretical Physics;
Technische Universität Berlin

18 The Martingale Theory of Bubbles: Implications for the
Valuation of Derivatives and Detecting Bubbles 493
Robert A. Jarrow; Philip Protter
Cornell University and Kamakura Corporation;
Cornell University

PART VI LESSONS FOR INVESTORS 513

19 Managing through a Crisis: Practical Insights and Lessons
Learned for Quantitatively Managed Equity Portfolios 515
Peter J. Zangari
Goldman Sachs

20 Active Risk Management: A Credit Investor's Perspective 545
Vineer Bhansali
PIMCO

21 Investment Strategy Returns: Volatility, Asymmetry, Fat Tails
and the Nature of Alpha 565
Arthur M. Berd
Capital Fund Management

Index 595

About the Editor

Arthur M. Berd is the head of macro volatility strategies at Capital Fund Management, a hedge fund specialising in systematic investment management, headquartered in Paris. He is a well-known industry expert in credit risk modelling, quantitative investment strategies and portfolio and risk management.

Before joining CFM, Arthur was the head of quantitative market strategies at BlueMountain Capital Management, a leading credit hedge fund in New York. Before that, he was a senior vice president at Lehman Brothers, where he was responsible for a variety of quantitative credit models and strategies across corporate bonds and credit derivatives, and was instrumental in portfolio and risk advisory activities for the firm's largest clients. Before joining Lehman Brothers in 2001, he was a vice president at Goldman Sachs Asset Management, focusing on risk management and quantitative portfolio analysis.

Arthur holds a PhD in physics from Stanford University, is the author of more than 30 publications in refereed journals and industry publications, and a frequently invited speaker at major industry conferences. He is a member of the editorial board of *the Journal of Credit Risk*, and the coordinator of the quantitative finance section in www.arXiv.org, a global electronic research repository.

About the Authors

Edward I. Altman is the Max L. Heine professor of finance at the Stern School of Business, New York University, and director of the credit and fixed income research program at the NYU Salomon Center. He has an international reputation as an expert on corporate bankruptcy, high yield bonds, distressed debt and credit risk analysis. He was named Laureate 1984 by the Fondation Hautes Etudes Commerciales in Paris for his accumulated works on corporate distress prediction models and procedures for firm financial rehabilitation, and awarded the Graham & Dodd Scroll for 1985 by the Financial Analysts Federation for his work on default rates and high yield corporate debt. He was inducted into the Fixed Income Analysts Society Hall of Fame in 2001 and elected president of the Financial Management Association (2003) and a Fellow of the FMA in 2004, and was among the inaugural inductees into the Turnaround Management Association's Hall of Fame in 2008. In 2005, Edward was named one of the "100 Most Influential people in Finance" by Treasury & Risk magazine and he is frequently quoted in the popular press and on US network television. He is an advisor to many financial institutions, including Citigroup, Concordia Advisors, Paulson and Company, Investcorp and RiskMetrics, and was an investment advisor to the New York State Common Retirement Fund, as well as being on the Boards of the Franklin Mutual Series Funds and Automated Trading Desk Inc. He is chairman of the academic advisory council of the Turnaround Management Association.

Kartik Anand is a post-doctoral fellow in economics at the Technische Universität Berlin, working in the collaborative research centre "Economic Risk". Kartik graduated with a PhD in applied mathematics from Kings College London, specialising in the mathematics of complex systems. Previous work assignments include a stint as a researcher at the Bank of England and a post-doctoral fellowship at the Abdus Salam Centre for Theoretical Physics in Trieste, Italy.

Vineer Bhansali is a managing director and portfolio manager in the Newport Beach office, where he oversees PIMCO's quantitative investment portfolios. From 2000, he also headed PIMCO's firmwide analytics department. Before joining PIMCO in 2000, he was a proprietary trader in the fixed-income trading group at Credit Suisse First Boston and in the fixed income arbitrage group at Salomon Brothers in New York. Previously, he was head of the exotic and hybrid options trading desk at Citibank in New York. Vineer is the author of numerous scientific and financial papers and of the books *Pricing and Managing Exotic and Hybrid Options* and *Fixed Income Finance: A Quantitative Approach*. He serves as an associate editor for the *International Journal of Theoretical and Applied Finance*. He has 20 years of investment experience and holds a PhD in theoretical particle physics from Harvard University. He has a Master's degree in physics and an undergraduate degree from the California Institute of Technology.

Lisa Borland is director of derivatives strategies at Evnine & Associates Inc, a San Francisco-based hedge fund. She received her Doctorate in theoretical physics from the University of Stuttgart, Germany, but has been working in to the field of finance for over 10 years. Her most notable work has probably been the development of a theory for non-Gaussian option pricing. However, her main interest is in developing trading strategies and risk control methodologies in various financial markets.

Jean-Philippe Bouchaud was appointed chairman and chief scientist of Capital Fund Management (CFM) in October 2001. At CFM, together with Marc Potters, he supervises the research team, and contributes by maintaining strong links between CFM's research and the academic world. He is also professor at École Polytechnique. After studying at the French Lycée in London, Jean-Philippe graduated from the École Normale Supérieure in Paris, France, where he obtained his PhD in theoretical physics. He was then appointed as a researcher by the Centre National de la Recherche Scientifique (CNRS) until 1992. After a year at the Cavendish Laboratory at the University of Cambridge, he joined the Service de Physique de l'État Condensé at the Commissariat à Energie Atomique at Saclay in France. Jean-Philippe became interested in theoretical and empirical finance in 1991. His research in quantitative finance led him to found the research company Science & Finance SA in 1994; this merged with CFM in July 2000. Jean-Philippe is today a well-known authority within the field of "econophysics". He was awarded the

IBM Young Scientist prize and the CNRS Silver Medal. He is also the editor-in-chief of *Quantitative Finance*.

Damiano Brigo is Gilbart professor of financial mathematics at King's College London. Formerly managing director and global head of the quantitative team in Fitch Solutions, Damiano was also visiting professor at the department of mathematics at Imperial College. He has published more than 50 works in top journals for mathematical finance, systems theory, probability and statistics, and books that have become field references in stochastic interest rate and credit modelling. Damiano is managing editor of the *International Journal of Theoretical and Applied Finance* and is a member of the Fitch Academic Advisory Board and is part of scientific committees for academic conferences occurring at MIT and other institutions. Damiano's interests include pricing, risk measurement, credit and default modelling, counterparty risk and stochastic dynamical models for commodities and inflation. He obtained a PhD in stochastic filtering with differential geometry in 1996 from the Free University of Amsterdam.

Ashish Das is a managing director and the head of research in Moody's Research Labs in New York. Previously, he was a vice president in the prime brokerage group at Morgan Stanley. Before this, he spent six years at Moody's KMV heading the portfolio group that was responsible for the correlation research (Gcorr) and portfolio risk modelling (Portfolio Manager/Risk Frontier). Ashish has a PhD in finance from the Kellogg School of Management, an MBA from the Thunderbird School of Global Management, and a Bachelor's degree in chemical engineering from the Indian Institute of Technology, Kanpur, India. He has published in prestigious journals, including *The Journal of Finance* and *Journal of Credit Risk*.

Vladislav Dubikovsky is a senior research associate at MSCI, where his focus is on short-horizon risk modelling. He is a principal research analyst in the Barra Integrated Model (BIM) Daily and PowerVaR initiatives. Before joining MSCI, Vladislav was a research and development engineer at Silvaco International, where he specialised in the numerical modelling of complex optoelectronic devices. He holds a PhD in physics (optics) from the Center for Research and Education in Optics and Lasers at the University of Central Florida, and he earned his MS in Applied Physics at Kiev State University. He has written research articles in the fields of physics, signal processing and finance.

Jean-David Fermanian is professor of finance and statistics at CREST–ENSAE in Paris. Previously, he was senior credit derivatives quant at BNP-Paribas in London. Just prior to joining BNP-Paribas, he was the head of risk methodologies at Ixis CIB in Paris. His research interests include in particular survival analysis, credit portfolio modelling and copulas. He has published numerous articles in economics, statistics and financial econometrics. Jean-David is a graduate of the École Normale Supérieure and ENSAE, and has a PhD in statistics from the University Paris 6.

Lisa R. Goldberg is executive director and global head of risk analytics at MSCI and adjunct professor of statistics at the University of California, Berkeley. Before joining MSCI in 1993, Lisa was a professor of mathematics at UC Berkeley and City University of New York, and she has held positions at The Institute for Advanced Study, Institut des Hautes Études Scientifiques and The Mathematical Sciences Research Institute. She received a PhD in mathematics from Brandeis University in 1984 and has received numerous academic awards, including the prestigious Sloan Fellowship. Lisa's research interests include extreme risk analysis, statistical evaluation of financial models, credit, index construction and green investing. She is the primary architect of MSCI Barra's extreme risk and credit models and she has been awarded three patents. She publishes and lectures extensively in both financial economics and mathematics and serves on the board of the JOIM Conference series and the editorial board of two Springer book series, and as a moderator for arXiv Quantitative Finance. She is co-author of *Portfolio Risk Analysis*, published in 2010 in the Princeton University Press Finance Series.

Dale F. Gray is the senior risk expert in the monetary and capital markets department at the IMF. He has developed frameworks for financial and sovereign risk analysis. Dale has worked for investment banks, rating agencies, World Bank, governments and MFRisk Inc, as well as advising investors and governments on macro risk analysis, integration of finance with macroeconomics and systemic risk analysis tools. He has worked in over 30 countries and is a frequent lecturer. He has numerous publications and is co-author of the book *Macrofinancial Risk Analysis* (with a foreword by Robert Merton). He has a PhD from MIT, an MS from Stanford, and is a certified financial risk manager.

Michael Y. Hayes is a senior associate at MSCI Barra, and a principal architect of Barra Extreme Risk (BxR) and Power VaR. He is currently focusing on how to incorporate extreme risk into portfolio construction, and is developing a new paradigm for empirical stress testing and scenario analysis using Barra factors. Michael earned his PhD in chemical physics from the University of Colorado, and his BA from Princeton University. He has authored more than a dozen research papers in the fields of chemistry, physics and finance.

John C. Hull is the Maple financial professor of derivatives and risk management at the Joseph L. Rotman School of Management, University of Toronto. He is an internationally recognised authority on derivatives and risk management. Recently his research has been concerned with credit risk, executive stock options, volatility surfaces, market risk and interest rate derivatives. He was, with Alan White, one of the winners of the Nikko–LOR research competition for his work on the Hull–White interest rate model. He has acted as consultant to many North American, Japanese and European financial institutions. He has written three books: *Risk Management and Financial Institutions* (now in its second edition), *Options, Futures and Other Derivatives* (now in its seventh edition) and *Fundamentals of Futures and Options Markets* (now in its seventh edition). The books have been translated into many languages and are widely used in trading rooms throughout the world. He was voted Financial Engineer of the Year in 1999 by the International Association of Financial Engineers.

Robert A. Jarrow is the Ronald P. and Susan E. Lynch professor of investment management at the Johnson Graduate School of Management, Cornell University and director of research at Kamakura Corporation. He is a co-creator of both the Heath–Jarrow–Morton model for pricing interest rate derivatives and the reduced form credit risk models employed for pricing credit derivatives. In commodities, his research was the first to distinguish between forward/futures prices, and he is the creator of the forward price martingale measure. He has been the recipient of numerous prizes and awards including the CBOE Pomerance Prize for Excellence in the Area of

Options Research, the Graham and Dodd Scrolls Award, the 1997 IAFE/SunGard Financial Engineer of the Year Award, and *Risk Magazine*'s Lifetime Achievement Award. He is on the advisory board of *Mathematical Finance*: a journal he co-founded in 1989. He is also an associate or advisory editor for numerous other journals and serves on the board of directors of several firms and professional societies. He is currently both an IAFE senior fellow and a FDIC senior fellow. He is included in both the Fixed Income Analysts Society Hall of Fame and the *Risk Magazine*'s 50-member Hall of Fame. He has written four books as well as over 145 publications in leading finance and economic journals.

Andreas (Andy) Jobst is a mid-career economist at the monetary and capital markets department of the IMF in Washington, DC. His work focuses on structured finance, risk management, sovereign debt management and financial regulation. As a member of IMF Article IV missions, he has been responsible for the financial sector coverage of several large mature and emerging market economies. He recently completed the stress test of the US financial sector for the IMF's Financial Stability Assessment Program. Andy is one of the main authors of the *Global Financial Stability Report* published by the monetary and capital markets department. He also contributes to both the early warning and vulnerability exercises (for both advanced and emerging economies) in collaboration with the Financial Stability Board and teaches courses on banking regulation, risk management, derivatives and systemic risk analysis at the IMF Institute. So far, he has published more than 25 articles in peer-reviewed journals and contributed to 10 books. He holds a PhD in finance from the London School of Economics.

René Kallestrup is a PhD student in the department of finance at the Copenhagen Business School. Throughout the banking crisis in Iceland, he worked at the Central Bank of Iceland, where his main responsibilities were analysing foreign exchange and credit markets. Before his job at the Central Bank he was a currency strategist at Danske Bank. He holds a Master's degree in economics from the University of Aarhus.

Brenda Karlin is a research associate within the credit and debt markets research program at the NYU Salomon Center for the Study of Financial Institutions, Stern School of Business. Brenda has eight years of fixed income product experience, having been previously employed by institutions such as TD Securities and Greenwich Natwest/Natwest Capital Markets as an analyst in credit derivatives and structured derivatives products. Her current research with Edward Altman, also of the NYU Salomon Center, focuses primarily on bankruptcy analysis and prediction and defaulted debt analysis.

David Lando is professor of finance and head of the finance department at the Copenhagen Business School. He holds a Master's degree from the joint mathematics–economics programme at the University of Copenhagen and a PhD in statistics from Cornell University. His main area of research in finance is credit risk modelling and risk management and some of his work has appeared in *Econometrica*, *The Journal of Financial Economics* and *Review of Financial Studies*. David is the author of a monograph on credit risk modelling published by Princeton University Press. He has been a visiting scholar at among other places Princeton University, the Federal Reserve Board in Washington, The Federal Reserve Bank of New York and he is currently a member of Moody's Academic and Advisory Research Committee. Before joining the Copenhagen Business School, he was a professor at the department of applied mathematics and statistics at the University of Copenhagen.

Robert (Bob) Litterman is the co-developer, along with the late Fischer Black, of the Black–Litterman global asset allocation model. Bob retired in 2009 after working for 23 years at Goldman Sachs. He was head of the firmwide risk department from 1994 to 1998, after which he became head of the quantitative group in the asset management division. Before joining the firm in 1986, Bob was an assistant vice president in the research department of the Federal Reserve Bank of Minneapolis and an assistant professor in the economics department at the Massachusetts Institute of Technology. In May 2008, Bob was honoured by the CFA Institute Board with the Nicholas Molodovsky Award, which is presented periodically to individuals "who have made outstanding contributions of such significance as to change the direction of the profession and to raise it to higher standards of accomplishment". Bob was also the recipient of the 2008 International Association of Financial Engineers (IAFE)/SunGard Financial Engineer of the Year Award, which recognises individual contributions to the advancement of financial engineering technology. He earned a BS in human biology from Stanford University in 1973 and a PhD in economics from the University of Minnesota in 1980.

Alexander Lipton is co-head of the Global Quantitative Group at Bank of America Merrill Lynch and visiting professor, Imperial College London. Prior to his current roles, Alexander was global head of credit analytics at Merrill Lynch. Earlier, he was a managing director and head of capital structure quantitative research at Citadel Investment Group in Chicago. He has also worked at Credit Suisse, Deutsche Bank and Bankers Trust. Previously, Alexander was a full professor of mathematics at the University of Illinois at Chicago and a consultant at Los Alamos National Laboratory. His current interests include industrial-strength pricing of derivatives, as well as technical trading strategies. In 2000 Alexander was awarded the first Quant of the Year Award by *Risk Magazine*. Alex is the author of two books (*Magnetohydrodynamics and Spectral Theory* and *Mathematical Methods for Foreign Exchange*) and the (co)editor of four more (including *The Oxford Handbook of Credit Derivatives*).

Ming Liu is an associate modeller in the sales and trading division at Morgan Stanley. He holds MS and PhD degrees in industrial engineering and management sciences from Northwestern University, where he won the Arthur Hunter Academic Excellence Award. The topic of his PhD thesis was "Efficient Simulation in Financial Risk Management". His paper on "Estimating Expected Shortfall with Stochastic Kriging", co-authored with Jeremy Staum, received the Best Student Research Paper Award from the INFORMS Financial Services Section and the Best PhD Student Paper Award from the INFORMS Simulation Society.

Matteo Marsili is a research scientist at the Abdus Salam ICTP, Trieste. He received his PhD in physics at SISSA. He has authored more than 100 scientific publications and two books. He has made important contributions to non-equilibrium statistical physics, to interdisciplinary applications of statistical mechanics to complex systems and to economics and finance in particular. Matteo is coordinator of the programme on Environmental and Ecological Economics (EEE) at ICTP and of several research grants. He is scientific director of *Journal of Statistical Mechanics* and editor of *Journal of Economic Interaction and Coordination*, *European Journal of Physics* Series B and *Physical Review* Series E.

ABOUT THE AUTHORS

Paul McCulley is a managing director, generalist portfolio manager and member of the investment committee at PIMCO in Newport Beach, CA. In addition, he heads PIMCO's short-term bond desk, leads PIMCO's cyclical economic forums and is author of the monthly research publication *Global Central Bank Focus*. Prior to joining PIMCO in 1999, he was chief economist for the Americas at UBS Warburg. During 1996–98, he was named to six seats on the Institutional Investor All-America fixed income research team. Paul has 27 years of investment experience and holds an MBA from Columbia Business School. He received his undergraduate degree from Grinnell College.

Andrea Pallavicini is head of financial engineering at Banca Leonardo in Milan. Previously, he worked as head of equity and hybrid models in Banca IMI, working also on dynamical loss models, interest-rate derivatives, smile modelling and counterparty risk. Over the years he has published several academic and practitioner-oriented articles in financial modelling, theoretical physics and astrophysics. He has taught Master's courses in finance at the universities of Pavia and Milan. He obtained a first degree in astrophysics, and a PhD in theoretical and mathematical physics from the University of Pavia.

Philip Protter received his BA from Yale University in 1971 and his PhD from the University of California, San Diego in 1975. After teaching at Duke University and Purdue University, he joined Cornell University in 2000, where he is a professor of operations research. He was director of financial engineering at Cornell University from 2000 to 2007. He is a fellow of the Institute for Mathematical Statistics, and he was a Fulbright Distinguished Chair in Paris, France, in 2007. His research focus is in the area of theoretical and applied probability. Areas of research include mathematical finance theory (asset pricing, liquidity risk, credit risk, etc), stochastic numerical analysis, stochastic analysis and its applications, weak convergence, Markov process theory and filtering theory. Philip has a longstanding interest in stochastic calculus and stochastic differential equations. His research focus also encompasses simulation and approximation of solutions for stochastic differential equations. He is the author of three books.

Jeffrey (Jeff) Rosenberg is a managing director and head of global credit strategy research at Bank of America Merrill Lynch. In this role, he is responsible for global macro credit strategy across high-grade, high-yield and credit derivatives as well as coordination of US fixed income strategy. This department is consistently top ranked in investor surveys, taking top three positions in the 2010 Institutional Investor polls for high grade, high yield and general strategy. Jeff joined Bank of America in 2002 from Credit Suisse First Boston, where he was the US investment-grade strategist. Previously, he worked on derivative pricing and risk management models at Bankers Trust. Prior to that, he was a mortgage trader and fixed-income analyst for a money management firm. He earned a Bachelor's degree in business from the University of Wisconsin–Madison, a Bachelor's degree in mathematics from the University of Minnesota and a Master's degree in computational finance from Carnegie Mellon University. He has been a chartered financial analyst since 1997.

David Shelton is director and co-head of credit derivatives research at Bank of America Merrill Lynch. Within credit research, David's main interests are pricing and hedging of CDOs and correlation products, counterparty risk and dynamic models of credit risk. Since 1998 he has worked as a quantitative analyst on FX, hybrid FX interest rate and credit products. Prior to his current role, David worked at Natwest, Citigroup and Barclays Capital. Before that he was a postdoctoral theoretical physicist in Canada and Oxford for two years, after receiving a DPhil in theoretical physics from the University of Oxford.

Alexander Sokol is the founder and CEO of CompatibL, a software and custom development company specialising in trading and risk management applications, financial analytics and technical computing. Before starting CompatibL in 2003, he was the founder and chief technology officer of Numerix, the leading provider of derivatives pricing software, where from 1996 to 2003 he was responsible for the entire research and development effort, including quant research and product development. Alexander's academic career included faculty positions in theoretical physics at the University of Illinois at Urbana-Champaign and the L. D. Landau Institute for Theoretical Physics (Moscow). He holds a PhD in theoretical physics from the

L. D. Landau Institute and an MSc in physics (with distinction) from the Moscow Institute of Physics and Technology. He is the author of more than 45 academic publications and one patent in the areas of physics, high performance computing and financial mathematics, and is the winner of the USSR Academy of Sciences Award and Medal for the Best Student Research of the Year.

Roger M. Stein is the president of Moody's Research Labs in New York. He has been actively engaged in developing new approaches to applied credit risk modelling for over 20 years. As the co-head of Moody's KMV's research and product development he led the development of commercial risk management tools that have been adopted widely by leading financial institutions globally. Before that he led Moody's risk management services' research group. He has authored numerous professional and academic articles and serves on the editorial boards of several finance-related journals. Roger's most recent book is *Active Credit Portfolio Management in Practice*, in which he and his co-author provide a handbook for practitioners on applied corporate credit risk management. He has a PhD from the Stern School of Business, New York University.

Roberto Torresetti is portfolio manager for Quaestio Capital covering mainly tactical asset allocation and volatility strategies. Previously, he was responsible for structured credit derivatives at BBVA and a senior quantitative analyst in credit derivatives at Banca IMI and equity derivatives at Lehman Brothers. He was also a quantitative fund manager at San Paolo IMI Asset Management. Roberto holds a Bachelor's degree in economics from Università Bocconi in Milan and completed his MA in economics at Università Bocconi and MS in financial mathematics at the University of Chicago.

Stuart M. Turnbull is the Bauer Chair professor of finance at the Bauer College of Business at the University of Houston. He is senior advisor to GlobeOp Financial Services, Ltd, a major provider of risk analytics for hedge funds and asset managers. He was a senior vice president, fixed income research, Lehman Brothers, New York. Before joining Lehman Brothers, he was vice president, risk management division, Canadian Imperial Bank of Commerce, Toronto, Ontario.

Peter J. Zangari is a managing director and head of risk management for the quantitative investment strategies (QIS) business at

Goldman Sachs Asset Management. Over the past 12 years at Goldman Sachs, he held various senior level positions within QIS with responsibilities spanning portfolio management, risk management, infrastructure and analytics. Before joining Goldman Sachs, Peter was a vice president at J. P. Morgan, where he was part of the original team that built RiskMetrics. He holds a BA from Fordham University and a PhD from Rutgers University.

Introduction

The ongoing global financial crisis has dramatically affected many aspects of our profession, even calling into question the very existence of institutions that have long been among the pillars of the capital markets. The main objective of this book is to uncover the roots of the financial crisis and to highlight the new realities that have emerged and insights that were gained from it. The book features topics ranging from tracking of the history of the crisis and its impact on the structure and functioning of capital markets to the analysis of the fundamental sources of market instabilities and offers new quantitative methodologies designed to withstand the test of future crises. Among the contributors are some of the best-known researchers from both academia and industry, whose expertise ranges from risk management to macroeconomics, from derivatives modelling to investment management.

DEBATING THE ORIGINS, OUTCOMES AND LESSONS OF THE FINANCIAL CRISIS

Many researchers have noted that the current crisis is bigger than just a single burst credit market bubble: it involves many interconnected markets, from real estate to sovereign debt, from commodities to equities, and almost everything in between. It has affected all participants in the financial system: banks, insurers, hedge funds, regulators and rating agencies, to name a few.

Why is that so? Why have so many markets frozen up or broken down in unison? This is not the first time this has happened, but it is certainly the deepest and longest crisis in many generations, globally. Is it even relevant to call the current situation just a "credit crisis", or should we be instead talking of an "economic crisis" like the Great Depression of the 1930s?

I believe the answer to the last question is that the crisis is indeed primarily about credit, but there are fundamental reasons why it spilled over to other markets once it grew too large. To reflect this, we have characterised it by a broader term of "financial crisis" in the title of the book; we believe it is a crisis of the financial system, but not necessarily of the economic system.

The root of the problem, as I see it, is that "credit" is not just an asset class or a market encompassing specific securities (commercial paper, bonds, loans) or derivatives (CDSs, CDOs). Credit risk in general is also a universal metric for all risks, because all risks are eventually transformed into a risk of holding the obligations of an entity that is carrying these other risks. To use a software analogy, the credit risk is the "interface" through which market participants interact with each other. If the base risk is geopolitical, it gets transformed into sovereign credit risk. If it is market risk, it gets transformed into the counterparty risk of market participants. If it is economic risk, it gets transformed into the credit risk of corporations and other real economy participants. Therefore, when this interface breaks down, the holders of any other form of risk have no choice but to reduce their exposures, because all of a sudden the formerly netted low-risk transactions become open-ended high-risk transactions.

This brings to the forefront the role of intermediaries in the credit markets, because it is the intermediaries that operate on this interface, aggregate the vast majority of the financial transactions and rely the most on netting and diversification to manage the risks on their books. By tracing the evolution of the financial intermediaries and the changing competitive landscapes among them, we can understand the driving forces behind the growth and bursting of the great financial bubble over the past several decades.

Traditionally, only banks were able to play the role of such intermediaries. Moreover, the transactions which accumulated on their books were, until the 1970s, mostly straightforward loan-type exposures to their clients, which were funded in an even simpler way: via deposits. The multiplier effect in such a system was relatively stable and explicitly regulated by the standard capital adequacy requirements. In other words, the system operated with considerable yet stable leverage.

Gradually, however, the landscape of the intermediation of credit risk changed. Investment banks and non-bank entities entered the intermediation business and gradually came to dominate it, while the traditional banks lagged behind for quite a few years (in the US this was partly due to Glass–Steagall Act constraints). The emergence of this "shadow banking system" has been among the most important developments in the past 30 years (see a detailed analysis of this phenomenon in Paul McCulley's chapter).

INTRODUCTION

One of the most important features of these new players in financial markets was that they operated with higher and more variable (or even uncertain) leverage, made possible by their aggressive use of derivatives and off-balance-sheet securitisation vehicles. This produced a gap in competitiveness, and correspondingly a gap in profits between non-bank entities and commercial banks. To level the playing field, the traditional banks pressed for deregulation, as a result of which formerly staid organisations like Citibank were given a chance to compete with the likes of Lehman Brothers, Merrill Lynch and Bear Stearns for a slice of the securitisation and derivatives markets. The results of this competition turned out not to be so good for most of the parties involved.

A lot of attention after the peak of the crisis has focused on over-the-counter (OTC) derivatives, particularly swaps and CDSs, and their risk (mis-)management as the proximate causes of the crisis. But these instruments, like their simpler brethren, exchange-traded futures and options, were originally intended as means for risk management, not risk amplification. The same could be said about the process of securitisation, which for years was an essential tool for bank risk management, until it became a profit centre in its own right and caused excessive risk taking and subsequent blow-ups. So, it makes sense to focus not just on the tools of the market, such as OTC derivatives, but on the users of these tools, in order to understand what went wrong and why.

Let us first look back in history. Perhaps the biggest watershed event of the modern finance era was the invention of the swap contract at Salomon Brothers in 1981. In this first transaction, the three-currency US dollar versus Deutschmark and Swiss franc swap between IBM and the World Bank (International Bank for Reconstruction and Development), the express objective was the mitigation of the counterparty risk compared with a simple cash loan. Indeed, the bilateral netting agreement typical in all swap contracts makes the counterparties exposed to only the small fraction of the notional loss in case of default. This feature, together with the attraction of the no-upfront-cash requirements of most swap transactions, has led to an explosive growth of the size of this market. According to the Bank for International Settlements (BIS), as of December 2008, the interest rate swaps, currency swaps, credit default swaps and equity- and commodity-linked contracts have grown to a total notional of US$591 trillion. A better measure of the OTC market size, its gross market value (defined as the aggregate replacement value by BIS), is estimated to be US$57 trillion. This is roughly equal to the aggregate world GDP (US$54 trillion) and the vast majority of these transactions were concentrated on the books of relatively few financial intermediaries!

Note that I intentionally do not make much distinction between interest rate or currency swaps and CDSs. Even though the CDSs have received a bad press recently, I do not believe that they themselves pose a much bigger risk to the system than all the other types of swap transactions. The problem is not in what type of risk is swapped, but in the off-balance-sheet nature of the swap transaction and the fact that a large notional amount is reduced to a small cashflow requirement and a small risk weight under most typical risk management methodologies. In other words, the swap contracts have allowed the financial system to vastly expand its leverage because of the belief that the risks were mitigated. Of course, the asymmetry of the CDSs payout and associated counterparty risk is substantially larger than that of interest rate or currency swaps, but it is alleviated by the variable margins usually required when selling CDS protection. The residual payments in addition to already posted margins are large only if the default was truly unexpected, like in fraud-driven defaults of Enron or Parmalat, or if the market was hoping for a bailout or some other resolution of the impending credit event, as in the case of Lehman Brothers.

So, the swap contracts (and the whole OTC derivatives market that grew out of them) that were hailed as the solution to the problem of counterparty risk became so successful that they now posed an even greater risk problem than the initial plain-vanilla transactions. In essence, the OTC market, instead of dispersing the counterparty risk of market participants, concentrated it in the hands of intermediaries and thus transformed it into pseudo-systemic risk. This was not necessarily a bad thing, as it produced several decades of accelerated growth and prosperity by freeing up other market participants from the clutches of credit risk. Unfortunately, instead of recognising this metamorphosis, the regulators thought that the risks were being self-contained and thus failed to foresee or prepare for the current crisis.

The story above makes is sound almost inevitable that the systemic crisis would occur as a result of increased use of OTC derivatives. It ignores, however, the role of skewed economic incentives and regulatory constraints in promoting the mis-use of these derivatives. As in any detective investigation, we must not only find the smoking gun, but also answer the question "who had the incentive?"

Consider, for example, the genesis of the troubles in AIG, Ambac, MBIA and some other insurance companies. In their drive for market share, broker–dealers gradually reduced their margin requirements and thus allowed greater and greater levels of leverage to accumulate for their most important counterparties (among which these large insurance companies were at the time). In some cases, such as AIG, with its "iron-clad" AAA ratings, there were no margins required whatsoever, making even a transaction earning a few basis points a winning trade, given virtually infinite leverage. Of course, the abuse of this special status led to the accumulation of unjustified risks on AIG's books and to its eventual fall from AAA status. The resulting margin calls appeared to be so severe precisely because any reasonable margin requirement is infinitely large when compared with zero, and therefore the borrower is unprepared to meet it (unless of course they have an internal discipline to set aside sufficient cash reserves and self-insure, like Warren Buffett's Berkshire Hathaway is used to doing).

Yes, it was the derivatives usage that enabled AIG and other insurers to build up the leverage. But it was the lax credit policies of their counterparties and the market practices dealing, in general, with long-term risks that made this not only feasible but also very (short-term) profitable. The very same derivatives, if used in the context of prudent risk management and capital requirements, would not have led to a similar meltdown of these companies. After all, not every financial institution that traded CDOs blew up in 2008; some were able to properly hedge their positions and some even made positive returns without taking huge directional bets or teetering on the brink of disastrous margin calls due to spiralling leverage combined with illiquid positions.

The irresistible attraction of high leverage stimulated in counterparties by low margin requirements is not really that different from the irresistible urge to buy a home we cannot really afford, stimulated by the proliferation of subprime mortgages. Ironically, both the least sophisticated and the most sophisticated market participants seem to have fallen ill with the same symptoms: the unchecked desire of immediate satisfaction overshadows prudent assessment of future risks and costs. Perhaps it is just down to fallible human nature, and financial sophistication and derivatives usage matters only in the form of its expression rather than in its substance.

But blaming human nature is too easy, even if it is right. There were particular constituents of the financial system that participated in the build-up of the financial excesses more than the others. Fingers have been pointed to greedy CEOs, near-sighted risk managers, complicit rating agencies, reckless traders and devious short-sellers, to name a few. There is plenty of blame to go around, without a doubt. What worries me, however, is that often the judging party is also not without a hand in the crisis, and the whole exercise smacks more of a blame-shifting and diversion of public anger than of a true quest for the roots of the problems.

I would like to focus here on one frequent notion that arose towards the end of the crisis: did the quants do it? After all, it was quants who designed the risk management systems, the quants who wrote the CDO pricing and credit rating models, the quants who ran the real estate growth forecasts. So are they to blame for all this mess? The CEOs, traders and politicians would like to know. I cannot clear the quants of all the blame, but I would simply point out that in the vast majority of situations, the quants had no decision-making power and were only (willing) accomplices of various flawed policies and practices. Yes, their oversimplified models enabled a lot of bad behaviour, but they did not cause it. At the same time, there were other, much better models available which, if used, would have alerted the investors and traders to looming risks or insufficiency or capital cushions. The causality actually ran in the opposite direction: the decision makers who were intent on pursuing the flawed policies chose the models which allowed them to justify their objectives. The incentives were skewed towards making the deals, and a quant model could always be found that would make the deals look attractive. Just as nuclear physicists should not be confused with the military strategists planning atomic wars, the quants should not be confused with the salespeople and traders making deals that use models for their justification.

The one incident in which quants squarely take the blame is the "Quant Crunch" episode of August 2007. In this case, it was actually the quantitative investment managers who were indeed the decision makers, and the quant models were not just enablers but the drivers of the process. As discussed in the illuminating chapters written by Bob Litterman and Peter Zangari, the prior success of quant strategies led to overinvesting in this space, and to the eventual sudden unwinding of the "crowded trade". The mechanism which caused the Quant Crunch was the same as that in the case of any bursting bubble, via forced unwinding of the excess leverage. The new twist was that this could happen in strategies that were believed to be well diversified and therefore specifically designed to be immune from such events. And the most important differentiating point between the quants after the Quant Crunch and bankers and traders after the Credit Crunch is that the quants have actually learned their lesson and have been hard at work devising better and more robust methodologies to avoid such debacles in the future: something that cannot be universally said about the other constituents of the financial system.

We would imagine that the near-catastrophic conditions of the world financial markets between September 2008 and March 2009 would have had a sobering and long-lasting impact on the policy makers. It is rather telling, however, that much of the new regulation and risk management rules and best practices promoted in the wake of the crisis have been directed at making the market mechanisms even more rather than less centralised. We appear to be fighting the systemic crisis by adopting new rules that make the financial system increasingly rigid, all the while pumping trillions of dollars of new capital into it via various programmes like TARP, TALF, PPIP, quantitative easing, etc. This is akin to getting burned by the hot steam from a boiling steamer, and then deciding to close its valve completely while still increasing the stove temperature; sure, this would give us a few minutes of "peace" without the pesky steam, but I would not want to stand near that steamer when its hinges finally give way and the whole thing blows up with all that pent-up energy.

The drive to put all derivatives into central counterparty (CCP) entities, or push them to exchanges, might seem like a good solution if we believe that it was the opacity that blew up Lehman or

AIG. Indeed, a centrally cleared swap contract has a lot more transparency than the one which resides on dealer's books. But will this transparency force more or less volatility in the behaviour of the market participants? It is quite possible that such transparency will bring about greater interdependencies between various traded risks, as the market participants and risk managers will not be able to ignore the flare-up of volatility in the neighbouring market. Larger numbers of observable warning signs can cause a trigger-finger syndrome in internal risk managers and those setting margin rules, potentially amplifying what might have been a minor localised event in one market into a self-reinforcing wave of risk reduction across the board (see Jeff Rosenberg's chapter for more in-depth analysis of the potential consequences of the new regulatory structure for trading markets and their liquidity).

Of course, the bigger benefit of the CCP design is the apparent reduction of the counterparty risk compared with more vulnerable prime brokerage setup. But what if, despite the safety of the margin requirements, a large failure occurs, or, worse yet, a sequence of failures caused by sequentially tightening margin calls? Would the CCP entity be sufficiently capitalised to deal with this? Good news if it is, but what if it is not? It seems to me that we are elevating the problem to yet another level of concentration, where the failure of the central counterparty is completely unthinkable due to its designated central role in the financial system and therefore it absolutely has to be supported by a government guarantee. It does not matter whether that guarantee is explicit or implicit; the threat of complete disarray and breakdown of the financial system will be so large that bailing out such a CCP will be a self-preservation move for any government. We have transformed the too-big-to-fail problem into a too-central-to-fail one.

Therefore, it seems logical to me that the only consistent way to introduce a reliable CCP mechanism in the securities markets is to explicitly nationalise these CCPs and to essentially run them as government agencies in collaboration with, or perhaps simply from within the regulatory agencies. This would remove the false pretense of allowing private companies to essentially manage the entire financial system and ignoring the obvious moral hazard of such a setup. It would also simultaneously solve the problem of derivatives market oversight, because the regulators would actually own all the trading records (and even the records for trades attempted but not consummated).

The government-owned CCP can be immunised from the fallout of a member failure if it demands variable risk margins that make the residual loss in case of such failure tolerable with respect to its reserve capital, or at least makes the likely bailout of the CCP less costly than the direct bailout of a member bank. Such a bailout could be arranged in the following manner: The Fed (or another appropriate agency) could lend necessary excess capital to the CCP and allow it to temporarily expand its balance sheet by accepting the failed member's trades on its own books. These trades would need to be either held to maturity (if the maturity is not too far) or gradually unwound. If the CCP is actually an exchange, the unwinding process can proceed smoothly because the exchange can work its inventory through the general market trading over time. If the CCP is only a clearing entity, then another management entity must be appointed to take over the unwinding of this portfolio of trades.

The sticking point in this design is that the CCP is not likely to charge margins differently depending on the member firm's counterparty risk. The margin rules are most likely to be based on the estimates of market risk of the contracts rather than their counterparty value adjustments. This phenomenon would produce an adverse selection, because the margin rates would need to be set high enough to cover average losses, which would make them too high for creditworthy counterparties and too low for credit-risky ones. Thus, the risky counterparties will essentially enjoy a funding arbitrage at the expense of low-risk ones.

The same adverse selection would occur in case of other systemic risk designs, such as those that require the members of the CCP entity to post large insurance premiums, akin to banks posting Federal Deposit Insurance Corporation (FDIC) premiums, or make transaction tax payments to fund the future bailouts. In any such schemes, where payments are made on the *pro rata* basis rather than real risk basis, a bank with less risky business would pay the same rate for protection as the bank with more risk, and therefore it would suffer in competitive advantage with respect to the latter. Again, it would become possible to arbitrage the system by playing dangerously close to the brink of permitted leverage (or by finding ways to go beyond that brink) and essentially gain in return on capital at the expense of more prudent investors. This skew in incentives versus constraints is too similar to the situation we had before 2008 to give us much comfort.

A different, and equally worrisome, point is that all these "rainy day" funds will be held by regulators and we will be reduced to putting our trust in the government agencies rather than professional investment managers for preserving and disbursing them in a judicious manner. This strikes me as a rather weak choice for society: whether to trust bankers, who have already demonstrated their inability to cope with the risks in the face of competing financial incentives, or the politicians, who have also demonstrated many times their proclivity to misdirect public funds in the face of competing political incentives. Indeed, while 2007 and 2008 were mostly the years of worry about banks and private financial system in general, in 2009 and, in particular, 2010, attention has turned to public finances, where the deficits and asset–liability imbalances are even bigger and harder to fix.

The intertwining of the political and economic life of societies with the financial life of markets has been highlighted by some pundits as potentially a sign of a much bigger crisis in society than just the financial one we all worry about. Notable thinkers with a deep understanding of markets and economy, including people as diverse in their opinions as George Soros, Paul Krugman and Bill Gross, have been quoted wondering aloud whether the recent crisis is also a crisis of the capitalist society. If these were merely some fringe pundits, we would easily dismiss such questions. After all, the capitalist society has not vanished and continues to churn out profits even after the worst of the crisis is over.

But the questions raised are indeed deeper. Capitalism has long been associated with free markets and globalisation, and all regulations and restraints on those have been thought of as vestiges of inefficiency, the price that society has to pay because it is not sufficiently free or advanced. However, the free flow of capital across industries and countries requires the system of financial intermediaries to take a dominating role; this is precisely the system that momentarily ceased to function in 2008. If the financial system is the lifeblood of the capitalist society, then what happened in 2008 was indeed a cardiac arrest, and we still live with its consequences, not knowing for sure yet whether it was caused by external causes or by innate deficiencies. What if it is a birth defect, in which case the problem will surely resurface again?

I do not know the answer to this question, but I do believe that it is a question worth asking and that we should not limit our search to finding a more stable design of the financial system, but should also look for a more stable and balanced design of the larger society to go hand in hand with a better economic framework. And if the long-term stability is considered a desirable feature of this design, then I can venture a guess that the system cannot be rigid and over-regulated; local rigidity and long-term stability cannot coexist. This is as much a law of Nature as it is a Zen principle.

I am far from suggesting that regulation is not necessary or is harmful. But the regulation must be directed at controlling the market participants' behaviour in a soft manner, with ability to judge the intent as well as the fact of the regulatory breach, rather than simply imposing rigid rules and hoping that the compliance with those will do the trick. I believe that an intentional vagueness in regulation and an ability to make *post factum* interpretations would go a long way toward thwarting abusive avoidance by market participants. Business managers, especially in the mainstream financial industry, tend to be risk averse when they cannot hide behind the formal compliance with the letter of regulation. A possibility of future censure based on the intent of their actions will force them to discipline themselves better than any capital requirements designed under Basel II, III, IV, or whichever iteration happens to be current by the time the next "Lehman-like" failure occurs.

As a reasonable model, I would suggest looking at the Prudent Man Rule,[1] and the more recent Prudent Investor Act (1990) which have a long history of ensuring proper fiduciary behaviour in the trust management industry. They work well precisely because they are vague: there is no bullet-point list of what constitutes the prudent man rule which could be gamed by a sinister trustee, and any dispute around it can be properly handled on the basis of common sense and up-to-date industry standards. At the time of writing, the Prudent Investor Act contains references to portfolio theory and diversification, but I am sure that, should the newly understood lessons of liquidity management find their place in the industry mainstream, they too will become a part of the Prudent Investor Act, ensuring its continued relevance.

Of course, enforcing such flexible regulation requires a lot more work than just coming up with a set of immutable rules, the compliance with which can be checked like a high-school multiple-choice exam. They actually require an understanding of what the market participants do and why. But the benefit is that they adapt to the times. While some new derivative can always be invented that would allow a regulatory arbitrage under a fixed set of rules, it would not be possible under a guidance-based regulation such as the Prudent Man Rule, because an alert regulator can always dispute the intent of the invention and judge it to be "imprudent".

Another important insight that has come out of the financial crisis, is that the belief in the absolute power of efficient markets in particular and efficiency in general has been finally put into serious doubt (see Part V of the book for several chapters dealing with this issue on a much deeper level). Efficiency is not always good. Efficiency kills evolution, and we need evolution to ensure progress. The concept of equilibrium is useful for closed systems, but rarely works well for open and exponentially complex systems like the capitalist economy. Not only that, but it also seems counterproductive in a social sense, as it envisions a world where there is not much progress. I would say that if it was possible to choose between two perfectly working economies, one which has an equilibrium and one that does not but instead has Darwinian forces fully enabled, we should choose the latter, because choosing thus would result in a better future for us and our children. Take the red pill, Neo, and let's escape The Matrix, even if it means facing up to the painful reality of the world that does not follow the academic dogmas!

STRUCTURE OF THE BOOK

The book is organised in six parts, whose subjects progress from exploration of the roots of the financial crisis and its impact on markets to insights for risk management, quantitative modelling and analysis of market stability and efficiency, and concluding with lessons for investment management.

Part I of the book is devoted to understanding the root causes of the financial crisis, and to tracing its origins in a few different markets.

Chapter 1 by John Hull, a leading authority in quantitative modelling of derivatives in general and credit risk in particular, gives a broad overview of the credit crisis, starting with the developments in the US housing market and showing how securitisation exacerbated the lax lending practices, particularly for subprime borrowers. He demonstrates how the more complex transactions, asset-backed-security collateralised debt obligations (ABS CDOs), have in fact served as conduits for capital to support the subprime securitisation and lending, thanks to risk estimates for the senior tranches of such CDOs that were too optimistic. He correctly highlights that the biggest problem with ABS CDOs was that they were constructed from the tranches of ABSs, which themselves represent large pools of mortgages. Thus, most idiosyncratic risk had already been diversified at the ABS level, and therefore when these were combined into CDOs it was wrong to assume that there would be any additional diversification benefit.[2]

Chapter 2 by Ashish Das and Roger Stein of Moody's Research Labs investigates thoroughly the roles of underwriting standards versus the changing macro-economic factors in the subsequent subprime losses; they discern substantial differences between the earlier and more recent vintages of subprime mortgages in terms of their performance. While the economic conditions, including the changes in prices of real estate, are shown to be the main driving factor behind the subprime losses, Das and Stein attribute a portion of these losses to the quality of underwriting at the time of origination.

Paul McCulley of PIMCO was among the first market practitioners to spot the dangers of the overgrowth in the financial sector, and is widely credited with popularising the phrase "shadow banking system" in his speech at 2007 Fed Jackson Hole conference. In Chapter 3, he presents an overview of this phenomenon and describes how the shadow banking system came into existence and why its dominance threatened the stability of the financial system, eventually contributing to the crisis that unfolded. He draws parallels with Hyman Minsky's theories of progression from stable to speculative financing to Ponzi schemes and shows how they explain the endemic boom–bust cycles in the financial system. These insights carry especial weight, coming from a portfolio manager who invests hundreds of billions of dollars in credit markets.

In their detailed analysis of the collapse of the Icelandic banking system in 2008 (Chapter 4), René Kallestrup and David Lando of the Copenhagen Business School examine this as an almost perfect example of how a dysfunctional and overstretched financial system can sink a country into a deep systemic crisis. They follow step by step the growth of the unmistakable bubble of banking in Iceland, analyse the flawed policies and procedures that misled international creditors, rating agencies and regulators into believing that these banks were indeed worthy of an investment grade (let alone Aaa) ratings, and sort through the aftermath of their collapse to gather lessons for others on how to avoid the fate of the Icelandic banking system.

Bob Litterman recalls in Chapter 5 his experience running the Quantitative Resources Group at Goldman Sachs Asset Management, which encompassed both quantitative hedge funds and long-only equity portfolios, through the early crisis years of 2007–8. In particular, he describes in great detail the events of early August 2007, which have come to be known as the "Quant Crunch". While the larger investment community remained relatively unscathed, many of the quantitatively run long/short equity fund managers were shaken during this short period by massive losses that, in the context of their portfolios, were the equivalent of a 10-sigma market crash. Although the market overall did not do anything particularly dramatic during that period, almost anyone invested in model-driven equity portfolios saw an incredible behaviour as virtually all the stocks they were short rallied and all the stocks they were long fell in unison. Litterman ascribes this to the likely effect of an unwinding of a large portfolio, coupled with a concentration of most quant funds in similar strategies and a relatively high leverage maintained prior to this event due to the perception of well-hedged risks. The result was similar to a short squeeze, except this was not in a single instrument, but rather in the entire strategy portfolio. He goes on to draw important lessons from this experience for the future of quantitative investing, which readers will surely find illuminating.

Part II of the book is about the impact that the financial crisis had on the structure and functioning of the markets that were among the most affected by the financial crisis: the OTC derivatives and the distressed credit.

In Chapter 6, Jeffrey Rosenberg, who heads the credit strategy group at Bank of America Merrill Lynch and has a vantage point very close to the credit market ebbs and flows, examines the impact of the financial crisis on the OTC derivatives market. He notes that the OTC market is still in the midst of significant changes of the regulatory regime, which are likely to affect both its structure and the potential uses of OTC derivatives. He outlines the trade-offs that the market is facing in trying to deal with the systemic risks associated with OTC derivatives, in particular the impact of the emergence of the central clearing requirements on the liquidity of the derivatives market. He concludes that we are likely to face a bifurcated liquidity, which will be dominated by simpler standardised derivatives and benchmark indexes, at the expense of lower liquidity in the off-the-run, non-benchmark and bespoke instruments.

In Chapter 7, Edward Altman and Brenda Karlin of the NYU Stern School of Business highlight the re-emergence of distressed exchanges in corporate restructurings. As a widely recognised pioneer of credit risk analysis, Altman can draw on his vast personal experience as well as his thoroughly compiled database of corporate credit events in order to pinpoint the important structural changes in the distressed credit market. Altman and Karlin show that 2008–9 saw a dramatic increase in distressed exchanges as companies tried to stave off a formal bankruptcy filing, with this trend eventually slowing down in late 2009 and early 2010. However, they warn investors that, even though the recovery rates in such exchanges are much higher than in bankruptcy, the probability of eventual bankruptcy and additional losses is very high.

Part III is dedicated to the lessons for risk management and regulation. These chapters cover the most challenging questions of risk management that have confounded both practitioners and regulators during the crisis: what to do with complex financial instruments that get created every day in the investment banks and do not readily fit the pre-existing frameworks, how to measure and understand the systemic risks on the national and global level and how to practically deal with the extreme risks which seem to get realised much more often these days.

In Chapter 8, Dale Gray and Andreas Jobst of the International Monetary Fund model the systemic and sovereign risks using the new framework of the systemic contingent claims analysis (CCA). They draw on the success of Merton's structural model of credit risk for corporate entities in order to build an extended methodology that can be applied to the balance sheets of entire economies and countries. With insights including the importance of inclusion of explicit and implicit government guarantees, financial sector exposures and sensitivity to foreign exchange risks, they obtain a holistic picture of sovereign risks through such metrics as risk-adjusted economic output and CCA balance sheets. Using the techniques from option pricing models, they calibrate their model to market observables and thereby obtain a much more dynamic picture of systemic risk than the traditional ones focused on slowly revealed economic data. Among the important features of their model is its ability to describe the positive and negative feedback effects between the systemic risks and the key players in the financial system.

Stuart Turnbull's chapter (Chapter 9) on measuring and managing risks in innovative financial instruments complements the topic by examining the difficult challenges facing both internal risk managers and external regulators when it comes to modern financial companies. Turnbull, who is one of the pioneers of quantitative credit risk and credit derivatives pricing models, gives us a road map to understanding the different dimensions of risks, model uncertainties and ties all these to specific instrument design and market characteristics. He goes on to give specific prescriptions for best practices in using and critically testing the models and estimating the risks of complex financial products.

In Chapter 10, the MSCI Barra research team of Vladislav Dubikovsky, Michael Hayes, Lisa Goldberg and Ming Liu focuses on the difficult problem of forecasting the extreme risks. Using the multifactor methodology and focusing on the fundamental equity factors, they develop a specialised model for estimating the extreme (multi-standard deviation) risks in equity portfolios. They demonstrate that the conventional statistical assumptions fail to describe the behaviour of the fundamental factor returns, especially in the tail of the distribution. Therefore, to be able to use extreme risk management tools such as shortfall optimisation accurately, they propose the new Barra extreme risks model (BxR), which empirically adjusts the "normal" estimates of factor covariance matrix to correctly fit the likelihood of rare extreme events. They demonstrate the superior forecasting accuracy of this new model, both for factor tilt portfolios and for factor-neutral pair portfolios.

Part IV is devoted to advances in quantitative modelling of derivatives after the financial crisis. The crisis revealed the most critical issues in uses of quant models in the areas of modelling structured products (both credit and ABSs), and pricing of OTC derivatives in the context of increased counterparty risks.

In Chapter 11, Damiano Brigo, Andrea Pallavicini and Roberto Torresetti give a thorough critique of the conventional pricing methodologies for structured credit products, in particular the implied credit correlation metric used in conjunction with the copula pricing methods. They explain the progression of industry standards, from compound correlation to base correlation to implied copula, and then introduce the expected tranche loss methodology as a model-independent approach to CDO tranche pricing. While the limitations of the implied correlation were pointed out by many, including Brigo *et al*, prior to the crisis on both theoretical and practical grounds, it was the severe price moves in the CDO market during the crisis that really brought this question to the attention of practitioners. The authors analyse the "in-crisis" performance of various models, confirming largely the breakdown of conventional models, especially in hedging of tranches. They conclude that the institutional rigidity of many trading organisations has probably played a role in keeping the over-simplified models at the core of their systems, despite ample room for improvement.

In Chapter 12, Jean-David Fermanian looks at pricing of mortgage-backed securities and CMOs and CDOs of asset-backed securities. We are introduced to some of the key types of securities at the centre of the financial crisis. The MBSs and collateralised mortgage obligations CMOs were obviously key in the subprime real-estate crisis. The CDOs epitomised the growth of the structured credit market, and the ABSs represented the outreach of the structured finance to other pools of securities, such as credit cards, car leases or even collections of other structured products. Fermanian explains the difficulties in analysing these complex securities from first principles, compounded by their sometimes highly complex cashflow rules, embedded credit enhancements, etc. He then proceeds to offer a unified treatment of all these complex structures with a top-down model focusing on aggregate observables such as total exposures, losses and prepaid amounts. Fermanian is careful to point out various assumptions that are necessary to justify his approach and discusses their applicability in real life situations.

Turning to the other big challenge for the post-crisis era, Alexander Lipton and David Shelton of Bank of America Merrill Lynch offer in Chapter 13 a sophisticated analytical model of the counterparty and collateral adjustments for pricing of derivative securities, using a portfolio of single-name CDSs and credit-linked notes (CLNs) as a relevant example that exhibits the key feature of "wrong way risk". Pricing models that take into account the counterparty credit risk have been known for some time. However, they mostly considered the issue statically, without the context of dynamic collateral adjustment, especially in the portfolio setting. Lipton and Shelton tackle this difficult problem in an reduced-form affine Cox-process framework, with large common intensity jumps that account for cross-credit correlations. They derive the pricing formulas for fully collateralised credit default swaps and for the counterparty value adjustments for single-name CDSs. They also derive the adjustments for CLNs, which became an increasingly popular way of raising capital among the banks before the crisis.[3]

In Chapter 14, continuing the important theme of the counterparty value adjustment (CVA), Alexander Sokol presents us with a complementary practitioner's view on implementing potential future exposure (PFE) and credit value adjustment calculations in the context of very large derivatives portfolios typical for major banks. Drawing on his consulting experience advising various clients on incorporating these computations into their existing risk systems, Sokol approaches the problem from another angle: how to get close to accurate results with reasonable speed of computation and without the need to completely rewrite the bank's risk systems. After reviewing the practical challenges, he proposes as a solution the exposure sampling method, which allows a set of market Monte Carlo simulations to be maintained and combined with separately modelled credit events. The resulting methodology is shown to be both accurate and fast, and actually requires fewer assumptions than many of the more complex numerical frameworks.

In Part V, we focus on the crucial issue of market efficiency and stability. The "noughties" have seen financial bubbles across the markets all over the world; these have raised questions over the conventional narrative of steady, stable and efficient markets that dominated financial thought since the 1970s. By trying to understand these phenomena not as rare outliers, but rather as an inherent feature of the financial markets, our contributors offer deep and complementary views on these important questions.

In Chapter 15, Jean-Philippe Bouchaud considers the endogenous dynamics of markets and investigates the role played by trading activity itself (as opposed to fundamental value) in the formation of the asset prices. He argues that exogenous news plays only a minor role in driving the dynamics of asset prices, which correspondingly exhibit features quite different from those assumed within an efficient-market framework. In fact, these statistical features are best understood if the market is described as a statistical system close to a critical point. The volatility of markets is shown to be very sensitive to random fluctuations in the order flow, which in fact dominate the impact of news in the short and medium term. The resulting decoupling of the short-term market dynamics from the fundamental value may be both a symptom and a cause of market bubbles and crises.

In Chapter 16, Lisa Borland zooms in on the specific statistical patterns of stock price returns to diagnose an ongoing market panic. She hypothesises that the markets undergo a self-organisation and that this is reflected in peculiar changes in the cross-sectional dispersion, kurtosis and the dynamics of correlations. In particular, she notes that, at times of panic, the dispersion is high but the kurtosis is low: an observation that confounds the proponents of the "black swan" description of market panic that simply asserts that tail events are less rare than believed and that they arise suddenly and unpredictably, without warning. Borland proposes a phenomenological model, which describes a spontaneous phase transition of stock dynamics to a highly correlated state at the onset of market panic. This model exhibits quite a remarkable qualitative agreement with real data, which shows that the dynamic effects play an important role in the genesis of market crises.

A complementary view on the intrinsic origins of market instabilities and their deviations from equilibrium is presented by Matteo Marsili and Kartik Anand in Chapter 17. They study the increased complexity of the financial markets, including the proliferation of derivative instruments, securitisation techniques and trading strategies. This complexity (which is often taken as a synonym for market completeness), they argue, is one of the root causes of the increased instability of the markets. What seemed a sign of greater efficiency turns out to be the exact opposite, due to dangerous levels of market degeneracy, where the same basic exposure can be achieved in many different ways, and with potentially many different levels of leverage. The stabilising effects actually emerge not from the attempts to achieve the elusive market efficiency, but from better understanding of its inefficiencies and from taking into account the effects of illiquidity and impact of our own trades on the market. Marsili and Anand go even further and introduce agent-based models of market participant behaviour to elucidate the notion of "trust" which is central to finance in general and banking in particular. The model allows us to qualitatively describe the sudden phase transition from a well-functioning market where participants trust each others' promises (credit obligations), to the dysfunctional one where trust "evaporates".

In Chapter 18, Robert Jarrow and Philip Protter show how to make sense of bubbles and non-equilibrium market states within the martingale pricing framework which is usually associated with the notions of rational expectations, precise market efficiency and equilibrium. They show that asset price bubbles, defined as market configurations in which asset prices diverge from their fundamental values given by the expected present value of future cashflows, can be studied in the context of the "no free lunch with vanishing risk" hypothesis, which is a weaker form of the strict no-arbitrage assumption. With an addition of the "no dominance" condition, Jarrow and Protter show that many classical option pricing results, such as put–call parity, continue to hold, even without imposing the assumption of equilibrium for asset price processes. Within their martingale theory, asset price bubbles can exist for underlying assets, their forwards and futures and other derivatives, but only in incomplete markets (eg, if we assume an asset price process with stochastic volatility driven by a non-tradeable source of randomness). They can be detected by means of statistical analysis of pricing relationships for assets and their derivatives. Jarrow and Protter conclude with a discussion of the implications of asset price bubbles for risk management and regulatory policy.

Finally, Part VI presents insights for investors and asset managers, with contributions devoted to equity portfolio management, credit investing and hedge fund strategies.

In Chapter 19, Peter Zangari shares his insights on how to cope with unpredictable and turbulent crisis conditions when managing equity portfolios in a quantitative, systematic manner. From his vantage point of overseeing the quantitative equity model implementation and portfolio analysis at one of the largest asset managers, Goldman Sachs Asset Management, he recalls the formidable challenges faced by the quants during the crisis. Starting from the August 2007 "Quant Crunch", and continuing almost unabated through the financial crisis years 2007–9, the quantitative equity strategies weathered a series of storms, of which each could deserve the title of the "storm of the century". Zangari critically examines and offers his conclusions on a host of important practical aspects of the quantitative investment process that have been affected by these experiences. They range from the renewed importance that should be given to modelling the market impact of your own trades to improved risk management methodologies including better forecasting of near-term risks and not only managing market risk (P&L volatility) but also explicitly controlling drawdowns, liquidity and contagion risks, and focusing on operational risk controls, especially for large portfolios near their capacity. On the strategy development side, he predicts a trend towards using more proprietary, less commonly known, predictive factors to avoid crowded strategies, and towards using cutting-edge technology to get access to information previously unavailable to investors (natural language processing, image processing, real-time news processing, etc). These and many other insights on how to handle the large and complex task of quantitative management of portfolios though crisis conditions, make this chapter an indispensable read for many practitioners.

In Chapter 20, Vineer Bhansali of PIMCO shares the buy-side perspective on active risk management. PIMCO, which is one of the largest asset management organisations in the world, was able to successfully navigate the credit crisis despite its size and inevitable exposure to every type of fixed income asset, partly due to its adherence to consistent and proactive tail-risk management, liquidity management and realistic assessment of common risk factors not distorted by their pre-crisis calm behaviour. Bhansali explains how they have recognised the presence of the systemic risk in their investment portfolios, how they have estimated the need for hedges and their added value and how an investor can pragmatically go about building such umbrella hedges over time. He explains that active risk management is not just a defensive tool for portfolio managers, but also an offensive tool because it allows the reduction of the sunk costs and preservation of buying power for when it has the most value: right after the crisis. What is remarkable in this chapter is that none of this appears to be extremely complicated or require the implementation of some advanced model. Rather, Bhansali's insight is that we must carefully think through the most important exposures and analyse the most relevant loss scenarios, paying more attention to practical issues than to esoteric questions of estimation of scenario probabilities. The ability to see the wood for the trees is what distinguished almost every one of the winning investors during the crisis.

Finally, in Chapter 21, Arthur Berd presents a stylised model of hedge fund returns that elucidates the relationship between the important statistical characteristics of their returns (time-varying volatility, asymmetry, fat tails) and their expected returns, that is, "alpha". Starting with an econometric model, an extended version of Garch which incorporates both asymmetric volatility response and asymmetric fat-tailed periodic returns, he applies it to sub-strategies of the Lehman Brothers Hedge Fund Index. The results are remarkable in their uniformity: the vast majority of investment strategies exhibit a negative dependence of expected returns on their own volatility; in other words, they are "short vol" strategies whose alpha is mainly earned from the premium of selling their volatility. The few notable exceptions are the CTA trend-following strategies, where the volatility exposure is positive and the "true alpha" is actually negative, signifying that these strategies earn their returns despite the negative carry associated with maintaining a long vol bias, as well as FX and certain fixed income strategies where both true alpha and the volatility exposure are positive, signifying that these strategies appear to be capable of buying vol cheaply enough to still generate positive carry. Berd gives a plausible fundamental explanation for this phenomenon and outlines the lessons for long-term investors for capital allocation across multiple hedge fund strategies.

ACKNOWLEDGEMENTS

In conclusion, on behalf of all the authors in this book, I would like to thank Risk Books for the opportunity to publish our views on the financial crisis and, in particular, the editors Lewis O'Sullivan, Lucie Carter and Sarah Hastings, for their efficient organisation of the editorial process. In addition, I thank Emma Dain (T&T Productions Ltd) for help with the editorial process and project management. Owing to the outstanding insights from my colleagues who contributed the chapters to this book, I am confident that it will become a "must read" reference for anyone trying to comprehend the recent financial crisis and to draw correct conclusions from it. I also hope that it will give a new impetus to many other researchers for their own quest towards a better understanding of the complex issues facing modern financial markets.

Arthur M. Berd
Paris, November 2010

> The opinions expressed in this introduction are those of the author and do not necessarily reflect the opinions of his present or past employers.

1. The Prudent Man Rule is based on common law stemming from the 1830 Massachusetts court decision, Harvard College v. Armory 9 Pick (26 Mass) 446, 461 (1830). The prudent man rule directs trustees "to observe how men of prudence, discretion and intelligence manage their own affairs, not in regard to speculation, but in regard to the permanent disposition of their funds, considering the probable income, as well as the probable safety of the capital to be invested."

2. This point highlights a big difference between ABS CDOs and more conventional corporate CDOs or collateralised loan obligations (CLOs). In the latter case, there is still a lot of idiosyncratic risk in the underlying pool components and therefore the securitisation makes sense. I would venture to predict that traditional fully funded CDO and CLO markets, unlike the ABS CDOs, will eventually revive and will actually provide investors with valuable return opportunities in the post-crisis recovery.

3. By selling a CLN to an investor, the bank not only gives the investor access to the particular asset wrapped in the note, but also essentially issues a promissory note that is an equivalent of selling its own bonds to the investor.

Part I

The Roots of the Crisis

1

The Credit Crunch of 2007: What Went Wrong? Why? What Lessons Can be Learned?

John C. Hull
Rotman School of Management, University of Toronto

Starting in 2007, the US experienced the worst financial crisis since the 1930s. The crisis spread rapidly from the US to other countries and from financial markets to the real economy. Some financial institutions failed. Many more had to be bailed out by national governments. There can be no question that the first decade of the 21st Century has been a disastrous one for the world's financial institutions and for the financial sector in general.

This chapter examines the origins of the crisis, what went wrong and why it went wrong. It also provides some observations on how similar crises can be avoided in the future.

THE US HOUSING MARKET

A natural starting point for any discussion of the credit crunch of 2007 is the US housing market. Figure 1.1 shows the S&P/Case–Shiller Composite-10 Index for house prices in the US between January 1987 and February 2009. Between 2000 and 2005, house prices rose much faster than they had in the previous decade. The very low level of interest rates between 2002 and 2005 was an important contributory factor but the increase was for the most part fuelled by mortgage lending practices.

The 2000–2006 period was characterised by a huge increase in what is termed subprime mortgage lending. Subprime mortgages are mortgages that are considered to be significantly more risky than average. Before 2000 most mortgages classified as subprime were second mortgages. After 2000 this changed as financial

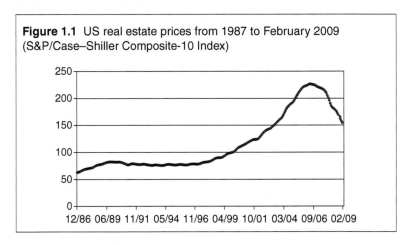

Figure 1.1 US real estate prices from 1987 to February 2009 (S&P/Case–Shiller Composite-10 Index)

institutions became more comfortable with the notion of a subprime first mortgage.

Mortgage lenders started to relax their lending standards in around the year 2000. This made house purchases possible for many families that had previously been considered to be not sufficiently creditworthy to qualify for a mortgage. These families increased the demand for real estate and prices rose. To mortgage brokers and mortgage lenders, the combination of more lending and higher house prices was attractive. More lending meant bigger profits. Higher house prices meant that the lending was well covered by the underlying collateral. If the borrower defaulted, the resulting foreclosure would not lead to a loss.

How could mortgage brokers and mortgage lenders keep increasing their profits? Their problem was that as house prices rose it was more difficult for first-time buyers to afford a house. In order to continue to attract new entrants to the housing market, they had to find ways to relax their lending standards even more and this is exactly what they did. The amount lent as a percentage of the house price increased. Adjustable rate mortgages (ARMs) were developed, where there was a low "teaser" rate of interest that would last for two or three years and be followed by a rate that was much higher.[1] A typical teaser rate was about 6% and the rate after the end of the teaser-rate period was typically 6% in excess of the six-month London Interbank Offered Rate (Libor). However, teaser rates as low as 1 or 2% have been reported. Lenders also became more cavalier in the way they reviewed mortgage applications. Indeed, the applicant's income and other information reported on the application form were frequently not checked.

Why was the government not regulating the behaviour of mortgage lenders? The answer is that the US government had been trying to expand home ownership since the 1990s, and had been putting pressure on mortgage lenders to increase loans to people with low and moderate income. Some state legislators (such as those in Ohio and Georgia) were concerned about what was going on and wanted to curtail what they considered to be predatory lending.[2] However, the courts decided that national standards should prevail.

A number of terms have been used to describe mortgage lending during the period leading up to the credit crunch. One is "liar loans", because individuals applying for a mortgage, knowing that no checks would be carried out, sometimes chose to lie on the application form. Another term used to describe some borrowers is "Ninja" (no income, no job, no assets). To quote from Krinsman (2007):

> In 2005 and 2006 lenders made it easier for borrowers to obtain subprime loans. For example, the typical subprime borrower with a FICO credit score between 450 and 680 could obtain a loan with little or no down payment, provide little or no documented proof of income or assets, obtain a loan with a low initial "teaser" interest rate that reset to a new, higher rate after two or three years.

Mortgages where the borrower had a Fair Isaac Corporation (FICO) credit score of less than 620 were typically classified as subprime but, when the down payment was low, 680 was sometimes used as the subprime cutoff.

Mian and Sufi (2008) have carried out research confirming that there was a relaxation of the criteria used for mortgage lending. Their research defines "high denial zip codes" as zip codes where a high proportion of mortgage applicants had been turned down in 1996 and shows that mortgage origination grew particularly fast for these zip codes between 2000 and 2007. Moreover, their research shows that lending criteria were relaxed progressively through time rather than all at once because originations in high denial zip codes are an increasing function of time during the 2000–2007 period. Zimmerman (2007) provides some confirmation of this. He shows that subsequent default experience indicates that mortgages originated in 2006 were of a lower quality than those originated in 2005, and these were in turn of lower quality than the mortgages originated in 2004.

Standard & Poor's has estimated that subprime mortgage origination in 2006 alone totalled US$421 billion. AMP Capital Investors estimate that there was a total of US$1.4 trillion of subprime mortgages outstanding in July 2007.

One of the features of the US housing market is that mortgages are non-recourse in many states. This means that when there is a default the lender is able to take possession of the house but other assets of the borrower are off-limits. Consequently, the borrower has a free American-style put option. They can sell the house at any time to the lender for the principal outstanding on the mortgage. (During the teaser interest rate period this principal often increased, making the option more valuable.) Market participants realised belatedly how costly the put option could be. If the borrower had negative equity, the optimal decision was to exchange the house for the outstanding principal on the mortgage. The house was then sold, adding to the downward pressure on house prices.

It would be a mistake to assume that all mortgage defaulters were in the same position. Some were unable to meet mortgage payments and suffered greatly when they had to give up their homes. But many of the defaulters were speculators who bought multiple homes as rental properties and chose to exercise their put options. It was their tenants who suffered. There are also reports that some house owners (who were not speculators) were quite creative in extracting value from their put options. After handing the keys to their houses to the lender, they turned around and bought (sometimes at a bargain price) other houses that were in foreclosure. Imagine two people owning identical houses next to each other. Both have mortgages of US$250,000. Both houses are worth US$200,000 and in foreclosure can be expected to sell for US$170,000. What is the owners' optimal strategy? The answer is that each person should exercise the put option and buy the neighbour's house. (There were ways of doing this without getting a bad credit rating.)

As Figure 1.1 illustrates, the bubble burst during the 2006–7 period. Many mortgage holders found they could no longer afford mortgages when teaser rates ended. Foreclosures increased. House prices declined. This resulted in other mortgage holders, who had borrowed 100% (or close to 100%) of the cost of a house, having negative equity. Some exercised their implicit put options and "walked away" from their houses and their mortgage obligations. This reinforced the downward trend in house prices.

The US was not alone in experiencing declining real estate prices. Prices declined in many other countries as well. The UK was particularly badly affected.

SECURITISATION

The originators of mortgages in many cases chose to securitise mortgages rather than fund the mortgages themselves. Securitisation has been an important and useful tool in financial markets for many years. It underlies the "originate-to-distribute" model that was widely used by banks prior to 2007.

Securitisation played a part in the creation of the housing bubble. Research by Keys *et al* (2008) shows that there was a link between mortgage securitisation and the relaxation of lending standards. When considering new mortgage applications, the question was not "Is this a credit we want to assume?" Instead it was "Is this a mortgage we can make money on by selling it to someone else?"

When mortgages were securitised, the only useful information received about the mortgages by the buyers of the products that were created from them was the loan-to-value ratio (ie, the ratio of the size of the loan to the assessed value of the house) and the borrower's FICO score. The reason why lenders did not check information on things such as the applicant's income, the number of years the applicant had lived at their current address, and so on was that this information was considered irrelevant. The most important thing for the lender was whether the mortgage could be sold to others, and this depended primarily on the loan-to-value ratio and the applicant's FICO score.

It is interesting to note in passing that both the loan-to-value ratio and the FICO score were of doubtful quality. The property assessors who determined the value of a house at the time of a mortgage application sometimes succumbed to pressure from the lenders to come up with high values. Potential borrowers were sometimes counselled to take certain actions that would improve their FICO scores.[3]

We now consider the products that were created from the mortgages.

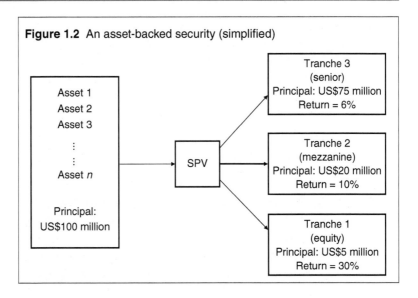

Figure 1.2 An asset-backed security (simplified)

Asset-backed securities

The main securities created from pools of mortgages were asset-backed securities (ABSs). Figure 1.2 shows a simple example illustrating the features of an asset-backed security. A portfolio of risky income-producing assets is sold by the originators of the assets to a special purpose vehicle (SPV) and the cashflows from the assets are allocated to tranches. In Figure 1.2 there are three tranches: the senior tranche, the mezzanine tranche and the equity tranche. The portfolio has a principal of US$100 million. This is divided as follows: US$75 million to the senior tranche, US$20 million to the mezzanine tranche and US$5 million to the equity tranche. The senior tranche is promised a return of 6%, the mezzanine tranche is promised a return of 10% and the equity tranche is promised a return of 30%.

The equity tranche is much less likely to realise its promised return than the other two tranches. An ABS is defined by specifying what is known as a "waterfall". This defines the rules for allocating cashflows from the income-producing assets to the tranches. Typically, cashflows from the assets during a particular time period are allocated to the senior tranche until the senior tranche has received its promised return. Assuming that the promised return to the senior tranche is made in full, cashflows are then allocated to the mezzanine tranche. If the promised return to the mezzanine tranche is made in full and cashflows are left over, they are allocated to the equity tranche. The precise waterfall rules are outlined in a legal document that is usually several hundred pages long. If any cash-flows remain after the equity tranche holders have received their promised returns, they are usually used to repay principal on the senior tranche.

When an ABS is created from a pool of mortgages it typically lasts for the whole life of the mortgages. The weighted average life of the mortgage pool depends on prepayments and defaults. At some stage, principal payments are made to tranches. The extent to which the tranches get their principal back depends on losses on the underlying assets. In Figure 1.2 the first 5% of losses are borne by the principal of the equity tranche. If losses exceed 5%, the equity tranche loses all its principal and some losses are borne by the principal of the mezzanine tranche. If losses exceed 25%, the mezzanine tranche loses all its principal and some losses are borne by the principal of the senior tranche.

There are, therefore, two ways of looking at an asset-backed security. One is with reference to the waterfall rules. Cashflows go first to the senior tranche, then to the mezzanine tranche and then to the equity tranche. The other is in terms of losses. Losses of principal are first borne by the equity tranche, then by the mezzanine tranche and then by the senior tranche.

The ABS is designed so that the senior tranche is rated AAA/Aaa. The mezzanine tranche is typically rated BBB/Baa. The equity tranche is typically unrated. Unlike the ratings assigned to bonds, the ratings assigned to the tranches of an asset-backed security are what might be termed "negotiated ratings". The objective of the creator of the ABS is to make the senior tranche as big as possible without losing its AAA/Aaa credit rating. (This maximises the profitability of the structure.) The ABS creator examines information published by rating agencies on how tranches are rated and may present several structures to rating agencies for a preliminary evaluation before choosing the final one.

ABS collateralised debt obligations

Finding investors to buy the AAA-rated senior tranches created from subprime mortgages was not difficult for the creators of an asset-backed security. Equity tranches were typically retained by the originators of the mortgages or sold to a hedge fund. Finding investors

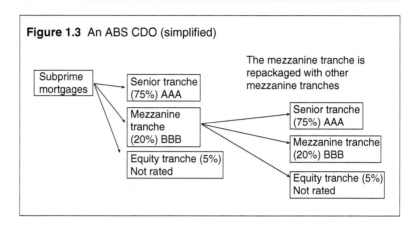

Figure 1.3 An ABS CDO (simplified)

for the mezzanine tranches was relatively difficult. This led financial engineers to be creative (arguably too creative). Financial engineers created an asset-backed security from the mezzanine tranches of different ABSs that were created from subprime mortgages. This is known as an asset-backed security collateralised debt obligation (ABS CDO) and is illustrated in Figure 1.3.

The senior tranche of the ABS CDO is rated AAA/Aaa. This means that the total of the AAA-rated instruments created in the example that is considered here is 90% (75% plus 75% of 20%) of the principal of the underlying mortgage portfolio. This seems high but, if the securitisation were carried further with an asset-backed security being created from the mezzanine tranches of ABS CDOs (and this did happen), the percentage would be pushed even higher.

In the example in Figure 1.3, the AAA-rated tranche of the ABSs would probably have been downgraded in the second half of 2007. However, it is likely to receive its promised return if losses on the underlying mortgage portfolio are less than 25% because all losses of principal would then be absorbed by the more junior tranches. The AAA-rated tranche of the ABS CDO in Figure 1.3 is much more risky. It will get paid the promised return if losses on the underlying portfolio are 10% or less because in that case mezzanine tranches of ABSs have to absorb losses equal to 5% of the ABS principal or less. As they have a total principal of 20% of the ABS principal, their loss is at most 5/20 or 25%. At worst this wipes out the equity tranche and mezzanine tranche of the ABS CDO but leaves the senior tranche unscathed.

Table 1.1 Examples of losses to AAA tranches of ABS CDO

Losses to subprime portfolios (%)	Losses to mezzanine tranche of ABS (%)	Losses to equity tranche of ABS CDO (%)	Losses to mezzanine tranche of ABS CDO (%)	Losses to senior tranche of ABS CDO (%)
10	25	100	100	0
15	50	100	100	33.3
20	75	100	100	66.7
25	100	100	100	100

The senior tranche of the ABS CDO suffers losses if losses on the underlying portfolios are more than 10%. Consider, for example, the situation where losses are 20% on the underlying portfolios. In this case, losses on the mezzanine tranches are 15/20 or 75% of their principal. The first 25% is absorbed by the equity and mezzanine tranches of the ABS CDO. The senior tranche of the ABS CDO therefore loses 50/75 or 66.7% of its value. These and other results are summarised in Table 1.1.

ABSs and ABS CDOs in practice

Figure 1.3 illustrates the nature of the securitisations that were carried out. In practice, more tranches were created and many of the tranches were thinner (ie, they corresponded to a narrower range of losses) than those in Figure 1.3. Figure 1.4 shows a more realistic example of the structures that were created. This is taken from an illustration by Gorton (2008), which was in turn taken from UBS (2007).

Two ABS CDOs are created in Figure 1.4. One is created from the BBB-rated tranches of ABSs (similarly to the ABS CDO in Figure 1.3). This is referred to as a Mezzanine ABS CDO (or Mezz ABS CDO). The other is from the AAA, AA and A tranches of ABSs. This is referred to as a High Grade ABS CDO. There is also a third level of securitisation, based on the A and AA tranches of the Mezz ABS CDO.

Many of the tranches in Figure 1.4 (for example, the BBB tranches of the ABS that cover losses from 1% to 4% and are used to create the Mezz ABS CDO) seem to be very risky. In fact, they are less risky than they appear when the details of the waterfalls of the underlying

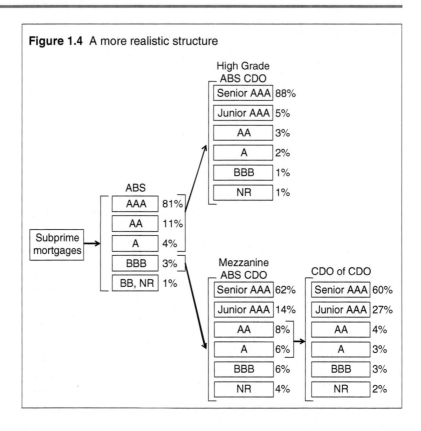

Figure 1.4 A more realistic structure

ABSs are taken into account. In the arrangement in Figure 1.4 there is some overcollateralisation, with the face value of the mortgages being greater than the face value of the instruments that are created by the ABSs. There is also what is termed "excess spread". This means that the weighted average of the returns promised to tranche holders is less than the weighted average of the interest due on the mortgages. If, because of these features, there are cashflows left over when all ABS tranches have received their promised returns, the cashflows are used to reduce the principal on the senior tranches.

Many banks have lost money investing in the senior tranches of Mezz ABS CDOs. The investments were typically financed at Libor and promised a return quite a bit higher than Libor. Because they were rated AAA, the capital requirements were minimal. In July 2008 Merrill Lynch agreed to sell senior tranches of Mezz ABS CDOs that had previously been rated AAA and had a principal of US$30.6 billion to Lone Star Funds for 22 cents on the dollar.[4]

RATINGS

The rating agencies played a key role in the securitisation of mortgages. The traditional business of rating agencies is of course the rating of bonds. This is based largely on judgement. The rating process for instruments such as the tranches of ABSs and ABS CDOs was different from the rating of bonds because it was based primarily on models. The rating agencies published their models. Interestingly, different rating agencies used different criteria. Moody's criterion was expected loss. If a tranche has a similar expected loss to an Aaa bond, it was rated Aaa. The S&P criterion was probability of loss. If the probability of loss for a tranche was similar to the probability of default for an AAA bond, it was rated AAA.

Many traders relied on the AAA/Aaa ratings of senior tranches without developing their own models or carefully examining the assumptions on which the models of the rating agencies were based. Risk weights for the tranches were low (typically 7% of the tranche principal) and the promised return was much higher than that obtainable on other assets rated AAA/Aaa.

Were the ratings unreasonable? Hull and White (2009) have examined this question. They conclude that the AAA/Aaa ratings for the senior tranches of ABSs were not too unreasonable. However, the AAA/Aaa ratings awarded to the senior tranches of Mezz ABS CDOs are much less easy to defend. Although the BBB tranches from which Mezz ABS CDOs were created have no higher expected losses or probabilities of loss than bonds that are rated BBB, the probability distribution of their loss is quite different and this has implications for the riskiness of the tranches of Mezz ABS CDOs.[5]

Two key factors determining the riskiness of the tranches of ABS CDOs are the thickness of the underlying BBB tranches and the extent to which defaults are correlated across the different pools used to create the Mezz ABS CDO. Consider an extreme situation where the tranches are very thin and the mortgages in all pools have the same default rate. The BBB tranches of all the underlying ABSs then have a certain probability, say p, of being wiped out and a probability $1 - p$ of being untouched. All tranches of the ABS CDO are then equally risky. They also have a probability p of being wiped out and a probability $1 - p$ of being untouched. It would be appropriate to give all of them the same rating as the underlying BBB tranches. This is an extreme example but it illustrates why BBB tranches should not be treated in the same way as BBB bonds for the second level of securitisation.

AVOIDING FUTURE CRISES

Many factors contributed to the financial crisis that started in 2007 (see, for example, Hull 2008, 2009). Mortgage originators used lax lending standards. Products were developed to enable mortgage originators to profitably transfer credit risk to investors. The products bought by investors were complex, and in many instances investors and rating agencies had inaccurate or incomplete information about the quality of the underlying assets. Rating agencies moved from their traditional business of rating bonds to rating structured products and assigned an AAA rating to tranches that were in some cases highly dependent on the structure of the correlation between the underlying assets.

The returns earned on AAA/Aaa tranches were high (eg, Libor plus 120 basis points) and they required very little capital because of the AAA rating. Traders loved the products because they gave good returns on regulatory capital and therefore led to high bonuses.

How can future crises be avoided? Here are a few observations.

Agency costs: originators and investors

Agency cost is a term used by economists to describe the cost in a situation where the interests of two parties in a business relationship are not perfectly aligned. It should be clear from the discussion earlier in this chapter that there were agency costs in the US mortgage market because the interests of the originators of mortgages and the interests of investors were not perfectly aligned. The present crisis might have been less severe if the originators of mortgages (and other assets where credit risk is transferred) were required by regulators to keep, say, 20% of each tranche created. This would have better aligned the interests of originators with the interests of the investors who bought the tranches. The market for structured products virtually disappeared during the credit crisis. However, the finance sector has a short memory. The market is likely to reappear at some future time. Regulators and rating agencies should be sensitive to situations where the interests of parties are not aligned.

The most important reason why originators should have a stake in all the tranches created is that this encourages the originators to make the same lending decisions that the investors would make. Another reason is that the originators often end up as administrators of the mortgages (collecting interest, making foreclosure decisions, etc). It is important that their decisions as administrators are made in the best interests of investors.

The originators of mortgages did sometimes keep the equity tranches of ABSs. This aligned their interests somewhat with the interests of the investors who purchased these tranches. However, the equity tranche was often regarded as a "free good". The originators had obtained adequate compensation for the mortgages from the sales of the other tranches to investors. Furthermore, once the equity tranche had been wiped out, mortgage originators had no stake at all in the performance of the mortgages.

It is important to note that there is a difference between a mortgage lender securitising 80% of its portfolio and a mortgage lender securitising 100% of its portfolio while keeping 20% of each tranche. In the first case, there will always be a suspicion that the better loans have been retained by the originator and that screening was lax on the rest. Rating agencies might reasonably assign a higher rating to tranches of a portfolio where a percentage of each tranche has been retained. However, the regulatory capital for the whole portfolio of mortgages that is originated should be the same in both cases.

This idea might have reduced the market excesses during the period leading up to the credit crunch of 2007. However, it should be acknowledged that one of the ironies of the credit crunch is that securitisation did not in many instances get the mortgages off the books of originating banks. Often AAA-rated senior tranches created by one part of a bank were bought by other parts of the bank. Because banks were both investors in and originators of mortgages, a reasonable alignment of the interests of investors and originators might be expected. But the part of the bank investing in the mortgages was usually far removed from the part of the bank originating the mortgages and there appears to have been little information flow from one to the other.

European Union regulators have made proposals similar to the one here (with 10% instead of 20% of each product created in a credit transfer arrangement being retained). Unsurprisingly, they have been met with a great deal of opposition from the banks, as pointed out by Rhode (2008). However, many banks have received huge capital injections from the government and may not be in a strong position to oppose the proposal.

Agency costs: financial institutions and their employees

Another source of agency costs concerns financial institutions and their employees. Employee compensation falls into three categories: regular salary, end-of-year bonus and stock or stock options. Many employees at all levels of seniority in financial institutions, particularly traders, receive much of their compensation in the form of end-of-year bonuses. This form of compensation tends to focus the attention of the employee on short-term results.

If an employee generates huge profits one year and is responsible for severe losses the next year, the employee will receive a big bonus the first year and will not have to return it the following year. The employee might lose their job as a result of the second year losses, but even that is not a disaster. Financial institutions seem to be surprisingly willing to recruit individuals with losses on their résumés.

Imagine you are an employee of a financial institution buying tranches of ABSs and ABS CDOs in 2006. Almost certainly you would have recognised that there was a bubble in the US housing market and would expect that bubble to burst sooner or later. However, it is possible that you would decide to continue trading. If the bubble did not burst until after December 31, 2006, you would still get a nice bonus at the end of 2006.

It is not necessarily the case that salaries on Wall Street are too high. Instead, it is the case that they should be calculated differently. It would be an improvement if annual bonuses reflected performance over a longer period of time than one year (say, five years). One idea is the following. At the end of each year a financial institution awards a "bonus accrual" (positive or negative) to each employee, reflecting the employee's contribution to the business. The actual cash bonus received by an employee at the end of a year would be the average bonus accrual over the previous five years or zero, whichever is higher. For the purpose of this calculation, bonus accruals would be set equal to zero for years prior to the employee joining the financial institution (unless the employee manages to negotiate otherwise) and bonuses would not be paid after an employee leaves it. Although not perfect, this type of plan would motivate employees to use a multi-year time horizon when making decisions.

Transparency

An ABS or an asset-backed security CDO is typically defined by a legal document several hundred pages long. As already mentioned, many investors did not analyse this document carefully when they bought AAA-rated tranches of the structured products. They relied on the AAA label. Once the tranches were perceived as risky it became almost impossible to trade them. This was because potential investors did not understand enough about the underlying portfolio and the algorithm used to determine the cashflows received by the various tranches.

ABSs, and particularly ABS CDOs, are arguably among the most complex credit derivatives that are traded. Lawyers should move with the times and define these instruments using software rather than words. In addition to providing a data file with the attributes of the mortgages and other instruments underlying the derivatives, lawyers should provide software enabling the cashflows realised by different tranches in different circumstances to be calculated. The user's inputs to the software would define a possible outcome concerning interest and principal payments on the underlying instruments each year. The outputs would be the cashflows realised by each tranche holder each year. The problems of defining structures like ABS CDOs where tranches are defined in terms of many other tranches could be handled efficiently with the software tools that exist today. The creators of tranches should be required to publish information about the performance of the underlying assets and tranches in a way that is compatible with the software.

There are companies that provide investors with detailed information about tranches of the sort suggested here. However, the information is expensive and not widely available to researchers and financial commentators. Ensuring that the information is widely available would be advantageous for the functioning of markets.

Investors and independent researchers would be able to run scenario analyses and form their own opinions about the values of different tranches. It is likely that this would have led to the illiquidity of the ABS and ABS CDO market in 2007 and 2008 not being as severe as it was. (Indeed, investors might have better understood the risks in the ABS CDO market in the first place.) A good case can be made for defining many derivatives (particularly the more complex ones) using software rather than written confirmations because the latter are very cumbersome as a description of how the products work.

The need for models

Normally, financial institutions do not trade instruments unless they have satisfactory models for valuing them. Typically there is a group within a financial institution that has the responsibility of vetting the model used for valuing a product and the product cannot be traded in any volume until the model has been approved. What is surprising about the subprime crisis is that financial institutions were prepared to trade senior tranches of an asset-backed security or an asset-backed security CDO without a model. Possibly it was thought that a model is unnecessary for valuing an AAA-rated instrument. But the lack of a model makes risk management almost impossible and causes problems when the instrument is downgraded.

The readiness of financial institutions to trade ABS CDOs is particularly surprising. An ABS CDO is similar in structure to what is called a CDO squared in the synthetic CDO market. CDO squareds are recognised by traders in the synthetic CDO market as highly risky products that are difficult to price. The market for them is much reduced for this reason. A tranche of an asset-backed security CDO is no less risky and no less difficult to price than a tranche of a CDO squared, but it was nevertheless considered by many financial institutions to be a good investment. Because models were not developed, the key role of correlation in valuing ABSs and (particularly) ABS CDOs was not well understood.

How models are used

Having the models to value ABS and ABS CDOs would have helped, but it would not by itself have been enough to mitigate the subprime crisis. To understand how models might have helped we have to consider how they should have been used.

The risk measures used by regulators, and by financial institutions themselves, are largely based on historical experience. For example, value-at-risk (VaR) measures for market risk are typically based on the movements in market variables seen over the last two to four years. Credit risk measures are based on default experience stretching back over 100 years. Stress testing often involves looking at the largest market moves experienced over the last 10, 20 or 30 years.

There can be no question that historical data provides a useful guide for risk managers. But historical data cannot be used in conjunction with models in a mechanistic way to determine if risks are acceptable. In risk management it is important that models be supplemented with human judgement. A risk management committee consisting of senior managers should meet regularly to consider the key risks facing a financial institution. Stress tests should be based on the scenarios generated by these managers in addition to those generated from historical data. The risk committee should be particularly sensitive to situations where the market appears to be showing bouts of "irrational exuberance".[6]

One of the lessons from past financial crises is that correlations increase in stressed market conditions. Using standard techniques to estimate correlations from past data and assuming that those correlations will apply in stressed markets is not appropriate. One of the roles of the risk management committee would have been to recognise the bubble in house prices and insist that stress tests where default rates simultaneously rise in all parts of the country be carried out. Of course, it is also important that key decision makers within the bank actually listen to risk managers and the risk management committee, particularly during periods of irrational exuberance. There is some evidence that they are reluctant to do this.

REGULATORY CHANGES

There can be little doubt that once financial institutions recover from the current crisis the regulatory environment will change. Banks and other financial institutions will be given less discretion to assess risks for themselves. The replacement of Basel I by Basel II was a trend toward self-regulation. It is likely that this trend will be reversed.

The most important thing that regulators can do is insist that all transactions, regardless of the credit ratings of the two sides to the transactions, are collateralised. In some cases, the collateralisation will involve clearinghouses. In other cases it will involve two-way collateralisation agreements with zero thresholds. It will hopefully never again be possible for a financial institution such as AIG to take a huge exposure without posting collateral.

CONCLUSIONS

The credit crisis that started in 2007 had a devastating effect on financial markets throughout the world. Its origins can be found in the US housing market. The US government was keen to encourage home ownership. Interest rates were low. Mortgage brokers and mortgage lenders found it attractive to do more business by relaxing their lending standards. Products for securitising mortgages had been developed so that the investors bearing the credit risk were not necessarily the same as the original lenders. Rating agencies gave an AAA rating to senior tranches that were created by securitisation. There was no shortage of buyers for the AAA-rated securities that were created because their yields were higher than the yields on other AAA-rated securities. Banks thought the "good times" would continue and, because compensation plans focused their attention on short-term profits, chose to ignore the housing bubble and its potential impact on the very complicated products they were trading.

House prices rose as both first-time buyers and speculators entered the market. Some mortgages had included a low "teaser rate" for two or three years. After the teaser rate ended, there was a significant increase in the interest rate for many borrowers. Unable to meet the higher interest rates, they had no choice but to default. This led to foreclosures and an increase in the supply of houses being sold. The price increases between 2000 and 2006 began to be reversed in 2006 and 2007. Speculators and others who found that the amount owing on their mortgages was less than the value of their houses (ie, they had negative equity) defaulted. This accentuated the price decline.

There are a number of steps that need to be taken to avoid future crises. The interests of the originators of loans should be aligned with the interests of those who ultimately bear the credit risk. This could be achieved by requiring originators of loans to keep a stake in each instrument created from the loans. The compensation plans within financial institutions should be changed so that there is much less emphasis on short-term performance. Some banks, such as UBS, moved in this direction in late 2008 and early 2009. The products that are traded should be made more transparent so that their risks are widely understood. Risk management should involve a heavy dose of managerial judgement, not just the mechanistic application of models. Finally, collateralisation, either through clearinghouses or through bilateral collateralisation agreements, should become a compulsory feature of derivatives markets.

> The author is grateful to Richard Cantor and Roger Stein for useful comments on an earlier draft. All views expressed are the author's own. First published as part of *The Journal of Credit Risk* Special Issue on "Lessons from the Credit Crisis" in summer 2009.

1   If real estate prices increased, lenders expected the borrowers to prepay and take out a new mortgage at the end of the teaser rate period. This would have been profitable for the lenders. Prepayment penalties, often zero on prime mortgages, were quite high on subprime mortgages.
2   "Predatory lending" describes the situation where a lender deceptively convinces borrowers to agree to unfair and abusive loan terms.
3   One such action might be to make regular payments on a credit card for a few months.
4   Merrill Lynch agreed to finance 75% of the purchase price. When the value of the tranches fell below 16.5 cents on the dollar, Merrill Lynch found itself owning the assets again.
5   Given that Mezz ABS CDOs accounted for a small percentage of the investment in the products created for mortgages, the rating agencies are not as blameworthy as is sometimes supposed.
6   "Irrational exuberance" was a term coined by Alan Greenspan during the bull market of the 1990s.

REFERENCES

Gorton, G., 2008, "The Panic of 2007", Working Paper, Yale School of Management.

Hull, J. C., 2008, "The Financial Crisis of 2007: Another Case of Irrational Exuberance", in *The Finance Crisis and Rescue: What Went Wrong? Why? What Lessons Can Be Learned?* (University of Toronto Press).

Hull, J. C., 2009, *Risk Management and Financial Institutions*, Second Edition (Upper Saddle River, NJ: Pearson).

Hull, J. C., and A. White, 2009, "The Risk of Tranches Created from Subprime Mortgages", Working Paper, University of Toronto.

Keys, B. J., T. Mukherjee, A. Seru and V. Vig, 2008, "Did Securitization Lead to Lax Screening? Evidence from Subprime Loans", Working Paper, University of Michigan.

Krinsman, A. N., 2007, "Subprime Mortgage Meltdown: How Did It Happen and How Will It End?" *Journal of Structured Finance*, Summer, pp. 13–19.

Mian, A., and A. Sufi, 2008, "The Consequences of Mortgage Credit Expansion: Evidence from the 2007 Mortgage Default Crisis", Working Paper, Graduate School of Business, University of Chicago.

Rhode, W., 2008, "Keep What You Sow", *Risk Magazine* **21**(10), pp. 56–58.

UBS, 2007, "Market Commentary", December 13.

Zimmerman, T., 2007, "The Great Subprime Meltdown", *Journal of Structured Finance*, Fall, pp. 7–20.

2

Underwriting versus Economy: A New Approach to Decomposing Mortgage Losses

Ashish Das, Roger M. Stein
Moody's Research Labs

Recent events in the mortgage market have led market participants and observers to discuss the role of underwriting standards in the 2007–9 market crisis. This chapter presents some stylised facts based on a series of *ex post* simulation experiments that were conducted using loan-by-loan data on 136 subprime mortgage pools underlying US residential mortgage-backed securities (RMBSs) issued between 2002 and 2007. The goal of these experiments is to provide some sense of the degree to which shifts in underwriting standards and the changing economic environment affect subsequent pool performance. In order to accomplish this decomposition, an instrument based on the transformation of a readily available Federal Reserve (hereafter simply referred to as "Fed") series is used that exogenises underwriting explicitly. This exogeneity is particularly convenient in settings where underwriting standards and the future state of the economy are evolving in tandem, as it permits a separation of these two effects. An attractive feature of this measure is that it can be observed in real time, and thus may be useful for forecasting subsequent mortgage performance for newly originated mortgages before any performance history is available on the mortgages.

While these findings are stylised, the experiments suggest that underwriting quality is an important contributor to abnormal pool loss levels, though it contributes far less than the dramatic changes in the economy do. Underwriting quality can lead directly to losses, as in the case of higher default rates for borrowers, or can affect losses in conjunction with declines in the economy, as in the case of a loan-to-value (LTV) ratio that turns out to be higher than reported due to more lenient verification standards, but that becomes more important as home prices decline further, increasing the LTV.

To give some sense of the results, one set of experiments suggests that from 2005 Q4 to 2007 Q1 (considered by many to include some of the poorest quality vintages), about 33%, in relative terms,[1] of the abnormal losses could be explained either by the direct impact of underwriting quality or by the indirect effect of underwriting quality that became evident in declining economic conditions. (Abnormal losses are defined more fully in what follows.)

At first glance, it would appear that statistics describing declining pool quality, in terms of measures such as average FICO scores or combined loan-to-value (CLTV), would be sufficient measures of underwriting quality. However, recent research in this area suggests that such may not be the case. For example, Demyanyk and Van Hemert (2008) point out that relative risk associated with given CLTV levels, by these authors' measures, increased during the period 2001 to 2007. In other words, the same value of CLTV implied different risk in different vintages. Demyanyk and Van Hemert develop a model of expected loan performance based on CLTV and other common factors and measure deviations over time of realised performance from expected performance. Based on this model, they go on to assert that "loan quality – adjusted for observed characteristics and macroeconomic circumstances – deteriorated monotonically between 2001 and 2007". This is true despite their remark that observed loan characteristics were not sufficiently different from those over the prior five years to explain the performance.

A number of other papers attempt to link the increased losses on subprime mortgage loans in 2006 and 2007 to the increase in securitisation and the resulting decrease in underwriting rigour among some market participants. Mian and Sufi (2008) construct a supply and demand argument and then use detailed postal-code level data to show that the sharp increase in mortgage defaults occurred in zip codes with disproportionately large numbers of subprime borrowers as of 1996. These zip codes subsequently experienced unprecedented relative growth in mortgage credit (pent-up demand) despite sharply declining relative income growth. Through arguments that eliminate income growth or the expectation of higher house prices as potential reasons for the sharp growth in mortgage credit, the authors provide some evidence, which they characterise as suggestive, that greater moral hazard on the part of originators may be the cause of the decline in the underwriting conditions.

Keys et al (2007) also provide evidence of differential underwriting standards using a large loan-level data set. They relate this decline to moral hazard introduced as a result of securitisation. Using the industry rule of thumb that loans to borrowers having a FICO score of 620+ are more likely to be securitised than otherwise, the authors demonstrate that losses on loans with FICO scores just below 620 (low securitisation probability) have substantially lower default rates than those with FICO scores of 621 (just above the cutoff and therefore having higher securitisation probability). Because the FICO scores (which the authors assume to be a proxy for credit quality) are quite close, the lower default rates on unsecuritised (retained) mortgages suggest that additional screening may have been done for the loans that had a lower probability of securitisation. In other words, lenders appeared less likely to scrutinise the soft characteristics of a borrower with a FICO score of 620+ given the substantially higher probability that the loan would be securitised. In a related article, Dell'Ariccia et al (2008) focus on a number of explanations for poor performance of subprime loans, one of which relates to the securitisation rate within different Metropolitan Statistical Areas. The authors provide some evidence that lending standards (as measured primarily by mortgage application denial rates) declined more in areas with higher mortgage securitisation rates. Rajan et al (2008) examine the incentives for lenders to seek and evaluate "soft" information in addition to the measures used for securitisation (eg, FICO score, CLTV, etc). Using an approach that is similar in concept to that of Demyanyk and Van Hemert (2008), they assert that statistical default models fitted in a low securitisation period that use standard financial factors systematically underpredict default for borrowers in a high securitisation period in environments in which the underwriters begin not to screen for valuable soft information.

In addition to the failure of lenders to monitor soft information about borrowers, evidence has also begun to appear supporting the incidence of outright fraud (Federal Bureau of Investigation 2008). Drawing on a number of third-party sources, the authors report that between 30% and 70% of early payment defaults may be linked to borrower misrepresentation on loan applications. Further, they report that the list of the top 10 states with the highest mortgage foreclosure rates also contained seven of the top 10 states for reported mortgage fraud.

While these studies provide suggestive evidence of reduced underwriting quality for residential mortgages and link this to increased loss rates, it would be useful to characterise more precisely the impact of this behaviour. In light (*ex post*) of the role of underwriting standards in influencing losses, whether due to loosening standards by banks or other behaviours by participants in the mortgage granting process, it is useful not only to estimate the impact of this change in underwriting quality on subsequent pool losses but also to determine the relative contribution to losses from underwriting conditions compared with the relative contribution from the economic environment.

Disentangling the effects of changes in key economic factors, such as home prices and the effects of underwriting standards, poses identification issues since both are time varying and endogenous to a model. In a study that is closest in objective to this one, Anderson *et al* (2008) use aggregate foreclosure data to estimate the differential role played by underwriting and changes in the economy to explain aggregate foreclosure levels. These authors estimate a model of aggregate foreclosures based on average pool-level loan quality statistics and a proprietary index of the "favourability of the economic environment" for subprime borrowers. By including a fixed effect for each vintage, they develop an (endogenous) index of implied vintage effects not explained by the quality of the mortgages or the state of the economy. They interpret this fixed effect as a measure of underwriting quality and report that in their model, underwriting quality explains about half of the increased foreclosures experienced in recent subprime vintages, while the economic downturn explains the remaining half.

The experiments presented here differ from Anderson *et al* (2008) in three important ways. Firstly, the index proposed by Anderson *et al* is necessarily a lagging one. The use of fixed effects implies the need to observe foreclosures in the periods following a particular vintage in order to assess the effect of underwriting during that vintage. For example, in order to estimate the underwriting quality of the 2009 Q3 vintage we would need to wait until the performance of loans originated in 2009 Q3 became available, which could take a year or more (though once the mortgages were seasoned, economic forecasts could be used to project losses from that point forward). In contrast, the instrument used here, which is described more fully later (see page 33 onwards), is a real-time measure that can be observed almost concurrently with the origination of the loans affected by underwriting quality. Secondly, the metric is a direct measure of underwriting quality that is exogenous to the data, rather than an endogenous one inferred from fixed effects or divergence between model and realised performance (which may be explained by a number of variables). As such, it is less likely to be contaminated by other economic factors. Finally, this metric is used in the study of loan-level rather than aggregate data. As a result, the model used here explicitly incorporates the behaviour associated with different loan structures and borrower incentives in addition to the heterogeneous nature of many mortgage pools, which often contain loans from a number of underwriting periods.

The presence of inherent optionality associated with mortgage loans in the US market that entitle the borrower to prepay the mortgage at any time, can confound inferences based on aggregate pool-level data. This is because portfolio-level summary statistics do not typically provide enough high-resolution information about the structure of the loans in the portfolio to account for features such as prepayment optionality. For example, when low foreclosure rates are observed in a portfolio over time, it is unclear whether these rates are low because the inherent default risk of the pool (unconditional default probability) is low or because a high prepayment rate for certain types of loans or borrowers allowed risky borrowers to prepay before they would have defaulted (conditional default probability) in a particular state of the world. Though foreclosure rates might appear the same in both cases, in the second case, observed foreclosure rates could jump suddenly if prepayment were no longer available or attractive to borrowers (due to, for example, increased interest rates).

In addition to the prepayment behaviour, it can be important to consider the joint distributions of factors rather than the marginal summaries provided at the pool level. For example, consider two pools with identical mean CLTVs and identical percentages of high- and low-documentation loans. In one pool all borrowers have the same CLTV, while in the other the borrowers are clustered into high- and low-CLTV groups. In the second pool, it also turns out that the highest CLTV loans are also those that are made to the low-documentation borrowers, while the low CLTV loans are all made to full-documentation borrowers. The second pool may have a different risk profile from the first, particularly in stress cases. However, without detailed loan-level information, it is often not possible to ascertain whether in the second pool the risk associated with higher leverage is compounded by low documentation while in the first pool it is not.

The experiments reported in this chapter make use of a newly introduced simulation tool that utilises loan- and borrower-specific attributes to decompose mortgage losses into those related to conditional prepayment probability, those related to conditional default probability and those related to conditional loss given default (LGD). This decomposition permits the introduction of an additional factor, related only to underwriting quality at the time of origination, which differentially affects loss-related behaviour. Importantly, this approach exogenises underwriting quality rather than inferring it from subsequent performance (as in, for example, Anderson *et al* (2008), Mian and Sufi (2008) or Rajan *et al* (2008)). Thus, it is possible to explicitly characterised the levels of underwriting quality at the time loans were originated and use these levels to decompose pool losses directly rather than inferring underwriting quality indirectly from the performance itself.

This chapter makes a first attempt at using loan-by-loan data and tools that reflect the optionality inherent in loans of different types in order to gauge the effect of underwriting versus the effect of changes in the economy on loan losses.

The informal nature of the experiments reported here must be emphasised. The authors hope that these preliminary findings will encourage other researchers to explore this phenomenon further and also provide some initial directional guidance to market participants interested in these effects. Because the chapter's goal is to provide stylised observations rather than rigorous mathematical results, the models used are not discussed in detail. However, the next section provides some background information in order to put the experiments into context. Interested readers can find more detail on the models in Kothari and Forster (2008).

The remainder of this chapter is structured as follows. The next section describes the structure of the commercial model used in the experiments. We then describe the factor used to measure underwriting quality in different vintages and presents some evidence that it provides information not present in either loan- and borrower-level measures of portfolio quality or measures of the state of the macroeconomy. Next we describe the design of the experiments and the data used in them. We then present the main results of the chapter and finally present some conclusions and directions for future work.

THE MODEL AND DATA

A new portfolio-based simulation tool called "Moody's mortgage metrics" was used for the experiments. A fuller description of the tool can be found in Kothari and Forster (2008).[2] The tool was released in November 2008. To provide context for these experiments, this section gives a brief description of this portfolio tool.

Model overview

Losses in a mortgage pool can be conceptually explained through two dominant measures of loss: the probability of default and the severity of losses in the event of default. However, in addition to these processes, understanding the prepayment behaviour of borrowers, given the type of mortgage they hold, is also helpful in understanding pool losses. A shift in prepayment rates does not change an individual borrower's credit quality. However, the exposure of a particular mortgage pool to risky borrowers is reduced by prepayments since borrowers that prepay cannot default in the current pool.

The simulator used in the experiments is a portfolio tool that assesses the credit risk of subprime residential mortgage portfolios by explicitly modelling the prepayment, default and severity behaviour of individual mortgages as a function of the loan characteristics and the values of macroeconomic factors (at the state and Metropolitan Statistical Area level). The simulator uses a multi-step Monte Carlo engine to simulate possible economic paths. For each of the loans in a mortgage portfolio, loan-level models calculate default and prepayment probabilities each quarter over a 10-year projection period. Defaults and prepayments are simulated based on these probabilities and, for loans that default, severity (LGD) is also calculated conditional on the loan-level and macroeconomic factors. The simulated losses for all loans in the portfolio are aggregated to obtain pool-level losses in each of the simulated economic paths, thereby producing a distribution of losses. Thus, pool losses are a result of the correlated behaviours (default, prepayment and severity) associated with loan-level characteristics (loan structure, borrower type, etc) as well as with macroeconomic factors.

The remainder of this section gives a high-level outline of the main features of the specific components of the simulator.

The economic models: term structure, home price appreciation and unemployment

The risk-free interest rates are simulated using a two-factor Cox–Ingersoll–Ross term-structure model (Cox *et al* 1985). The subprime market rate (which is important for calculating quantities such as the mortgage premium or incentive of borrowers to refinance for rate reduction) is also simulated as a function of the aggregate borrower-specific characteristics and the prevailing interest rate environment. Home price appreciation (HPA) and unemployment models are autoregressive models (which use the last two quarters of unemployment and home price movement, respectively, as well as the current level of 10-year Treasury Bonds). The simulator uses separate models for national HPA and unemployment, state-level HPA and unemployment and, for many Metropolitan Statistical Areas, Metropolitan Statistical Area-level HPA and unemployment.

Loan-level models

The loan-level models incorporate borrower- and loan-specific factors such as the FICO score, CLTV, documentation type, coupon rate, property type, loan type, loan purpose, loan size, legal jurisdiction, etc. Some factors (eg, CLTV and coupon rate) are updated as economic factors (eg, local home prices and London Interbank Offered Rate (Libor), respectively) change.

The models for predicting the two types of loan termination, prepayment and default, share a common probability framework. They are of the class of hazard rate or survival models based on time-to-event data. The implementation uses a Cox hazard model.

Unlike either the prepayment or default processes, the severity (or LGD process) is not described by a probability, but rather by a ratio: the proportion of the total amount of the loan that is lost when a borrower defaults. As a result, the LGD calculations follow a regression approach that assumes that the dependent variable is beta distributed.

Simulation algorithm

The various economic factor and loan-level behaviour models are integrated through a multi-step Monte Carlo simulation by using the following (highly summarised) algorithm:

1. For each iteration
    a. Generate one realisation of each economic scenario (40 quarters)
        i. For each quarter
            1. For each non-defaulted, non-prepaid state of the simulated loan
                a. Determine the loan status this quarter
                      i. If default
                          1. mark loan as defaulted
                          2. determine loan-level severity
                          3. record a loss
                      ii. If prepay mark loan as prepaid
            2. End for loan
        ii. End for quarter
        iii. Sum losses for pool in period 40
    b. End for economic scenario
2. End for iteration
3. Calculate loss distribution based on the final losses for each pool in each scenario (there will be one point in the distribution for each scenario that represents the pool losses under that scenario).

The data

The experiments described in the remainder of the chapter make use of a data set of mortgage pools from 136 mortgage-backed transactions issued between 2002 and 2007. Particular interest is given to the performance of late-vintage mortgage pools. For the purposes of this chapter late-vintage pools are defined as those pools in the sample that underlie RMBS transactions originated in 2006 and 2007.

For each transaction, the experimental data set included loan-by-loan information on individual mortgages for all fields that were required in order to run the portfolio simulation. Importantly, in addition to the origination date of the RMBS transaction, each loan record also contained the origination date of the mortgage (often one or more quarters prior to the deal closing date of the RMBS), which allowed the identification of the quarter in which the underwriting environment should be observed for this loan.

In addition to data on the loans at origination for each transaction, lifetime-loss estimates for each transaction were compiled, based on Moody's analysis of current pool performance.[3] Importantly, these estimates were developed based on actual pool performance and projections about likely defaults and losses of loans that were already delinquent or performing. This contrasts with the simulator used for estimating loss distributions on new mortgage transactions without pool performance history. This data provides estimates of lifetime losses on mortgage pools that are still outstanding.

For clarity, Rocco (2009) reports two sets of forecasts: those that assume impact from government intervention and those that do not. Since it is difficult to model government intervention, the latter were more relevant in this exercise.

At this point it is useful to note that views on lifetime losses, both from an average-per-vintage perspective and from a transaction-specific perspective, vary widely among market participants, many of whom are examining the same or similar data. In reality, future losses cannot be observed, so estimates of these future losses are forecasts by their nature. That said, at the time these experiments were conducted (April 2009), the general consensus in terms of the order of magnitude of losses seems to cluster around levels that are not qualitatively dissimilar from the Moody's estimates. Of course even small differences in opinions about pool losses can translate into economically meaningful differences in losses at tranche level and in security valuation. However, since the goal in this exercise is to provide stylised observations about the drivers of these losses rather than precise economic quantities, even market participants with different views on lifetime losses due to differing assumptions or differing information sets may still find the results reported here to be of interest.

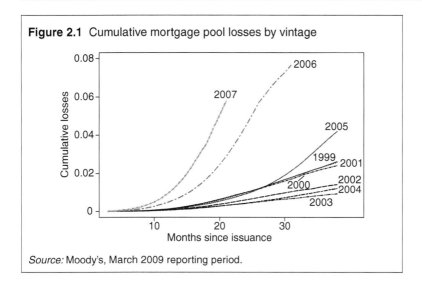

Figure 2.1 Cumulative mortgage pool losses by vintage

Source: Moody's, March 2009 reporting period.

INCORPORATING AN ASSESSMENT OF UNDERWRITING QUALITY

It is generally agreed that the quality of underwriting can vary over time. In hindsight, some periods, such as 2006 and 2007, appear to have been characterised by particularly lenient lending for a variety of reasons. Not surprisingly, the rates of delinquency and the values of severity for pools originated during these vintages are particularly high. This can be seen clearly in Figure 2.1, which shows average cumulative losses by vintage for subprime mortgage pools. The high loss rates of the late-vintage pools stands in stark contrast to the more modest levels of earlier vintages.

However, while the figure shows marked differences in performance between vintages, it does not provide much insight into the drivers of these changes. For example, the property values underlying many late-vintage loans have also deteriorated substantially, and have done so rapidly. This could explain a good deal of the higher losses. On the other hand, the anecdotal evidence, supported by some of the research mentioned in the introduction, suggests that there could also have been time-varying underwriting quality effects driving portions of this performance. Endogenous measures like the fixed effects associated with the vintage cannot always provide sufficient information to parse these factors. Thus, it was appealing to use an exogenous measure of underwriting quality in the current

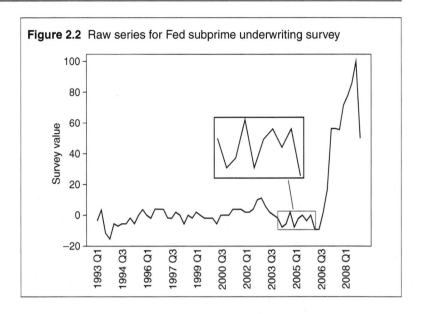

Figure 2.2 Raw series for Fed subprime underwriting survey

experiments. The simulator uses this factor to shift the default probabilities and the severity values to reflect the underwriting quality at the time the loan was originated. The factor is a variant on a data series provided by the Fed.

The series reports the results of a survey of bankers that The Fed conducts periodically in which it asks loan officers at various lending institutions whether their institutions are more or less likely to tighten their underwriting criteria in various asset classes, including mortgage loans, in the coming months. The Fed aggregates these responses and compiles a series that reflects net tightness of underwriting conditions based on this survey as the net percentage of the number of respondents who indicate tightening versus loosening.[4] For example, if the net tightness number is positive, it means that the underwriting quality is likely to tighten, whereas a negative number for net tightness means that the banks are likely to loosen the underwriting criteria. A variant of this measure was also used at the pool level in Hughes (2007). Before 2007 Q2, there was no subprime version of this series. In fact, The Fed initially reported a single series for all mortgages but switched in 2007 Q2 to separate series for prime and subprime markets. In order to create a contiguous series prior to this point, the newly released subprime series is adjusted to stitch it to the historical all-mortgage lending series.

Figure 2.2 shows the value of the raw series. From this figure, it is clear that the quarterly raw series is quite volatile. For example, note that in 2004 Q4, the series actually shows a tightening of standards, despite the loosening in the periods immediately before and after (boxed and inset in Figure 2.2), and the bankers reported tightening in 2006 Q3. This volatility is characteristic of the behaviour of the raw series. In early experiments, the raw series demonstrated little predictive power when used on its own. However, suitably smoothing this series (using, in this case, an eight-quarter moving average) appears to produce a factor that has greater explanatory power compared with the raw series. The experiments used a normalised version of the series, adjusted so that average underwriting tightness had a value of zero: positive values imply tighter underwriting reports and negative values imply looseness.

The results of the smoothing and the historical estimation used together produce a series that appears to be more predictive than the raw series. The smoothed series is shown in Figure 2.3.

To provide some context, three lagged economic series are also shown and each is compared with the lagged survey series. Visually, none of the three macro-series appear to have a strong pattern of co-movement with the underwriting series, although there is some commonality in the behaviour during some periods.

Examining the relationship of this series to losses on late-vintage pools provides some sense of the impact of underwriting on losses in general and this can be used to incorporate the impact of underwriting into the simulations. As shown in the next section, analysis using this underwriting quality factor enhanced the fits of estimated pool performance to projected lifetime pool performance. In other words, the underwriting quality factor appears to provide information beyond the economic factors used in the simulations. Importantly, it does so without requiring *a priori* assumptions about issues such as the length or shape of the credit cycle, etc.

For default and severity this factor is only relevant at the point of mortgage origination. The tightness of underwriting reflects an estimate of the leniency that the banking community overall reported exercising in underwriting loans at that time. Once the terms of the loan are set and the borrower is granted a loan, changes in underwriting will not affect the quality of underwriting for that specific loan. For this reason, while the behaviour of this factor is observed

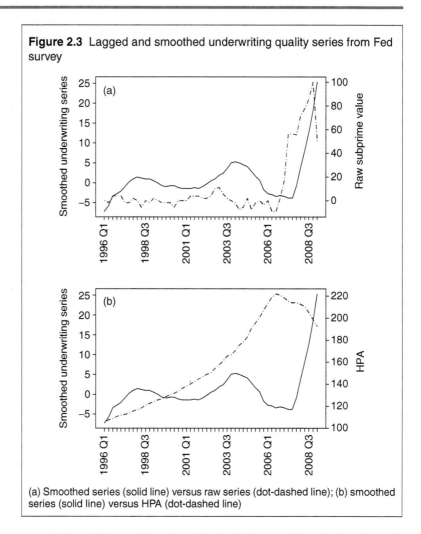

Figure 2.3 Lagged and smoothed underwriting quality series from Fed survey

(a) Smoothed series (solid line) versus raw series (dot-dashed line); (b) smoothed series (solid line) versus HPA (dot-dashed line)

quarterly and is used to adjust the default rate and severity for each loan in a given vintage, there is no need to simulate the vintage factor into the future, since all loans in a portfolio will already have closed and future changes in underwriting practices will not affect them.

Average loss estimates with and without underwriting quality adjustments

The remainder of this chapter describes experiments that rely on the simulation tool discussed in the previous section (see page 29 onwards). These experiments are augmented with the underwriting quality factor (described in this section) to decompose loss drivers

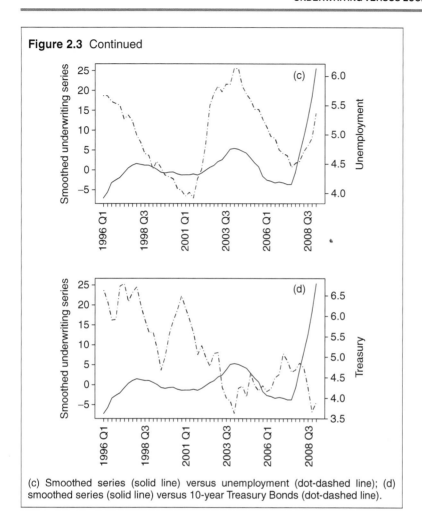

Figure 2.3 Continued

(c) Smoothed series (solid line) versus unemployment (dot-dashed line); (d) smoothed series (solid line) versus 10-year Treasury Bonds (dot-dashed line).

into those associated with generic mortgage pool quality, those associated with changes in the macroeconomic environment and those attributable to changes in underwriting quality during the period of study. In order to provide some sense of the effect of the underwriting quality factor, it is first necessary to demonstrate the general role of this factor in establishing a better fit to the estimated lifetime losses than appears possible using loan quality and economic factors alone.

To give some notion of this, the simulator estimates the lifetime mean loss rate for a pool using a 10-year horizon from the date of closing. More specifically, the simulator divides the 10-year loss

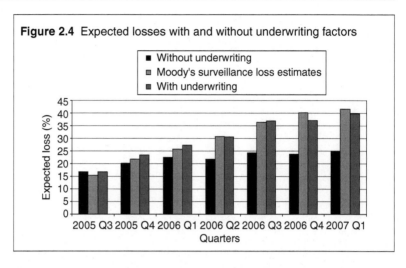

Figure 2.4 Expected losses with and without underwriting factors

horizon for a seasoned pool into two periods. The first period comprises the time span from the given transaction's closing to the start of the simulation (typically the current date). The losses for this period are estimated using original pool composition and the actual realised economic factors until the current date. Thus, some portion of the portfolio will default or prepay in the simulation based on the realised economy (though the affected loans in the simulation may not be the same as the loans that have actually defaulted and prepaid in the subsequent performance data). The second period is populated by simulating many paths for the economy from today to the end of the time remaining in the 10-year period. Estimated mean loss for the pool in any given economic path is simply the sum of the mean losses from the first period and the second period.

Note that the historical macroeconomic data used in these experiments was data on home prices, unemployment and interest-rate levels through 2008 Q4, which is the last reported period at the time of the experiments.

Figure 2.4 shows the estimated mean percentage losses[5] of the model for the 2005 Q3–2007 Q1 vintages with and without the underwriting factor. The light-grey bar in each group represents Moody's forecasted lifetime losses based on observed pool performance,[6] while the black bar represents simulation results based only on the realised economy without using the Fed underwriting factor. Finally, the dark grey bar shows the current model including the Fed underwriting factor.

Note that, in the case of the simulations that do not include the factor, simulated losses may agree reasonably well with a specific vintage (eg, 2005 Q3), but losses simulated on the other vintages are much lower (higher) than the realised losses. However, when including the transformed value of the Fed factor, realised losses on many vintages can be matched reasonably well. Note also that the difference between the simulated lifetime losses (without the underwriting factor) and empirical lifetime-loss estimates varies substantially. For example, in 2006 Q4, the relative gap is about 40%, while in 2005 Q4 it is only about 10%. This suggests that a simple multiplicative or additive adjustment will not capture the time-varying components of the loss process.

In hindsight, the behaviour of the model with this factor makes sense if, as most market participants and a number of researchers believe, there were changes in the information in various measures of loan quality and the rigour with which these were collected, verified and calculated. Thus, examining the performance of loan pools based solely on these criteria may miss the change in meaning of these factors.

THE EXPERIMENTS AND DATA

The method used for estimating the mean loss rate for a pool from an earlier vintage using a 10-year horizon simulation was described in the previous section. To recap, the simulator divides the 10-year loss horizon for an old vintage into two periods. The first period estimates the losses arising from the realised economy through the current date, and the second part projects losses based on simulated economies.

For the next set of experiments, it is necessary to run simulations in another way. For some of these experiments it is useful to net out the effect of the realised (abnormal) economy so it is convenient to estimate future losses of a pool based strictly on the information available at the origination of the transaction. In other words, the economic factors are simulated from the start of the transaction's closing for the subsequent 10 years, based only on the economic data available at that time rather than by using the realised economy up until the present and only simulating thereafter. Losses on the pool are then estimated using the 10 years of simulated economic factors. This method of estimating losses based on 10 years of simulated economic factors can be termed the "as of" method, while the other method of estimating losses based partly on the realised economy and the rest on the simulated economy may be termed the "combined" method. The key distinction is that the "as of" method represents an unconditional estimate of losses, while the "combined" method represents a conditional estimate of losses, where conditioning is done based on the realisation of the economy through the current period.

These two approaches can be used to try to understand the relative impact of the economic environment and the quality of underwriting on future lifetime losses by first considering what the expected losses would be in an economy-neutral and underwriting-neutral setting then comparing these with the losses obtained when these factors are introduced. For example, if the unconditional expected losses (ELs) are estimated to be 5% without economy and underwriting factors, but when these effects are included, the figure becomes 11%. The remaining 6% (= 11 − 5) of losses can be explained in terms of either abnormal economic conditions or abnormal underwriting.

In order to try to disentangle the components of the average loss for a given pool losses were simulated on 136 pools, originated between 2002 Q3 and 2007 Q1, in four different ways.

1. "As of" without underwriting (unconditional EL):[7] "as of" simulations are run without including the underwriting factor. Conceptually, this assumes that nothing about the realised economy is known and the underwriting condition is taken to be approximately "average" at origination. This estimate represents the unconditional EL for the pool where the losses are not conditioned on either underwriting quality or severe economic conditions. Thus, it is a baseline against which realised losses will be compared.

2. Combined path without underwriting (abnormal economy only): combined-path simulations are run without including the underwriting factor. Conceptually, this assumes that the realised economy is factored into the losses but that the underwriting condition at the origination of the transaction is not factored into the losses.

3. "As of" with underwriting (abnormal underwriting only): the full "as of" simulations including the underwriting factor are run. Conceptually, this assumes that no knowledge of

the realised economy was available but that the underwriting standard, as it was reported at the time, is factored into the losses.

4. Combined path with underwriting (conditional EL): full combined-path simulations including the underwriting factor are run. Conceptually, this is the most informed case in which the realised economy and the underwriting standard, as it was reported at the time, are factored into the losses.

Turning different sources of information on and off in each case attempts to control the effects of each component of losses in different ways and thus to isolate the effects of each component of losses.

The contribution of abnormal economic conditions towards EL is defined as the difference in the ELs for the combined case (ie, with realised economy) without underwriting (2) and the "as of" case (ie, without realised economy) without underwriting (1). This attempts to isolate the degree to which knowledge of the more-adverse-than-expected realised economy to date adds to the overall forecast of EL

abnormal economy effect = (combined without underwriting)
$$- (\text{"as of" without underwriting})$$

The direct contribution of abnormal underwriting towards EL is defined as the difference between the EL for the as of case with underwriting effect, (3), and the "as of" case without underwriting effect (unconditional losses), (1)

abnormal underwriting effect = ("as of" with underwriting)
$$- (\text{"as of" without underwriting})$$

Losses that incorporate both the realised economy and the underwriting effect (4) can now be decomposed into four components: losses that do not incorporate realised economy or underwriting effect, plus the contribution of economy, plus the direct contribution of underwriting, plus some (typically small) residual part that captures the non-linearities arising from the interaction of underwriting and economy (that is, $\{(4) - [(1) + ((3) - (1)) + ((2) - (1))]\}$). This simplifies to $[((4) - (2)) - ((3) - (1))]$

total losses = (unconditional EL) + (abnormal economy)
$$+ (\text{abnormal underwriting}) + \text{residual}$$

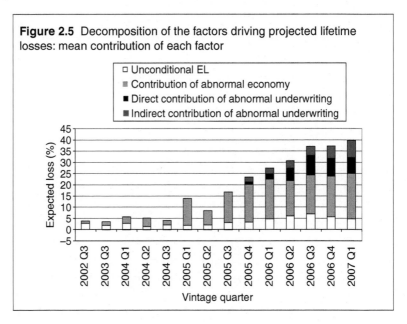

Figure 2.5 Decomposition of the factors driving projected lifetime losses: mean contribution of each factor

The abnormal losses are defined as the conditional EL minus the unconditional EL

$$\text{abnormal losses} = (\text{conditional EL}) - (\text{unconditional EL})$$

Finally, the percentage impact of the underwriting effect on the EL is measured by dividing the sum of direct and indirect underwriting effects by the total abnormal losses (ie, the total losses above the unconditional EL). This is equivalent to isolating the total contribution of underwriting, (4) − (2), and dividing this by the total contribution of underwriting and economy, (4) − (1)

percentage contribution of underwriting

$$= \frac{(\text{underwriting} + \text{interaction of underwriting and economy})}{(\text{abnormal losses})}$$

The next section presents the results of these calculations in the simulation experiments.

RESULTS: THE IMPACT OF UNDERWRITING ON SUBPRIME LOSSES

While these results are informal and therefore only intended to be directional, they are fairly straightforward and can be seen graphically in Figure 2.5. In the figure, the bars represent the mean projected lifetime losses of the pools of a specific vintage, with the height of each bar showing the average loss of the loans in the sample for each vintage. The bars are made up of four components. The first component, "unconditional EL", shows the amount of losses that can be attributed (approximately) to the baseline quality of the pools in that vintage in typical underwriting environments, given the economy at the time of origination. The second component, "abnormal economy", shows the amount of losses that can be attributed to changes in the economy between origination and the current period, then from the current point through the rest of the simulation. (These losses are overwhelmingly due to declines in home prices.) The third component, "abnormal underwriting", shows the contribution of the underwriting environment at the time of origination. Finally, the last component is a residual, which is labelled as the indirect contribution of underwriting. This last component can reasonably be characterised as the combined effect of declining home prices and more lax underwriting in which lax underwriting compounds the effect of a declining economic environment.

A number of things are apparent from the figure. Looking first at the baseline quality of the pools originated in each vintage, evidence of some drift in pool quality can be seen given the economic environment prior to origination, as denoted by the relatively higher loss levels associated with this component of losses in later vintages. However, in examining this component it also becomes clear that these shifts in quality were neither the dominant cause of losses nor a consistent proportion of losses. Note in particular that the mean value of the "unconditional EL" component is almost identical in 2004 Q1 and in 2005 Q4, though the projected lifetime losses for each are quite different. Importantly, this component is measured slightly differently in each period due to the starting point of the simulation in each case (the state of the economy at the time the RMBS transaction closed) so care should be taken when interpreting it.

Turning to the second contributor, the impact of the abnormal economy, a sudden and dramatic increase in the size of the losses in this component can be seen for transactions that contain loans originated closer and closer to the peak of real-estate prices in 2006 (recall that mortgages in a particular transaction are typically originated one to two quarters before the closing of the transaction itself).

Table 2.1 Expected losses and contributions under various combinations of realised economy effect and underwriting effect (mean)

Vintage quarter	1	2	3	4	5	6	7	8
2002 Q3	2.79	3.81	2.83	3.86	1.02	0.04	0.01	4.67
2003 Q3	1.82	3.46	1.80	3.44	1.64	−0.02	0.00	−1.23
2004 Q1	2.70	5.76	2.66	5.69	3.06	−0.04	−0.03	−2.34
2004 Q2	1.39	5.12	1.36	5.06	3.73	−0.03	−0.03	−1.63
2004 Q3	1.98	4.05	1.95	4.00	2.07	−0.03	−0.02	−2.48
2005 Q1	1.86	13.81	1.84	13.69	11.95	−0.02	−0.10	−1.01
2005 Q2	2.12	8.44	2.09	8.35	6.32	−0.03	−0.06	−1.44
2005 Q3	3.11	16.76	3.10	16.71	13.65	−0.02	−0.03	−0.36
2005 Q4	3.31	20.16	4.47	23.41	16.85	1.15	2.10	16.18
2006 Q1	4.75	22.51	7.16	27.37	17.76	2.41	2.45	21.48
2006 Q2	6.01	21.80	11.56	30.61	15.80	5.55	3.26	35.81
2006 Q3	7.00	24.36	15.60	36.97	17.36	8.60	4.01	42.08
2006 Q4	5.65	23.76	13.60	37.22	18.11	7.95	5.51	42.63
2007 Q1	4.70	25.07	11.81	39.78	20.36	7.11	7.61	41.95

1, unconditional EL; 2, abnormal economy only; 3, abnormal underwriting only; 4, conditional EL; 5, contribution of abnormal economy $(= 2 − 1)$; 6, direct contribution of abnormal underwriting $(= 3 − 1)$; 7, indirect contribution of abnormal underwriting $(= 4 − 2) − (3 − 1)$; 8, percentage contribution of abnormal underwriting $(= 6 + 7) / (4 − 1)$.

The third component of losses, the impact of abnormal underwriting quality, which is the major area of focus in this study, shows a marked pattern as well. A dramatic increase in the size of this factor's impact for later vintage pools can be observed. For example, the mean contribution of underwriting quality to losses from 2003 to 2005 was very small (negative). In contrast, the mean contribution from 2005 Q4 to 2007 Q1 was about 33%. The details of these calculations are given for each vintage in Table 2.1.

In addition, the contribution to the abnormal losses of abnormal underwriting is summarised as

Percentage contribution of underwriting

$$= \frac{(\text{underwriting} + \text{interaction of underwriting and economy})}{(\text{abnormal losses})}$$

and presented in column 8.

To give some basic sense of the economic impact, shifts in underwriting quality accounted for an average of about 33% (relative) of abnormal projected late-vintage subprime losses under this analysis. In these simulations, if underwriting quality had been closer to the historical mean levels, then lifetime losses on these pools might have been in the 20–25% (absolute) range, rather than the 24–40% range that the simulations currently suggest based on 2008 Q4 data.

CONCLUSION

This chapter has attempted to delve a bit deeper into the effects of the underwriting environment and subsequent pool performance. In doing so, a new application of a readily available (transformed) Fed series has been introduced, which exogenises underwriting and thereby facilitates the decomposition of the components of losses. This is particularly useful in settings where underwriting standards and the state of the economy are evolving in tandem. An attractive feature of this measure is that it can be observed in real time, and thus may be useful in forming forecasts of subsequent mortgage performance for newly originated mortgages before any performance history is available on the mortgages.

Though the experiments discussed in this chapter are preliminary and informal, a number of stylised observations can be made.

Firstly, it would appear that, as many commentators believe heuristically, underwriting quality has substantially altered the risk profile of subprime mortgage pools in the years leading up to the market crisis of 2007–9. While many market participants appeared aware of the general trend towards loosening (as evidenced by the survey levels), it would appear that even those in the retail banking community (ie, lending officers who reply to the Fed survey) did not fully appreciate the degree to which the standards had changed. For example, the quarterly underwriting quality survey actually reported credit standard tightening in 2006 Q4, one of the worst-performing vintages of recent history. There is some evidence that standards were in fact loosening during this period and, indeed, the smoothed series shows this more clearly. This can also be seen in the experiments which show that in 2006 Q4, the increase in the loss estimate due only to abnormal underwriting relative to the unconditional EL (Table 2.1, (6)/(1)) was about 140%, compared with about 122% in the preceding quarter.

Secondly, based on these experiments, there is some evidence of the detrimental role of the looser underwriting standards in subsequent projected losses. Based on this analysis it would appear that about 33% (relative) of abnormal late-vintage subprime losses can be attributed either directly or indirectly to the reported quality of underwriting at the time of loan origination. For reference, this implies that if reported underwriting quality were closer to the historical mean levels, simulated lifetime losses on these pools could have been in the 20–25% (absolute) range, rather than the 24–40% range that the model estimates based on 2008 Q4 economic data.

Finally, there appears to be some evidence that a portion of the high loss levels that are currently forecast is due to the interaction of reduced underwriting standards and concomitant declines in the economic environment. This would be the case, for example, if CLTV were understated because of less rigorous appraisals and this additional (unseen) leverage became magnified due to home price declines. Thus, the lax underwriting would exacerbate the increase in losses due to declines in the economy.

In all, while these findings are suggestive, the goal here was to provide directional evidence rather than precise quantitative guidance on the impact of underwriting on subsequent pool losses. There are many limitations to the approach (for example, data on the relationships described here is available for a limited number of years: the underwriting series itself required a fair amount of transformation and also required the realisation of high loss levels on existing mortgage pools before the relationships became clear; and the distribution of mortgage pools that is shown here is less well populated in the earliest vintages).[8] The authors hope that other researchers who find this topic to be of interest will extend this research stream in the future and propose additional measures of underwriting quality. Hopefully, the instrument used (the transformed Fed survey series) will also aid researchers both in academia and in industry to better understand and characterise the complicated relationship between mortgage risks on the one hand and loan characteristics, underwriting quality and the state of the economy on the other.

> The authors thank Darrell Duffie for helpful discussions during the early phases of this research and for ideas on structuring some of the experiments described in this chapter. Jipil Ha, Jigar Patel and Ajit Thomas provided research assistance and programming

support during the running of the experiments described in this chapter. The authors are also grateful for comments from Navneet Agarwal, Richard Cantor, Kumar Kanthan and Andrew Kimball. The chapter also benefited greatly from general discussions with members of Moody's Academic Advisory and Research Committee. The content of this chapter is copyrighted material by Moody's Investors Service Inc and/or its licensors and affiliates (together, "MOODY'S"). First published as part of *The Journal of Credit Risk* Special Issue on "Lessons from the Credit Crisis" in summer 2009.

1   Note that this is relative to the total amount of the abnormal losses, the rest of which are attributable to declines in the economy in this analysis.

2   Note that in the experiments that follow, the core model is used without the supplementation of the originator assessment, servicer quality rating or third-party review analytics described in Kothari and Forster (2008).

3   See Rocco (2009) for a summary of these estimates.

4   See www.federalreserve.gov/boarddocs/snloansurvey/200902/chartdata.htm.

5   All losses in this chapter are expressed as a percentage of the original pool balance.

6   Note that because only a sample of pools is used for each vintage and the pool-specific lifetime-loss estimate is used for each, the average loss numbers shown in this informal study may not agree in all cases with the overall mean vintage loss estimates published in Rocco (2009).

7   Note here that even the unconditional estimates are based on a new simulation methodology implemented after the onset of the crisis, and therefore do not represent estimates of what the loss forecasts might have been at the actual time the RMBS was issued. For clarity, the simulator used for the experiments reported here was released in November 2008 and used components that were calibrated based on the recent subprime experience and macroeconomic dynamics.

8   Note also that the experiments do not control for the possibility of outright mortgage fraud, though this would certainly influence the results if it could be confirmed and measured.

REFERENCES

Anderson, C. D., D. R. Capozza and R. Van Order, 2008, "Deconstructing the Subprime Debacle Using New Indices of Underwriting Quality and Economic Conditions: A First Look", Working Paper, University Financial Associates LLC and University of Michigan. URL: http://papers.ssrn.com/sol3/papers.cfm?abstract_id=1160073.

Cox, J. C., J. E. Ingersoll and S. A. Ross, 1985, "A Theory of the Term Structure of Interest Rates", *Econometrica* 53, pp. 385–407.

Dell'Ariccia, G., D. Igan and L. Laeven, 2008, "Credit Booms and Lending Standards: Evidence from the Subprime Mortgage Market", Working Paper, International Monetary Fund.

Demyanyk, Y. S., and O. Van Hemert, 2008, "Understanding the Subprime Mortgage Crisis", Working Paper, Federal Reserve Bank of Cleveland and New York University. URL: http://papers.ssrn.com/sol3/papers.cfm?abstract_id=1020396.

Federal Bureau of Investigation, 2008, "2007 Mortgage Fraud Report", Federal Bureau of Investigation, Washington, DC.

Hughes, T., 2007, "Regional Economy Review", URL: http://www.economy.com, February.

Keys. B. J., T. Mukherjee, A. Seru and V. Vig, 2007, "Did Securitization Lead to Lax Screening? Evidence from Subprime Loans", paper presented at The European Finance Association Annual Meeting 2008, URL: http://papers.ssrn.com/sol3/papers.cfm?abstract_id=1093137.

Kothari, D., and Y. Forster, 2008, "Moody's Approach to Rating US Residential Mortgage-Backed Securities", in *Structured Finance Rating Methodology* (New York: Moody's Investors Service).

Mian, A. R., and A. Sufi, 2008, "The Consequences of Mortgage Credit Expansion: Evidence from the US Mortgage Default Crisis", Working Paper, National Bureau of Economic Research, URL: http://papers.ssrn.com/sol3/papers.cfm?abstract_id=1072304.

Rajan, U., A. Seru and V. Vig, 2008, "The Failure of Models that Predict Failure: Distance, Incentives and Defaults", Research Paper 08-19, Chicago Graduate School of Business.

Rocco, J., 2009, "Subprime RMBS Loss Projection Update", In *Structured Finance Rating Methodology* (New York: Moody's Investors Service).

3

The Shadow Banking System and Hyman Minsky's Economic Journey

Paul McCulley
PIMCO

As we look for answers about the financial crisis, it is clear that creative financing played a massive role in propelling the global financial system to hazy new heights, before leading the way into the depths of a systemic crisis. But how did financing get so creative? It did not happen within the confines of a regulated banking system, which submits to strict regulatory requirements in exchange for the safety of government backstopping. Instead, financing got so creative through the rise of a "shadow banking system", which operated legally, yet almost completely outside the realm of bank regulation. The rise of this system drove one of the biggest lending booms in history, and collapsed into one of the most crushing financial crises we have ever seen.

Perhaps the most lucid framework for understanding this progression comes from the work of Hyman P. Minsky, the mid-20th-century American economist whose theory on the nature of financial instability proved unnervingly prescient in explaining the rise and fall of shadow banking, and the dizzying journey of the global financial system over the past several years.

THE NATURE AND ORIGIN OF THE SHADOW BANKING SYSTEM

The term "shadow banking system" was coined by this author in August 2007 at the Federal Reserve's annual symposium at Jackson Hole, WY. Unlike conventional regulated banks, unregulated shadow banks fund themselves with uninsured short-term funding, which may or may not be backstopped by liquidity lines from real banks. Since they fly below the radar of traditional bank regulation, these levered-up intermediaries operate in the shadows without backstopping from the Federal Reserve's discount lending window or access to Federal Deposit Insurance Corporation (FDIC) deposit insurance.

The allure of shadow banking over since the late 1990s is unambiguous: there is no better way for bankers to maximally leverage the inherent banking model than by becoming non-bank bankers, or shadow bankers. And they did this in droves, running levered-up lending and investment institutions known as investment banks, conduits, structured investment vehicles, hedge funds, etc.[1] They did so by raising funding in the non-deposit markets, notably unsecured debt such as interbank borrowing and commercial paper, and secured borrowing such as reverse repo and asset-backed commercial paper. And usually (but not always) such shadow banks maintained a reliance on conventional banks with access to The Fed's window.

SHADOW BANKING'S RELATIONSHIP WITH REGULATORS AND RATING AGENCIES

Since shadow banks do not have access to the same governmental safety nets that real banks have; they do not have to operate under meaningful regulatory constraints, notably for the amount of leverage they can use, the size of their liquidity buffers and the type of lending and investing they can do. To be sure, shadow banking needed some seal of approval, so that providers of short-dated funding could convince themselves that their claims were *de facto* "just as good" as deposits at banks with access to the US government's liquidity safety nets. Conveniently, the friendly faces at the rating agencies, paid by the shadow bankers, stood at the ready to provide such seals of approval. Moody's and Standard & Poor's would put an A-1/P-1 rating on the commercial paper, which in turn would be bought by money market funds. Of course, it is inherently an unstable structure. The rating agencies face an in-built problem of putting ratings on new innovations, because they have not had a chance to observe a historical track record, ie, to see their performance over a full cycle.

The bottom line is that the shadow banking system created explosive growth in leverage and liquidity risk outside the purview of The Fed. And it was all grand while ever-larger application of leverage put upwards pressure on asset prices. There is nothing like a bull market to make geniuses out of levered dunces.

SHADOW BANKING VERSUS CONVENTIONAL BANKING

Despite the extraordinary Keynesian public life-support system that was born of necessity to keep banks alive (and capitalism as a going concern), capitalist economies usually want their banking systems to be owned by the private sector. As private companies, banks make loans and investments on commercial terms in the pursuit of profit, but also in the context of prudential regulation, to minimise the downside to taxpayers of the moral hazard inherent in the two safety nets (FDIC deposit insurance and The Fed's discount window). But, as is the wont of capitalists, they love levering the sovereign's safety nets with minimal prudential regulation. This does not make them immoral, merely capitalists.

Since the 1970s, the growth of "banking" outside formal, sovereign-regulated banking has exploded, and it was a great gig so long as the public bought the notion that such funding instruments were "just as good" as bank deposits.

Keynes provides the essential (and existential) answer to why the shadow banking system became so large; the unravelling of this lies at the root of the current global financial system crisis. It was a belief in a convention, undergirded by the length of time that belief held: shadow bank liabilities were viewed as "just as good" as conventional bank deposits not because they are, but because they had been. And the power of this conventional thinking was aided and abetted by both the sovereign and the sovereign-blessed rating agencies, until, of course, convention was turned on its head, starting with a run on the asset-backed commercial paper (ABCP) market in August 2007, the near death of Bear Stearns in March 2008, the *de facto* nationalisation of the Federal National Mortgage Association (FNMA) and the Federal Home Loan Mortgage Corporation (FHLMC) in July 2008, and the actual death of Lehman Brothers in September 2008. Maybe, just maybe, there was and is something special about a real bank, as opposed to a shadow bank! And indeed that is unambiguously the case, as evidenced by the ongoing partial re-intermediation of the shadow banking system back into the sovereign-supported conventional banking system, as well as the mad scramble by remaining shadow banks to convert themselves into conventional banks, so as to eat at the same sovereign-subsidised capital and liquidity cafeteria as their former stodgy brethren.

MINSKY SHEDS LIGHT ON SHADOW BANKING

The shadow banking system, from its explosive growth to its calamitous collapse, followed a path that may have looked quite familiar to the economist Hyman P. Minsky. He passed away in 1996, but his teachings and writings echo today. Building from the work of many economists before him, most notably Keynes, Minsky articulated a theory on financial instability that describes in almost lurid detail what happened in the shadow banking system, the housing market and the broader economy that brought us to the depths of financial crisis; and he published this theory in 1986! So the first thing we do when we discuss Minsky is show reverence. He studied at Harvard and taught at Brown University, Berkeley and Washington University in St Louis. After his retirement in 1990, he continued writing and lecturing with the Levy Economics Institute, which now hosts an annual symposium in his honour.

Minsky may well have considered himself a Keynesian economist (he published his analysis and interpretation of Keynes in 1975), but Minsky's own theories headed off in a new direction. Keynes is, of course, a solid place to start any adventure in economic theory. Remember that Keynes effectively invented the field of macroeconomics, which is founded on the proposition that what holds for the individual does not necessarily hold for a collection of individuals operating as an economic system. This principle is sometimes called the "fallacy of composition", and sometimes called the "paradox of aggregation". But we need not resort to fancy labels to define the common sense of macroeconomics. Anybody who has ever been a spectator at a crowded football game has witnessed the difference between microeconomics and macroeconomics: from a micro perspective, it is rational for each individual to stand up to get a better view; but from a macro perspective, each individual acting rationally will produce the irrational outcome of everybody standing up but nobody having a better view.

THE FINANCIAL INSTABILITY HYPOTHESIS

Minsky took Keynes to the next level, and his huge contribution to macroeconomics comes under the label of the "Financial Instability Hypothesis". Minsky openly declared that his hypothesis was "an interpretation of the substance of Keynes's General Theory". Minsky's key addendum to Keynes's work was really quite simple: providing a framework for distinguishing between stabilising and destabilising capitalist debt structures. Minsky summarised the hypothesis beautifully in 1992:

> Three distinct income-debt relations for economic units, which are labeled as hedge, speculative, and Ponzi finance, can be identified.
>
> Hedge financing units are those which can fulfill all of their contractual payment obligations by their cash flows: the greater the weight of equity financing in the liability structure, the greater the likelihood that the unit is a hedge financing unit. Speculative finance units are units that can meet their payment commitments on "income account" on their liabilities, even as they cannot repay the principal out of income cash flows. Such units need to "roll over" their liabilities (eg, issue new debt to meet commitments on maturing debt)....
>
> For Ponzi units, the cash flows from operations are not sufficient to fulfill either the repayment of principal or the interest due on outstanding debts by their cash flows from operations. Such units can sell assets or borrow. Borrowing to pay interest or selling assets to pay interest (and even dividends) on common stock lowers the equity of a unit, even as it increases liabilities and the prior commitment of future incomes....
>
> It can be shown that if hedge financing dominates, then the economy may well be an equilibrium-seeking and -containing system. In contrast, the greater the weight of speculative and Ponzi finance, the greater the likelihood that the economy is a deviation-amplifying system. The first theorem of the financial instability hypothesis is that the economy has financing regimes under which it is stable, and financing regimes in which it is unstable. The second theorem of the financial instability hypothesis is that over periods of prolonged prosperity, the economy transits from financial relations that make for a stable system to financial relations that make for an unstable system.
>
> In particular, over a protracted period of good times, capitalist economies tend to move from a financial structure dominated by hedge finance units to a structure in which there is large weight to units engaged in speculative and Ponzi finance. Furthermore, if an economy with a sizeable body of speculative financial units is in an

inflationary state, and the authorities attempt to exorcise inflation by monetary constraint, then speculative units will become Ponzi units and the net worth of previously Ponzi units will quickly evaporate. Consequently, units with cash flow shortfalls will be forced to try to make position by selling out position. This is likely to lead to a collapse of asset values.

(Minsky 1992, pp. 6–8)

Those three categories of debt units – hedge,[2] speculative and Ponzi – are the straws that stir the drink in Minsky's Financial Instability Hypothesis. The essence of the hypothesis is that stability is destabilising because capitalists have a herding tendency to extrapolate stability to infinity, putting in place ever-more risky debt structures, up to and including Ponzi units, that undermine stability.

The longer people make money by taking risk, the more imprudent they become in risk-taking. While they are doing that, it is self-fulfilling on the way up. If everybody is simultaneously becoming more risk-seeking, that brings in risk premiums, drives up value of collateral, increases the ability to lever and the game keeps going. Human nature is inherently pro-cyclical, and that is essentially what the Minsky thesis is all about. He says:

from time to time, capitalist economies exhibit inflations and debt deflations which seem to have the potential to spin out of control. In such processes the economic system's reactions to a movement of the economy amplify the movement – inflation feeds upon inflation and debt-deflation feeds upon debt-deflation

(Minsky 1992, p. 1)

This pro-cyclical tendency applies to central banks and policy makers as well; it is hard for this author to avoid the conclusion that too much success in stabilising goods and services inflation, while conducting an asymmetric reaction function to asset price inflation and deflation, is a dangerous strategy. Yes, it can work for a time. But precisely because it can work for a time, it sows the seeds of its own demise. Or, as Minsky declared, stability is ultimately destabilising, because of the asset price and credit excesses that stability begets. in other words, stability can never be a destination, only a journey to instability.

Minsky's hypothesis richly explains the endemic boom-bust cycles of capitalism, including the bubbles in property prices, mortgage finance and shadow banking that characterise the recent bust. You may ask: why all these endemic boom-bust cycles? Is capitalism not driven by Adam Smith's invisible hand, where markets are efficient and always find just the right prices for things through what people like us call a "discovery process"? Well, much of the time that is right; but not all the time. Indeed, the most interesting, and profitable, times to be involved in investment management are when Smith's invisible hand is visibly broken. What Minsky's Hypothesis did was provide a framework for how and when Smith's hand would break.

MINSKY'S ECONOMIC JOURNEY: FORWARD AND REVERSE

In Minsky's theory, economic cycles can be described by a progression (a journey, if you will, in forward or reverse) through those three debt units: "hedge" financing units, in which the buyer's cashflows cover interest and principal payments; "speculative" finance units, in which cashflows cover only interest payments; "Ponzi" units, in which cashflows cover neither and depend on rising asset prices to keep the buyer afloat.

The forward Minsky journey, this time around anyway, was the progression of risk-taking in the financial markets represented by the excess of subprime loans, structured investment vehicles (SIVs) and other shady characters inhabiting the shadow banking system. Their apparent stability begat ever-riskier debt arrangements, which begat asset price bubbles. And then the bubbles burst, in something this author dubbed (years ago, in fact, when looking back on the Asian credit crisis) a "Minsky moment". We can quibble about the precise month of the moment in our present Minsky journey: while August 2007 seems favourite, we would not argue strenuously with you about three months either side of that date.

Whatever moment you pick, we have since been travelling the reverse Minsky journey: moving backwards through the three-part progression, with asset prices falling, risk premiums moving higher, leverage getting scaled back and economic growth getting squeezed. Minsky's "Ponzi" debt units are only viable as long as the levered assets appreciate in price. But when the price of the assets decline, as we have seen in the US housing market, Minsky tells us we must go through the process of increasing risk-taking in reverse, with all its consequences.

The recent Minsky moment comprised three bubbles bursting: in property valuation in the US, in mortgage creation, again, principally in the US, and in the shadow banking system, not just in the US but around the world. The blowing up of these three bubbles demanded a systemic re-pricing of all risk, which was deflationary for all risk asset prices. These developments are, as Minsky declared, a prescription for an unstable system, to wit, a system in which the purging of capitalist excesses is not a self-correcting therapeutic process but a self-feeding contagion: debt deflation.

THE US HOUSING MARKET'S MINSKY JOURNEY

The bubble in the US housing market provides a plain illustration of the forward Minsky journey in action, as people bet that prices would stably rise forever and financed that bet with excessive debt. Indeed, the mortgage debt market followed Minsky's three-step path almost precisely. The first type of debt, the hedge unit, is actually quite stable: the borrower's cashflow is sufficient to both fully service and amortise the debt. In the mortgage arena, this is known as an old-fashioned loan, like our parents had, as well as the one the author used to have. Every month, you write a cheque that pays the interest and nibbles away at the principal, *et voilà*, when the last payment is made many years down the road, usually 30, the mortgage simply goes away and you own the house free and clear. You may even throw a little party and ritually burn the mortgage note.

The next, more risky unit of debt, the speculative unit, comes about when people are so confident in stably rising house prices that they find the hedge unit to be, let us say, boring. Technically, Minsky defined the speculative unit as a loan where the borrower's cashflow is sufficient to fully service the debt, but not amortise the principal. Thus, when the loan matures, it must be refinanced. In the mortgage arena, this type of loan is called an interest only (IO) loan, with a balloon payment at maturity equal to the original principal amount. Thus, these types of borrowers are speculating on at least three things at the time of refinancing: the interest rate has not risen; terms and conditions, notably the down payment, have not tightened and, perhaps most importantly, the value of the house has not declined.

Minsky taught that, when credit is evolving from hedge units to speculative units, there is no fear, as the journey increases demand for the underlying assets that are being levered, and drives up their prices. Think about it this way: most people do not mentally take out a mortgage for X dollars, even though they literally do, but rather take out a mortgage that requires Y dollars for a monthly payment. In the mortgage arena, that means that a speculative borrower can take on a larger mortgage than a hedge borrower, because the monthly payment is lower for the speculative borrower: they are paying only interest, not that extra amount every month to pay off the principal over time. Thus, the speculative borrower can pay a higher price for a house than a hedge borrower with the same income. Accordingly, as the marginal mortgage is taken down by a speculative borrower, it drives up home prices, truncating the risk that the value of the house will fall before the balloon payment comes due.

Of course, speculative financing makes sense only so long as there is an infinite pool of speculative borrowers driving up the price, *de facto* collectively validating the speculative risk they took. Sounds like a recipe for a bubble, no? Demographics assure us there is a finite pool of home buyers. In this case, expectations of stably rising home prices ultimately run into the reality of affordability, but that does not in and of itself stop the game.

There is a final leg to a forward Minsky journey, thanks to the reality that humans are not inherently "value investors", but "momentum investors". Humans are not wired to buy low and sell high; rather, they are wired to buy that which is going up in price. This seems to make no sense, particularly when there is a known limit to size and affordability constraints; why would rational people buy a house for a higher price than other folks in the same financial circumstances could afford to pay? However, we are talking not about rationality here, but human nature. They are not one and the same thing. Humans are not only momentum investors, rather than value investors, but also inherently both greedy and suffering from hubris about their own smarts. It is sometimes called a bigger fool game, with each individual fool thinking they are slightly less foolish than all the other fools. And yes, a bigger fool game is also sometimes called a Ponzi scheme.

Fittingly, the last debt unit on the forward Minsky journey is called a Ponzi unit, defined as a borrower who has insufficient cashflow to even pay the full interest on a loan, much less pay down the principal over time. Now, how and why would such a borrower ever find a lender to make him a loan? Simple: as long as home prices are universally expected to continue rising indefinitely, lenders come out of the woodwork offering loans with what is called negative amortisation, meaning that if you cannot pay the full interest charge, that is okay; they will just tack the unpaid amount on to your principal. At the maturity of the loan, of course, the balloon payment will be bigger than the original loan.

As long as lenders made loans available on virtually non-existent terms, the price did not really matter all that much to borrowers; after all, housing prices were going up so fast that a point or two either way on the mortgage rate did not really matter. The availability of credit trumped the price of credit. Such is always the case in manias. It is also the case that once a speculative bubble bursts, reduced availability of credit will dominate the price of credit, even if markets and policy makers cut the price. The supply side of Ponzi credit is what matters, not the interest elasticity of demand.

Clearly, the explosion of exotic mortgages (subprime, interest only, pay-option, with negative amortisation, etc) in recent years have been textbook examples of Minsky's speculative and Ponzi units. But they seem okay, as long as expectations of stably rising home prices are realised. Except, of course, they cannot forever be realised. At some point, valuation does matter! How could lenders ignore this obvious truth? Because while it was going on they were making tons of money. Tons of money does serious damage to the eyesight, and our industry's moral equivalent of optometrists, the regulators and the rating agencies, are human too. As long as the forward Minsky journey was unfolding, rising house prices covered all shameful underwriting sins. Essentially, the mortgage arena began lending against asset value only, rather than asset value plus the borrowers' income. The mortgage originators, who were operating on the originate-to-distribute model, had no stake in the game (no active interest) because they simply originated the loans and then repackaged them.

But who they distributed these packages to, interestingly enough, were the shadow banks. So we had an originate-to-distribute model and no stake in the game for the originator, and the guy in the middle was being asked to create product for the shadow banking system.

The system was demanding product. Well, if you have got to feed the beast that wants product, how do you do it? You have a systematical degradation in underwriting standards so that you can originate more. But as you originate more, you bid up the price of property, and therefore you say, "These junk borrowers really are not junk borrowers. They are not defaulting." So you drop your standards once again and you take prices up. And you still do not get a high default rate. The reason this system works is that you, as the guy in the middle, had somebody bless it: the credit rating agencies. A key part of keeping the three bubbles (property valuation, mortgage finance and the shadow banking system) going was that the rating agencies thought the default rates were low because they were, in fact, low. But they were low because the degradation of underwriting standards was driving up asset prices.

Both regulators and rating agencies were beguiled into believing that the very low default rates during the period of soaring home prices were the normalised default rates for low quality borrowers, particularly ones with no down payment skin in the game. The rating agencies' Mister Magoo act was particularly egregious, because the lofty ratings they put on securities backed by these dud loans were the fuel for explosive growth in the shadow banking system, which issued tons of similarly highly rated commercial paper to fund purchases of the securities.[3]

It all went swimmingly, dampening volatility in a self-reinforcing way, until the bubbles created by financial alchemy hit the fundamental wall of housing affordability. Ultimately, fundamentals do matter! We have a day of reckoning: the day the balloon payment becomes due, the margin call, the Minsky moment. If the value of the house has not gone up, then Ponzi units, particularly those with negatively amortising loans, are toast. And if the price of the house has fallen, speculative units are toast still in the toaster. Ponzi borrowers are forced to "make position by selling out position", frequently by stopping (or not even beginning!) monthly mortgage payments, the prelude to eventual default or "jingle mail".[4] Ponzi lenders dramatically tighten underwriting standards, at least back to Minsky's speculative units: loans that may not be self-amortising, but at least are underwritten on evidence that borrowers can pay the required interest – not just the teaser rate, but the fully indexed rate on adjustable rate mortgages.

From a microeconomic point of view, such a tightening of underwriting standards is a good thing, albeit belated. But from a macroeconomic point of view, it is a deflationary turn of events, as serial refinancers, riding the presumed perpetual home price appreciation, are trapped long and wrong. And in this cycle, it is not just the first-time home buyer (God bless them!) that is trapped, but also the speculative Ponzi long: borrowers who were not covering a natural short[5] but rather betting on a bigger fool to take them out ("make book", in Minsky's words). The property bubble stops bubbling, and, when it does, both the property market and the shadow banking system go bust.

When the conventional basis of valuation for the originate-to-distribute (to the shadow banking system) business model for subprime mortgages was undermined, the asset class imploded "violently". And the implosion was not, as both Wall Street and Beltway mavens predicted, contained. Rather it became contagious, first on Wall Street, with all "risk assets" re-pricing to higher risk premiums, frequently in violent fashion, and next on Main Street, with debt-deflation accelerating in the wake of a mushrooming mortgage credit crunch, notably in the subprime sector, but also up the quality ladder.

Yes, we are now experiencing a reverse Minsky journey, where instability will, in the fullness of time, restore stability, as Ponzi debt units evaporate, speculative debt units morph after the fact into Ponzi units and are severely disciplined if not destroyed, and even hedge units take a beating. The shadow banking system contracts implosively as a run on its assets forces it to de-lever, driving down asset prices, eroding equity, and forcing it to de-lever again. The shadow banking system is particularly vulnerable to runs: commercial paper investors refusing to re-up when their paper matures, leaving the shadow banks with a liquidity crisis; a need to tap their back-up lines of credit with real banks or to liquidate assets at fire sale prices. Real banks are in a risk-averse state of mind when it comes to lending to shadow banks, lending when required by back-up lines but seeking not to proactively increase their footings to the shadow banking system but, if anything, reduce them. Thus, there is a mighty gulf between The Fed's liquidity cup and the shadow banking system's parched liquidity lips.

The entire progression self-feeds on the way down, just like it self-feeds on the way up. It is incredibly pro-cyclical. The regulatory response is also incredibly pro-cyclical. You have a rush to laxity on the way up, and you have a rush to the opposite on the way back down. And essentially, on the way down, you have the equivalent of Keynes's paradox of thrift: the paradox of de-levering. It can make sense for each individual institution, for a shadow bank or even a real bank, to de-lever, but, collectively, they cannot all de-lever at the same time.

POLICY REACTIONS TO THE REVERSE MINSKY JOURNEY

Along the way, policy makers have slowly recognised the Minsky moment followed by the unfolding reverse Minsky journey. But I want to emphasise "slowly", as policy makers, collectively, tend to suffer from more than a thermos full of denial. Part of the reason is human nature: to acknowledge a reverse Minsky journey, it is first necessary to acknowledge a preceding forward Minsky journey (a bubble in asset and debt prices) as the marginal unit of debt creation morphed from hedge to speculative to Ponzi. That is difficult for policy makers to do, especially ones who claim an inability to recognise bubbles while they are forming and, therefore, do not believe that prophylactic action against them is appropriate. But framing policies to mitigate the damage of a reverse Minsky journey requires that policy makers openly acknowledge that we are where we are because they let the invisible, if not crooked, hand of financial capitalism go precisely where Minsky said it would go, unless checked by the visible fist of counter-cyclical, rather than pro-cyclical, regulatory policy.

That is not to say that Minsky had confidence that regulators could stay out in front of short-term profit-driven innovation in financial arrangements. Indeed, he believed precisely the opposite:

> In a world of businessmen and financial intermediaries who aggressively seek profit, innovators will always outpace regulators; the authorities cannot prevent changes in the structure of portfolios from occurring. What they can do is keep the asset-equity ratio of banks within bounds by setting equity-absorption ratios for various types of assets. If the authorities constrain banks and are aware of the activities of fringe banks and other financial institutions, they are in a better position to attenuate the disruptive expansionary tendencies of our economy.
>
> (Minsky 2008, p. 281)

Minsky wrote those words in 1986! Years later, we can only bemoan that his sensible counsel was ignored and the economy experienced the explosive growth of the shadow banking system, or what Minsky cleverly called "fringe banks and other financial institutions".

Minsky's insight that financial capitalism is inherently and endogenously given to bubbles and busts is not just right, but spectacularly right. We have much to learn and relearn from the great man as we collectively restore prudential common sense to bank regulation, for both conventional banks and shadow banks.

Meanwhile, we have a problem: we are on a reverse Minsky journey. The private sector wants to shrink and de-risk its balance sheet, so someone has to take the other side of the trade to avoid a depression: the sovereign. We pretend that The Fed's balance sheet and Uncle Sam's balance sheet are in entirely separate orbits because of the whole notion of the political independence of the central bank in making monetary policy. But when you think about it, not from the standpoint of making monetary policy but of providing balance sheet support to buffer a reverse Minsky journey, there is no difference between Uncle Sam's balance sheet and The Fed's balance sheet. Economically speaking, they are one and the same.

I think we are pretty well advanced along this reverse Minsky journey, and it is a lot quicker than the forward journey for a very simple reason. The forward journey is essentially momentum driven; there is a systematic relaxation of underwriting standards and all that sort of thing, but it does not create any pain for anybody. The reverse journey, however, does create pain, otherwise known as one giant margin call. The reverse journey comes to an end when the full faith and credit of the sovereign's balance sheet is brought into play to effectively take the other side of the trade. No, your author is not a socialist, just a practical person. You must have somebody on the other side of the trade. The government not only steps up to the risk-taking and spending that the private sector is shirking, but goes further, stepping up with even more vigour, providing a meaningful reflationary thrust to both private sector risk assets and aggregate demand for goods and services.

Thus, policy makers have a tricky balancing act: let the deflationary pain unfold, as it is the only way to find a bottom of undervalued asset prices from presently overvalued asset prices, while providing sufficient monetary and fiscal policy safety nets to keep the deflationary process from spinning out of control. Debt deflation is a beast of burden that capitalism cannot bear alone. It is not rich enough; it is not tough enough. Capitalism's prosperity is hostage to the hope that policy makers are not simply too blind to see.

As long as we have reasonably deregulated markets and a complex and innovative financial system, we will have Minsky journeys, forward and reverse, punctuated by Minsky moments. That is reality. You cannot eliminate them. It is a matter of having the good sense to have in place a counter-cyclical regulatory policy to help modulate human nature.

> The opinions expressed in this chapter are those of the author and do not necessarily reflect the opinion of Pacific Management Investment Company LLC. This chapter is based on McCulley (2009).

1   This list is representative, not exhaustive.
2   No relation to hedge funds.
3   To describe the full circularity of this process would require an endlessly circular sentence. Let me start: the issuance of this additional commercial paper created yet more demand for the services of the ratings agencies, which, remember, are paid by the issuer....
4   "Jingle mail" (because of the sound made by house keys) is the return of collateral to the lender.
5   Remember, you are born short a roof over your head, and must cover, either by renting or buying.

REFERENCES

McCulley, P., 2009, "The Shadow Banking System and Hyman Minsky's Economic Journey" in, L. B. Siegel (ed), *Insights into the Global Financial Crisis*, December, URL http://www.cfapubs.org/doi/pdf/10.2470/rf.v2009.n5.15.

Minsky, H. P., 1992, "The Financial Instability Hypothesis", Jerome Levy Economics Institute Working Paper 74, URL: http://www.levy.org/pubs/wp74.pdf.

Minsky, H. P., 2008, *Stabilizing an Unstable Economy* (New York: McGraw-Hill; first published in 1986 by Yale University Press, New Haven, CT).

4

The Collapse of the Icelandic Banking System

René Kallestrup; David Lando

Danmarks Nationalbank, Copenhagen Business School;
Copenhagen Business School

The collapse of Iceland's three largest banks in late September and early October 2008 was the biggest banking failure relative to the size of an economy in modern history. Financial crises are of course always easier to spot with the benefit of hindsight, but it is fair to say that there were many indications that the fall of the Icelandic banking system was an accident waiting to happen. Not only were commonly used early warning indicators of banking crises very strong in the case of Iceland, but there had in fact already been a mini funding crisis in early 2006. In this chapter we list the warning indicators and document how the Icelandic banks managed to continue their aggressive growth despite the funding crisis in 2006. Strong reported financial key figures masked the true riskiness of the Icelandic business model and the extreme concentration risk in the financial system. In addition, investors and rating agencies overestimated the value of potential sovereign support from a country whose fiscal capacity was limited compared with the size of the banks' assets. Helped by strong credit ratings and implicit sovereign guarantees, the banks were able to fund their risky business model through foreign deposits and by accessing bond markets outside of Europe. While central bank liquidity facilities have been critical in saving the global banking system, the Icelandic case study also reveals how such facilities may prolong a crisis, make it deeper and ultimately contribute to a crash of a floating exchange rate.

The chapter is organised as follows: the next section describes the severity of the banking crisis, the currency crisis and the public debt crisis. We then focus on early warning indicators of a financial crisis in Iceland. The subsequent section documents the fact that the focus

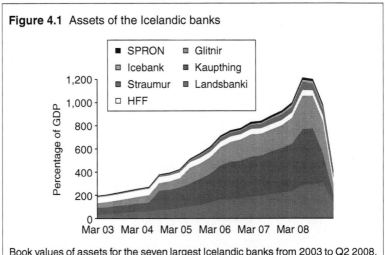

Figure 4.1 Assets of the Icelandic banks

Book values of assets for the seven largest Icelandic banks from 2003 to Q2 2008. In Q3–Q4 2008, data is based on information from the accounting firm Deloitte LLP and the consulting firm Oliver Wyman. The values of assets after write-downs are shown in Q4 2008.
Source: Consolidated financial accounts and the Special Investigation Commission.

of regulators and rating agencies on apparently strong financial key figures downplayed the true riskiness of the banks' business model. In the next section we analyse the asset side of the balance sheet and show the extreme concentration risk in the Icelandic financial system. We then document how the banks were able to fund their risky business model by accessing bond markets, through foreign deposits and using central bank liquidity facilities. Sovereign support and credit ratings probably played an important role in this process. We give our conclusion in the final section.

Our analysis is based on a wide range of publicly available statistics and information. Institutions such as the Central Bank of Iceland (2009a, 2010), the IMF (2008b) and the OECD (2009) have also published reports on the crisis in Iceland. Verbal reviews can also be found in Fridriksson (2009), Jännäri (2009) and Jónsson (2009). In April 2010, the Icelandic Parliament's Special Investigation Commission published a report on the collapse of the Icelandic banking system (Special Investigation Commission 2010). The report, which runs to more than 2,000 pages, documents the fact that the banks did not comply with the domestic laws and regulations, and this may eventually lead to prosecutions. Although we will describe some

THE COLLAPSE OF THE ICELANDIC BANKING SYSTEM

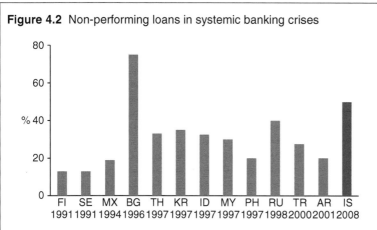

Figure 4.2 Non-performing loans in systemic banking crises

The highest level of non-performing loans is shown as percentage of total loans during the years $[t, t+5]$, where t is the initial year of the crisis. In Iceland, the share of non-performing loans is assessed to be around 50%. FI, Finland; SE, Sweden; MX, Mexico; BG, Bulgaria; TH, Thailand; KR, Korea; ID, Indonesia; MY, Malaysia; PH, Philippines; RU, Russia; TR, Turkey; AR, Argentina; IS, Iceland. For example, FI is at 13% in 1991, which means the peak in non-performing loans in the period from 1991 to 1996 is 13%.

Source: Laeven and Valencia (2008) and Andersen (2009).

questionable business practices, our focus is mainly on using the data that was available to supervisors or the public. We consider only the history up to the collapse in early October 2008.

A TRIPLE CRISIS IN ICELAND

As a starting point, we briefly describe the extent of the triple crisis which culminated in the default of the three largest banks in October 2008.

At its peak in March 2008, the book assets of three banks, Kaupthing, Landsbanki and Glitnir, stood at more than 1,000% of GDP (Figure 4.1).[1] The banks maintained branches and subsidiaries in more than 20 countries, but they focused primarily on Iceland, the UK, Denmark and Norway. When the three largest banks collapsed, they accounted for around 85% of the Icelandic banking system. Six months later, when savings and loan funds (Reykjavik Savings Bank and Icebank) as well as the investment bank Straumur-Burdaras were in financial trouble, more than 90% of the banking system was in wind-up proceedings. The write-downs were very large. As of October 2008, independent auditors assessed asset values of the

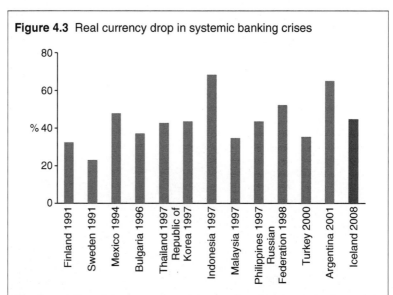

Figure 4.3 Real currency drop in systemic banking crises

The depreciation of the domestic real (onshore) exchange rate is shown. It is measured as the fall from the peak to the trough. The year of the systemic banking crisis (which may be different from the year of the exchange rate crisis) is shown.
Source: Bank for International Settlements.

three banks after write-downs to be around 300% of GDP, down from book values of assets around 835% of GDP. The write-downs as a percentage of assets were 69.4, 65.2 and 54.2 for Kaupthing, Glitnir and Landsbanki, respectively. Write-downs on loans to holding companies and the banks' largest customers were the biggest contributors. The share of non-performing loans was very high compared with other recent systemic banking crises, as shown in Figure 4.2. This is, of course, in part due to the fact that the failure of the Icelandic banks took place during the most serious international financial crisis since the Great Depression.

In addition to the systemic banking crisis, large market pressure to sell assets denominated in the Icelandic króna (IKr) put heavy pressure on the currency. Ultimately there was an effective collapse of the freely floating exchange rate. The sharp depreciation posed a risk for the small open economy depending on imports and domestic households as well as companies with foreign currency denominated loans. The IMF therefore, as part of a rescue package, recommended capital controls to stabilise the exchange rate at a higher level than determined in the free market. In Figure 4.3 we show

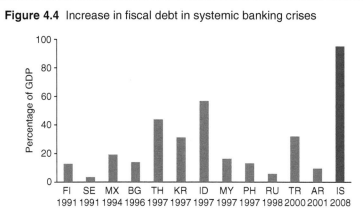

Figure 4.4 Increase in fiscal debt in systemic banking crises

The increase in gross government debt is shown as a percentage of GDP over the period $[t, t+5]$, where t denotes the starting year of the crisis. The data for Iceland is based on the Central Bank of Iceland's 2012 forecast. The year of the systemic banking crisis (which may be different from the year of the sovereign debt crisis) is shown. The net fiscal cost, which includes the recovery proceeds over the same period, is not shown.
Source: Laeven and Valencia (2008) and the Central Bank of Iceland.

the drop in the real exchange rate and compare it with other drops in banking crises after 1990. Later, we will see that the drop in the exchange rate in the "offshore market", ie, the market for Icelandic króna outside of Iceland, was much larger.

The high gross cost of recapitalising the banking system and future public deficits will also lead to a strong increase in public sector debt. As seen in Figure 4.4, the rise in public sector debt relative to GDP is higher for Iceland than other countries experiencing a systemic banking crisis. The Republic of Iceland avoided a sovereign default because the government had an initial low debt burden and a balanced public budget prior to the crisis.

In terms of non-performing loans, drop in exchange rate and relative increase in public debt, the Icelandic crisis was arguably the worst triple crisis since 1990.[2]

EARLY WARNING CRISIS INDICATORS

Reinhart and Rogoff (2009) note that

> economists do not have a terribly good idea of what kinds of events shift confidence and of how to concretely assess confidence vulnerability. What one does see, again and again, in the history of financial crises is that when an accident is waiting to happen, it eventually does.

While each crisis is different, there do exist a number of indicators which signal that a systemic banking crisis is waiting to happen. Important indicators are a rapid expansion of the banking system, a private-sector credit boom, a large rise in equity and property prices, a rapid real exchange rate appreciation in combination with balance sheet mismatches in the economy, a large current account deficit and a large external short-term debt build-up.[3] In the sections below, we briefly recall why these indicators are relevant predictors of banking crises and we document that the indicator levels in the case of Iceland were exceptionally high compared with both non-crisis and crisis countries.

Large bank balance sheets relative to the economy

We first look at the growth and the size of the Icelandic banks' balance sheets relative to the domestic GDP in the years leading up to the crisis. The sizes of the assets are measured relative to the Icelandic GDP, since around one-third of the banks' loans were to Icelandic entities according to the banks' reported balance sheets.[4] Rapid organic growth can be a signal of problems because it is often accompanied by lower asset quality (ie, riskier loans) and growth through acquisitions is associated with a risk of overpaying for assets. The rapid rise in the Icelandic banks' balance sheets relative to GDP has been without historical precedent. The banks' assets expanded from around 100% of GDP in 2003 to more than 1,000% of GDP by 2008. In the period from 2003 to 2008, the primary driver behind the expansion of the banks' balance sheets was the growth in existing activities (internal growth), whereas external growth through acquisitions accounted for around 160% of GDP. The latter was especially pronounced in 2004 and 2005, when Kaupthing acquired the Danish bank FIH Erhvervsbanks and the British bank Singer & Friedlander, respectively.

The overall size of the banking sector relative to the domestic GDP is also a relevant indicator, since it may reflect the sovereign's contingent liabilities in times of financial trouble. On this scale, the size of the Icelandic banking system was large but broadly similar to that of Ireland and Switzerland (Figure 4.5). The main difference, however, was that the large Swiss banks were assessed to be systemically important outside of Switzerland, as demonstrated, for example, by the liquidity swap facilities in foreign currency provided by the European Central Bank and the Federal Reserve to the

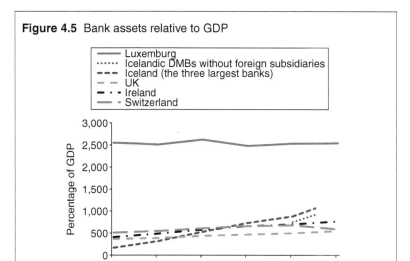

Figure 4.5 Bank assets relative to GDP

The end-of-year assets of domestically registered banks (excluding assets of foreign subsidiaries) in countries with large banking systems are shown relative to GDP. The three largest Icelandic banks' consolidated assets (ie, including the assets of the banks' foreign subsidiaries) are shown from 2003 to Q2 2008. Data on the assets of domestically registered Icelandic banks is only available from Q2 2007.

Source: OECD (2009).

Swiss National Bank. In contrast, the Icelandic banking system was not assessed as too big to fail outside of Iceland. Interestingly, the relative size of the Icelandic banking system was much smaller than in Luxembourg, a country which did not face severe banking problems in 2008. As shown in Figure 4.6, the banks' assets in Luxembourg primarily belonged to subsidiaries of foreign banks and this may lower the sovereign's willingness to assist these banks in the case of financial problems. Later we will also see that both Switzerland and Luxembourg were large net external creditor nations, whereas Iceland was a large net external debitor.

Iceland's private sector credit boom

The rapid growth of the banks' assets was partly a result of a rapid expansion of credit to the private sector in Iceland.[5] As with the growth in assets, this is an indicator of lower marginal asset quality of the banks' loan portfolios, but deteriorating marginal asset quality is particularly likely in a small, less diversified country like Iceland.

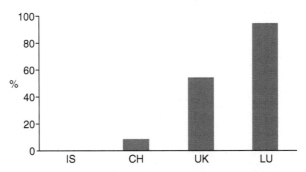

Figure 4.6 Banking systems: the share that is 50% or more foreign owned

The capital of the Icelandic banks was domestically owned, whereas the banks in Luxembourg were primarily owned by foreigners (year-end 2005 data). IS, Iceland; CH, Switzerland; UK, United Kingdom; LU, Luxembourg.
Source: World Bank.

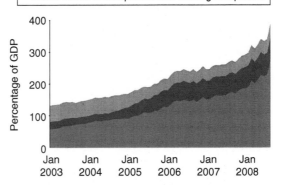

Figure 4.7 Bank and the HF Fund's credit to the private sector

Icelandic deposit money banks' (DMBs) credit to Icelandic households and companies (including holding companies) is shown. Credit provided by the Housing Financing Fund is also shown.
Source: The Central Bank of Iceland, OECD and the authors' calculations.

Domestic credit provided by deposit money banks to households and companies as well as holding companies accounted for around 250% of GDP by year-end 2007. In addition, the state-guaranteed mortgage lender, the HF Fund, provided credit to households for

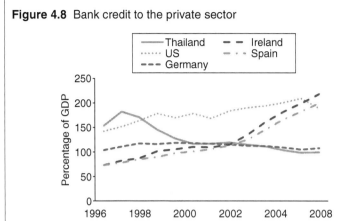

Figure 4.8 Bank credit to the private sector

Countries with high stocks of domestic credit to the private sector and non-financial public sector enterprises provided by deposit money banks are shown. Data for Iceland is shown Figure 4.7.
Source: Fitch Ratings.

around 40% of GDP (Figure 4.7).[6] The bank credit expansion to residents in Iceland has been without historical precedence, as seen in Figure 4.8, where we see countries with a high amount of bank credit to GDP.

A rapid rise in stock prices and house prices

A rapid rise in stock prices and house prices is often associated with more collateralised borrowing, which fuels further increases in asset prices. When the market turns, there is the danger of a negative price spiral in which collateral value erodes because of forced asset sales and unwinding of positions.

The banks' lending to the private sector in Iceland was channelled into the domestic equity market. Remarkably, a large part of this rise was driven by domestic demand. The Special Investigation Commission (2010) has documented that the large increase of stock prices until mid-2007 was driven by the increasing domestic leverage in stock purchases (see also the next section). Foreign capital was also channelled into the stock market but the foreign ownership was estimated at only around 10 to 15% in mid-2007 (IMF 2007). The Icelandic stock market benchmark index rose by close to 500% between January 2003 and July 2007, when it peaked with a market capitalisation around 270% of GDP (Figure 4.9).

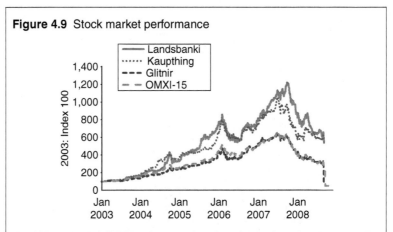

Figure 4.9 Stock market performance

The OMX Iceland 15 (OMXI-15) was the benchmark index based on 15 companies with the highest market capitalisation. Trading was suspended in the banks on October 6, 2008.
Source: Bloomberg.

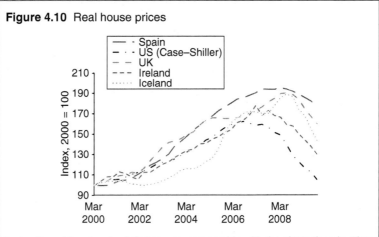

Figure 4.10 Real house prices

Iceland's real house price inflation was comparable with the sharp rises in other developed economies.
Source: OECD.

The banks' lending to the private sector in Iceland was also channelled into non-tradeable sectors, which triggered price and wage inflation and thus a general loss of competitiveness. Real house prices rose by more than 80% over eight years to the peak in year-end 2007. It was especially pronounced in 2005 after the banks started to expand their mortgage lending (Figure 4.7). That said, the rise

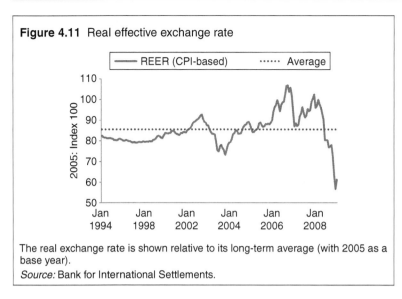

Figure 4.11 Real effective exchange rate

The real exchange rate is shown relative to its long-term average (with 2005 as a base year).
Source: Bank for International Settlements.

in house prices in Iceland was similar to the rise in other advanced economies (Figure 4.10).

Real exchange-rate appreciation

Domestic households and companies had large amounts of loans indexed to foreign currency despite mainly owning króna-denominated assets. This asset–liability mismatch made households and companies vulnerable to a depreciation of the domestic currency.

The banks' massive domestic lending to the private sector in Iceland, combined with investment projects, large wealth effects and tax cuts, resulted in a consumption boom. This was the main reason why, in order to curb the rise in inflation, the Central Bank of Iceland repeatedly raised its policy rate, which eventually reached double figures in early 2006. Inflation remained well above its trading partners though. An unfortunate by-product of the tight monetary policy was the attractiveness of currency carry trading. The high interest resulted in a massive inflow of capital into Iceland as well as further borrowing in foreign currency by households and companies and a strengthening of the real exchange rate relative to its recent trend.[7] As shown in Figure 4.11, the domestic currency experienced two episodes of rapid appreciation in the years leading up to the crisis. The inflow of capital was of course a by-product of the large current account deficit, as seen in the next subsection. In mid-2007, it was estimated that foreigners held around 25–30%

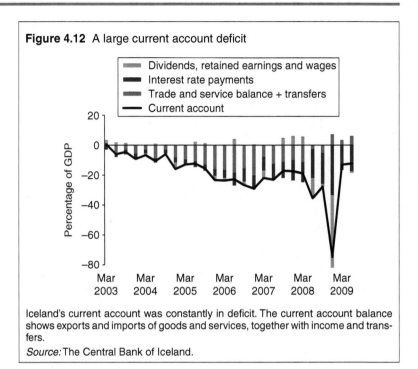

Figure 4.12 A large current account deficit

Iceland's current account was constantly in deficit. The current account balance shows exports and imports of goods and services, together with income and transfers.
Source: The Central Bank of Iceland.

of the fixed income market (IMF 2007). In addition, there were a large number of other high-yielding instruments available for the currency carry trader such as króna-denominated Eurobonds, FX swaps, etc. Later in this chapter we take a closer look at borrowing in foreign currency.

A persistent current account deficit

The consumption spree in Iceland and the strong currency were the main factors behind the increased demand for foreign goods.[8] As of 2006, the current account deficit was more than 20% of GDP and the largest in the world. It reflected a deficit on goods and services (a trade deficit) and interest rate payments on the country's external debt (see the items in Figure 4.12).[9] In 2003–5 interest rate payments to foreigners accounted for around 2–5% of GDP and they rose to more than 20% in 2008.

A country with a current account deficit is running down its net foreign asset position. The net international investment position (NIIP), ie, the sum of external assets minus the stock of external liabilities, for Iceland was −131% of GDP at year-end 2007, as seen

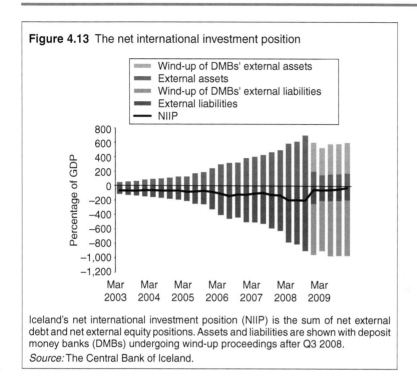

Figure 4.13 The net international investment position

Iceland's net international investment position (NIIP) is the sum of net external debt and net external equity positions. Assets and liabilities are shown with deposit money banks (DMBs) undergoing wind-up proceedings after Q3 2008.
Source: The Central Bank of Iceland.

in Figure 4.13. The negative NIIP increased as a result of the accumulation of current account deficits and valuation effects on the external assets and debt. Iceland's high net debt burden clearly reflected an unsustainable position and the economy was vulnerable to a sudden capital flow reversal. Macroeconomic theory predicts that countries with a large negative NIIP should experience a depreciation of real exchange in order to generate a trade surplus to pay interest rates on the external liabilities. In Iceland, a depreciation of the currency would have the unfortunate effect of increasing the cost of servicing debt for households and companies that had loans indexed to foreign currency. We will return to this point later.

It is common to exclude the net external equity position in the NIIP. Iceland's net external debt (the stock of external debt minus the stock of external assets) amounted to around 230% of GDP at year-end 2007. According to Fitch data, Iceland's net external debt was the second highest level in the world (the highest being in Bermuda), whereas the gross debt was higher in a few other countries (Bahrain, Ireland, Bermuda and Luxembourg). Figures 4.14

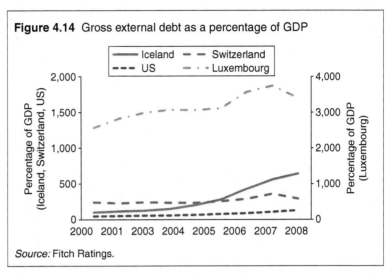

Figure 4.14 Gross external debt as a percentage of GDP
Source: Fitch Ratings.

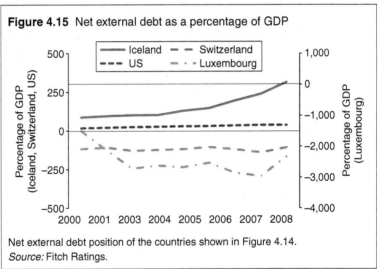

Figure 4.15 Net external debt as a percentage of GDP
Net external debt position of the countries shown in Figure 4.14.
Source: Fitch Ratings.

and 4.15 compare debt in Iceland with that in selected countries with high gross external debt levels.

A high amount of short-term external debt

Rolling over short-term debt in foreign currency exposes the banks to funding risk in foreign exchange markets. Iceland's gross external debt (liabilities of residents to foreigners) reached around 520% of GDP in year-end 2007, while Icelandic deposit money banks

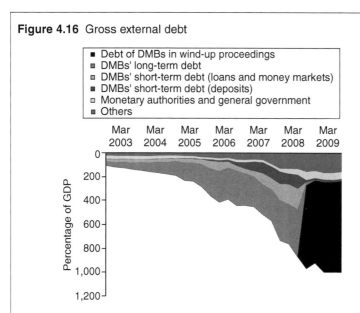

Figure 4.16 Gross external debt

- Debt of DMBs in wind-up proceedings
- DMBs' long-term debt
- DMBs' short-term debt (loans and money markets)
- DMBs' short-term debt (deposits)
- Monetary authorities and general government
- Others

DMBs accounted for the majority of Iceland's gross external debt (according to parent company data). Short-term debt is defined as an original maturity of less than one year. The banks' liabilities being wound up are shown separately after Q3 2008. Direct investments are included in the "others" component.
Source: The Central Bank of Iceland.

accounted for around 455% of GDP.[10] After the onset of the global credit crisis in 2007, the banks' share of short-term external debt rose sharply, as seen in Figure 4.16. This reveals the large exposure of the banks' parent companies to potential foreign exchange funding liquidity risk. The banks' external short-term debt covers deposits in foreign branches and loans, where repurchase agreements are treated as loans. We return to Iceland's short-term external debt later.

The mini crisis of early 2006

The strong economic imbalances, almost all of which were public knowledge, were not ignored by the markets. In late 2005 and early 2006, doubts about the Icelandic banks' business models began to emerge. Market participants were worried about the banks' growth pace and their underlying asset quality, the high dependence on bond financing in the European market and their low deposit base as well as cross-shareholding between the banks themselves and between banks and major financial undertakings. In February 2006, the rating agency Fitch changed the outlook from stable to negative on the sovereign, stating that it had been "triggered by a material deterioration in Iceland's macro-prudential risk indicators, accompanied by an unsustainable current account deficit and soaring net external indebtedness." In March 2006, doubts over Icelandic vulnerabilities turned into fears. Merrill Lynch's (2006) banking report stated

> we think the banks should be compared less with other European banks and more with emerging market banks, since the systemic risks we see in Iceland have much more in common with emerging markets.

Danske Bank's (2006) macro report stated

> we look at early warning indicators for financial crises and conclude that Iceland looks worse on almost all measures than Thailand did before its crisis in 1997, and only moderately more healthy than Turkey before its 2001 crisis.

The negative "publicity" resulted in a re-evaluation of the risk associated with the Icelandic banking system. Access to the European bond markets effectively closed and several money market funds refused to roll over the banks' extendable notes in March 2006 (see, for example, *The Times* 2006). It resulted in a significant downward pressure on the currency and equity market as well as wider credit default swap (CDS) spreads on the banks.[11] It was named the mini crisis of 2006. But why did this mini crisis not grow into a much more severe crisis? It is hard to document econometrically, but there is certainly evidence to suggest that reassurances from different sources played a large role.

Reports from other investment banks pointed to an overreaction towards credit fears in Iceland, and Moody's (2006) issued a special comment in April with the title "Iceland's Solvency and Liquidity Are Not at Risk" stating

> Iceland is well positioned to deal with any potential claims on government resources that might emanate from a systemic problem in any sector of the economy.... Our Aaa rating for Iceland is compatible with such an extreme scenario.

Furthermore, a strong counterattack was provided in a report by Herbertsson and Mishkin (2006), sponsored by the Iceland Chamber of Commerce. The report analysed a few early warning crisis indicators in Iceland. In particular, the focus was on the very low net government debt relative to GDP as well as the banks' (moderate) exposure to Icelandic households and businesses. In the words of the authors:

> our analysis indicates that the sources of financial instability that triggered financial crisis in emerging market countries in recent years are just not present in Iceland, so that comparisons of Iceland with emerging market countries are misguided.

They concluded that the probability of an emerging-market-style financial crisis was very low in light of Iceland's developed economy and floating exchange rate. That said, they also mentioned the risk of a self-fulfilling prophecy by investors pulling away from Icelandic exposure en masse.

After reviewing the Mishkin report, Morgan Stanley (2006) analysts, for example, concluded that there was no risk of a financial crisis in Iceland and recommended investing in Tier 1 capital of the banks. It is difficult to establish a direct causal link, but the banks' CDS spreads subsequently narrowed and the mini crisis ended in May 2006. It did have some lasting effects, however. The CDS spreads on the Icelandic banks stabilised at a higher level than on other Nordic banks. Also, in response to the international criticism, the Icelandic banks decided to diversify their funding mix: a strategy made possible by the banks' relatively strong credit ratings (see the next section). Furthermore, the banks tried to scale down their opaque cross-ownership structures.

It is interesting to note that, at the time of the mini-crisis in early 2006, market participants were concerned that the size of the three banks stood at between five and six times GDP and the banks' gross external debt at three times GDP. At the time of the collapse in 2008, these two figures had, in fact, doubled.

HOW CAN BANK FUNDAMENTALS LOOK SOUND DESPITE PROBLEMS?

In this section we take a closer look at arguments behind the high ratings assigned to the three largest Icelandic banks. We focus on Moody's setup, since Standard & Poor's only rated one of the banks and Fitch consistently rated the banks 'A' in the period from 2003 to 2007. Moody's bank senior debt and deposit rating is a function of

Figure 4.17 Moody's stand-alone assessment of the Icelandic banking sector

Moody's assessment of the banks' quantitative and qualitative fundamentals in Icelandic and in the Nordic region. Quantitative financial fundamentals are profitability, capital, liquidity, efficiency and asset quality, whereas qualitative fundamentals are franchise value, risk positioning and regulatory as well as operating environment.
Source: Moody's (2007b).

the "bank financial strength rating" (BFSR), reflecting an opinion of a bank's stand-alone financial strength relative to other rated banks globally, and an assessment of the degree of sovereign or other support in the event of financial distress. A bank's final credit rating may thus be higher than its BFSR. Moody's BFSR scorecard assigns equal weighting to quantitative financial fundamentals and qualitative indicators in mature markets like Iceland. Figure 4.17 shows Moody's (2007b) assessment of fundamental and qualitative indicators for the Icelandic banks in November 2007. Iceland's overall credit risk assessment was less benign than their average Nordic peers, but it did not signal any immediate cause for concern. In the sections below, we investigate in detail Moody's assessment of quantitative financial fundamentals and qualitative indicators, as well as sovereign support factors.

Window dressing quantitative financial fundamentals

Moody's five factors behind financial quantitative fundamentals are asset quality, profitability, total capital, liquidity and efficiency. At first sight, traditional indicators of these factors for the Icelandic banks were relatively favourable right up to the crash of the banking system. How could this happen? Below, we address this question for

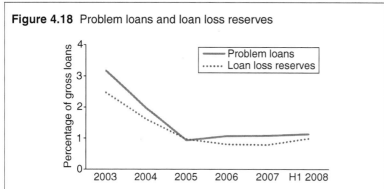

Figure 4.18 Problem loans and loan loss reserves

The average share of loan loss reserves made by the three banks. Problem loans are defined as the sum of doubtful and non-performing loans.
Source: Moody's.

all factors except "efficiency", which plays a smaller role in assessing the risk of bank failure. In summary, we argue that Moody's indicators of "asset quality" were based on the banks' (backward-looking) loan loss reserves and therefore did not capture the deteriorating asset quality. Inadequate loan loss reserves inflated profitability, and total capital was grossly exaggerated because of overestimation of asset value and failure to account for "weak capital", ie, bank-funded purchases of their own stocks. "Liquidity" was based on the banks' own estimates which, similar to banks in other countries, failed to account for the drastic dry-up in market liquidity during the crisis. In Iceland, the banks were also dependent on smoothly functioning foreign exchange markets. Some of these issues were problems of rating methodology and an over-reliance on figures reported by the banks themselves. Others, such as the problem with "weak capital", point to a weakness in financial supervision which, for example, should have detected the extent of weak capital.

Remarkably modest problem loans

In 2006 and 2007, the three banks' average loan loss reserves for future asset quality deteriorations were less than 1% of the gross outstanding loans. These tracked the banks' historical strong credit performance. The amount of reported problem loans, ie, the sum of doubtful and non-performing loans, was broadly in line with their Nordic peers. As shown in Figure 4.18, the number of problem loans was in fact lower in 2005–8 than in 2003–4. The implementation of the

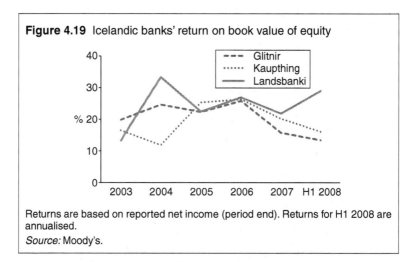

Figure 4.19 Icelandic banks' return on book value of equity

Returns are based on reported net income (period end). Returns for H1 2008 are annualised.
Source: Moody's.

new accounting standard explains the decline in loan loss reserves in 2004–5: the International Financial Reporting Standard (IFRS), which applied to Icelandic banks from 2005, required the banks to recognise loan loss reserves only after a loss or trigger event was identified. However, the drastic write-downs in asset values after the collapse suggest that there must also have been misreporting of loan performance. To quote the Special Investigation Commission (2010),

> When the banks collapsed there was an inevitable and significant reduction in the value of their assets. It is, however, the Commission's finding that the quality of loan portfolios had started to erode at least 12 months before the collapse and continued to erode until the collapse, even though this was not reported in the banks' financial statements.

The same commission reports that loan "renegotiations" had been common for large loans in order to avoid the need to report them as non-performing.

Reported high returns on equity

According to their published financial statements, the Icelandic banks appeared to be very profitable despite the high capital ratios. The average return on equity (ROE) was higher than in the rest of the Nordic region, as can be seen in Figures 4.17 and 4.19. *Ex post*, it is clear that the high ROE was boosted by the insufficient loan loss reserves and insufficient recognition of problem loans.

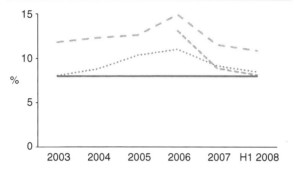

Figure 4.20 Total capital ratios and Tier 1 capital

– – Captial ratio (simple average)
······ Tier 1 ratio (simple average)
--- Capital ratio corrected with deductions of weak equity
——— Minimum (total capital ratio)

Icelandic banks' total capital and Tier 1 capital to risk-weighted assets (RWAs). The Tier 1 capital is shareholder equity minus intangible assets plus hybrid core capital. The Icelandic regulators allowed Tier 1 capital to include up to 33% of hybrid capital. Weak equity is defined as the direct financing by the banks of their own shares. Total capital is measured as Tier 1 capital plus subordinated loans excluding hybrid core capital. RWAs are reported by the banks.
Source: Moody's and the Special Investigation Committee.

Capital ratios and leverage

The published regulatory capital ratios stated by the Icelandic banks ranked them among the best-capitalised banks in the world. Although an IMF (2009) study documents that the capital ratios for eventually failing banks before 2008 were higher than for non-failing banks, high capital ratios are normally associated with financial robustness. As seen in Figure 4.20, the Icelandic banks' average total capital ratio was around 13% in the period between 2003 and mid-2007. In 2008, it dropped slightly but remained well above the statutory minimum requirements at 8% (ie, the total capital base divided by risk-weighted assets). The banks had internal targets of total capital ratios of 10–11%. If we trust that assets were worth par, as recorded by the Icelandic banks (which certainly was not the case), the leverage ratio on the total capital base was around 12. The ratio of asset to shareholder equity was around 17 and the ratio of asset to shareholder equity minus intangible assets was around 26. Hence, the banks' leverage, which is not influenced by the banks'

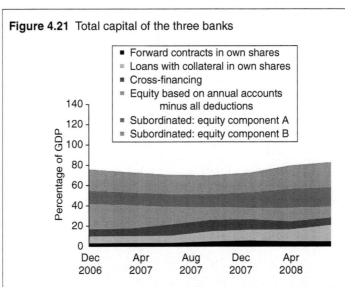

Figure 4.21 Total capital of the three banks

The total capital base of the three Icelandic banks was around 83% of GDP in Q2 2008. Subordinated debt represented around 53% of the capital base. The banks' direct financing by the banks of their own shares and cross-financings of shares accounted for around 34% of the capital base. Equity based on annual accounts minus the above-mentioned deductions accounted for the remaining 13% of the capital base.

Source: The Special Investigation Commission.

reported risk-weighted assets, appeared to be moderate. The average Tier 1 capital, which is closest to equity but includes hybrid capital, was also relatively high. In the next section, we will consider underestimation of risk when the banks computed risk-weighted assets. Below, we focus on the low quality of the banks' reported capital.

After the onset of the global financial crisis, the banks extended their direct loans with collateral in their own shares and raised the positions of forward contracts on their own shares. The direct financing by the banks of their own shares can be called "weak equity" (Special Investigation Commission 2010). In Figure 4.21 we see the weak equity relative to the total capital. In mid-2008, it represented around 25% of the combined capital base or more than 50% of the core capital (total capital base excluding subordinated loans). Cross-financing in stocks between the banks peaked in 2007. If we include cross-financing in the "weak equity" measure, it amounted to around 34% of total capital and more than 70% of core capital in mid-2008.

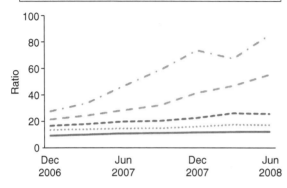

Figure 4.22 Leverage of the three banks

The banks' real leverage based on different measures of capital, which are defined in Figure 4.21. Leverage is defined as assets divided by equity.
Source: The Special Investigation Commission and the authors' calculations.

It is also interesting to take a close look at the banks' leverage. The leverage on book equity minus all deductions (own and cross-financing equity financing as well as subordinated debt) stood around 85 in mid-2008, as seen in Figure 4.22. Therefore, the *de facto* equity cushion of the banks did not offer much protection to the banks' creditors. In fact, the banks had reduced their economic capital without it being apparent in their balance sheets.

Prudential supervision by the Icelandic Financial Supervisory Authority would have required that loans exclusively secured with the banks' shares were subtracted from the capital. In Figure 4.20 we see that this factor alone would have pulled capital towards the 8% statutory minimum requirement in mid-2008 (for Landsbanki the ratio was below the 8% ratio in mid-2007). In addition, individual capital requirement for the banks should have been raised on the back of the higher risks associated with the banks' investment banking activities and the elevated risk of an economic downturn in Iceland (and thus higher loan losses). Stricter capital rules are allowed within the Basel II rules.

Future bank regulation is likely to partly address the issue. The Basel III bank regulation proposes raising the quality, consistency and transparency of the capital base as well as promoting the stability of the financial system as a whole. In the words of the Basel Committee on Banking Supervision (2009):

> The reforms strengthen bank-level, or microprudential, regulation, which will help raise the resilience of individual banking institutions to periods of stress. The reforms also have a macroprudential focus, addressing system wide risks that can build up across the banking sector as well as the procyclical amplification of these risks over time. Clearly these two micro and macroprudential approaches to supervision are interrelated, as greater resilience at the individual bank level reduces the risk of system wide shocks.

Micro-prudential capital requirements would have excluded the Icelandic banks' subordinated capital in the calculations of Tier 1 capital. Furthermore, macro-prudential capital requirements would have been raised in the light of the three banks' contribution to systemic risk in the economy. The capital requirements would have been very high given the three banks' systemic importance in the economy.

Satisfactory liquidity positions

The Icelandic banks' reported maturity mismatch between assets and liabilities was not extensive relative to other global banks. The maturity profile of the banks' assets and liabilities is illustrated in Figure 4.23. In addition to the liquid assets shown, the banks' longer-term asset portfolio and undrawn committed credit facilities were important sources of liquidity. Following the mini crisis of early 2006, the Icelandic banks decided to have liquidity policies that ensured sufficient liquid funds if the banks were unable to access capital markets or interbank markets over at least the next 12 months (but with an assumption of stable deposits). As of year-end 2007, the Icelandic banks reported that they passed Moody's 12-month liquidity test even with a partial run on retail and corporate deposits.

Banks may pledge securities (like government bonds and other related securities) as collateral in return for central banks, investment banks and money market funds providing short-term funding

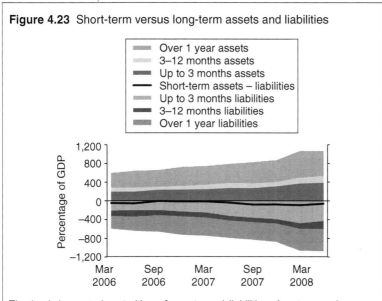

Figure 4.23 Short-term versus long-term assets and liabilities

The banks' reported maturities of assets and liabilities. Assets are shown as positive and liabilities as negative numbers. The black line shows the difference between assets and liabilities with a maturity of less than one year. Deposits are shown as short-term liabilities even though they are typically not required to be repaid in a short period of time.

Source: annual and interim reports.

(see also the penultimate section). Also, committed lines of credit can in principle be drawn up to their maximum. In reality, however, lines of credit are not totally committed liquidity insurance. In Iceland, many of the credit lines were contingent upon a minimum credit rating (Moody's Baa2). Furthermore, the liquidity facility provider to the Icelandic banks was often allowed to set the yield on the loans according to quotes in the CDS market (Special Investigation Commission 2010). The main risks for the Icelandic banks were that creditors would not roll over the debt (or refinance at much wider credit spreads) and repo lenders as well as trading counterparties required more collateral before long-term assets fully matured. *Ex post*, it was evident that the banks severely underestimated funding liquidity risk in foreign currency, but this problem was not unique to the Icelandic banks. Furthermore, the banks' reported liquidity pools, like the sale of bonds and subsidiaries of the banks, turned out to be very difficult to monetise in a distressed market environment.

Qualitative fundamentals below their Nordic peers

We now turn to Moody's assessment of the Icelandic banks' qualitative factors: franchise value, regulatory environment and operating environment, as well as risk positioning. The first three factors were assessed as "moderate" but with the banks' risk position having a low score. Moody's "franchise value" consists of an assessment of four sub-factors: market share and sustainability, geographical diversification, earnings stability and earnings diversification. The banks' earnings were considered unstable, as economic stability was assessed to be more volatile in Iceland (exacerbated by large macroeconomic imbalances). That said, the loan portfolio was judged to be partly diversified, as foreign operations of the banks accounted for a growing share of the total assets. Icelandic regulation and enforcement of regulation was not a cause for concern for the credit rating agencies since it was in line with Basel and EU regulation. Furthermore, the level of corruption was very low. Moody's "risk positioning" score consists of an assessment of corporate governance, controls and risk management, financial reporting transparency, credit risk concentration, liquidity management and market risk appetite. Moody's considered the overall "risk positioning" score to be low. The banks' credit scores on qualitative and quantitative fundamentals in the "polygon" (Figure 4.17) can be used to understand the BFSR by year-end 2007.

The Icelandic banks' way in to the Aaa league

It is illustrative to take a closer look at Moody's rating of Kaupthing, the largest of the three Icelandic banks, over time (Figure 4.24). The ratings of the two other Icelandic banks broadly followed the same pattern. Before 2003, Kaupthing had been an unrated investment bank, but as the bank merged with the Icelandic retail bank, Búnaðarbanki Íslands ("the agricultural bank") it received a long-term deposit and debt A3 credit rating from Moody's. Later it was upgraded to A2 by Moody's to "reflect... the bank's successful execution of the merger of the two predecessor entities in May 2003, resulting in a well diversified and dominant market player with healthy financial fundamentals." After the acquisition of Danish FIH Erhvervsbanks, where consolidated assets approximately doubled, the bank was upgraded to A1 to "reflect... the bank's leading position in its domestic market in Iceland, the fact that it is one of the

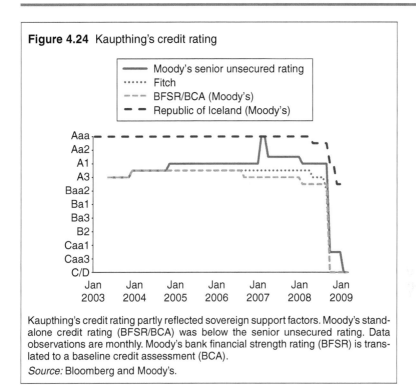

Figure 4.24 Kaupthing's credit rating

Kaupthing's credit rating partly reflected sovereign support factors. Moody's stand-alone credit rating (BFSR/BCA) was below the senior unsecured rating. Data observations are monthly. Moody's bank financial strength rating (BFSR) is translated to a baseline credit assessment (BCA).
Source: Bloomberg and Moody's.

country's largest institutions, and its healthy financial fundamentals." In 2005, Kaupthing acquired the London-based investment bank Singer & Friedlander. Moody's A1 rating reflected the strong likelihood of state support in the event of systemic shock, with the BFSR remaining unchanged at A2. In fact, the stand-alone rating was downgraded to A3 in the second half of 2006.

In February 2007, Moody's (2007a,c) incorporated additional financial support into its bank ratings trough its joint-default analysis (JDA). The Icelandic banks were thus temporarily upgraded to Aaa. A refinement of its bank rating methodology in April 2008 modified ratings to Aa3 after heavy criticism of the JDA. Each of the banks thus "only" received a three-notch uplift in its debt/deposit ratings from its stand-alone credit rating. Moody's justification for the new Aa3 rating of the banks was explained in its publication on the Icelandic banking system outlook. To quote Moody's (2008a):

> Each bank individually accounts for at least 25% of the system. We believe that the default of any one of these three banks would pose a substantial risk to the Icelandic economy, the consequences of

which would be far greater than the cost of rescuing a failing bank. Therefore, in Moody's judgment, there is a very high probability that the Icelandic authorities would support each of the rated banks in a period of financial distress.

Hence, the Icelandic banks were rated as if the sovereign was able to bail them out in a worst case scenario. We return to the sovereign support issue in the penultimate section.

The rating agencies were not alone in giving a positive review of Icelandic banks. In November 2007, Baldursson and Portes (2007) issued a report, again sponsored by the Iceland Chamber of Commerce, which was even more optimistic than the credit rating agencies. In their assessment:

> The banks have negligible exposure to the US subprime market, structured finance products, and related financial vehicles that have hit many financial institutions hard recently. Most fundamental, the banks exploit strong competitive advantage, arising from their entrepreneurial management, flat management structures, and unusual business models.
>
> Yet in spite of their strong performance, Icelandic banks have lower ratings than their Nordic peers, and a much higher risk premium is being placed on their debt during the present turmoil. We see no justification for this in their risk exposure. This suggests that either the markets are not fully aware of their situation or markets place a country premium on the banks.

In the next section we will take a look at the financial markets' view on the Icelandic banks relative to their credit ratings.

Low market-implied credit rating

Was the market better than credit ratings at capturing the risks of the Icelandic banking system? The answer depends on whether we consider equity, bond or CDS markets' assessment. Equity-implied credit ratings, based on the performance of the equity using Moody's KMV expected default frequency measure, were not factoring in immediate financial distress for the Icelandic banks in 2008 (see Kaupthing's implied rating in Figure 4.25).[12] As previously noted, the banks' market capitalisation was an unreliable indicator of the true valuation. In fact, the Special Investigation Commission (2010) documents manipulation of stock values.

It was more difficult for the banks to influence the CDS market directly. CDS-implied ratings, ie, ratings implied from CDS spreads,

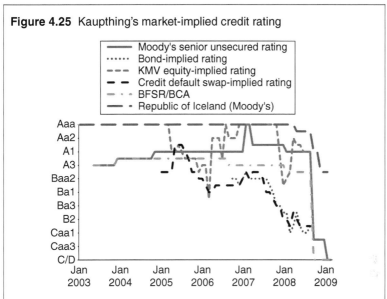

Figure 4.25 Kaupthing's market-implied credit rating

Kaupthing's CDS-implied credit rating was lower than the official rating. Moody's CDS-implied ratings are derived from five-year CDS quotes. For further information please Moody's (2010). Data observations are monthly.
Source: Bloomberg and Moody's.

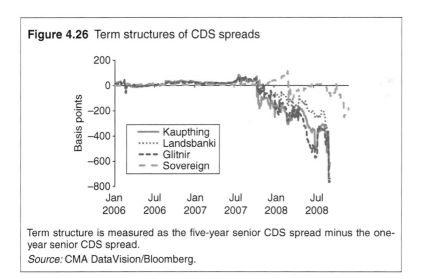

Figure 4.26 Term structures of CDS spreads

Term structure is measured as the five-year senior CDS spread minus the one-year senior CDS spread.
Source: CMA DataVision/Bloomberg.

were much lower than senior unsecured ratings and ratings based on equity prices. Since CDS spreads tend to move in tandem with credit spreads on bonds, it is not surprising that the bond-implied

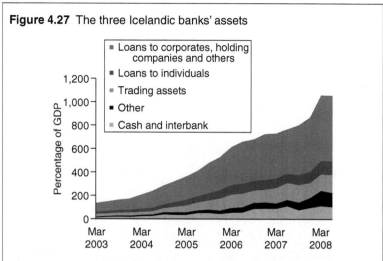

Figure 4.27 The three Icelandic banks' assets

Composition of the three largest banks' assets. Loans to corporations and holding companies were the largest item on the banks' balance sheets. Further items include loans to individuals, trading assets and cash and interbank loans. The item "other" measures all other assets not included in the aforementioned categories.
Source: Bloomberg and interim accounts.

rating was similar to the CDS-implied rating. The interesting observation is that worries about the asset quality of Icelandic banks and doubts on the sovereign support spurred a demand for credit protection. Hedge-fund speculation may also have contributed to a further widening of the CDS spreads Furthermore, as seen in Figure 4.26, the term structures of CDS spreads for the three major banks started to invert in the autumn of 2007: a typical sign that the market is worried that the issuer may face financial distress. In summary, the CDS markets and the ratings derived from CDS spreads were the perhaps the clearest early warning signals of the banking crisis.

THE BANKS' ASSET QUALITY

In this section we take a closer look at the banks' asset composition and quality. In summary, several factors contributed to the decline in asset quality. The rapid expansion of the banking book, which covers loans to the corporate sector and individuals, in itself indicated a deteriorating asset quality. In addition, many Icelandic customers had loans denominated in foreign currency and they were therefore vulnerable to a depreciation of the Icelandic króna. The corporate loan book was of course sensitive to a downturn in the Icelandic and international economy, but the banks were particularly sensitive to such a downturn because they were also heavily exposed to listed and unlisted domestic equities. Finally, the banks had weak corporate governance and a high concentration of risk in their loan portfolios. Below, we take a closer look at the composition of the banks' assets shown in Figure 4.27.

Loans to the corporate sector rising sharply

The biggest item on the banks' balance sheet was corporate loans, whose share of total lending was approximately 83% in 2007–8. The banks' large volume of loans to the corporate sector was in part driven by the reliance on the simplest approach to assessing the risk-weighted assets in the banking book (the so-called "standardised approach" in the Basel II framework) rather than the development of their own internal rating-based models (IRBs). In the standardised approach, each group of customers has a fixed capital charge per unit of exposure in the calculations of risk-weighted assets (20% to 150% depending on the credit assessment). A well-known weakness in this framework is that banks have an incentive to exploit the risk weights and acquire the riskiest corporate assets. This seems to have been the case in Iceland. An example is the Icelandic banks' acquisition and leveraged finance (ALF) portfolios. The banks were rather open about their exposures, with Glitnir noting in its official securities note document:

> we have exposure to credit risk related to acquisition finance loans, which typically involve higher degrees of leverage than general corporate borrowing and make these borrowers more exposed to increases in interest rates and downturns in the economy.

Glitnir reported that the leveraged loan portfolio accounted for approximately 9.2% of its total loan portfolio as of Q2 2008. For Kaupthing, the ALF portfolio was reported to represent 17% of its customers' loans at the end of Q2 2008.

Before the onset of the global financial crisis, the Icelandic banks expanded into new markets where there was already fierce competition. The banks saw the expansion outside of Iceland as a way to diversify their loan portfolios and improve their credit ratings. In Figure 4.28 we see that around two-thirds of the banks' loans were to outside of Iceland in 2008. The competition for loans to customers, however, prohibited the Icelandic banks, which faced a larger credit

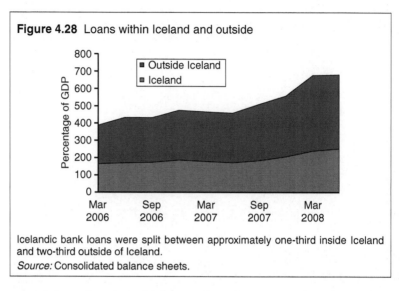

Figure 4.28 Loans within Iceland and outside

Icelandic bank loans were split between approximately one-third inside Iceland and two-third outside of Iceland.
Source: Consolidated balance sheets.

spread, from charging a higher credit-risk premium than their global competitors. To quote the chief economist of Kaupthing, Jónsson (2009):

> the three Icelandic banks could pass the premium on to their domestic clients, but that option did not exist with foreign clients, who might be lost to banks of other nations.

The Icelandic banks' relatively strong liquidity positions subsequent to the mini crisis in 2006 made the banks better prepared for the onset of global financial crisis in mid-2007 than many other international banks. In fact, the Icelandic banks saw the global financial crisis as a way to capture market shares from their competitors. This explains why the Icelandic banks continued to expand their balance sheets even as the global crisis started in mid-2007 (Figure 4.27). In August 2007, Kaupthing also announced its intention to acquire the Dutch merchant bank NIBC, which would have increased Kaupthing's balance sheet by two-thirds.[13] In fact, lending to foreign parties increased by more than 100% of Iceland's GDP within a year. In the words of the Special Investigation Commission (2010):

> The increase was so substantial that it can be assumed that many of these new clients had turned to the Icelandic banks after other banks were beginning to slow their lending, and that these clients had thus been rejected by other banks…. The Icelandic banks thus

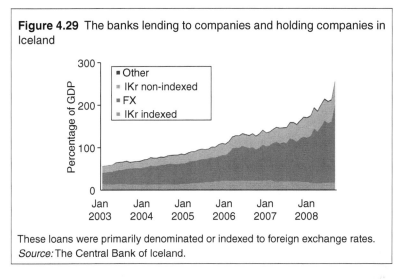

Figure 4.29 The banks lending to companies and holding companies in Iceland

These loans were primarily denominated or indexed to foreign exchange rates.
Source: The Central Bank of Iceland.

lent substantial amounts while experiencing considerable liquidity problems at the same time.

In Iceland, the banking system extended its total lending to the domestic corporate sector to more than 170% of GDP by year-end 2007 (Figure 4.29). In particular, lending to holding companies grew rapidly in the second half of 2007. The banks were also lending for stock purchases and often took domestic stocks as collateral.[14] Loans collateralised with equities increased the banks' exposure to (indirect) market liquidity risk in case the borrower was unable to fulfil the loan contract. As the crisis struck in Iceland, the collateral sales related to contractual margin calls increased and this resulted in a downward pressure on equity prices. The Special Investigation Commission (2010) documents that these margin calls were abandoned, as the banks were reluctant to realise credit losses on the loan portfolio and start a fire sale in the domestic equity market.

The double-digit interest rates from early 2006 in Iceland (and a stable currency) increased the incentive for the Icelandic companies to finance themselves in foreign low-interest-rate currencies. Approximately 70–75% of bank loans to corporations were foreign-exchange linked, which was an important indirect credit risk for the Icelandic banks. The banks were fully hedged against currency risk but their customers were left with open foreign-currency exposure. The banks had fewer assets than liabilities denominated in foreign currency, which implied a short (spot) position in foreign exchange

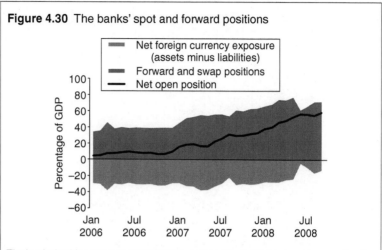

Figure 4.30 The banks' spot and forward positions

The banks had fewer assets than liabilities denominated in foreign currency (equivalent to a short foreign exchange position). However, the banks established a long foreign exchange position through forward and currency swaps. Hence, their overall net open position was long foreign exchange.
Source: The Central Bank of Iceland.

market (Figure 4.30). Without hedging, a depreciation of the domestic currency would deteriorate the banks' capital adequacy ratios. However, the banks hedged themselves against such a depreciation with a long foreign currency position through derivatives (currency swaps, etc). In fact, the banks not only were protected against a depreciation of the Icelandic króna, but they also used derivatives to increase their open long foreign exchange position in order to gain on a depreciation of the króna.[15] The net positive foreign exchange balance was around 40% of GDP at year-end 2007, partly reflecting the fact that the banks' customers had short foreign exchange positions.

A part of the Icelandic corporate sector's foreign exchange risk was naturally hedged, but the majority of the companies were still dependent on króna earnings to repay the debt and interest rate payments in foreign currency. In the event of a sharp depreciation of the domestic currency, it could easily result in loan losses on the asset side of the banks if the underlying borrower was unable to repay the larger foreign-exchange-denominated debt. In Iceland, the foreign-currency-indexed debt of the corporate sector was substantially higher than in other systemic banking and currency crises (Figure 4.31). With the sharp depreciation of the Icelandic currency in

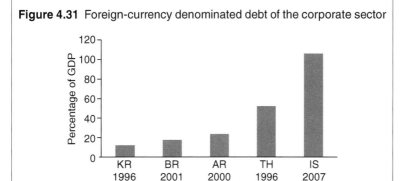

Figure 4.31 Foreign-currency denominated debt of the corporate sector

Foreign-currency-denominated (or indexed) debt of the corporate sector in countries facing financial crises. The data was collected prior to the systemic banking crisis. KR, Republic of Korea; BR, Brazil; AR, Argentina; TH, Thailand; IS, Iceland. *Source:* Rosenberg *et al* (2005) and the Central Bank of Iceland.

2008, the majority of the firms in Iceland were technically bankrupt. This was also the case in Thailand in the late 1990s.

Loans to the household sector in Iceland

Loans to individuals in Iceland constituted a smaller part of the banks' balance sheets. The three banks entered the Icelandic mortgage market in Q3 2004, when they started competing aggressively with the state-supported HF Fund (which used to be the dominant player in the retail mortgage sector). This competition set the foundations for an underpricing of risk, since the banks would never be able to offer competitive interest against a state-sponsored institution over an extended period of time (the HF Fund's interest rate set the lower bound, as seen in Figure 4.32). The banks gained a competitive edge against the government guarantee by granting more liberal criteria for mortgages, eg, attractive loan-to-value ratios (OECD 2009). This resulted in households refinancing their mortgages and switching to the banks. Hence, the HF Fund's lending relative to GDP fell sharply (Figure 4.33).

As the HF Fund offered domestic currency loans only (indexed to the consumer price index), the banks later promoted low-interest foreign-currency loans. This resulted in a sharply increasing share of foreign-currency-indexed loans to households (around 15% of GDP in 2008). As with corporate loans, the foreign-currency lending was an indirect credit risk for the banks, as few households would

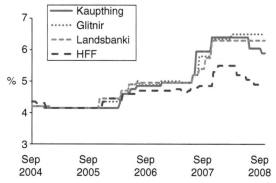

Figure 4.32 Real interest rates on indexed housing loans

Real interest rates on inflation-indexed housing loans set by the three largest banks and the Housing Financing Fund. The state-supported HF Fund's interest rate set the lower bound for interest rates in Iceland.
Source: The Central Bank of Iceland.

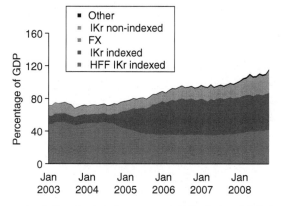

Figure 4.33 Domestic banks and HF Fund lending to households

Deposit money banks' lending by category: non-inflation indexed, inflation indexed, indexed to the foreign exchange rate and others. The HF Fund provided only inflation-indexed loans.
Source: The Central Bank of Iceland.

have a natural hedge against a sharp depreciation of the domestic exchange rate. The banks' lending to the Icelandic household sector reached slightly more than 100% of GDP or 200% of disposable income by year-end 2007, as seen in Figures 4.33 and 4.34. It is a rather large amount, but it was partly mitigated by relatively modest loan-to-value ratios. It suggests that the fall in Icelandic house

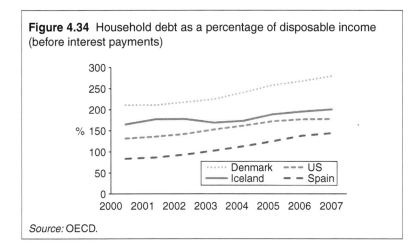

Figure 4.34 Household debt as a percentage of disposable income (before interest payments)

Source: OECD.

Table 4.1 Loan-to-value ratio of mortgage loans

LTV ratio	Year-end 2006	Year-end 2007
0–50	20	34
50–70	22	25
70–90	34	23
90–100	8	5
100+	8	4
Unknown	8	9

The banks' reported loan-to-value ratios of mortgage loans were moderate going into the crisis (based on parent company data). This indicated that the banks had a cushion before they would start to lose money.
Source: The Icelandic Financial Supervisory Authority and the Central Bank of Iceland.

prices in 2007–8 was not the primary culprit of the banking crisis in Iceland, since there were relatively stringent loan-to-value ratios on mortgage loans to the household sector (see also Table 4.1).[16]

The banks' trading assets were larger than those of their peers

In the period 2003–8, the three banks' trading portfolios accounted for 15–16% of total assets on average (Figure 4.27). The main part of the marketable securities was in the form of bonds, whereas the equity holdings (both listed and unlisted equity exposures) accounted for approximately 2–3% of total assets. According to the IFRS, changes in market value of trading assets are required to be reflected in the income statement on a mark-to-market basis. In the

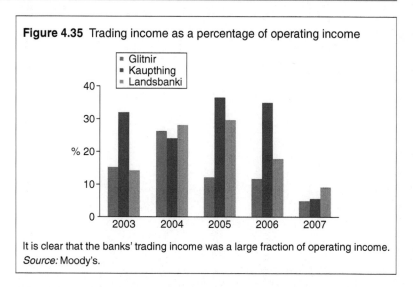

Figure 4.35 Trading income as a percentage of operating income

It is clear that the banks' trading income was a large fraction of operating income.
Source: Moody's.

years of rising stock markets (2003 to mid-2007), the strong profits of the bank were buoyed from trading income (Figure 4.35). However, when the price of risky assets fell after the onset of the global financial crisis in mid-2007, the strong income from long trading positions was clearly not sustainable.

Poor corporate governance and leveraged bank owners

The primary worries regarding the Icelandic banks were the large extent of related party lending, their large exposures to single customers and the opaque nature of their cross-ownership structures. This was noted by several investment banks in 2006 and onwards. The findings were repeated in an IMF (2008a) study:

> Icelandic banks have a relatively high concentration of exposure to large borrowers and connected parties, with the top 20 borrowers representing between 250 percent and 300 percent of Tier I capital.

In addition, it was common knowledge that the controlling shares in the banks were owned by highly leveraged interconnected companies and they were sensitive to a fall in share prices. After the collapse of the banking system, the Special Investigation Commission (2010) revealed that the lending to related parties in interim accounts was grossly understated in financial statements. In fact, each of the banks had total lending to related parties exceeding the maximum of 25% of capital stated in EU regulations on large risk exposures.

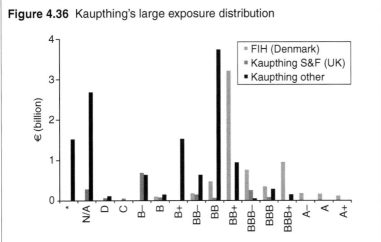

Figure 4.36 Kaupthing's large exposure distribution

The distribution of Kaupthing's subjective credit ratings based on exposures larger than €0.045 billion (as of September 25, 2008). The figure shows the parent company and the two subsidiaries, FIH Erhvervsbanks and Kaupthing Singer & Friedlander. "N/A" indicates the data was not available and the asterisk indicates that the loan taker is on a special list without a need for a credit rating.
Source: http://wikileaks.org/.

The banks circumvented the rule by using a very narrow definition of connected risk to related parties. In addition, many of the banks' customers had large loans from several banks, which resulted in a concentration of risk in the system. For instance, the three banks' total lending to Baugur Group at the highest level constituted 53% of the three banks' equity base. The commission also found that

> The operations of the banks were in many ways characterised by their maximising the benefit of majority shareholders, who held the reins in the banks, rather than by running reliable banks with the interests of all shareholders in mind and to show due responsibility towards creditors.

After the collapse of the Icelandic banks, a document was leaked which provided a snapshot of Kaupthing's pre-crisis loan book of large exposures. We have aggregated the data in Figure 4.36 according to the internal risk ratings scale based on an individual assessment of customers. The bank's rating scale is to some extent related to the official rating agencies' but with the bank's internal assessment of the probability of default that within 12 months the customer will be unable to meet his financial obligation.[17] According to the bank's

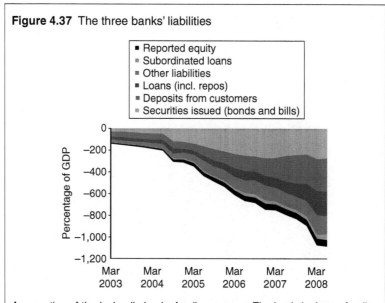

Figure 4.37 The three banks' liabilities

Aggregation of the Icelandic banks funding sources. The banks' primary funding source was issuances of commercial paper and bonds. The second most important funding source was foreign wholesale and retail deposits. Third in line were loans. The item "other liabilities" measures all other liabilities not included in the previous categories.
Source: Bloomberg and interim accounts.

internal assessment, the asset quality of the large exposures was predominantly non-investment grade. This seems to largely contradict a statement by Kaupthing in September 2008 that there are "signs of an improved loan portfolio despite the substantial growth of the portfolio since 2003" under the headline "sound asset quality".[18] The loan book revealed very dubious lending and governance practices. There were loans given to holding companies and individuals with low or no collateral, or loans to entities with the only purpose of buying stocks in Kaupthing. For example, Kaupthing's loans to companies related to Exista, which was the biggest shareholder with a 23% stake, amounted to more than 25% of Kaupthing's capital.

HOW DID THE BANKS GET FUNDING AFTER 2006?

It is remarkable that the Icelandic banks managed to continue their aggressive growth despite the mini funding crisis in early 2006. We now show how they were able to fund themselves up to the collapse of the banking system. Figure 4.37 shows the funding sources

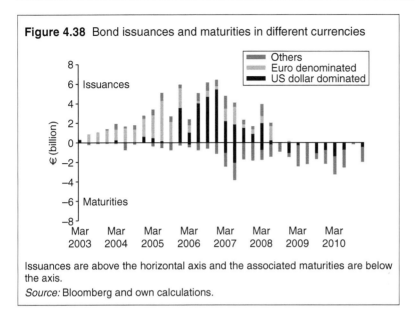

Figure 4.38 Bond issuances and maturities in different currencies

Issuances are above the horizontal axis and the associated maturities are below the axis.

Source: Bloomberg and own calculations.

divided into broad categories from January 2003 to June 2008. The banks' most important funding source was issuances of commercial paper and bonds. The second most important funding source was foreign wholesale and retail deposits. A third source of funding was from bilateral and syndicated loans as well as access to money market lines from relationship banks. These include short-term collateralised loans from central banks and investment banks. We now take a closer look at these funding sources and discuss the role played by the government and central bank in securing this funding.

Unsecured securities as the primary funding source

Leading up to the mini crisis in 2006, the Icelandic banks borrowed heavily in foreign security markets at low credit spreads in order to finance their asset growth. Initially, the Icelandic banks focused on unsecured bond issuances under their Euro Medium Term Notes programmes (Figure 4.38). The bonds typically had a maturity of three to five years. The Icelandic banks' debt had high credit ratings and could therefore easily enter the balance sheets of international banks and other institutional investors who also saw Icelandic risk as means of diversifying their portfolios.

After the mini crisis of early 2006, the Icelandic banks seemed unable to access European debt securities markets and they shifted to the US debt securities markets. The opening in the US was primarily caused by a strong demand for cash collateralised debt obligations (CDOs) with Icelandic bank securities as the underlying assets. These securities were attractive to use as collateral in CDOs, as they offered higher yields than other credit institutions with similar ratings. The Icelandic banks were also used as reference securities in synthetic CDOs, and the selling of credit protection caused by this may have contributed to a narrowing of CDS spreads on the banks. According to Bloomberg (2008), relying on Standard & Poor's documentation, the three Icelandic banks were included in 376 CDOs worldwide and another 297 CDOs had made bets on two of the three banks as of October 2008. After mid-2007, a part of the general widening of CDS spreads on the Icelandic banks was likely to have been caused by buying of protection to hedge existing CDOs. During the mini crisis in 2006, the banks also returned to issuances in króna. In order to repay liabilities in foreign currency, the banks thus relied on a liquid functioning foreign exchange spot or swap market.

Finally, implicit sovereign support through the silent acceptance of the growing banking system had calmed the senior bond investors. The common understanding among investors is best summarised by the investment bank, Merrill Lynch (2006):[19]

> in the event of a systemic crisis, we would be expecting the Treasury to support the banks [...] such is the dependence of the banks on external funding that we would expect some provision to ensure that shorter term, senior obligations at the very least continued to be serviced in an orderly fashion.

The Icelandic banks are likely to have found it impossible to rollover their liabilities if government officials had explicitly dismissed the implicit guarantee on the banks' liabilities.

Deposit finance outside of Iceland

We now turn to the banks' funding through foreign deposits. Before the onset of the mini crisis of 2006, deposits constituted a relatively low proportion of the banks' total liabilities (around 20%) and the average ratio of loans to deposits was around 3. This implied a very high dependency on market funding relative to their Nordic

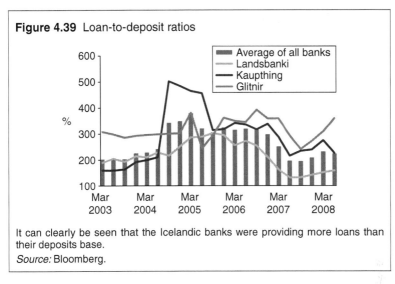

Figure 4.39 Loan-to-deposit ratios

It can clearly be seen that the Icelandic banks were providing more loans than their deposits base.
Source: Bloomberg.

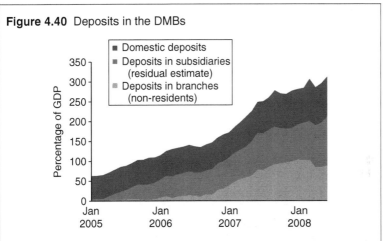

Figure 4.40 Deposits in the DMBs

The composition of deposits from January 2005 to June 2008. Deposits in subsidiaries are calculated as the difference between total deposits according to interim accounts and deposits in branches according to data from the Central Bank of Iceland.
Source: The Central Bank of Iceland and the authors' calculations.

peers. On the back of the mini crisis, the rating agencies encouraged the banks to increase their deposit base, since it was considered to be a more reliable funding source than bond financing. Deposits of ordinary Icelanders were never going to be enough to fund the banks. The integration of financial markets in the European Economic Area (EEA),[20] however, enabled the Icelandic banks to expand rapidly in the European market. Icelandic banks could easily establish subsidiaries and branches in the EEA, based on the principles of home country control and mutual recognition. Deposits in subsidiaries and branches abroad became an important funding base in 2007 and early 2008. As a result, the ratio of deposits to total liabilities rose to around 30% and the average ratio of loans to deposits fell to around 2 (Figures 4.37 and 4.39). In 2006, some of the banks' foreign subsidiaries already offered so-called wholesale deposits (often deposits based on specific agreement between intermediaries, including interest rates and duration). Landsbanki also offered accounts through their branches, as seen in Figure 4.40.

In October 2006, Landsbanki launched Internet-based retail deposit accounts through their UK branch, paying higher interest rates than many competitors were offering. The accounts were named IceSave. EU/EEA rules stipulate that branches are a part of the parent company (located in Iceland) and operations should be supervised by the (Icelandic) supervisory authority. Furthermore, the UK Financial Services Authority was to supervise the liquidity management and was authorised to intervene in the branch. A branch was an Icelandic legal entity and deposits were thus covered by the Icelandic Depositors and Investors' Guarantee Fund up to €20,887 to each depositor (or €20,000 according to the European Deposit Guarantee Directive).[21] The Icelandic insurance scheme only had assets amounting to around 0.5% of deposits in October 2008, and it had insufficient funds to cover even domestic deposits in the case that one of the three banks failed. This can be said of other countries with large banks (relative to GDP) as well, however. But the foreign deposits in branches represented a large foreign currency potential liability of the sovereign, which could have been avoided if regulators had demanded a transfer of the deposits of the branch to a UK subsidiary. We return to the sovereign's contingent liabilities in the penultimate section. The deposit accounts were marketed in the UK and later in the Netherlands with reference to the systemic importance of Landsbanki in Iceland, the Republic of Iceland's Aaa rating as well as the deposit insurance backed by Icelandic authorities.[22] IceSave was named a "clear genius" by the management of Landsbanki, as it was a cheap way to get funding when the funding cost on new senior debt issuances was rising (as reflected in the CDS

THE COLLAPSE OF THE ICELANDIC BANKING SYSTEM

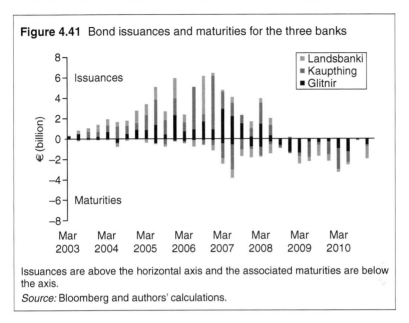

Figure 4.41 Bond issuances and maturities for the three banks

Issuances are above the horizontal axis and the associated maturities are below the axis.
Source: Bloomberg and authors' calculations.

spread on the bank). In Figure 4.41 we see that Landsbanki lowered its debt issuance since the bank was so successful in gathering deposits.

In November 2007 Kaupthing also launched an Internet-based savings account through Kaupthing Edge, deposit accounts offering relatively high interest rates. Kaupthing's stand-alone subsidiary in the UK, Kaupthing Singer & Friedlander, was an independent foreign legal entity under the supervision of the UK FSA and depositors were covered by the UK deposit guarantee scheme (the Financial Services Compensation Scheme).[23] In June 2008, Glitnir also opened a retail account under the name "Save & Save". Landsbanki, with its high deposit ratios, was considered less risky by the market, since insured depositors have few incentives to fear the safety of their deposit (at least as long as the insurance is credible). However, the relatively strong funding position of Landsbanki changed over the period February to April 2008 with negative coverage of the Icelandic banks in the UK press. It resulted in an outflow of wholesale and, to a lesser extent, retail deposits in the UK branch. It was close to causing the failure of Landsbanki in early 2008. Nonetheless, the return of retail deposits was later used to repay the outflow of wholesale deposits (Special Investigation Committee 2010).[24] Landsbanki thus was surviving on the back of insured deposits.

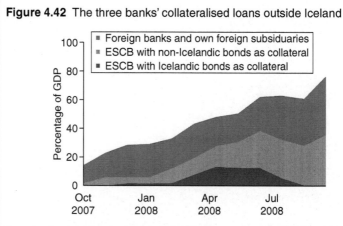

Figure 4.42 The three banks' collateralised loans outside Iceland

Data for the three banks' collateralised loans with foreign banks and their own foreign subsidiaries as well as at the European System of Central Banks (ESCB). The data covers the period from October 31, 2007, to September 30, 2008 and was disclosed after the collapse of the banking system. Data on Landsbanki's collateralised loans made through the UK is not available.
Source: Special Investigation Commission.

Short-term collateralised loan and the collapse of the exchange rate

The banks' external maturity profile shortened substantially after the onset of the global financial crisis. Repurchase agreements ("repos") or collateralised loans turned into an important short-term funding source. In September 2008, collateralised loans from outside Iceland amounted to at least 70% of Iceland's GDP. As seen in Figure 4.42, repo transactions with non-central banks (for example, Royal Bank of Scotland) accounted for the main part of the collateralised loans.[25] The securities that were secured against the loans were typically the banks' foreign bonds and Icelandic securities.

Central banks provide (last resort) liquidity facilities against eligibility collateral to banks with capital above the statutory minimum requirements. Bagehot's (1873) famous dictum states that "to avert panic, central banks should lend early and freely (without limit), to solvent firms, against good collateral, and at 'high rates'." Obviously, solvency turned out to be a problem, but central banks also accepted dubious collateral. The Icelandic banks owned subsidiaries in Luxembourg and thus had access to collateralised loans through the Central Bank of Luxembourg (CBL) from the European System of Central Banks (ESCB). In the latter part of 2008, the CBL was a

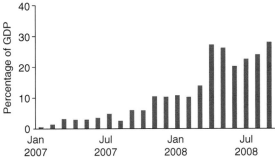

Figure 4.43 The banks' holdings of other Icelandic banks' bonds

It is clear that the Icelandic banks were buying their own and other Icelandic banks' bonds in 2007 and 2008.
Source: The Central Bank of Iceland.

major provider of liquidity to the Icelandic banks, with the banks achieving close to 40% of GDP in collateralised loans through the CBL. Central bank rules prevent banks from posting their own debt as collateral, but during 2008 the three banks circumvented this by posting each other's bonds as collateral at the CBL. This procedure is popularly referred to as issuing "love letters". At the end of July 2008, the CBL prohibited this way of funding with reference to the strong interconnection among the Icelandic banks. This reduction is clearly seen in Figure 4.42.

Fortunately for the banks, the "love letters" were more readily accepted at the Central Bank of Iceland (CBI). In 2008, the Icelandic banks issued debt to the savings bank, Icebank, which then used the debt as collateral at the CBI. Figure 4.43 shows the rapid growth in the banks' holdings of bonds issued by other Icelandic banks and Figure 4.44 demonstrates that these bonds were used to a large extent as collateral at the CBI. Collateralised loans at the CBI amounted to around 20% of GDP. Kaupthing and Glitnir also issued covered bonds used for collateralised loans at the CBI.

The CBI's domestic liquidity provision made the upcoming crisis worse by contributing to a collapse of the exchange rate. The CBI only provided liquidity in Icelandic króna, whereas the CBL provided liquidity in euro, in compliance with rules on liquidity. Since the Icelandic banks primarily needed foreign currency, they exchanged the króna into foreign exchange in the spot or currency swap markets. In Figure 4.30, we see that the banks constantly raised their

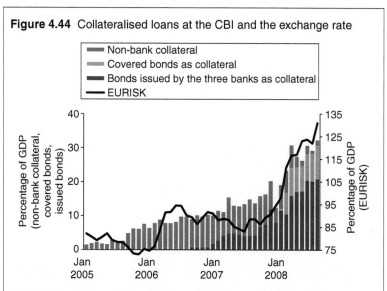

Figure 4.44 Collateralised loans at the CBI and the exchange rate

The Icelandic banks collateralised loans at the Central Bank of Iceland from January 2005 to September 2008. The CBI accepted bonds issued by the three banks. A rise in EURISK is an appreciation of the euro against the (onshore) Icelandic króna.

Source: Central Bank of Iceland and the Special Investigation Commission.

short positions against the domestic currency. The one-way flow in the currency market was exacerbated by currency carry traders liquidating their existing positions.[26] Figure 4.45 shows the simultaneous sharp rise in sovereign credit risk and the drop in the exchange rate. It was followed by a further sharp drop in the off-shore exchange rate after the implementation of exchange rate controls in October 2008.

In 2008, the CBI's rules for the credit standards of eligible collateral were broadly similar to the rules in the ESCB, stating that unsecured bonds and bills were required to have a minimum long-term rating of "A−" by Standard & Poor's or Fitch Ratings or of "A3" by Moody's as well as having securities trading on a regulated market in the EEA. However, the credit agencies' ratings of the Icelandic banks reflected the high probability of sovereign support to the banking system. The CBI might reasonably, as a minimum, have based its liquidity facilities against eligible collateral on an assessment of a bank's stand-alone financial strength credit rating and/or supplemented by market implied credit ratings. According to Moody's

THE COLLAPSE OF THE ICELANDIC BANKING SYSTEM

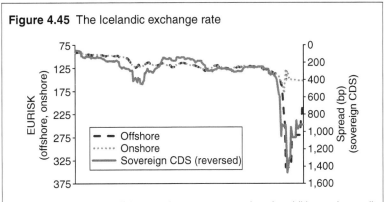

Figure 4.45 The Icelandic exchange rate

Icelandic onshore and offshore exchange rates are given in addition to the credit default swap on the Republic of Iceland. A rise in EURISK is an appreciation of the euro against the króna. The rise in credit risk co-moved with a depreciation of the króna.
Source: Reuters and the Central Bank of Iceland.

stand-alone BFSR or CDS-implied credit ratings, the Icelandic banks were not qualified for collateralised lending in February 2008.

The sovereign's inability to help the banking sector

All access to funding of the banks was facilitated by or even depended on implicit or explicit sovereign support. Throughout the expansion of the banking system, official statements indeed indicated a willingness to support the three largest banks. In fact, the country's prime minister, Geir Haarde, was very proud of the banking sector and actually wanted it to expand further. In his words (Haarde 2008):[27]

> The financial sector has become one of the most important sectors in the country. I see it as very important that it will be in a position to continue its growth [...]. The Treasury is in a strong position and can therefore borrow sizeable amounts if necessary. There is no doubt that the Treasury and the Central Bank could provide assistance if a serious situation were to emerge in the banking system.

However, Iceland clearly faced a huge mismatch between the foreign currency roll-over risk of the banking sector and the sovereign's ability to provide foreign currency. The banking sector's foreign currency liabilities far exceeded Iceland's fiscal capacity.

After the onset on the global credit crisis in mid-2007, the appetite for Icelandic bonds declined sharply and the bonds were issued

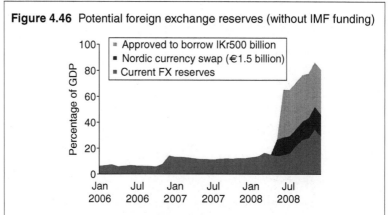

Figure 4.46 Potential foreign exchange reserves (without IMF funding)

Iceland's foreign exchange reserves and potential funding in foreign currency. In June 2008, the government's debt management office was allowed to borrow up to IKr500 billion to bolster the foreign currency reserves. However, they were unable to borrow at attractive credit spreads.
Source: Bloomberg.

with higher yields. The main worry was the total bond refinancing need in 2008 and the following years. In 2009 alone, it accounted for 100% GDP and €35 billion in foreign bonds needed refinancing through 2012, corresponding to more than 300% of GDP. Glitnir had the largest rollover risk among the banks in Q4 2008 and Q1 2009 (Figure 4.41). The significant fall in the banks' new bond issuances combined with the fast pace of lending magnified the medium-term refinancing risks. The banks were gambling that the funding markets would open up again as they had done after the mini crisis of early 2006.

The banks' short-term gross external debt rose from around 190% of GDP in Q4 2007 to around 290% of GDP in Q3 2008. In 2008, it reflected deposits in overseas foreign branches at around 117% of the GDP and loans (including repurchase agreements) at 173% of the GDP. The short-term debt was extremely high relative to Iceland's foreign currency reserves, which amounted to around 30% of GDP, as seen in Figure 4.46.[28] In May 2008, the Central Bank of Iceland entered a currency swap agreement of €1.5 billion with the Central Banks of Denmark, Sweden and Norway which increased the sovereign's potential foreign exchange reserves to around 50% of GDP. A large gap has often occurred in countries prior to systemic banking and currency crises between the short-term external debt and foreign exchange reserves. But, as seen from Figure 4.47,

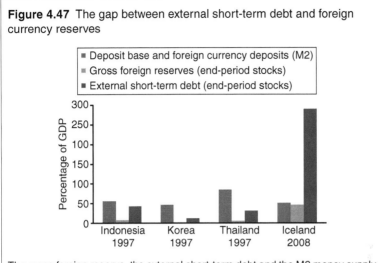

Figure 4.47 The gap between external short-term debt and foreign currency reserves

The gross foreign reserve, the external short-term debt and the M2 money supply are shown for Indonesia, Korea, Thailand and Iceland in the year of the systemic banking crisis. Gross foreign exchange reserves are net of forwards and swaps for Thailand.
Source: Allen *et al* (2002) and the Central Bank of Iceland.

Iceland's "external gap" was enormous. The CBI's foreign currency reserves were far too low to provide liquidity directly in foreign currency and it was clearly not a credible lender of last resort in foreign currency. In reality, the Icelandic banking system was "doomed", as the CBI's requests for currency swaps from the European Central Bank, Bank of England and the US Federal Reserve were rejected.

CONCLUDING REMARKS

There are many features of the Icelandic banking system leading up to the collapse that are very similar to previous banking crises. The warning signals that have preceded banking crises in the past (Reinhart and Rogoff 2009) were present in Iceland as well. As we have shown, some were more extreme than in any other previous banking crises when measured against the size of the Icelandic economy. It is, however, astonishing that the build-up of the banking system could reach such proportions given the fact that in 2006 the system was already under heavy pressure from markets. Then, some investors had already questioned both the business models of Icelandic banks and the huge imbalances in the Icelandic economy.

There were several factors that made the continued build-up possible. First, sovereign support, in terms of both promised government support and central bank liquidity provision against dubious collateral, played a key role. Second, the supervision of banks in Iceland was extremely weak and did not react to questionable business practices that the authority could have detected at the time. These practices, for example, meant that real leverage was much higher than reported. Third, credit ratings were too high, in part because the agencies overestimated the value of the sovereign support and because they relied on accounting reports, in which assets and profitability were inflated because of inadequate loan loss provisioning. Investors, as in many other cases in the 2007-9 financial crisis, failed to question the high ratings, even when market indicators pointed to much weaker credit quality. High ratings and investors' over-reliance on ratings secured access to financing from foreign lenders, in part indirectly from securitisation of Icelandic bank debt through the CDO markets. In defence of the rating agencies, sovereign support has played a key role in saving hundreds of banks in other countries, many of which also had very large risks in the banking system compared with GDP. Also, rating agencies maintain that they are not in the business of verifying accounting reports and other information which passes the regulatory review and due diligence procedures.

Iceland is a textbook example of the high risk for government of providing guarantees and not being prepared for extreme events. Sovereign support may help to alleviate a systemic banking crisis, but regulatory forbearance to keep systemically important institutions afloat can have severe consequences as well.

> The views expressed in this chapter are those of the authors and do not necessarily reflect the position of Danmarks Nationalbank. The authors thank Ásgeir Daníelsson, Kim Abildgren, Rune Mølgaard and Martin Seneca for helpful comments. Any remaining errors are the responsibility of the authors.

1 Assets are henceforth measured as consolidated assets, meaning the assets of the parent company including the assets of foreign subsidiaries (except if mentioned otherwise). The rapid rise in assets relative to GDP in 2008 was partly caused by the depreciation of the domestic currency relative to the rise in the domestic price level. The value of foreign currency assets measured in domestic currency is calculated using the onshore exchange rate, whereas the GDP is measured in current prices. In foreign currency terms, the three banks' balance sheets peaked in euro terms at more than €120 billion in Q4 2007. At the same time Iceland's annual GDP was more than €14 billion.

2   It is difficult to compare output losses across countries when banking crises reflect unsustainable economic developments before the crises.

3   See also Borio and Lowe (2002), Bordo and Jeanne (2002), Borio and Drehmann (2009) as well as Reinhart and Rogoff (2009, 2010).

4   That said, the location of the assets is complicated by the fact that the banks lent large sums to holding companies that operated both in Iceland and outside the country.

5   According to stated financial reports, around one-third of the banks' loans were to Icelandic entities.

6   The Housing Financing Fund (the HF Fund) is a residential mortgage lender with an explicit state guarantee and an objective to support the government's housing policy.

7   An assessment of the central bank's interest rate policy is beyond the score of this chapter. See Special Investigation Commission (2010) for further comments.

8   Large investments in aluminium and power also accounted for a part of the deficit. (See also Figure 4.16.)

9   The largest ever quarterly deficit was recorded at 78% of GDP in Q4 2008, fuelled by losses by Icelandic entities on a foreign exposure (which is registered as a negative dividend and/or retained earnings).

10 Gross external debt is the stock of all debt of residents to non-residents. In 2008, a large part of the increase relative to GDP can be attributed to depreciation of the króna relative to the domestic price level (see the explanation in endnote 1).

11 The depreciation of the króna sparked an unwinding of the currency carry trades around the world, for instance in the high-yielding New Zealand dollar. In fact, the króna achieved the nickname "the canary in the coal mine", as a sell-off in the króna signalled investors' elevated risk aversion in the currency markets.

12 See Moody's (2010) on market implied credit ratings.

13 Nevertheless, the announcement backfired, with a sharp widening in CDS spreads on the bank to 800–1,000 basis points. In January 2008, Kaupthing made a statement that the proposed acquisition of NIBC was abandoned. Ironically, NIBC had accepted losses due to exposure to subprime mortgages, whereas Kaupthing had not accepted upcoming losses on its loan portfolio.

14 According to the Central Bank of Iceland (2008) around 13% of the parent banks' total lending to customers was against share collateral at the end of 2007. At year-end 2007, 39% of the shares used as collateral for loans were listed on the OMX Exchange in Iceland (and valued at nearly 17% of the total year-end market value).

15 In fact, "hedging" gains were a primary driver behind the banks' reported profits in 2008.

16 Nonetheless, with a 90% loan-to-value on a marginal mortgage, the bank naturally starts to lose money when prices fall by more than 10% (if margin calls are impossible, eg, due to a very high debt service). As of June 2009, the Central Bank of Iceland (2009b) assessed that only around 2.5% of homeowners had both a negative equity position and a heavy debt service.

17 Bond ratings are based on expected long-term risk of default and thus are not intended to change over the business cycle. The subjective rating scale can take collateral as well as covenants into account and can be adjusted rapidly.

18 See "Kaupthing Bank Company Profile, September 2008" at http://www.kaupthing.com/lisalib/getfile.aspx?itemid=17423.

19 Several financial analysts also referred to liquidity support by the Nordic central banks in the so-called Memorandum of Understanding (MoU) dated June 2003. The MoU makes clear that the central banks will not intervene to prop up an insolvent bank, but a bank facing liquidity problems could be offered support from the group.

20 The 27 EU countries as well as Switzerland, Norway and Iceland.

21 It was less desirable for the Landsbanki to transfer IceSave deposit accounts from the branch to its subsidiary, Heritable Bank, since the UK rules on large exposures placed considerable

limitations on the transfer of funds to other parts of the banking group, including to Iceland (Special Investigation Commission 2010). The Dutch rules of transfer were less restrictive.

22 See an official letter by Landsbanki to its employees at http://blog.eyjan.is/helgavala/files/2009/07/staff_letter_150208_-_final.PDF.

23 Kaupthing also offered Edge through its branch in Germany. However, the majority of the Edge accounts were offered through subsidiaries.

24 The sluggish reaction of retail depositors is similar to the Northern Rock case, as documented by Shin (2009): "The Northern Rock depositor run, although dramatic on television, was an event in the aftermath of the liquidity crisis at Northern Rock, rather than the event that triggered its liquidity crisis.... Indeed, the irony of the images of Northern Rock's retail customers standing in line to withdraw deposits is that retail deposit funding is perhaps the most stable form of funding available."

25 Collateralised loans explain a large part of the increase in short-term external loans seen in Figure 4.16. They include securities to repos with Kaupthing's subsidiary, Singer & Friedlander (KSF). The parent company directed repos through KSF and achieved funding. In early October 2008 these transactions were seen by the UK FSA as a way for the parent company to reach the deposits of Kaupthing Edge (Special Investigation Commission 2010).

26 The malfunctioning foreign exchange swap market resulted in the low FX swap-implied króna yields and lowered the attraction of the currency carry trade implemented through FX swaps.

27 Even after the Icelandic government stepped in to rescue Glitnir, an economic advisor to the prime minister, Tryggvi Herbertsson, said in an interview with the BBC (British Broadcasting Corporation 2009): "It's obvious that the banking system in Iceland is very large compared with the economy, but still we think we can maintain the problem, you know, because the balance sheet of the bank is after all very good." To the question "If one of them did get into difficulties, despite what you say, could you afford to rescue it?" he responded " Definitely we would come to the rescue of the bank, definitely".

28 With the bankruptcy of Landsbanki, the minimum reimbursement limited the potential bill to the Icelandic deposit insurance scheme; the bill was "only" around €4 billion, or 40% of GDP.

REFERENCES

Allen, M., C. Rosenberg, C. Keller, B. Setser and N. Roubini, 2002, "A Balance Sheet Approach to Financial Crisis", IMF Working Paper 210.

Andersen, G., 2009, Speech by the Director General of the Icelandic Financial Supervisory Authority (FME) at the Annual General Meeting of the Icelandic Financial Services Association, May 14.

Bagehot, W., 1873, *Lombard Street: A Description of the Money Market*, URL: http://www.gutenberg.org/etext/4359.

Baldursson, F. M., and R. Portes, 2007, "The Internationalisation of Iceland's Financial Sector", Report, November, URL: http://faculty.london.edu/rportes/Iceland%20final.pdf.

Basel Committee on Banking Supervision, 2009, "Strengthening the Resilience of the Banking Sector", Consultative Document, December.

Bloomberg, 2008, "CDOs Imperiled by Collapse of the Iceland Bank, S&P says", October 16.

British Broadcasting Corporation, 2009, "Money Box", Paul Lewis (Presenter), Transcript (first broadcast October 4, 2008).

Bordo, M. D., and O. Jeanne, 2002, "Monetary Policy and Asset Prices: Does 'Benign Neglect' Make Sense?", *International Finance* 5(2), pp. 139–64.

Borio, C., and M. Drehmann, 2009, "Towards an Operational Framework for Financial Stability: 'Fuzzy' Measurement and Its Consequences", BIS Working Paper 284.

Borio, C., and P. Lowe, 2002, "Asset Prices, Financial and Monetary Stability: Exploring the Nexus", BIS Working Paper 114.

Central Bank of Iceland, 2008, "Financial Stability Report", May.

Central Bank of Iceland, 2009a, "Financial Stability Report", October.

Central Bank of Iceland, 2009b, "The Situation of Icelandic Households Following the Banks' Collapse", Report, June.

Central Bank of Iceland, 2010, "The Financial Crisis in Iceland and the Fault Lines in Cross-border Banking", presented by Már Gudmundsson, Proceedings of FIBE Conference, Bergen, Norway, January 7.

Danske Bank, 2006, "Iceland: Geyser Crisis", Research Publication, March 21. URL: http://sic.althingi.is/pdf/RNAvefVidauki3Enska.pdf.

Flannery, M. J., 2009, "Iceland's Failed Banks: A Post-Mortem", Report, Special Investigation Commission.

Fridriksson, I., 2009, "The Banking Crisis in Iceland in 2008", Report, The Central Bank of Iceland.

Haarde, G. H., 2008, Speech to the Annual Meeting of the Central Bank of Iceland, March 28, URL: http://eng.forsaetisraduneyti.is/media/Raedur_og_greinar_radherra/Rada_rh._a_ensku_Sedlabanka.pdf.

Hellmann, T., K. C. Murdock and J. E. Stiglitz, 2000, "Liberalization, Moral Hazard in Banking and Prudential Regulation: Are Capital Requirements Enough?", *American Economic Review* 90, pp. 147–65.

Herbertsson, T. T., and F. S. Mishkin, 2006, "Financial Stability in Iceland", Report, May, URL: http://v3.moodys.com/sites/products/ProductAttachments/MIRFrequentlyAskedQuestions.pdf.

IMF, 2007, "Iceland: Selected Issues", Report, August.

IMF, 2008a, "Iceland: Financial System Stability Assessment – Update", December.

IMF, 2008b, "Iceland: Request for Stand-By Arrangement – Staff Report", IMF Country Report 08/362.

IMF, 2009, "Global Financial Stability Report: Detecting Systemic Risk", Chapter 3.

Jännäri, K., 2009, "Banking Regulation and Supervision in Iceland: Past, Present and Future", Report.

Jónsson, A., 2009, *Why Iceland? How One of the World's Smallest Countries Became the Meltdown's Biggest Casualty* (London: McGraw-Hill).

Laeven, L., and F. Valencia, 2008, "Systemic Banking Crises: A New Database", IMF Working Paper 08/224.

Merrill Lynch, 2006, "Icelandic Banks: Not What You Are Thinking", Report, March 7.

Moody's, 2006, "Moody's Says that Iceland's Solvency and Liquidity Are Not at Risk", Comment, April 4.

Moody's, 2007a, "Bank Financial Strength Ratings: Global Methodology", Report, February.

Moody's, 2007b, "Icelandic Banks vs Nordic Peers", Presentation, Reykjavik, November 27.

Moody's, 2007c, "Incorporation of Joint-Default Analysis into Moody's Bank Ratings: A Refined Methodology", Report, March.

Moody's, 2008a, "Iceland: Banking System Outlook", Report.

Moody's, 2010, "Market Implied Ratings", Report.

Morgan Stanley, 2006, "European Banks – Icelandic Banks: Seeing the Facts through the Frenzy", Report, May 12.

OECD, 2009, *OECD Economic Surveys: Iceland*, Volume 2009/16, September.

Reinhart, C. M., and K. S. Rogoff, 2009, *This Time is Different: Eight Centuries of Financial Folly* (Princeton University Press).

Reinhart, C. M., and K. S. Rogoff, 2010, "From Financial Crash to Debt Crisis" NBER Working Paper 15795.

Rosenberg, C., L. Halikias, B. House, C. Keller, J. Nystedt, A. Pitt and B. Setser, 2005, "Debt-Related Vulnerabilities and Financial Crises: An Application of the Balance Sheet Approach to Emerging Market Countries", IMF Occasional Paper 240.

Shin, H. S. 2009, "Reflections on Northern Rock: The Bank Run that Heralded the Global Financial Crisis", *Journal of Economic Perspectives* 23(1), pp. 101–19.

Special Investigation Commission, 2010, "Report from the Special Investigation Commission", Report to Althingi (Icelandic Parliament), April 12.

The Times, 2006, "Icelandic Banks Refused Extensions on Loans", March 25.

5

The Quant Crunch Experience and the Future of Quantitative Investing

Bob Litterman
Goldman Sachs (Partner, retired), Commonfund (Trustee)

One of the more fascinating stories to come out of the investment world in recent years is that of quantitative investing. After a decades-long evolution, this approach to investing grew enormously over the 10 years prior to the events of July and August 2007. In the author's view that is not the end of the story, but, rather, the beginning of a new chapter. Let us take a closer look.

To start with a definition, we like to think that quantitative asset management draws on the best knowledge from the academic theory of finance, which tells us that return should be commensurate with risk, to take advantage of systematic opportunities in the marketplace. Some risks are better than others, of course. Quantitative investors, just like all other investors, attempt to identify investments offering a premium that more than justifies the risk. A recent example occurred in early 2009 when the premium on credit risk seemed very high. The stock market was clearly on the mend by the end of April, but credit spreads remained quite wide. Many investors thought the nation faced a prolonged recession. Coming out of a severe crunch, credit spreads were wider than at almost any time in history, including at the height of the Great Depression. So, for investors willing to take credit risk, there was an opportunity to be well rewarded.

While there is a certain amount of commonality among quants, they do not all do the same thing. Some work at a very high frequency, trading thousands of times a day. They seek to take advantage of short-term movements in securities that are driven by other investors. A low-frequency quant (as the author was at Goldman

Sachs Asset Management prior to retirement) also looks for patterns in data, but at much longer time intervals. We can think of value investing as a simple example of low-frequency quantitative investing.

In that context, let us focus on the difference between a quant and a fundamental value investor. A quant looks at hundreds of metrics of value, such as price-to-book or price/earnings ratios. Basically, quants employ the scientific method to test various hypotheses and determine if a particular metric would have historically forecast returns consistently above those justified by the risk. These historical patterns serve as an indicator that there is some market failure: perhaps a behavioural bias or an institutional feature that results in the set of securities with this characteristic being consistently mispriced.

When they find these patterns, and assuming these patterns are consistent with what would be expected given economic analysis, quantitative investors will construct a portfolio with exposure to that "factor", for example, by overweighting high book/price stocks and underweighting low book price stocks. Quants like to use the term "factor", and what they mean by it is something that forecasts something else. Quants generally look for these factors and invest in them. Quants also typically do considerable analysis of risk and transactions costs and try to use the results and these analyses and computerised trading to improve the net returns of the portfolio.

Fundamental managers are doing something similar, but not in the quant's systematic way. Instead, fundamental managers may look at the price-to-book ratio of 1,000 stocks and posit that there must be a reason why some seem to be cheap. They will then go to work to understand what makes certain companies different. They are trying to bring something to the table that either is not public or is public and not widely appreciated.

Fundamental research is not systematic and, therefore, it is not easy to replicate. This is an important point. Because what quants do is systematic, it is actually fairly easy to replicate. That was not true in the 1990s, but two decades later the barriers to entry have come down. We can imagine that anyone with a computer, a database and some simple programs can take advantage of the well-documented approaches that rely on standard techniques and databases. And anything that is that easy to take advantage of is eventually going to go away. This brings us to what happened in August 2007.

In brief, there was so much money flowing into the quant space that it became crowded. There was also a lot of risk in the market owing to the credit crunch that started in 2006 with subprime mortgages. As the subprime problem grew, it created a lot of anxiety, particularly among hedge funds with exposure to the mortgage sector. As the anxiety spread, it eventually spilled over into quantitative investing. While nobody knows exactly how that happened, we get the sense is that it started with the multi-strategy hedge funds. These funds employ lots of different strategies, each designed to take advantage of one or more anomalies in the marketplace. In the years leading up to 2006, big hedge funds had raised billions of US dollars and were looking for strategies that could accommodate a large amount of capital. Quant was one of them. Because quantitative investing is relatively simple to replicate, it was possible to hire a few quants to put together a portfolio that could try to add alpha, returns from risk uncorrelated with the market, to billions of dollars.

Multi-strategy hedge funds also allocate capital among different strategies. For example, they might have some of their capital devoted to fixed income, credit and mortgages, and some to quantitative equity strategies. When a strategy looks particularly attractive, they give it more capital and vice versa. So, capital flowed into quantitative strategies. For those who were already in the space, it was a nice tailwind. The performance of standard quant strategies was good, even though those strategies were based mostly on standard factors.

Our quant strategies had very high Sharpe ratios. The highly levered, pure version of our equity strategies had done very well since inception in 2003, and had to be capped at US$6 billion in capital under management. In June 2007 it was up another 15% for the year. The fund had positions in over US$20 billion each of long and short equities. Every risk we could hedge we did, while at the same time we maximised our exposure to quantitative factors. By the time the year was over the fund was down 30%.

The spillover to the quant space began with the subprime problem. As it grew, investors started to get nervous. Liquidity began to dry up and managers who had fixed positions in mortgages and/or credit started to feel some pressure. Some high-profile hedge funds got into trouble. Soon, we believe, the multi-strategy hedge funds decided they did not want to be in positions that could be difficult to exit, and as funds lost money in mortgage bets, and later in credit positions, they were forced to raise capital by selling out of other more liquid positions such as quantitative equities.

We, of course, also worried about exiting positions, but our portfolios were very liquid and each position was designed to be held for months at a time. And we had no direct exposure to mortgages or to the level of the stock market; we did not have any particular anxiety about our portfolios.

Given the growth in assets, the quant group had expected the returns from quantitative investing to decay over time. We thought there might only be a few more really good years. What we did not expect was an implosion.

So it was that in July 2007 some significant quant investors started to liquidate their positions. The factors made small moves lower almost every day that month, and that pattern is consistent with a controlled liquidation or reduction in risk of quant portfolios. That action, in itself, caused quants to experience a very bad month and towards the end of July investors who were probably relatively new to quant began to panic, leading to an implosion in quant portfolios in the first week of August. It is a strange thing to talk about movement in quant factors because you cannot go to a Bloomberg screen to see it. One of the author's colleagues said that in order to see what was going on as the quant space de-levered in a panic, you had to be wearing "quant-goggles".

The overall movement of factors generating returns is typically pretty small. In August 2007, factors started moving 10 times as much as they usually did, and their moves were all in the wrong direction. So, every factor in quant portfolios went the wrong way at the same time, and by a factor of 10.

The whole episode only lasted about a week and was largely concentrated in the equity markets. By Friday of the second week in August, four days after quant factors fell off a cliff, all the factors started coming back very strongly.

Surely every quant must have felt that they were at the centre of the storm, and, being the chairman of the quant group at Goldman Sachs Asset Management, this author was no exception. Gary Cohn, one of the co-presidents of Goldman Sachs at the time, spent a lot of time on our floor that week. Our highly levered quant equity hedge fund was running dangerously low on capital. On Wednesday we decided to de-lever our portfolio by raising new capital for the fund. By Thursday evening the firm had put together a group of investors who would join the firm in injecting US$3 billion of new capital into the fund, effectively halving its leverage. The capital came in at Friday's close. The quant rebound began on Friday morning.

Nonetheless, the damage was done. There were several factors that made the quant strategies susceptible to this liquidity shock. One was the fact that they were so disciplined. Unlike most investors, quants minimised exposure to the idiosyncratic components of a portfolio and maximised exposure to their factors, many of which were well known and used by many other quants. This commonality across quant funds was a second key reason why quant strategies were susceptible to the August 2007 shock and subsequent de-leveraging. Correlations across different quant portfolios were not especially high before "the event", so the risk was not so obvious. It is like equity markets around the world: day to day they are not that highly correlated, but in a big move they can become very highly correlated. That is what happened to quants. Since August 2007, there has been an ongoing de-leveraging of the quant space. Now, instead of riding a tailwind, quants are bucking a headwind.

What does this mean going forward? Clearly, one lesson is that, when there is a crisis, it will tend to spill over from one market to others, just as subprime did, even if they are unrelated, like quant. Another lesson is crowded trades. Those of us who had been managing assets using quantitative techniques for many years did not think of what we did as "a trade". But, because we were competing against managers who did think of it as a trade, it became a trade. In July 2007 it was a case of hot money leaving the space, and once that became clear it was a race to get out.

Those employing high-frequency strategies were also hurt badly, but they were set up to move quickly, and they did. Historically, the high-frequency quants were providers of liquidity. But when the de-leveraging turned ugly they too began to demand liquidity. The price impacts of trades were exaggerated by this collapse of liquidity provision.

Because the technology and knowledge behind quantitative strategies is now widely available, if an opportunity is too obvious or easy, it will quickly disappear. So, to be successful going forward, what quants need to do is avoid the "recipe approach" by doing original research and concentrating on more subtle opportunities. They will not be able to hold on to well-known factors and expect that they will work well. The opportunities are likely to be much smaller because, as soon as an opportunity is significant, money is going to flow in and take it away. Personally, the author believes that markets are not perfectly efficient, and, as long as they are not, there will be opportunities for quants to exploit.

How should institutional investors now think about quantitative investing? Quant is really just like any other strategy in that you want skilled managers with a particular approach or process that you believe has the potential to deliver alpha. Obviously, you would like them to be smaller rather than larger because they are going to be able to take advantage of more opportunities that way. And the opportunities themselves are likely to be smaller. Nonetheless, we expect that there will be many successful quant managers following different strategies as the future of quantitative investing unfolds.

Just like many other fields, investing is becoming more quantitative over time. Quant strategies did fail in 2007, spectacularly in some cases, and the overall size of the quantitative space has shrunk dramatically since then. Nonetheless, at the same time many quant strategies have done very well since the crisis, by taking advantage of disrupted markets and the resulting opportunities (such as the credit spreads discussed earlier). The lesson from the crisis is not that systematic analysis of data and the disciplined scientific/quantitative mode of analysis no longer work, but rather that this analysis needs to be employed in a more thoughtful way. Quants need to search for factors that are not well known, and they need to keep their fund sizes smaller, allowing them to be more dynamic. They also need to be more cognisant of the impact that other market participants, particularly other quants, may have on their portfolios. Investors who employ good quantitative analysis in this way are the ones who will succeed going forward.

Part II

The Impact on the Markets

6

No Margin for Error: The Impact of the Credit Crisis on Derivatives Markets

Jeffrey Rosenberg
Bank of America Merrill Lynch

Bear Stearns, Lehman Brothers and AIG: three key events of the 2007–9 credit crisis were at their core related to troubled mortgage exposure. Derivatives played varying roles in each of these cases and dramatic changes in the structure and economics of the global derivatives markets stand as a consequence of the crisis. During the summer of 2010, the Dodd–Frank Wall Street Reform and Consumer Protection Act enshrined the legislative legacy of this era to be followed by the phase of regulatory implementation. While that contributes substantial uncertainty as to the exact impact of these reforms, the broad implications are clear: create greater transparency of the over-the-counter (OTC) market, reduce the counterparty risk of the OTC market through centralised clearing and limit the speculative capacity of derivatives to create systemic risk.

MORTGAGE MARKET AND DERIVATIVES

The rapidly growing mortgage market, particularly the expansion of the non-agency mortgage market, both fuelled a housing market boom and fed a growing demand from investors for yield. Figure 6.1 highlights this growth. Behind the key events of Bear Stearns, Lehman and AIG (and the Federal National Mortgage Association and Federal Home Loan Mortgage Corporation before these), this growth led to an overexposed balance sheet when coupled with short-term funding inability, and tipped each event over towards insolvency and government intervention. Derivatives, primarily in the form of credit default swaps linked to collateralised debt obligations (CDOs) with non-agency residential mortgages as their

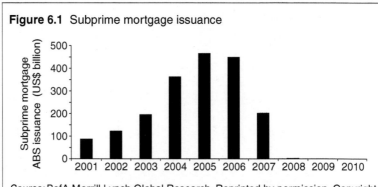

Figure 6.1 Subprime mortgage issuance

Source: BofA Merrill Lynch Global Research. Reprinted by permission. Copyright © 2010 Bank of America Corporation.

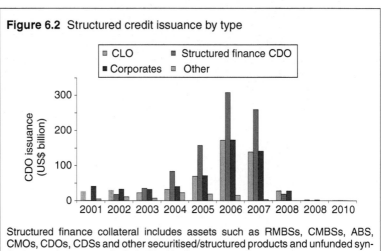

Figure 6.2 Structured credit issuance by type

Structured finance collateral includes assets such as RMBSs, CMBSs, ABS, CMOs, CDOs, CDSs and other securitised/structured products and unfunded synthetic tranches are not included in this data.
Source: SIFMA.

primary form of collateral, played a role in expanding these firms' exposures to the credit losses that ultimately would push them towards insolvency. Figures 6.1 and 6.2 highlight the rapid growth of both cash and structured finance (CDO) exposures linked to the growth of the mortgage market.

THE ROLE OF CREDIT DERIVATIVES IN THE CREDIT CRISIS

Mortgage market exposures and their related derivatives played a key role in the credit crisis. But, leading up to the crisis, all derivatives markets exhibited high growth rates. Figure 6.3 highlights the

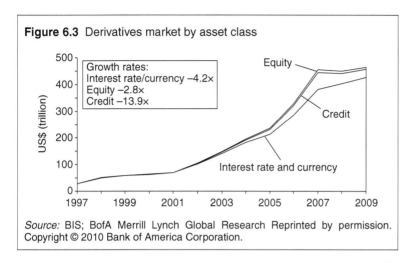

Figure 6.3 Derivatives market by asset class

Growth rates:
Interest rate/currency −4.2×
Equity −2.8×
Credit −13.9×

Source: BIS; BofA Merrill Lynch Global Research Reprinted by permission. Copyright © 2010 Bank of America Corporation.

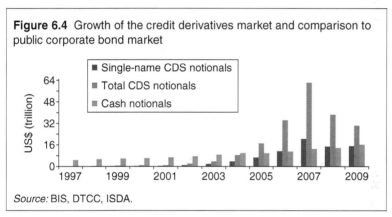

Figure 6.4 Growth of the credit derivatives market and comparison to public corporate bond market

Source: BIS, DTCC, ISDA.

growth in notional amounts of derivatives by broad asset class. And unique in its contribution to the crisis stands the growth of the credit derivatives market.

From 2002 to 2009, credit derivatives expanded at just under 14×: the largest growth rate of any derivative asset class. Figures 6.4–6.6 highlight the growth of credit derivatives relative to the cash credit market, a relatively recent breakdown of credit derivatives by product type and a comparison of growth trends in cash credit markets, respectively. As a result of both the rapid pace of growth in credit derivatives and a discussion below on their role in the credit crisis, much of what follows will focus on the particular impact from and changes to the credit derivatives market.

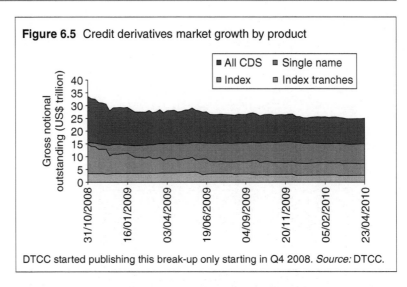

Figure 6.5 Credit derivatives market growth by product

DTCC started publishing this break-up only starting in Q4 2008. *Source:* DTCC.

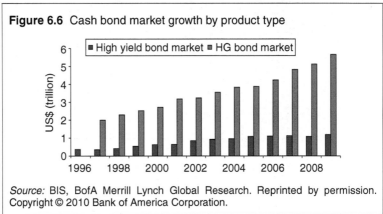

Figure 6.6 Cash bond market growth by product type

Source: BIS, BofA Merrill Lynch Global Research. Reprinted by permission. Copyright © 2010 Bank of America Corporation.

Single tranche CDO contribution to corporate credit default swap growth

Another feature of the pre-crisis credit derivative markets is the role single-tranche collateralised debt obligations (STCDOs) played in the overall corporate credit default swap (CDS) market growth. STCDOs represented a key evolution in the application of financial engineering technology. But the key to the growth of these markets fuelled by this technology was its ability to meet the pressing demands of investors at the time for high-quality, high-yielding assets. The broad investment backdrop of the years leading up to the credit crisis was associated with falling risk-free yields and

NO MARGIN FOR ERROR

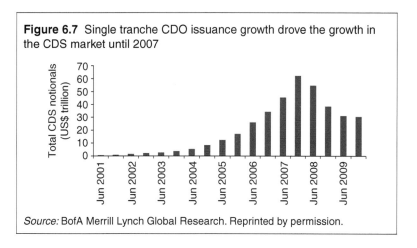

Figure 6.7 Single tranche CDO issuance growth drove the growth in the CDS market until 2007

Source: BofA Merrill Lynch Global Research. Reprinted by permission.

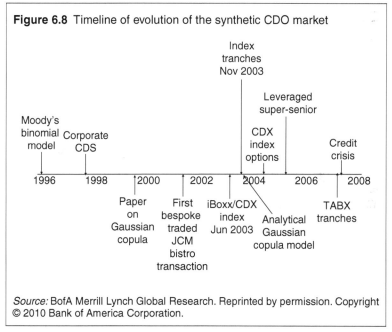

Figure 6.8 Timeline of evolution of the synthetic CDO market

Source: BofA Merrill Lynch Global Research. Reprinted by permission. Copyright © 2010 Bank of America Corporation.

compression in credit spreads. The result was a lack of yield from traditional sources of investment. The persistence of this environment led broadly to the search for yield. STCDOs meet these needs and as a result boomed. Figure 6.7 shows the growth of the CDS market driven by the issuance in STCDOs and Figure 6.8 highlights some of the key innovations in the development of the product along the way that contributed to this growth.

In its simplest form, the STCDO enabled the end-user investor access to leveraged exposure to an underlying portfolio of investment grade exposures. The leverage magnified the yield and mark-to-market risk, without (in the view of the rating agencies at the time) increasing the default risk of the investment. The end result was a high-spread, highly rated investment. For the growth of the single-name-CDS market, the leverage meant that every US$1 issued in tranche notional created, on average, about US$10 of notional risk hedging requirements, assuming a 10× levered tranche. In hindsight, however, it is now clear that these high ratings and high spreads were not achieved without a cost as the leverage that magnified yields as spreads compressed amplified market risk as spreads widened, exhibiting a volatility of return wholly inconsistent with the rating.

Innovation outpaced understanding

Among the many poorly understood aspects of the credit crisis, the role of derivatives ranked amongst the highest. How was it that Lehman Brothers could fail so rapidly? Or Bear Stearns before it? How could AIG lose so much money so quickly? And how could the losses increase so dramatically over such a short period of time? For each of those critical questions along the path of the crisis, derivatives often (rightly or wrongly) were singled out as the source. A lack of understanding of the derivatives market, and particularly the OTC credit derivatives market, contributed to the uncertainty of their role in precipitating the credit crisis. As a result, one of the key legacies of the credit crisis is the regulatory and structural reforms placed on the derivatives market that are intended to increase the transparency, and by doing so the understanding, of these markets.

Innovation outpaced regulation

The years leading up to the credit crisis contained a flurry of innovations in credit derivative markets. Figure 6.9 highlights this rapid pace of development, during which time over eight different asset class or indexes of CDSs were introduced. And while the entirety of the CDS market is frequently lumped together, Figure 6.1 highlights that, far from being one generic CDS market, the term "CDS" rightly represents a contractual form of risk transfer (a bilateral agreement where the payout is linked to a binary event) that the market found increasingly broad forms of application.

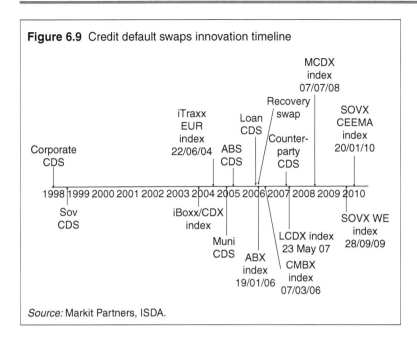

Figure 6.9 Credit default swaps innovation timeline

Source: Markit Partners, ISDA.

Table 6.1 Credit default swaps by asset and related index

CDS type	CDS inception	Asset class	Related index
CDS	1998	Corporations	CDX, iTraxx
LCDS	2006	Loans	LCDX
Sov CDS	1998	Sovereigns	SovXWE, SovXCEEMA
MCDS	2004	US Municipals	MCDX
ABS CDS	2005	ABS	ABX, CMBX
CCDS	2007	Counterparty risk	—
Recovery swap	2006	Corporations	—

Source: ISDA, Markit Partners.

The regulatory reform aftermath of the credit crisis is likely to broadly affect all derivative markets. The centre of the credit crisis – subprime residential mortgage exposure – and its related derivatives contributed in important ways to the crisis, especially in the case of AIG. Counterparty risk featured prominently in that case, and also in issues related to other monoline insurance exposures as well as exposures to structured investment vehicles (SIVs). We will first address the environment of derivatives pre-crisis and then look at those issues and the impact on the derivatives market outlook post-crisis.

Pre-crisis changes to the OTC derivatives market practices

Before the onset of the credit crisis, the derivatives market was undergoing its own, voluntary, industry-led restructuring. The rapid growth rate of the derivatives market trading outpaced the development of back-office systems to support the volumes creating "operational" risk. This risk was first addressed formally by regulators in 2005. That focus resulted in industry agreements to address the main areas of concern at that time: the backlog of unconfirmed trades, many arising from the practice of "novation". Under the derivatives practice of the time, trades could be "assigned" from one counterparty to another or "novated" without agreement from the remaining party to the trade. That resulted in a backlog of unconfirmed "novations", leading to the operational risk that the remaining party to a CDS might not immediately know its counterparty: a risk especially problematic in the event of a counterparty default. The appendix on "novation and operational risks of derivatives pre-crisis" (see page 163) describes the details surrounding this issue. Figure 6.10 highlights the timeline of pre-crisis derivatives structural reforms and Figure 6.2 shows key infrastructure reforms and milestones.

By March 2008, goals for CDS operations management expanded to include: consistent use of electronic confirmation platforms (that replaced the previous manual process that contributed to confirmation backlogs), submission by one day post trade, accuracy goals and trade matching by five days post trade.

SYSTEMIC RISK ISSUES OF DERIVATIVES PRE-CRISIS

While before the crisis the focus of derivatives market reform was to reduce "operational" risks arising from the markets' rapid growth, after the crisis the focus of reform changed to addressing more fundamental issues of concern arising from the role derivatives might have played in the crisis. Critically, that focus turned to the role of transparency, counterparty risk and leverage implicit in the OTC derivatives market.

Table 6.2 A timeline of infrastructure development initiatives by the industry

Date	Type	Description
September 27, 2006	Achievements	Ended the market practice of assigning trades without obtaining prior consent of counterparties
		Reduced the number of all confirmations outstanding by 70% and confirmations outstanding for more than 30 days by 85%
		Doubled the share of trades that are confirmed on an electronic platform to 80% of total trade volume
		Agreed on a protocol for the settlement of a credit event
November 1, 2007	Achievements	A few major dealers began calculating and settling fees and coupons centrally via DTCC rather than bilaterally
	Commitments	Most are committed to be live for the Sept 2008 roll
March 27, 2008	Achievement	Electronic processing of more than 90% of trades
	Commitments	Automated novations processing by the end of 2008
		Universal use of standard reference data
		Full implementation of centralised settlement among major dealers by Sept 2008
		90% $T + 1$ submission
		90% submitted accurately, matching without amendment
		92% matched by $T + 5$

Source: Federal Reserve, New York and TriOptima.

Table 6.2 (*Cont.*)

Date	Type	Description
June 9, 2008	Commitments	Increasing standardisation and automation of credit derivatives trade processing with the objective of $T + 0$ matching
		Developing a central counterparty for CDS to reduce systemic risk
		Incorporating an auction based settlement into CDS documentation
		Reducing the volume of outstanding credit derivatives trades by multilateral trade terminations to help reduce operational risk
October 31, 2008	Commitments	Institute a central counterparty for CDSs
		Reduce levels of outstanding trades via portfolio compression (tear-ups)
		Enhance market transparency: DTCC to publish aggregate market data
		Continue operational improvements
	Achievement	US$24 trillion of CDS trade notional amounts have been eliminated
March 4, 2009	Achievement	ICE becomes a member of Federal Reserve System
April 8, 2009	Achievement	Big Bang protocol
		Standardisation of coupons
		Hardwiring of auction settlement
September 8, 2009	Commitments	Each dealer commits to submitting 95% of new eligible trades for central clearing by October 2009
		Clearing 80% of all eligible trades beginning October, 2009

Source: Federal Reserve, New York and TriOptima.

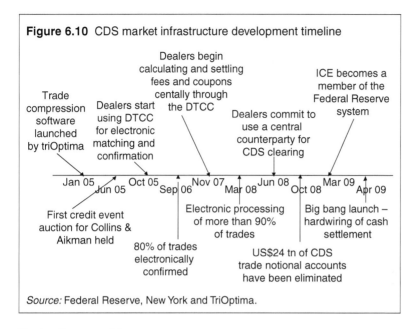

Figure 6.10 CDS market infrastructure development timeline

Source: Federal Reserve, New York and TriOptima.

Derivatives and leverage

A key to understanding the systemic risk potential of derivatives is their relationship to leverage. CDS market participants promise in a bilateral agreement to exchange cashflows following a potential "credit event". There are no hard assets set aside to guarantee payment. Thus, should the "protection seller" (the party to the transaction looking to provide that payment in the event of an occurrence of a "credit event") default on its obligation to pay the required cashflows post-credit event, the protection buyer simply becomes a general creditor of the protection seller.

No margin for error: initial and variation margin's role in limiting the systemic risk of derivatives

To reduce counterparty risk, counterparties are required to post collateral against the risk of their default. This collateral takes two forms, termed "initial margin" and "variation margin". Generally, both initial and variation margin are required of counterparties, but this practice varies both by firm and according to the perceived default risk of the counterparty.

Initial margin represents the initial capital held against the risk of loss in a derivatives trade. Variation margin represents the subsequent counterparty risk exposure over the life of the trade arising

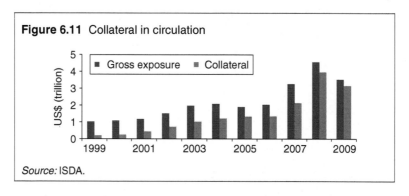

Figure 6.11 Collateral in circulation

Source: ISDA.

from changes in the market value of derivative ("mark-to-market" risk). In theory, by keeping variation margin as close to zero as possible and by holding an adequate amount of initial margin, the counterparty default risk of a derivative trade can be eliminated. As we will discuss, the practical reality and challenges in implementation of such a policy in the years leading up to the crisis led to rising levels of counterparty risk in the system.[1] Practices surrounding the collateral requirements of AAA rated counterparties in particular contributed to the systemic risks of derivatives during the credit crisis. These represent significant legacy issues in the management of counterparty risk and likely will evolve considerably from their pre-crisis market application. As of year-end 2009, across all derivatives categories, the International Swaps and Derivatives Association (ISDA) estimates that there was approximately US$3.1 trillion of collateral in circulation, down from US$3.9 trillion in 2008 but up from US$2.1 trillion at the end of 2007 (Figure 6.11).

Determinants of initial margin

Initial margin is based on both risk of a particular trade and the risk of a counterparty default. Hence, in theory selling protection at 500bp should entail a higher initial margin than selling protection at 200bp, irrespective of the creditworthiness of the counterparty. Additionally, higher risk counterparties would pay more margin than low-risk counterparties. The intersection of these two principals would result in a matrix approach to counterparty risk management such as depicted in Table 6.3.

Before the credit crisis, when the risk of counterparty default was presumed to be from non-dealers only, generally only hedge funds were required to post initial margin. Real money accounts such

Table 6.3 Hypothetical initial margin estimates for CDS trade

CDS spread	Client sells protection		Client buys protection	
	Strong rating (%)	Weak rating (%)	Strong rating (%)	Weak rating (%)
100	1.6	4.0	No margin	2.0
500	8.0	20.0	2.0	4.0
1,000	14.0	35.0	3.5	7.0

Source: BofA Merrill Lynch Global Research. Reprinted by permission. Copyright © 2010 Bank of America Corporation.

as pension funds, mutual funds, or insurance companies generally did not have to post initial margin, as the counterparty risk facing the dealer was typically that associated with the assets of the fund rather than the risk of the management firm. Additionally, given that spreads before the credit crisis were relatively tight, little risk was perceived in further tightening. Hence initial margin was generally required only on trades where hedge funds were selling protection (and therefore faced the risk of rising spreads).

Framework for setting initial margin

Initial margin represents the "cushion" over and above the regular mark-to-market risk for which variation margin provides protection. Consider the case where a dealer believes it would take approximately two weeks to discover that a counterparty were no longer creditworthy, decide to unwind that counterparty, obtain the necessary approvals and effect an unwind. Initial margin then would reflect the dealer's expected loss over a two-week period, with respect to that counterparty's portfolio.[2]

An unresolved question in the current market environment, and the subject of significant attention, is how best to measure the magnitude and volatility of expected losses. The difficulty, of course, is that the expected loss is both a function of the spread movement on the underlying contract and the probability of a counterparty default. But, as the Lehman Brothers example so clearly illustrated, those two events are highly correlated. That is, in the case where the counterparty default risk is rising, the exposure to the counterparty is also increasing.

Estimates of potential spread widening might be based on historical volatility or experience during the crisis. Note, however, that pre-crisis, a historical volatility approach might have understated the initial margin required, as, leading up to the crisis, volatility of spreads was significantly muted. In many cases risk managers would simply scale-up the required margin in order to provide better counterparty protection.

Initial margin and leverage

The initial margin represents the upfront cost to the counterparty to enter the CDS transaction. To the extent that no further cushion was to be held by the counterparty of the CDS, that initial margin represents the "equity" of the trade. On a return on equity perspective, the reciprocal of the initial margin percentage represents the implicit leverage of the CDS contract.

A race to the bottom

However, the largely subjective nature of determining the initial margin left open the possibility of competitive "devaluations" in initial margin. This occurs as some clients seek out not only the best price for a CDS transaction but also the best terms, in this case the initial margin, as, by lowering the initial margin, leverage and hence return on equity could be maximised. Alternatively, minimising the initial margin may have been desirable in order not to maximise leverage but to deploy equity capital to other attractive investments or to hold the margin amounts in higher yielding forms than those available through dealer margins, which typically paid only Fed funds. In this case, minimising the initial margin held at dealers and holding sufficient capital against derivatives positions to limit the degree of leverage overall in the fund would make sense, as other higher yielding assets could be employed for the "capital" amounts, resulting in overall better returns on capital for the fund.

During the period of stable to declining spread and volatility leading up to the credit crisis, credit risk appeared to be declining. In this environment, pressure to reduce the initial margin resulted in compression in initial margin over time. Figure 6.12 highlights the

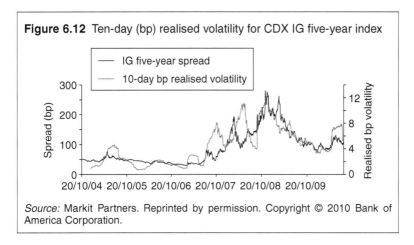

Figure 6.12 Ten-day (bp) realised volatility for CDX IG five-year index

Source: Markit Partners. Reprinted by permission. Copyright © 2010 Bank of America Corporation.

declining volatility of spreads pre-crisis. As a result of this compression, declines in initial margin may not have appeared to be increasing counterparty risk (as they were being offset by the perception of declining risk of the underlying exposure). Of course, in hindsight the failure to maintain a minimum floor for initial margin in the face of such market pressures contributed to a potential decline in counterparty risk protections, adding to the systemic risk potential from counterparty defaults.

SIVs, monolines and AIG before the crisis

In this environment of perceived declining credit risk, the seeds of the SIV, monoline and AIG events were sown. In each case, declining market risk created the perception of declining counterparty risk of those three broad classes of market participants. And in such an environment, declining market risk contributed to the erosion in counterparty protections: practices related to initial and variation margin in the case of monolines and AIG, and the failure to recognise the liquidity risks inherent in the SIV business model. In each case, the dealer community perceived that selling-off credit exposure (particularly exposures associated with non-agency residential mortgages and their derivatives) would be effective in reducing their own exposures. Monolines and AIG provided explicit credit wraps or guarantees, often using the CDS form of contract to effect the risk transfer. And SIVs provided an outlet to sell, if only on a short-term basis, the AAA cash bond exposures arising primarily out of structuring non-agency residential mortgages into CDOs. The first phases of the credit crisis revealed the failure of those counterparties' business models to meet the obligations of risk transfer. As a result, much of the credit risk came back on to the balance sheets of the dealers, and dealer counterparty risk became the focal point of the crisis.

The transfer of risk back to the dealer community contributed to the next phase of systemic risk: the counterparty risk of the dealer community. This stands in contrast to an earlier era of systemic risk: that posed by the default of the hedge fund firm Long Term Capital Management in 1998. Moreover, despite a relatively recent history of dealer defaults or near defaults[3] dealers generally did not post initial margin to either other dealers or to clients, contributing to the systemic risks of rising mortgage exposures on the balance sheets of dealers.

Note that the lack of posting of initial margin, however, was somewhat compensated for by the practice of variation margin, whereby daily mark-to-market exposures on derivative counterparty exposures by both dealers and clients required collateral posting. However, in the case of correlated default risk, whereby large losses on the reference derivative contribute or cause the default of a counterparty and/or where subsequently the default of a counterparty results in further losses on the derivative, the lack of sufficient initial margin can (and in the case of Lehman Brother's likely did) exacerbate losses and systemic risk. Additionally, the Lehman episode exposed the systemic risks of "rehypothecation": the market practice of using customer securities posted as margin from a hedge fund to a dealer as collateral for the dealer's own borrowings.[4] Those concerns have led to the establishment of post-credit-crisis practices of "segregation" (legally separating client collateral from dealers' usage) and "portability" (the ability to transfer collateral from one counterparty to another in the event of a counterparty default) of customer margin accounts, fixtures of the structure of the post-crisis role of central clearing discussed further below.

The contribution of asymmetric collateral posting to the systemic risk during the credit crisis
The ability of highly rated counterparties (AAA rated entities) to demand or extract through the competitive marketplace[5], as was frequently the case for AIG, monoline insurance companies and

derivative product companies (DPCs), would play a critical role in exacerbating the systemic risk of counterparties with exposure to derivatives tied to subprime exposure. This, of course, describes in essence the issue of AIG.

The legacy of asymmetric collateral posting in a post-crisis derivatives world

The legacy of such events for the future of the derivatives market stands in the limitation posed to the two forms of asymmetric collateral posting. Today both dealers and presumed high quality counterparties are required to post collateral, or will be required to post collateral as derivatives shift to central clearing regimes. And in a world of higher credit spreads and more-symmetric risks to assets from both price declines as well as increases, initial margin is now generally required or likely to become required (again under the shift to central clearing) for both long and short risk positions.

POST-CRISIS DERIVATIVES REFORM AND THE ROLE OF CENTRAL COUNTERPARTY CLEARING

Derivative market reform now centres on the key issues of transparency, counterparty risk and leverage. More broadly, the issues of post-crisis derivative reform create distinctions between speculative and hedging usage and limits on the former's ability to result in manipulation.[6] Below, we briefly review the regulatory history of derivatives and address one consequence of the financial regulatory reform bill establishing central counterparty clearing as the one of the main structural reforms to be mandated by this legislation. We discuss the basics of the central clearing model and how this model affects the economics of derivatives through changing the structure of counterparty risk mitigation techniques. In particular, in order to reduce the systemic risk potential of the clearinghouses themselves, the market follows a diversification approach to central clearing whereby different products clear at different clearinghouses. This reduction in risk through diversification, however, comes at a cost, as the prospect for risk reduction across products (and hence across clearinghouses) is lost. The economic gain of reduced counterparty risk under the clearinghouse model (as opposed to the bilateral model prevalent before the crisis) comes with the trade-off of higher costs of derivatives usage.

Finally, clearinghouses themselves can clear only what can reasonably be priced by clearinghouse members. While clearinghouses can contribute to transparency, in themselves clearinghouses do not create liquidity[7] but rather require liquidity in order to clear. Clearinghouses represent an important step in the evolution of the infrastructure for derivatives and in particular for the relatively newer credit derivative asset class. However, given that much of the non-standardised derivatives are unlikely to be able to be cleared, this part of the market is likely to remain OTC. Changes in capital requirements for dealers may encourage greater usage of standardised, clearable derivatives. But the trade-off between cost and customisation in determining the direction of future trading volumes in the broad derivative market and specifically to the credit derivative market remains uncertain and subject to the specific implementation phase of regulatory reform following the passage of the Dodd–Frank legislation in summer 2010.

A condensed history of US derivative regulation

Exchange-traded derivative regulation dates back to the 1930s. The US Commodity Futures Trading Commission (CFTC) and the Securities and Exchange Commission (SEC) have historically regulated these markets.

The state of OTC derivative regulation immediately preceding the financial regulatory reform of 2010 reflects the 1999 report of The President's Working Group on Financial Markets. Prior to the paper and the ensuing legislation, there was uncertainty around the legal enforceability of derivative contracts traded outside of exchanges because the Commodity Exchange Act (CEA) effectively said that contracts traded outside of regulated exchanges are legally unenforceable. The paper recommended that the bilateral transactions between sophisticated counterparties be excluded from the CEA. Non-financial commodities of finite supply (like corn or grain) would remain under the CEA.

The working group felt that financial institutions trading OTC derivatives were sophisticated and would act in their own self-interest. In addition, they put the responsibility on the regulators who oversaw those institutions to monitor their OTC derivatives traded by them. The quote below highlights that view:

> The members of the Working Group agree that there is no compelling evidence of problems involving bilateral swap agreements that would warrant regulation under the CEA; accordingly, many types of swap agreements should be excluded from the CEA. The sophisticated counterparties that use OTC derivatives simply do not require the same protections under the CEA as those required by retail investors. In addition, most of the dealers in the swaps market are either affiliated with broker–dealers or FCMs [Futures Commission Merchants] that are regulated by the SEC or the CFTC or are financial institutions that are subject to supervision by bank regulatory agencies. Accordingly, the activities of most derivatives dealers are already subject to direct or indirect federal oversight.
>
> (The President's Working Group on Financial Markets 1999, p. 15)

The report also recommended enhancement of electronic trading, the development of a clearinghouse and greater market transparency. The Commodities and Futures Modernization Act of 2000 put some of these recommendations into law. The OTC market now had a firm legal footing on which to grow, spurring the exponential volume increases that markets would see over the following nine years up to the credit crisis.

THE CREDIT CRISIS AND THE IMPETUS FOR REGULATORY CHANGE
AIG Financial Products

Clearly, losses associated with AIG and its CDS exposures through AIG Financial Products (AIGFP) prompted much criticism of the CDS market. Taken at its most basic level, AIGFP's CDS book had a relatively straightforward strategy. During the height of the subprime residential mortgage boom, AIGFP would sell protection in CDS on a wide variety of CDO products referencing subprime assets. By selling protection, they were agreeing to receive a small fee (say, 0.30% of the notional value of the CDS) on an annual basis in exchange for agreeing to pay their counterparty up to the full notional of the CDS contract if the underlying CDO defaulted.[8] Stripping away the complex layers of financial engineering, this meant that effectively AIG guaranteed the default risk of subprime mortgages.

However, the sheer size of the market exposures to AIG highlighted critical flaws in counterparty risk management. As we describe in the section above, during the pre-crisis period, high quality counterparties were frequently able to demand margin terms

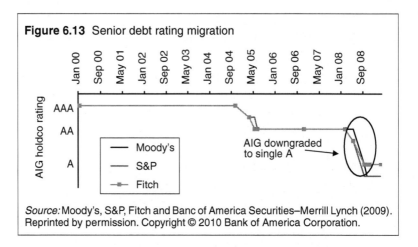

Figure 6.13 Senior debt rating migration

Source: Moody's, S&P, Fitch and Banc of America Securities–Merrill Lynch (2009). Reprinted by permission. Copyright © 2010 Bank of America Corporation.

from counterparties that had the effect of reducing initial and even variation margin payments. For AIG, this improved the capital efficiency of its business but at the cost of raising counterparty risk not only to their counterparty, but (in hindsight, as the practice was repeated across multiple counterparties to AIG) to the entire system.

AIG financial products and collateral postings

AIG, through its financial products subsidiary AIGFP, provided risk transfer through the CDS contract on losses on primarily super senior CDOs referencing primarily subprime mortgages. For the purchasers of this protection, the risk of holding these securities on their balance sheet was effectively swapped for the counterparty risk of AIG: its ability to pay on any losses the securities might realise. At the time, as a AAA rated counterparty, counterparties perceived this risk to be low.

However, since the counterparties faced risks not only of ultimate losses but also of mark-to-market losses (given mark-to-market accounting requirements), they needed a form of risk transfer that mitigated those mark-to-market risks as well. The CDS contract provided that form of protection, effectively shifting that mark-to-market loss to AIG through "collateral" posting arrangements. Here, the obligation of one of the counterparties to pay another is recognised through daily "mark-to-market" valuations. These valuations reflecting the anticipated or potential losses (based on market pricing) on the "reference" instrument created the obligation of AIG to make collateral payments to its counterparties.

AIG's requirement to make these substantial collateral payments stemmed from two sources. First, the plunging value of the reference securities created huge "mark-to-market" losses. Second, the deteriorating counterparty credit condition of AIG based on the growing liability from these losses led to credit rating downgrades (Figure 6.13). Those downgrades in turn led to even greater collateral posting requirements (Table 6.4). Here we should note that, in practice, the inability to agree on a market price added considerably to the uncertainty and counterparty risk in the system. In theory, well-functioning markets will have prices that clear and are readily available. In reality, in the run-up to the credit crisis subprime mortgage exposures had anything but those characteristics making the practice of securing variation margin (collateral payments), and reducing counterparty risk, difficult.

Those collateral payments effectively transferred the mark-to-market risk to AIG. If AIG based its exposures on its estimates of ultimate loss realization, the risk it faced was in reality the mark-to-market risk of the securities. However, since some collateral posting requirements only kicked in *after* a downgrade, it is possible that both AIG and its counterparties, having viewed this likelihood as low at the time, assumed that the mark-to-market risk issue for AIG (and hence the counterparty risk each counterparty to AIG faced) was correspondingly low. In hindsight, the collateral posting requirements created a "springing" mark-to-market risk for which AIG had not sufficient liquidity. That event resulted in the government intervention which subsequently led to the focus of derivatives, and particularly credit derivatives regulatory reform.

Lehman Brothers

Lehman Brothers presented a real-world test of the derivatives close out procedures. These procedures laid out in the ISDA Master Agreement govern the requirements and actions to be taken in the even of a default by a counterparty. Again, the need for practicing these procedures was well documented at the time.[9] And while the default caused considerable uncertainty, eventually the market completed the process according to the contractual obligations, if not without some difficulty. Those difficulties would expose some additional risks that market participants understated, particularly in the case

Table 6.4 AIG collateral dynamics

Date (as of)	Total	Regulatory capital (US)	Arbitrage multi-sector (US)	Arbitrage corporations (US)	Comment
30/06/2007	0.0	0.0	0.0	0.0	No collateral posting requirements on AIGFP's CDS portfolio
31/12/2007	2.9	0.0	2.7	0.2	Market value declines and rating downgrades of underlying CDOs
31/03/2008	8.2	0.2	7.6	0.4	Market value declines and rating downgrades of underlying CDOs
30/06/2008	13.8	0.3	13.2	0.3	Market value declines and rating downgrades of underlying CDOs
31/07/2008	16.1	—	—	—	Market value declines and rating downgrades of underlying CDOs
31/08/2008	22.0	—	—	—	Market value declines and rating downgrades of underlying CDOs
30/09/2008	32.8	0.4	31.5	0.9	Due to rating downgrades (all three agencies) on 15 September and market value declines
5/11/2008	37.3	—	—	—	Market value declines and rating downgrades of underlying CDOs
31/12/2008	8.8	1.3	5.1	2.3	Decrease due to settlements via Maiden Lane III

Source: Company Filings and Banc of America Securities–Merrill Lynch (2009). Reprinted by permission. Copyright © 2010 Bank of America Corporation.

of rehypothecated collateral, bankruptcy trigger clauses in structured credit derivative transactions and in the long process of settling bankruptcy claims arising from derivative counterparty exposures.

Though these issues contributed to an overall environment of uncertainty, the market systemic risk from Lehman Brothers' default event at the time arguably had more to do with the failure of the Reserve Fund than derivatives exposures to Lehman. The Reserve Fund, as a result of holding a large percentage of its money market fund in Lehman Brother's commercial paper, was unable to maintain the US$1 net asset value on its funds. This "breaking the buck" precipitated a panic in the short-term money markets. While Lehman Brothers' default contributed to an overall period of uncertainty in the market, the panic in the short-term markets created a collapse in the inter-bank funding markets. That collapse, rather than any failures in counterparty derivatives exposures, created the need for government intervention to forestall the liquidity crisis that precipitated the collapse in global equity markets in autumn 2008. Nevertheless, the lack of transparency of derivatives exposures and the uncertainty of the potential systemic risk from counterparty default risks gave rise to many of the structural reforms emphasising transparency in the market. Moreover, the greater transparency is intended to give regulators and market participants greater understanding of the structure of derivatives exposures and limit the potential that opacity in the market has to grow systemic risk uncertainty.

STRUCTURAL REFORM OF DERIVATIVES MARKETS AFTER THE CRISIS

Subsequent to the US Treasury's proposal on May 13, 2009, legislative bills aimed at achieving these regulatory goals were passed in both the House and the Senate:

- the Over-the-Counter Derivatives Markets Act, passed by the House Financial Services Committee on October 15, 2009 ("HFSC Bill");

- the Derivatives Markets Transparency and Accountability Act, passed by the House Committee on Agriculture on October 21, 2009 ("HAG Bill");

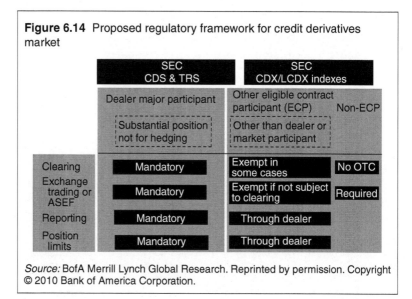

Figure 6.14 Proposed regulatory framework for credit derivatives market

Source: BofA Merrill Lynch Global Research. Reprinted by permission. Copyright © 2010 Bank of America Corporation.

- the Restoring American Financial Stability Act of 2009, introduced by Senator Christopher Dodd in the Senate Banking Committee on November 10, 2009 ("SBC Bill");
- the combined bill was signed into law by President Barack Obama on July 21, 2010 as part of the broader financial regulatory reform bill, the "Dodd–Frank Wall Street Reform and Consumer Protection Act".

These bills, while being structurally similar to the US Treasury proposal, propose details around implementation of the reform. Figure 6.14 shows the proposed broad framework for derivatives regulation. Below we highlight some of the broad themes part of the final legislation. However, the details of the implementation of the legislation will determine the exact economic and structural changes to the derivatives markets. Note that the following discussion is based on our interpretation of the language in the bills and should not be construed as either definitive or legal advice.

Regulators

The CFTC and SEC are expected to regulate the derivatives markets with separate jurisdictional authorities. With the caveat that their jurisdictions could change, CFTC is expected to regulate broad-based credit indexes (eg, CDX indexes), while SEC is expected to regulate single-name CDSs (including LCDSs) and narrow-based credit indexes.

Participants

Market participants are classified into four categories to distinguish regulation applicable to different entities. For example, entities that are systemically important and those that can significantly impact the stability of the financial system may need closer monitoring and regulation than others. The broad classification proposed is as follows:

- dealers;
- major participants, with a substantial net position in derivatives or whose outstanding positions create substantial net counterparty exposure;
- eligible contract participants (ECPs), a broad range of market participants using derivatives for the purpose of hedging their business/commercial risks;
- Non-ECPs, ie, small, under-capitalised municipalities and certain private individuals.

Clearing

Derivatives are required to be cleared unless an exemption is provided by CFTC/SEC. CFTC/SEC may provide an exemption from clearing if

- it is not accepted by a derivatives clearing organisation/clearing agency or
- one of the counterparties is not a dealer or Major Participant and it can demonstrate its capability to meet its financial obligations for non-cleared trades.

Trading on an exchange or alternate swap execution facility

If a trade is required to be cleared, it also must be executed on an exchange or an alternate swap execution facility (ASEF). All trades with a non-ECP as a counterparty must be executed on an exchange or an ASEF. A trade is exempt from this requirement if and only if there is no exchange or ASEF available for the particular kind of swap.

Segregation of collateral

Segregation of collateral is required to ensure portability of funds upon a default of a dealer or clearing member. Collateral may be segregated at the clearinghouse or via a separate third-party custodian account at the clearing member/dealer.

SEC and CFTC may work with the Financial Institutions Regulatory Administration (FIRA) to set position limits, margin and capital requirements. Furthermore, reporting is mandatory, in the case of a non-cleared trade, to a repository or the SEC or CFTC.

As of October 5, 2009, Intercontinental Exchange (ICE0 declared that it had cleared US$3 trillion of dealer index trades globally. Buy-side participants are also working with clearinghouses/exchanges regarding the mechanics of client-clearing currently and hope to kick start client-clearing in 2010. While specifics around some of the aspects of the above regulation are bound to be discussed and developed over the next few months, the framework discussed here should broadly help understand the regulatory guidelines.

Centralised clearinghouses

A centralised clearinghouse[10] (also termed a "central counterparty" or "CCP") is an entity that interposes itself between the seller and buyer of protection in a cleared trade. Both counterparties will face a clearinghouse such that if one of the counterparties cannot "make good" on its contract, the other counterparty will not be affected. A clearinghouse applies multilateral netting of trades and requires that counterparties post margin, thus reducing systemic risk and minimising cashflows between counterparties. We reuse a simplified example of netting and trade compression and CCP settlement from a recent IMF working paper.[11]

Each counterparty is labelled with a letter and "E" stands for the maximum counterparty exposure of each. The arrows represent the direction of credit exposure sized at US$5 in each case. Figure 6.15 shows the example of bilateral exposures. Each counterparty holds margin up to the maximum of their potential exposure. For example, counterparty C would face maximum losses in the event that both A and D default, resulting in a potential loss of US$10. Figure 6.16 shows the resulting exposures for the example under central clearing. Here each bilateral trade is replaced with a central clearing trade and exposure. Now, in the case of C, the original exposures from A,

Figure 6.15 Original exposures without a centralised clearinghouse

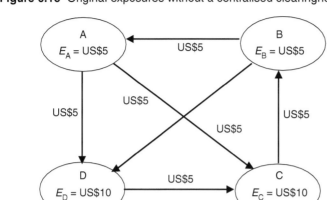

Source: IMF, BofA Merrill Lynch Global Research. Reprinted by permission. Copyright © 2010 Bank of America Corporation.

Figure 6.16 Resulting exposures due to a centralised clearinghouse

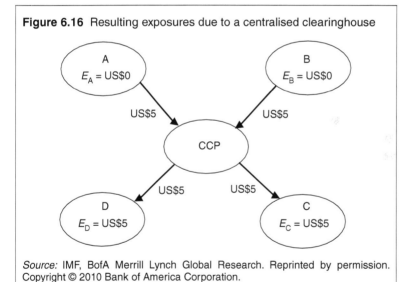

Source: IMF, BofA Merrill Lynch Global Research. Reprinted by permission. Copyright © 2010 Bank of America Corporation.

D and to B are netted leaving only an exposure of US$5. The economic advantage of such a model is clear in reducing the bilateral counterparty risks and reducing margin required to be held against offsetting trades. In this simple example, C's maximum counterparty exposure would decline from US$10 under the bilateral settlements to US$5 under the central clearing model.

LIMITATIONS OF CLEARINGHOUSES

Despite the focus of reform on the establishment of clearinghouses, clear limitations on this structural reform exist that limit the absolute level of risk reduction possible under a clearinghouse model. These limitations fall under two broad categories: limits to what can be cleared and limits to portfolio margining.

Limits to what can be cleared

A critical component of a successful central clearing model is price transparency and liquidity. A clearinghouse requires both but creates neither. A frequent misconception of clearinghouses is that by moving derivatives settlements towards clearinghouses both transparency and liquidity will improve. Transparency improvements can be accomplished separately through trade reporting and repository mechanisms irrespective of the how the settlement of a derivative works. That leaves the issue of liquidity. Liquidity is a function of capital and trading volumes applied to a given derivative. It is also a function of the degree of heterogeneity or homogeneity of the underlying risk being expressed through the derivative. To the extent that the underlying risk is highly customised, derivatives will tend to be more specific leading to the effect of distributing the trading volumes in a broad class of risks into specific types and definitions of derivatives resulting in lower liquidity in each.

A key question for the development of derivative markets will be the extent to which the costs of a customised derivative outweigh its benefits. To the extent that a more generic derivative can accomplish the goals of the user, the greater trading volume can be concentrated into fewer contracts. The increased liquidity that results can lead to that derivative being eligible for central clearing. However, some degree of customisation may remain desirable for end users, and these contracts by their nature will be likely to fail to display sufficient liquidity to enable central clearing. Thus, some portion of the derivatives market, even under central clearing, is likely to remain bilaterally cleared, as it was before the crisis.[12]

Trade-offs of diverse central clearing: diversification for cost

Central clearing however also results in greater costs. The cost "increase" is in terms of the loss of cost reduction possible under a bilateral settlements system. Costs of derivative trading can be reduced when the risks of a counterparty's trades can be considered as a portfolio rather than individually. To the extent diversification helps to reduce the risk of the overall portfolio, economically speaking the required margin to minimise counterparty risk would be less than the sum of the individual positions. This ability, however, is lost under a diversified central clearinghouse model, as counterparty risk is considered at each clearinghouse invalidating the ability to consider the counterparty's total portfolio of risks regardless of the clearinghouse. Such a trade-off results from a strategy of diversifying clearinghouse risk to reduce the systemic risk potential of the clearinghouses themselves. But that reduction in systemic risk comes at the cost of raising the costs of derivative trading.[13]

CONCLUSIONS

The derivatives markets face fundamental structural changes after the credit crisis. This regulatory reform accelerates the pace of changes that were already underway before the crisis. And while the Dodd–Frank legislation provides broad guidance as to how the market will change in key areas of regulation, transparency and structure, the exact form and hence implications of these changes remains very much uncertain. A few key conclusions, however, can be drawn as to the post-credit-crisis derivatives world. The trade-off for achieving a reduction in the potential systemic risk of the OTC derivatives markets will be greater costs of trading. The expansion of central clearing will reduce system risk but will not in itself increase liquidity. The strategy to limit the potential systemic risk of the clearinghouses themselves through diversification results in greater costs of derivative usage through the loss of a portfolio view of counterparty risk. Changes in capital charges faced by dealers in OTC derivatives and the costs of customised derivatives through both these charges and the lack of central clearing will need to be weighed by end users against the benefits of customised exposures. To the extent that those costs outweigh the benefits, greater trading volumes in derivatives may become concentrated into a few "benchmark" contracts, with higher liquidity in these "benchmarks" but lower liquidity and higher costs for more customised derivatives.

1   We note that such concerns were well documented at the time. For example, the Counterparty Risk Management Policy Committee, a voluntary industry group, published recommendations addressing counterparty risk in the period leading up to the crisis (July 2005) and at the height of the crisis (August 2008).

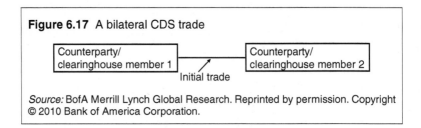

Figure 6.17 A bilateral CDS trade

Source: BofA Merrill Lynch Global Research. Reprinted by permission. Copyright © 2010 Bank of America Corporation.

2   Note we are thinking here of a small, private hedge fund as counterparty, not, say, a large broker–dealer such as Lehman Brothers. In the latter case, the default event was immediate; for the former it may be less transparent.
3   Drexel (1990), Kidder Peabody (sold to Paine Webber in 1994) and Barings (1995).
4   For more discussion on this issue see, for example, Singh and Aitken (2010).
5   That is, restrictions or outright waivers on the practice of posting initial margin (and in some cases even variation margin).
6   This context was argued by Duffie (2010).
7   Here liquidity is defined as the ability to trade at a given size with limited impact on price.
8   In most cases, they would end up paying their counterparty less than the full notional by the amount of the recovery on the asset post default.
9   See, for example, the Counterparty Risk Policy Committee reports (http://www.crmpolicygroup.org/).
10 For a more detailed description of clearinghouse mechanics, please see the first appendix.
11 This example was discussed in Kiff *et al* (2009).
12 A more detailed discussion of this issue can be found in Duffie *et al* (2010).
13 A detailed description of this effect can be found in Duffie and Zhu (2009).

APPENDIX: CENTRAL COUNTERPARTY CLEARING DETAILS

Central counterparty (CCP) clearing has become so ingrained in the exchange-traded portion of the derivatives market that even experts in those products are sometimes unsure of CCP mechanics. This is particularly true for client clearing. The details around client clearing, as well as the CCPs that will clear trades, are still being sorted out for products like interest rate swaps and credit default swaps. Below, we highlight a few general examples of clearing from both members' and clients' perspectives to shed some light on this sometimes confusing process. The exact methodologies could change somewhat as the details are rolled out.

Clearing among clearinghouse members

Figure 6.17 shows a bilateral trade between two dealers that are also clearinghouse members. If one were to default, the trade would be

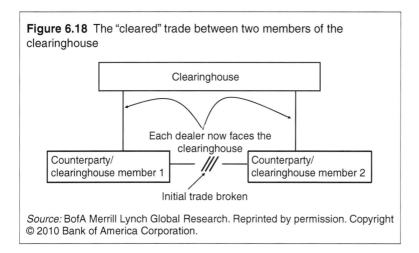

Figure 6.18 The "cleared" trade between two members of the clearinghouse

Source: BofA Merrill Lynch Global Research. Reprinted by permission. Copyright © 2010 Bank of America Corporation.

broken and the surviving counterparty would have to file a claim for any money owed.

Figure 6.18 shows the trade after clearing via the CCP. Note that the original trade is broken and each dealer now faces the clearinghouse. If dealer 1 were to default, its counterparty would still face the clearinghouse thus mitigating counterparty risk for dealer 2.

In order to face the clearinghouse directly, both dealers need to be clearinghouse members. As members they capitalise the CCP. In addition to capital commitments, the two clearinghouse members would post initial and variation margin. The margin and capital are used in that order to cover member defaults.

Client clearing

Now we shall look at a few examples of client clearing. Client clearing is simply the use of segregated accounts to clear non-clearinghouse members via a member of the CCP.

Separate clearing agent and trade counterparty

Figure 6.19 shows an example OTC trade.[14] The client would like to clear the trade but does not want to clear it via its trading counterparty. This is important, as the trading counterparty will not necessarily be a member of the clearinghouse. See the initial trade below.

Figure 6.20 illustrates the transactions associated with client clearing. Note that the margin is deposited in a segregated account. The

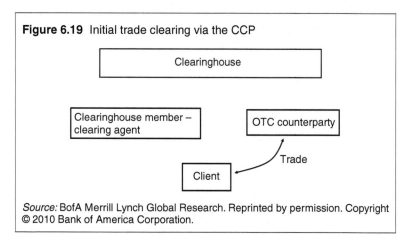

Figure 6.19 Initial trade clearing via the CCP

Source: BofA Merrill Lynch Global Research. Reprinted by permission. Copyright © 2010 Bank of America Corporation.

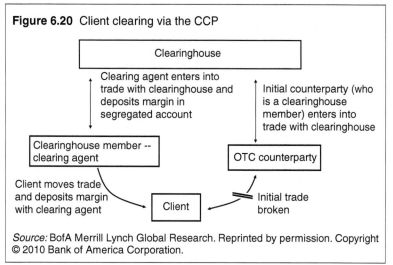

Figure 6.20 Client clearing via the CCP

Source: BofA Merrill Lynch Global Research. Reprinted by permission. Copyright © 2010 Bank of America Corporation.

account will hold initial and variation margin associated with the trade.

If the clearing agent defaults (Figure 6.21), then the money held in the separate account would be transferred to another clearinghouse member who would become the new clearing agent. This highlights the concept of "portability". The client's funds are held separately in the CCP so that if a member defaults, they can be moved to another agent.

In this arrangement, the clearing agent is exposed to the risk that the client may default leaving them with a naked position facing the clearinghouse. Accordingly, the agent is likely to hold some margin

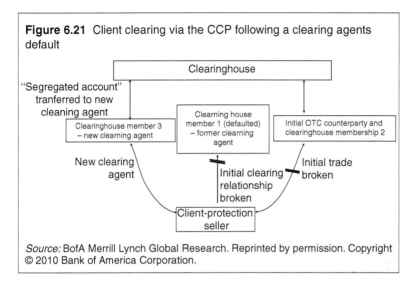

Figure 6.21 Client clearing via the CCP following a clearing agents default

Source: BofA Merrill Lynch Global Research. Reprinted by permission. Copyright © 2010 Bank of America Corporation.

greater than that held in the segregated account. This margin will not be portable, but should only be a fraction of the margin held at the CCP.

Segregated accounts resolve one of the counterparty issues that was important during the Lehman bankruptcy. Since the margin was held at Lehman, it was not bankruptcy remote. The bankruptcy judge had to approve the release of these accounts. This can take time. Investors minimise this risk via the segregated, portable accounts at the CCP.

Same clearing agent and trade counterparty

Let us now look at a different example. Here the clearing agent and the counterparty are the same.

Figure 6.23 highlights the set of transactions that would now occur in order to clear the client's trade. Note that they are very similar to the above example, where the clearing agent and counterparty are separate. This is because a clearing agent within the counterparty institution will enter into the same transaction.

If the initial clearing agent and counterparty goes bankrupt (Figure 6.24), then the account is transferred to another agent (again highlighting portability).

Again, the mechanisms we highlight above are in line with clearinghouses in the various options markets. Clients can reduce counterparty risk via a clearinghouse even if they are not a member. If

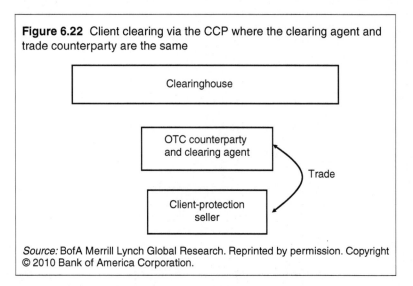

Figure 6.22 Client clearing via the CCP where the clearing agent and trade counterparty are the same

Source: BofA Merrill Lynch Global Research. Reprinted by permission. Copyright © 2010 Bank of America Corporation.

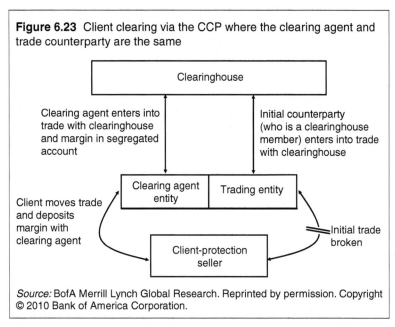

Figure 6.23 Client clearing via the CCP where the clearing agent and trade counterparty are the same

Source: BofA Merrill Lynch Global Research. Reprinted by permission. Copyright © 2010 Bank of America Corporation.

at some point clients are able to become members, they will have to assess whether the reduced counterparty risk associated with joining a clearinghouse outweighs the costs associated with capitalising it. In other markets cleared via a CCP, the majority of participants do not become clearinghouse members.

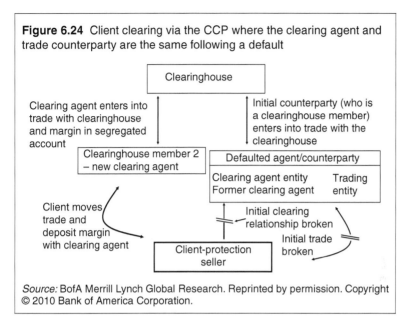

Figure 6.24 Client clearing via the CCP where the clearing agent and trade counterparty are the same following a default

Source: BofA Merrill Lynch Global Research. Reprinted by permission. Copyright © 2010 Bank of America Corporation.

APPENDIX: NOVATION AND OPERATIONAL RISKS OF DERIVATIVES PRE-CRISIS

A key aspect of the pre-crisis derivatives market was the practice of "novation". Since OTC derivatives are bilateral agreements, without a process for "assignment "of trades, the only means to close out of an OTC derivative would be to unwind the trade with the original dealer. That would, however, significantly limit the liquidity of the market. So the practice of assignment developed.

An assignment involves three parties: the "remaining party", who remains on the CDS contract even after the assignment takes place; the "transferor", who assigns (transfers) liability for the contract; and the "transferee", to whom the contract is assigned (transferred).

Technically, an assignment may not occur unless the remaining party agrees to face the transferee. This is because the original CDS contract was a bilateral agreement between the remaining party and the transferor. To remove the transferor from the original CDS contract and replace it with the transferee, the transferor must obtain permission from the remaining party.

However, historically, assignments were executed without the permission of the remaining party. This was one of the concerns highlighted by market regulators. Consider an original trade between a broker–dealer and a client, which is then assigned by the client to a different broker–dealer. This often resulted in a decrease in counterparty risk, because the new broker–dealer was viewed as more creditworthy than the client (eg, a hedge fund). Expecting that the original broker–dealer (the remaining party) would agree to the assignment, the client (transferor) and the new broker–dealer (transferee) have simply assigned the trade, and later sought permission from the remaining party.

Operationally, this resulted in a backlog of assignments, where remaining parties may not know which counterparty they face for months at a time. Should a "credit event" occur before the assignment backlog is completed, the remaining party may contact the wrong counterparty for payment. Moreover, should either the transferor or transferee file for bankruptcy, the remaining party may not know its exact credit exposure for some time.

In September 2005, the Federal Reserve and 14 dealers met to discuss risks to the credit derivatives market. On October 24, 2005, the 2005 Novation Protocol took effect for the CDS market. This protocol requires the following:

> The transferee must receive consent from the remaining party by 6 pm, in the location of the transferee, on the day an assignment is agreed to. If the transferee does not receive consent by 6 pm, the assignment will instead be booked as a new trade.

By booking the attempted assignment as a new trade, the transferor (the hedge fund) remains with both trades facing the original counterparty (the remaining party) and the new trade (facing the transferor). This is operationally and economically less attractive, as the counterparty risk that the hedge fund faces actually increases, and the margin for both trades needs to be held, even though economically the hedge fund faces no net increase in exposure. The margin held on both trades created the incentive to ensure that assignments are agreed to, and resulted in a rapid reduction in unconfirmed assignments.

REFERENCES

Banc of America Securities–Merrill Lynch, 2009, "AIG: Initiation of Coverage", Report, March 17,

Duffie, D., 2010, "In Defense of Financial Speculation", *Wall Street Journal*, February 24.

Duffie, D., and X. Zhu, 2009, "Does a Central Clearing Counterparty Reduce Counterparty Risk?", Stanford Graduate School of Business Research Paper, February.

Duffie, D., A. Li and Th. Lubke, 2010, "Policy Perspectives on OTC Derivatives Market Infrastructure", Federal Reserve Bank of New York Staff Reports, January (Revised March).

Kiff, J., J. Elliott, E. Kazarian, J. Scarlata and C. Spackman, 2009, "Credit Derivatives: Systemic Risks and Policy Options", IMF Working Paper, November.

The President's Working Group on Financial Markets, 1999, "Over-the-Counter Derivatives Markets and the Commodity Exchange Act", URL: http://www.ustreas.gov/press/releases/reports/otcact.pdf.

Singh, M., and J. Aitken, 2010, "The (Sizable) Role of Rehypothecation in the Shadow Banking System", IMF Working Paper 10/172.

7

The Re-Emergence of Distressed Exchanges in Corporate Restructurings

Edward I. Altman, Brenda Karlin

NYU Salomon Center

In 2008 and 2009, bondholders of ailing companies were affected by a re-emergence of an important corporate restructuring strategy, known as a "distressed exchange" (DE). This tactic is usually an attempt by an ailing firm to avoid bankruptcy by proposing a fundamental change in the contractual relationship between a debtor and its various creditor classes and is "voluntarily" agreed upon by a sufficient percentage (usually 90% or more) of relevant creditor claims. While one of the most common and dramatic DEs involves a substitution of lower priority equity securities for debt claims, DEs can also result from a reduction of the effective interest rate on the debt, a subordination of claims, an extension of time to repay the debt or a package of new securities, cash and other securities, that have a total value that is less than the face value of the original debt claim. Another critical component is the condition that the original claim is selling at a distressed price at the time of the DE announcement, usually below 70 cents on the US dollar. The resulting situation is still called a DE even if the price of the existing debt increases after the announcement. The recovery rate to bondholders participating in distressed exchanges since 1985 is significantly higher than recoveries on other, more dramatic types of default – namely payment defaults and bankruptcies. Nevertheless, there is no guarantee that a distressed exchange will permanently immunise the firm against further distress, with almost 50% of all companies completing distressed exchanges prior to 2008 ultimately filing for bankruptcy.

The first instances of DEs in the modern high-yield bond era were the so-called 3(a)9 exchange championed by Drexel Burnham

Lambert in the 1980s. These exchanges were particularly attractive to the distressed firms because they did not require Securities and Exchange Commission review and could be accomplished quickly (usually in less than a month). A second critical element was that the exchange was tax free, even if the new securities had a combined value of less than the original claim. This tax-free exemption changed in the early 1990s, when the reduction in debt was considered a taxable event. This revised tax ruling is still in effect at the time of writing in 2009, regardless of whether or not the company is in a distressed condition. Hence, there is little incentive for a highly solvent firm to exchange its debt for equity and reduce its leverage when the consequence would be a meaningful increase in taxes. As such, these exchanges will usually only take place when a firm is desperately trying to avoid an even more costly bankruptcy, and also usually where it has sufficient tax-loss credits to offset the taxable exchange.

In a preliminary discussion of DEs (Altman and Karlin 2009), it was proposed that it was time to revisit this tax ruling, since the de-leveraging of corporate America is a meaningful objective. Very soon afterwards, we learned that the economic stimulus legislation that passed Congress in February 2009 contained important relief for companies seeking to restructure debt by deferring most cancellation of debt "income" in 2009 and 2010 until 2014, then amortising over a five-year period from 2014 to 2018. For a more detailed description of this new legislation, including whether it may pay for a company to take advantage of this tax deferral while in bankruptcy, see Kirkland and Ellis LLP (2009).

While a few earlier studies, such as Gilson *et al* (1990), showed that out-of-court restructurings were considerably less costly than bankruptcies to the debtor firm, in many cases the DE was followed by a bankruptcy anyway. Our own results, discussed below, show that out of 57 DEs completed prior to 2008 at least 26 (46%) were followed by a bankruptcy filing, and the majority of others resulted in a change of ownership of the debtor (ie, were acquired).

IMPLICATIONS OF DISTRESSED EXCHANGES

Distressed exchanges have important implications for credit markets. Firstly, just about all instances of DEs are now categorised as a "default" in the calculations of default rates, including in our own calculations. There is still some debate, however, as to whether the entire debt issue involved in a DE should be counted as a default or only the actual amount tendered in the exchange. Another debatable issue is the date on which the debt should be considered in default: when the DE is announced or when it is completed. This is particularly relevant for the computation of the recovery rate of the default event. The policy is to count a DE that has been accepted by the requisite proportion of claimants at the time the announcement of the tender offer took place, unless there were changes in the terms of the exchange or other material events took place, as in the case of GMAC (discussed below). In addition, we only count the face value amount of claims that are tendered, not the total outstanding amount of the debt issue.

DISTRESSED EXCHANGE DEFAULTS IN THE CREDIT DEFAULT SWAP MARKET

An important consequence of a completed DE had been that it was possible, but not likely, that it would trigger a default event in the credit default swap (CDS) market. This is known as a modified restructuring (MOD-R) default. Since this market began developing in the late 1990s, there has been a recurring ambiguity over whether a DE or other significant negative firm development would trigger a default and unwinding of the transaction. Evolving formalisation of CDS contracts by the International Swaps and Derivatives Association (ISDA) have reduced these controversies and resulted in certain guidelines. Furthermore, as of April 2009, DEs were no longer considered a default event, eliminating one possible negative event that could constitute a default and trigger a payout. This change constitutes a reduction in the insurance potential of a CDS hedging contract.

In the past, triggers for DEs that changed the terms of existing debt included an equity for debt swap, a drop in coupon, extension of maturity or creation of contractual subordination, but only if it is within the context of the existing bond or loan.[1] In the case of the GMAC in 2008, where less than 60% of the par value amount of the issue was bound by the exchange, a CDS default was not triggered. The same was true in all of the 2008 DEs. The corporate market has not recently experienced any distressed exchanges that could trigger a default in the CDS market, although they have been observed in the sovereign market (eg, Argentina). Outside of a prepackaged Chapter 11, US corporations have found it extremely difficult to affect an exchange which would qualify as a default under ISDA guidelines. As noted above, a proposal to eliminate a "modified exchange" as a default trigger in CDS contracts was adopted in order to avoid confusion and costly lawsuits. Therefore, since March 2009, only a failure to pay interest or a bankruptcy qualifies.

The distinction between a default in the primary market (and what investors believe will be their ultimate recovery) and what triggers a payout in the CDS market helps to explain why CDS spreads have recently been tighter for many distressed credits than CDS spreads in the bond market. Other reasons for tighter spreads are liquidity and funding differences, but it is difficult to isolate each factor.

DISTRESSED EXCHANGES IN 2008

To say that a resurgence in the incidence of DEs was observed in 2008 is a gross understatement. Indeed, the number of DEs in 2008 (14) was almost double the number for any year since 1984 (see Table 7.1). The total amount of DEs (US$30.3 billion) was more than twice the total amount from 1984–2007 combined. Firms appeared to have been scrambling to avoid bankruptcy like never before and, due to their significant tax-loss credits, they were not concerned about the taxable nature of the debt reductions.[2] In addition, since debtor-in-possession (DIP) loans and equity infusions were constrained due to the 2007–9 credit crisis, the usual benefits of bankruptcy were lessened and the prospect of liquidation in bankruptcy heightened. Creditors, on the other hand, are less likely to resist a DE tender because the likely recovery after a DE is greater than either in bankruptcy reorganisation or in liquidation. Of course, initial DE proposals can be challenged by creditors in the hope that the debtor will sweeten the offer. Several instances of this occurred in 2008, the most publicised of which was the recently completed GMAC exchange. If the DE goes through despite some proportion that is not tendered, those not tendering will continue to have a claim of full face value should a bankruptcy subsequently occur subsequently.

The saga of the 2008 GMAC/Residential Capital exchange is exceptional for several reasons. It involved the US government in a material way and it is by far the largest DE in history. The initial

DE offer was a complicated package of cash, new debt and preferred stock that was advertised as needing a tender of at least 75% of the outstanding debt amounts of both GMAC and Residential Capital, a subsidiary of GMAC. The 75% was the amount supposedly necessary for the Federal Reserve to grant GMAC status as a bank holding company, thereby giving it access to The Fed's discount window and its low-cost debt borrowings.

It appeared that the 75% was not going to be achieved, although the bank holding company status was formally announced subject to the requisite amount of new equity capital being raised, ostensibly in the equity-for-debt swap from the DE. When it became obvious that the 75% was not going to be achieved, the US government trumped that requirement by investing US$5 billion directly in preferred stock of GMAC and loaning an additional US$1 billion to GM for the purpose of that firm's purchase of additional preferred securities. Hence, the 75% exchange was not necessary and GMAC accepted the 59% of GMAC bonds tendered as well as the 39% tendered to Residential Capital. *De facto*, the usual 90% requirement, or even the 75% stated in the objective, was not relevant and the DE was achieved.

The irony of the GMAC DE is that all creditors (both those that tendered and those that did not) were pleased with the exchange, since the prices on all existing bonds spiked significantly due to the government's enormous equity "bailout" infusion. The upfront premium on the CDS of the remaining GMAC bonds also dropped dramatically from about 44% as of the day before the firm won Federal Reserve approval (actually the equity infusion) to become a bank holding company, to about 10.5% on January 2, 2009. Most of the drop occurred after the announced equity infusion on December 29, 2008. Bond prices increased by about 30 points after that announcement.

DEs in 2008 amounted to about 22% of the defaulted issuers (14 of 64) but as much as 60% of the US dollar amount of defaults.[3] These statistics attest to the domination of 2008 in the DE phenomenon. For the period 1984–2009, however, DEs only accounted for about 10.6% of all defaulting issuers and 12.0% of all default dollar amounts (see Table 7.1).

Table 7.1 High-yield bond distressed exchange default and recovery statistics 1984–2009

Year	DE defaults ($)	Total defaults ($)	% DE defaults to total US$	DE defaults (# issuers)	Total defaults (# issuers)	% DE defaults to total # issuers	DE recovery rate (%)*	All default recovery rate (%)**	Difference between DE and all default recovery rate (%)
2009	23,212.60	123,823.79	18.7	46	120	38.3	42.68	36.13	6.55
2008	30,329.42	50,763.26	59.7	14	64	21.9	52.41	42.50	9.91
2007	146.83	5,473.00	2.7	1	19	5.3	85.17	66.65	18.52
2006	0.00	7,559.00	0.0	0	0	0.0	N/A	N/A	N/A
2005	0.00	36,209.00	0.0	0	34	0.0	N/A	62.96	N/A
2004	537.88	11,657.00	4.6	5	39	12.8	58.05	57.72	0.33
2003	1,034.94	38,451.00	2.7	7	86	8.1	78.52	45.58	32.94
2002	764.80	96,858.00	0.8	3	112	2.7	61.22	25.30	35.92
2001	1,267.60	63,609.00	2.0	5	156	3.2	33.12	25.62	7.50
2000	50.00	30,295.00	0.2	1	107	0.9	77.00	26.74	50.26
1999	2,118.40	23,532.00	9.0	6	98	6.1	65.39	27.90	37.49
1998	461.10	7,464.00	6.2	2	37	5.4	17.34	40.46	(23.12)
1997	0.00	4,200.00	0.0	0	0	0.0	N/A	N/A	N/A
1996	0.00	3,336.00	0.0	0	0	0.0	N/A	N/A	N/A
1995	0.00	4,551.00	0.0	0	0	0.0	N/A	N/A	N/A

*Weighted-average recovery rates for each year. **Arithmetic average of the weighted-average annual recovery rates; only those years with DEs counted. The arithmetic average of each individual DE (116) for the entire sample period was 48.24% and the average for the non-DE defaults (983 observations) was 36.72%.

Source: Authors' compilation from the NYU Salomon Center Master Default Database.

DISTRESSED EXCHANGES

Table 7.1 Continued

Year	DE defaults ($)	Total defaults ($)	% DE defaults to total US$	DE defaults (# issuers)	Total defaults (# issuers)	% DE defaults to total # issuers	DE recovery rate (%)*	All default recovery rate (%)**	Difference between DE and all default recovery rate (%)
1994	0.00	3,418.00	0.0	0	0	0.0	N/A	N/A	N/A
1993	0.00	2,287.00	0.0	0	0	0.0	N/A	N/A	N/A
1992	0.00	5,545.00	0.0	0	0	0.0	N/A	N/A	N/A
1991	76.00	18,862.00	0.4	1	62	1.6	31.30	40.67	(9.37)
1990	1,044.00	18,354.00	5.7	7	47	14.9	43.15	24.66	18.49
1989	548.90	8,110.00	6.8	7	26	26.9	44.53	35.97	8.56
1988	390.30	3,944.00	9.9	3	24	12.5	28.40	43.45	(15.05)
1987	33.60	7,486.00	0.4	2	15	13.3	40.70	66.63	(25.93)
1986	114.80	3,156.00	3.6	4	23	17.4	47.68	36.60	11.08
1985	323.30	992.00	32.6	2	19	10.5	55.04	41.78	13.26
1984	100.10	344.00	29.1	1	12	8.3	44.12	50.62	(6.50)
Totals/averages	69,460.74	580,279.05	12.0	117	1,100	10.6	51.81**	42.00**	9.82

Blanks denote that data is unavailable. *Weighted-average recovery rates for each year. **Arithmetic average of the weighted-average annual recovery rates; only those years with DEs counted. The arithmetic average of each individual DE (116) for the entire sample period was 48.24% and the average for the non-DE defaults (983 observations) was 36.72%.

Source: Authors' compilation from the NYU Salomon Center Master Default Database.

Table 7.2 Difference in means test between recovery rates: all non-distressed exchange defaulting issuers versus distressed exchanges 1984–2009

	All defaults excluding DE	Distressed exchanges
Sample size	2,239	269
Mean recovery rate	36.72	48.24
Standard deviation	25.95	23.59
Variance	673.63	556.27
t-test*		7.48755

$$*t = \frac{\bar{x}_T - \bar{x}_C}{\sqrt{\text{var}_T/n_T + \text{var}_C/n_C}}.$$

Source: Authors' compilation from NYU Salomon Center master default database.

RECOVERY RATES ON DISTRESSED EXCHANGES

Since DEs are not as dramatic a testimony to the firm's distressed status as is a bankruptcy or non-payment of cash interest on the debt, we might expect that the recovery rate on DE defaults will be higher than other, more serious distressed situations. Indeed, the data backs this up. Table 7.1 shows that the arithmetic average recovery rate on all DE defaults was 51.81% for 1984–2009 compared with 42.00% for all defaults and 36.7% for all non-DE defaults (see Table 7.2). In 2008, DEs recovered 52.4%, while non-DE defaults recovered only 27.1%. Although not as striking a difference, DEs in 2009 recovered 42.68%, while non-DE defaults recovered only 34.56%.

In Table 7.2, we calculate a difference in means test between the arithmetic average recovery rate (48.2%)[4] on the 117 DEs over the period 1984–2009 compared with the average recovery rate on all non-DE defaults (36.7%) over the same period. We find that, given the above, the DE recovery rate is significantly higher ($t = 7.49$) at the 1% confidence level. It is not surprising that bondholders will choose, in many instances, to accept a recovery with certainty from a DE rather than take the chance of holding out for an uncertain, and probably lower, recovery in bankruptcy. Our results do not include data for situations when a DE offer is rejected. It is safe to assume, however, that most of these scenarios would be associated with a subsequent bankruptcy petition. Investors still must decide, given the completion of a DE, whether to hold on to the new set of securities

Table 7.3 Distressed exchanges completed by quarter, 2009

Quarter	DE defaults (# issuers)	DE defaults ($)
1	11	4,696.97
2	17	11,122.28
3	15	5,556.69
4	9	1,836.65
Total	52*	23,212.60

*This total exceeds the 46 listed in Table 7.1, since several issuers completed more than one distressed exchange in 2009.

from the exchange or to sell as quickly as is feasible. It can safely be said that if a bankruptcy takes place subsequent to a DE, then the default recovery after bankruptcy will be considerably lower than it would have been had the investor sold immediately after the DE (perhaps by about 20%). What is not known is the likely positive average return on those situations when a bankruptcy is permanently avoided after the DE.

SUBSEQUENT PERFORMANCE OF DE FIRMS

An important follow-on question to the DE restructuring strategy is over the subsequent performance of the firm and its securities. This has been assessed by tracking the firms that completed a DE prior to 2008,[5] separating them into several categories as of March 2009, including "still operating", "acquired" and "bankrupt" (Chapter 7 or 11). Obviously, a DE that results in a subsequent bankruptcy proved to be an unsuccessful restructuring, and the DE merely delayed the eventual demise of the firm.

The subsequent fate of 57 DEs in the period 1984–2007 is listed in Tables 7.4–7.8. Of the 57 DEs, 26 (45.6%) eventually went bankrupt (20 Chapter 11 reorganisations and six Chapter 7 liquidations). The time from the completion of the DE to bankruptcy ranged from less than one month to 18 years, with the median being about two years. Seventeen (30.0%) DE firms were eventually acquired, while 11 (19.3%) were still operating in 2009. We could not find subsequent data on three firms. In conclusion, almost half of our DE sample declared bankruptcy subsequent to the exchange and the remaining were still operating as a going concern in one form or another in

Table 7.4 Subsequent development of distressed exchanges (1984–2007)

Issuer name	DE date	Exch. type	Subseq. devel.	Bank-ruptcy date	Years from DE to b'ruptcy	Amount exch. (US$M)
@Track Commun.	15/02/01	D	Ch 11	02/02/04	3.00	94.33
Abraxas Petrol. Corp	01/11/99	D	Still op.			258.60
Advantica Restaurant Group Inc	01/03/02	D	Still op.			529.60
After Six Inc	28/08/89	U	Ch 7	26/02/99	3.50	20.00
Aircoa Hospitality Services	15/09/90	C	Acq'd			34.00
Alamosa Holdings Inc	12/09/03	D/E	Acq'd			750.00
Alpine Group	14/09/89	D/E	Still op.			43.70
American Cellular Corp	15/07/03	E/C	Acq'd			11.70
American Telecasting Inc	13/05/98	D	Acq'd			276.90
AMF Bowling Worldwide Inc	28/06/99	C	Ch 11	03/07/01	2.08	476.00
Anchor Adv. Products, Inc (Moll Industries)	08/08/00	D	Acq'd; Subseq. Ch 11	19/09/02	2.08	50.00
Charter Commun.	24/08/05	D	Ch 11	27/03/09	3.67	6,861.00
Continental Global Group Inc	04/10/04	D	Acq'd			120.00
Dailey Intl Inc	21/05/99	E	Ch 11	28/05/99	0.02	275.00
Darling Delaware Co	15/09/90	D/E	Still op.			175.00
Dart Drug Stores Inc	01/07/87	D/E	Ch 7	10/08/89	2.08	28.60
Focal Commun. Corp	31/10/01	E	Ch 11	19/12/02	1.17	510.20
Forstmann & Co	14/08/90	D	Ch 11	22/09/95	5.08	100.00

D, debt; C, cash; E, equity; U, undetermined.

Table 7.4 Continued

Issuer name	DE date	Exch. type	Subseq. devel.	Bankruptcy date	Years from DE to b'ruptcy	Amount exch. (US$M)
Foster Wheeler Ltd	22/09/04	E	Still op.			7.88
G&G Retail Inc	18/03/04	E	Ch 11	15/01/06	1.83	107.00
Gaylord Container Corp	04/03/02	D	Acq'd			85.20
General Defense Corp	01/02/88	E/C	Acq'd			87.50
Golden Ocean Group Ltd	20/09/99	E	Ch 11	14/01/00	0.33	200.00
Hall-mark Electronics Corp	01/03/90	D	Acq'd			112.00
Harborside Healthcare Corp	06/04/01	D	Acq'd			137.31
Heafner Tire Group Inc	26/03/02	C	Acq'd			150.00
Home Group Funding Inc	15/01/91	D	Acq'd			76.00
Int'l Controls Corp	15/06/90	U	Info not found			288.00
Iron Age Holdings Corp	02/12/03	C	Ch 7	22/01/07	3.08	45.18
J Crew Group Inc	08/05/03	D	Still op.			21.70
JL French Automotive Castings Inc	24/08/04	E	Ch 11	10/02/06	1.50	28.00
Jordan Indust. Inc	24/02/04	D	Still op.			275.00
Kane Indust. Inc	01/01/90	D/C	Ch 11	18/03/94	4.17	70.00
Kenai Corp	15/10/84	E	Info not found			100.10

2009. (Tables 7.4–7.5 show the subsequent performance of 57 firms that went through a distressed exchange prior to 2008. Tables 7.6–7.8 show the subsequent performance of 22 firms that went through a distressed exchange after 2007.)

Table 7.4 Continued

Issuer name	DE date	Exch. type	Subseq. devel.	Bankruptcy date	Years from DE to b'ruptcy	Amount exch. (US$M)
Metropol. Broadcast.	12/10/89	D/C				135.20
Miramar Marine Corp	05/12/89	U	Ch 11	15/04/91	1.33	125.00
Na-Churs Plant Food	01/05/86	U	Still op.			20.00
New World Pictures Inc	12/08/88	U	Acq'd			285.00
North Atlantic Holding Co	09/05/07	D	Still op.			146.83
NTEX Inc	17/05/01	E	Still op.			35.78
Oak Indust.	29/03/85	D/E	Acq'd			115.00
Ponderosa, Inc	06/12/89	U	Acq'd; Subseq. Ch 11	22/10/08	18.83	125.00
Roma Restaur't Holdings Inc: Romacorp Inc	01/07/03	D/C	Ch 11	06/11/05	2.33	57.00

THE TREND OF DISTRESSED EXCHANGES

As expected, DEs continued without abatement in 2009, with three times as many firms completing at least one distressed exchange within the year when compared with 2008. This was due to the record number of distressed companies as well as changes in the Bankruptcy Code in 2005 that made it more difficult to reorganise successfully (ie, to emerge as a going concern at the end of the reorganisation process). As noted earlier, we observed an unprecedented appetite in 2008 and in early 2009 to restructure out of court rather than risk bankruptcy and liquidation.[6] No doubt, the difficulty in raising debtor-in-possession loans and exit-financing influenced the decision to file for bankruptcy. Indeed, prior to 2008, our statistics (Altman and Hotchkiss 2006) found that as much as 60–65% of large Chapter 11s in the 20 years prior to 2008 were successful in emerging from the bankruptcy process as a "going concern", although a

Table 7.4 Continued

Issuer name	DE date	Exch. type	Subseq. devel.	Bankruptcy date	Years from DE to b'ruptcy	Amount exch. (US$M)
Savin Corp	01/02/86	D/E	Ch 11; subseq. acq'd	14/12/93	7.83	58.70
Service Control Corp	15/07/89	U	Acq'd			100.00
Specialty Foods Acquisition Corp	10/06/99	D	Ch 11	18/09/00	1.25	793.80
Sunbeam Corp	01/02/88	U	Ch 11	20/02/88	0.05	17.80
Telesyst. Int'l Wireless Inc	06/07/01	D/C	Ch 7			489.95
Texas Int'l Co	22/08/85	U	Ch 11	26/04/88	2.67	208.30
Tultex Corp	13/05/99	D/C	Ch 7	03/12/99	0.58	115.00
UbiquiTel Inc	21/02/03	D/C	Acq'd			107.30
Univision Holdings Inc	01/02/90	C	Acq'd			265.00
Western Union Telegraph Co	01/11/87	D/C	Ch 11	04/02/93	5.25	5.00
Wickes Inc	27/02/03	D	Ch 7	20/01/04	0.92	63.24
Wilshire Financial Services Group Inc	13/11/98	E	Ch 11	03/03/99	0.33	184.20
XM Satellite Radio Inc	28/01/03	D	Acq'd			24.00
Zapata Corp	01/11/86	C	Still op.			36.10

non-significant number (about 200) ultimately filed again (Altman et al 2009).

In addition to the lack of Chapter 11 financing in the two years since 2008, the Bankruptcy Code of 2005 clearly tilted the negotiating process towards favouring creditors. As Miller (2009) pointed out, creditors had strong lobbyists arguing their point of view in the discussions leading up to the 2005 Code, while debtors did not. Leases are now more difficult to reject and certain claims, such as swaps and securities, are now exempt from the "automatic stay". Additionally, creditors can now wait for the exclusivity period to run out after 20

Table 7.5 Summary of information for Table 7.4

Exchange type		Subsequent development		Years from distressed exchange to bankruptcy	
Debt		18	Bankruptcy: Ch 7	6 Count	57
Cash		6	Bankruptcy: Ch 11	18 Mean	3
Equity		9	Acquired	17 Median	2.08
Debt/equity		6	Still operating	11 Max.	18.83
Debt/cash		7	Acquired: subseq. Ch 11	2 Min.	0.02
Equity/cash		2	Other	3	
Undetermined		9			

(18 + 2) months and then propose their own reorganisation plan. All of these factors encourage debtors to try to restructure out of court; hence the relatively strong showing of DEs in 2009. However, as can be seen in Table 7.3, interest in using DEs as a financing vehicle waned somewhat near the end of 2009, as general market conditions improved and other avenues of re-financing became available. The 11 DEs completed in the first-quarter of 2009 alone were only slightly less in number than the total completed in all of 2008 (14). Despite increasing momentum through the second quarter, by the fourth quarter of 2009 the number of DEs completed on a quarterly basis had dropped significantly from mid-year. Through the first quarter of 2010 we have seen relatively few DEs brought to market, and expect that the slowdown experienced in the second-half of 2009 will continue throughout 2010 as well.

CONCLUSION

The purpose of this study is to highlight the re-emergence of a type of distressed restructuring strategy known as a distressed exchange. The combination of an elevated fear of liquidations in bankruptcy, sizeable net operating losses to offset debt forgiveness taxes, and increased aggressiveness on the part of corporate advisors had motivated a significant increase in DE activity in 2008 and 2009. Indeed, DEs in 2008 and 2009 combined comprise slightly more than 50% of the total number completed in our 26-year sample (1984–2009), with over US$50 billion in debt forgiveness.

DISTRESSED EXCHANGES

Table 7.6 Subsequent development of distressed exchanges (2008–9)

Issuer name	DE date	Exch. type	Subseq. devel.	Bankruptcy date	Years from DE to bankruptcy	Amount exchanged (US$ M)
Ainsworth Lumber Co, Ltd	29/07/2008	D/E	Still op.	N/A	N/A	823.54
American Achievement Group Holding Corp	25/02/2009	D	Still op.	N/A	N/A	104.3
Clear Channel Communications	23/12/2008	D	Still op.	N/A	N/A	252.40
Clear Channel Communications Inc	23/12/2008	D	Still op.	N/A	N/A	102.24
CMP Susquehanna Corp	03/04/2009	D/E*	Still op.	N/A	N/A	175.46
Finlay Fine Jewelry Corp	25/11/2008	D	Still op.	N/A	N/A	139.64
Ford Motor Co	03/04/2009	D/C	Still op.	N/A	N/A	3,353.91
Freescale Semiconductor Inc	10/03/2009	D	Still op.	N/A	N/A	3,040.67
GMAC, LLC	29/12/2008	D,C,E**	Still op.	N/A	N/A	14,985.80
Harrah's Operating Co Inc	08/04/2009	D/C	Still op.	N/A	N/A	5,550.78
Harrah's Operating Co Inc	19/12/2008	D/C	Still op.	N/A	N/A	1,789.36
Hovnanian Enterprises Inc	24/11/2008	D	Still op.	N/A	N/A	71.46
Intelsat Ltd	12/02/2009	C	Still op.	N/A	N/A	460.61
Metaldyne Corp	26/11/2008	C	Ch 11	27/05/2009	0.50	361.34
Neff Corp	16/12/2008	D	Still op.	N/A	N/A	196.00
NXP BV	30/03/2009	D	Still op.	N/A	N/A	420.00
OSI Restaurant Partners, LLC	20/03/2009	C	Still op.	N/A	N/A	240.00
Primus Telecommunications Group Inc	22/05/2008	D/C	Ch 11	16/03/2009	0.83	54.30
RH Donnelley Corp	20/06/2008	D	Ch 11	28/05/2009	0.92	594.31
Residential Capital, LLC	04/06/2009	D/C	Still op.	N/A	N/A	
Sensata Technologies BV	30/03/2009	C	Still op.	N/A	N/A	109.99
Six Flags Inc	11/06/2008	D	Still op.	N/A	N/A	530.70
Tekni-Plex Inc	02/06/2008	E	Still op.	N/A	N/A	303.35

D, debt; C, cash; E, equity; U, undetermined. *Preferred & warrants; **Preferred.

Table 7.7 Summary information for Table 7.6 (2008–9)

Exchange type		Subsequent development		Years from distressed exchange to bankruptcy	
Debt	10	Bankruptcy: Ch 11	3	Count	23
Cash	4	Still operating	20	Mean	0.75
Equity	1			Median	0.83
Debt/Equity	2			Maximum	0.92
Debt/Cash	5			Minimum	0.50
Debt/Equity/Cash	1				

Table 7.8 Summary information for Table 7.6 (1984–2009)

Exchange type		Subsequent development		Years from distressed exchange to bankruptcy	
Debt	28	Bankruptcy: Ch 7	6	Count	80
Cash	10	Bankruptcy: Ch 11	21	Mean	2.76
Equity	10	Acquired	17	Median	1.96
Debt/equity	8	Still operating	31	Maximum	18.83
Debt/cash	12	Acquired: subseq. Ch 11	2	Minimum	0.02
Equity/cash	2	Other	3		
Debt/equity/cash	1				
Undetermined	9				

Please do not quote without permission from authors. All correspondence should be sent to ealtman@stern.nyu.edu. The authors thank Viral Acharya, Sanjiv Das, Max Holmes and Harvey Miller for their valued comments, and Abhimanyu Gupta for his computational assistance. This chapter is an update of the article of the same name published in *The Journal of Credit Risk* Special Issue on "Lessons from the Credit Crisis" in summer 2009.

---

14 Note that, at the time of writing, the ICE CDS clearinghouse does not offer client clearing. The June 2, 2009, letter to the New York Federal Reserve Bank committed to offer client clearing by December 15, 2009.

1 That is, if it has the same Committee on Uniform Security Identification Procedures (CUSIP) security identifier. It is in a form that binds all holders of the obligation and it is "voluntary" in that only investors who accept and tender their bonds are subject to what the issuer proposes. Hence, there was no default event even if those not accepting had their priority subordinated vis-à-vis those accepting.

2   Debt forgiveness which gives rise to income may be offset by net operative losses (NOLs) in an out-of-court restructuring. In a bankruptcy, debt forgiveness is generally excluded from income regardless if any NOLs are relevant, but at the end of the year the debtor must still generally reduce any available favourable tax attributes by the amount of the excluded debt forgiveness. The same tax treatment may be accomplished out of bankruptcy if the debtor is deemed to be "insolvent" immediately before the debt forgiveness; the amount is limited to the amount of insolvency. New legislation, however, defers any taxes regarding certain debt forgiveness income incurred in 2009 and 2010.

3   For a detailed report on defaults in 2008, see Altman and Karlin (2009).

4   The average of the annual weighted average DE recovery rates was 50.9% (see Table 7.1).

5   The 14 DE firms in 2008 have not been tracked because their DE is too recent to assess with regard to their ultimate fate.

6   In 2008 and through February 2009, there were 22 Chapter 11s that were converted to Chapter 7 liquidations (New Generation Research 2009), approximately 10% of all large (more than US$100 million in liabilities) Chapter 11 filings in the three-year period 2006–8.

REFERENCES

Altman, E., and E. Hotchkiss, 2006, "Corporate Financial Distress and Bankruptcy", Third Edition (Hoboken, NJ: John Wiley & Sons).

Altman, E., and B. Karlin, 2009, "Defaults and Returns in the High-Yield Bond Market: The Year 2008 in Review and Outlook in 2009", Special Report, NYU Salomon Center, February 13.

Altman, E., T. Kant and T. Rattanaruengyot, 2009, "Post-Chapter 11 Bankruptcy Performance: Avoiding Chapter 22", *Journal of Applied Corporate Finance* 21(3), pp. 53–64.

Gilson, S., K. John and L. Lang, 1990, "Troubled Debt Restructurings: An Empirical Study of Private Reorganization of Firms in Default", *Journal of Financial Economics* 27, pp. 315–53.

Kirkland and Ellis LLP, 2009, "Economic Stimulus Legislation Provides New Deferral Rules for Debt Cancellation Income, Kirkland Alert, February, URL: http://www.kirkland.com/siteFiles/Publications/7AA5935BC6CCB550732CF562DE9A17D.pdf.

Miller, H., 2009, "Keynote Address", 2009 Daily Bankruptcy Review Restructuring and Turnaround Summit, New York, February 12.

New Generation Research, 2009, *The 2009 Bankruptcy Yearbook and Almanac* (Boston, MA: New Generation Research).

Part III

Risk Management and Regulation

8
Modelling Systemic and Sovereign Risks

Dale F. Gray, Andreas A. Jobst
International Monetary Fund

The complex interactions, spillovers and feedbacks of the global crisis that began in 2007 remind us how important it is to improve our analysis and modelling of financial crises and sovereign risk. This chapter provides a broad framework to examine how vulnerabilities can build up and suddenly erupt in a financial crisis with potentially disastrous feedback effects for sovereign debt and economic growth. Traditional macroeconomic analysis overlooks the importance of risk, which makes it ill suited to examine interconnectedness and transmission mechanisms in response to common shocks. Against this background, the chapter discusses lessons from the crisis and new directions for research on modelling financial crises and sovereign risk. It shows how risk management tools and contingent claims analysis (CCA) can be applied in new ways to measure and analyse financial system and sovereign risk. A new framework ("Systemic CCA") is presented, which can help the measurement, analysis and management of financial sector systemic risk, tail risk and associated government implicit and explicit guarantees (contingent liabilities).

Since October 2008, unprecedented and sweeping government interventions appear to have stabilised the global financial system, but the potential of a resumption of asset impairments and the unresolved moral hazard problem of large complex financial institutions (LCFIs) implies large contingent liabilities for the public sector. Such contingent liabilities may imperil fiscal sustainability, as they increase the susceptibility of public finances to the potential impact of systemic distress ("tail risk").

This chapter begins with a brief overview of the crisis of 2007–9, which describes key features and market events, the actions of the authorities and feedbacks from the markets to the real economy. This is followed by a section on what has been missing in the measurement and analysis of financial crises and sovereign risk. This includes a discussion of the need for better measurement and analysis of analysis of risk exposures and their impact on interconnectedness and contagion. Conceptual frameworks that can better analyse risk exposures and risk-adjusted balance sheets are presented. It shows how risk management tools and CCA can be applied in new ways to the financial system, to economic sectors and the national economy. CCA is a valuable tool to improve systemic financial sector and sovereign risk management. A new framework ("Systemic CCA") is presented in the first appendix (see page 215), which can help the measurement, analysis and management of financial sector systemic risk and associated government implicit and explicit guarantees (contingent liabilities). An example of the application of Systemic CCA to a large Group of Twenty country is provided. (The second appendix provides a taxonomy of types of different systemic risk models in relation to Systemic CCA). The next section shows how it can be used to analyse potential (non-linear) destabilising feedback processes between the financial sector and the sovereign balance sheet. Finally, the systemic risk dynamics are interlinked with important new measures of risk-adjusted economic output value via the application of CCA.

SOME KEY FEATURES OF THE CRISIS OF 2007–9

To understand the origin of the crisis we must look at the huge growth in what was termed "subprime mortgage lending" between 2000 and 2006.[1] As lending grew, housing prices rose, and creative ways were devised to attract new buyers by offering inviting "teaser rates" that were low for the first two or three years but then increased sharply afterwards.[2]

The mortgage market structure changed after 2003, as Wall Street firms moved aggressively to issue "private label" mortgage-backed securities (MBSs): these grew from 24% of the market in 2003 to 57% by mid-2006. The "private label" MBSs expanded into subprime mortgages via securitisation, which pooled a large number of mortgages together in new structure called asset-backed securities (ABSs). The surge in new credit created in this way contributed to the upward spiral of higher house prices, and eventually to speculation and a bubble in the housing market. Poor regulation meant discipline in mortgage lending was eroded by a loosening of lending standards.[3] As initial low "teaser" rates expired and adjustable rate mortgage interest payments increased, many households could not afford to pay their mortgages. Eventually, the surge of house prices slowed, and borrowers owing more than their house was worth ("negative equity") defaulted.

The regulatory rules for banks gave them an incentive to put structured assets into off-balance-sheet vehicles since these avoided the need to hold so much capital. Structured finance and regulatory rules created incentives for regulatory arbitrage which allowed for a reduction in the capital cushion across the financial system. The strategy of creating such off-balance-sheet vehicles was part of the "originate and distribute" model that allowed banks to hold less capital than if the assets were held on-balance sheet. These structured assets were financed by very short-term funding. The commercial paper market provided a large portion of this short-term funding. The funding was rolled over every week, essentially turning loans to these off-balance-sheet vehicles into the equivalent of a short-term deposit.

While the crisis started with a credit shock from defaults by subprime borrowers in mid-2007, there were additional features which amplified the subprime credit shock and turned it into such a serious crisis. The beginning of the crisis in 2007 can be thought of as a run on the parallel banking system. The sufficient conditions for a run are

- a negative credit shock from subprime borrowers,
- illiquid structured credit without transparent values,
- very short-term funding of longer maturity assets (maturity transformation),
- the lack of a lender of last resort to key institutions in what had grown into a very sizeable "parallel banking system" (outside the regulated banking sector) (Loeys and Cannella 2008).

The build-up in leverage, financed by wholesale short-term funding, was a key contributing factor to the severity of the crisis. The leverage in securitised products comes not from the products themselves but from how they are funded (collateralised debt obligations themselves merely redistribute risk). By 2007, short-dated funding of longer maturity assets outside of the regulated banking world was worth about US$5.9 trillion (Loeys and Cannella 2008).[4] Overall this maturity transformation amounted to 40% of the total maturity transformation in the US financial system in 2007. Yet there was no official lender of last resort to this "parallel banking system". The vulnerabilities were building from 2003 to 2007, but did not erupt into a full-blown crisis until mid-2007, when lenders stopped providing short-dated funding to structured investment vehicles (SIVs), conduits and asset-backed commercial papers (ABCPs). This was similar to a run. Figure 8.1 shows the linkage of key risk transfer between balance sheets at the initial stages of the crisis in the US.

In July 2008 it became evident that the mortgage defaults were affecting the Federal Home Loan Mortgage Corporation and Federal National Mortgage Association. On September 11, 2008, financial markets and the rating agencies decided Lehman Brothers was near bankruptcy. The US Treasury tried to arrange financial support but decided not to participate in a bailout or facilitate an orderly workout for Lehman. AIG was also in discussions with the authorities for emergency help over the same weekend. On September 14, 2008, Lehman declared bankruptcy: the largest bankruptcy in history by a factor of six (Rotman School of Management 2008). Prime money market funds (MMFs) that held the US$4 billion Lehman commercial paper and US$20 billion short-term debt had to write down these assets when Lehman went bankrupt. This led one money market fund to "break the buck",[5] shaking confidence in the supposedly safe prime MMFs and prompting intense redemption pressures from institutional investors. Falling confidence led to a precipitous pullback from MMFs, engendering a downward spiral in confidence in the financial system. World stock markets plunged, wiping out US$1 trillion in market value. The crisis rapidly spilled over internationally. Several banks in the UK, Belgium and other countries were taken over by their governments. Depositors started a run on an Icelandic bank, the Icelandic krona fell by over 60% and the three largest Icelandic banks had to be nationalised, triggering a sovereign debt crisis (Iceland had a "triple" crisis).

Extensive government support via liability guarantees, capital injections and economic stimulus packages were used to counteract the sharp recession caused by the spillovers from the crisis globally.

Figure 8.1 Interlinkages between households, banks and various agents in the securitisation market

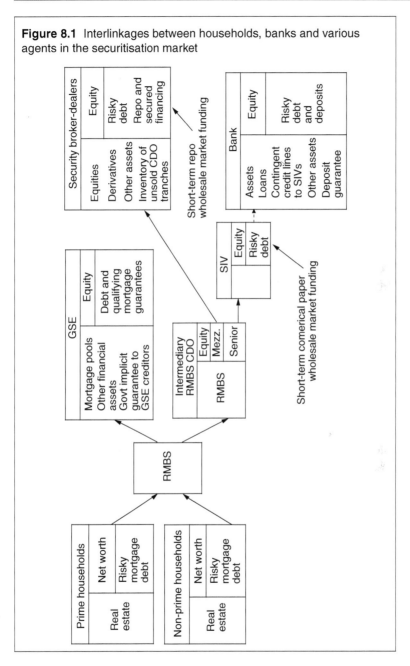

Many governments significantly increased their borrowing, raising sovereign debt levels at the same time as tax revenues were declining, and expenditures and fiscal deficits were increasing.

The next stage of the crisis emerging in 2010 was the sovereign debt crisis in the Eurozone (Greece, Spain, Portugal and Ireland) and raised serious concern about UK and US debt sustainability. Sovereign debt and fiscal issues and banking sector risks are intertwined: as sovereign credit risks rise, the value of government support to banks becomes more uncertain and sovereign spreads spill over increasing banking borrowing costs. Large-scale banking rollover and refinancing needs and high sovereign borrowing needs occurred simultaneously in 2010 in many countries.

Across the globe people asked how such a crisis could have happened. A sober analysis was provided by Martin Wolf (2008):

> we need to ask ourselves whether we could have done a better job of understanding the processes at work. The difficulty we had was that we all look[ed] at one bit of the clichéd elephant in the room. Monetary economists looked at the monetary policy. Financial economists looked at risk management. International macroeconomists looked at global imbalances. Central bankers focused on inflation. Regulators looked at Basel capital ratios and then only inside the banking system. Politicians enjoyed the good times and did not ask too many questions.... One big lesson of this experience is that economics is too compartmentalised and so, too, are official institutions. To get a full sense of the risks we need to combine the worst scenarios of each set of experts.

What has been missing in the measurement and analysis of financial crises and sovereign risks?

What is needed are better frameworks to model macro financial risk transmission, macroeconomic flows and financial and sovereign risks together in an integrated way. Wolf talks about monetary economists, financial economists, international macroeconomists, central bankers, regulators and politicians. What is clearly missing from this list are macro financial risk economists.[6] Where were the macro financial risk experts that (should have been) working for the central banks, ministries of finance, regulatory bodies and international institutions? These experts should be constantly measuring and analysing

- risk exposures and risk-adjusted balance sheets at the aggregate sector and sovereign level, including off-balance-sheet risks in the system,
- the integration of financial sector risks with monetary policy models,

- financial contagion and interconnections.

To mitigate and manage financial sector and sovereign risk, new tools and regulatory framework are needed.[7] Below we take a closer look at what has been missing in the areas mentioned above.

RISK EXPOSURES AND RISK-ADJUSTED BALANCE SHEETS

Traditional macroeconomic and banking models do not adequately measure risk exposures of financial institutions and sovereigns and cannot be used to understand the transmission and amplification of risk within and between balance sheets in the economy. Traditional macroeconomic analysis of the governments and central banks is based almost entirely on flow or accounting balance sheets. Sovereign debt analyses focus on debt sustainability (stocks and flows). A fundamental point is that such analyses do not indicate a risk exposure, which is forward-looking, from an accounting balance sheet or from a flow of funds.[8] A risk exposure measures how much can be lost over a forward-looking time horizon with an estimated probability.

One key risk that macroeconomists have left out of their models is default risk. As pointed out by Charles Goodhart:[9]

> the study of financial fragility has not been well served by economic theory. Financial fragility is intimately related to probability of default. Default is hard to handle analytically being a discontinuous, nonlinear event so most macro models [and their underlying] transversality assumptions exclude the possibility of default.

Default risk models and risk-adjusted balance sheets are needed to analyse financial fragility, including that of the sovereign. Not only is there an absence of credit risk modelling in macroeconomics, but there is an absence of models that integrate credit, market and liquidity risks in financial and sovereign crisis models into one framework.

INTERCONNECTIONS, CONTAGION AND DESTRUCTIVE-FEEDBACK LOOPS

Despite a wide range of financial sector reform initiatives that have surfaced in response to the 2007–9 global financial crisis, regulatory proposals under discussion at the time of writing in autumn 2010 have so far failed to address systemic risk as a result of both solvency and liquidity constraints amid agency problems arising from insufficient prudential oversight.

Given the elusive nature of systemic risk, policy makers recognise the need for a multi-faceted approach comprising complementary measures in areas of regulatory policies, supervisory scope and resolution arrangements as part of a sustainable solution towards a more resilient financial sector. Some measures under discussion include more stringent prudential standards (such as limits on leverage and higher capital requirements as a way to limit the scale and scope of banking activities), a broader adoption of contingent capital initiatives (and related proposals of "bail-ins"), designing "living wills", strengthening resolution processes for LCFIs (possibly in combination with the establishment of a specialised supervisor of systemically important firms) and the creation of a dissolution fund to finance potential future bailouts. In particular, proposals for financial sector reform foresee surcharges in the form of taxes or levies on "too-big-to-fail" firms which would be directly related to their contribution to systemic risk as a result of their sources and term structure of funding, their leverage and their relationships with other financial firms.

So far, however, most policy efforts have not focused in a comprehensive way on assessing network externalities caused by the interconnectedness within financial institutions and financial markets and their effect on systemic risk. Such efforts would be motivated by the belief that systemic crises result from inadequate reserves for exposures to

- contingent claims on other institutions (off-balance-sheet activities),
- the cyclicality of volatility-based margin requirements and haircuts in wholesale funding markets that amplifies exposure to common asset price shock,
- the negative correlation between asset prices and funding costs during times of stress.

In this regard, the size, interconnectedness and complexity of individual financial institutions (with varying degrees of leverage and maturity mismatches) create vulnerabilities to system risk in the financial sector, which can adversely affect real economic activity in the absence of sufficient redundancies.

In particular, coordination failure can impede liquidity transformation in poorly risk-proofed areas of the financial system, with negative consequences for solvency. During the credit crisis, a rise in system-wide counterparty risk,[10] which is a combination of credit risk and liquidity risk, affected all financial institutions holding similar assets on their balance sheets. While funding shocks reduce leverage, and thus the probability of insolvency, the liquidation of assets under fire sale conditions depresses asset prices and fuels confidence-induced downward liquidity spirals and funding. Reduced risk appetite among investors and a rush to safer government securities would further result in contagion. Regulators, governments and central banks also did not pay attention to the linkages between financial sector risk exposures and sovereign risk exposures and their potential interactions and spillovers to other sectors in the economy or internationally. Frameworks for analysing cross-border liquidity and contagion need improvement.

There should be more emphasis on the use of system-wide stress-testing approaches to evaluate vulnerabilities and the potential impact of what Merton calls "destructive-feedback loops". Improvements are needed in modelling destabilisation processes and destructive-feedback loops caused by situations where a guarantor provides a guarantee, the obligations of which the guarantor may not be able to meet precisely in those states of the world in which the guarantor is called on to pay (Merton 2008).

CONTINGENT CLAIMS ANALYSIS

Contingent claims analysis stems from the option pricing theory pioneered by Black and Scholes (1973) and Merton (1973), and, thus, is forward-looking by construction, providing a consistent framework based on current market conditions rather than on historical experience.[11] When applied to the analysis and measurement of credit risk, CCA is commonly called the "Merton Model", which is predicated on the following three principles:

(i) the values of liabilities (equity and debt) are derived from assets;

(ii) liabilities have different priorities (ie, senior and junior claims);

(iii) assets follow a stochastic process.

Assets (present value of income flows, proceeds from assets sales, etc) are stochastic and, over a certain time horizon, may be above or below promised payments on debt, which constitute a default barrier. When there is a chance of default, the repayment of debt is considered "risky", to the extent that it is not guaranteed in the event of default (risky debt is equal to risk-free debt minus a guarantee against default).

CCA can help central banks analyse and manage the financial risks of the economy. The basic analytical tool is the risk-adjusted (CCA) balance sheet, which shows the sensitivity of the enterprise's assets and liabilities to external "shocks". At the national level, the sectors of an economy can be viewed as interconnected risk-adjusted balance sheets with portfolios of assets, liabilities and guarantees, some explicit and others implicit. Traditional approaches have difficulty analysing how risks can accumulate gradually and then suddenly erupt in a full-blown crisis. The CCA approach is well suited to capturing such "non-linearities" and to quantifying the effects of asset-liability mismatches within and across institutions. Risk-adjusted CCA balance sheets facilitate simulations and stress testing to evaluate the potential impact of policies to manage systemic risk.

The CCA model assumes that the total market value of assets, A, at any time t is equal to the sum of its equity market value, E, and its risky debt, D, maturing at time T. The asset value is stochastic and may fall below the value of outstanding liabilities, which constitutes the bankruptcy level ("default threshold" or "distress barrier") B. B is defined as the present value of promised payments on debt discounted at the risk-free rate.[12] The value of risky debt is equal to the default-free debt minus the present value of expected loss due to default. The standard normal density of the volatility-adjusted balance-sheet leverage defines the "distance to default" relative to the firm value. Default occurs when the asset value is insufficient to meet the amount of debt owed to creditors at maturity, ie, $A < B$. Equity value is the value of an implicit call option on the assets, with an exercise price equal to default barrier. It can be computed as the value of a call option. The expected potential loss due to default can be calculated as the value of a put option, P, on the assets with an exercise price equal to B. The equity value can be computed as the value of a call option

$$E(t) = A(t)N(d_1) - Be^{-rT}N(d_2)$$

$$d_1 = \frac{\ln(A/B) + (r + \frac{1}{2}\sigma^2)T}{\sigma\sqrt{T}}, \quad d_2 = \frac{\ln(A/B) + (r - \frac{1}{2}\sigma^2)T}{\sigma\sqrt{T}}$$

where r is the risk-free rate, σ is the asset return volatility and $N(d)$ is the cumulative probability of the standard normal density function below d. In its basic concept, the model assumes that the implicit options are of the European variety, and set the time until expiry, T, equal to the time horizon of interest (usually between one and five years).

The present value of market-implied expected losses associated with outstanding liabilities can be valued as an implicit put option, which is calculated with the default threshold B as strike price on the asset value A of each institution. Thus, the present value of market-implied expected loss can be computed as

$$P_E(t) = Be^{-rT}N(-d_2) - A(t)N(-d_1)$$

Several widely used techniques have been developed to calibrate the CCA models using a combination of balance-sheet information and forward-looking information from equity markets. The market value of assets of corporations and financial institutions cannot be observed directly but it can be implied using financial asset prices. From the observed prices and volatilities of market-traded securities, we can estimate the implied values and volatilities of the underlying assets in financial institutions.[13] Also, in some cases asset and asset volatility can be estimated directly and can be used to calibrate risk-adjusted balance-sheet models. In the traditional Merton (1973) model, the calibration requires knowledge about the value of equity, E, the volatility of equity, σ_E, and the distress barrier as inputs into the equations

$$E = A_0 N(d_1) - Be^{-rT}N(d_2) \quad \text{and} \quad E\sigma_E = A\sigma_A N(d_1)$$

in order to calculate the implied asset value A and implied asset volatility σ_A.[14] In our case, we also derive the so-called "state-price density" (SPD) of implied asset values from equity option prices. This requires the estimation of the risk-neutral density (RND) function of the underlying asset price using the parameters of a mixture of lognormal densities to match the observed option prices (Melick and Thomas 1997) and non-parametric regression (Aït-Sahalia and Lo 1998).

Once the asset value and asset volatility are known, together with the default barrier, time horizon and the discount rate r, the values of the implicit put option, $P_E(t)$, can be calculated. Since $P_E(t)$ can be decomposed into the probability of default (PD) and loss given default (LGD)

$$P_E = N(-d_2) \underbrace{\left(1 - \frac{N(-d_1)}{N(-d_2)} \frac{A}{Be^{-rT}}\right)}_{\text{LGD}} Be^{-rT}$$

there is no need to introduce a potential inaccuracy by assuming a certain LGD. Alternatively, it is possible to go back to the relation

$$s = -T^{-1} \ln\left(1 - \frac{P_E(t)}{Be^{-rT}}\right)$$

between the implicit put option and some debt spread s. The spread is a function of the implicit put option and the present value of the default barrier, B, and can thus be written as a function of the risk-neutral default probability (RNDP) and LGD, so that

$$s = -T^{-1} \ln(1 - \text{RNDP} \times \text{LGD})$$

Note that this specification does not incorporate skewness, kurtosis or stochastic volatility, which can account for implied volatility smiles and skews of equity prices, in order to maintain an analytical form. For robustness,[15] however, we can also employ the closed-form Gram–Charlier extension (Backus *et al* 2004) to the Merton model, which allows for kurtosis and skewness in returns and does not require market option prices in order to be implemented, but is constructed using the same diffusion process for stock prices as the Black–Scholes model.[16]

MEASURING EXPECTED LOSSES AND CONTINGENT LIABILITIES FROM THE FINANCIAL SECTOR

The implicit put option calculated for each financial institution from equity market and balance-sheet information using CCA can be combined with information from CDS markets to estimate the government's contingent liabilities. If guarantees do not affect equity values in a major way (especially when firms are close to the default barrier), CDS spreads should capture only the expected loss retained by the bank (and borne by unsecured senior creditors) after accounting for the implicit guarantee. Hence, the scope of the government guarantee is defined as the difference between the total expected loss (ie, the value of a put option $P_E(t)$ derived from the bank's equity price) and the value of an implicit put option derived from the firm's CDS spread.[17]

$P_{CDS}(t)$ reflects expected losses associated with default net of any financial guarantees, ie, residual default risk on unsecured senior debt and can be written as

$$P_{CDS}(t) = \left(1 - \exp\left(-\left(\frac{s_{CDS}}{10,000}\right)\frac{RMV}{RFV}T\right)\right)Be^{-rT}$$

with the ratio between recovery at face value (RFV) and recovery at market value (RMV) as adjustment factor, which decreases (increases) the CDS spread s (in basis points) in the case of a positive (negative) difference ("basis") with the corresponding bond spread. $P_{CDS}(t)$ is derived by rearranging the specification of the CDS spread

$$s_{CDS} = -\frac{1}{T}\ln\left(1 - \frac{P(t)_{CDS}}{Be^{-rt}}\right) \times \frac{RMV}{RFV} \times 10,000$$

under the risk-neutral measure, assuming a survival probability

$$1 - \bar{p} = \exp\left(-\int_0^t h(u)\,du\right) = e^{-ht}$$

at time t with cumulative default rate $\bar{p}$, constant hazard rate $s_{CDS} \approx h$ and the implied yield to maturity on the risky debt, $y = h - r$, defined by

$$D = Be^{-yt} \rightarrow e^{-yt} = \frac{D}{B} = \left(Be^{-rt} - \frac{P(B)}{B}\right)$$

so that $1 - \bar{p} \approx 1 - P_{CDS}(t)/Be^{-rt}$.

We use $P_{CDS}(t)$ to determine the fraction α of total potential loss due to default, $P_E(t)$, covered by implicit guarantees that depress the CDS spread below the level that would otherwise be warranted for the option-implied default risk. In other words, $\alpha P_E(t)$ is the fraction of bank default risk covered by the government (ie, its contingent liability) and $(1 - \alpha)P_E(t)$ is the risk retained by the banks and reflected in the CDS spreads. Using this relation, it can be seen that

$$\alpha(t) = 1 - \frac{P_{CDS}(t)}{P_E(t)}$$

Thus, this definition, if applied to daily data, allows us to measure the time pattern of the government's contingent liability and the retained risk in the banking sector.[18]

THE SYSTEMIC CCA METHODOLOGY

Our interest in contingent liabilities from the financial sector (and the systemic risk stemming from multiple institutions with "too-big-to-fail" properties) warrants measurement of the joint, or systemic, financial sector risk via the implicit put options in financial institutions. However, a simple summation presupposes that the correlation between them is 1. In addition, conventional (bivariate) correlation is ill suited for systemic risk analysis when extreme events occur jointly (and in a non-linear fashion). To address this issue, we view the financial sector as a portfolio of individual contingent claims (with individual risk parameters), whose joint implicit put option value is defined as the multivariate density of each financial institution's individual marginal distribution of market-implied contingent liabilities and their time-varying dependence structure.[19]

We apply the so-called Systemic CCA framework, which quantifies systemic risk of market-implied contingent liabilities from the financial sector based on the conceptual underpinnings of the CCA methodology. More specifically, this framework combines financial market data and accounting information to infer the risk-adjusted balance sheets for individual financial institutions and the dependence between them in order to estimate the joint market-implied contingent liabilities as point estimates of a multivariate distribution (Gray and Jobst 2010; Gray *et al* 2010). More specifically, we assume that the marginal distributions of individual contingent liabilities fall within the domain of the generalized extreme value (GEV) distribution, which identifies possible limiting laws of asymptotic tail behaviour of normalised extremes in order to quantify the possibility of common extreme shocks (Pickands 1981; Coles *et al* 1999; Poon *et al* 2003; Jobst 2007). The dependence function is estimated iteratively on a unit simplex that optimises the coincidence of multiple series of cross-classified random variables, similar to a χ-statistic that measures the statistical likelihood of observed values differing from their expected distribution (see below).

As opposed to the traditional (pairwise) correlation-based approach, this method of measuring "tail dependence" is better suited to analysing extreme linkages of multiple (rather than only two) entities, because it links the univariate marginal distributions in a way that formally captures both linear and non-linear dependence over time while explicitly accounting for joint tail behaviour. The choice of the empirical distribution function of the underlying data to model the marginal distributions avoids problems associated with using specific parameters that may or may not fit these distributions well: a problem potentially exacerbated during stressful periods (Gray and Jobst 2009).

By accounting for the dependence structure of individual bank balance sheets and associated contingent claims, this approach can be used to quantify the contribution of specific institutions to the dynamics of the components of systemic risk (at different levels of statistical confidence),[20] how this systemic risk affects the government's contingent liabilities and how policy measures may influence the size and allocation of this systemic risk over time. Since point estimates of systemic risk are time-varying in this model, it is arguably more comprehensive than the current exposition of both CoVaR (Adrian and Brunnermeier 2008) and marginal expected shortfall (MES) (Acharya et al 2009) (as well as extensions thereof, such as Huang et al 2010).

The amount of estimated government contingent liabilities from the financial sector can also inform the computation of a fair value price of a systemic risk surcharge or guarantee fee. The fair value (in basis points) of a risk-based surcharge that would compensate for the average contingent liabilities at any point of time during the sample period can be written as

$$-\frac{1}{T}\ln\left(1 - \frac{1}{\sum_j^m B_j e^{-rT}} \frac{G^{-1}_{\mu,\sigma,\xi}(a; \alpha P_{m,T})}{T}\right) \times 10{,}000$$

where B represents the aggregate default barrier of all m-institutions in the sample, r is the risk-free rate, T is time horizon of the surcharge, and $G^{-1}_{\mu,\sigma,\xi}(\cdot)$ is the multivariate density function of individual contingent liabilities as a time-varying fraction α of expected losses $P_{m,T}$ (equity put option) of an m number of financial institutions in the system (see the next subsection).

CASE STUDY: EXPECTED LOSSES AND CONTINGENT LIABILITIES FOR FINANCIAL INSTITUTIONS IN A LARGE GROUP OF SEVEN COUNTRY

This section describes the results from applying the Systemic CCA framework (see the appendix on Systemic CCA (page 215)) to the financial sector of the US (IMF 2010b). It uses market and balance-sheet information of commercial banks, investment banks, insurance companies and special purposes financial institutions using daily data between January 1, 2007 and the end of January 2010.[21] We apply the enhanced version of the Merton model (see above) with implied asset volatility derived from equity options to determine the CCA-based risk-adjusted balance sheets and one-year CDS spreads as the basis for calculating associated market-implied contingent liabilities. Figures 8.2–8.5 show the analytical progression from the summation of individual contingent liabilities derived from implicit put option values to their multivariate distribution, together with a decomposition of individual contributions to the change of joint contingent liabilities by groups of financial institutions.

Total expected losses (area) and contingent liabilities (line) are highest between the periods just after the Lehman collapse in September 2008 and end of July 2009 (Figure 8.2). The analysis suggests that markets expected that on average more than 50% of total expected losses could have been transferred to the government in the event of default. A simple summation of expected losses and contingent liabilities, however, ignores the fact that individual defaults do not happen concurrently, ie, they do not capture intertemporal changes in the dependence structure between this "portfolio" of financial institutions.

The median of the joint distribution is much lower than the simple summation of individual contingent liabilities, which underscores the importance of accounting for the dependence structure when measuring systemic risk. With the dependence structure included, the median value of joint contingent liabilities is much lower than the total contingent liabilities obtained from summation. There are two 50th percentile lines in Figure 8.2. The solid line shows results for the case where government-sponsored financing agencies were *de facto* nationalised (which warranted their exclusion from the sample on September 8, 2008, which is marked by the sharp drop in the line before Lehman Brothers declared bankruptcy a little more than a week later). Controlling for the time-varying dependence structure between sample firms, the expected joint contingent liabilities peaked at about 1% of GDP at the end of March 2009, averaging 0.5% of GDP over the sample period. The second, dashed, 50th percentile line shows the case where these government-sponsored financing

Figure 8.2 US financial sector: total contingent liabilities and multivariate density of contingent liabilities ("Systemic CCA")

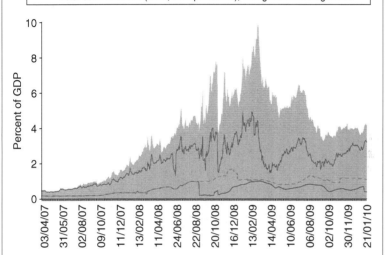

Sample period: January 3, 2007–January 29, 2010 (743 observations) of individual put option values (ie, expected losses) conditional on the endogenous alpha factor of implicit guarantees of 36 sample banks, insurance companies and other financial institutions. The multivariate density is generated from univariate marginals that conform to the generalized extreme value (GEV) distribution and a non-parametrically identified time-varying dependence structure. The marginal severity and dependence are estimated over a window of 60 and 250 working days (with daily updating) via the LRS method and the optimisation of an unit simplex that optimises the coincidence of multiple series of cross-classified random variables respectively (see the appendix on Systemic CCA (page 215)).

agencies are left in the sample (note that daily equity prices were still available but it can be argued that data at such frequency might be too noisy and, thus, less informative).

After the collapse of Lehman Brothers, the extreme tail risk in the system increased sharply. The point estimates of the 95th percentile expected shortfall of extreme risk jumped to more than 20% of GDP in the months after the Lehman collapse (Figure 8.3). The shaded bands show the one and two standard deviation bands around the estimate. In other words, during this period of exceptional systemic distress, market prices implied a minimum loss of 20% of GDP with

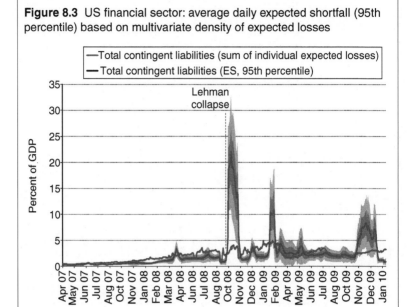

Figure 8.3 US financial sector: average daily expected shortfall (95th percentile) based on multivariate density of expected losses

Sample period: January 3, 2007–January 29, 2010 (743 observations) of individual put option values (ie, expected losses) of 36 sample banks, insurance companies and other financial institutions. The black line shows the expected shortfall (ES) for the entire sample at a 95th percentile threshold within a confidence band of one and two standard deviations (pale grey areas). The multivariate density is generated from univariate marginals that conform to the generalized extreme value distribution and a non-parametrically identified time-varying dependence structure. The marginal severity and dependence are estimated over a window of 60 and 250 working days (with daily updating) via the LRS method and the optimisation of an unit simplex that optimises the coincidence of multiple series of cross-classified random variables, respectively (see the appendix on Systemic CCA (page 215)).

a probability of 5% over a one-year time horizon. The magnitude of such tail risk dropped to under 2% of GDP during 2009.

The joint tail risk measure of contingent liabilities shows spikes in April 2008 and October 2008, indicating a high government exposure to financial sector distress. After controlling for the market perception (via CDS prices) about the residual risk retained in the financial sector, we find that the potential tail risk transferred to the government exceeded 9% of GDP in April 2008 (in the wake of the Bear Stearns rescue) and reached almost 20% of GDP in October 2008 (Figure 8.4). The black line shows the 95th percentile expected shortfall within a confidence band of one and two standard deviations (pale grey areas). The spike in April 2008 is absent in Figure 8.3, which shows expected losses, illustrating the distinction between expected

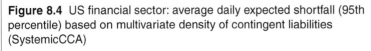

Figure 8.4 US financial sector: average daily expected shortfall (95th percentile) based on multivariate density of contingent liabilities (SystemicCCA)

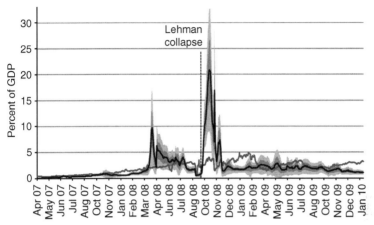

Sample period January 3, 2007–January 29, 2010 (743 observations) of individual put option values (ie, expected losses) conditional on the endogenous alpha factor of implicit guarantees of 36 sample banks, insurance companies, and other financial institutions. The red line shows the expected shortfall (ES) for the entire sample at a 95th percentile threshold within a confidence band of one and two standard deviations (pale grey areas). The multivariate density is generated from univariate marginals that conform to the generalized extreme value (GEV) distribution and a non-parametrically identified time-varying dependence structure. The marginal severity and dependence are estimated over a window of 60 and 250 working days (with daily updating) via the LRS method and the optimisation of an unit simplex that optimises the coincidence of multiple series of cross-classified random variables respectively (see the appendix on Systemic CCA (page 215)).

losses and contingent liabilities for the purpose of systemic risk measurement. The bailout of Bear Stearns led to expectation of public support and induced highly correlated expectations of government support across numerous institutions, while residual risk outside anticipated public sector support was considered less susceptible to co-movements in asset prices.

The systemic risk from contingent liabilities was considerable during the credit crisis. For the whole period from March 1, 2007 to January 29, 2010, the average contingent liabilities at the 50th and the 95th percentile levels amounted to 0.5% and 1% of GDP, respectively. Failed and bailed-out firms contributed the largest share to these contingent liabilities, especially prior to the collapse of Lehman Brothers (Figure 8.5). Note that 50th percentile estimate can be used with the sum of the default barriers for all institutions to calculate a

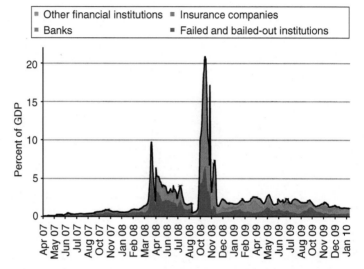

Figure 8.5 US financial sector: decomposition of average daily expected shortfall (95th percentile) based on multivariate density of contingent liabilities ("Systemic CCA")

Sample period: March 1, 2007 to January 29, 2010 (743 observations) of individual put option values (ie, expected losses) conditional on the endogenous alpha value of 36 sample banks, insurance companies, and other financial institutions. The chart shows the group-wise contribution to expected shortfall (ES) at a 95th percentile threshold. The multivariate density is generated from univariate marginals that conform to the generalized extreme value (GEV) distribution and a non-parametrically identified time-varying dependence structure. The marginal severity and dependence are estimated over a window of 60 and 250 working days (with daily updating) via the LRS method and the optimisation of an unit simplex that optimises the coincidence of multiple series of cross-classified random variables, respectively (see the appendix on Systemic CCA (page 215)).

price of a systemic risk surcharge or guarantees fee (see the previous section).

MACRO RISK ANALYSIS OF FINANCIAL CRISES AND INTERACTIONS WITH SOVEREIGN RISK AND ECONOMY-WIDE RISK

The history of financial crises indicates a widening of the safety net provided by the government to the financial sector in times of stress. After the Great Depression, the US introduced deposit insurance, which was subsequently adopted by over 100 countries. Events in the run-up to the 2007–9 crisis indicate that the incentive structures facing owners of banks encourage finding ways to increase bank equity returns (privatising the gains) in good times, while socialising the losses by shifting risk to the government in bad times. According to Alessandri and Haldane (2009), "state support stokes future risk-taking incentives, as owners of banks adapt their strategies to maximize expected profits". They list five strategies to exploit the asymmetric payouts of equity (and limited) liability:

(i) create much higher leverage;
(ii) increase the proportion of assets held in bank trading books;
(iii) diversify assets in a way that increases systemic risk;
(iv) originate assets that have asymmetric returns (with high payouts in good states of the world and high defaults in bad states of the world);
(v) sell protection via CDS market that earns premiums in the good states of the world but create massive losses in bad states of the world.

The previous discussion and illustration of Systemic CCA points out the importance of measuring the government's contingent liabilities to banks and accounting for the dependence structure of the portfolio of such contingent liabilities using a framework that can capture time variation and tail risk. There are additional risk exposures of the government to the financial sector beyond the liability guarantees discussed in the previous section. The full set of interlinked risk exposures between the government and financial sector should be analysed in a comprehensive framework.

A stylised framework starts with the economic, ie, risk-adjusted, balance sheets of the financial sector (portfolio of financial institutions) and is then linked to, and interacts with, the government's economic balance sheet.[22] For example, distressed financial institutions can lead to large government contingent liabilities, which in turn reduce government assets and lead to higher risk of default on sovereign debt. Table 8.1 shows the key linkages between the financial sector and the government; the economic balance-sheet items in italics reflect the risk exposures of the government to the financial sector. The government has provided financial guarantees associated with expected losses due to default, it may have provided asset guarantees, it may have injected capital and have an equity stake in the banks. All of these are the government's risk exposures to the

Table 8.1 Linkages between the financial sector and sovereign balance sheets

Financial sector	Government
Assets	
Assets/loans	Present value of (fiscal surplus
+ liquid assets/reserves	and guarantee fees)
+ asset guarantees	+ equity (government owned)
	+ other assets
Liabilities	
− equity (non-government)	− credit owed to Central Bank
− equity (government-owned)	− asset guarantees
− Default-free debt and deposits	
$+(1-\alpha)*$ expected losses due to default	$-\alpha*$ expected losses due to default
− Present value of guarantee fees	− default-free sovereign debt
	+ expected losses due to sovereign default
Assets minus liabilities	
0	0

financial sector. Note that these risk exposures consist of a portfolio financial institutions. These in turn affect the economic value of the government's assets and may affect the government's own default risk and borrowing spreads. Risk interactions and feedbacks can be analysed with this type of framework.

A vicious destructive-feedback loop could arise in the situation where the financial system is large compared with the government's holdings and distress in the financial system triggers a large increase in government financial guarantees/contingent liabilities. Potential costs to the government, due to the guarantees, can lead to a rise in sovereign spreads. Bank's spreads depend on retained risk, which is lower given the application of government guarantees, and also on the creditworthiness of the sovereign (as a result of fiscal sustainability and debt service burden), as investors view the bank's and sovereign risk as intertwined. Concern that the government balance sheet will not be strong enough for it make good on guarantees could lead to deposit withdrawals or a cut-off of credit to the financial sector, triggering a destructive feedback where both bank and sovereign spreads increase.[23] In some situations, this vicious cycle can spiral out of control, resulting in the inability of the government to provide sufficient guarantees to banks and leading to a systemic financial crisis and a sovereign debt crisis (see below).

Interaction and feedback between sovereign CCA balance sheet and the financial sector: potential destabilisation processes

The CCA framework can be used to calibrate sovereign balance sheets and integrated with banking sector balance sheets in simple but illustrative framework to show the interaction and potential destabilisation of values of spreads and risks in both the sovereign and banking sectors. In the absence of measurable equity and equity volatility, such as in the case of a developed country sovereign, including where the assets and debt are all in the same currency, the term structure of sovereign spreads can be used to estimate implied sovereign assets and asset volatility and calibrate market-implied sovereign risk-adjusted balance sheets.

Sovereign spreads are related to the sovereign implicit put option and sovereign default barrier (or threshold that debt restructuring is triggered) in the following way. Rearranging the formula for the sovereign implicit put option gives

$$\frac{P_{Sov}}{B_{Sov}e^{-rT}} = N(-d_2) - \frac{A_{Sov}}{B_{Sov}} \frac{1}{e^{-rT}} N(-d_1)$$

Inserting this equation into the equation for sovereign spreads and using both an estimate of the sovereign default barrier from debt data and the full term structure of the sovereign CDS (CDS for years 1, 3, 5, 7 and 10) can be used to find and estimate of implied sovereign assets, A_{Sov}, and implied sovereign asset volatility, σ_A, which most closely matches the sovereign spread term structure. The sovereign asset value can be broken down into its key components: reserves (R), net fiscal asset or present value of the primary fiscal surplus (PVPS), implicit and explicit contingent liability (αPut_{Bank}) and "other" remainder items, ie, $A_{Sov,t=0} = R + \text{PVPS} - \alpha \text{Put}_{Bank} + \text{Other}$. The value of the foreign currency reserves can be observed and the contingent liabilities can be estimated from the banking sector CCA models (ie, Systemic CCA). Subtracting these from the implied sovereign asset and subtracting an estimate of the present value of the expected primary surplus allows us to calculate the residual (Other). There are a number of government assets and various unrealised liabilities, pension and health-care obligations, which are not known but are aggregated in "Other", which may include contingent financial support from other governments or multilaterals or other backstop assets (eg, land or other public sector assets of value). We can use this valuation formula to evaluate the effects of changes in reserves, the primary fiscal balance and the implicit banking sector guarantee on the sovereign asset value. This can be used with changes in the composition of short-term and long-term debt for stress tests to evaluate changes in sovereign credit spreads and other values and risk indicators.

The spreads for the banks can be seen as a function of the implicit put option (derived from equity information) times the fraction of risk retained by the banks (as described in the Systemic CCA section above) plus a premium (δ) if high sovereign spreads spill over to increase bank spreads

$$s_{Bank} = -\frac{1}{T}\ln\left(1 - \frac{(1-\alpha)P_{Bank}}{B_{Bank}e^{-rT}}\right) + \delta$$

This simple model shows the ways in which sovereign and bank spreads can interact and potentially lead to a destabilisation process. If sovereign spreads increase this can lead to an increase in bank spreads because

(i) the credibility of sovereign guarantees decreases (alpha goes down),

(ii) the implicit bank put option could increase as the value of the bank's holdings of government debt decrease,

(iii) the bank default barrier may increase due to higher borrowing costs as the premium (δ) increases (and if banks cannot rollover debt).

Prospects of a much more fragile banking system can feed back on sovereign spreads via several possible channels, eg, increasing large bank guarantee/bailout costs that may overwhelm the budget, reduced ability of sovereigns to borrow from banks and potential crowding out effects.

Fiscal, banking and other problems can cause distress for the government which can transmit risk to holders of government debt. Holders of sovereign debt have a claim on the value of the debt minus the potential credit loss, the value of which is dependent on the level of assets of the sovereign.[24] A sudden stop in access to foreign funding (inability to rollover short-term debt and to borrow) can dramatically increase credit spreads for the sovereign and for banks. A vicious spiral of increasing bailout costs for banks (possibly currency devaluation) and inability of sovereign to borrow can lead to default of both banks and the sovereign.

In a currency union, such as the Eurozone, devaluation of one country is not a policy option if the union is to continue. Analysing, let alone managing sovereign risk and financial sector risk in a currency union with unclear contingency lines, is especially complex. If a medium-sized country were to default on its sovereign debt, this could spread losses to banks in many countries, causing contagion to the financial sector and other sovereigns, and even threatening the euro currency union. New architecture for managing fiscal risk and sovereign risk within the currency union is needed. Such a new framework could benefit from the analysis of interlinked risk-adjusted balance sheets to aid in the design of fiscal rules, risk mitigation strategies and lender-of-last-resort and guarantee guidelines.

ECONOMY-WIDE CCA INTERLINKED BALANCE SHEETS RELATING SYSTEMIC RISK AND NEW MEASURE OF RISK-ADJUSTED ECONOMIC OUTPUT VALUE

Three important sets of interrelated accounts in the economy, which are somewhat similar to those in large modern financial institutions, are income/flow accounts, mark-to-market balance sheets and risk exposure measures, whose combination gives rise to a fair measure of profitability. Risk managers would find it difficult to analyse risk exposures by relying solely on the income and cashflow statements while ignoring (mark-to-market) balance-sheet assessments or information on their institution's derivatives or option positions. The country risk analysis that relies only on the macroeconomic flow-based approach is deficient in a similar way, given that the traditional analysis does not take into account the volatility of assets (and, even more importantly, its change over time) and does not capture credit risk and risk transmission.

However, CCA balance sheets for key sectors of an entire economy can be integrated together into an economy-wide balance sheet. For each sector, the assets, plus contingent assets (or minus contingent liabilities), minus equity/junior claims, minus risky debt, sum to zero. In these "mark-to-market" risk-adjusted balance sheets there are values of claims and consumption and investment are treated like "dividend payments" out of the relevant sector asset.[25] The interlinked economic balance sheets demonstrate the interdependence among sectors. Whenever one sector is "long" a certain implicit option, another sector is "short" the same implicit option. For example, the economic balance sheet of the banking sector has assets consisting of corporate loans (default-free debt minus the value of a put option). The banking sector also includes contingent liabilities (implicit put options) from the government as an asset, which is an obligation (short put option) on the government's economic balance sheet for each sector.[26]

Something quite similar to the traditional macroeconomic income accounts can be derived from a specific, static case of the general macrofinancial contingent claim equations. If the asset volatility in the CCA formulas in all sectors is set to zero and a change in the between periods is calculated, it becomes the standard flow-of-funds framework.[27] The traditional flow of funds is a special case of the risk-adjusted balance-sheet framework when volatility is set to zero. Macroeconomic flow accounts cannot capture credit risk exposures (measured by implicit put options) and thus fail to measure risk-adjusted equity or net worth across the economy.

The CCA macroeconomic balance sheet can be used to derive the important new measure of economic output value, which adjusts the traditional flow-based measures of GDP, and its components, for the level of risk. Note that the above relationships for the CCA risk-adjusted economy-wide balance sheet, or CCA-based economic output (EO_{CCA}), are based upon the put–call parity equations relating sector assets and liabilities, in conjunction with the cross-ownership structure of sector liabilities. An important implication of this is that changes in the sector-implicit put options have a counterpart in the changes of the sector-implicit call options, or "equity". CCA-based economic output (EO_{CCA}) is what might be called the present value of "risk-adjusted GDP".

One way to understand the importance of this concept is to think about a corporate contingent claims balance sheet where there are assets, equity, risky debt value and dividend and interest payments (the "flows" out of the balance sheet over a given horizon). If the traditional macroeconomic approach was taken to analyse this corporate, only the flows would be measured, ie, the dividend and interest payments. The totality of the (macroeconomist views) of the corporate would be the dividend and interest flows, ignoring equity and risky debt value. The shortcomings of macroeconomics in not measuring values such as equity-like claims and not measuring debt values (default free value minus expected loss due to default), when viewed this way, is astonishing. CCA can be used to remedy this situation by calculating the economy-wide values of equity-claims and of risky debt and expected losses, with the (dividend-like) flows out of the balance sheets included as well.

The systemic risk dynamics are interlinked with the new measures of risk-adjusted economic value via the CCA balance sheets and put–call parity relationships. Systemic risk can be analysed using a portfolio of implicit put options in the financial sector and for the sovereign contingent liabilities (as described earlier) using a multivariate dependence structure, appropriate for fat-tailed distributions, to analyse average risk and tail risk.

In order to measure the CCA-based economic output (EO_{CCA}) correctly, the call options/net worth value cannot simply be summed; the correlation/dependence structure needs to be included. Since conventional (bivariate) correlation is ill suited when extreme events occur jointly (and in a non-linear fashion), one way forward is to generate the multivariate density of individual net worth according to our specification as described above. As opposed to the traditional (pairwise) correlation-based approach, this method of measuring "tail dependence" is better suited to analysing extreme linkages of multiple (rather than only two) entities, because it links the univariate marginal distributions in a way that formally captures both linear and non-linear dependence over time. EVT can be used in a framework for the analysis of risk-adjusted economic output (EO_{CCA}), based on a multivariate limiting distribution that formally captures the potential of extreme realisations within and across sectors.

During the recession, the value of tax revenues declined, expenditures expanded due to the stimulus and government guarantees increased dramatically, as did direct financial support measures. The dependence between these components is an important factor affecting the sovereign asset level. Higher borrowing increased the distress barrier, which in combination with lower assets, continued to raise sovereign risk. The impact on CCA-based economic output (EO_{CCA}), due to the persistence of depressed sector asset values, was exacerbated by escalating contingent liabilities from the financial sector. The riskiness of the financial sector, and the extent to which it informs our assessment of economic growth, is central in this regard. The framework allows the identification of marginal sensitivity of risk-adjusted economic output to aggregate contingent liabilities of the financial sector, which illustrates that the financial sector can be both a risk absorber and a risk driver. Thus, we can define the contribution of the financial sector to economic output (based on interlinked balance sheets and dynamic dependence structure) conditional on the public cost of the joint contingent claim of financial sector activity.

CONCLUSIONS AND NEW DIRECTIONS

The financial crisis that began in 2007 has its roots in excessive leverage and maturity transformation in the shadow banking system, which led to large-scale risk transmission and spillovers and ultimately large-scale risk transfer to the sovereign. One reason for not seeing the potential seriousness of the crisis at the time lies in the shortcomings of macroeconomic analysis which do not include default or risk transmission. What is needed going forward is much better macrofinancial risk analysis with risk-adjusted balance sheets based on CCA.

We have presented a new framework ("Systemic CCA") which can help the measurement, analysis and management of financial sector systemic risk, tail risk and associated government implicit and explicit guarantees (contingent liabilities). An example of Systemic CCA applied the US financial sectors delivers useful insights about the magnitude of potential public sector costs from market-implied expected losses. In particular, the ability to assess contributions of individual institutions to systemic tail risk and to analyse the risk retained in the financial system in relation to the risk taken on by the government via large contingent liabilities makes the Systemic CCA framework a useful methodology for analysing potential (non-linear) destabilising feedback processes between the financial sector and the sovereign balance sheet. This makes it ideal for analysis of the interaction of spillover effects between the sovereign and financial sector spillovers.

Moreover, the systemic risk dynamics are interlinked with important new measures of risk-adjusted economic output value via the

CCA balance sheets and put–call parity relationships. Going forward, this approach could inform more accurate representation of the impact of the systemic risk dynamics on financial stability and economic growth. Future research would ideally explore the use of CCA-based economic output value and Systemic CCA to promote economic growth and financial stability and the relationship to fiscal and debt management dynamics.

APPENDIX: SYSTEMIC CCA – CALCULATING SYSTEMIC MARKET-IMPLIED EXPECTED LOSSES AND CONTINGENT LIABILITIES

The Systemic CCA framework is predicated on the quantification of the systemic financial sector risk from implicit guarantees to the financial sector in situations of market stress. We apply the concept of Extreme Value Theory (EVT) in order to specify a multivariate limiting distribution that formally captures the potential of extreme realisations of contingent liabilities. More specifically, we derive the joint a multivariate distribution generated from the relative magnitude of individual implicit equity option values (after accounting for guarantees) and their linear and non-linear time-varying dependence. Such an approach allows us to determine expected and unexpected losses from systemic financial sector risk, as well as measures of extreme (or residual) risk. Note here that the aggregation of contingent claims (rather than their underlying assets and liabilities) is crucial to preserve individual balance-sheet risk.

Let us define the individual put option values associated with m financial sector entities as the vector-valued series

$$X_{i,j} \equiv \alpha_i' P_{i,j} = (\alpha_1 P_1^n, \ldots, \alpha_m P_m^n)$$

of independent and identically distributed observations. We specify the individual asymptotic tail behaviour of all elements of $X_{i,j}$ as the limiting law of an n-sequence of normalised maxima, such that the probability of the order statistic

$$\lim_{n \to \infty} \Pr \left(\frac{x_{m:m}^1 - g_m^1}{h_m^1}, \ldots, \frac{x_{m:m}^n - g_m^n}{h_m^n} \right)$$

converges to the non-degenerate limit distribution

$$F_n(X) = \lim_{n \to \infty} \Pr \left(\frac{x - g_m^n}{h_m^n} \leqslant y \right) = [F(h_m^n y + g_m^n)]^n \to G(x)$$

for a choice of constants $g_m^n > 0$, $h_m^n \in \mathbb{R}$, and the ith univariate marginal

$$y_j = y_j(x_j) = \left(1 + \frac{\xi_j(x - \mu_j)}{\sigma_i}\right)_+^{-1/\xi_j} \quad (\text{for } j = 1, \ldots, m)$$

lies in the domain of attraction of the GEV distribution for

$$F_n^{[h_n x + g_n]}(x) \approx G(x)$$

where $1 + \xi_j(x - \mu_j)/\sigma_j > 0$, the scale parameter $\sigma_j > 0$, the location parameter is denoted by μ_j and the shape parameter by ξ_j.[28] The higher the absolute value of the shape parameter, the larger the weight of the tail and the slower the speed at which the tail approaches its limit.[29] All raw moments of $G(\cdot)$ are estimated by means of the linear combinations of ratios of spacings (LRS) estimator. We derive the natural estimator of the shape parameter ξ from the linear combination

$$\hat{\xi} = \left(\frac{n}{4}\right)^{-1} \sum_{i=1}^{(n/4)} \hat{\xi}_i$$

of $\hat{\xi}_i = -\log(\hat{v}_i)/\log(c)$, where

$$\hat{v}_i = \frac{x_{n(1-q):n} - x_{nq^c:n}}{x_{nq^c:n} - x_{nq:n}} \quad \text{and} \quad c = \sqrt{\frac{\log(1-q)}{\log(q)}}$$

for quantile $q = i/n$. Since $x_{nq:n}$ is the point estimate of $G_{\xi,\mu,\sigma}^{-1}(q)$, the following approximation holds

$$\hat{v}_i \approx \frac{G_\xi^{-1}(1-q) - G_\xi^{-1}(q^c)}{G_\xi^{-1}(q^c) - G_\xi^{-1}(q)} = c^{-1+\xi}$$

Second, as an alternative to a general copula function that links the marginal distributions using only a single (and time-invariant) dependence parameter, we specify the multivariate dependence structure of joint tail risk as the function $A(\omega_1, \ldots, \omega_{m-1})$, which is derived non-parametrically by expanding the bivariate logistic method proposed by Pickands (1981) to the multivariate case and adjusting the margins according to Hall and Tajvidi (2000) so that

$$A(\omega) = \min\left(1, \max\left\{n\left\{\sum_{i=1}^n \bigwedge_{j=1}^m \frac{y_{ij}/\hat{y}_{\cdot j}}{\omega_j}\right\}^{-1}, \omega, 1-\omega\right\}\right)$$

where $\hat{y}_{\cdot j} = \sum_{i=1}^{n} y_{ij}/n$ and $0 \leqslant \max(\omega_1,\ldots,\omega_{m-1}) \leqslant A(\omega_j) \leqslant 1$ for all $0 \leqslant \omega_j \leqslant 1$, subject to the optimisation of the $(m-1)$-dimensional unit simplex

$$S_m = \left\{(\omega_1,\ldots,\omega_{m-1}) \in \mathbb{R}_+^n : \omega_i \geqslant 0, 1 \leqslant j \leqslant m-1; \sum_{j=1}^{m-1} \omega_j \leqslant 1 \text{ and } \omega_m = 1 - \sum_{j=1}^{m-1} \omega_j\right\}$$

S_m establishes the degree of coincidence of multiple series of cross-classified random variables similar to a χ-statistic that measures the statistical likelihood of observed values differing from their expected distribution. $A(\cdot)$ represents a convex function on $[0,1]$ with $A(0) = A(1) = 1$, ie, the upper and lower limits of $A(\cdot)$ are obtained under complete dependence and mutual independence, respectively.

Finally, after estimation of the marginal distributions and the dependence structure, we obtain the multivariate distribution

$$G_{t,\mu,\sigma,\xi}(x) = \exp\left\{-\left(\sum_{i=1}^{m} y_{it}\right)A(\omega)\right\}$$

and the corresponding joint density

$$G_{\xi,\hat{\mu},\hat{\sigma}}^{-1}(a) = \int_0^a g(x)\,dx$$

at quantile $q_a = 1 - a$ at any point in time t (and estimation period τ), using the maximum likelihood estimation

$$\hat{\theta}_{\text{MLE}} = \arg_\theta \max \prod_{i=1}^{n} g(x;\theta)$$

with lognormal likelihood function

$$\ell(x) \propto \sum_{i=1}^{n} -\left(\sum_{i=1}^{m} y_{it}\right)A(\omega)$$

so that we obtain the point estimate

$$\hat{x}_{a,m,t} = G_{t,\hat{\xi},\hat{\mu},\hat{\sigma}}^{-1}(a) = \hat{\mu}_j + \frac{\hat{\sigma}_j}{\hat{\xi}_j}\left(\left(-\frac{\ln(a)}{A(\omega)}\right)^{-\hat{\xi}_j} - 1\right)$$

of the joint implicit put option value as expected total contingent liabilities from expected losses $\mathbb{E}[P_{i,j}]$. We then obtain the expected shortfall (ES) (or conditional value-at-risk (VaR)), as risk measure for

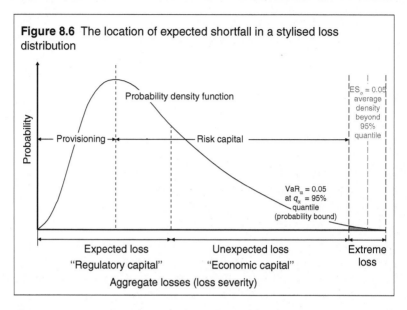

Figure 8.6 The location of expected shortfall in a stylised loss distribution

the aggregate implicit put option of the financial sector, reflecting the probability-weighted residual risk beyond a pre-specified threshold probability $1 - q = a$ (say, 95th percentile level for $a = 0.05$) of maximum losses.[30] Thus, we can write the average daily ES for a total sample of m institutions as

$$\text{ES}_{a,t} = -\mathbb{E}[P_{m,t} \mid P_{m,t} \geqslant G^{-1}_{t,\mu,\sigma,\xi}(a) = \text{VaR}_{q_a,t}]$$

for every day t within the sample time period T for threshold quantile value

$$\text{VaR}_{q_a,t} = \sup\{G^{-1}_{t,\mu,\sigma,\xi}(\cdot) \mid \Pr[P_{p,t} > G^{-1}_{t,\mu,\sigma,\xi}(\cdot)] \leqslant a = 0.05\}$$

assuming a statistical confidence level of $1 - a = 0.95$. Figures 8.2–8.5 show an example of using the proposed methodology to derive the time-varying estimate of the 95% ES of expected losses and contingent liabilities for the financial sector of the US (IMF 2010b).

Since this approach also considers the time-variation of point estimates due to a periodic updating, it is more comprehensive than alternative (conditional) measurement approaches to systemic risk, such as CoVaR (Adrian and Brunnermeier 2008), CoRisk (Chan-Lau 2010) and systemic expected shortfall (SES) (Acharya et al 2009) (as well as extensions thereof, such as in Huang et al 2010). Neither approach applies a multivariate density estimation like Systemic CCA, which allows the determination of the marginal contribution of an individual institution to concurrent changes of both the severity of systemic risk and the dependence structure across any combination of sample institutions for any level of statistical confidence and at any given point in time. In contrast, CoVaR, CoRisk and SES examine incremental effects that cover only a fraction of available data that could be usefully integrated to assess the system-wide sensitivity of contingent liabilities to individual default risk of banks (and the associated cost to governments upon realisation states of distress).

APPENDIX: COMPARING SYSTEMIC CONTINGENT CLAIMS ANALYSIS ("SYSTEMIC CCA") WITH OTHER SYSTEMIC RISK MEASURES

The goal of financial systemic risk measures is to determine the contribution of individual financial institutions to systemic risk including capturing contagion between institutions. The ultimate objective is to assess how this contribution could be internalised through special taxes, risk-based surcharges and/or insurance premiums that mitigate excessive risk-taking. Four of the main systemic risk models proposed are CoVaR, systemic expected shortfall (SES), distress insurance premium (DIP) and the Systemic CCA. A short description of each is given below (see also Table 8.2).

CoVaR (Adrian and Brunnermeier 2008). The CoVaR quantifies how financial difficulties of one institution can increase the tail risk of others. CoVaR for a certain institution is defined as the VaR of the whole sector conditional on a particular institution being in distress. More specifically, the CoVar of bank X is the conditional VaR of bank Y, after conditioning that bank X is in difficulty (bank X's marginal contribution to systemic risk is then computed as the difference between its CoVar and the financial system's VaR). The methodology uses quintile regression analysis to predict future CoVaR on a quarterly basis, which are then related to particular characteristics (eg, leverage) and observed market risk factors (eg, CDS spreads). The model relies on infrequent bank-specific VaRs and there are methodological short-comings in the estimation of system VaR.

Systemic expected shortfall (SES) (Acharya *et al* 2009). The marginal expected shortfall (MES) specifies historical expected losses,

Table 8.2 Comparison of systemic risk measures

	CoVaR	SES	DIP	Systemic CCA
Dimensionality	Multivariate	Bivariate	Bivariate	Multivariate
Frequency	Quarterly	Quarterly	Daily	Daily
Conditionality	Percentile of individual default risk	Percentile of total default risk	Percentile of total default risk	Both individual and joint default risk
Dependence measure	Linear, parametric	Empirical	Linear, parametric	Non-linear, non-parametric
Method	Panel quantile regression	Empirically derived expected shortfall	Conditional correlation (DCC Garch)	Various option pricing and RND estimation methods, multivariate GEV
Data input	Asset returns	Equity returns	Equity returns and CDS implied default probabilities	Expected losses ("implicit put option")
Macro/micro control factors	Macro state variables in panel estimation	Leverage ratio as scaling factor of SES	N/A	Reduced-form estimation in balance sheet identities of CCA and implicit put option
Reference	Adrian and Brunnermeier (2008)	Acharya et al (2009)	Huang et al (2010)	Gray and Jobst (2010)

conditional on having breached some high systemic risk threshold. Adjusting MES by the degree of firm-specific leverage and capitalisation yields the systemic expected shortfall (SES). MES measures only the average, linear, bivariate dependence. It does not consider interaction between subsets of banks and is limited to cases when the entire banking sector is undercapitalised.

Distress insurance premium (DIP) (Huang *et al* 2010). This approach to measuring and stress-testing the systemic risk of a banking sector extends the approach in Huang *et al* (2010) to identifying various sources of financial instability and to allocating systemic risk to individual financial institutions. The systemic risk measure, called the DIP, is defined as the insurance cost to protect against distressed losses in a banking system and is a summary indicator of market perceived risk that reflects expected default risk of individual banks and correlation of defaults. It combines estimates of default risk backed out of CDS spreads with correlation backed out of bank equity returns.

Systemic CCA (Gray and Jobst 2010, Forthcoming; IMF 2010c). This framework combines financial market data and accounting information to infer the risk-adjusted balance sheets of financial institutions and the dependence between them in order to estimate the joint market-implied expected losses and contingent liabilities. Information from equity and CDS markets is used to calculate individual contingent liabilities to generate a conditional, non-linear metric of systemic contingent liabilities. This measure provides three distinct benefits:

(i) by applying a multivariate density estimation, it helps to quantify the marginal contribution of an individual firm to the magnitude of potential risk transfer to the government, while accounting for rapidly changing market valuations of balance-sheet structures;

(ii) it can be used to value systemic risk charges, guarantees or insurance within a consistent framework for estimating potential losses based on current market conditions rather than on historical experience (Khandani *et al* 2009);

(iii) it is more comprehensive and flexible than CoVaR or MES, which can be seen as different subsets of the Systemic CCA.

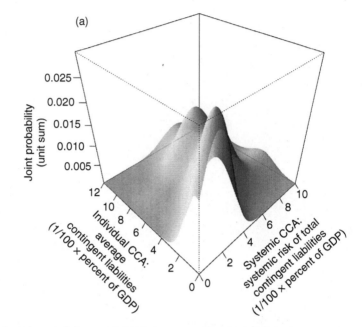

Figure 8.7 Bivariate kernel density function of individual contingent liabilities and systemic risk from joint contingent liabilities (Systemic CCA)

Sample period: January 3, 2007–January 1, 2010 (743 observations) of individual and aggregate put option values (ie, expected losses) of 36 sample banks, insurance companies and other financial institutions. Note: the chart shows the bivariate probability distribution of (i) the average contingent liabilities (α value* implicit put option) in percent of GDP (as of end-2008) (y-axis) and (ii) average contribution to systemic risk from contingent liabilities at the 95th percentile relative to GDP (x-axis) over a sample period between January 2, 2008 and October 20, 2009. Kernel density estimation with Epanechnikov kernel and linear binning, using an empirically derived bandwidth.

The expected shortfall metric in the SES model is an improvement over VaR. ES is a coherent risk measure, but conditioning ES on the most severe outcomes for the entire sample of banks ignores the potential optionality that a wide range of underlying asset values below the ES threshold could increase the magnitude of tail events. But, similarly to CoVaR, the parametric specification of SES/MES conditional on quarterly estimated data (eg, the necessity to estimate a leverage ratio from quarterly available data) is insensitive to rapidly changing market valuations of balance-sheet structures and requires re-estimation with the potential of parameter uncertainty.

Figure 8.7 Continued

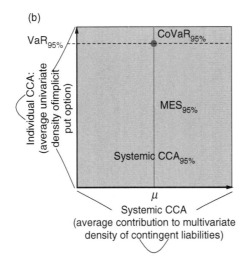

Sample period: January 2, 2008–October 19, 2009 (482 observations) of individual put option values of sample banks in a small advanced economy in Europe. Note: the chart is a stylised representation of the bivariate probability distribution (see part (a)) of (i) the average contingent liabilities (α-value* implicit put option) in percent of GDP (as of end-2008) (y-axis) and (ii) average contribution to systemic risk from contingent liabilities at the 95th percentile relative to GDP (x-axis). CoVaR $= \frac{1}{2}\int_{0.95}^{1}\int_{0.95}^{1} xy\,dx\,dy$; MES$_{95\%} = \frac{1}{2}\int_{0.95}^{1}\int_{0}^{1} xy\,dx\,dy$; Systemic CCA$_{95\%} = \frac{1}{2}\int_{0}^{1}\int_{0}^{1} xy\,dx\,dy$.

MES measures only average, linear, bivariate "dependence". There is a similarity to contingent claims analysis (CCA) where the implicit put option (either using default barrier or using default barrier plus minimum capital) is a function of leverage (market value of asset and barrier) and tail risk distribution, but it gets rolled into one key risk severity measure (and high frequency, dynamic dependence measures can be calculated).

DIP has similarities to SES in the sense that correlations from equity market returns are used but default probabilities are backed out of credit default swap (CDS) spreads. The price of CDSs reflects the retained risk in the bank since the price of credit protection is affected by government liability guarantees. Compared with Systemic CCA measures, total risk and splits out government contingent liabilities and retained risk. The dependence structure in systemic CCA captures tail risk and average risk in a more sophisticated way than simple correlation. Combining individual contingent liabilities (derived from CCA analysis using the α-value) with a measure of joint contingent liabilities (using Systemic CCA) generates a conditional, non-linear metric of systemic risk sensitivity to individual firms. Estimating the empirical bivariate density of both vectors over the entire distribution of expected losses (rather than a specific quantile, like CoVaR) returns the marginal rate of substitution (MRS) between the individual and the joint impact of expected losses on contingent liabilities (see Figure 8.7). Since this approach also considers the time-variation of point estimates of systemic risk (without re-estimation), it is more comprehensive than CoVaR and SES if these methods were to be applied to measure systemic risk from contingent liabilities across different levels of statistical confidence at daily frequencies.

Both SES and CoVaR cover only a fraction of available data that could be usefully integrated to assess the system-wide sensitivity of contingent liabilities to the default risk of banks (and the associated cost to governments upon realisation states of distress). The chart in Figure 8.7(b) shows, in a stylised form, the relation between individual contingent liabilities and systemic risk from total contingent liabilities derived from the Systemic CCA framework. CoVaR represents the average systemic risk at a given percentile of individual contingent liabilities only: a threshold that is set irrespective of whether high levels of systemic risk did actually coincide with increases of higher individual default risk of systemically important financial institutions. In contrast, MES, as a key element of SES, defines an expected shortfall measure conditional on a defined percentile threshold that is defined by the historical density and not by the variation of a density function of systemic risk. Neither approach applies multivariate density estimation like Systemic CCA, which would allow the determination of the marginal contribution of an individual institution to changes of both the severity of systemic risk and the dependence structure across institutions of contingent liabilities for any level of statistical confidence and at any given point in time.

---

1   Subprime mortgages are mortgages to people with low incomes and few assets, which allow them to purchase houses with small down payments and low initial interest rates.

2   See Zandi (2009).

3   Recall the term "Ninja" (No Income, No Job or Assets) loans.

4 The US$5.9 trillion was composed of: broker–dealers funding through repos and customer deposits (US$2.2 trillion); commercial paper issued by ABS issuers, finance companies (US$1.4 trillion); auction rate securities (US$900 billion) and repo funding by hedge funds (US$1.3 trillion).

5 Breaking the buck refers to closing with a net asset value less than US$1.

6 The financial economists he mentioned looked at risk management, but he is referring primarily to private sector risk managers at the level of the individual financial institution.

7 This is similar to what some central bankers call a "macroprudential approach" to financial stability.

8 Merton (2002) pointed out that "Country risk exposures give us important information about the dynamics of future changes that cannot be inferred from the standard 'country accounting statements', either the country balance sheet or the country income flow-of-funds statements".

9 Charles Goodhart in a conference presentation at the IMF, Washington, DC, in 2005.

10 The crisis made it clear to many risk managers, regulators and policy makers that counterparty risk coming from the credit default swap (CDS) market needs to be addressed. The introduction of a central clearinghouse is under discussion at the time of writing.

11 Although market prices are subject to market conditions not formally captured in this approach, they endogenise the capital structure impact of government interventions.

12 Moody's KMV (MKMV) defines this barrier as being equal to the total short-term debt plus one-half of long-term debt.

13 An implied value refers to an estimate derived from other observed data. Techniques for using implied values are widely practised in options pricing and financial engineering applications.

14 Note that all input variables are calculated from market prices, with the exception of the default barrier, which is derived from discounting the so-called "adjusted liabilities" (ie, short-term debt plus one-half of the long-term debt) provided by MKMV for each sample firm.

15 These results are not reported in this chapter, but can be provided by the authors upon request.

16 Further refinements of this model would include various simulation approaches at the expense of losing analytical tractability. The ad hoc model of Dumas et al (1998) is designed to accommodate the implied volatility smile and is easy to implement, but requires a large number of market option prices. The Heston (1993) and Heston and Nandi (2000) models allow for stochastic volatility, but the parameters driving these models can be difficult to estimate. Many other models have been proposed in order to incorporate stochastic volatility, jumps and stochastic interest rates. Introducing jumps in asset prices leads to small improvements in the accuracy of option prices. Other option pricing models include those based on copulas, Lévy processes, neural networks, Garch models and non-parametric methods. Finally, the binomial tree proposed by Cox et al spurned the development of lattices, which are discrete-time models that can be used to price any type of option: European or American, plain vanilla or exotic.

17 We approximate the change in recovery value based on the stochastic difference between the standardised values of the fair value CDS (FVCDS) spread and the fair value option adjusted spread (FVOAS) reported by MKMV. Both FVOASs and FVCDSs are credit spreads (in basis points) over Libor for the bond CDS of a particular company, calculated by the MKMV valuation model based on duration (term) of t years (where $t = 1$ to 10 in one-year increments). Both spreads imply an LGD determined by the industry category. In practice, this adjustment factor is very close to unity for most cases, with a few cases where the factor is within a 10% range (0.9–1.1).

18 Note that the estimation of the alpha value depends on a variety of assumptions that influence the assessment of the likelihood of government support, especially at times of extreme stress during the credit crisis. The extent to which the put option values of the Merton model differ from those implied by CDS spreads might reflect distortions stemming from the modelling choice (and the breakdown of efficient asset pricing in situations of illiquidity), changes in market conditions and the capital structure impact of crisis interventions, such as equity dilution in the wake of capital injections by the government, beyond the influence of explicit or implicit guarantees. See IMF (2010b,c) for more details.

19 Note here that the aggregation of individual contingent claims (rather than their underlying assets and liabilities) is crucial to preserve individual balance-sheet risk.

20 The contribution to systemic (joint tail) risk is derived as the partial derivative of the multivariate density relative to changes in the relative weight of the univariate marginal distribution of each bank at the specified percentile. More specifically, the total expected shortfall can be written as a linear combination of the expected shortfalls of individual contingent liabilities, where the relative weights (in the weighted sum) are given by the second-order cross partial derivatives of the inverse of the joint probability density function to changes in both the dependence function and the marginal distribution of individual contingent liabilities.

21 Key inputs used were the daily market capitalisation of each firm (from Bloomberg), the default barrier estimated for each firm based on quarterly financial accounts (from Moody's KMV CreditEdge), the risk-free rate of interest (at 3%), a one-year time horizon and one-year CDS spreads (from MarkIt). Outputs were the expected losses (ie, the implicit put option value over a one-year horizon) and the contingent liabilities (ie, α^* implicit put option).

22 There are three types of accounts for any entity (including a financial institution or a government): flow/income accounts, accounting balance sheets and economic risk-adjusted balance sheets. All three need to be analysed. In the economic risk-adjusted balance sheet of financial institutions or government, assets always equal liabilities. In simple terms assets + guarantees − equity − (default-free debt − expected loss due to default) = 0.

23 The Iceland crisis of 2008 is a case in point.

24 See Gapen et al (2005) and Gray and Malone (2008) for more detail on sovereign CCA models.

25 From a macroeconomic perspective, the net worth of each sector is tantamount to the intertemporal budget constraint that lies at the core of the flow-of-funds calculation. If all consumption and investment expenditures are taken as discretionary, for simplicity, then, at any time, the net worth of the sector is equal to the present value of consumption and investment expenditures.

26 See Gray and Malone (2008), Gray et al (2008, 2010) and Gray and Jobst (2009) for details on the structure and calibration of economy-wide CCA balance sheets.

27 We highlight only the main points of the argument here, and refer the interested reader to Gray and Malone (2008) for a lengthier discussion.

28 The upper tails of most (conventional) limit distributions (weakly) converge to this parametric specification of asymptotic behaviour, irrespective of the original distribution of observed maxima (unlike parametric VaR models).

29 The shape parameter also indicates the number of moments of the distribution, eg, if $\zeta = 2$, the first moment (mean) and the second moment (variance) exist, but higher moments have a finite value. This is of practical importance since many results in for asset pricing in finance rely on the existence of several moments.

30 Expected shortfall is an improvement over VaR, which, in addition to being a pure frequency measure, is "incoherent", ie, it violates several axioms of convexity, homogeneity and subadditivity found in coherent risk measures. For example, subadditivity, which is a mathematical way of saying that diversification leads to less risk, is not satisfied by VaR. In contrast, ES is a coherent risk measure, but conditioning ES on the most severe outcomes for the entire sample of banks ignores the potential optionality that a wide range of underlying asset values below the ES threshold could increase the magnitude of tail events.

REFERENCES

Acharya, V. V., L. Pedersen, T. Philippon and M. Richardson, 2009, "Regulating Systemic Risk", in V. V. Acharya and M. Richardson (eds), *Restoring Financial Stability: How to Repair a Failed System* (New York: John Wiley & Sons).

Adrian, T., and M. K. Brunnermeier, 2008, "CoVaR", Staff Reports 348, Federal Reserve Bank of New York.

Aït-Sahalia, Y., and A. W. Lo, 1998, "Nonparametric Estimation of State-Price Densities Implicit in Financial Asset Prices, *The Journal of Finance* 53, pp. 499–547.

Alessandri, P., and A. Haldane, 2009, "Banking on the State", Paper Presented at Federal Reserve Bank of Chicago Twelfth Annual International Banking Conference on "The International Financial Crisis: Have the Rules of Finance Changed?", September 25.

Backus, D. K., S. Foresi and L. Wu, 2004, "Accounting for Biases in Black–Scholes", Working Paper, New York University, Goldman Sachs Group and Baruch College.

Bakshi, G., C. Cao and Z. Chen, 1997, "Empirical Performance of Alternative Option Pricing Models", *The Journal of Finance* 52(5), pp. 2003–49.

Black, F., and M. Scholes, 1973, "The Pricing of Options and Corporate Liabilities", *Journal of Political Economics* 81(3), pp. 637–54.

Board of Governors of the Federal Reserve System, 2009a, "The Supervisory Capital Assessment Program: Design and Implementation", April 24, URL: http://www.federalreserve.gov/bankinforeg/scap.htm.

Board of Governors of the Federal Reserve System, 2009b, "The Supervisory Capital Assessment Program: Overview of Results", May 7, URL: http://www.federalreserve.gov/bankinforeg/scap.htm.

Chan-Lau, J. A., 2010, "Regulatory Capital Charges for Too-Connected-to-Fail Institutions: A Practical Proposal", IMF Working Paper 10/98, International Monetary Fund, Washington, DC.

Coles, S. G., J. Heffernan and J. A. Tawn, 1999, "Dependence Measures for Extreme Value Analyses", *Extremes* 2, pp. 339–65.

Congressional Oversight Panel, 2010, "February Oversight Report: Commercial Real Estate Losses and the Risk to Financial Stability", February, URL: http://cop.senate.gov/reports/library/report-021110-cop.cfm.

De Jong, P., 1988, "The Likelihood for a State Space Model", *Biometrika* 75, pp. 165–9.

De Jong, P., 1991, "The Diffuse Kalman Filter", *Annals of Statistics* 19, pp. 1073–83.

Dumas, D., J. Fleming and R. E. Whaley, 1998, "Implied Volatility Functions: Empirical Tests", *The Journal of Finance* 53(6), pp. 2059–2106.

Gapen, M. T., 2009, "Evaluating the Implicit Guarantee to Fannie Mae and Freddie Mac Using Contingent Claims", in *Credit, Capital, Currency and Derivatives: Instruments of Global Financial Stability or Crisis?*, International Finance Review, Volume 10 (Bingley: Emerald Books).

Gapen, M. T., D. F. Gray, C. H. Lim and Y. Xiao, 2005, "Measuring and Analyzing Sovereign Risk with Contingent Claims", IMF Working Paper 05/155, International Monetary Fund, Washington, DC.

Gray, D. F., 2009, "Modeling Financial Crises and Sovereign Risk", *Annual Review of Financial Economics* 1, pp. 117–44.

Gray, D. F., and A. A. Jobst, 2009, "Higher Moments and Multivariate Dependence of Implied Volatilities from Equity Options as Measures of Systemic Risk", in *Global Financial Stability Report*, Chapter 3, pp. 128–31 (Washington, DC: International Monetary Fund).

Gray, D. F., and A. A. Jobst, 2010, "New Directions in Financial Sector and Sovereign Risk Management", *Journal of Investment Management* 8(1), pp. 23–38.

Gray, D. F., and A. A. Jobst, Forthcoming, "Systemic Contingent Claims Analysis (Systemic CCA): Estimating Potential Losses and Implicit Government Guarantees to Banks", IMF Working Paper.

Gray, D. F., A. A. Jobst and S. Malone, 2010, "Quantifying Systemic Risk and Reconceptualizing the Role of Finance for Economic Growth", *Journal of Investment Management* 8(2), pp. 90–110.

Gray, D. F., and S. Malone, 2008, *Macrofinancial Risk Analysis* (New York: John Wiley & Sons).

Gray, D. F., R. C. Merton and Z. Bodie, 2007, "Contingent Claims Approach to Measuring and Managing Sovereign Credit Risk", *Journal of Investment Management* 5(4), pp. 5–28.

Gray, D. F., R. C. Merton and Z. Bodie, 2008, "A New Framework for Measuring and Managing Macrofinancial Risk and Financial Stability", Working Paper 09-015, Harvard Business School.

Hall, P., and N. Tajvidi, 2000, "Distribution and Dependence-Function Estimation for Bivariate Extreme Value Distributions", *Bernoulli* 6, pp. 835–44.

Heston, S. L., 1993, "A Closed-Form Solution for Options with Stochastic Volatility with Applications to Bond and Currency Options", *Review of Financial Studies* 6(2), pp. 327–43.

Heston, S. L., and S. Nandi, 2000, "A Closed-Form Garch Option Valuation Model", *Review of Financial Studies* 13(3), pp. 585–625.

Huang, X., H. Zhou and H. Zhu, 2010, "Assessing the Systemic Risk of a Heterogeneous Portfolio of Banks during the Recent Financial Crisis", Working Paper, January 26, URL: http://ssrn.com/abstract=1459946.

IMF, 2008a, *Global Financial Stability Report: Containing Systemic Risks and Restoring Financial Soundness*, World Economic and Financial Surveys (Washington, DC: International Monetary Fund).

IMF, 2008b, *Global Financial Stability Report: Financial Stress and Deleveraging Macro-Financial Implications and Policy*, World Economic and Financial Surveys (Washington, DC: International Monetary Fund).

IMF, 2008c, "United States: Staff Report for the 2009 Article IV Consultation", Country Report SM/08/216, International Monetary Fund, Washington, DC.

IMF, 2009a, *Global Financial Stability Report: Responding to the Financial Crisis and Measuring Systemic Risks*, World Economic and Financial Surveys (Washington, DC: International Monetary Fund).

IMF, 2009b, *Global Financial Stability Report: Navigating the Financial Challenges Ahead*, World Economic and Financial Surveys (Washington, DC: International Monetary Fund).

IMF, 2009c, "United States: Staff Report for the 2009 Article IV Consultation", Country Report SM/09/187, International Monetary Fund, Washington, DC.

IMF, 2010a, *Global Financial Stability Report: Meeting New Challenges to Stability and Building a Safer System*, World Economic and Financial Surveys (Washington, DC: International Monetary Fund).

IMF, 2010b, "United States: Publication of Financial Sector Assessment Program Documentation: Financial System Stability Assessment", Country Report No. 10/247 (July 30), International Monetary Fund, Washington, DC.

IMF, 2010c, "United States Financial Sector Assessment Program Technical Note on Stress Testing", July, International Monetary Fund, Washington, DC.

Jaynes, E., 1957, "Information Theory and Statistical Mechanics", *Physical Review* 106, pp. 620–30.

Jobst, A. A., 2007, "Operational Risk: The Sting Is Still in the Tail but the Poison Depends on the Dose", *Journal of Operational Risk* 2(2), pp. 1–56.

Khandani, A., A. W. Lo and R. C. Merton, 2009, "Systemic Risk and the Refinancing Ratchet Effect", Working Paper, Harvard Business School.

Kullback, J., 1959, *Information Theory and Statistics* (New York: John Wiley & Sons).

Kullback, S., and R. Leibler, 1951, "On Information and Sufficiency", *Annals of Mathematical Statistics* 22, pp. 79–86.

Kumhof, M., and D. Laxton, 2007, "A Party without a Hangover? On the Effects of US Fiscal Deficits", IMF Working Paper 07/202.

Loeys, J., and M. Cannella, 2008, "How Will the Crisis Change Markets?", Global Asset Allocation and Alternative Investments, J. P. Morgan (April 14), p. 8.

Lunn, D. J., A. Thomas, N. Best and D. Spiegelhalter, 2000, "WinBUGS: A Bayesian Modelling Framework. Concepts, Structure and Extensibility", *Statistics and Computing* 10(4), pp. 325–37.

Melick, W., and C. Thomas, 1997, "Recovering an Asset's Implied PDF from Option Prices: An Application to Crude Oil during the Gulf Crisis", *Journal of Financial and Quantitative Analysis* 32, pp. 91–115.

Merton, R. C., 1973, "Theory of Rational Option Pricing", *The Bell Journal of Economics and Management Science* 4(1), pp. 141–83.

Merton, R. C., 1974, "On the Pricing of Corporate Debt: The Risk Structure of Interest rates", *The Journal of Finance* 29, pp. 449–70.

Merton, R. C., 1977, "An Analytic Derivation of the Cost of Loan Guarantees and Deposit Insurance: An Application of Modern Option Pricing Theory", *Journal of Banking and Finance* 1, pp. 3–11.

Merton, R. C., 2002, "Future Possibilities in Finance Theory and Finance Practice", in H. Geman, D. Madan, S. Pliska and T. Vorst (eds), *Mathematical Finance: Bachelier Congress 2000* (Springer).

Merton, R. C., 2008, "Observations on Risk Propagation and the Dynamics of Macro Financial Crises: A Derivatives Perspective", Keynote Speech, ECB, December 1.

Merton, R. C., and Z. Bodie, 1992, "On the Management of Financial Guarantees", *Financial Management Journal* 21, pp. 87–109.

Pickands, J., 1981, "Multivariate Extreme Value Distributions", in *Proceedings of the Forty-Third Session of the International Statistical Institute*, Volume 2, Pp. 859–878 (The Hague: ISI).

Poon, S.-H., M. Rockinger and J. Tawn, 2003, "Extreme Value Dependence in Financial Markets: Diagnostics, Models, and Financial Implications", *The Review of Financial Studies* 17(2), pp. 581–610.

Rotman School of Management, 2008, *The Finance Crisis and Rescue: What Went Wrong? Why? What Lessons Can be Learned?*, p. 7 (Toronto: Rotman/UTP Publishing).

Swiston, A., 2008, "A US Financial Conditions Index: Putting Credit Where Credit Is Due", IMF Working Paper 08/161.

Tarashev, N., C. Borio and K. Tsatsaronis, 2009, "The Systemic Importance of Financial Institutions", *BIS Quarterly Review*, September, pp. 75–87.

Wolf, M., 2008, "A Time for Humility", *Financial Times*, December 29, URL: http://blogs.ft.com/economistsforum/2008/11/.

Zandi, M., 2009, *Financial Shock* (New Jersey: Pearson Education/FT Press).

9

Measuring and Managing Risk in Innovative Financial Instruments

Stuart M. Turnbull
C. T. Bauer College of Business

In the 2007–9 credit crisis, the issues of improper valuation and inadequate risk management in the use of credit derivatives were at the centre of the credit market turmoil. There has been much discussion about the use of such instruments as mortgage-backed securities, collateralised debt obligations (CDOs) and credit default swaps (CDSs). The crisis has raised the question of how we measure the risks of innovative financial products and manage those risks. Innovative financial instruments are typically illiquid and pose several challenges for their valuation and the measurement and management of the risks associated with them. Measuring risk at some specified time horizon requires the ability to price different assets in future states and to compute different risk measures. Managing risk requires the means to alter a risk profile, through either contractual mechanisms such as master agreements or institutions such as clearinghouses or via the use of hedging instruments. This chapter addresses some of the many issues that arise when a new form of financial instrument is introduced.

Innovation in financial instruments takes two forms: variations on existing types of instruments and instruments introduced for new classes of risk. Examples of the first type of innovation are swaptions, lookback options and exchange options, and, for the second type, credit derivatives, catastrophe bonds and derivatives on volatility. In the first case there are developed markets for the underlying assets, while in the second case the markets are new. The different forms of innovation introduce their own sets of issues. Here we will focus mainly on the instruments introduced for new classes of risk and address the questions of how we price such instruments and perform risk management.

To illustrate the many different issues that arise when considering a new form of financial innovation, we consider a particular example of an innovation. However, we stress that the focus is on general issues that arise and the analysis is applicable for any form of instrument. Given that credit derivatives were the catalyst for the credit crisis, we consider the issues that arise in the pricing of credit derivatives written on a portfolio of obligor related assets. For example, the portfolio could be residential mortgages, credit cards, bonds or derivatives. Each asset will generate a cashflow provided that default does not occur. The event of default will generate a terminal payment. The focus of this chapter will be on the general issues that arise and not on the minutiae of contract details.

We start with issues relating to pricing, similar issues being relevant for risk management. For a CDO, there are two different approaches: bottom-up and top-down. The bottom-up approach models the individual assets in the collateral pool of the CDO. In order to model the cashflows generated by the collateral pool it is necessary to model the default dependence between the assets. This was the Achilles' heel for valuation and risk management in the crisis. The top-down approach directly models the cashflows from the collateral pool, ignoring the explicit constituents of the collateral pool. There is often limited data available for innovations, implying that models used for either pricing or risk management cannot be too complicated. There is a real trade-off between the need to estimate parameters and the availability of data.

The design characteristics of an instrument affect both the demand side and the supply side. End users will use an instrument if it provides some service at a lower cost than instruments that are currently available. To stimulate the supply side, there should be mechanisms to offset the risk. The design affects the cost of hedging. In turbulent conditions, certain features in the design may make an instrument unusually sensitive to shocks in the economy or market disruptions. Design characteristics are discussed later in the chapter.

With any new innovation there will initially be limited liquidity. We discuss the factors that influence the level of liquidity. There are many factors (such as the ability to grow both the supply and demand, the ease of pricing, the transparency of the pricing process, the existence of hedging tools, the costs associated with hedging and the ability to observe posted prices on a regular basis) that provide investors with information about liquidity and market depth. The ability to hedge and speculate makes an instrument attractive to a wide range of investors. However, participation in the market by some investors will be sensitive to macroshocks. If these investors are forced to leave a market, unwinding positions will increase price volatility and affect liquidity.

Counterparty risk affects all contracts. With an innovation, the difficulties in estimating the effects of this form of risk are increased. First, there is little information available to help in specifying the joint distribution that models default between the innovation and the counterparty. Second, for an innovation there is the need to develop the back-office facilities to handle trades and keep track of the different counterparties. Third, if collateral has been posted, it is necessary to consider how the value of the collateral varies with the creditworthiness of the counterparty. We discuss these issues, as well as the use of master agreements and clearinghouses.

Risk management requires the ability to generate the probability distribution describing the value of a portfolio of assets at some future specified time horizon. There is usually limited data for an innovation, which restricts the complexity of models. If the parameter values are set so that model prices match a subset of extant prices (that is, they are calibrated), then the effects of model misspecification and limited liquidity are compounded into the parameter values, increasing the variability of these parameters. Limited data also means that model testing will be difficult. While a model may be calibrated to match a subset of prices, there is no guarantee that the model will be useful for hedging. If a model is deficient, stress testing may give the risk manager a false sense of security. Scenario analysis is one way to address the uncertainty surrounding model valuation. However, this requires managers to think outside the confines of their modelling framework.

There are a number of managerial issues that can greatly impact on the risk management function. When an innovation is introduced, an existing accounting system is often used without regard for whether it will generate perverse incentives for traders. A trader might undertake a trade that enhances a bonus, though it may not be in the best long-term interests of the firm. In an environment where there is a constant flux of innovations, senior managers are often ignorant about the exact nature of the innovations and refuse to acknowledge their lack of knowledge, relying on their traders and quants for guidance. This affects their ability to exercise independent judgement about the risk characteristics of an innovation. There are many costs arising from the operational and legal risks associated with an innovation that are neglected when it is marked-to-model, implying that the innovation is overvalued. Risk management issues are discussed in below.

For certain types of instruments, a credit rating is often a prerequisite in order to increase the marketability of the innovation. For risk managers or investors not involved in any issuer/rater discussions, the methodology used to determine the ratings is not transparent. In the credit crisis we have seen that rating agencies did a poor job in assessing the creditworthiness of recent innovations. This implies that if ratings are used, it is essential that risk managers understand what they mean, how they are derived and the accuracy of the methodology. For innovations there is no history, so the challenge is to interpret what information a rating actually conveys and to decide how to use this information. We address these issues in the penultimate section. The last section summarises our conclusions.

PRICING

At the centre of the credit crisis has been the issue of how to price different types of CDOs. Here we consider some general form of CDO structure and identify some of the different issues that must be addressed for both pricing and hedging. For a CDO there are two ways to tackle the issue of pricing: a bottom-up approach and a top-down approach. A bottom-up approach starts by modelling the event of default and the loss given default (LGD) for the individual assets in the collateral pool of the CDO.[1] The use of any form of realistic model requires the estimation of model parameters, implying that there is a trade-off between the complexity of the model and the availability of data. The ability to model the behaviour of individual assets in the collateral pool depends on the nature of the assets. In some cases the assets may be derivatives, and this adds a new layer of complexity. A simple case would be a CDS written on a bond or a loan. A far more complicated case would be mortgage-backed bonds issued by a mortgage trust. While the bottom-up approach is a logical starting point, for some types of assets the approach is infeasible, as either the data requirements become overwhelming or the underlying assets become too complex. This necessitates taking a top-down approach.

Basic setup

We start with the basic setup. Initially we work in a continuous-time framework, though a discrete-time approach could also be employed. In simulations, a discrete-time framework is usually employed. We assume a probability space $(\Omega, \mathcal{F}, Q)$ and a filtration $(\mathcal{F}_t; t \geqslant 0)$ satisfying the usual conditions (Protter 1993). A stopping time has an intensity process $\lambda(t)$ with

$$\int_0^t \lambda(s)\,ds < \infty \quad \text{for all } t$$

Given no default up to time t, the probability of default over the next interval Δt is approximately $\lambda(t)\Delta t$. A default time for obligor k generates a default process $N_k(t)$ that is 0 before default and 1 after default. The probability of obligor k surviving until time t is given by

$$P[\tau_k > t] = E^Q\left[\exp\left(-\int_0^t \lambda_k(s)\,ds\right) \mid \mathcal{F}_0\right] \quad (9.1)$$

Default can arise from events that are unique to the obligor or sector, or through dependence on common economic factors. For example, in the credit crisis the fall in house prices was one of the major drivers of default. The collapse of Enron was due to factors unique to the firm: in this case, fraud. We assume that default for obligor k, $k = 1,\ldots,m$, depends on a set of measurable covariates denoted by the vector $X_k(t)$ (Lando 1994, 1998). The probability of no default over the period $[0,t]$ is given by

$$P[\tau_k > t] = E\left[\exp\left(-\int_0^t \lambda_k(X_k(s))\,ds\right) \mid \mathcal{F}_0\right] \quad (9.2)$$

The value of a zero coupon bond that pays US$1 at time T if there is no default and zero otherwise is given by

$$\bar{B}_k[0,T] = E^Q[A(T)\mathbf{1}_{\{\tau_k > t\}} \mid \mathcal{F}_0] \quad (9.3)$$

where $\mathbf{1}_{\{\tau_k > t\}}$ is an indicator function that equals 1 if $\tau_k > t$ and 0 otherwise, and $A(T)$ is the numéraire appropriate for the pricing measure Q. If the numéraire is the money market account, then we have

$$\bar{B}_k[0,T] = E^Q\left[\exp\left(-\int_0^T r(u) + \lambda_k(u)\,du\right) \mid \mathcal{F}_0\right] \quad (9.4)$$

where $r(u)$ is the instantaneous spot interest rate.[2] To evaluate the above expression we must make assumptions about the distributions that describe the evolution of the spot rate and intensity function.

Modelling assumptions

For the instantaneous spot interest rate, the standard assumptions are either Gaussian, Feller diffusion processes, possibly with jumps (Dai *et al* 2007), or Lévy processes (Eberlein and Ozkan 2003). For the intensity process, Gaussian processes have been assumed, as they facilitate easy-to-compute closed-form solutions. However, they do imply that the intensity function can be negative. Duffie and Singleton (1999) assume that both the spot interest rate and the intensity rate are described by Feller processes. These assumptions imply that, given parameter restrictions, these processes are strictly positive. Eberlein *et al* (2006) describe the intensity function using Lévy processes. Lando (1994, 1998) models the intensity function as a Cox process, a typical example being

$$\lambda_k(t) = \sum_{j=1}^{m} b_{k,j} x_j(t) \quad (9.5)$$

where $\{b_{k,j}\}$ are coefficients and $\{x_j\}$ covariates. Restrictions must be placed on the processes for $\{x_j(t)\}$ to ensure that they are positive. If the coefficients $\{b_{k,j} > 0\}$ are positive, then the intensity is positive. These sign restrictions greatly complicate empirical estimation and consequently are often ignored. For references to the existing literature see Schönbucher (2003). Instead of Feller processes, a quadratic formulation can be applied

$$\lambda_k(t) = \left[\sum_{j=1}^{m} b_{k,j} x_j(t)\right]^2 \quad (9.6)$$

where $\{x_j\}$ are covariates described by Gaussian processes. For empirical estimation, no restrictions need be placed on the signs of the coefficients.

Bottom-up approach

Pricing the tranches of a CDO requires modelling the cashflow generated by the assets in the collateral pool. In a bottom-up approach, the process describing the event of default and the LGD must be estimated for each asset in the collateral pool. Modelling the cashflow generated by the assets in the collateral pool necessitates considering how the event of default by one asset will affect the remaining assets. The state of the economy will in general affect the creditworthiness of obligors. Similarly, events in a particular sector will affect the obligors belonging to that sector. Default by one obligor may be beneficial to remaining obligors due to the reduced competition or it may signal the perilous state of a particular sector of the economy. The issue is how to model the default dependency among the assets.

The factor model described by Equation 9.6 is one possible way to model default dependence if some of the covariates $\{x_j\}$ are common to all assets, describing either the macro state of the economy or a sector. A popular alternative is to use a copula function to model the joint distribution for defaults. The basic model used for pricing and risk management has been the normal copula. CreditMetrics generalised the Merton (1974) model to describe the probability of n obligors defaulting. Li (2000) showed that the model could be formulated in terms of a normal copula. Copula functions knit together the marginal distribution functions to give the joint distribution.[3] The normal copula is defined as

$$c(u_1,\ldots,u_n) = \Phi_{n,\Sigma}(\Phi^{-1}(u_1),\ldots,\Phi^{-1}(u_n))$$

where u_i, $i = 1,\ldots,n$, are realisations of uniform random variables and $\Phi_{n,\Sigma}$ is the n-dimensional multivariate normal cumulative distribution function with zero mean and correlation matrix Σ. The critical issue for application is the specification of this correlation matrix. In the Merton (1974) model, it is the correlation of asset returns. The attraction of the normal copula is its simplicity.

Once the correlation matrix is specified, it is possible to generate the distribution of the default times for the n obligors. From the distribution multivariate normal distribution with zero mean and correlation matrix Σ, draw realisations $x_1,\ldots,x_n$ and then map onto the unit interval $u_i = \Phi(x_i)$. For risk management, a credit rating transition matrix can be used to infer the new credit class for each obligor. For pricing, the marginal distribution describing the event of default for each obligor is inferred from CDS prices. The default time can then be inferred (Schönbucher 2003, p. 331). For pricing different tranches on a credit index, it is usually assumed that all correlations are the same and the representative correlation is taken as an input parameter and calibrated to match the price of the equity tranche. Unsurprisingly, the other tranches are misplaced, giving rise to a skew in what is called base correlation. To address the existence of this skew, a whole family of latent factor models has been introduced.[4] The marginal distributions are calibrated to match existing credit default prices. The default dependency among obligors is described by the common latent factors. This use of factor models reduces the number of parameters that must be estimated.[5]

We know from the work of Acharya *et al* (2003) and Altman *et al* (2005) that recovery rates depend on more than one factor and vary with the state of the economy. This affects the loss distribution, as default probabilities and recovery rates are negatively correlated; if the state of the economy is declining and the frequency of defaults increasing, recovery rates decrease. This means that it is necessary to jointly model the probability of default and the LGD. This is a non-trivial undertaking. Dullmann and Trapp (2004) test a number of different latent factor models.

The event of an obligor defaulting will in general affect the creditworthiness of other obligors. The effects may be positive or negative depending on the nature of the default, the size of the obligor and the relationship of the obligor with other firms. If the default reduces competition, then it may be beneficial if remaining obligors are competitors. If the remaining obligors are suppliers to the defaulting obligor, then the effects of the default may be negative. This implies that modelling the effects of default on other obligors requires a detailed analysis. There are many papers that have developed models describing the consequences of default on other obligors.[6] The challenge with these types of models is that they are difficult to calibrate, implying that their predictions are problematic. To date, we have no extensive empirical results for these models.

The central issue, for either pricing or risk management, is whether modelling at the level of the obligor is capable of generating a realistic loss distribution for the whole portfolio.

Top-down approach

A top-down approach directly models the cashflows generated by the portfolio of assets in the collateral pool without explicit identification of individual assets, thus reducing the magnitude of the problems associated with parameter estimation identified in the last section. The typical formulation assumes that there are a number of different types of event that cause a loss to occur. Each time an event occurs, the portfolio suffers a loss; the size of the loss depends on the type of event. The arrival of each type of event is modelled by Poisson processes. The intensity of arrival is assumed to be stochastic. With this approach, the number of parameters that must be estimated is greatly reduced. For example, in Longstaff and Rajan (2008) there are three types of events. The interpretation of these events is that the first type of event models default by individual obligors, the second type of event models sector or group defaults and the third type of event models economy-wide defaults. In the simplest form of the model there are six parameters to estimate: three jump sizes and three volatilities. The benefit of this parsimony is that models can usually be calibrated, while the cost is that the model may do a poor job in describing the dynamics of the prices of different structures over time.

Implications for new innovations

For new financial products there is a real trade-off between the complexity of models and the availability of data. A bottom-up approach is a logical starting point to model the loss distribution generated by a portfolio of obligors. The critical issue is that of modelling default dependence.

The copula approach is simple, though static. The use of the normal copula is perhaps the least demanding in terms of the number of parameters that must be estimated. For risk management, a credit rating transition matrix and a multi-factor equity return model are used to generate the correlation matrix. For pricing, CDS prices are used to infer the intensity for each obligor. It is usually assumed that the recovery rate is some fixed known value. Often equity returns are used to generate the correlation matrix, though there is little theoretical justification. Alternatively, the correlation matrix is assumed to be described by one parameter that is calibrated so that the model price matches the price of one tranche, usually the equity tranche. In practice, for pricing, both the bottom-up and top-down approaches rely on calibration. The limitation of this approach is that model imperfections and the lack of liquidity of prices are compounded into the calibrated parameters.

The reduced-form approach introduces default dependence via the specification of the intensity function. If a Cox process is assumed for the intensity function, then a time series of CDS prices is required to allow estimation. Consider a simple Cox process of the form

$$\lambda_k(t) = b_{k,0} + b_{k,1} x_1(t) + b_{k,2} x_2(t)$$

where $x_1(t)$ and $x_2(t)$ are covariates described by some type of stochastic process and $b_{k,0}$, $b_{k,1}$ and $b_{k,2}$ are coefficients. Simple types of processes usually require three parameters to be estimated for each covariate plus a correlation coefficient, giving seven parameters. There are three coefficients, so a total of 10 parameters must be estimated. In a credit default index, the constituent members belonging to the index change every six months, meaning that there are approximately 128 trading days. There is a real trade-off between the complexity of the model, and hence the number of parameters, and the availability of data. This is especially the case when the collateral pool is composed of bonds written on either subprime mortgages or credit cards and issued by an asset-backed trust. This introduces a lot of complications. The underlying assets in the pool are asset-backed bonds. However, the behaviour of these bonds depends on the type of mortgages or credit cards in the trust and the waterfall that divides the cashflows generated by the trust to the different tranches. It becomes very difficult to model the behaviour of the asset-backed bonds, especially as these bonds are rarely traded. Data about the underlying assets for the bonds (for example, subprime mortgages or credit cards) is often not available.

In some cases a model is calibrated to match the prices of tranches on an index where the asset pool is different from the assets in the pool of the CDO under consideration, making parameter calibration even more unreliable. This difficulty arises because of the lack of data for the new product.

Summary
In this section we have discussed some of the issues that arise when trying to price new financial products. A bottom-up approach is a logical starting point for modelling the event of default and the LGD for individual obligors in the collateral pool. Modelling the cashflows generated by the collateral pool requires describing the nature of the default dependence among the assets. However, the limited availability of data constrains the complexity of models. In an attempt to reduce the problems of limited data, a top-down approach directly models the cashflows generated by the collateral pool.

Often models are calibrated to a subset of extant prices. The limited liquidity of prices and the deficiencies of the model are impounded into model parameters. The limited data means that there is little, if any, empirical evidence about the accuracy of a model and its ability to hedge. For new products, data limitations mean that even if models are calibrated to match a subset of prices, there is uncertainty about posted model prices, especially for products that are highly illiquid. This affects not only trading but also risk management.

DESIGN CHARACTERISTICS

The design of an instrument defines its risk-sharing characteristics and its appeal to different potential users.[7] To stimulate usage, the design should attempt to anticipate features that will appeal to end users. On the demand side it should help to reduce the costs of achieving some service, such as altering the risk profile facing an investor. On the supply side it should be designed to reduce the costs associated with hedging, for example, by meshing with the features of extant instruments that can be used for hedging. For example, the rollover dates for CDS indexes match the International Monetary Market dates. This matching of maturities helps if the London Interbank Offered Rate (Libor) futures are used as a hedging tool.

The design of the innovation directly affects its risk characteristics. Identifying the risk characteristics of a new instrument requires identifying the conditions under which different features of an instrument affect its risk profile. Certain design features may make an instrument extremely sensitive to underlying factors and market disruptions. We demonstrate the first point via a simple example that produced a domino effect in mortgage CDOs and the second point by examining asset-backed commercial paper (ABCP).

Factor sensitivity

We consider how the design of subprime CDO tranches made the tranches quite sensitive to the state of the housing market. The nature of the risks involved in holding an AAA-rated super-senior tranche of a subprime CDO was completely missed by all the players: rating agencies, regulators, financial institutions and investors.

The underlying assets in a subprime CDO were mortgage-backed bonds. These bonds were created by placing subprime mortgages into a trust and dividing the aggregate cashflows into tranches.[8] A typical subprime trust is usually composed of several thousand individual mortgages, typically around 3,000–5,000 mortgages for a total amount of approximately US$1 billion. The distribution of cashflows generated by the mortgage pool is tranched into different classes of mortgage-backed bonds, from the equity tranche, typically created through overcollateralisation, to the most senior tranche, rated AAA. A typical subprime CDO has a pool of assets composed of mortgage-backed bonds rated BB to AA, with an average rating of BBB.

There was a characteristic in the design that made the tranches quite sensitive to mortgage defaults. The problem was that the initial level of subordination for a BBB bond was relatively small, between 3% and 5%, and the width of the tranche was very thin, between 2.5% and 4%. As prepayments occurred, the level of subordination of the lower tranches increased in relative terms over time. Assuming a recovery of 20% on the foreclosed homes means that a default rate of 20% on subprime mortgages, which was realistic during the credit crisis, will most likely hit most of the BBB tranches, causing default. The typical collateral pool of a CDO would normally contain bonds from different locations, giving geographic diversification. The premise is that downturns in local housing markets would be isolated events and the national market would continue to flourish.

The rolling over of subprime mortgages was dependent in large part on rising house prices so that the borrower could refinance. The fall in house prices occurred in states right across the US. Compounding the severity of the problems was the recessionary economic environment. Under these circumstances, the loss correlations across all the mortgage-backed bonds in the collateral pool will be close to one. As a consequence, if one mortgage-backed bond is hit, it is most likely that most of the mortgage-backed bonds will also be hit during the same period. And, given the thin width of the tranches, it is most likely that if one mortgage-backed bond is wiped out, they will all be wiped out at the same time, wiping out the super-senior tranche of the subprime CDO.

In other words, we are in a binary situation, where either the cumulative default rate of the subprime mortgages remains below the threshold where underlying mortgage-backed bonds are untouched and the super-senior tranches of subprime CDOs will not incur any loss, or the cumulative default rate breaches this threshold and the super-senior tranches of subprime CDOs could all be wiped out.

Market disruptions

Special investment vehicles invested in long-term assets and financed their purchases by issuing ABCP. With the fall in house prices and increased uncertainty about the value of the underlying collateral, vehicles had to reduce the amount of ABCP, forcing them to sell assets in order to meet claims. The uncertainty about collateral valuation increased, and investors eventually refused to purchase new ABCP. The rating agencies had anticipated market disruptions and insisted on vehicles having multiple backstop lines of credit. What they had not anticipated were the effects of "wrong way" feedback. The valuation of the collateral became increasingly difficult as the value of the vehicle's assets (mostly illiquid assets) declined. This triggered the selling of illiquid assets, causing further price declines.

If the ABCP had been issued with a clause stating that if the vehicle was unable to roll over its debt, the maturity of the paper could be extended by one or two years, then this would have reduced some of the pressure on the hedge funds.

Summary

Both of these examples illustrate how design features affected the performance of instruments. For new innovations, the challenge is to identify the features in the design that affect its risk profile and the ability of investors to hedge.

LIQUIDITY

With any new innovation there will initially be limited liquidity. Liquidity for an innovation depends on many factors such as the ability to grow both the supply and demand, the ease of pricing the innovation, the transparency of the pricing process, the existence of hedging tools and the costs associated with hedging.[9] The ability to hedge and speculate makes an instrument attractive to a wide range of investors.[10] An innovation will attract certain types of investors on the demand and supply sides and the actions of these different groups affect the level and the stability of liquidity in the market. The level of liquidity will depend on the state of the sector and economy. If macroshocks to the economy or to a sector adversely affect investors' confidence, causing them to exit positions, this will decrease the level of liquidity.

Education

With the launch of a new innovation comes the need to build both supply and demand by educating potential users about the usefulness of an innovation and its risk–return characteristics and identifying any accounting or regulatory issues that might impede adoption. The range of possible uses will affect the size of both supply and demand and thus the size of the group of investors willing to trade the instrument and thus its liquidity.

The complexity of an innovation also affects its appeal to different clienteles and the amount of education required to reach end users. A CDS is a simple contract to shift credit risk. It protects one party (the protection buyer) from the loss from par on a specified face value of bonds of a specified seniority following the default of the reference obligor specified in the contract. When these instruments were introduced, many institutions devoted much effort explaining to investors the uses of the instruments, how they could be hedged and the general pricing methodology. In this case, many investors such as banks and fixed income portfolio managers found the innovation attractive, as it offered an alternative way to limit their exposure to default risk. A CDO is a complex product. Each CDO has its own unique structure defining how cashflows from the underlying assets are allocated to the different tranches over the life of the instrument. The complexity of this class of instruments limits their appeal (at least in an ideal world[11]) to investors with the ability to analyse the risk profile and to understand the frailty of the underlying assumptions.[12]

To ensure liquidity, it is necessary to grow the supply side of the transaction. Depending on the type of innovation, there may be a natural clientele for whom the product provides a convenient way to adjust their risk exposure. The supply side may grow if the risk–return characteristics of the innovation are attractive to investors and there are hedging instruments.

In any new form of financial instrument, there is the possibility of ambiguity in the contract terms and procedure, giving rise to legal and settlement risk. To minimise these costs, it is desirable that contracts become standardised, meaning that there should be some form of master contract where the terms and procedures are stated unambiguously. The number of terms and procedures generally increases with the complexity of an instrument. The more complex an instrument, the more difficult it will be to develop a standardised form of contract. The benefit of adopting a standardised contract, such as an International Swaps and Derivatives Association master agreement, is a lowering of transaction costs associated with legal and settlement risk and consequently this is a major contributor to improving an instrument's liquidity.

The ease of pricing a new product

Investors' ability to analyse and price a new product is directly affected by the nature of the assets underlying the product, the complexity of the design and the availability of data. If it is relatively easy to determine the price, this aids investors' understanding of the roles different factors have upon price and helps to increase their confidence in the model prices and hence liquidity. The structure of an innovation plays an important role in the ease of pricing. If an innovation references a constant portfolio of underlying assets, then this reduces the costs of acquiring data and analysis. For example, a CDS references a bond type of a given seniority issued by a company. If the reference portfolio is complex and the structure of the innovation is too, as is the case for CDOs, then this greatly increases the data requirements and analytical skills needed to understand the complexity of the structure.

In some cases the data requirements can be formidable, as is the case for subprime-backed bonds. Data on the subprime mortgages supporting the bonds may be difficult to access and the bonds are illiquid. This adversely affects the ability to price the instrument. Portfolios of these bonds are often used for securitisation and their illiquidity compounds the difficulties of pricing mortgage-backed CDOs. Data about CDOs can be purchased, though it is incomplete and not always timely. This contributes to the inability to reliably price these assets and hence liquidity.

For pricing we need to address the following issues: data requirements; the ability to calibrate models; the complexity of the innovation. Valuing path-dependent instruments, such as CDOs, requires the use of Monte Carlo simulation.[13] But before the simulation can be performed, it is necessary to calibrate the model. This involves specifying the marginal distributions for each of the underlying assets, describing the joint default dependency and the LGD for each asset. However, without reliable prices for each of the underlying assets, each of these tasks becomes problematic. In a top-down approach, the prices of different tranches can be used for calibration. These are usually very illiquid. If calibration is not easy it will be detrimental to liquidity, as this increases the uncertainty about the accuracy of the model price. In a bottom-up approach, it is necessary to calibrate using the prices of the underlying assets if such prices are available. Without the prices of tranches, specification of default dependence is challenging.

For complex products, many investors do not have the in-house ability to address all the data issues and perform model valuations and have relied on the credit rating as a guide to the inherent risk and what should be an acceptable price by comparing yields of instruments of similar risk. The credit rating has been used as a risk measure, even though it measures only one dimension of creditworthiness. The inability to readily analyse such structures increases uncertainty about the valuation and decreases the liquidity of the bonds. However, some investors have stepped into the valuation "fog" to engage in credit rating "arbitrage".[14]

Hedging a new product

The existence of a secondary market provides investors with the ability to exit a position, and this option directly affects the liquidity of the primary market. For a new product, limited liquidity increases the risk in entering into a position and the costs of exiting the position. Many institutions recognise this, and, in order to grow the market, agree to make a secondary market on request. This exposes the institution and also the investor to increased risk, for while there may be a market allowing an investor to exit, the price may not be competitive.

For any position, the ability to hedge provides an avenue to reduce the risk exposure of a position. It also increases the attractiveness of investing in the innovation. For a new innovation, the task is to find other instruments that are natural hedging tools. The costs associated with hedging can be reduced if the characteristics of the innovation synchronise with the institutional features of the hedging instruments. A simple example would be where the rollover dates of the innovation match the maturity dates of the hedging instruments.

An innovation might be a catalyst for further innovations. If a bank sells credit protection using CDSs, it is exposed to two types of risk. If the creditworthiness of the reference entity underlying a CDS deteriorates, the bank will be forced to write down the value of the CDS and in extreme cases if default occurs the bank must compensate the protection buyer for the loss. One way for the bank to hedge this type of risk is to sell a portfolio of different CDSs to a special purpose vehicle and to buy protection on the portfolio of CDSs, creating what is called a "synthetic CDO". This second form of innovation provides a way for the bank to hedge its risk and helps the supply of individual CDSs, improving liquidity.

Transparency

New financial instruments trade in the over-the-counter market. Buyers and sellers must contact dealers to obtain bid–ask quotes and judge the depth of the market. The ability of investors to see posted bid–ask quotes on a regular basis via a third-party screen helps to improve the transparency of the pricing process, especially for less sophisticated investors. It also provides information about the depth of the market. In the autumn of 2002, dealers in the CDS market realised this and agreed to trade an index on a portfolio of 125 investment grade obligors. Dealers posted bid–ask quotes daily on a third-party screen. This greatly helped to improve the liquidity of the market. It allowed investors to take views on the market as a whole and also provided a means for them to calibrate their models.

Summary

In this section we identified some of the factors that determine liquidity for a new product. The process of building both demand and supply requires educating end users about the uses of a new product and its risk–return characteristics and addressing any accounting and regulatory issues. The ease of pricing will depend on the complexity of the product and data availability. The ability to hedge will depend on what other instruments are available. The cost associated with hedging will depend on the compatibility of the innovation's design with respect to the institutional features of the hedging instruments. The ability to observe posted prices on a regular basis will provide investors with information about liquidity and market depth.

COUNTERPARTY RISK

Counterparty risk is the risk that a party to a contract might fail to perform when called upon to honour its contractual commitments. It exposes the other party to the contract to a mark-to-market risk.[15] To determine the effects of counterparty risk on the value of a contract first requires identifying the nature of the counterparty risk. In some cases it could be default by the counterparty. In other cases it could be the risk of the counterparty being downgraded and its inability to post additional collateral.

If the underlying asset is a credit risky asset and the risk event for the counterparty is default risk, then determining the impact of counterparty risk requires modelling the joint distribution of the default times for the underlying asset and the counterparty. If the underlying asset defaults first, the risk is in whether the counterparty will default prior to settlement. If during the life of the contract the counterparty defaults first, it is necessary to price a new contract with the same premium.

The event of the counterparty defaulting will in general affect the probability distribution of the reference asset subsequently defaulting.[16] Default by the counterparty can occur at any time and Monte Carlo simulation is usually employed to model this process. When default occurs, it is necessary to price a new contract. For complex instruments such as CDOs, a separate simulation is required, meaning that it is necessary to perform a simulation within a simulation. The total number of simulations needed to ensure reasonable accuracy becomes prohibitive, implying that for complex instruments different types of approximations must be employed.[17]

Reducing counterparty exposure

Steps to mitigate counterparty risk span a wide spectrum, including limiting total exposure to individual counterparties, exposure to particular sectors, master contract agreements that facilitate netting, "haircuts" in pricing, posting of collateral and payment in advance. Some of these approaches are model independent. Limiting the total exposure to a particular obligor requires only information systems that can keep track of the total exposure. For some types of instruments, this requirement may not be possible. For example, for synthetic CDOs, the same obligor may appear in many different tranches. Unless the names of the obligors in the different assets are known, it is impossible to determine the total exposure.

If there are already a number of contracts with the same counterparty that are covered under a master agreement, then the effects of counterparty risk on the valuation of contracts are non-linear. For example, let X and Y denote the value of two contracts to some investor I. These contracts have the same counterparty C. Without a master agreement, the exposure to counterparty C is

$$\max(0, X) + \max(0, Y)$$

With a master agreement, the exposure to counterparty C is

$$\max(0, X + Y)$$

but

$$\max(0, X + Y) \leqslant \max(0, X) + \max(0, Y) \qquad (9.7)$$

implying that a master agreement lowers the exposure, as expected.

A new product will not be covered under a master agreement. Let Z denote the value of the innovation to investor I; the contract is with the same counterparty C. The exposure to counterparty C is given by

$$\max(0, X + Y) + \max(0, Z)$$

To lower counterparty risk, it is in the interest of dealers to attempt to standardise the contract as quickly as possible so that the contract can be covered under a master agreement (see Equation 9.7).

One way to lower counterparty risk is for investors to clear trades in the innovation through a clearinghouse. The clearinghouse steps in and becomes the counterparty to the investor I. Note that the clearinghouse is exposed to investor I and the counterparty. A clearinghouse concentrates counterparty risk and requires careful risk management and adequate capital to prevent failure.

Implications for an innovation

For a new innovation the difficulty of estimating the effects of counterparty risk are compounded due to limited data and liquidity. First, there is limited information available to help in specifying the joint distribution describing the occurrence of the risk event for the counterparty and the reference asset. Second, for a new product, the financial institutions offering the product need to develop the necessary back-office facilities to keep track of the counterparties associated with the product. Third, the financial institution needs to carefully consider whether there is wrong way dependence. The posting of collateral provides protection if the value of the collateral is not positively dependent on the same factors that affect the counterparty. If conditions in the economy adversely affect the creditworthiness of the counterparty and the value of the posted collateral, then it becomes necessary to increase the posted collateral. The posting of additional collateral may further weaken the creditworthiness of the counterparty.[18] It is important to recognise *ex ante* this form of wrong way dependence. Another issue is whether the collateral is traded in a liquid market. If not, then questions about the valuation of the collateral can arise, especially if there is wrong way dependence.

For a new innovation it is necessary to establish the legal identity of the counterparty and to know the judicial system governing any disputes with the contract. Different legal systems may accord different treatments for the contract.

Summary

In this section we have identified some of the additional issues that arise in assessing the effects of counterparty risk associated with innovations: firstly, data limitations, making it challenging to estimate the joint distribution between the underlying asset and the counterparty; secondly, the need to develop the back-office support; thirdly, the need to recognise the possible existence of wrong way dependence if collateral is posted; fourthly, the need to standardise the contractual terms and develop a master agreement; finally, the treatment of the contract under different legal systems.

RISK MANAGEMENT

Risk management entails being able to measure and manage risk over specified time intervals, such as a day, a week or a year.[19] Measuring the risk at a specified time horizon requires the ability to generate the probability distribution describing the value of an instrument or portfolio. There are two steps in this operation. The first step is to price the instrument or portfolio at the horizon. This involves using the pricing (risk-neutral) probability distribution. The second is to estimate risk measures such as VaR or expected shortfall, using the natural probability distribution. Risk management always involves using both the natural and risk-neutral probability distributions. Managing the risk profile requires the ability to hedge risk exposures. This often involves calculating partial derivatives of the price with respect to certain variables (the so-called Greeks) to construct a hedge. If the pricing model is misspecified, then the partial derivatives will be misspecified and hedging will be ineffective.

Successful risk management requires anticipating the risks generated by an instrument. With any new form of instrument, there are additional factors that can cause risk. The usual starting point is the pricing of the instrument, which raises the following questions.

- What type of model should be used?
- Does data exist that facilitates the estimation or calibration of the model's parameters?
- How sensitive is the pricing to certain parameters?
- How effective is the model for hedging?
- What are the costs associated with hedging?

There are many additional dimensions to risk that are difficult to quantify. These hidden dimensions are known as "dark risk". For example

- What is the best way to address the estimation of model parameters in a non-stationary environment, given limited data?
- How does the complexity of an instrument and parameter uncertainty affect the pricing and risk management?[20]
- Are there legal and/or settlement risks associated with the contract?
- Is there any way to test the model?

There are other dimensions of dark risk arising from managerial considerations. The first issue is understanding how an accounting system can generate incentives for traders to undertake trades where the prime purpose of the trades is to enhance their bonuses. In an environment where there is a constant flux of innovations, senior management is often ignorant of the exact nature of the innovations. This affects their ability to judge the risk characteristics and to understand all the costs that an innovation generates.

Model parameters

Data availability influences the choice of model. If data is limited, this restricts the types of models that can be employed, since it is necessary to calibrate the model. This implies that the model cannot be too sophisticated. Typically, a methodology that can be calibrated and used for products that depend on a subset of the factors that affect the new innovation is modified so that it can be applied to the new innovation. This usually necessitates additional assumptions. For example, the issue of modelling default dependence is addressed in risk management in order to meet the requirements of the Basel II Accord. A similar type of modelling approach is used to price multi-name credit derivatives, though the calibration procedures are quite different. Without sufficient data, time series analysis of the properties of the price dynamics is limited. This also implies that the ability to test the model will be limited.

For pricing, a model is usually calibrated to match extant prices. For new innovations, markets are illiquid and the spread due to the lack of liquidity is incorporated into the parameters of the pricing model. It is assumed that the determinants of the liquidity in the market are the same as the determinants of the value of the innovation. There is no reason why this should be the case. However, without a model to describe how liquidity varies, the modeler has no choice but to compound the determinants of liquidity and value. This increases the variability of the parameter estimates.

A typical pricing or risk management model takes a number of inputs and estimated parameters to produce an estimate of either a price or a risk measure. There may be certain inputs and parameters that can cause significant changes in the output. For example, in stock option models uncertainty about volatility can have a first-order effect on price. For multi-name credit derivatives, specification of the default dependency can significantly affect both the price and risk measures. Knowledge about these types of sensitivities can provide important information to risk managers for stress testing. However, it is important to remember that stress testing assumes the validity of the underlying model and simply stresses the variables in the model. If the model is deficient, the risk manager may have a false sense of security.

Testing a model

Any form of model should be tested for accuracy. If a model's parameters are calibrated so that the model matches existing prices on a particular day, as is standard practice, the issue is whether the model is useful for hedging. Many models can match price and yet do a poor job hedging, implying that they are misspecified and of limited value for risk management. The issue of judging the hedging performance of a model, even when there is adequate data available, is not straightforward. Hedging is performed in discrete time and is subject to bid–ask spread issues and hence the hedging errors will be described by a distribution that has a finite non-zero mean.[21] Judging the relative performance of model specifications is equivalent to judging between different distributions. This can be done, given additional assumptions. With limited data, such an exercise is problematic.

If it is impossible to establish a way of judging a model for a new innovation, we can still perform some useful risk management exercises, although this does require risk managers to think about all of the possible factors that might affect risk and not simply those used in their risk models. For example, consider a CDO on residential mortgage bonds. Each bond is written on a portfolio of residential mortgages. The bonds are chosen from different geographic areas in order to increase the level of diversification. The correlation of residential mortgage default rates across states has typically been quite low during the period of rising house prices. We know that these bonds are related to both economy-wide and regional factors, implying that default dependence can vary with the state of the economy. At the start of 2006 the rate of increase in house prices started to decrease across many major states. The US car industry has been experiencing troubles for many years, and with rising petrol prices the demand for cars would decrease, causing further economic difficulties for the industry and its associated suppliers. These types of considerations raise questions of how the risk of the CDO would be affected if

- there is an increase in mortgage default rates and
- there is an increase in the default dependency across states.

However, the ability of the risk manager to ask such questions requires an environment that encourages managers to think about the risk drivers and how changing conditions affect the relative importance of the drivers and the overall risk. These broader considerations cannot be achieved by simply relying on the mechanical stress testing of models.

There are other dimensions of risk that are not usually mentioned in discussions about risk management and yet can have a major impact on the risk associated with an innovation. For example, when considering the availability of hedging instruments and the ease of hedging, the risk manager needs to identify how the ability to hedge varies with the state of the economy. Additionally, certain instruments may require the posting of collateral, depending on the risk of the underlying reference entity and/or the creditworthiness of the writer of the contract. The conditions triggering the collateral calls and the determination of the amounts need to be easily identifiable. For both pricing and risk management, it is necessary to estimate the probability of a call and the additional amount of collateral required. Another example would be an innovation that requires the rolling over of short-term debt. The lender of the debt may require collateral of a certain value. The risk lies in how the value of the collateral and the innovation are related. If the value of the collateral decreases, it may become necessary to post additional collateral, thereby lowering the value of the innovation. In the extreme case the market may cease to function, meaning that it is impossible to roll over the debt. This form of wrong way dependence poses a major risk. The role of the risk manager is to recognise its existence, identify the consequences and assign a probability of occurrence as conditions change. For a new innovation, it is essential to identify these considerations in order to understand the risk of the innovation in changing economic conditions.

Unintended consequences

The introduction of a new innovation may generate a series of unintended consequences. For example, the introduction of subprime mortgage-backed CDOs was initially profitable for the issuers. This created a demand for these types of mortgages. To ensure an adequate supply, originators lowered their underwriting standards, as they were rewarded on the basis of volume and shifted the risk of mortgage defaults to the arrangers (the issuers of the CDOs).[22] This lowering of underwriting standards increased the probability of default for the mortgages contained in mortgage-backed bonds. However, the data used to model the risk of the CDOs was from a prior period and did not reflect the changing conditions.[23] A risk manager needs to look not just at an innovation in isolation but also at the incentives facing different players that contribute to the innovation and the consequences of the incentives.

The risk manager also needs to recognise that holding different examples of an innovation may result in a concentration of risk. For example, holding different types of mortgage-backed CDOs may result in a concentration of risk if the same bond appears in different CDOs. Standard & Poor's reports that just 35 different borrowers appear in nearly half of the 184 collateralised loan obligations that it rates (Sakoul 2009). The risk manager needs the ability to identify the underlying assets in an innovation. This means that data about the underlying assets must be available.

Accounting incentives

When an innovation is introduced, often an existing accounting framework for another security is adopted to account for trades in the innovation. Traders are familiar with the characteristics of the existing accounting scheme and "fit" the new product into its framework. Traders' incentives are inherently short term in nature, given the typical way of determining bonuses that concentrates on the profits generated over the accounting year. They have incentives to engage in trading activities that generate profits over the short term at the expense of long-term profits. In the long term they may not continue to be employed by the same institution, or they may hope to offset future losses.

The challenge for risk managers is to understand the incentives generated by the accounting system and the types of trades that it encourages traders to undertake. Risk managers must try to distinguish between trades that generate short-term profits and those that are in the best interests of the firm. Risk managers face another obstacle: that of ignorance on the part of senior management.

Senior management

When an innovation is introduced, senior management may not understand the nature of the innovation, its risk characteristics and how the accounting treatment fits the innovation and the incentives generated by the accounting system. They often refuse to acknowledge their ignorance and rely on the traders and their quants to characterise the profitability and risk.[24] However, the incentives of the trading desk are usually not aligned with those of senior management. Traders are rewarded on the basis of the profitability of their desk over the accounting year, while senior management personnel are rewarded on the basis of their business. Bonuses are paid in the form of cash and deferred shares, vested over a few years. If the cash part is large enough and the vesting period short enough, then the long-term outlook is relatively unimportant for traders.

Diligent risk managers may object to certain trades on the grounds that they are not in the best interests of the firm, being instead driven by the desire to increase bonuses. For the risk managers' objections to be enforced, support by senior management is required. Risk managers are unlikely to receive support if senior management personnel are ignorant and do not understand the issues, relying on the traders and quants for guidance.[25] Regulators are often in the same position as senior management. They have far fewer incentives than senior management to understand the complexities and subtleties of an innovation. Hence, they fail to provide risk managers with the necessary support.

Mark-to-model

In recording the value of an illiquid asset, a model price is usually used. We have already discussed the issues arising from calibration. Here we focus on some of the additional costs and risks that are usually neglected when determining the value of an innovation. For an innovation, the operational risks are greater than those associated with a seasoned product. The list of potential areas of risk is long and includes such issues as the accounting incentives generated by the accounting system, model risk, complexity risk (the more complex a product the greater the risk of pricing and trading errors), settlement risk and legal risk.[26] To determine the value of an innovation, these operational costs should be included.

Summary

In this section we have discussed some of the many additional problems that an innovation causes in risk management. Given data and model limitations, risk managers need to take a broader view of risk determinants. They also need to consider whether an innovation generates perverse incentives to different players and the resulting consequences of such incentives.

CREDIT RATING AGENCIES

For certain types of instruments a credit rating is often a prerequisite for increasing the marketability of the innovation. The determination of a rating for an innovation typically involves detailed discussion between the issuer of the innovation and the credit rating agency about the availability of data and the methodology the agency will employ to determine a rating. This is often an interactive process, resulting in refinements of the instrument to ensure appropriate ratings. The assessment of a rating may involve both quantitative and qualitative considerations.

For a risk manager or investors not involved in these issuer/rater discussions, the methodology used to determine the ratings is not transparent. The rating agencies publish much general information about their methodologies, but precise information does not appear to be available. For risk managers and investors, transparency in the rating process is necessary in order to understand how a rating is defined, and the type of data and methodology used.

Understanding a rating

The first requirement is to understand what criteria a rating agency are using as a measure of creditworthiness. A rating scheme is an ordinal ranking: an instrument with an AAA rating has in some sense less credit risk than an instrument with an AA rating. A rating may be either an assessment of a probability of a defined event occurring or the expected loss if the defined event occurs. Given a particular definition, the agency may assign the quantitative part of the rating based on some form of average rating over some time horizon, to give a "through the cycle" assignment. How the average is computed, how the qualitative part is assigned and how the quantitative and qualitative parts are combined are all unclear.

A credit rating is not a sufficient statistic for measuring the risk of an asset (Brennan *et al* 2009; Crouhy *et al* 1999). This implies that the value and risk of an asset may change without any change in the credit rating, even with continuous monitoring. Rating agencies do not continuously monitor the creditworthiness of an asset, so a credit rating is often an outdated assessment of creditworthiness. In practice, a rating is some form of time average of the creditworthiness of the asset over the life of the contract. The rating overestimates creditworthiness in bad times and underestimates it in good times. A rating measures one aspect of credit risk. Investors and risk managers need to understand the different factors that affect the value of an innovation and its creditworthiness.

The second requirement is to understand the methodology. This necessitates identifying the factors that affect the creditworthiness of the innovation and matching this list against the factors that have been considered in the rating assessment. In the current credit crisis investors learned that the valuation of collateral assets was not considered in assessing the rating of a special investment vehicle. Knowledge about the methodology allows for the identification of the model assumptions and the opportunity to examine their robustness. However, the ability to test or judge robustness requires knowledge about the market. This may be missing for new innovations, meaning that risk managers will have to rely on professional judgement.

The third requirement is to know the type of data employed when determining a rating. In the credit crisis the rating agencies accepted the data from the originators without checking whether distributional assumptions had changed. They ignored information about the increasing misrepresentation of borrower characteristics. The nature of the data greatly influences the distributional assumptions. Is a long time series necessary for estimation? What assumptions are made about the stationarity of the coefficients? Is there enough empirical evidence to justify the assumed distributional assumptions? Without sufficient data it is difficult to test the robustness of assumptions.

Implications

For innovations, data availability and the nature of the distributional assumptions are important issues that must be addressed in order to estimate different risk measures over arbitrary time horizons. In the absence of sufficient data about the innovation, data pertaining to the underlying assets in a structure may be available and can be used to extract information about the range of parameters used to measure the risk of the innovation. Often the availability of this data is limited. For synthetic CDOs, the underlying assets are CDSs. The market for these assets has only been in existence for a relatively short period, making it difficult to infer behaviour in different economic conditions. Consequently, much professional judgement must be used in specifying the assumptions with respect to the probabilities of default, default dependence and recovery rates when trying to assess the creditworthiness of a structure.

For risk managers and investors the challenge is to interpret what information a rating actually conveys. Consider a rating on a mezzanine tranche of a mortgage-backed CDO. For risk managers a useful risk measure would be the expected loss for each tranche over each year spanning the maturity of the structure. Presumably, a rating is an assessment of the average expected loss over the life of the CDO. The pattern of expected losses may fluctuate over the life of the contract. By using some form of time average, information about the fluctuations is suppressed, yet information about fluctuations would be of benefit.

What use is a rating?

Given the limitations of credit ratings, how can risk managers use ratings in risk management? In CreditMetrics, bonds and loans are allocated to credit risk classes and the change in credit quality over a one-year horizon is modelled by using a transition matrix that describes the probabilities of rating transitions. In this approach all bonds within a rating class are treated as homogeneous. If a new innovation can be classified as having the same credit risk characteristics as an existing instrument, then this might provide a way to use the same risk management tools. If this is not the case, the challenge is to determine how ratings can be usefully employed.

Risk managers also need to consider whether conflicts of interest that rating agencies face have affected their objectivity, especially as rating agencies have little legal exposure, given their use of a First Amendment defence (Coffee 2008).[27] Without independent verification, investors face a "market for lemons" situation; the rating is probably too generous. The rating agencies publish tables detailing how different rating classes for bonds and loans have performed with respect to their credit performance. For bonds and loans, the agencies have data extending back many decades.

This is not the case for structured products. These products necessitate modelling the cashflows generated by the assets in the collateral pool. This means that it is necessary to model default dependence. Until recently there was little empirical information about the performance of the agencies' models. For a new innovation the rating methodology is untested. Risk managers and investors need to remember the tentative nature of the methodology.

Summary

In this section we have discussed some of the issues that arise in the use of credit ratings for innovations. For investors and risk managers, the first issue is determining the precise meaning of a rating. Next is understanding the methodology behind the quantitative and qualitative aspects of a rating and the data requirements. The final issue is that, for an innovation, the rating methodology is tentative and untested, implying that whatever information a rating conveys should be treated with caution.

CONCLUSIONS

In this chapter we have discussed some of the diverse challenges of measuring and managing the risk of innovative financial products. Measuring risk requires an ability to first identify the different dimensions of risk that an innovation introduces. The list of possible factors is long: model restrictions, illiquidity, limited ability to test models, design characteristics, counterparty risk and related managerial issues. For measuring some of the different dimensions of risk, the implications of limited available data must be addressed. Given the uncertainty about model valuation and estimated risk metrics, how can risk managers respond? Stress testing a model of unknown validity may generate a false sense of security. For a scenario analysis to be useful, risk managers need to understand the different factors that affect the product. This requires the ability to think outside the confines of their limited pricing models, something that was missing in the credit crisis. The use of credit ratings for an innovation is problematic for two reasons. First, the meaning of a rating is unclear; second, the rating agencies are faced with the same data and measurement issues, implying that any credit risk measure should be treated with great caution. All parties within a company (senior management, traders and risk managers) have important roles to play in assessing, measuring and managing the risk of new products. The company's directors also have a responsibility to ensure that these duties are being fulfilled.

The problems facing regulators following the introduction of an innovation range from the problems with an individual institution to systemic effects. In the current credit crisis regulators placed (and continue to place) too much faith in rating agencies. For an innovation, a rating is a rough measure of some poorly defined credit metric. Regulators need to question whether ratings should be used for innovations in determining capital. For innovations, especially complex products such as CDOs, detailed information about an innovation has often been unavailable to investors. Regulators can require that data about each innovation be available to investors and regulators on a timely basis. This would allow for independent testing. In order to measure systemic risk, all major institutions, including hedge funds, need to come under regulatory monitoring. Regulators need the ability to measure the holding of an innovation by different institutions and the buildup of concentrated holdings.

> The author is grateful for comments and suggestions from M. Crouhy, R. Jarrow, C. Pirrong, D. Rowe, C. Smithson, L. Wakeman and seminar participants at the Bauer College and the 2009 "Financial Innovation and Crisis" Conference, organised by the Federal Reserve Bank of Atlanta. This chapter was first published as part of *The Journal of Credit Risk* Special Issue on "Lessons from the Credit Crisis" in summer 2009.

1 We leave the precise nature of the assets unspecified. Examples of possible candidates would be mortgages, asset-backed securities or CDSs on asset-backed securities.

2 This approach for pricing credit risky assets, called the reduced-form approach, was first introduced by Jarrow and Turnbull (1995).

3 For an introduction to the use of copula functions applied to finance, see Schönbucher (2003, Chapter 10) and O'Kane (2008, Chapter 14).

4 See Andersen (2006) for a description of these models and references to extant literature.

5 See Burtschell *et al* (2005) for an analysis of the performance of widely used copulas for pricing.

6 For a description of these types of models see Jarrow and Yu (2001), Gagliardini and Gourieroux (2003) and Yu (2007).

7 There is a large literature about security design (Allen and Gale 1995).

8 A subprime CDO is in fact a CDO squared on subprime mortgages.

9 The interaction between market and funding liquidity is discussed in Brunnermeier and Pedersen (2009).

10 During the 2007–9 credit crisis, some commentators recommended that the purchase of CDSs be restricted to investors who own the underlying asset. This would greatly reduce the liquidity of the CDS market.

11 From the credit crisis, it is clear that many investors failed to understand the risk characteristics of these instruments.

12 The issue of complexity is discussed in Rowe (2005).

13 An alternative would be to use scenario analysis. For pricing it is necessary to specify the probability (under the pricing measure) of the occurrence of each scenario.

14 This refers to tranches with the same credit rating, trading with different yields. To quote one trader: "Pick the one with highest yield. It is a no-brainer".

15 Consider the case of a CDS where there is the risk that the protection seller might default. For simplicity we assume that there is no risk that the protection will default. If the protection seller defaults before the reference obligor, then to restore the protection buyer to the position prior to default necessitates pricing a swap with the same premium. If the creditworthiness of the reference obligor has deteriorated, then the value of the swap to the protection buyer would be positive, implying a mark-to-market loss. If the reference obligor defaults and the protection seller defaults prior to settlement, the protection buyer is exposed to the full loss from the reference obligor (Turnbull 2005).

16 See Gagliardini and Gourieroux (2003) for a detailed discussion.

17 See Pykhtin (2005) for a survey of the different approaches that are used in practice.

18 In the current credit crisis, concern has been expressed about the consequences of AIG being downgraded and whether it had the ability to post collateral arising from all the contracts it had written.

19 The limitations of traditional risk measures such as VaR are well known and will not be discussed here (McNeil *et al* 2005).

20 Some of these issues are discussed by Rowe (2009).

21 In continuous time and for zero bid–ask spreads, the pricing error should be zero if the model is correctly specified.

22 For a more detailed analysis of the associated incentives, see Crouhy *et al* (2008).

23 The rating agencies had a policy of accepting data from originators without any form of auditing to check the reliability of their assumptions about the default data.

24 Arrogance and ignorance were the prime drivers behind the collapse of Barings Bank in 1995 (Board of Banking Supervision 1995).

25 The role of risk managers versus traders is discussed in Blankfein (2009).

26 A good introduction to operational risk is given in Crouhy *et al* (2001, Chapter 13).

27 The rating of credit structures has been a very profitable business for the rating agencies. Moody's reported in 2006 that 43% of total revenues came from rating structured products.

REFERENCES

Acharya, V., S. Bharath and A. Srinivasan, 2003, "Understanding the Recovery Rates on Defaulted Securities", Working Paper, London Business School.

Allen, F., and D. Gale, 1995, *Financial Innovation and Risk Sharing*, Second Edition (Cambridge, MA: MIT Press).

Altman, E., A. Resti and A. Sironi, 2005, "Default Recovery Rates in Credit Modeling: A Review of the Literature and Empirical Evidence", *Journal of Finance Literature* 1, pp. 21–45.

Andersen, L., 2006, "Portfolio Losses in Factor Models: Term Structures and Intertemporal Loss Dependence", *The Journal of Credit Risk* 2(4), pp. 3–31.

Blankfein, L., 2009, "Do Not Destroy the Essential Catalyst of Risk", *Financial Times* February 9.

Board of Banking Supervision, 1995, "Inquiry into the Circumstances of the Collapse of Barings", Report, Bank of England.

Brennan, M. J., J. Hein and S.-H. Poon, 2009, "Tranching and Ratings", Working Paper, Anderson School, UCLA.

Brunnermeier, M. K., and L. H. Pedersen, 2009, "Market Liquidity and Funding Liquidity", *Review of Financial Studies* 22(6), pp. 2201–38.

Burtschell, X., J. Gregory and J.-P. Laurent, 2005, "A Comparative Analysis of CDO Pricing Models", Working Paper, BNP-Paribas.

Coffee, J. C., 2008, "Turmoil in the US Credit Markets: The Role of the Credit Rating Agencies", Testimony before the United States Senate Committee on Banking, Housing, and Urban Affairs on April 22, URL: http://banking.senate.gov/.

Crouhy, M. G., S. M. Turnbull and L. Wakeman, 1999, "Measuring Risk Adjusted Performance", *The Journal of Risk* 2(1), pp. 5–35.

Crouhy, M. G., D. Galai and R. Mark, 2001, *Risk Management* (New York: McGraw-Hill).

Crouhy, M. G., R. A. Jarrow and S. M. Turnbull, 2008, "Insights and Analysis of Current Events: The Subprime Credit Crisis of 2007", *Journal of Derivatives* 16(1), pp. 81–110.

Dai, Q., K. J. Singleton and W. Yang, 2007, "Regime Shifts in a Dynamic Term Structure Model of US Treasury Bond Yields", *Review of Financial Studies* 20(5), pp. 1669–706.

Duffie, K., and K. Singleton, 1999, "Modeling Term Structures of Defaultable Bonds", *Review of Financial Studies* 12, pp. 687–720.

Dullmann, K., and M. Trapp, 2004, "Systematic Risk in Recovery Rates: An Empirical Analysis of US Corporate Credit Exposure", Working Paper, Deutsche Bundesbank, Frankfurt.

Eberlein, E., and F. Ozkan, 2003, "The Defaultable Lévy Term Structure: Rating and Restructuring", *Mathematical Finance* 13, pp. 277–300.

Eberlein E., W. Kluge and P. Schönbucher, 2006, "The Lévy Libor Model with Default Risk", *The Journal of Credit Risk* 2(3), pp. 3–42.

Gagliardini, P., and C. Gourieroux, 2003, "Spread Term Structure and Default Correlation", Working Paper, Lugano and University of Toronto.

Jarrow, R. A., and S. M. Turnbull, 1995, "The Pricing and Hedging of Options on Financial Securities Subject to Credit Risk", *Journal of Finance* 50(1), pp. 53–85.

Jarrow, R. A., and F. Yu, 2001, "Counterparty Risk and the Pricing of Defaultable Securities", *Journal of Finance* 56(5), pp. 555–76.

Lando, D., 1994, "Three Essays on Contingent Claims Pricing", PhD Thesis, Cornell University.

Lando, D., 1998, "On Cox Processes on Credit Risky Securities", *Review of Derivatives Research* 2, pp. 99–120.

Li, D., 2000, "On Default Correlation: A Copula Function Approach", *Journal of Fixed Income* 9(1), pp. 43–51.

Longstaff, F. A., and A. Rajan, 2008, "An Empirical Analysis of the Pricing of Collateralized Debt Obligations", *Journal of Finance* 63(2), pp. 529–63.

McNeil, A. J., R. Frey and P. Embrechts, 2005, *Quantitative Risk Management* (Princeton University Press).

Merton, R. C., 1974, "On the Pricing of Corporate Debt: The Risk Structure of Interest Rates", *Journal of Finance* 29, pp. 449–70.

O'Kane, D., 2008, *Modelling Single Name and Multi-Name Credit Derivatives* (New York: John Wiley & Sons).

Protter, P., 1993, *Stochastic Integration and Differential Equations*, Second Edition (Berlin: Springer).

Pykhtin, M., 2005, *Counterparty Credit Risk Modelling* (London: Risk Books).

Rowe, D., 2005, "The Danger of Complexity", *Risk Magazine* 18(4), p. 91.

Rowe, D., 2009, "Second-Order Uncertainty", *Risk Magazine* 22(4), p. 85.

Sakoul, A., 2009, "S&P Sees New Systemic Risk in CLO Defaults", *Financial Times*, February 16.

Schönbucher, P. J., 2003, *Credit Derivatives Pricing Model* (New York: John Wiley & Sons).

Schönbucher, P. J., and D. Schubert, 2001, "Copula Dependent Default Risk in Intensity Model", Working Paper, University of Bonn.

Turnbull, S. M., 2005, "The Pricing Implications of Counterparty Risk for Non-Linear Credit Products", *The Journal of Credit Risk* 1(4), pp. 3–30.

Yu, F., 2007, "Correlated Defaults in Intensity Based Models", *Mathematical Finance* 17, pp. 155–73.

10

Forecasting Extreme Risk of Equity Portfolios with Fundamental Factors

Vladislav Dubikovsky, Michael Y. Hayes, Lisa R. Goldberg, Ming Liu
MSCI Risk Analytics

Extreme events are an important source of financial risk, but they present special challenges in quantitative forecasting. This chapter describes an empirical approach to forecasting extreme risk and evaluates its accuracy out-of-sample on a range of factor-based strategies and pair trades. The results show that for a large majority of strategies the empirical model is more consistent with market behaviour than a conditional normal model.

Like volatility, shortfall comes equipped with a standard portfolio management toolkit that includes risk budgets, betas and correlations (Goldberg *et al* 2010). Shortfall optimisation can be formulated as a linear programming problem, and it is therefore a suitable risk measure for portfolio construction, as described in Rockafellar and Uryasev (2000, 2002) and Bertsimas *et al* (2004). This optimisation framework has been applied in Bender *et al* (2010) as a constraint in the active management context, and for asset allocation in Sheikh and Qiao (2009). On the other hand, important questions remain about the practical application of shortfall in the investment process. One question is the role of estimation error, which has been studied extensively in the context of volatility, but it presents an even greater challenge for shortfall, as discussed in Kondor *et al* (2007). A more basic issue is the accuracy of a shortfall forecast, which affects both optimisation and risk reporting. Underforecasts of risk can lead to inadequate capital reserves, making institutional investors vulnerable to liquidity traps in turbulent markets. Overcautious forecasts of risk are no less dangerous, as illustrated by a car travelling at half the

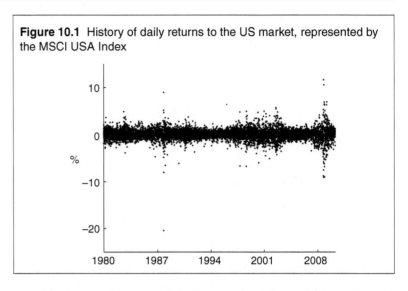

Figure 10.1 History of daily returns to the US market, represented by the MSCI USA Index

speed limit on a freeway. The efficacy of a risk model is contingent on its accuracy.

Extreme measures such as shortfall present a formidable challenge in quantitative forecasting. Recent data does not provide enough detail to describe severe outcomes: you cannot say what the worst loss in 100 looks like based on only 20 observations. Extreme risk forecasts based on recent data thereby require extrapolation from an assumed distribution. On the other hand, it is not obvious how data from the distant past is relevant to risk today: a long historical window in the early throes of the 2007–9 credit crisis would have predicted historically low levels of risk.

Figure 10.1 shows broad irregularity in daily return dynamics over four decades (1972–2009). The market was calm for periods of varying length, punctuated by violent eruptions characterized by high volatility and large outliers. However, a closer examination reveals subtle regularity: relative to the prevailing level of volatility, there are extreme events in both calm and turbulent periods. One of the most visible outliers since 2003 occurred on February 27, 2007, when the market still exhibited historically low levels of volatility. Such observations suggest that a long history may contain information relevant to a range of risk climates.

This is the main insight behind Barra Extreme Risk (BxR), which is a new model that forecasts the risk of extreme gains and losses for a broad class of equity portfolios. BxR is based on fundamental

Figure 10.2 Exposure of Google to Barra fundamental factors since 2004, showing how the characteristics of individual stocks can change

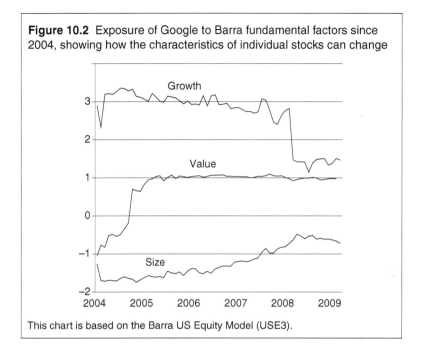

This chart is based on the Barra US Equity Model (USE3).

factors, and reflects historical behaviour due to portfolio characteristics rather than holdings. It adapts historical factor and asset-specific returns to the current market environment, thereby expanding the set of data that is relevant to the problem of forecasting extreme risk.

THE BARRA EXTREME RISK MODEL

Barra fundamental factors describe common characteristics among similar stocks over time. For example, the Value factor reflects common characteristics of all value stocks throughout history, while individual stocks commonly change from Growth to Value (see Figure 10.2).

Given a sufficiently long history prior to an analysis date, fundamental factors can provide a detailed picture of risk without requiring any parametric (eg, normal) assumptions. A longer history provides more examples of the portfolio's behaviour on bad days, and it satisfies basic sample-size criteria that enable statistical analysis of large losses.

The empirical use of factor returns naturally captures a wide range of real market behaviour. Some factors exhibit a higher degree of asymmetry and a higher proportion of extreme returns (for example, the Barra Global Equity Model (GEM2) Leverage and Momentum factors), while others are more symmetric or have a smaller proportion of extreme returns (such as the GEM2 Value factor; see Goldberg and Hayes 2010).

The Barra fundamental factor models express asset or portfolio return in terms of fundamental factor returns (f) and asset-specific returns (u)

$$R_t = X \cdot f_t + h \cdot u_t \qquad (10.1)$$

where R_t is the synthetic return on historical date t, X is a vector of the current portfolio exposures to common factors, f_t is a vector of common factor returns, h is a vector of current asset holdings and u_t is a vector of asset-specific returns.

Equation 10.1 describes the historical dynamics of a hypothetical portfolio with characteristics of today's portfolio. The Barra model data history covers a wide range of market climates, persistent periods of high and low volatility and several major financial crises. Statistically, this implies that the history contains returns generated from a variety of covariance matrices: market volatility rises and falls, as do correlations among factors (see Figure 10.3).

To use this long history to forecast risk today, BxR normalises the history to account for prevailing market conditions in the past, and then updates the normalised history to reflect market conditions on the analysis date. This is accomplished by "dividing" the historical factor returns by the square root of the historical Barra Integrated Model (BIM) daily covariance matrix, and multiplying by the square root of the current BIM daily covariance matrix

$$\begin{aligned}\hat{R}_t &= X \cdot \hat{f}_t + h \cdot \hat{u}_t \\ &= X \cdot (F_T^{1/2} \cdot F_t^{-1/2}) \cdot f_t + h \cdot (\Delta_T^{1/2} \cdot \Delta_t^{-1/2}) \cdot u_t \qquad (10.2)\end{aligned}$$

Further refinements are made to account for bias in the inversion of the factor covariance matrix, the impact of outliers in the specific volatility estimation and missing asset-specific returns. The one-day BxR returns are aggregated to longer horizons by repeatedly sampling with replacement from the one-day returns and summing. This procedure is equivalent to a discrete convolution of the one-day return distribution, and it accounts for the changing shape of risk at longer horizons. The complete BxR methodology is documented in Hayes and Knight (2010). To summarise, the key model

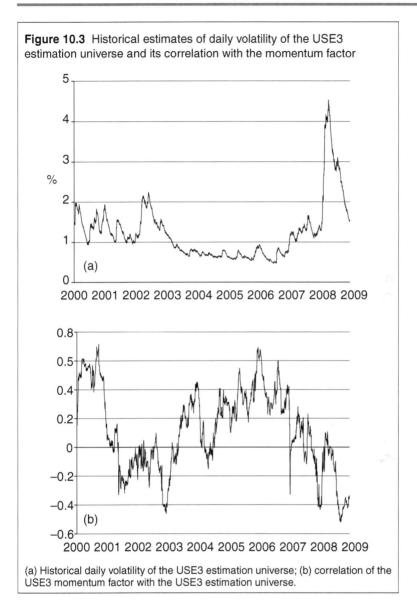

Figure 10.3 Historical estimates of daily volatility of the USE3 estimation universe and its correlation with the momentum factor

(a) Historical daily volatility of the USE3 estimation universe; (b) correlation of the USE3 momentum factor with the USE3 estimation universe.

assumption is that the BxR returns, $\hat{R}_t$, are identically distributed, but there is no assumption made about the nature of the distribution. This facilitates a direct connection between the empirical data and the risk forecasts, and it distinguishes BxR from parametric models and the generalised autoregressive conditional heteroscedasticity (Garch) models.

STATISTICAL TESTS OF FORECAST ACCURACY

This section compares the forecasting power of BxR and an industry-standard conditional normal model. The two models are evaluated out-of-sample in a broad spectrum of practical situations: industry and style tilts, as well as pair portfolios, in the US, UK and Japan equity markets. The study runs over a two-black-swan era (April 2000–December 2009) and evaluates forecasts over the entire period and by regime. The results show that under a wide range of circumstances BxR offers a greater degree of forecast accuracy than a comparably calibrated conditional normal model.

The simplest measures of extreme risk are shortfall, s, and gain, g. These are expected losses and gains in excess of a threshold,[1] and they are expressed as follows

$$\left.\begin{array}{l} s = E[-R \mid -R > \text{loss threshold}] \\ g = E[R \mid R > \text{gain threshold}] \end{array}\right\} \quad (10.3)$$

where R denotes portfolio return, and the loss and gain thresholds are expressed as quantiles of the loss and return distributions. Here "loss threshold" is used as a synonym for "value at risk", although there is no market vernacular for "gain threshold".

Models

BxR forecasts of portfolio shortfall and gain and their thresholds are compared with an industry-standard conditional normal model. Although the normal distribution has been much maligned in the risk literature dating back to Mandelbrot (1963), a well-calibrated conditional normal model yields a surprisingly high degree of accuracy, especially at the 95% confidence level (Pafka and Kondor 2001). In general, it is not possible to statistically reject a conditional model unless the test period spans several years (Barbieri et al 2009).

The volatility of the conditional normal model is estimated from the BIM daily covariance matrix and specific risk model. In this model (and in all normal models), shortfall and gain at a given confidence level are fixed multiples of volatility. For example, at the 95% confidence level, the multiplier is 2.04. By contrast, BxR offers an empirical view of market history using a long daily history of Barra factor returns and BIM daily covariance matrices. Both models adjust to the current covariance environment, using a 21-day half-life exponential weighting and Equation 10.2.

Test portfolios

Test portfolios are based on the Barra US Equity Model (USE3), Barra UK Equity Model (UKE7) and Barra Japan Equity Model (JPE3), which have 68, 54 and 53 factors, respectively. Factor histories begin in January 1981 for the US market and in January 1994 for the UK and Japan markets. The history of asset-specific returns begins in January 2000.

Each market is represented by one portfolio for each industry factor, two portfolios for each style factor and 50 randomly generated pair portfolios. An industry tilt is composed of all firms with non-zero industry exposure. A style portfolio includes top- or bottom-decile firms based on their ranking by exposure. Industry and style portfolios are capitalisation weighted, and their composition is updated monthly. Each pair portfolio consists of 50 pairs of stocks that are in the estimation universe for the entire out-of-sample period. A pair portfolio is constructed by selecting an industry at random and then randomly choosing a long stock from this industry. The short stock is randomly chosen among the stocks that best offset the industry exposure of the long stocks. Both long and short stocks are drawn without replacement.

Test statistics

In the evaluations below, all forecasts are at the 95% confidence level and a one-day horizon. Standard errors for each portfolio and each forecast are computed as described in the appendix. The standard errors are then aggregated by market into histograms. If the standard errors were independent and followed a standard normal distribution, we would expect 19 out of 20 to fall in the interval $[-2,2]$, so that the bars in the unshaded region at the centre of each panel would account for 95% of the observations. As explained in the appendix, the assumptions of independence and normality are out of reach, so the $[-2,2]$ interval is only a guide intended to facilitate comparison. All else being equal, a model is preferred if its distribution of standard errors is more centred and more concentrated in the interval $[-2,2]$.

The baseline accuracy tests span the 10-year out-of-sample period of April 2000–December 2009. This period includes two turbulent regimes, the Internet bubble (2000–2) and the financial crisis of 2007–9, as well as the low-volatility bull market fuelled by the US housing

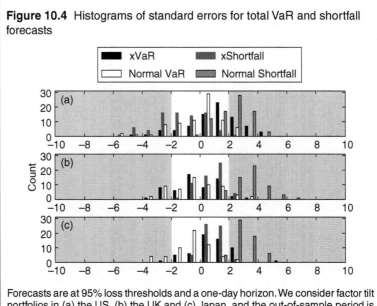

Figure 10.4 Histograms of standard errors for total VaR and shortfall forecasts

Forecasts are at 95% loss thresholds and a one-day horizon. We consider factor tilt portfolios in (a) the US, (b) the UK and (c) Japan, and the out-of-sample period is April 2000–December 2009. Relative to BxR, the conditional normal model tends to underforecast shortfall.

bubble (2003–6). In the next section we first evaluate both total risk forecasts of the tilt portfolios and their active risk against a benchmark before considering a breakdown by regime. Analogous studies are made for the pair portfolios.

RESULTS
Total and active risk of tilt portfolios

Figures 10.4–10.6 display histograms of standard errors corresponding to VaR and shortfall forecasts for factor tilt portfolios. Figure 10.4 concerns total risk in the loss tail, Figure 10.5 concerns total risk in the gain tail and Figure 10.6 concerns active risk in the loss tail.

In each figure, panels (a)–(c) correspond to the US, UK and Japan markets, respectively. Across the nine panels, the conditional normal shortfall and gain histograms are consistently shifted to the right, indicating a bias towards underforecasting. To a lesser extent, there is a tendency to underforecast the loss (VaR) and gain thresholds in both models. BxR shows a slight tendency to overforecast total shortfall in the US. This is analysed further in the next subsection.

Figure 10.5 Histograms of standard errors for gain threshold and gain forecasts

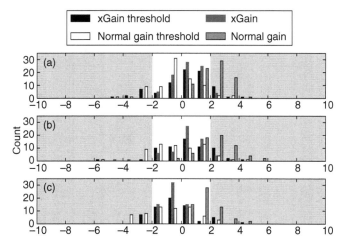

Forecasts are at 95% gain thresholds and a one-day horizon. We consider factor tilt portfolios in (a) the US, (b) the UK and (c) Japan, and the out-of-sample period is April 2000–December 2009. For several portfolios, the gain threshold is substantially underforecast by both models.

Figure 10.6 Histograms of standard errors for active VaR and shortfall of factor tilt portfolios against market benchmarks

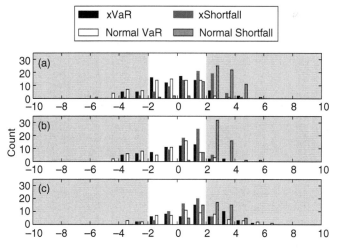

Forecasts are at 95% loss thresholds and a one-day horizon. We consider active factor tilt portfolios in (a) the US, (b) the UK and (c) Japan, and the out-of-sample period is April 2000–December 2009. Relative to BxR, the conditional normal model tends to underforecast shortfall.

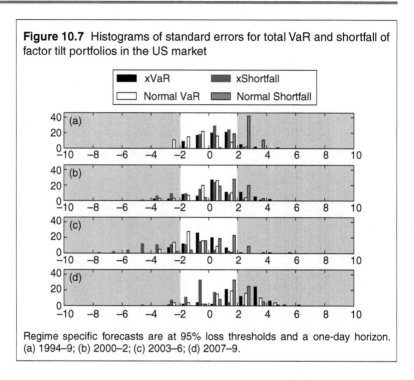

Figure 10.7 Histograms of standard errors for total VaR and shortfall of factor tilt portfolios in the US market

Regime specific forecasts are at 95% loss thresholds and a one-day horizon. (a) 1994–9; (b) 2000–2; (c) 2003–6; (d) 2007–9.

TOTAL RISK OF TILT PORTFOLIOS BY REGIME

Figures 10.7–10.9 evaluate forecasts of VaR and shortfall for tilt portfolios in different regimes in the US, UK and Japan markets: the Internet bubble (April 2000–December 2002), the low-volatility bull market (January 2003–December 2006) and the financial crisis (January 2007–December 2009). As in the previous examples, the conditional normal model shows a pronounced bias towards underforecasting shortfall, and both models tend to overforecast VaR to a lesser extent.

Notably, BxR overforecasts shortfall in the US market during the bull market, while the conditional normal model slightly underforecasts shortfall. This is an exceptional case: the profile of centred BxR histograms and biased conditional normal forecasts of extreme risk persists during the bull market in the UK and Japan markets. Furthermore, as shown in Figure 10.7(a), this profile is also obtained in the US for an earlier, low-volatility regime, January 1994–December 1999.[2] The source of the exception may be explained by Figure 10.10, which shows 40-year histories of daily returns to the Japan, UK and US markets. Relative to other calm regimes in the three markets

FORECASTING EXTREME RISK OF EQUITY PORTFOLIOS WITH FUNDAMENTAL FACTORS

Figure 10.8 Histograms of standard errors for total VaR and shortfall of factor tilt portfolios in the UK market

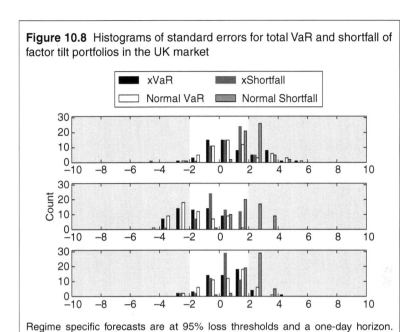

Regime specific forecasts are at 95% loss thresholds and a one-day horizon. (a) 2000–2; (c) 2003–6; (d) 2007–9.

Figure 10.9 Histograms of standard errors for total VaR and shortfall of factor tilt portfolios in the Japan market

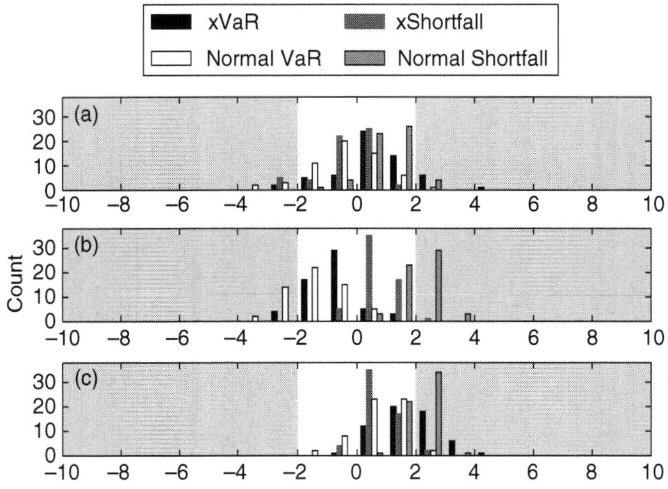

Regime specific forecasts are at 95% loss thresholds and a one-day horizon. (a) 2000–2; (c) 2003–6; (d) 2007–9.

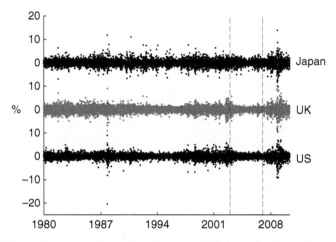

Figure 10.10 Time series of daily returns to three developed markets during the period January 1980–April 2010

Volatility regimes, extreme events and asymmetry between losses and gains are evident. Outliers can be observed in most periods of low volatility. A notable exception is the housing bubble in the US market, January 2003–December 2006 (between dashed lines), which had relatively few outliers.

shown, returns to the US market between January 2003 and December 2006 exhibit an unusually high degree of symmetry and relatively few outliers. In other words, this period in US history seems to be more "normal" than usual.

PAIR PORTFOLIOS

The standard error histograms in Figure 10.11 correspond to pair portfolios in the US, UK and Japan markets. Unlike tilt portfolios, pair portfolios tend to be dominated by idiosyncratic risk, so the accuracy of specific risk forecasts is under scrutiny in this final set of tests. As in all previous evaluations, the conditional normal model shows a pronounced bias towards underforecasting shortfall.

CONCLUSION

> Those who cannot remember the past are condemned to repeat it.
> Santayana, *The Life of Reason*, Volume 1

Variations on Santayana's sentiment have appeared in numerous *post mortem* analyses of the 2007–9 financial crisis. This is both a

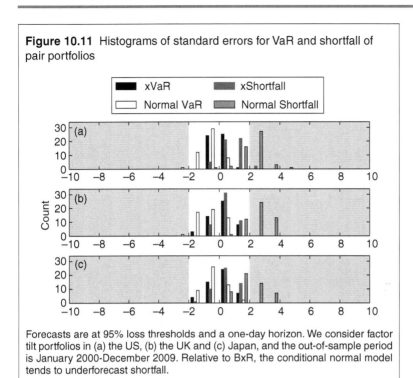

Figure 10.11 Histograms of standard errors for VaR and shortfall of pair portfolios

Forecasts are at 95% loss thresholds and a one-day horizon. We consider factor tilt portfolios in (a) the US, (b) the UK and (c) Japan, and the out-of-sample period is January 2000-December 2009. Relative to BxR, the conditional normal model tends to underforecast shortfall.

philosophical and a practical point: long histories of data, suitably modified to reflect the current market, are a crucial ingredient of extreme risk forecasts, as they satisfy the stringent data requirements of extreme risk while obviating extrapolation.

This chapter has shown that forecasts informed by a long view of history are more consistent with market behaviour than those extrapolated from a normal distribution. Under a wide range of market conditions and for a broad class of portfolios, the conditional normal model underforecasts extreme risk compared with BxR. This result is consistent with the observation that extreme events are much more commonplace in financial markets than in a world of normally distributed returns.

These results open the door to applications of extreme risk analysis in the investment process. Shortfall and gain can shed light on aspects of financial risk that may be neglected by volatility. Institutional investors can use extreme risk measures to help allocate economic capital, to better construct and optimise portfolios, and to reveal investment opportunities and hedges.

APPENDIX: MEASURING FORECAST ACCURACY

For each portfolio, define a time series z_t as the difference between shortfall forecasts s_t and realised losses L_t

$$z_t = s_t - L_t \qquad (10.4)$$

The standard error of the portfolio is the mean of z_t over the τ periods when the realised loss exceeds a VaR threshold, normalised by standard deviation

$$z = \frac{1}{\sigma\sqrt{\tau}} \sum_{\{t|L_t > \text{loss threshold}\}} z_t \qquad (10.5)$$

The parameter σ is approximated by the sample standard deviation of z over τ. Formula 10.5 is in the form of a standard error, but its distributional properties are unknown. Two subtleties related to the interpretation of the standard errors are discussed next.

First, the number of periods when the realised loss L_t exceeds the loss threshold (VaR) is much smaller than the total number of periods T. Consider a relatively data-rich situation in which there are $T = 2,500$ realisations and forecasts. This represents an out-of-sample period consisting of 10 years of daily data. For the modest goal of assessing an extreme risk forecast at the 99% confidence level, z is based on approximately 25 data points. This small sample may undermine the standard confidence interval of $[-2,2]$, which is based on assumptions of independence and normality.[3] Therefore, it is difficult to assess the accuracy of extreme forecasts for a particular model, although it is possible to make meaningful comparisons between models as in the section describing our results.

Second, the definition of z depends on the forecast loss threshold (VaR). The evaluation of shortfall is thereby contingent on the accuracy of the associated VaR forecast. Value-at-risk accuracy can be measured using the Kupiec statistic. Over the T periods for which there are realisations and forecasts, compute the fraction of violations, $\hat{v}$, when the realisation exceeds the VaR forecast. If the confidence level is p, then the expected value of $\hat{v}$ is equal to $v = (100 - p)/100$, and the statistic

$$z = \frac{T - (\hat{v} - v)}{\sqrt{T \cdot v \cdot (1-v)}} \qquad (10.6)$$

is binomially distributed and scaled to have mean zero and standard deviation 1. For moderate values of T, the binomial converges rapidly to the normal, so the confidence interval is approximated by the normal confidence interval.

The authors thank Jeff Knight for his valuable editorial feedback on this chapter.

1   Goldberg and Hayes (2010) highlight the significant benefits of convex measures, such as shortfall and gain, over their non-convex thresholds (eg, value-at-risk). Unlike value-at-risk (VaR), shortfall and gain lead to relatively simple and transparent optimisation, and they never penalise diversification.

2   In this study (as in all others concerning the US), the factor return history begins in January 1981. Unlike the other studies, the specific return history begins in January 1994.

3   The guideline is based on finite variance versions of the Central Limit Theorem, and for many reasons it may fail even for a sample that is much larger than 25. This point and its relevance to the accuracy of financial forecasts are discussed in Barbieri *et al* (2010).

REFERENCES

Barbieri, A., K. Chang, V. Dubikovsky, J. Fox, A. Gladkevich, C. Gold and L. Goldberg, 2009, "Modeling Value at Risk with Factors", MSCI Barra Research Paper 2009-39.

Barbieri, A., V. Dubikovsky, A. Gladkevich, L. R. Goldberg and M. Y. Hayes, 2010, "Central Limits and Financial Risk", *Quantitative Finance*, in press.

Bender, J., J.-H. Lee and D. Stefek, 2010, "Constraining Shortfall", MSCI Barra Research Paper 2010-15.

Bertsimas, D., G. J. Lauprete and A. Samarov, 2004, "Shortfall as a Risk Measure: Properties, Optimization and Applications", *Journal of Economic Dynamics and Control* 28, pp. 1353–81.

Goldberg, L. R., and M. Y. Hayes, 2010, "The Long View of Financial Risk", *Journal of Investment Management*, First Quarter.

Goldberg, L. R., M. Y. Hayes, J. Menchero and I. Mitra, 2010, "Extreme Risk Analysis", *Journal of Performance Measurement*, Spring.

Hayes, M. Y., and J. Knight, 2010, "The BxR Analytics Guide", MSCI Barra Extreme Risk Documentation.

Kondor, I., S. Pafka and G. Nagy, 2007, "Noise Sensitivity of Portfolio Selection under Various Risk Measures", *Journal of Banking and Finance* 31, pp. 1545–73.

Mandelbrot, B., 1963. "The Variation of Certain Speculative Prices", *Journal of Business* 36, pp. 394–419.

Pafka, S., and I. Kondor, 2001, "Evaluating the RiskMetrics Methodology in Measuring Volatility and Value-at-Risk in Financial Markets", *Physica* A 299, pp. 305–10.

Rockafellar, R. T., and S. Uryasev, 2000, "Optimization of Conditional Value-at-Risk", *The Journal of Risk* 2, pp. 493–517.

Rockafellar, R. T., and S. Uryasev, 2002, "Conditional Value-at-Risk for General Loss Distributions", *Journal of Banking and Finance* 26, pp. 1443–71.

Sheikh, A. Z., and H. Qiao, 2009, "Non-Normality of Market Returns: A Framework for Asset Allocation Decision Making", Advisory Paper, J. P. Morgan Asset Management.

Part IV

Quantitative Modelling

11

Limits of Implied Credit Correlation Metrics Before and During the Crisis

Damiano Brigo; Andrea Pallavicini; Roberto Torresetti
King's College London; Banca Leonardo; Quaestio Capital Management

In this chapter we analyse the limits of popular models or pseudo-models (mostly quoting mechanisms) that in the past have been extensively used to mark-to-market and risk manage multi-name credit derivatives. This chapter presents a compendium of results we first published before the crisis, back in 2006, pointing out the dangers in the modelling paradigms used at the time in the market, and showing how the situation has even worsened subsequently by analysing more recent data. The analysis also points out that the current paradigm had been heavily criticised before the crisis, referring to works by us and other authors addressing the main limitations of the current market paradigm well before popular accounts such as Salmon (2009), Jones (2009) and Lohr (2009) appeared.

We will present a comparison of how a selected set of credit derivatives models fared before and during the crisis, pointing to the fact that the problems plaguing both compound and base implied correlation worsened with the advent of the credit crunch.

To develop the above comparison, we first introduce the Gaussian copula, which represents a common way to introduce dependence in credit derivatives modelling. Typically, a Gaussian copula is postulated on the exponential random variables triggering defaults of the pool names according to first jumps of Poisson processes. We cannot do justice to the huge copula literature in credit derivatives here. We only mention that there have been attempts to go beyond the Gaussian copula introduced in the collateralised debt obligations (CDOs) world by Li (2000) and leading to the implied (base and compound) correlation framework, some important limits of which have been pointed out in Torresetti et al (2006b). Li and Hong Liang (2005) also proposed a mixture approach in connection with CDO squared. For results on sensitivities computed with the Gaussian copula models see, for example, Meng and Sengupta (2008). One of the key problems of the copula approach is that it cannot be extended in a simple way to a fully dynamical model in general.

An alternative to copulas is to insert dependence among the default intensities of single names.[1] Joshi and Stacey (2006) resort to modelling business time to create default correlation in otherwise independent single names defaults, using an "intensity gamma" framework. Similarly, but in a firm value-inspired context, Baxter (2007) introduces Lévy firm value processes for CDO calibration.

Albanese et al (2006) introduce an approach, based on structural model ideas, that can be made consistent with several inputs under both the historical and pricing measures and that succeeds in calibrating CDO tranches.

The models above are bottom-up models, in that they model single default times and connect them through some dependence structure, as opposed to top-down models, ie, models that start by modelling the loss as an aggregate object.

In this chapter, building on Torresetti et al (2006b), we start with the net present value (NPV) of synthetic CDO tranches on pools of corporate credit references in its original layout: the compound correlation framework. We highlight the three main problems of this approach, namely the non-invertibility of a number of tranches both before and during the crisis, the flattening of 7,750 possibly different pairwise correlation parameters into a single one for each tranche and the typical non-smooth behaviour of the compound correlation, making interpolation for pricing bespoke (non-standard attachment–detachment) CDO tranches rather difficult.

We then introduce the next step the industry took,[2] namely the introduction of base correlation, as a solution to problems in compound correlation given the fact that the resulting map is much smoother (thus facilitating the pricing of bespoke tranche spreads from liquid index tranches) and, until early 2008, the heterogeneous pool one-factor Gaussian copula base correlation had been consistently invertible from index market tranche spreads.

Nevertheless, we expose some of the known remaining weaknesses of the base correlation framework, namely that, depending on the interpolation technique being used, tranche spreads could not be arbitrage free. In fact, for senior tranches it may well be that the expected tranche loss plotted versus time is initially decreasing. Moreover, inverting correlation for senior and super senior tranches is often impossible, and finally we have the related inconsistency at single-tranche valuation level, where two components of the same trade are valued with models having two different parameter values. The 7,750-into-1 parameter flattening also remains a problem.

We then abandon base correlation and summarise the concept of "implied copula", introduced by Hull and White (2006) as the "perfect copula". This is a non-parametric model that can be used to deduce the shape of the risk-neutral pool loss distribution from a set of market CDO spreads spanning the entire capital structure. We applied this model in Torresetti *et al* (2006c) to compare the risk-neutral and physical/historical distributions of default rates in the iTraxx Index. The general use of flexible systemic factors was later generalised and improved by Rosen and Saunders (2009), who also discuss the dynamic implications of the systemic factor framework. In the context of one-factor models with a more econometric flavour, Berd *et al* (2007) interpret the latent factor as the market return governed by an asymmetric Garch model, and introduce the implied correlation surface as a mapping between the given loss-generating model and a Gaussian benchmark.

We then introduce a model-independent approach to CDO tranche pricing and interpolation where expected tranche losses (ETLs) for different detachment points and maturities can be viewed as the building blocks on which synthetic CDO formulas' components are built with linear operations. We explain in detail how the payouts of credit indexes and tranches are valued in terms of ETLs. This methodology, first illustrated (pre-crisis) in Torresetti *et al* (2006a), is reminiscent of Walker's (2006) earlier work and of the formal analysis of the properties of expected tranche loss in connection with no arbitrage in Livesey and Schlögl (2006).

We also mention some further references which appeared later and deal with the evolution of this technique: Parcell and Wood (2007) consider carefully the impact (again pre-crisis) of different kinds of interpolation, whereas Garcia and Goossens (2007) compare ETLs between the Gaussian copula and Lévy models.

Finally, we will present the "in-crisis" performance of the various models analysed pre-crisis: implied correlation, implied copula and expected tranche loss surface.

We close here by mentioning our earlier articles and recent book, namely Brigo et al (2006a,b, 2007, 2010) and Torresetti and Pallavicini (forthcoming), for further discussion, results and references regarding dynamical loss models that achieve consistent pricing of CDO tranches with different attachments and maturities, surpassing the limits highlighted here for the Gaussian copula.

MARKET QUOTES

For single names our reference products will be credit default swaps (CDSs).

The most liquid multi-name credit instruments available in the market are instead credit indexes and CDO tranches (eg, DJ-iTraxx, CDX). We discuss them in the following.

The index is given by a pool of names $1, 2, \ldots, M$, typically $M = 125$, each with notional $1/M$ so that the total pool has unitary notional. The index default leg consists of protection payments corresponding to the defaulted names of the pool. Each time one or more names default, the corresponding loss increment is paid to the protection buyer, until final maturity $T = T_b$ arrives or until all the names in the pool have defaulted.

In exchange for loss increase payments, a periodic premium with rate S is paid from the protection buyer to the protection seller, say at times $T_1, T_2, \ldots, T_b = T$, until final maturity T_b. This premium is computed on a notional that decreases each time a name in the pool defaults, and decreases by an amount corresponding to the notional of that name.

We denote by $\bar{L}_t$ the portfolio cumulated loss and by $\bar{C}_t$ the number of defaulted names up to time t divided by M. Since at each default part of the defaulted notional is recovered, we have $0 \leqslant d\bar{L}_t \leqslant d\bar{C}_t \leqslant 1$. The discounted payout of the two legs of the index is given as follows

$$\text{DefLeg}(0) := \int_0^T D(0,t)\, d\bar{L}_t$$

$$\text{PremLeg}(0) = S_0 \sum_{i=1}^{b} \delta_i D(0, T_i)(1 - \bar{C}_{T_i})$$

where $D(s,t)$ is the discount factor (often assumed to be deterministic) between times s and t and $\delta_i = T_i - T_{i-1}$ is the year fraction. In the second equation the actual outstanding notional in each period would be an average over $[T_{i-1}, T_i]$, but we have replaced it with the value of the outstanding notional at T_i for simplicity.

The market quotes the values of S_0 that, for different maturities, balances the two legs. Assuming deterministic default-free interest rates, if we have a model for the loss and the number of defaults, we may require that the loss and number of defaults in the model, when plugged into the two legs, lead to the same risk-neutral expectation (and thus price)

$$S_0 = \frac{\int_0^T D(0,t)\, d\mathbb{E}_0[\bar{L}_t]}{\sum_{i=1}^{b} \delta_i D(0, T_i)(1 - \mathbb{E}_0[\bar{C}_{T_i}])} \tag{11.1}$$

Synthetic CDO with maturity T are contracts involving a protection buyer, a protection seller and an underlying pool of names. They are obtained by "tranching" the loss of the pool between the points A and B, with $0 \leqslant A < B \leqslant 1$

$$\bar{L}_t^{A,B} := \frac{1}{B-A}[(\bar{L}_t - A)\mathbf{1}_{\{A<\bar{L}_t\leqslant B\}} + (B-A)\mathbf{1}_{\{\bar{L}_t>B\}}]$$

An alternative expression that is useful is

$$\bar{L}_t^{A,B} := \frac{1}{B-A}[B\bar{L}_t^{0,B} - A\bar{L}_t^{0,A}] \tag{11.2}$$

Once enough names have defaulted and the loss has reached A, the count starts. Each time the loss increases, the corresponding loss change re-scaled by the tranche thickness $B - A$ is paid to the protection buyer, until maturity or until the total pool loss exceeds B, in which case the payments stop.

The discounted default leg payout can then be written as

$$\text{DefLeg}_{A,B}(0) := \int_0^T D(0,t)\, d\bar{L}_t^{A,B}$$

As usual, in exchange for the protection payments, a premium rate $S_0^{A,B}$, fixed at time $T_0 = 0$, is paid periodically. Part of the premium can be paid at time $T_0 = 0$ as an upfront $U_0^{A,B}$. The rate is paid on the "surviving" average tranche notional. If we further assume payments are made on the notional remaining at each payment date T_i, rather than on the average in $[T_{i-1}, T_i]$, the premium leg can be written as

$$\text{PremLeg}_{A,B}(0) := U_0^{A,B} + S_0^{A,B}\,\text{DV01}_{A,B}(0)$$

$$\text{DV01}_{A,B}(0) := \sum_{i=1}^{b} \delta_i D(0, T_i)(1 - \bar{L}_{T_i}^{A,B})$$

When pricing CDO tranches, we are interested in the premium rate $S_0^{A,B}$ that sets to zero the risk-neutral price of the tranche. The tranche value is computed taking the (risk-neutral) expectation (in $t = 0$) of the discounted payout consisting of the difference between the default and premium legs above. Assuming deterministic default-free interest rates, we obtain

$$S_0^{A,B} = \frac{\int_0^T D(0,t)\,d\mathbb{E}_0[L_t^{A,B}] - U_0^{A,B}}{\sum_{i=1}^{b} \delta_i D(0, T_i)(1 - \mathbb{E}_0[\bar{L}_{T_i}^{A,B}])} \qquad (11.3)$$

The above expression can be easily recast in terms of the upfront premium $U_0^{A,B}$ for tranches that are quoted in terms of upfront fees.[3]

GAUSSIAN COPULA MODEL

The Gaussian copula model is a possible way to model dependence of random variables and, in our case, of default times. As the default event of a credit reference is a random binary variable, the correlation between default events is not an intuitive object to handle. Rather, we need to focus our attention on default times. We denote by τ_i the default time of name i in a pool of M names. Default times of different names need to be connected. The copula formalism allows us to do this.

Indeed, if $p_i(t) = \mathbb{Q}\{\tau_i \leqslant t\}$ is the default probability of name i by time t, we know that the random variable $p_i(\tau_i) = U_i$ is a uniform random variable. Copulas are multivariate distributions on uniform random variables. If we call $C(u_1, \ldots, u_n)$ a multivariate uniform distribution, and $U_1, \ldots, U_M$ is a multivariate uniform with distribution C, then a possible multivariate distribution of the default times with marginals p_i is

$$\tau_1 := p_1^{-1}(U_1), \ldots, \tau_M := p_M^{-1}(U_M)$$

where for simplicity we assume the p are strictly invertible. Clearly, since the $U_1, \ldots, U_M$ variables are connected through a multivariate distribution C, we have a dependence structure on the default times.

The Gaussian copula enters the picture when we assume that

$$[U_1, \ldots, U_M] = [\Phi(X_1), \ldots, \Phi(X_M)]$$

where the X_i are standard Gaussian random variables and $[X_1, \ldots, X_M]$ is a given multivariate Gaussian random variable with a given correlation matrix. Φ is the cumulative distribution function of the one-dimensional standard Gaussian. In the Gaussian copula model the default times are therefore linked via normally distributed latent factors X.

A particular structure is assumed for the default probabilities p_i. The default probabilities of single names are supposed to be related to hazard rates λ. In other terms

$$p_i(t) = 1 - \exp\left(-\int_0^t \lambda_i(s)\,ds\right)$$

We define

$$\Lambda_i(t) := \int_0^t \lambda_i(s)\,ds$$

$S_0^{A,B}$ (spread) or $U_0^{A,B}$ (upfront) would be provided by the market and a correlation number ρ characterising a Gaussian copula with a correlation matrix where all entries are equal to ρ (in this case we will say the correlation matrix is "flat to ρ") would be implied from the market quote. Indeed, Formula 11.3 defined the market quotes in terms of expectations of the tranched loss $\bar{L}^{A,B}$; in turn, the loss to be tranched at a given time is defined in terms of single default times as

$$\bar{L}_t = \sum_{i=1}^M \frac{1}{M}(1-R_i)\mathbf{1}_{\{\tau_i \leqslant t\}} = \sum_{i=1}^M \frac{1}{M}(1-R_i)\mathbf{1}_{\{\Phi(X_i) \leqslant p_i(t)\}} \quad (11.4)$$

where the X_i are multivariate Gaussian random variables with correlation matrix flat to ρ and R_i are the recovery rates associated to each name.

The correlation parameter ρ is therefore affecting the tranche price, since it is a key statistical parameter contributing to the tranched loss distribution whose expectation will be used in matching the market quote.

We will first introduce the general one-factor Gaussian copula model. Then we will introduce the finite pool (where M is finite) homogeneous ($p_1 = p_2 = \cdots = p_M$ and $R_1 = R_2 = \cdots = R_M$) one-factor Gaussian copula model. We will show how the loss probability formulas can be computed in this case.

In this chapter we stay with the homogeneous version, since this is enough to highlight some of the key flaws of implied correlation, and leave the detailed derivation of the formulas for the heterogeneous and large pool versions to Brigo et al (2010). Note that in practice, due to the necessity of computing hedge rations with respect to single names, the heterogeneous version is used, even if spread dispersion across names, leading possibly to very different p_i values, complicates matters.

One-factor Gaussian copula model

A one-factor copula structure is a special case of the Gaussian copula above where

$$X_i = \sqrt{\rho_i}S + \sqrt{1 - \rho_i}Y_i$$

where Y_i and S are standard independent Gaussian variables. S is a systemic factor affecting default times of all names. Y_i is an idiosyncratic factor affecting just the ith name. ρ_i are non-negative and less than or equal to 1.

This parameterisation would lead to a correlation between Gaussian factors X_i and X_j given by $\sqrt{\rho_i \rho_j}$. However, consistent with the flat correlation assumption and the homogeneity assumption, all pairwise correlation parameters collapse to a single common value, ie, $\rho_i = \rho$ for all i.

Assuming the deterministic and possibly distinct recovery rate R_i upon default, we are able to simulate the pool loss at any time t starting from the simulation of the Gaussian variables X_i starting from Equation 11.4.

Thus, we are able to simulate the NPV of the premium and default leg of any tranche.

Calculating the NPV of a derivative instrument via simulations can be necessary but may lead to intensive numerical effort. Introducing the assumption of homogeneity, it turns out that the Gaussian copula model yields a semi-analytical formula to calculate the distribution of the pool loss.

Assume we know the realisation of the systemic factor S. In this case, conditional on S, the default events of the pool of credit references are independent. The default by time T conditional on the realisation of the systemic factor S of each single credit reference in the pool is a Bernoulli random variable with the same event probability of default

$$\mathbb{Q}\{\tau_i < T \mid S\} = \mathbb{Q}\{X_i < \Phi^{-1}(p_i(T)) \mid S\}$$
$$= \Phi\left(\frac{\Phi^{-1}(1 - \exp(-\Lambda(T))) - \sqrt{\rho}S}{\sqrt{1-\rho}}\right)$$

The number of defaulted entities in the pool by time T conditional on the realisation of the systemic factor S is the sum of M independent identically distributed Bernoulli variables and thus is binomially distributed

$$\mathbb{Q}\left\{\bar{C}_T = \frac{n}{M} \mid S\right\}$$
$$= \frac{M!}{n!(M-n)!}\mathbb{Q}\{\tau_i < T \mid S\}^n(1 - \mathbb{Q}\{\tau_i < T \mid S\})^{M-n} \quad (11.5)$$

where we point out that the $\mathbb{Q}\{\tau_i < T \mid S\}$ are the same for all i, since we are dealing with a homogeneous pool assumption.

We can now integrate the expression in Equation 11.5 to get the unconditional probability of n defaults occurring in the standardised pool of M credit references before time T, leading to

$$\mathbb{Q}\left\{\bar{L}_T = (1-R)\frac{n}{M}\right\} = \int_{-\infty}^{+\infty} \mathbb{Q}\left\{\bar{C}_T = \frac{n}{M} \mid S\right\}\varphi(S)\,dS \quad (11.6)$$

By computing the integral in Equation 11.6 for $n = 1,\ldots,M$ we obtain the unconditional distribution of the pool loss rate that we need in order to compute the theoretical tranche spread $S_0^{A,B}$ (or upfront $U_0^{A,B}$) in Equation 11.3.

The integral in Equation 11.6 does not allow for a closed-form solution, whereas all other quantities can be calculated analytically. Hence, the name "semi-analytical" (analytical up to the calculation of the integral) for the finite-pool homogeneous one-factor Gaussian copula model formula for theoretical tranche spread in Equation 11.3.

Compound correlation

Compound correlation is a first paradigm for implying credit default dependence from liquid market data. This approach consists in linking defaults across single names through a Gaussian copula where all the correlation parameters are collapsed to one parameter.

Given this correlation parameter and the desired declination of the one-factor Gaussian copula, we can compute the loss distribution on a given set of dates. Thus, we can compute the expectations contained in Equation 11.3, and with them the fair tranche spread.

A key step that will allow us to distinguish compound from base correlation is the decomposition of the tranche loss according to Equation 11.2. Since the default leg and premium leg (in particular the dollar value of a basis point (DV01)) defining Equation 11.3 are linear in the tranched loss $\bar{L}_t^{A,B}$, by Equation 11.2 this becomes linear in base tranched losses $\bar{L}_t^{0,B}$ and $\bar{L}_t^{0,A}$.

Now one key step is that, when we evaluate the expected $\bar{L}_t^{A,B}$ through Equation 11.2, we can use two different copula correlations for the two pieces $\bar{L}_t^{0,A}$ (correlation ρ_A) and $\bar{L}_t^{0,B}$ (correlation ρ_B). As a consequence, the final formula reads

$$\mathbb{E}_0[\bar{L}_t^{A,B}](\rho_A, \rho_B) := \frac{1}{B-A}[B\mathbb{E}_0[\bar{L}_t^{0,B}](\rho_B) - A\mathbb{E}_0[\bar{L}_t^{0,A}](\rho_A)]] \quad (11.7)$$

A similar decomposition holds for the DV01, which is a linear combination of such objects.

Consider the DJ-iTraxx tranches, for example, to clarify the procedure. For a given maturity in 3, 5, 7 or 10 years, consider the market quotes

$$U^{0,3\% \text{ Mkt}} + 500\text{bp running}, \quad S^{3,6\% \text{ Mkt}}, S^{6,9\% \text{ Mkt}}, S^{9,12\% \text{ Mkt}}, S^{12,22\% \text{ Mkt}}$$

To obtain the implied correlation we proceed as follows.

First solve in $\rho_{3\%}$ for the equity tranche

$$\text{DefLeg}_{0,3\%}(0, \rho_3, \rho_3) = 500\text{bp DV01}_{0,3}(0, \rho_3, \rho_3) + U^{0,3\% \text{ Mkt}}$$

Then, in moving on, we have two choices: retain ρ_3 from the earlier tranche calibration and solve

$$\text{DefLeg}_{3,6}(0, \rho_3, \rho_6) = S^{3,6\% \text{ Mkt}} \text{DV01}_{3,6}(0, \rho_3, \rho_6)$$

in ρ_6 (base correlation) or solve

$$\text{DefLeg}_{3,6}(0, \bar{\rho}_{3,6}, \bar{\rho}_{3,6}) = S^{3,6\% \text{ Mkt}} \text{DV01}_{3,6}(0, \bar{\rho}_{3,6}, \bar{\rho}_{3,6})$$

in a new $\bar{\rho}_{3,6}$ (compound correlation). The next step will again be similar, and we iterate until we reach the end of the capital structure.

Compound correlation is more consistent at the single-tranche level, since we value the whole payout of the tranche premium and default legs with one single copula (model) with parameter $\bar{\rho}_{3,6}$.

Table 11.1 DJ-iTraxx Europe S5 10-year tranche quotes on August 3, 2005

Tranche (%)	Running (bp)	Upfront (%)
0–3	500	49
3–6	360	0
6–9	82	0
9–12	46	0
12–22	31	0

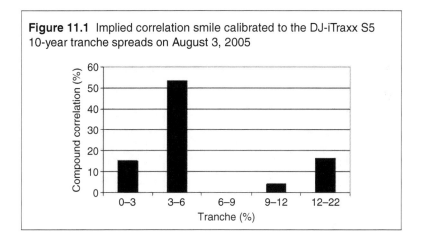

Figure 11.1 Implied correlation smile calibrated to the DJ-iTraxx S5 10-year tranche spreads on August 3, 2005

Base correlation is inconsistent at the single-tranche level: we value different parts of the same payout with different models, ie, part of the payout (involving $L_{0,3}$) is valued with a copula in ρ_3, while a different part (involving $L_{0,6}$) of the same payout is valued with a copula in ρ_6.

We shall focus on implications for base correlation later on, and now deal with compound correlation. The market data we take as inputs is detailed in Table 11.1. The equity tranche is quoted up front (0.49 means 49%) and all other tranches are quoted in number of running basis points (360 means 3.60% per annum). In Figure 11.1 we present the compound correlation smile we imply from this set of market data. We notice that there is no bar corresponding to the 6–9% tranche: from the market spread of the tranche we cannot infer a compound correlation. We see in the following how this problem is not atypical, and the reason why this problem surfaces is illustrated

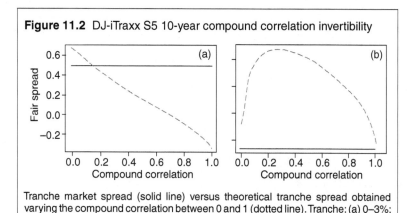

Figure 11.2 DJ-iTraxx S5 10-year compound correlation invertibility

Tranche market spread (solid line) versus theoretical tranche spread obtained varying the compound correlation between 0 and 1 (dotted line). Tranche: (a) 0–3%; (b) 6–9%.

in Figure 11.2. The solid horizontal line is the level of the market spread.

Further, we notice that

- for certain tranches, from the unique market spread we can imply more than one compound correlation, although this does not happen in our example of Figure 11.2, where the solid line crosses the dotted line at most at one point,

- given a market spread, we are not always guaranteed that we can infer a compound correlation, as we see, for example, in the 6–9% tranche of Figure 11.2 (there is no intersection between the solid line and the dotted line).

We have seen that on August 3, 2005, we cannot infer a compound correlation for the 6–9% tranche. In Figure 11.3, taken from Torresetti *et al* (2006b), we see how this problem is not limited to a sporadic set of dates but, rather, is affecting clusters of dates.

From March 2005 to November 2006 (the sample on which the analysis in Torresetti *et al* (2006b) is based), the non-invertibility of the compound correlation concerned the 10-year 6–9% tranche for DJ-iTraxx, and the 10-year 7–10% tranche and, marginally, the 10-year 10–15% for CDX.

Base correlation

Here we will illustrate base correlation and we will see how compound correlation problems are overcome but at the expense of introducing a deeper inconsistency.

LIMITS OF IMPLIED CREDIT CORRELATION METRICS

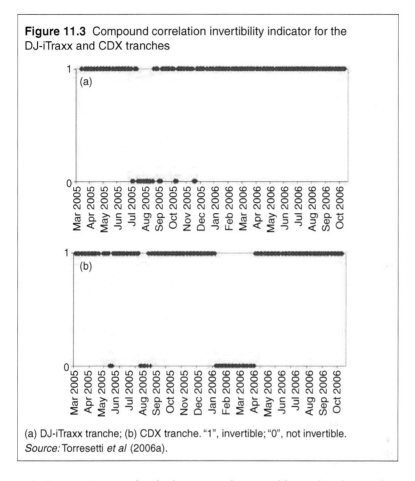

Figure 11.3 Compound correlation invertibility indicator for the DJ-iTraxx and CDX tranches

(a) DJ-iTraxx tranche; (b) CDX tranche. "1", invertible; "0", not invertible.
Source: Torresetti *et al* (2006a).

In Figure 11.4 we plot the base correlation calibrated to the market data in Table 11.1 and the expected equity tranche loss for the various detachment points as a function of time

$$\mathbb{E}_0[\bar{L}_t^{0,B}], \quad B = 3\%, 6\%, 9\%, 12\%, 22\%$$

From these expectations, using Equations 11.2, we can compute the expected tranche loss $\mathbb{E}_0[\bar{L}_t^{A,B}]$, plotted in Figure 11.5 as a function of time.

From Figure 11.4 we note that the base correlation is a much smoother function of detachments than compound correlation. Also, to price a non-standard tranche, say a 4–15% tranche, we can interpolate the non-standard attachment 4% and detachment 15%, whereas with the compound correlation we do not know exactly what to

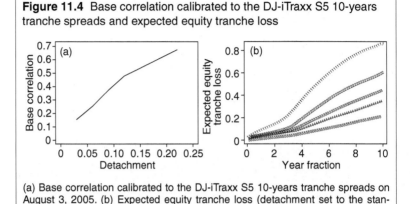

Figure 11.4 Base correlation calibrated to the DJ-iTraxx S5 10-years tranche spreads and expected equity tranche loss

(a) Base correlation calibrated to the DJ-iTraxx S5 10-years tranche spreads on August 3, 2005. (b) Expected equity tranche loss (detachment set to the standardised tranches detachment) corresponding to the calibrated base correlation. 1, 0–3%; 2, 3–6%; 3, 6–9%; 4, 9–12%; 5, 12–22%.

Figure 11.5 Expected tranche loss as a function of time derived from the base correlations calibrated to the DJ-iTraxx S5 10-year tranche spreads on August 3, 2005

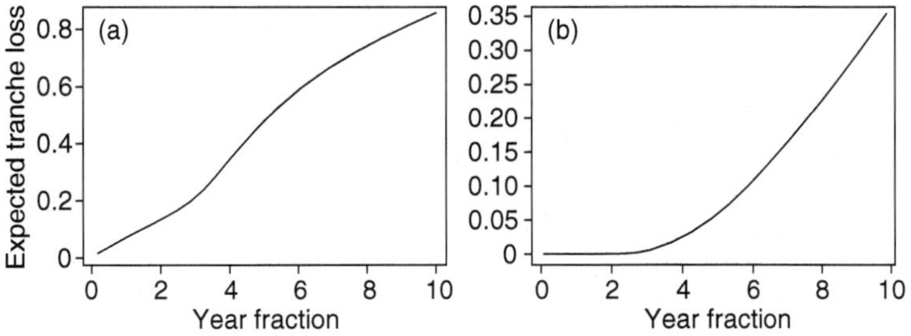

interpolate. Should the 4–15% DJ-iTraxx tranche compound correlation be a weighted average of the 3–6%, 6–9%, 9–12% and 12–22% tranches? Why, and using what weights? This problem stems from the fact that compound correlation is associated with two points rather than a single point.

As we can see from our examples, the base correlation approach is also not immune from inconsistencies. In fact in Figure 11.7 we note that in 2005, taking the 6–9% tranche as an example, the expected tranche loss becomes initially slightly negative. This inconsistency arises from the different base correlations we use in Equation 11.2 to compute the two expected tranche loss terms in A and B.

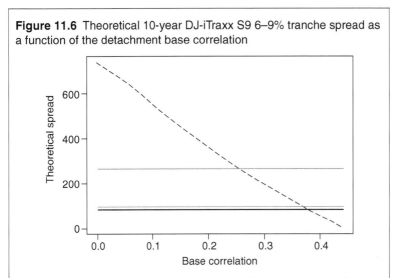

Figure 11.6 Theoretical 10-year DJ-iTraxx S9 6–9% tranche spread as a function of the detachment base correlation

The attachment base correlation (dotted line), market tranche spread (horizontal black line) and minimum and maximum tranche spread invertible from the compound correlation (solid grey lines) are fixed.

Summary on implied correlation

Is base correlation a solution to the problems of compound correlation?

The answer is in the affirmative and this can be clearly seen, for example, in Figure 11.6, where we plot the fair tranche spread as a function of the base correlation on the detachment point for each tranche, given the base correlation on the attachment point set equal to the calibrated base in Figure 11.4(a).

This gives us an idea of the range of the tranche spread we can calibrate using base correlation. The plots of Figure 11.6 are similar to those in Figure 11.2, showing the fair tranche spread as a function of compound correlation. In Figure 11.6 the solid black line is horizontal at the level of the market spread for the tranche. The two grey lines are the minimum and maximum spread we are able to obtain by varying compound correlation.

We note that for each tranche the fair spread is a monotonic function of the base correlation on the detachment point and also that the range of market spreads that can be attained by varying base correlation is much wider than the corresponding one for compound correlation. However, this comes at a price.

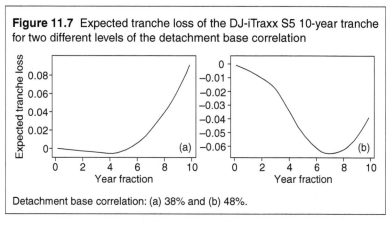

Figure 11.7 Expected tranche loss of the DJ-iTraxx S5 10-year tranche for two different levels of the detachment base correlation

Detachment base correlation: (a) 38% and (b) 48%.

Consider, for example, the 6–9% tranche. In Figure 11.7 we plot in the abscissas the year fraction of the tranche payment dates and in the ordinates the expected tranche (6–9%) loss. For both graphs in Figure 11.7 the tranche attachment correlation is the calibrated base on the 6% detachment. The tranche detachment (9%) correlation is set to the calibrated base in part (a) (38.07%) and to an arbitrarily high level (48%) on the graph in part (b).

We can see a markedly negative profile for the expected tranched loss, which clearly violates the no-arbitrage constraints. Indeed, the loss must be non-negative and non-decreasing in each path through time, and tranching does not alter that. More simply, the tranched loss at a given point in time is a non-negative random variable, and its expected value needs to be non-negative itself. This does not happen in our example, in that the basic non-negativity constraint is violated. This is a strong drawback of the base correlation paradigm at a very basic level.

There are, overall, two major problems with the use of implied correlation as a parameter in a Gaussian copula model as we described it above, even if we are willing to accept the flattening of 7,750 parameters into one: first, the model parameter changes every time we change tranche, implying very different and inconsistent loss distributions on the same pool. Second, there is a total lack of dynamics in the notion of copula. We address the first problem in the next section, showing that the financial literature was trying to overcome such limitations well before the crisis started in 2007. We will not address the second problem here but will rather refer the reader to Brigo *et al* (2006a,b, 2007, 2009, 2010).

CONSISTENCY ACROSS CAPITAL STRUCTURE: IMPLIED COPULA

In the implied-copula approach, a factor-copula structure is assumed, which is similar to the one-factor Gaussian copula approach seen earlier. However, this time we do not model the copula explicitly, but instead model default probabilities conditional on the systemic factor S of the copula. The copula will then be "hidden" inside these conditional probabilities, which will be calibrated to the market; hence the name "implied" copula. In illustrating the implied copula we will also assume a large pool homogeneous model, in that the default probabilities of single names will all be taken equal to each other and the pool of credit references is assumed to be comprised of an infinite number of credit references.

Let us consider, for simplicity, survival probabilities that are associated to a constant-in-time hazard rate. We know that if we have a constant-in-time (possibly random) hazard rate λ for name i, then the survival probability is

$$\mathbb{Q}(\tau_i > t) = \mathbb{E}[\exp(-\lambda t)]$$

The implied-copula approach postulates the following "scenario" distribution for the hazard rate λ conditional on the systemic factor S

$$\lambda \mid S \sim \begin{Bmatrix} \text{Conditional} \\ \text{hazard} & \text{Systemic} & \text{Scenario} \\ \text{rate} & \text{scenario} & \text{probability} \\ \lambda_1 & S = s_1 & p_1 \\ \lambda_2 & S = s_2 & p_2 \\ \vdots & \vdots & \vdots \\ \lambda_h & S = s_h & p_h \end{Bmatrix}$$

This way the default probability for each single name $i = 1, \ldots, M$ is, conditional on the systemic factor S

$$\mathbb{Q}(\tau_i < t \mid S = s_j) = 1 - \exp(-\lambda_j t)$$

Compare this with the Gaussian factor-copula case

$$\mathbb{Q}(\tau_i < T \mid S = s_j) = \Phi\left(\frac{\Phi^{-1}(1 - \exp(-\Lambda(T))) - \sqrt{\rho}s_j}{\sqrt{1-\rho}}\right)$$

Unconditionally, the implied copula yields the default probabilities

$$\mathbb{Q}(\tau_i < t) = \sum_{j=1}^{h} p_j \mathbb{Q}(\tau_i < t \mid S = s_j)$$

$$= \sum_{j=1}^{h} p_j (1 - e^{-\lambda_j t})$$

Conditional on S, all default times are independent, have the same hazard rate and their hazard rates are given by the above scenarios.

By resorting to the infinite pool approximation, fully illustrated in Brigo et al (2010), for the Gaussian factor copula in the LHP version, we have that

$$\bar{C}_T^M(s_j) := \frac{1}{M} \sum_{i=1}^{M} \mathbf{1}_{\{\tau_i < T \mid S = s_j\}} \to \mathbb{E}\mathbf{1}_{\{\tau_i < T \mid S = s_j\}}$$

$$= \mathbb{Q}\{\tau_i < T \mid S = s_j\} = 1 - e^{-\lambda_j T}$$

when M tends to ∞.

This way we avoid taking expectations, except the final one with respect to S, since, conditional on $S = s_j$, all randomness has been ruled out according to the spirit of the law of large numbers: both the pool default rate and the loss are replaced by their expected value.

We will assume, in line with the market convention, that the protection payment will be calculated on the average outstanding notional between any two protection premium payment dates. Conditional on the systemic factor realisation $S = s_j$, the premium leg tranche value will be

$$\text{PremLeg}_{A,B}^j := U_0^{A,B} + S_0^{A,B} \, \text{DV01}_{A,B}^j$$

$$\text{DV01}_{A,B}^j := \sum_{i=1}^{b} \delta_i D(0, T_i)(1 - L(0.5(T_i + T_{i-1}))_{A,B}^j)$$

$$L(t)_{A,B}^j := \frac{\min(B - A, \max(((1 - R_j)(1 - \exp(-\lambda_j t)) - A, 0))}{B - A}$$

where $U_0^{A,B}$ and $S_0^{A,B}$ are the market mid upfront and running spread for the tranche A, B with maturity T_b.

We will discretise the loss increments, entering the calculation of the discounted default leg payout, on the same set of dates of the discounted premium leg payout calculation: the protection premium payment dates. We will also assume that on average the loss increment arrives at the middle of each time interval $[T_{i-1}, T_i]$

$$\text{DefLeg}_{A,B}^j := (1 - R_j) \sum_{i=1}^{b} D(0, 0.5(T_i + T_{i-1}))(L(T_i)_{A,B}^j - L(T_{i-1})_{A,B}^j)$$

where R_j is a deterministic function of the probability of default conditional on the realisation of the systemic factor S, $R_j = a \log(1 - \exp(-\lambda_j 5y))$. This particular function corresponds to the empirical observation that recoveries are lower during periods when default rates are high. The coefficient a is estimated fitting issuer weighted recovery rate senior unsecured to the issuer weighted all rated bond default rate using data from Moody's from 1982 to 2004.

In the case of the index the above definitions are still valid, except for the DV01, which becomes

$$\text{DV01}_{0,1}^j := \sum_{i=1}^{b} \delta_i D(0, T_i) \left(1 - \frac{L(0.5(T_i + T_{i-1}))_{0,1}^j}{1 - R_j} \right)$$

We will call $\text{PremLeg}_{A,B}$ and $\text{DefLeg}_{A,B}$ the column vectors that stack respectively all discounted premium leg and default leg values conditional on the systemic factor s states

$$\text{PremLeg}_{A,B} = (\text{PremLeg}_{A,B}^1, \ldots, \text{PremLeg}_{A,B}^h)^T$$
$$\text{DefLeg}_{A,B} = (\text{DefLeg}_{A,B}^1, \ldots, \text{DefLeg}_{A,B}^h)^T$$

Then, we integrate against S, simply summing over all possible hazard rate scenarios and multiplying by the scenario probability, to obtain the tranche unconditional price. In matrix notation, the receiver tranche value can be rewritten as

$$\text{NPV}_{A,B} := P^T (\text{PremLeg}_{A,B} - \text{DefLeg}_{A,B})$$

where $P := (p_1, \ldots, p_h)^T$ is the column vector with the systemic factor probability distribution.

Calibration of implied copula

When calibrating all the five-year DJ-iTraxx tranches, we end up minimising a constrained sum of squares. If we call NPV the matrix with all tranches (columns) discounted payout for all possible states (rows)

$$\text{NPV} = \begin{bmatrix} \text{NPV}_{0\%,3\%}^1 & \cdots & \text{NPV}_{22\%,100\%}^1 \\ \vdots & \ddots & \vdots \\ \text{NPV}_{0\%,3\%}^h & \cdots & \text{NPV}_{22\%,100\%}^h \end{bmatrix}$$

then calibration becomes simply

$$\operatorname*{argmin}_{P=(p_1,\ldots,p_h)^T} P^T \operatorname{NPV} \operatorname{NPV}^T P \qquad (11.8)$$

subject to

$$\sum_{i=1}^{h} p_i = 1, \quad p_i \geqslant 0, \ i = 1, \ldots, h$$

Note that for the base correlation calibration the market tranches had to have consecutive adjacent attachment and detachment points spanning the whole capital structure; if that was not the case, some base correlation interpolation assumption had to be introduced. With the implied copula this is not necessary, in that the tranches to be calibrated need not span the whole capital structure or be adjacent.

In the implied-copula framework, Hull and White (2006) calibrate the scenario probabilities p while pre-assigning the hazard rate scenarios λ_j exogenously. The number of hazard rate scenarios λ_j can be seen empirically to be quite large (up to $h = 30$), in order to be able to fit market data with a good precision. In this case the above optimisation has too many degrees of freedom, which might result in a very good fit but quite an irregular scenario probability distribution. In order to cope with this problem, Hull and White (2006) propose to add to the target function a quantity that penalises changes in convexity in the patterns of the scenario probabilities plotted against the default probabilities associated to each scenario.

Torresetti *et al* (2006c) propose a different approach from Hull and White (2006), in which there is no need to select a regularisation coefficient. A two-stage optimisation will make sure that all tranches are priced within the bid–ask spread without the need to choose a regularisation coefficient. The numerical solution of the first-stage optimisation, ie, the solution to the problem set out in Equation 11.8, can be expressed as a deviation of each theoretical tranche spread from the market mid quote. The theoretical spread of the tranche can be computed given the vector P of the systemic factor probability distribution. If the standardised mispricing is between -1 and $+1$, then the vector of systemic state probabilities P results in a calibration of the theoretical tranche spread $\operatorname{NPV}_{A,B} / \operatorname{DV01}_{A,B}$ that lies within the bid–ask spread. The solution to the first-stage optimisation gives a numerical starting point to the second-stage optimisation problem,

Table 11.2 CDX.NA.IG five-year tranche quotes on June 6, 2006

Tranche (%)	Mid	Bid	Ask
0–3	32.40%	31.50%	33.60%
3–7	106.5bp	100bp	113bp
7–10	23.5bp	22bp	25bp
10–15	10bp	9.3bp	10.7bp
15–30	5.5bp	5.1bp	5.9bp

Figure 11.8 Optimal pool default counting C_{5y} distribution resulting from the two-stage optimisation

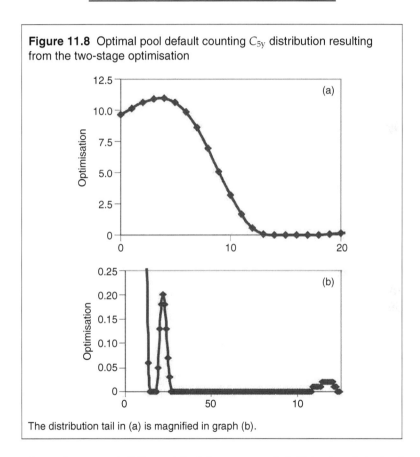

The distribution tail in (a) is magnified in graph (b).

where the second differential of the state probabilities is minimised while the standardised mispricing is kept within the $[-1, 1]$ interval.

We consider the market quotes in Table 11.2 for the CDX.NA.IG five-year tranches on June 6, 2006, while in Figure 11.8 we plot the optimal distribution resulting from the two-stage optimisation as outlined in Torresetti *et al* (2006c).

Index and tranche NPV as a function of ETL

Let us assume that we are given the market spreads of a set of tranches spanning the entire capital structure. Moreover, let us assume that we have the market spreads of a set of k tranches with attachments A_j and detachments B_j with $j = 1, \ldots, k$ where $A_1 = 0$, $B_k = 1$ and $A_{i+1} = B_i$ for $i = 1, \ldots, k-1$.

We call $f(t, h, k)$ the ETL at time t of the tranche with attachment h and detachment k. To simplify the notation we will often identify the seniority of the tranche in the capital structure of the CDO only through the detachment point k, writing $f(t, h, k) = f(t, k)$ when h is clear from the context given the adjacent attachment and detachment points

$$f(t, A, B) := \mathbb{E}_0[\bar{L}_t^{A,B}]$$

By assuming interest rates and default times to be independent and discretising the integrals entering the NPV of the premium and default leg in Equation 11.3 on the tranche payment dates, we obtain

$$S_{T_b}^{A,B} = \frac{\sum_{i=1}^{b} D(0, T_i)(f(T_i, A, B) - f(T_{i-1}, A, B))}{\sum_{i=1}^{b} \delta_i D(0, T_i)(1 - f(T_i, A, B))} \tag{11.9}$$

Then, since the tranches are adjacent, the expected portfolio loss is the summation of the ETL multiplied by the tranche depth (detachment minus attachment), namely

$$f(t, 0, 100\%) = \sum_{i=1}^{k} \mathbb{E}[\bar{L}_t^{A_i, B_i}](B_i - A_i) = \mathbb{E}[\bar{L}_t]$$

Once given the expected portfolio loss $\mathbb{E}[\bar{L}_t]$ and the recovery rate R, we can compute the expected portfolio default rate as $\mathbb{E}[\bar{L}_t]/(1 - R) = f(t, 0, 100\%)/(1 - R)$. Hence, the index spread becomes

$$S_{T_b} = \frac{\sum_{i=1}^{b} D(0, T_i)(f(T_i, 0, 100\%) - f(T_{i-1}, 0, 100\%))}{\sum_{i=1}^{b} \delta_i D(0, T_i)(1 - f(T_i, 0, 100\%)/(1 - R))} \tag{11.10}$$

We will seek to calibrate tranches (the entire capital structure except the super-senior tranche) and indexes for the 3-, 5-, 7- and 10-year maturities in terms of all the unknown $f(t, A, B)$ terms.

The set of all $4 \times 10 \times 6 = 240 f$ needed to price all tranches, except the super senior, and the index (one f for each maturity, quarterly payment date and tranche) is created by interpolating the $4 \times 6 = 24$ basic nodal $f(t, k)$ (one for each maturity and for each detachment).

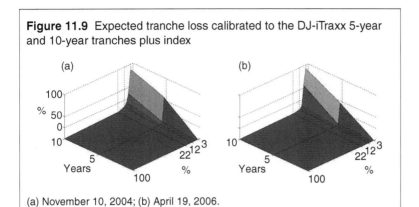

Figure 11.9 Expected tranche loss calibrated to the DJ-iTraxx 5-year and 10-year tranches plus index

(a) November 10, 2004; (b) April 19, 2006.

The target of the optimisation will be to find the f values that set the NPV of the $24 = 4 \times (5+1)$ instruments (five tranches and one index for each maturity) as close to zero as possible whilst maintaining the following constraints

$$\underset{\{f(3y,3\%),\ldots,f(10y,100\%)\}}{\mathrm{argmin}} \sum_{T} \sum_{(A,B)} \mathrm{MisprStdz}^2_{T,A,B} \qquad (11.11)$$

subject to

$$\left. \begin{array}{l} 0 \leqslant f(t,k) \leqslant 1 \\ f(t_i,k) \geqslant f(t_{i-1},k) \\ f(t,k_{j-1}) \geqslant f(t,k_j) \end{array} \right\} \qquad (11.12)$$

where

$$\mathrm{MisprStdz}_{T_b,A,B} = \frac{S^{A,B}_{T_b} - S^{A,B,\mathrm{mid}}_{T_b}}{(S^{A,B,\mathrm{ask}}_{T_b} - S^{A,B,\mathrm{bid}}_{T_b})/2} \qquad (11.13)$$

and the double summation in the objective function is taken with respect to all four (3-, 5-, 7- and 10-year) maturities and all available instruments, tranches plus the index.

Note that the ETLs $f(t,k)$ enter the standardised mispricing equation (Equation 11.13) of the tranches and indexes via Equations 11.9 and 11.10, respectively.

In Figure 11.9 we plot the ETL $f(t,k)$ resulting from the optimisation for the two dates November 10, 2004, and April 19, 2006.

We note that with this method we rest assured that the time inconsistencies of the base correlation are overcome:

- negative expected tranche losses are ruled out and

Table 11.3 Percentage of sample repriced outside the bid–ask range

	CDX		DJ-iTraxx	
Interpolation (%)	Linear (%)	Spline (%)	Linear (%)	Spline (%)
$\text{Mispr}_{\text{Bid-Ask}} > 1$	1.0	2.6	0.2	1.3
$\text{Mispr}_{\text{Bid-Ask}} > 1.2$	0.8	0.2	0.2	0.2
$\text{Mispr}_{\text{Bid-Ask}} > 1.4$	0.0	0.0	0.2	0.0
$\text{Mispr}_{\text{Bid-Ask}} > 1.6$	0.0	0.0	0.0	0.0
Number of dates	616	616	473	473

Sample data for CDX range from November 13, 2003, to June 14, 2006, while those for DJ-iTraxx range from June 21, 2004, to May 23, 2006.

- the same expected tranche loss on a given date is used to price tranches with different maturity (the 0–3% expected tranche loss with one-year horizon entering the NPV of the 5- and 10-year tranche can be quite different depending on whether we are computing it with the attachment and detachment 5- or 10-year base correlations).

Numerical results

Our pre-crisis sample goes from November 13, 2003, to June 14, 2006, for the CDX and from June 21, 2004, to May 23, 2006, for DJ-iTraxx. From Table 11.3 we note that, except for the DJ-iTraxx pool with a linear interpolation, in all cases we find a solution where the theoretical spread exceeds the bid–ask spread by less than one-fifth (0.4/2) of the bid–ask range. In the case of the DJ-iTraxx pool with a linear interpolation, we find only one date where all instruments cannot be priced within the bid–ask range: in this case the theoretical spread is outside the bid–ask spread by less than one-third (0.6/2) of the bid–ask range.

In all cases we find only a few dates where we could not calibrate an ETL surface within the bid–ask spread of each tranche plus the index. The few dates where market instruments could not be priced exactly show a standardised mispricing that is extremely small. The highest mispricing was obtained for the DJ-iTraxx using a linear interpolation, the mispricing being only 0.3 times the bid–ask spread: $0.3 = (1.6 - 1)/2$.

The notion of ETL surface across maturity and tranche attachments is as close to a model independent notion of implied dependence as possible, since it focuses on one of the most direct market objects embedded in market quotes, when assuming default-free interest rates to be independent of default (or even deterministic).

Rather than going through implied correlation, based on the arbitrary assumption of a Gaussian copula connecting defaults across names and leading to inconsistencies in the temporal axis, we consider directly quantities entering the valuation formula and infer them from market quotes given minimal interpolation assumptions. To make sure that interpolation does not interfere excessively, we carry out the calibration through two different interpolation techniques (linear and splines).

While in our framework the bid–ask spreads of the instruments enter the target function we aim at minimising in order to imply the surface, in Walker's (2006) framework the instruments NPVs must be exactly zero. By including bid–ask spreads as we do, the no-arbitrage constraints are satisfied across the vast majority of dates; in particular, we find fewer violations of the no-arbitrage condition than in Walker's framework.

The method appears to be helpful as a first model-independent procedure to deduce implied expected loss surfaces from market data, allowing analysis of basic no-arbitrage constraints in the market quotes. It is also of immediate use to value tranches with non-standard attachments and maturities and forward starting tranches, although excessive extrapolation is to be avoided.

APPLICATION TO MORE RECENT DATA AND THE CRISIS

In this chapter we check whether the critical features we have discussed about implied correlation and the subsequent elements coming from more advanced models were still present during the crisis, after mid-2007. We will observe that the features are still present and often amplified in the market after the beginning of the crisis.

Implied "in-crisis" correlation

We begin by extending the sample of the compound correlation invertibility analysis to see if the non-invertibility again arose during the market turmoil in 2007–9. As before, we resort to the homogeneous pool model.

LESSONS FROM THE CREDIT CRISIS

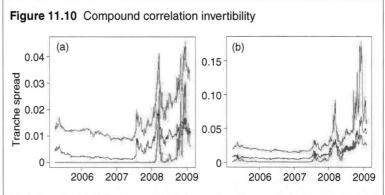

Figure 11.10 Compound correlation invertibility

Market spread (black line) versus minimum and maximum tranche spread obtained varying the compound correlation between 0 and 1 (grey lines). Black dots are highlighting the dates and market spread that were not invertible (black line lies outside the area within the two grey lines). Tranche: (a) 10-year 12–22%; (b) 10-year 10–15%.

After the credit crunch began in summer 2007, the problematic tranches changed. In fact, the non-invertibility issue moved toward the senior part of the capital structure with respect to the situation pre-crisis: mainly the 10-year 12–22% tranche for the DJ-iTraxx, and the 10-year 10–15% and, marginally, the 10-year 15–30% tranches for the CDX (see Figure 11.10).

Another relevant issue, besides the non-invertibility of compound correlation, is its non-uniqueness when invertible. We have seen in Figure 11.2 that on August 3, 2005, for some tranches the map between correlation and theoretical tranche spread is not monotonic. In particular, we have seen how this was the case for the DJ-iTraxx 10-year 6–9% tranche. Despite this map not being monotonic, on this particular date we did not encounter the problem of having more than one compound correlation implying the same theoretical spread.

We check whether there have been dates where a given tranche market spread could be mapped into more than one compound correlation (and we did a similar analysis for the CDX). In Figure 11.11 we plot the market spread and highlight with dots the dates when the market spread was invertible into two different compound correlations for a couple of mezzanine tranches.

The problem of the non-uniqueness of the compound correlation is particularly acute for several mezzanine tranches, some of which are shown in Figure 11.11, for both (5- and 10-year) maturities, and

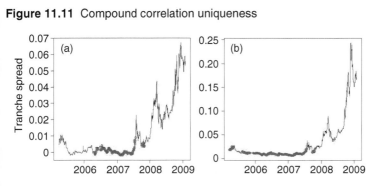

Figure 11.11 Compound correlation uniqueness

Dots highlight the dates where more than one compound correlation could reprice the tranche market spread. Tranche: (a) iTraxx 10-year 6–9%; (b) CDX five-year 3–7%.

for both regions (DJ-iTraxx and CDX). Also, for a given tranche, the problem of non-uniqueness of the compound correlation can span a relevant time window: for example, the five-year DJ-iTraxx 3–6% compound correlation (not shown here) was not uniquely invertible from March 2005 to October 2007.

Now we move on to base correlation. Overall, it surpassed compound correlation and prevailed over more sophisticated dynamic loss models pre-crisis because

(i) it could be calibrated to almost all market conditions experienced pre-crisis,

(ii) it resulted in a smooth map, thus allowing for pricing of bespoke tranches via interpolation;

(iii) it could be used to define sketchy correlation mapping methods used for pricing tranches on Bespoke CDO portfolios, where no other correlations were available,[4] and

(iv) in its heterogeneous version it provided traders with easy to calculate hedge ratios.

"In-crisis" this perception was quite shaken. For example, the finite pool heterogeneous one-factor Gaussian copula base correlation often could not be calibrated to the five-year CDX Series 9 tranches during 2008.

The inability to calibrate the 15–30% tranche spread happens because the 30% detachment base correlation cannot be sufficiently increased: the minimum attainable theoretical 15–30% tranche

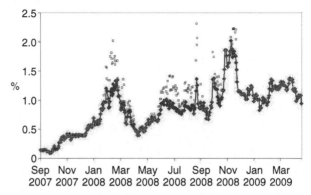

Figure 11.12 Market spread and minimum attainable spread via heterogeneous base correlation calibration for the five-year CDX 15–30% tranche

Open squares, 15–30% minimum attainable spread; filled diamonds, 15–30% market spread.

spread obtained for a 30% detachment base correlation of 100% is above the 15–30% market tranche spread. This in turn occurs because the 15% detachment base correlation is already so high that the 100% upper bound for correlation values becomes a binding constraint.

In this respect we plot in Figure 11.12 the CDX five-year Series 9 15–30% tranche market spread (solid line with diamonds) and the minimum tranche spread (open squares) that could be calibrated using the finite pool heterogeneous one-factor Gaussian copula base correlation from September 2007 to May 2009.

We have thus seen that the heterogeneous base correlation had calibration problems on those dates where the 100% upper bound for the correlation became a binding constraint. If we move to a homogeneous assumption, the homogeneous copula could calibrate all the capital structure, whereas the heterogeneous copula could not. In fact, allowing heterogeneity may change the shape of the loss distributions considerably.

In Figure 11.13 we plot the five-year CDX homogeneous and heterogeneous base correlation calibrated to the market spread on December 7, 2007. We note that heterogeneous base correlation could not calibrate the 15–30% tranche and we also note that the homogeneous base correlation is smaller than the heterogenous base so that the 100% upper bound for correlation was not reached.

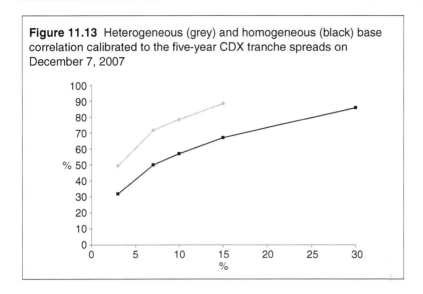

Figure 11.13 Heterogeneous (grey) and homogeneous (black) base correlation calibrated to the five-year CDX tranche spreads on December 7, 2007

We mention that the deterministic recovery assumption, whilst being computationally very convenient, does not help in the above set-up. This has been addressed in the base correlation framework by Amraoui and Hitier (2008) and Krekel (2008), among others, who introduce random recovery. However, even with this update, base correlation remains flawed and may still lead to negative loss distributions, and anecdotally there are dates during the crisis where the heterogeneous pool base correlation with random recovery cannot fit the market if such random recovery is imposed to be consistent with single name CDSs.

In summary, the heterogeneous version of the base correlation failed during the recent credit crisis, as market participants were not able to calibrate it for a considerable amount of time.

"In-crisis" implied copula

Here we analyse the implied-copula framework described in the previous section (see page 299 onwards).

In Figure 11.14 we show the implied distribution for the default counting process, calibrated to the CDX and DJ-iTraxx tranches (the entire capital structure except the super-senior tranche) and the index for the 10-year maturities from March 2005 to January 2009. We note how, since the beginning of the crisis, the probability mass underlying the implied loss distribution shifted towards a higher

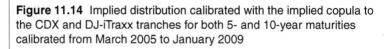

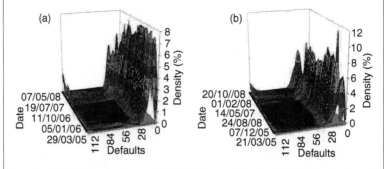

Figure 11.14 Implied distribution calibrated with the implied copula to the CDX and DJ-iTraxx tranches for both 5- and 10-year maturities calibrated from March 2005 to January 2009

Tranche: (a) DJ-iTraxx 10-year; (b) CDX 10-year. The implied distribution is calibrated with the implied copula via a two-stage optimisation as in Torresetti et al (2006c). See Brigo et al (2010) for more details.

number of defaults for both the DJ-iTraxx and the CDX and for maturities of both five and 10 years. This can be interpreted as an increased perceived default riskiness in general.

Also, we note how, since the start of the crisis, the probability mass associated to a catastrophic or Armageddon event, ie, the default of the entire pool of credit references, has increased dramatically.

"In-crisis" expected tranche loss surface

The performance of the expected tranche loss surface model during the crisis was not as egregious as that pre-crisis. This was in part due to the fact that with the super-senior tranche available the system became overdetermined. In fact the capital structure was completed[5] and the super-senior expected loss had not only to fit the index spread, via the deterministic recovery, but to retrieve both the index and the super-senior tranche.

Adding the super-senior tranche to the set of market instruments in the optimisation of Equation 11.11 does not add any degrees of freedom in the variables whose function is being optimised, while adding two instruments, one for each maturity.

With the addition of the super-senior tranche the unknown ETL of the 22–100% tranche, for example, will not be calibrated to the index assuming a deterministic recovery but will be calibrated instead directly to the super-senior tranche spread. The index will then be a by-product of the calibration of all other tranches if we assume a deterministic recovery.

We will modify the ETL approach to calibrate all tranches including the super-senior plus the index, by implying a deterministic recovery which is piecewise constant in time. We set

$$(1 - R_t)\, d\bar{C}_t = d\bar{L}_t; \quad R_t := R_{5y}\ \forall t \leqslant T_{5y}, \quad R_t := R_{10y}\ \forall t > T_{5y}$$

where R_{5y} and R_{10y} are deterministic constants to be determined.

Furthermore, the objective function will be changed to penalise deviations of the stepwise constant calibrated recovery from 40%, the market standard when pricing the recovery of Senior Unsecured CDSs, leading to

$$\underset{\{R_{5y}, R_{10y}, f(5y,3\%),\ldots,f(10y,100\%)\}}{\operatorname{argmin}} 100 \sum_T \sum_{A,B} (\text{MisprStdz}^{A,B})^2 + \sum_T (R_T - 0.4)^2 \tag{11.14}$$

subject to the constraints in Equation 11.12, where the standardised mispricing is given by

$$\text{MisprStdz}^{A,B} = \begin{cases} \dfrac{S_0^{A,B,\text{theor}} - S_0^{A,B,\text{bid}}}{S_0^{A,B,\text{ba}}} & \text{if } S_0^{A,B,\text{theor}} < S_0^{A,B,\text{bid}} \\[2mm] \dfrac{S_0^{A,B,\text{theor}} - S_0^{A,B,\text{ask}}}{S_0^{A,B,\text{ba}}} & \text{if } S_0^{A,B,\text{theor}} > S_0^{A,B,\text{ask}} \\[2mm] 0 & \text{otherwise} \end{cases}$$

with $S_0^{A,B,\text{ba}} := \tfrac{1}{2}(S_0^{A,B,\text{ask}} - S_0^{A,B,\text{bid}})$.

More particularly, on all dates where the optimisation set out in Equation 11.11 results in a standardised mispricing of any tranche or index for any maturity larger than zero, ie, the theoretical spread of any of the tranches or index for any of the two considered maturities is outside the bid–ask spread, we will run the optimisation set out in Equation 11.14, where, with respect to the optimisation equation (Equation 11.11), we will introduce the piecewise constant recovery rate, flat between time 0 and the five-year maturity and then between the 5- and 10-year maturities. This will give us two additional degrees of freedom in the optimisation.

In Figure 11.15 we plot for each date the calibrated piecewise constant recovery: the 5- and 10-year implied recoveries. We note that the above calibration implied a recovery lower than 40% for the first five years, on those dates where a single fixed recovery was not able

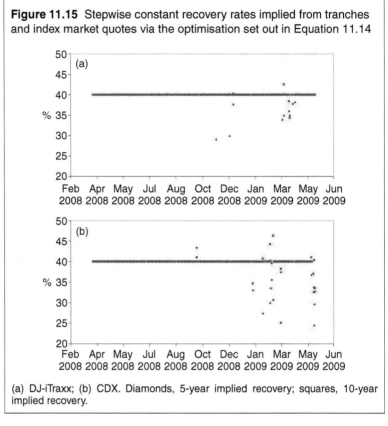

Figure 11.15 Stepwise constant recovery rates implied from tranches and index market quotes via the optimisation set out in Equation 11.14

(a) DJ-iTraxx; (b) CDX. Diamonds, 5-year implied recovery; squares, 10-year implied recovery.

to calibrate all tranches and the index. This is in line with the evidence that recovery rates depend on the business cycle, recovery rates being lower during periods of recession. It is also consistent with the forecasts of a slower than expected economic recovery as we move out of the recent crisis.

FINAL DISCUSSION AND CONCLUSIONS

This work is part of a long path we have followed for credit derivatives, and CDOs in particular. It stops before the introduction of the more advanced models, which have been presented in Brigo *et al* (2006a,b, 2007, 2010).

The criticism we presented regarding the use of the Gaussian copula and of compound and base correlation had all been published before the beginning of the credit crisis. Thus, the notion that quantitative analysts and academics had no idea of the limits and dangers underlying the copula model is simply false. There is even a book titled *Credit Correlation: Life after Copulas* (Lipton and Rennie 2007) that is the summary of talks given at a conference with the same name in 2006 in London.

Despite these warnings, at the time of writing, the Gaussian copula model is still being used in its base correlation formulation, although under some possible extensions such as random recovery, and using some simplifying tricks for generating the loss distribution.[6] The reasons for this are complex. First is the difficulty of all the "top-down" aggregated-loss models, improving the consistency issues, in accounting for single name data and to allow for single name sensitivities, although various degrees of progress in this area have been made.[7] While the aggregate loss is modelled so as to calibrate indexes and tranches satisfactorily, the model sees the loss dynamics, but not the single name defaults, as an aggregate object. Therefore, partial hedges with respect to single names are not possible. Furthermore, even the few models that could try to have single name consistency have not been sufficiently developed and tested to become operational on a trading floor. Indeed, a fully operational model with realistic run times and numerical stability is more than a prototype with some satisfactory properties that have been run in some "off-line" studies. Also, when one model has been coded in the libraries of a bank, changing the model implies a long path involving a number of issues that have little to do with modelling and more to do with IT problems and integration with other systems, to give just two examples. Therefore, unless a new model appears to be greatly promising in all aspects, there is reluctance to adopt it on the trading floor.

All these issues call for further research efforts. At the time of writing, there is no fully tested operationally satisfying and single-name-consistent dynamic model capable of a consistent calibration of indexes and CDO tranches across capital structure and maturity, although we have shown in Brigo *et al* (2006a,b, 2007, 2010) that steps forward have been made. More generally, while it is true that to some extent this is an unsolved problem, this does not mean that the quantitative community of practitioners and academics was unaware of the limitations of copula models before the crisis, as has been documented abundantly.

The views expressed in this chapter are the sole responsibility of
the authors and do not necessarily reflect those of their employers.

1   See, for example, Chapovsky et al (2007).

2   See, for example, McGinty and Ahluwalia (2004).

3   The tranches that are quoted on the market refer to standardised pools (DJ-iTraxx for Europe
    and CDX for North America), standardised attachment–detachment points $A-B$ (0–3%, 3–6%,
    6–9%, 9–12%, 12–22%, 22–100% for the DJ-iTraxx and 0–3%, 3–7%, 7–10%, 10–15%, 15–30%,
    30–100% for the CDX) and (3-, 5-, 7- and 10-year) standardised maturities.

4   See, for example, Bear Stearns and Lehman Brothers' reports by Reyfman et al (2004) and
    Baheti et al (2007).

5   The liquidity of the super-senior tranche since the end of 2005 allowed us to include it in the
    set of the calibration instruments.

6   See, for example, Andersen et al (2003).

7   See, for example, Giesecke et al (forthcoming), Brigo et al (2007), Halperin and Tomecek (2008)
    and Bielecki et al (2008).

REFERENCES

Albanese, C., O. Chen, A. Dalessandro and A. Vidler, 2006, "Dynamic Credit Correlation Modeling", Report, URL: http://www.defaultrisk.com.

Amraoui, S., and S. Hitier, 2008, "Optimal Stochastic Recovery for Base Correlation", Research Report, BNP Paribas.

Andersen, L., J. Sidenius and S. Basu, 2003, "All Your Hedges in One Basket", *Risk Magazine*, November 1.

Baheti, P., and S. Morgan, 2007, "Base Correlation Mapping", Lehman Brothers QCR Quarterly, Report, 2007 Q1.

Baxter, M., 2007, "Lévy Simple Structural Models", in A. Lipton and A. Rennie (eds), *Credit Correlation: Life after Copulas* (World Scientific).

Berd, A. M., R. F. Engle and A. B. Voronov, 2007, "The Underlying Dynamics of Credit Correlations", URL: http://ssrn.com/abstract=837824.

Bielecki, T., and M. Rutkowski, 2001, *Credit Risk: Modeling, Valuation and Hedging* (Heidelberg: Springer).

Bielecki, T., S. Crepey and M. Jeanblanc, 2008, "Up and Down Credit Risk", Working Paper, URL: http://www.defaultrisk.com.

Brigo, D., A. Pallavicini and R. Torresetti, 2006a, "The Dynamical Generalized-Poisson Loss Model, Part One: Introduction and CDO Calibration", URL: http://www.ssrn.com.

Brigo, D., A. Pallavicini and R. Torresetti, 2006b, "The Dynamical Generalized-Poisson Loss Model, Part Two: Calibration Stability and Spread Dynamics Extensions", URL: http://www.ssrn.com.

Brigo, D., A. Pallavicini and R. Torresetti, 2007, "Cluster-Based Extension of the Generalized Poisson Loss Dynamics and Consistency with Single Names", *International Journal of Theoretical and Applied Finance* 10(4), pp. 607–31.

Brigo, D., A. Pallavicini and R. Torresetti, 2009, "Credit Models and the Crisis, or How I Learned to Stop Worrying and Love the CDOs", http://ssrn.com/abstract=1529498.

Brigo, D., A. Pallavicini and R. Torresetti, 2010, *Credit Models and the Crisis: A journey into CDOs, Copulas, Correlations and Dynamic Models* (Chichester: John Wiley & Sons).

Chapovsky, A., A. Rennie and P. A. C. Tavares, 2007, "Stochastic Intensity Modelling for Structured Credit Exotics", in A. Lipton and A. Rennie (eds), *Credit Correlation: Life after Copulas* (World Scientific).

Garcia, J., and S. Goossens, 2007, "Base Expected Loss Explains Lévy Base Correlation Smile", URL: http://www.ssrn.com.

Giesecke, K., L. Goldberg and X. Ding, Forthcoming, "A Top-Down Approach to Multi-Name Credit", *Operations Research*.

Golub, H., and C. Van Loan, 1983, *Matrix Computation*, p. 384 (Baltimore, MA: Johns Hopkins University Press).

Halperin, I., and P. Tomecek, 2008, "Climbing Down from the Top: Single Name Dynamics in Credit Top Down Models", Working Paper, J. P. Morgan Quantitiative Research.

Hamilton, D., P. Varma, S. Ou and R. Cantor, 2005, "Default and Recovery Rates of Corporate Bond Issuers, 1920-2004", Report, Moody's Investors Service, Global Credit Research, January.

Hull, J., and A. White, 2006, "Valuing Credit Derivatives Using an Implied Copula Approach", *Journal of Derivatives* 14(2), pp. 8–28.

Jones, S., 2009, "Of Couples and Copulas: The Formula that Felled Wall St", April 24, 2009, *Financial Times*.

Joshi M. S., and A. M. Stacey, 2006, "Intensity Gamma: a New Approach to Pricing Portfolio Credit Derivatives", *Risk Magazine* 19(7), pp. 78–83.

Krekel, M., 2008, "Pricing Distressed CDOs with Base Correlation and Stochastic Recovery", Research Report, UniCredit.

Li, D. X., 2000, "On Default Correlation: A Copula Function Approach", *Journal of Fixed Income* 9(4), pp. 43–54.

Li, D. X., and M. Hong Liang, 2005, "CDO^2 Pricing Using Gaussian Mixture Model with Transformation of Loss Distribution", URL: http://www.defaultrisk.com

Lipton, A., and A. Rennie (eds), 2007, *Credit Correlation: Life after Copulas* (World Scientific).

Livesey, M., and L. Schlögl, 2006, "Recovery Rate Assumptions and No-Arbitrage in Tranche Markets", Lehman Brothers, London (Paper presented at the Summer School on Financial Derivatives, Imperial College, London).

Lohr, S. 2009, "Wall Street's Math Wizards Forgot a Few Variables", *New York Times*, September 12.

McGinty, L., and R. Ahluwalia, 2004, "A Model for Base Correlation Calculation", Tehcnical Document, J. P. Morgan Credit Derivatives Strategy.

Meng, C., and A. N. Sengupta, 2008, "CDO Tranche Sensitivities in the Gaussian Copula Model", URL: http://www.defaultrisk.com/.

Morini, M., and D. Brigo, 2007, "No-Armageddon Arbitrage-Free Equivalent Measure for Index options in a Credit Crisis", e-print, arXiv:0812.4156.

Morini, M., and D. Brigo, 2009, "Last Option before the Armageddon", *Risk Magazine*, September.

Parcell, E., and J. Wood, 2007, "Wiping the Smile off Your Base (Correlation Curve)", Technical Report, Derivative Fitch.

Prampolini, A., and M. Dinnis, 2009, "CDO Mapping with Stochastic Recovery", URL: http://www.ssrn.com.

Reyfman, A., K., Ushakova and W. Kong, 2004, "How to Value Bespoke Tranches Consistently with Standard Ones", Educational Report, Bear Stearns.

Rosen, D., and D. Saunders, 2009, "Analytical Methods for Hedging Systematic Credit Risk with Linear Factor Portfolios", *Journal of Economic Dynamics and Control* 33(1), pp. 37–52.

Salmon, F., 2009, "Recipe for Disaster: The Formula that Killed Wall Street", *Wired Magazine*, Issue 17.03, URL: http://www.wired.com/.

Torresetti, R., and A. Pallavicini, Forthcoming, "Stressing Rating Criteria Allowing for Default Clustering: the CPDO case", in T. Bielecki, D. Brigo and F. Patras (eds), *Credit Risk Frontiers: Subprime Crisis, Pricing and Hedging, CVA, MBS, Ratings and Liquidity* (Chichester: John Wiley & Sons).

Torresetti, R., D. Brigo, and A. Pallavicini, 2006a, "Implied Expected Tranched Loss Surface from CDO Data", URL: http://www.ssrn.com.

Torresetti, R., D. Brigo and A. Pallavicini, 2006b, "Implied Correlation in CDO Tranches: A Paradigm to be Handled with Care", URL: http://www.ssrn.com.

Torresetti, R., D. Brigo and A. Pallavicini, 2006c, "Risk Neutral versus Objective Loss Distribution and CDO Tranches Valuation", *Journal of Risk Management in Financial Institutions* 2(2), pp. 175–92.

Walker, M., 2006, "CDO Models. Towards the Next Generation: Incomplete Markets and Term Structure", Report, URL: http://www.defaultrisk.com.

12

Another view on the pricing of MBSs, CMOs and CDOs of ABSs

Jean-David Fermanian
CREST–ENSAE

Since the 1980s, securitisation has fuelled the creation of multiple families of financial products that we will call "structures". The reasons for this boom are well known and have been widely studied in the literature: see, for example, Fabozzi and Kothari (2008) or Takavoli (2008). Apparently, most of these structures follow the same logic: gather more-or-less tradeable assets together in an ad hoc vehicle, create different tranches that would provide different risk/return profiles for different classes of investors and sell them.

Let us keep in mind the two icons of this business.

- Synthetic corporate collateralised debt obligations (CDOs), based on about 100 credit default swaps: the main underlying risks are the potential default events of the underlying firms, their spread variations and the recovery amounts after any default.

- Asset-backed securities (ABSs): cash instruments based on thousands of individual loans coming from retail banking. Here, losses can occur due to prepayment (some underlying assets can be repaid more quickly than expected, inducing a marked-to-market loss for investors) or to default risk (inability to reimburse some coupons or principal fully). When the underlying loans are related to mortgages, we use the term mortgage-backed securities (MBSs).

All these structures are exposed to an interest rate risk, but mortgages face particular exposure. Indeed, lower interest rates are an incentive to prepay current loans and to enter into new ones under better financial conditions. When interest rates rise, the weight of periodic reimbursements will become heavier for weak-floating-rate borrowers, pushing them to bankruptcy more easily.

In addition to CDOs and ABS, a lot of (more-or-less) exotic structures have appeared. They differ in the way risks are allocated between investors and as time passes. In particular, collateralised mortgage obligations (CMOs) borrow the "tranching" idea from CDOs, but apply it to mortgages. Moreover, there exists a menagerie of exotic corporate structures (forward-starting CDOs, leveraged super senior tranches, CPDOs, etc) exemplifying the imagination of structuring desks.

The children of securitisation share a common high degree of complexity and its corollary: the difficulty in assessing continuously their fair prices in any market environment and to measure and to understand their underlying risks. Moreover, their final payouts depend strongly on the tranching process that allocates risk among investors, and that generates the so-called "waterfalls" of payments. But beyond their visible similarities, such products show significant differences on the model side and in terms of practical management. In securitisation, two factors are particularly significant:

- the distinction between cash and synthetic structures;
- the number of underlyings.

Indeed, one of the key points in a cash structure is the full description of its future cashflows. Obviously, these cashflows will be random, due to possible future default events, prepayments, interest rate moves, etc. Otherwise, such a product would be risk free. But even in a fully deterministic environment, the task of cashflow calculation is painful. It often implies a significant cost in terms of IT infrastructure/systems. More seriously, the creativity of structurers and the risk appetite of clients have converged to complicate the picture. Now, a lot of structures involve non-linearities, triggers, tranching, optionalities (call rights), regular tests linked with external processes like ratings, etc. Thus, the degree of complexity can be so high that the formal pricing of any cash structure becomes a permanent challenge. Everybody knows the classical principles of derivatives valuation (to exhibit a relevant stochastic processes that would describe the underlyings and then the calculation of an expectation under a risk-neutral probability, possibly in closed form). Here, such an agenda appears inaccessible for most practitioners. This feeling has been strengthened with the latest avatars of the securitisation universe, the famous CDOs of ABS, which provide another level of securitisation. Formally, as "CDO squared", they produce securitisations of already securitised products, inducing highly complex modelling issues. The risk management of such structures is particularly challenging. These CDOs of ABS were under the spotlight during the financial crisis of 2007–9. The losses they suffered have offered arguments against the business of securitisation and its excesses.

Apparently, synthetic structures offer more guarantees. Indeed, their underlyings are derivatives, typically swaps, for which cashflows are simpler and relatively standardised. Then, there are some hopes the waterfalls of synthetic structures could be modelled explicitly, at least in the simplest cases. Indeed, this is often the case, particularly with corporate CDOs based on credit default swaps. For these products, the remaining challenge is the famous "correlation puzzle", or the way in which individual default risks may be correlated. This problem has generated a huge amount of literature. At the time of writing, the market standard is the so-called "Gaussian copula model" (Li 2000), an apparently static model that could be justified by some underlying credit-spread dynamics (Fermanian and Vigneron 2010). Its shortcomings are numerous and well known (Finger 2004; Lipton and Rennie 2007).[1] Its wide and rash use by practitioners is believed to be one of the sources of the 2007–9 credit crisis. Therefore, its key formula has been called "the formula that killed Wall Street" (Salmon 2009).

Actually, the "correlation puzzle" is still present for cash structures too. In the US, many mortgage-related products are implicitly guaranteed by an agency (eg, Federal National Mortgage Association, Federal Home Loan Mortgage Corporation, Government National Mortgage Association). They convey virtually no default risk, and academics have often considered credit risk as a second-order effect. As a consequence, the amount of academic literature that deals with prepayment issues is significantly larger than the stream of papers that focus on the default risk of borrowers. Unfortunately, the subprime crisis has illustrated the weaknesses of the standard risk management practices in such cash structures. After the dramatic increase of default risk in every category of US mortgages, it is no longer reasonable to leave credit risk aside. Note that default risk is far from being negligible in continental European structures too. There, prepayment incentives are a lot weaker than in the US (partly due to associated penalties) and loans are not guaranteed most of the time.

Strangely, these deep questions have been somewhat hidden by the first immediate challenge: to recover expected cashflows associated with the at-hand cash structure. In practice, engineers were a little obsessed by the management of huge amounts of loan-level information which created a smokescreen covering the major problems on the purely quantitative side: the way default and prepayment events would be dependent and would modify waterfalls. Ultimately, the main concern is to price and hedge such derivatives. But, as a consequence, and as noticed by Brigo *et al* (2010),

> [cash CDOs] are complex products with sophisticated and path-dependent payouts that are often valued with extremely simplistic models.

Therefore, two methodologies have been developed, largely independently, without any clear link between them: on the one hand, synthetic and relatively standardised synthetic structures (based on CDSs or ABCDSs, their counterparts for asset-backed securities), daily market quotes, "correlation trading" desks and financial engineers with the same background as quants on other derivatives (FX, interest rates, stocks) and, on the other hand, a less well-defined world of cash structures, mainly US and mortgage related, rather than buy-side oriented, where quantitative models are more econometric and crucially dependent on traders' inputs.

In our opinion, there are no theoretical reasons to justify such a discrepancy, merely practice and history. The fundamental modelling issues remain whatever the nature or number of the underlyings (particularly cash or synthetic). The cornerstone is dependence between all the underlying risks.

A few attempts have tried to adapt the usual models of synthetic corporate CDOs towards ABS: Lou (2007), Garcia and Goossens (2008a,b), Hull and White (2009), among others. These authors have amended the usual one-factor Merton model to deal with ABS-type structures. Such approaches will be outlined in the next section. Since the standard "static" Merton model does not focus on the underlying dynamics, these models cannot capture the uncertainty around the timing of cashflows without a heroic simplification of reality.

Another tempting approach is related to intensity-based models. Here, by building dependent individual default-intensity processes, we get a satisfying description of correlated default events and their timings to fit the CDO market. The extension of such reduced-form models to ABS structures seems to be particularly relevant. Indeed, duration models have become the standard framework for the latter products, since the publication of some seminal papers at the end of the 1980s (Richard and Roll 1989; Schwartz and Torous 1989). Thus, individual stochastic default and prepayment rate processes (possibly correlated) could be the main tools for pricing ABS. In addition, the associated formalism could be very close to the classical approach of stochastic intensity models, especially with use of the arsenal of affine jump-diffusion processes available (Duffie *et al* 2000). We outline such an approach later in the chapter (see page 325 onwards).

As an alternative to the previous bottom-up models, we present the top-down approach of Fermanian (2010), where total exposures, losses and prepaid amounts are correlated stochastic processes. Therefore, in a parsimonious framework and under reasonable assumptions, it is possible to get closed-form (or at least semi-analytical) pricing formulas for CMOs and even CDOs of ABS (see page 328). In the discussion section (see page 337), we discuss the relative advantages and shortcomings of all these approaches. Finally, we describe the skeleton of a core model to price every ABS-type structure. We quote some technical hurdles and difficulties that need to be overcome before we start to live in such a "perfect world" (see page 340).

THE MERTON MODEL AND ABS-TYPE PRODUCTS

As usual in a Merton-style approach (Merton 1974), a "default risk" asset value process $(X_{it})_{t>0}$ can be associated with any underlying i in a given pool, ie, with any debt (corporate, retail, other). The default event of i is recorded when its asset value falls below a debt threshold. Similarly, a "prepayment" asset value process $(Y_{it})_{t>0}$ can be built, and prepayment events would be generated exactly like default events. When the first of these two events occurs, the corresponding name leaves the pool and its current balance is removed.

It is theoretically possible to make all these processes dependent, to state relevant debt and prepayment boundaries and generate trajectories to get prices (by simulation, most of the time). Clearly, the lack of closed-form formulas and of instruments for calibration, the number of parameters and the huge number of underlying processes prevent such a "brute force" approach. Note that this difficulty already appears with most synthetic corporate CDOs, ie, in the case of default risk only and without amortisation features. Using Zhou (2001), we can check the complexity of pricing CDOs by dealing with multidimensional asset value processes. Thus, the consideration of even a single process per name which would generate the minimum of the latent default time and of the latent prepayment time is not yet a solution that can be used in practice.

Therefore, simplifying assumptions have to be made. The first tempting assumption is related to the definition of the default/prepayment events themselves. As in the market standard "base correlation" framework, we could consider that the default (respectively, prepayment) of i occurs before T when X_{iT} is below some threshold d_{iT} (respectively, e_{iT}), for every maturity T. It is well known that such a strategy allows relatively simple closed-form pricing formulas for synthetic CDOs. Nonetheless, in general, the "correlations" are different from one time horizon to another and it is impossible to simulate all the default events consistently at several times T. In other words, we need to assume that some defaulted names can be resurrected, to be calibrated to every portfolio loss distribution at every time T. This weakness of the base correlation technique is well known (Brigo et al 2010). In the case of ABS, it is particularly tricky, because the effect of time is even stronger than for (bullet) bond/CDS exposures. Moreover, the possibility of pricing by simulation is even more desirable, because it is most often the only way of integrating path-dependent features, or even to deal conveniently with amortisation schedules. Indeed, time after time, current notionals have to be calculated depending on some pre-specified amortisation schemes. Moreover, the latter can depend on many random events (triggers, tests, etc).

A shortcut would be to assume parametric profiles of amortisation and/or independence between amortization/prepayment and defaults. This is the solution proposed by Garcia and Goossens (2008a,b), for instance. Clearly, this approach is highly questionable for standard ABS, even if it could be accepted by default for CDOs of ABS, due to the number of underlyings and the complexity of exact cashflow calculations for the latter structures.

Since there are often thousands of names in many ABS-type products, the "infinitely granular assumption" seems to be natural: the proportion of an individual current balance is negligible with respect to the total current notional, as in Hull and White (2009). In this simplified framework, closed-form pricing formulas can be obtained, but only for bullet exposures, and the previous intertemporal inconsistency still remains in general. Consequently, this practical trick does not provide the magical tool we are looking for.

To summarise, only very approximate pricing models of ABS can be based on Merton's structural approach in practice, given the current state of the art.

STOCHASTIC INTENSITIES AND ABS-TYPE PRODUCTS

In addition to the structural approach, there exists another important stream of CDO pricing models, called "reduced-form" or "intensity-based" models. These are still bottom-up models, but, unlike Merton-style models, they concentrate only on the timing of defaults, particularly through stochastic intensities. There are no longer (relatively artificial) economic arguments that aim to explain firm behaviours as they can appear in most structural models. This difference is also standard in economics, between those authors who want to understand the fundamental underlying behaviours and those who concentrate on descriptions/predictions based on econometrics.

Bottom-up reduced-form models are now standard for pricing corporate CDOs; see Duffie and Garleanu (2001), Mortensen (2006), among others. These authors have proposed to associate a stochastic intensity process $(\lambda_{it})_{t>0}$ with every name i in a portfolio. At time t, the intensity λ_{it} can be seen as the "instantaneous" default likelihood of i, conditional on the information available at time t. In other words

$$P(\tau_i \in [t, t + \Delta t] \mid \tau_i > t, \mathcal{F}_t) \simeq \lambda_{it} \Delta t$$

where τ_i denotes i's (random) default time, and $\mathcal{F}_t$ denotes some amount of information that is available at time t (to be specified for each particular model).

Dependence between default events is obtained by building dependence between the default-intensity processes above, for instance, through factor models. As in the seminal paper by Duffie and Garleanu (2001), we can assume that there exists a common systemic (respectively, idiosyncratic) stochastic intensity $(\lambda_t)_{t>0}$ (respectively, $(\lambda_{it}^*)_{t>0}$) such that

$$\lambda_{it} = a_i\lambda_t + b_i\lambda_{it}^*$$

for some positive constants a_i and b_i. In other words, conditionally on the systemic process $(\lambda_t)_{t>0}$, the laws of default (and default events themselves) are independent.

Despite the large number of parameters and practical issues in terms of calibration, the merits of these models are certain and the fit to the market is acceptable most of the time (Eckner 2009; Chapovsky *et al* 2006). A natural idea would be to extend such reduced-form models towards ABS structures. Indeed, such a framework is more in line with the standard approach of ABS pricing than Merton-style models. The econometric point of view has become common practice in pricing ABSs/MBSs. Huge amounts of historical data about prepayment and now default are available and potentially allow the estimation of sophisticated duration models (but under the physical measure). Therefore, many authors have explained the duration of mortgages directly in reduced-form approaches.[2]

Note that standard corporate CDOs pricing models are calibrated to market data most of the time, especially those based on iTraxx and CDX. For such standardised baskets, there is a one-to-one mapping between default times/recovery rates and realised cashflows. Unfortunately, this is not the case for most ABS, and practitioners must rely on historical/econometrical procedures. For the latter, no sufficiently liquid and reliable instruments are available in the market to find (risk-neutral) estimates of the underlying model parameters. Moreover, it is very tempting to use the high level of information that is available in the pool descriptions for every loan and borrower: the Fair Isaac Corporation (FICO) score; the loan documentation level; the loan-to-value; the loan balance; the margin levels; whether the rate is fixed/floating; the US state of origination; the delinquency history, etc. Therefore, statistics and econometrics provide key tools for ABS, when stochastic calculus is suitable for synthetic corporate CDOs, even if both frameworks are reduced form (or intensity based).

Nonetheless, the development of credit risk models and stochastic intensities approaches have influenced the academic literature on ABS. Indeed, as Goncharov (2002) pointed out,

> [a]fter all, from a mathematical point of view nothing precludes one from interpreting prepayment as a "default" in the intensity-based approach to pricing credit risk.

Thus, it is tempting to introduce stochastic default intensities and prepayment intensities for every name in a given ABS pool. The techniques should be similar to those for corporate CDOs.

Actually, this is not entirely the case. A major difference is due to the competing risks feature of mortgages: the life of any loan is ended by default or prepayment, but only one of these two alternatives is observed. Possibly, right censoring can occur in practice, inducing another competing risk in models. When dealing with default and prepayment risks simultaneously and in the explicit framework of competing risk models, see, for example, Deng et al (2000) or Kau et al (2006).

As a consequence, the competing risk feature of MBS histories has to be taken into account, at least during the inference step. This apparently technical point changes the perspective, and has induced another significant gap between the two families of reduced-form models. The default intensities of corporate CDOs are associated explicitly with the underlying default times and there is a one-to-one relation between them. This is no longer the case with MBSs in general. Indeed, a well-known result of non-identifiability (Tsiatis 1975) states:

> Assume every individual is under the threat of two risks, whose associated underlying default times are denoted by τ and $\tilde{\tau}$. If we observe only realizations of the minimum of both times, ie, $Y = \min(\tau, \tilde{\tau})$ and of the nature of this event, ie, $\delta = \mathbf{1}(\tau \leqslant \tilde{\tau})$, then it is impossible to identify the joint law of τ and $\tilde{\tau}$.

Here, imagine that τ (respectively, $\tilde{\tau}$) is the "latent" default (respectively, prepayment) time of any borrower. In databases of loan histories, we observe only the liquidation or termination by prepayment of every loan, but never both events. Thus, in practice, either a parametric model for $(\tau, \tilde{\tau})$ is assumed and we recover identifiability, or a richer desirable semi-parametric approach is assumed. In the latter case (the more advanced one), the goal is no longer to identify stochastic intensity processes associated with an underlying default time τ and an underlying prepayment time $\tilde{\tau}$, but rather to be able to calculate quantities like

$$\lambda_{it}^* := P(\tau_i \in [t, t + \Delta t], \delta_i = k \mid \tau_i > t, \tilde{\tau}_i > t)\Delta t$$

and

$$\tilde{\lambda}_{it}^* := P(\tilde{\tau}_i \in [t, t + \Delta t], \delta_i = k \mid \tau_i > t, \tilde{\tau}_i > t)\Delta t$$

for every name i and $k \in \{0, 1\}$. The previous quantities λ_{it}^* and $\tilde{\lambda}_{it}^*$ are called case-specific rates (see, for example, Kalbfleisch and Prentice 1980). They are directly linked to data, but they no longer describe the law of (hypothetical) underlying default and prepayment times. Nevertheless, they are sufficient for inference and prediction.

Note that by putting the competing risks issue aside and trusting a risk-neutral calibration procedure it is theoretically possible to price ABS structures (even CDOs of ABS) in the formalism of stochastic intensities, exactly as with synthetic CDOs. In particular, this was proposed in Jäckel (2008), where the notional of any loan is reduced by default and/or prepayment continuously through fractional loss rates. Both of these rates follow Gamma processes. Notably, there is independence between fractional loss intensities due to default and those due to prepayment, even if dependence across the names in the pool is obtained by common factor processes. The substance of this bottom-up model is close to the ideas we develop in the next section.

A TOP-DOWN APPROACH FOR ASSET-BACKED SECURITIES AND COLLATERALISED DEBT OBLIGATIONS OF ASSET-BACKED SECURITIES

In contrast to "bottom-up" models that try to model every underlying individually, some authors have argued that it is not necessary to work name by name to price the most standard CDOs. Indeed, the payouts and the prices of most standard CDOs depend only on the behaviour of the aggregated loss process in the portfolio. Thus, the so-called "top-down" approach was developed for the pricing of corporate structured products (see, for example, Andersen et al 2008; Bennani 2005; Schönbucher 2005). These authors concentrate on the dynamics of a single continuous-time loss process. The idea is to evaluate options of different maturities that would be written on this loss. This method seems to be particularly relevant in the case of mortgage pools that put together thousands of underlying loans. The latter cannot be risk-managed individually, removing one of the main arguments in favour of "bottom-up" models. To the best of our knowledge, a "top-down" ABS pricing model was first proposed in Fermanian (2010). He built a random process around an "information summary", the mean amortisation profile. Similarly, the underlying default risk was tackled by the expected loss random process of the whole portfolio. Both processes were correlated with each other, and with the yield curve, which was considered as the main systemic driver. Independently, Lou's (2007) paper built up similar ideas, but mainly at the loan level and on terms too general to obtain analytical pricing formulas.

In this section, we describe in detail the model of Fermanian (2010). In practical terms, this approach is a lot cheaper than managing thousands of individual loan descriptions and their interdependencies inside micro-econometric models. The author assumes implicitly that the diversification in the underlying pool is large. Thus, a few macro-factors (mainly the moves of the interest rate curve) are sufficient to price and risk-manage ABS-type structures like CMOs. By exhibiting closed-form formulas, simulations are avoided. Therefore, it is a parsimonious and consistent way of dealing with the main underlying risks together. Note that, contrary to a large part of the literature that deals with conforming mortgages, default events are not neglected. In the structures we consider, they will constitute one of the main sources of risk in addition to prepayment.

Without loss of generality, we consider that the total notional amount of our pool of assets is 1. The assumed tranching process is related to several detachment points $K_0 < K_1 < \cdots < K_p$. We set $K_0 = 0$ and $K_p = 1$. At every time t, the outstanding notional of the whole portfolio will be denoted by $O(t)$ and the outstanding notional of the tranche $[0, K]$ by $O_K(t)$. Obviously, these quantities are random.

The notional amounts of these tranches can be reduced due to three different effects.

1. The "natural" amortisation process, which is deterministic for every underlying name and deduced from contractual terms.

The loans are amortised from the most senior tranches to the most junior ones ("top-down" amortisation).

2. The prepayment process. This also reduces the most senior tranches first. It can be seen as a randomisation of the previous amortisation profile.

3. The default process: failure to pay remaining coupons or nominals. This concerns the most junior tranches first ("bottom-up" notional reduction).

These features cover the most frequent specification of simple ABS structures (standard CMOs, for instance). Potentially, all these effects can apply to a given tranche simultaneously, at least from a certain time on.

For the sake of simplicity, we shall consider an asset-backed-security synthetic structure here. In this case, we do not have to take care of coupon payments even if complex notional repayment schedules can occur. Typically, we can keep in mind a synthetic CDO of an asset-backed security, whose underlyings are some CDSs on ABS tranches (the so-called ABCDSs). In this case, no initial fund is necessary to invest in such a structure. The cashflows come only from notional repayments and defaults. The main price driver here is default risk, as for the usual synthetic corporate CDOs. The case of the usual "cash" (coupon-bearing) structures like CMOs can be deduced relatively easily (Fermanian 2010).

Let $RA_{t,K}$ and $DL_{t,K}$ be respectively the time-t risky annuity and the default leg that are associated with the tranche $[0, K]$. The default leg is related to default event losses only. The spread associated with the tranche $[K_{j-1}, K_j]$ is denoted by $s_{t,j}$ and it satisfies, by definition

$$s_{t,j}\{RA_{t,K_j} - RA_{t,K_{j-1}}\} = DL_{t,K_j} - DL_{t,K_{j-1}} \qquad (12.1)$$

for every time t and every $j = 1,\ldots,p$. This identity is standard in credit derivatives, for the pricing of credit default swaps and CDOs. The first goal of our model will be to evaluate these risky annuities and these default legs. This can be done in closed form under reasonable assumptions.

Let us denote by T^* the maturity of our structure. It may be seen as the largest maturity date of all the underlyings, or as a contractual call date of the structure. By definition

$$RA_{t,K} = E\left[\int_t^{T^*} \exp\left(-\int_t^s r_u\, du\right) O_K(s)\, ds \,\Big|\, \mathcal{F}_t\right] \qquad (12.2)$$

and denoting by r_s the usual short interest rate process. We denote by $E_t[\cdot]$ expectations conditional on the market information $\mathcal{F}_t$ at time t and under a risk-neutral measure Q. The filtration $(\mathcal{F}_t)$ records all the past and current relevant information concerning the description of the cashflows and the underlyings: past payments, contractual features, interest rates, recorded losses, etc. Note that our risky annuity definition is homogeneous with a duration multiplied by a notional amount.

To fix these ideas, let us denote by $A(s)$ the portfolio amortised amount at time s. Moreover, let $A_K(s)$ be the same amount but related to the tranche $[0, K]$, ie, $A_K(s) = [A(s) - (1-K)]^+$. The latter quantity is the amount of money by which the tranche $[0, K]$ has been reduced from above, due to the amortisation process only. Actually, since this tranche is also reduced potentially from below by the default events, we have $O_K(s) = [K - L(s) - A_K(s)]^+$. We have introduced $L(s)$, the loss of the whole portfolio at time s; this is simply the accumulated amount that is due to default events. The same quantity, but related to the tranche $[0, K]$, is denoted by $L_K(s)$. Note that the latter quantity depends on the outstanding notional process of this tranche, and also on the amortisation profile. This feature complicates the asset pricing formulas significantly. Moreover, note that the portfolio outstanding notional $O(s)$ is related to the other quantities by the relation $O(s) = 1 - L(s) - A(s)$.

The loss process that refers to the tranche $[0, K]$ can be rewritten as

$$L_K(s) = L(s) \cdot \mathbf{1}(L(s) \leqslant K - A_K(s))$$

when the tranche $[0, K]$ has not been fully paid down. Otherwise, the loss amount is fixed, and keeps its last value (just before this tranche has been fully paid down). Consequently, we can write the default leg of the tranche $[0, K]$ as seen at time t as follows

$$\begin{aligned} \mathrm{DL}_{t,K} &= E_t\left[\int_t^{T^*} \exp\left(-\int_t^s r_u\, du\right) L_K(\mathrm{d}s)\right] \\ &= E_t\left[\int_t^{T^*} \exp\left(-\int_t^s r_u\, du\right) \mathbf{1}(L(s) + A_K(s) \leqslant K) L(\mathrm{d}s)\right] \end{aligned}$$
(12.3)

In practice, we need to evaluate the latter integral with some matrix of dates $T_0 = t, T_1, \ldots, T_p = T^*$. Therefore, by neglecting the accrued payments due to defaults between two successive dates, we consider that

$$DL_{t,K} \simeq \sum_{i=1}^{p} E_t\left[\exp\left(-\int_t^{T_i} r_u \, du\right) \right.$$
$$\left. \times \mathbf{1}(L(T_i) + A_K(T_i) \leqslant K)(L(T_i) - L(T_{i-1})) \right]$$

with a reasonable accuracy. To evaluate the functions $RA_{t,K}$ and $DL_{t,K}$ (and due to some elementary algebraic operations) it is sufficient to calculate the expectations

$$\mathcal{E}_1(s) = E_t\left[\exp\left(-\int_t^s r_u \, du\right)[K - L(s) - [A(s) - 1 + K]^+]^+ \right]$$
(12.4)

$$\mathcal{E}_2(s,\bar{s}) = E_t\left[\exp\left(-\int_t^s r_u \, du\right)\mathbf{1}\{L(s) + [A(s) - 1 + K]^+ \leqslant K\}L(\bar{s}) \right]$$
(12.5)

for every couple $(s,\bar{s})$, $t \leqslant \bar{s} \leqslant s \leqslant T^*$.

Thus, the evaluation of the previous expectations is sufficient to price such synthetic structures. Tractable formulas, possibly closed-form formulas, are highly desirable. Unfortunately, these expressions involve some tricky double indicator functions in general. To simplify the analysis, we could make the following assumption.

Assumption 12.1. The amortisation process and the prepayment process will reduce only the most senior tranche.

In other words, under Assumption 12.1, we consider only trajectories where the amortisation process is stopped (or the structure is repaid) before the most senior tranche is fully paid down from above. This assumption implies that $A_{K_j}(t, T_i) = 0$ for all dates $T_i \leqslant T^*$ and for all detachment points $K_j < 1$.

Typically, in such structures, the most junior tranches are very thin with respect to the most senior tranches. It is not unusual for the latter to be related to more than 90% of total initial portfolio nominals. Moreover, in practice, these structures are "called" when the amortisation process has reduced a large part of the pool (typically 90%). Therefore, Assumption 12.1 was particularly reasonable before the 2007–9 crisis and it is still relevant for most structures. Under Assumption 12.1, Fermanian (2010) has provided closed-form formulas for $\mathcal{E}_1(s)$ and $\mathcal{E}_2(s,\bar{s})$. In his paper, general semi-analytical formulas have been proved when this assumption is removed.

Note that, under Assumption 12.1, $\mathcal{E}_1(s)$ and $\mathcal{E}_2(s,\bar{s})$ are significantly simplified. For instance, for all the tranches except the most senior one, we now have

$$\mathcal{E}_1(s) = E_t\left[\exp\left(-\int_t^s r_u\, du\right)[K - L(s)]^+\right]$$

and

$$\mathcal{E}_2(s,\bar{s}) = E_t\left[\exp\left(-\int_t^s r_u\, du\right)\mathbf{1}\{L(s) \leq K\}L(\bar{s})\right]$$

The expectations $\mathcal{E}_1$ and $\mathcal{E}_2$ above can be deduced from the value of some options that are written on the loss process $L(\cdot)$. Basically, it is more relevant to work in terms of the (non-discounted) expected loss process itself, which is defined by

$$\mathrm{EL}(t,T) := E[L(T) \mid \mathcal{F}_t] = E_t[L(T)]$$

Indeed, this process takes into account all the forecasts in the market continuously. Therefore, it is more acceptable to set some diffusion processes on the expected losses than on the credit losses directly. Moreover, it allows us to specify a large variety of behaviours depending on the remaining time to maturity in a consistent way. The effect of time and maturities is strong for MBSs: at the beginning of the pool, default/prepayment rates are low, due to borrowers' selection processes (the so-called "seasoning effect"). Then, typically, these rates are upward sloping, and after some years they start to decrease. Indeed, the borrowers that have "bad" individual characteristics have already defaulted/prepaid, and only the relatively safest borrowers stay in the pool (the "burnout effect"). Finally, when the process L is essentially increasing, there is no such constraint on EL, which is a desirable property in terms of model specification.

Thus, these previous expectations can be rewritten as functions of the expected losses themselves by noting that $L(s) = \mathrm{EL}(s,s)$. For instance

$$E_1(s) = E_t\left[\exp\left(-\int_t^s r_u\, du\right)[K - \mathrm{EL}(s,s)]^+\right]$$

and

$$E_2(s,\bar{s}) = E_t\left[\exp\left(-\int_t^s r_u\, du\right)\mathbf{1}\{\mathrm{EL}(s,s) \leq K\}\,\mathrm{EL}(\bar{s},\bar{s})\right]$$

These expectations can be calculated as functions of the spot curve $EL(t, \cdot)$ and the model parameters only. From now on, we will consider only the expected loss process, which can be seen as our underlying. Similarly, we define the expected amortised amount process $A(t, T)$ by $A(t, T) := E_t[A(T)]$.

Moreover, to evaluate the functions $RA_{t,K}$ and $DL_{t,K}$, we have to take into account the randomness of interest rates. Indeed, it has long been observed that the price of mortgage-backed securities depends strongly on the interest rate curves (see, for example, Boudoukh *et al* 1997), at least through prepayment. But we go further. It is intuitively clear that default rates themselves depend on interest rates. All other things being equal, the higher the rates, the more numerous the default events should be. Indeed, such increases induce financial difficulties for the debtors that are involved in floating rate loans. It should be stressed that, due to central bank policies, interest rates tend to fall when default rates skyrocket during strong recessions. This could create an opposite trend. As a consequence, the sign of the correlation between interest rate and default rates moves may be ambiguous.

Now, we assume that the expected loss process is lognormal. Since $EL(\cdot, T)$ is a Q-martingale by construction, its drift is zero. That is, we make the following assumptions.

Assumption 12.2. For all times t and T

$$EL(dt, T) = EL(t, T)\sigma(t, T)\, dW_t$$

Obviously, $(W_t)_{t \in [0,T]}$ is an $\mathcal{F}$-adapted Brownian motion under Q. For the moment, we assume that we know the quantities $EL(t, \cdot)$ at the current time t, as they can be observed in the market. Now, let us deal with the interest rate process.

Assumption 12.3. Every discount factor $B(t, T)$ follows the dynamics

$$\frac{B(dt, T)}{B(t, T)} = (\cdots)\, dt + \bar{\sigma}(t, T)\, d\overline{W}_t$$

for all T and $t \in [0, T]$. Here, $(\overline{W}_t)$ is an $\mathcal{F}$-adapted Brownian motion under Q, and $E[dW_t \cdot d\overline{W}_t] = \rho\, dt$.

Similarly, we can tackle the amortisation process $A(t, T)$, which will be assumed to be lognormal.

Assumption 12.4. For all times t and T

$$A(\mathrm{d}t, T) = A(t, T)\tau(t, T)\,\mathrm{d}\overline{W}_t$$

All the previous volatility functions are assumed to be deterministic, in order to simplify calculations. But Assumption 12.4 could be weakened. Moreover, a perfect correlation between the amortisation process and the interest rate process has been assumed, essentially for convenience. This could be weakened at the cost of additional technicalities. The lognormal specification does not prohibit some strange features like $A(t,s) > 1$ or $EL(t,s) > 1$ for some dates (s,t) and with some (small) probability. Theoretically, such events are unlikely. This is the price to be paid in order to have a simple specification under Assumption 12.1, and such phenomena are common in asset pricing (think about Gaussian interest rate models). Actually, this issue will be significantly reduced with reasonable parameter values and without pricing very high tranches of the capital structure.

It should come as no surprise that the expected loss process $EL(\cdot, T)$ may decrease in time, for a given time horizon T. Indeed, this process is related partly to some expectations of future losses and partly to the current realised losses. Future expected losses could become smaller tomorrow if the market participants become more confident about the financial strength of the borrowers in the pool. Moreover, in the ABS world, it is even possible to recover some losses in the future. Indeed, recorded losses do not necessarily imply the closure of deals/tranches. These losses can be temporary, because they are based on some statistical models and projected cashflows. In other words, losses are not clearly identified with certainty before the formal termination of the distressed loans considered. Therefore, marked-to-model losses can be recorded one day and recovered at least partly afterwards. These temporary losses are clearly a source of difference with corporate CDOs.

Through some change-of-numéraire techniques, Fermanian (2010) has calculated the expectations $\mathcal{E}_1$ and $\mathcal{E}_2$, both under and without Assumption 12.1. In the former case, simple closed-form formulas were obtained. In the latter case, semi-analytical formulas were obtained: conditionally on the amortised amount at the relevant date, formulas of the "Assumption 12.1 case" can be applied and integrated with respect to the law of the random variable $A(s,s)$, for every s.

Now, assume the current time is t. To obtain t-prices of tranches, it remains to evaluate the t-spot expected losses $EL(t, T)$ and, for the most senior tranche, the expected amortised amount $A(t, T)$. Since they are not observed directly in the market, additional assumptions concerning the shape of the t-current profile $T \mapsto E(t, T)$ have to be made. For instance, we could state that, with a constant rate $\theta_t > 0$, we have

$$EL(t, dT) = \theta_t \cdot E_t[O(T)] \, dT$$

This constant θ_t has the status of a constant default rate, even if it is related to some expectations of losses. Note that the above relation induces a feedback of losses towards the amortisation process $A(\cdot, \cdot)$ through $O(\cdot, \cdot)$.

Formally, we could deal with the amortisation process as with the expected loss process itself. For the moment, we have merely to evaluate $A(t, T)$ knowing the information at time t. We will assume that

$$A(t, dT) = [\xi_{t,T} + b_t] \cdot E_t[O(T)] dT$$

where $\xi_{t,T}$ is the "theoretical" amortisation rate at time t for the T maturity, and b_t is a constant risk premium. The former quantity is the time-T rate of decrease in terms of the notional, assuming there will be no prepayments. This can be inferred from a description of the cashflows that are associated with the survival assets in the pool at time t. This rate $\xi_{t,T}$ is the global risk premium associated with both the prepayment process and the amortisation process. If $\xi_{t,\cdot}$ were a constant function, then $(\xi_{t,\cdot} + b_t)$ would be the t-amortisation rate and b_t could be seen as the so-called "constant prepayment rate" at time t. The constancy of b_t with respect to T has been made just for convenience. It is straightforward to extend the results to deal with (deterministic) term structures of prepayment rates. Since $E_t[O(T)] = 1 - A(t, T) - EL(t, T)$, we deduce that

$$E_t[O(dT)] = -A(t, dT) - EL(t, dT) = -(\theta_t + b_t + \xi_{t,T}) E_t[O(T)] \, dT$$

and therefore

$$E_t[O(T)] = O(t) \exp\left(-(\theta_t + b_t) \cdot (T - t) - \int_t^T \xi_{t,u} \, du\right)$$

Finally, we get

$$EL(t, T) = EL(t, t) + O(t) \theta_t \int_t^T \exp\left(-(\theta_t + b_t) \cdot (u - t) - \int_t^u \xi_{t,v} \, dv\right) du$$
(12.6)

Thus, at the current time t, the expected loss depends only on the "no-default, no-prepayment" amortisation profile and on some constants θ_t and b_t. We have replaced a whole unknown spot curve $\mathrm{EL}(t, \cdot)$ by a parameterisation of this curve, given by Equation 12.6. Obviously, other choices of spot EL curves are possible, even from a purely non-parametric point of view, if the data related to the pool are sufficiently rich. Note that Equation 12.6 does not contradict Assumption 12.2.

Similarly, we deduce the spot amortisation profile, ie, the curve $A(t, \cdot)$

$$A(t, T) = A(t, t) + O(t) \int_t^T (\xi_{t,u} + b_t) \\ \times \exp\left(-(\theta_t + b_t) \cdot (u - t) - \int_t^u \xi_{t,v}\, dv\right) du$$

Then we have obtained all the building blocks to price standard synthetic tranches.

DISCUSSION AND PRACTICAL ISSUES

The different approaches given above have their pros and cons. But besides theoretical arguments in favour of or against any of them, the practical implications are crucial, particularly in terms of calculation time. Indeed, any ABS bond contains at least hundreds (more often thousands) of individual loans, for which a lot of information is available: the history of past payments, the features of every loan and every borrower, etc. A first crucial decision is to know whether quants/modellers want to use all this information or just a relatively small part of it. In the former case, they will naturally build a "bottom-up" model. In the latter case, they will be attracted by "top-down" approaches.

Clearly, this decision has significant practical consequences. Actually, such a decision is related to the "infinitely granular" assumption, which was established by the famous "Basel II model" (Gordy 2003): any individual credit exposure in the pool is sufficiently small that some "law of large numbers" effect applies. In particular, all idiosyncratic behaviours are perfectly diversified, and the risk in the portfolio is driven entirely by the underlying systemic factors. Such a behaviour is likely in mortgages that include large pools of "not too dissimilar" loans. When most of the loans are of the same nature (fixed rate or ARM 2/28, for example) and when borrowers share similarities (all of them are poor quality subprime borrowers, or, alternatively, all of them are implicitly guaranteed by an agency), we accumulate arguments in favour of the "infinitely granular" assumption.

Actually, the distinction above between "bottom-up" and "top-down" approaches is not just a consequence of the potential granularity level. Indeed, in both frameworks we can find variable degrees of use of loan-per-loan static data and dynamic features: the current and past status of the borrowers, their time spent in delinquency or foreclosure states, and, more generally, all the individual loan histories. To be specific, a basic bottom-up model could not be calibrated precisely to all these features, and it will use only a few of them (for example, the default/prepayment probability conditional on the initial FICO score, or conditional on the current borrower state). It is particularly true for structural models. On the other hand, there is some space, at least in theory, for the building of very rich dynamic intensity-based processes for every loan, possibly with many explanatory variables. Apparently, a top-down model does not have to deal with numerous individual characteristics. But, in the previous section, we pointed out that these characteristics have to be managed in order to estimate the relevant mean default rates θ_t and mean prepayments rates b_t. In practice, under a historical calibration point of view, this may imply the estimation of individual default and prepayment rates followed by an aggregation stage over all the borrowers. Therefore, the calibration step of a top-down model often involves the management of loan-level information. Actually, this historical calibration procedure is the standard approach because of the lack of market instruments to calibrate top-down model parameters. Indeed, with the notable exception of ABX-type quotes, it is difficult to find sufficiently reliable quotes to lead a usual "risk-neutral" calibration with ABS structured products.

An important discrepancy between the corporate synthetic CDO world and the ABS/MBS world is hedging. Indeed, credit default swaps are available for a lot of corporate firms. They allow continuous (partial) hedging, and even perfect replication under some no-jump-to-default assumptions (Fermanian and Vigneron 2009). Even with top-down approaches, it may be possible to calculate hedge ratios (at least in theory) by the use of random thinning techniques

(Giesecke *et al* 2010). Unfortunately, micro-hedging is clearly a pipe dream for retail-based products (as it is for most ABSs), because no market instruments are available. Actually, management of loan-per-loan risk is virtually impossible with large pools (larger than several hundreds of names) in practice. This is particularly true for the securitisation of tranches, such as for CDOs of ABSs. In this case, the usual shortcut is to assume that every tranche behaves like a bond and we recover the usual CDO framework (see, for example, Jäckel 2008). It is clearly a strong assumption, because of the non-linearity of the credit risk of tranches. In theory, it would be necessary to model and price simultaneously and consistently every "first-level" tranche. But the IT and operational effort required is huge. Thus, it is not really a surprise that rating agency models and even most dealer models of CDOs of ABSs have been accused of using models/platforms that are too simplistic to manage such a level of complexity, especially during the stressed period of time we saw in 2007–9.

Another source of discrepancy is in the definition of default events themselves. Officially, a corporate default is realised when an announcement appears in a shortlist of financial newspapers. Even if the recovery process can take several weeks or even months, the default event is taken as certain and quoted recovery rates appear quickly in the market. Therefore, formally and in practice between dealers, a default event can be considered as a point in time with a slight approximation. This is clearly an advantage in terms of modelling. Unfortunately, for mortgages, it is not entirely the case. Default is progressive and there is no consensus in defining a particular point in time that would be called "default time": 30, 60 or 90 days of delinquency, or even more? What about foreclosure or real estate owned? In every case, the legal termination of a mortgage debt in trouble is the final stage of a relatively long process (several months at least), that often (but not always) finishes with the sale of a house, and during which cashflows continue due to servicers' activity. This uncertainty concerning default dates of mortgages is a source of noise and fragility in most pricing models, especially when we want them to mimic CDO models, which do not really suffer from this issue.

In the corporate world, it has been recognised for a long time that recovery rates cannot be considered to be constant over time.

Indeed, they vary significantly depending on the macro-economic environment. In particular, when the economy is plummeting and default rates surge, recovery rates tend to be smaller than their historical averages.[3] But, for a long time, corporate CDS and CDOs were priced with constant recoveries, essentially for the sake of simplicity. Recently, and as a result of the credit crisis in 2007–9, stochastic recoveries have been introduced in order to price synthetic CDOs. Particularly in the standard structural approach, recoveries are linked with the systemic factor.[4] Similar propositions have emerged in the same spirit for intensity-based CDO models.[5] This approach is clearly relevant for ABS products. In a certain sense, the link between recoveries (or severities) and some systemic factors is even stronger and more natural for ABSs than for corporate debt. Indeed, in the case of mortgages, the value of houses and their recovered values in case of liquidation are directly linked to the prices on the local housing market. Moreover, at least in the US, mortgage default likelihoods are closely related to the value of collaterals: when the market value of the collateral (the house) is larger then the value of the debt (the mortgage), the "negative equity" borrowers tend to default more frequently, all other things being equal; this is in line with rational behaviour. Therefore, when dealing with mortgages, the independence of recovery rates and default times is clearly not a reasonable assumption, when it is acceptable with corporate debt as a first approximation. Furthermore, the necessity for modelling jointly default, prepayment and severity adds another level of complexity to the pricing of ABSs and CMOs.

THE "PERFECT" WORLD

In theory, financial engineers can imagine a "perfect model" for pricing ABS-related structures, conditionally on the current historical and market information and on the existing information technology. Here we briefly propose some guidelines for pricing a CMO tranche, knowing that this programme can be extended to other ABSs including CDOs of ABSs.

(i) For every individual loan i in the pool, define a "latent" process $(X_{it})_{t>0}$ that drives i's default risk. Similarly, define a "latent" process $(Y_{it})_{t>0}$ that drives i's prepayment risk. These processes could be dealt with as classical asset values but they could also be stochastic intensities or other quantities that allow the calculation of default/prepayment durations.

(ii) Introduce dependency between all these processes. The most standard way of doing this is through factor models: split all these processes between systemic and idiosyncratic components; the former will be dependent, while the latter will be independent.

(iii) Generate a vector path of all the previous systemic factors. Draw individual trajectories of (X_{it}) and (Y_{it}) and then default and/or prepayment events.

(iv) Compute the associated projected cashflows, conditionally on the previous simulated scenario. Calculate the present value of these future cashflows.

(v) Repeat steps (iii) and (iv) multiple times. The price of the tranche is given by the average of all these present values.

Potentially, step (iii) is able to reflect all the features of any structure: changes of tranche ratings, moves on the house market, credit-trigger behaviour, etc. Obviously, such a program has to solve some technical issues. The first issue is simply the exact specification of all the above processes and their interdependency. Strangely, however, this point is not the most problematic, because an arsenal of potential models has been developed intensively by quants since the 1990s especially to price CDOs.

Calibration is more critical. Indeed, under this reduced-form point of view, financial engineers need an impressive amount of data to calibrate the thousands of underlying processes. Clearly, there are very few market quotes/prices, even if these few can provide valuable benchmarks. Thus, by default, historical calibration is mandatory, but under the implicit assumption that the borrower behaviours and the past explanatory variables will have the same effects in the future. Unfortunately, this assumption is highly questionable, particularly in the case of structural modifications in the market, as occurred in the US with the federal Home Affordable Modification Program (HAMP) during 2009–10.

Even if past history is relevant to explain the future behaviour of borrowers, the estimation of all the model coefficients is a statistical challenge. In theory, the literature on duration models (Kalbfleisch and Prentice 1980; Andersen *et al* 1993) and competing risks (Crowder 2001) is significant and we can rely on numerous estimation techniques. However, these techniques have been developed particularly in biology, where samples are small (at most a few hundred names). An even better source could be provided by the works of micro-econometricians who have studied individual strategies and behaviours on the labour market.[6] In every case, the identification and measurement of the underlying explanatory variable effects is far from straightforward. This task is complicated by the existence of unobservable latent variables, common factors, time-dependent covariates and by the treatment of right censoring and possibly left truncation.

Another significant hurdle is due to IT infrastructures and calculation times. Indeed, the computational power that is required to follow our "perfect model" program is impressive. To fix these ideas, imagine we want to price a mortgage-backed security that contains 1,000 loans with maturities of around 30 years. It is usual practice to use monthly time steps, because of monthly coupon payments. Moreover, in the world of derivatives, a realistic pricing by simulation cannot usually be based on less than 1,000 random paths. Thus, we will have to calculate a borrower state and its current balance at least 360 million times, at least. Furthermore, in the case of intensity models, it is necessary to estimate default/prepayment monthly rates through the lines above, before simulating these events, ie, to estimate laws before simulating realisations under these laws. It is well known this "Monte Carlo of Monte Carlo" procedure is particularly costly. Even with the most up-to-date computers, the computational challenge is significant and only a few dealers would be able to develop a sufficiently powerful pricing platform to follow our "perfect world" agenda.

CONCLUSION

Corporate collateralised debt obligations and structures based on asset-backed securities are clearly different products. They are traded in different markets, as proved by the determinants of their spread behaviours (Vink and Thibeault 2008). Nonetheless, their significant similarities in terms of payouts justify our comparison of their respective pricing models. We have argued that these two worlds have not sufficiently interacted in the past. We have tried to explain why and to what extent some models that have been developed by the quants on the one side could be adopted by the other side. Particularly, we have detailed an original one-factor "top-down" approach for ABS structures, in the same spirit as the models proposed for synthetic corporate CDOs in recent years. Finally, the discrepancies and particularities of both worlds have been discussed, particularly from a practical point of view (eg, calibration, data sets, IT platforms). Today, in order to obtain a "pure" pricing of ABS-related products, as may be done with other underlyings (rates or stock derivatives), the hurdles are numerous even if a theoretically ideal pricing framework can be described.

1 A complete picture of the historical debate is given in Brigo *et al* (2010).
2 See Deng (1997), Kariya and Kobayashi (2000), Kariya *et al* (2002), among others.
3 See, for example, Altman *et al* (2004, 2005) and Altman (2006).
4 See Andersen and Sidenius (2004), Amraoui *et al* (2009), among others.
5 See Christensen (2005, 2007), Karoui (2007), Dobranszky (2008), etc.
6 See, for example, Lancaster (1990).

REFERENCES

Altman, E., 2006, "Default Recovery Rates and LGD in Credit Risk Modeling and Practice: An Updated Review of the Literature and Empirical Evidence", Working Paper, New York University.

Altman, E., A. Resti and A. Sironi, 2004, "Default Recovery Rates in Credit Risk Modelling: A Review of the Literature and Empirical Evidence", *Economic Notes* 33(2), pp. 183–208.

Altman, E., B. Brady, A. Resti and A. Sironi, 2005, "The Link between Default and Recovery Rates: Theory, Empirical Evidence, and Implications", *Journal of Business* 78(6), pp. 2203–27.

Amraoui S., L. Cousot, S. Hitier and J.-P. Laurent, 2009, "Pricing CDOs with State Dependent Stochastic Recovery Rates", Working Paper.

Andersen L., and J. Sidenius, 2004, "Extension to the Gaussian Copula: Random Recovery and Random Factor Loadings", *Journal of Credit Risk* 1(1), pp. 29–70.

Andersen, L., V. Piterbarg and J. Sidenius, 2008, "A New Framework for Dynamic Credit Portfolio Loss Modeling", *Journal of Theoretical Applied Finance* 11, pp. 163–97.

Andersen, P. K., Ø. Borgan, R. D. Gill and N. Keiding, 1993, *Statistical Models Based on Counting Processes* (Springer).

Bennani, N., 2005, "The Forward Loss Model: A Dynamic Term Structure Approach for the Pricing of Portfolio Credit Derivatives", Working Paper, Royal Bank of Scotland.

Brigo, D., A. Pallavicini and R. Torresetti, 2010, "Credit Models and the Crisis: Or How I Learned to Stop Worrying and Love the CDOs", Working Paper, URL: http://ssrn.com/abstract=1529498.

Boudoukh, J., R. F. Whitelaw, M. Richardson and R. Stanton, 1997, "Pricing Mortgage-Backed Securities in a Multifactor Rate Environment: A Mutivariate Density Estimation Approach", *Review of Financial Studies* 10, pp. 405–46.

Chapovsky, A., A. Rennie and P. Tavares, 2006, "Stochastic Intensity Modelling for Structured Credit Exotics", Technical Report, Merrill Lynch, October.

Christensen, J. H. E., 2005, "Joint Estimation of Default and Recovery Risk: A Simulation Study", Working Paper, Department of Finance, Copenhagen Business School.

Christensen, J. H. E., 2007, "Joint Default and Recovery Risk Estimation: An Application to CDS Data", Working Paper, URL: http://www.fdic.gov/bank/.

Crowder, M., 2001, *Classical Competing Risks* (London: Chapman and Hall).

Deng, Y., 1997, "Mortgage Termination: An Empirical Hazard Model with a Stochastic Term Structure", *Journal of Real Estate and Economics* 14, pp. 309–31.

Deng, Y., J. M. Quigley and R. Van Order, 2000, "Mortgage Termination, Heterogeneity, and the Exercise of Mortgage Options", *Econometrica* 68, pp. 275–307.

Dobranszky, P., 2008, "Joint Modelling of CDS and LCDS Spreads with Correlated Default and Prepayment Intensities and with Stochastic Recovery Rate", Working Paper, URL: http://ssrn.com/abstract=1262217.

Duffie, D., and N. Garleanu, 2001, "Risk and Valuation of Collateralized Debt Obligations", *Financial Analysts Journal* 57(1), pp. 41–59.

Duffie, D., J. Pan and K. Singleton, 2000, "Transform Analysis and Asset Pricing for Affine Jump Diffusions", *Econometrica* 68, pp. 1343–76.

Eckner, T., 2009, "Computational Techniques for Basic Affine Models of Portfolio Credit", *Journal of Computational Finance* 13(1), Fall.

Fabozzi, F. J., and V. Kothari, 2008, *Introduction to Securitization* (Chichester: John Wiley & Sons).

Finger, C., 2004, "Issues in the Pricing of Synthetic CDOs", Working Paper 04-01, Riskmetrics.

Fermanian, J.-D., 2010, "A Top-Down Approach for Asset-Backed Securities: A Consistent Way of Managing Prepayment, Default and Interest Rate Risks", Working Paper, URL: http//www.ssrn.com.

Fermanian, J.-D., and O. Vigneron, 2009, "On Break-Even Correlation: The Way to Price Structured Credit Derivatives by Replication", Working Paper, URL: http://www.defaultrisk.com.

Fermanian, J.-D., and O. Vigneron, 2010, "Pricing and Hedging Basket Credit Derivatives in the Gaussian Copula", *Risk Magazine*, February, pp. 92–6.

Garcia, J., and S. Goossens, 2008a, "One Factor Models for the ABS Correlation Market: Pricing TABX Tranches", Working Paper, URL: http://ssrn.com/abstract=1274808.

Garcia, J., and S. Goossens, 2008b, "One Credit Event Models for CDO of ABS", Working Paper.

Giesecke, K, L. Goldberg and X. Ding, 2010, "A Top-Down Approach to Multi-Name Credit", Working Paper, URL: http://ssrn.com/abstract=1312275.

Gordy, M., 2003, "A Risk-Factor Model Foundation for Ratings-Based Bank Capital Rules", *Journal of Financial Intermediation* 12, pp. 199–232.

Goncharov, Y., 2002, "An Intensity-Based Approach to Valuation of Mortgage Contracts subject to Prepayment Risk", Working Paper, University of Illinois at Chicago.

Hull, J., and A. White, 2009, "The Risk of Tranches Created from Residential Mortgages", Working Paper.

Jäckel, P., 2008, "Gamma Loss and Prepayment", *Risk Magazine*, September.

Kalbfleisch, J. D., and R. L. Prentice, 1980, *The Statistical Analysis of Failure Time Data* (Chichester: John Wiley & Sons).

Kariya, T., and M. Kobayashi, 2000, "Pricing Mortgage Backed Securities (MBS): A Model Describing the Burnout Effect", *Asia–Pacific Financial Markets* 7, pp. 182–204.

Kariya, T., S. R. Pliska and F. Ushiyama, 2002, "A 3-Factor Valuation Model for Mortgage Backed Securities (MBS)", Working Paper, Kyoto Institute of Economic Research.

Karoui, L., 2007, "Modeling Defaultable Securities with Recovery Risk", Working Paper, McGill University.

Kau, J., D. Keenan and A. Smurov, 2006, "Reduced-Form Mortgage Pricing as an Alternative to Option-Pricing Models", *The Journal of Real Estate Finance Economics* 33(3), pp. 183–96.

Lancaster, T., 1990, *The Econometric Analysis of Transition Data* (Cambridge University Press).

Li, D., 2000, "On Default Correlation: A Copula Function Approach", *Journal of Fixed Income* 9(4), pp. 43–54.

Lipton, A., and A. Rennie (eds), 2007, *Credit Correlation: Life after Copulas* (World Scientific).

Lou, W., 2007, "Valuation of Subprime Mortgage-Backed Securities: A Portfolio Credit Derivatives Approach", Working Paper.

Merton, R., 1974, "On the Pricing of Corporate Debt: The Risk Structure of Interest Rates", *The Journal of Finance* 29(2), pp. 449–70.

Mortensen, A., 2006, "Semi-Analytical Valuation of Basket Credit Derivatives in Intensity-Based Models", Working Paper, URL: http://ssrn.com/abstract=663425.

Richard, F., and R. Roll, 1989, "Prepayment on Fixed-Rate Mortgage-Backed Securities" *Journal of Portfolio Management* 15, pp. 73–82.

Salmon, F., 2009, "Recipe for Disaster: The Formula That Killed Wall-Street", *Wired Magazine*, URL: http://www.wired.com/.

Schönbucher, P., 2005, "Portfolio Losses and the Term Structure of Loss Transition Rates: A New Methodology for the Pricing of Portfolio Credit Derivatives", Working Paper, ETH, Zurich.

Schwartz, E., and W. N. Torous, 1989, "Prepayment and the Valuation of Mortgage-Backed-Securities", *The Journal of Finance* 44, pp. 375–92.

Takavoli, J., 2008, *Structured Finance and Collateralized Debt Obligations: New Developments in Cash and Synthetic Securitization* (Chichester: John Wiley & Sons).

Tsiatis, A., 1975, "A Nonidentifiability Aspect of the Problem of Competing Risks", *Proceedings of the National Academy of Science of the United States of America* 72, pp. 20–2.

Vink, D., and A. E. Thibeault, 2008, "ABS, MBS and CDO Compared: An Empirical Analysis", *The Journal of Structured Finance* 14(2), pp. 27–45.

Zhou, C., 2001, "An Analysis of Default Correlations and Multiple Defaults", *The Review of Financial Studies* 14, pp. 555–76.

13

Pricing of Credit Derivatives with and without Counterparty and Collateral Adjustments

Alexander Lipton; David Shelton

Bank of America Merrill Lynch, Imperial College London;
Bank of America Merrill Lynch

Subsequent to the financial crisis of 2007–8, the credit value adjustment (CVA) for derivatives positions (that is, the adjustment to valuation required to account for the credit risk of one or both counterparties who have entered into a portfolio of transactions) has been an area of heightened focus for banks, regulators and politicians.

In this chapter we will concentrate on the particular case of a portfolio of single name credit default swaps (CDSs). This is a pertinent example since it exhibits so-called "wrong way risk" (Redon 2006); in other words, the size of the exposure is positively correlated with the likelihood of default of the counterparty, as well as being highly asymmetric with respect to the two counterparties. In order to capture this effect, we need to model the default correlation between issuers with a common factor. As we will see, in order to generate significant default correlation it becomes essential to incorporate jumps in this process, representing sudden economy-wide deterioration of credit quality.

Whatever the underlying political motivation for attempting to introduce one or more central clearing counterparties for CDSs, it is clear (Duffie and Zhu 2009) that counterparty risk will certainly not be eliminated and may in fact be increased, and hence the problem remains a relevant one.

CREDIT VALUE ADJUSTMENT FOR CREDIT DEFAULT SWAPS AND SHORTFALL FOR CREDIT-LINKED NOTES

Generally, in the presence of an International Swaps and Derivatives Association (ISDA) CSA (Credit Support Annex), it is necessary to consider an entire "netting set" of trades when evaluating the CVA, since the overall CVA is a function of the mark to market (MTM) of an entire portfolio of trades with a given counterparty when the default occurs. A good summary is presented in Pykhtin and Zhu (2006), Zhu and Pykhtin (2007) and Gregory (2009), although some of the ideas go back at least as far as Sorensen and Bollier (1994) and Duffie and Huang (1996) (see also Duffie 2001).

In order to capture this effect precisely for a margined portfolio, we need to incorporate information about not just the entire netting set of trades with a given counterparty, but also the rules governing triggering of collateral calls, the minimum transfer amount (MTA) and how long the counterparty has to post the collateral in the event that it is called for. In this chapter we shall not dwell on these specific details but rather present a general framework for computing the CVA for a portfolio of credit default swaps (CDSs). This provides a test case with which to understand the effect of default correlation and "wrong way risk" on the CVA of credit derivatives positions.

We will also consider the case of a credit-linked note (CLN) where the issuer (usually a trust or special purpose vehicle (SPV)) has sold CDS protection referencing a single credit. This is a case where there genuinely is no "netting set" or CSA since the position is fully collateralised up front, and hence treating a single trade in isolation makes sense. Since the CLN is collateralised with credit risky collateral which may exhibit changes in mark to market or default, there is the possibility of shortfall in a credit event. As a result of its limited recourse feature, the CLN is genuinely isolated from the credit risk of the noteholder. Here instead the credit risk of the collateral plays a role similar to that of the risky protection seller in a more conventional CDS CVA calculation.

Valuation of a portfolio of CDS positions

In general in this chapter, we denote "us" by credit 1, the risky counterparty by credit 2 and consider the value of a derivatives position referencing credits $3, \ldots, N$ from the point of view of counterparty 1. We denote the value of the theoretical fully collateralised position by $U^{\{3,\ldots,N\}}$.

In the case where one or other counterparty is risky and the position is not fully collateralised it is also useful to define a "collateral shortfall"

$$Z^{\{3,\ldots,N\}} = U^{\{3,\ldots,N\}} - C^{\{3,\ldots,N\}} \quad (13.1)$$

This is the theoretical fully collateralised value minus the value of the available collateral $C^{\{3,\ldots,N\}}$. By this definition, if $C^{\{3,\ldots,N\}} > 0$, counterparty 2 has net posted collateral to counterparty 1, and if $C^{\{3,\ldots,N\}} < 0$, counterparty 1 has net posted collateral to counterparty 2. In the event that $Z^{\{3,\ldots,N\}} \neq 0$ at the time of default of one or other counterparty, there can be a shortfall and hence a non-zero CVA.

We denote by $V^{\{2,3,\ldots,N\}}$ the value of the derivative position assuming credit 1 to be risk-free but incorporating the risk of credit 2 and by $V^{\{1,3,\ldots,N\}}$ the value of the position assuming credit 2 to be risk-free but incorporating the risk of credit 1. We define the corresponding unilateral CVAs

$$W^{\{2,3,\ldots,N\}} = V^{\{2,3,\ldots,N\}} - U^{\{3,\ldots,N\}} \quad (13.2)$$
$$W^{\{1,3,\ldots,N\}} = V^{\{1,3,\ldots,N\}} - U^{\{3,\ldots,N\}} \quad (13.3)$$

We denote the value of the position in which we incorporate the credit risk of both credit 1 and credit 2 by $V^{\{1,2,3,\ldots,N\}}$. We define the corresponding bilateral CVA

$$W^{\{1,2,3,\ldots,N\}} = V^{\{1,2,3,\ldots,N\}} - U^{\{3,\ldots,N\}} \quad (13.4)$$

Generally, we decompose the bilateral CVA into one contribution coming from the default of credit 1, and one from the default of credit 2

$$W^{\{1,2,3,\ldots,N\}} = W_1^{\{1,2,3,\ldots,N\}} + W_2^{\{1,2,3,\ldots,N\}} \quad (13.5)$$

Fully collateralised CDS

For a theoretical fully collateralised CDS position, there is no CVA. The time-t value $U^{\{i\}}(t)$ of a fully collateralised, notional η_i, T-expiry CDS referencing credit i, paying a (continuous) coupon $\eta_i c_i$ in exchange for receiving $\eta_i L_i$ on default of credit i can be expressed as

$$U^{\{i\}}(t) = \eta_i(U_{DL}^{\{i\}}(t) - U_{CL}^{\{i\}}(t)) \quad (13.6)$$

Here $U_{DL}^{\{i\}}(t)$ and $U_{CL}^{\{i\}}(t)$ denote the values of the default and coupon legs, respectively, for a unit notional CDS. These can be expressed in terms of following risk-neutral expectations

$$U_{DL}^{\{i\}}(t) = L_i D_t^{-1} \mathbb{E}_t[\mathbf{1}_{t<\tau_i\leqslant T} D_{\tau_i}], \qquad U_{CL}^{\{i\}}(t) = c_i A_t^{\{i\}}(t,T) \quad (13.7)$$

where $A_t^{\{i\}}(t,T)$ denotes the risky annuity

$$A_t^{\{i\}}(t,T) = D_t^{-1} \mathbb{E}_t\left[\int_t^T \mathbf{1}_{\tau_i>v} D_v\, dv\right] \quad (13.8)$$

Here

$$D_T = \exp\left(-\int_0^T r_u\, du\right)$$

is the stochastic discount factor to time T; we denote the default time of the ith credit by τ_i, the recovery by R_i, and $L_i = 1 - R_i$. Note that throughout this chapter, by a slight abuse of notation, we sometimes use R_i to denote the fractional recovery value of a derivatives position, and sometimes the recovery as a fraction of notional of debt of a specific subordination (as here): it should always be apparent which usage is intended.

The theoretical fully collateralised value of a portfolio of CDS can be expressed as

$$U^{\{3,\ldots,N\}}(t) = \sum_{j=3}^{j=N} U^{\{i\}}(t) \quad (13.9)$$

By assumption the corresponding "collateral shortfall" $Z^{\{3,\ldots,N\}}(t) \equiv 0$ at all times in this case, and hence the CVA is zero.

Uncollateralised CDS: unilateral CVA

We now consider a single CDS referencing credit 3, which has been executed between a counterparty who considers themselves risk-free and a risky counterparty, and for which no collateral has been posted by either counterparty. The unilateral CVAs $W^{\{1,3\}}(t) = V^{\{1,3\}}(t) - U^{\{3\}}(t)$ (where credit 2 considers themselves to be risk-free) and $W^{\{2,3\}}(t) = V^{\{2,3\}}(t) - U^{\{3\}}(t)$ (where credit 1 considers themselves to be risk-free) may be expressed as follows (Pykhtin and Zhu 2006)

$$W^{\{1,3\}}(t) = -D_t^{-1}\mathbb{E}_t[\mathbf{1}_{t<(\tau_1\wedge\tau_3)=\tau_1\leqslant T} L_1 D_{\tau_1}(U^{\{3\}}(\tau_1))_-] \quad (13.10)$$

$$W^{\{2,3\}}(t) = -D_t^{-1}\mathbb{E}_t[\mathbf{1}_{t<(\tau_2\wedge\tau_3)=\tau_2\leqslant T} L_2 D_{\tau_2}(U^{\{3\}}(\tau_2))_+] \quad (13.11)$$

Here and throughout we assume that the probability of simultaneous defaults is zero. Expression 13.11 is based on the assumption that if credit 2 defaults and the value of the position to counterparty 1 is positive, they only expect to recover a fraction R_2 of the theoretical fully collateralised value, while if the value of the position is negative, they are still liable for the full amount. In practice, as we will highlight later (see page 357 onwards), this may be an idealised assumption.

Uncollateralised CDS: bilateral CVA

This is the symmetric analogue of the unilateral expressions in Equations 13.10 and 13.11. This time we incorporate the credit risk of both credits 1 and 2, and the value of the position to the risky counterparty 1 can be expressed as

$$V^{\{1,2,3\}}(t) = U^{\{3\}}(t) + W_1^{\{1,2,3\}}(t) + W_2^{\{1,2,3\}}(t)$$

where the bilateral CVA contributions $W_1^{\{1,2,3\}}(t)$ (debit value adjustment: DVA) and $W_2^{\{1,2,3\}}(t)$ (CVA) can be expressed as follows

$$W_1^{\{1,2,3\}}(t) = -D_t^{-1}\mathbb{E}_t[\mathbf{1}_{t<(\tau_1\wedge\tau_2\wedge\tau_3)=\tau_1\leqslant T}L_1 D_{\tau_1}(U^{\{3\}}(\tau_1))_-] \quad (13.12)$$

$$W_2^{\{1,2,3\}}(t) = -D_t^{-1}\mathbb{E}_t[\mathbf{1}_{t<(\tau_1\wedge\tau_2\wedge\tau_3)=\tau_2\leqslant T}L_2 D_{\tau_2}(U^{\{3\}}(\tau_2))_+] \quad (13.13)$$

We note that the expressions in Equations 13.12 and 13.13 are not the same as the corresponding unilateral expressions (Equations 13.10 and 13.11), since the bilateral expectations involve the default time of all three credits, but they are qualitatively similar, and generally for two counterparties of similar credit risk and relatively symmetrical exposures we expect a degree of cancellation. For a summary of the underlying assumptions leading to these expressions, see Gregory (2009) or Brigo and Capponi (2010). We can see straight away from Equations 13.12 and 13.13 that the CVA is less than or equal to 0 while the DVA is greater than or equal to 0: according to these assumptions we can "benefit" from a deterioration of our own credit quality.

Partially collateralised CDS: unilateral and bilateral value adjustments

It is straightforward to generalise the unilateral expressions (Equations 13.10 and 13.11) and bilateral expressions (Equations 13.12 and 13.13) to incorporate partial collateralisation by making the replacement

$$U^{\{3\}}(t) \rightarrow Z^{\{3\}}(t) = U^{\{3\}}(t) - C^{\{3\}}(t) \quad (13.14)$$

In the case of the CDS, we assume that the posted collateral $C^{\{3\}}(t)$ is risk-free; hence, we can express the unilateral CVA as

$$W^{\{1,3\}}(t) = -D_t^{-1}\mathbb{E}_t[\mathbf{1}_{t<(\tau_1\wedge\tau_3)=\tau_1\leqslant T}L_1 D_{\tau_1}(Z^{\{3\}}(\tau_1))_-] \quad (13.15)$$

$$W^{\{2,3\}}(t) = -D_t^{-1}\mathbb{E}_t[\mathbf{1}_{t<(\tau_2\wedge\tau_3)=\tau_2\leqslant T}L_2 D_{\tau_2}(Z^{\{3\}}(\tau_2))_+] \quad (13.16)$$

Similarly, for the bilateral CVA we have

$$W_1^{\{1,2,3\}}(t) = -D_t^{-1}\mathbb{E}_t[\mathbf{1}_{t<(\tau_1\wedge\tau_2\wedge\tau_3)=\tau_1\leqslant T}L_1 D_{\tau_1}(Z^{\{3\}}(\tau_1))_-] \quad (13.17)$$

$$W_2^{\{1,2,3\}}(t) = -D_t^{-1}\mathbb{E}_t[\mathbf{1}_{t<(\tau_1\wedge\tau_2\wedge\tau_3)=\tau_2\leqslant T}L_2 D_{\tau_2}(Z^{\{3\}}(\tau_2))_+] \quad (13.18)$$

As we will see below, the CLN is analogous to a partially collateralised CDS. However, the situation is somewhat different, since the collateral itself can be credit risky, and as a result of the limited recourse feature there can be a shortfall when neither the collateral nor the swap counterparty has defaulted.

CLN: unilateral value adjustment

Credit-linked notes come in various guises and it is not possible to cover every possible contract. Instead, we consider typical examples that exhibit the most important features.

The issuer of a credit-linked note, generally an SPV or trust, takes the funds invested by the noteholders, purchases an issuer-2 bond $B^{\{2\}}(t)$ as collateral, and enters a CDS referencing issuer 3 to sell protection to counterparty 1. The collateral $C^{\{3\}}(t)$ and corresponding collateral shortfall $Z^{\{3\}}(t)$ (Equation 13.1) may therefore be written as

$$C^{\{3\}}(t) = B^{\{2\}}(t) \quad (13.19)$$

$$Z^{\{3\}}(t) = U^{\{3\}}(t) - B^{\{2\}}(t) \quad (13.20)$$

Shortfalls may occur if $Z^{\{3\}}(t)$ is positive (ie, the derivatives position is under-collateralised from the point of view of counterparty 1) when a default has occurred. Treating counterparty 1 as risk-free, the value of the swap $V^{\{2,3\}}(t)$ to counterparty 1 can be written, as before

$$V^{\{2,3\}}(t) = U^{\{3\}}(t) + W^{\{2,3\}}(t) \quad (13.21)$$

Generally, the issuer of the collateral, credit 2, plays a role similar to that of the risky counterparty in Equation 13.16: if the collateral defaults, the trade terminates and the swap counterparty can suffer

PRICING OF CREDIT DERIVATIVES

a shortfall if $Z^{\{3\}}(t) > 0$. Defining $\tau = \tau_2 \wedge \tau_3$, the expression for $W^{\{2,3\}}(t)$ is similar to Equation 13.16

$$W^{\{2,3\}}(t) = -D_t^{-1}\mathbb{E}_t[\mathbf{1}_{t<\tau\leqslant T}D_\tau(Z^{\{3\}}(\tau))_+] \qquad (13.22)$$

However, note that here there can be a shortfall even if both credit 1 and credit 2 remain solvent, since if credit 3 defaults, counterparty 1 has limited recourse in the event that the collateral is inadequate to cover the anticipated payout. We can therefore decompose the unilateral "CVA" equation (Equation 13.22) into two terms

$$W^{\{2,3\}}(t) = W_2^{\{2,3\}}(t) + W_3^{\{2,3\}}(t) \qquad (13.23)$$

$$W_2^{\{2,3\}}(t) = -D_t^{-1}\mathbb{E}_t[\mathbf{1}_{t<\tau=\tau_2\leqslant T}D_{\tau_2}(U^{\{3\}}(\tau_2) - R_2)_+] \qquad (13.24)$$

$$W_3^{\{2,3\}}(t) = -D_t^{-1}\mathbb{E}_t[\mathbf{1}_{t<\tau=\tau_3\leqslant T}D_{\tau_3}(L_3 - B^{\{2\}}(\tau_3))_+] \qquad (13.25)$$

By contrast, for a CDS directly executed with a solvent counterparty 2, there is no shortfall when $\tau = \tau_3$, since even if the collateral posted under the CSA is insufficient to cover the payout, counterparty 1 will be able to request payment of the full amount from counterparty 2. The way in which the recovery R_2 appears in Equation 13.24 also differs from Equation 13.16, where there is an overall pre-factor of $L_2 = 1 - R_2$, since in the CLN case R_2 represents the recovery value of the collateral as a fraction of notional rather than a fraction of the overall exposure as in conventional CVA calculations.

We note that this case is described contractually as the case where the swap counterparty does not bear the MTM risk of the collateral, in the sense that the note issuer must sell as much of the collateral as is necessary to meet their immediate cash obligation to the swap counterparty. One other common case is where the dealer "bears the MTM risk of the collateral". In this case, an obligation to pay the swap counterparty is met by delivering that amount in face value or notional of collateral. Thus, if the bond is above or below par, the dealer will experience a windfall or shortfall, respectively, with respect to the theoretical fully collateralised value

$$W_3^{\{2,3\}}(t) = -D_t^{-1}\mathbb{E}_t[\mathbf{1}_{t<\tau=\tau_3\leqslant T}D_{\tau_3}L_3(1 - B^{\{2\}}(\tau_3))] \qquad (13.26)$$

For the sake of definiteness, in this chapter we will always consider the case presented in Equation 13.25, although there is no difficulty in handling Equation 13.26 and we mention it because it is important in practice.

CLN: bilateral value adjustment

We now consider the case where we also incorporate the credit risk of the CDS counterparty 1. There are several possibilities here, depending both on the term sheet and on legal interpretation. We present here some common contractual terms for what happens in the event of dealer (credit 1) default:

1. collateral is liquidated and the noteholder receives the proceeds (or takes delivery) of the collateral;
2. collateral is liquidated and the noteholder receives the proceeds (or takes delivery) of the collateral, and the swap counterparty owes a "make whole" to the noteholder if the market value of the collateral is below par;
3. collateral is liquidated and the noteholder receives the proceeds (or the noteholder takes delivery) of the collateral, and also is owed any positive mark to market (MTM) to the SPV under the CDS by the swap counterparty;
4. collateral is liquidated and the swap counterparty is paid any positive MTM to it under the CDS, with the noteholder only receiving any surplus liquidation proceeds.

Cases 1–3 generally feature in rated deals, but may also be included in non-rated deals. They all correspond to a "flip clause" whereby, although in all other cases the swap counterparty is senior to the noteholder, in the case of dealer default the seniority "flips" from the swap counterparty to the noteholder: this feature is intended to isolate the noteholders from the risk of default of the swap counterparty. Case 4 only features in some non-rated deals and corresponds to the assumption that the swap counterparty retains seniority over the noteholders. However, as we will discuss later, at the time of writing there are questions as to the legal enforceability of the "flip clause" in some jurisdictions. If it were deemed unenforceable, the swap counterparty would presumably remain senior to the noteholders, and the payout in all cases would end up close to case 4.

We express the value of the swap $V^{\{1,2,3\}}(t)$ to counterparty 1 as

$$V^{\{1,2,3\}}(t) = U^{\{3\}}(t) + W^{\{1,2,3\}}(t) \tag{13.27}$$

$$W^{\{1,2,3\}}(t) = W_1^{\{1,2,3\}}(t) + W_2^{\{1,2,3\}}(t) + W_3^{\{1,2,3\}}(t) \tag{13.28}$$

Here, other than the definition of $\tau = \tau_1 \wedge \tau_2 \wedge \tau_3$, the terms $W_2^{\{1,2,3\}}(t)$ and $W_3^{\{1,2,3\}}(t)$ are identical to Equations 13.24 and 13.25

$$W_2^{\{1,2,3\}}(t) = -D_t^{-1}\mathbb{E}_t[\mathbf{1}_{t<\tau=\tau_2\leqslant T}D_{\tau_2}(Z^{\{3\}}(\tau_2))_+]$$
$$= -D_t^{-1}\mathbb{E}_t[\mathbf{1}_{t<\tau=\tau_2\leqslant T}D_{\tau_2}(U^{\{3\}}(\tau_2) - R_2)_+] \quad (13.29)$$
$$W_3^{\{1,2,3\}}(t) = -D_t^{-1}\mathbb{E}_t[\mathbf{1}_{t<\tau=\tau_3\leqslant T}D_{\tau_3}(Z^{\{3\}}(\tau_3))_+]$$
$$= -D_t^{-1}\mathbb{E}_t[\mathbf{1}_{t<\tau=\tau_3\leqslant T}D_{\tau_3}(L_3 - B^{\{2\}}(\tau_3))_+] \quad (13.30)$$

It is worth noting that, in the case of positive interest rates, we generally have $B^{\{2\}}(t) \geqslant R_2$, ie, the bond is worth more than its recovery value, and $U^{\{3\}}(t) \leqslant 1 - R_3$, ie, the CDS is worth at most its payout in default. Hence, it can be shown that if $R_2 + R_3 \geqslant 1$, the terms $W_2^{\{1,2,3\}}(t) \equiv 0$ and $W_3^{\{1,2,3\}}(t) \equiv 0$ identically. This interesting property is particular to the CLN and shows that these expectations are extremely sensitive to recovery assumptions.

We can express $W_1^{\{1,2,3\}}(t)$ as follows for each of the cases enumerated above

$$W_1^{\{1,2,3\}}(t) = -D_t^{-1}\mathbb{E}_t[\mathbf{1}_{t<\tau=\tau_1\leqslant T}D_{\tau_1}U^{\{3\}}(\tau_1)] \quad (13.31\,\text{a})$$
$$W_1^{\{1,2,3\}}(t) = -D_t^{-1}\mathbb{E}_t[\mathbf{1}_{t<\tau=\tau_1\leqslant T}D_{\tau_1}(U^{\{3\}}(\tau_1) + R_1(1 - B^{\{2\}}(\tau_1))_+)] \quad (13.31\,\text{b})$$
$$W_1^{\{1,2,3\}}(t) = -D_t^{-1}\mathbb{E}_t[\mathbf{1}_{t<\tau=\tau_1\leqslant T}D_{\tau_1}(L_1(U^{\{3\}}(\tau_1))_- + (U^{\{3\}}(\tau_1))_+)] \quad (13.31\,\text{c})$$
$$W_1^{\{1,2,3\}}(t) = -D_t^{-1}\mathbb{E}_t[\mathbf{1}_{t<\tau=\tau_1\leqslant T}D_{\tau_1}(L_1(U^{\{3\}}(\tau_1))_-$$
$$+ (U^{\{3\}}(\tau_1) - B^{\{2\}}(\tau_1))_+)] \quad (13.31\,\text{d})$$

Once again the adjustment term (Equation 13.29) is similar to the CVA for a partially collateralised CDS (Equation 13.18), but there is also a shortfall term (Equation 13.30) deriving from the case where reference entity 3 defaults first. The "own default" terms (Equation 13.31) differ from the typical DVA (Equation 13.17), which is always positive since the dealer always "benefits" from their own default. By contrast, we see from Equation 13.31 that, while in all four cases the dealer may benefit if the theoretical MTM $U^{\{3\}}(\tau)$ of the CDS is negative at the time of default, there are scenarios where the dealer loses and the noteholder benefits. In the first three cases (Equations 13.31 a–13.31 c), this is a direct result of the "flip clause". If the MTM of the CDS to the dealer was positive prior to the default, they will suffer an instantaneous loss on their own default because the noteholder has first recourse to the collateral; hence, there will be no money left to cover the MTM of the CDS. In the fourth case (Equation 13.31 d), the dealer may suffer a loss as a result of the limited recourse feature: although they retain the senior claim, there can still be a shortfall if the collateral is inadequate to cover the MTM of the CDS.

In summary, the value of the CDS with the SPV to the dealer can exhibit a higher CVA-like term than a regular CDS with a similar level of collateralisation, as a result of the limited recourse feature, which can result in a loss even when reference entity 3 defaults first. What is more, the DVA-like adjustment due to the dealer's own default may not act to reduce the net value adjustment and may in fact increase it as a result of either a "flip clause" or the limited recourse feature. Generally, as we will see later, the DVA for a CDS protection buyer is relatively small, as it is "right way" risk and the CDS payout is highly asymmetric. In the case of a CLN the contribution from the dealer's own default can be both large and of opposite sign to conventional DVA. These valuation adjustments may not technically be classified by accountants or lawyers as "CVA" but it is clear that from a mathematical point of view they are closely related.

One final case that can be important is where the swap counterparty 1 is also the issuer of the collateral 2. In this case we redefine $\tau = \tau_1 \wedge \tau_3$ and Equation 13.30 and 13.31 continue to hold for the shortfall in the event of default of either credit 1 or 3, with the proviso that wherever the bond price $B^{\{2\}}(t)$ appears in Equation 13.31 it must be replaced by its recovery value, R_1.

Finally, as a result of the symmetric nature of the problem, if we denote the value of the swap to the dealer by $V(t)$, the value of the CLN to the noteholder can be expressed as

$$\left. \begin{array}{l} \text{Value of swap to dealer: } V^{\{1,2,3\}}(t) \\ \text{Value of CLN to noteholder: } B^{\{2\}}(t) - V^{\{1,2,3\}}(t) \end{array} \right\} \quad (13.32)$$

This reflects the fact that the total collateral available to satisfy the claims of both the swap counterparty and the noteholders is simply $B^{\{2\}}(t)$; hence, the total value of both positions must equate to the present value of the collateral.

Practical issues and controversies

At this stage it is worth commenting on the applicability of this framework in the real world. An obvious test case for the default of a dealer counterparty is Lehman Brothers, for which the credit event determination date was September 16, 2008. One of the assumptions of CVA is that the undefaulted counterparty will continue to make contractual payments to the defaulted one. However, some counterparties who had bought credit protection from Lehman and were suffering significant cashflow issues themselves opted in the heat of the crisis to withhold premium payments for protection that they were unlikely ever to receive. The highly asymmetric nature of the CDS payout compared with the more balanced profile of, for example, an interest rate swap was thrown into high relief in these cases. We can therefore question whether assuming continuation of contractual payments to the defaulted counterparty is sufficiently conservative.

There has also been significant controversy over the "flip clause". The US bankruptcy court has ruled that the "flip clause" is unenforceable under the US bankruptcy code (Peck 2010); in other words, if the swap counterparty has a senior claim, they cannot suddenly flip to being junior upon their default. Meanwhile, in a parallel proceeding in the UK high court, it was ruled that the clause was valid as a matter of English law (Lord Neuberger of Abbotsbury 2009). Clearly, the outcome of this controversy could have significant impact on the valuation of some CLN positions.

Meanwhile, at the time of writing, the International Accounting Standards Board (IASB) is consulting on whether the bilateral value adjustment makes sense at all (IASB 2009; Upton 2009). This is related to the wider question of how liabilities such as an issuer's own debt should be accounted for on the balance sheet. Unlike derivatives pricing, the treatment of liabilities is not motivated by hedging arguments, although the concepts of fair value and replacement cost are conceptually related. Concerns were raised when a number of large dealers booked "profits" as a result of the worsening of their own credit quality during the financial crisis of 2008–9, which seemed counterintuitive to many. Unfortunately, the alternative proposals also have their own difficulties.

Finally, care should be taken over how the market value of the derivative contracts in default should be determined. In theory it should include CVA, since market value is usually understood to mean "replacement cost": the price at which another risky counterparty would be prepared to take over the obligations of the contract, which would clearly include CVA. In this chapter we sidestep the issue by simply defining the recovery to be a fraction of theoretical rather than replacement value.

The framework presented here should be sufficiently generic to accommodate any changes that arise as a result of accounting or regulatory changes.

AFFINE MODEL WITH COMMON AND IDIOSYNCRATIC FACTORS

In order to evaluate the various expectations introduced above we need to specialise to a particular model. This problem can be handled using structural models (Lipton and Sepp 2009), but in this chapter we consider a specific affine reduced-form approach along the lines introduced by Cox *et al* (1985) and subsequently developed by many others (see, for example, Chen and Filipovic 2007; Lipton 2010).

Affine framework

We consider a framework in which the intensity of the Cox default process of the ith credit is given by

$$X_i(t) = \alpha_i(t) + \beta_i X(t) \qquad (13.33)$$

The common intensity process $X(t)$ affects the creditworthiness of all credits, while the deterministic term $\alpha_i(t)$ represents idiosyncratic credit risk and provides a means of calibrating the term structure of CDS quotes for credit i. For analytical convenience (rather than for deeper reasons) it is customary to assume that the common intensity process $X(t)$ is governed by the square-root stochastic differential equation (SDE)

$$dX(t) = \kappa(\theta - X(t))\,dt + \sigma\sqrt{X(t)}\,dW_t + J\,dN_t \qquad (13.34)$$

where the jump process N_t has intensity λ and, in order to preserve tractability, the jumps are typically assumed to have an exponential distribution

$$\Pr(J = z)\,dz = \phi\exp(-\phi z)\,dz \qquad (13.35)$$

As we will see later, it is necessary for there to be jumps in the intensity process in order to generate an appreciable correlation between

PRICING OF CREDIT DERIVATIVES

the default events of individual credits. For practical purposes it is often more convenient to consider discrete jump distributions with jump values $J_m > 0, 1 \leq m \leq M$, occurring with probabilities $\pi_m > 0$; this can be more flexible than employing a parametric distribution because it allows for the placement of jumps precisely where they are needed.

Denoting the default time of the ith credit by $\tau_i > t$, in this framework the survival probability $q_t^i(T)$ and the discounted survival probability $Q_t^i(T)$ from time t to T can be written

$$q_t^i(T) = \mathbb{E}_t[\mathbf{1}_{\tau_i > T}]$$

$$= \mathbf{1}_{\tau_i > t} \mathbb{E}_t\left[\exp\left\{-\int_t^T X_i(v)\, dv\right\}\right]$$

$$= \mathbf{1}_{\tau_i > t} \exp\left\{-\int_t^T \alpha_i(v)\, dv\right\} \mathbb{E}_t\left[\exp\left\{-\beta_i \int_t^T X(v)\, dv\right\}\right]$$
(13.36)

$$Q_t^i(T) = \mathbb{E}_t\left[\exp\left\{-\int_t^T r_v\, dv\right\} \mathbf{1}_{\tau_i > T}\right] = P_t(T) q_t^i(T) \quad (13.37)$$

where we have assumed that the risk-free short rate r_t is deterministic and hence uncorrelated with the intensity process and we have defined the risk-free discount factor

$$P_t(T) = \exp\left\{-\int_t^T r_v\, dv\right\}$$

We may compute the quantity $Q_t^i(T)$ by solving the following pricing problem, consisting of a (backward) partial integro-differential equation (PIDE) and the appropriate boundary condition

$$(\partial_t + \mathcal{L})V(t, X, T) - (r_t + \alpha_i(t) + \beta_i X)V(t, X, T) = 0 \quad (13.38)$$

$$V(T, X, T) = 1 \quad (13.39)$$

where

$$\mathcal{L}V \equiv \kappa(\theta - X)V_X + \tfrac{1}{2}\sigma^2 X V_{XX} + \lambda\left[\phi \int_0^\infty V(X+J)e^{-\phi J}\, dJ - V(X)\right]$$
(13.40)

for the case of exponential jumps, or

$$\mathcal{L}V \equiv \kappa(\theta - X)V_X + \tfrac{1}{2}\sigma^2 X V_{XX} + \lambda\left[\sum_m \pi_m V(X + J_m) - V(X)\right] \quad (13.41)$$

for the case of discrete jumps. The corresponding solution can be written in the so-called affine form

$$V(t, X, T) = \exp\left\{-\int_t^T (r_v + \alpha_i(v))\, dv + a(t, T) + b(t, T) X(t)\right\} \quad (13.42)$$

Specialising to the case of the exponential distribution and $\beta_i = 1$, we obtain the following pair of non-linear ordinary differential equations

$$\frac{db(s)}{ds} = -1 - \kappa b(s) + \tfrac{1}{2}\sigma^2 b^2(s) \qquad (13.43)$$

$$\frac{da(s)}{ds} = \kappa \theta b(s) + \frac{\lambda \phi}{\phi - b(s)} \qquad (13.44)$$

where we have defined $s = T - t$. The non-linear Ricatti equation (Equation 13.43) may be reduced to linear form by making the substitution $b(s) = mc'(s)/c(s)$. Choosing $m = -2/\sigma^2$, we eliminate the non-linear term to obtain

$$c'' + \kappa c' - \tfrac{1}{2}\sigma^2 c = 0 \qquad (13.45)$$

Postulating solutions of the form $e^{\alpha s}$, applying the boundary condition $b(0) = 0$ and choosing a convenient normalisation, we find

$$c(s) = \frac{1}{2\gamma}\left((\gamma + \kappa)\exp\left\{\frac{\gamma - \kappa}{2}s\right\} + (\gamma - \kappa)\exp\left\{\frac{-\gamma - \kappa}{2}s\right\}\right) \qquad (13.46)$$

where we have defined $\gamma = \sqrt{\kappa^2 + 2\sigma^2}$. Back-substituting for b and integrating Equation 13.44, we obtain

$$b(s) = -\frac{2}{\sigma^2}\frac{c'(s)}{c(s)} = -\frac{2(e^{\gamma s} - 1)}{(\gamma + \kappa)e^{\gamma s} + (\gamma - \kappa)} \qquad (13.47)$$

$$a(s) = -\frac{2\kappa\theta}{\sigma^2}\ln(c(s)) + \frac{2\lambda s}{\phi(\gamma - \kappa) - 2} - \frac{2\lambda\phi}{\phi^2\sigma^2 - 2\phi\kappa - 2}$$
$$\times \ln\left(\frac{(\phi(\gamma + \kappa) + 2)e^{\gamma s} + (\phi(\gamma - \kappa) - 2)}{2\gamma\phi}\right) \qquad (13.48)$$

Coordinate transformation

In order to recover the corresponding expression for the case $\beta_i \neq 1$, we must make the following coordinate transformations

$$\theta \to \beta_i \theta, \qquad \sigma \to \sqrt{\beta_i}\sigma, \qquad \phi \to \frac{\phi}{\beta_i}, \qquad b \to \beta_i b \qquad (13.49)$$

The survival probability and its discounted counterpart then have the following form

$$q_t^i(T) = \exp\left\{-\int_t^T \alpha_i(v)\,dv + a(s) + b(s)X(t)\right\}$$
$$Q_t^i(T) = \exp\left\{-\int_t^T r_v\,dv\right\}q_t^i(T) \qquad (13.50)$$

Fully collateralised CDS pricing

The time-t value of a fully collateralised, notional η_i, T-expiry CDS as defined in Equation 13.6 referencing credit i, paying a (continuous) coupon $\eta_i c_i$ in exchange for receiving $\eta_i L_i = \eta_i(1 - R_i)$ on default of credit i is given by $U^{\{i\}}(t, X)$, which solves the pricing problem

$$(\partial_t + \mathcal{L})U^{\{i\}}(t, X, T) - (r_t + \alpha_i(t) + \beta_i X)U^{\{i\}}(t, X, T)$$
$$= c_i \eta_i - L_i \eta_i (\alpha_i(t) + \beta_i X) \quad (13.51)$$
$$U^{\{i\}}(T, X, T) = 0 \quad (13.52)$$

Using Duhamel's Principle and integration by parts, we obtain

$$U^{\{i\}}(t, X, T) = \eta_i \left(-c_i A_t^i(t, T) + L_i \left((1 - Q_t^i(T)) - \int_t^T r_v Q_t^i(v) \, dv \right) \right) \quad (13.53)$$

where $A_t^i(u, T)$ is the time-t value of a continuous risky annuity referencing credit i accruing between u and T

$$A_t^i(u, T) = \int_u^T Q_t^i(v) \, dv \quad (13.54)$$

If necessary, we can handle the case of a discrete coupon paid at times $\{T_j : j = 1, \ldots, N\}$ and accrual according to a chosen convention by making the following replacement in Equation 13.51

$$c_i \eta_i \rightarrow c_i \eta_i \sum_{j=1}^{N} (\delta(t - T_j) d(T_{j-1}, T_j) + \varphi d(T_{j-1}, t) \mathbf{1}_{T_{j-1} < t \leq T_j} (\alpha_i(t) + \beta_i X)) \quad (13.55)$$

Here $d(t, u)$ denotes the day count fraction between times t and u, $\varphi = 1$ if accrued is paid in default ($\varphi = 0$ otherwise) and $\delta(u)$ is the delta function. Via Duhamel's Principle, the annuity can then be written as

$$A_t^i(t, T) = \sum_{j=1}^{N} \mathbf{1}_{t \leq T_j < T} \left(d(T_{j-1}, T_j) Q_t^i(T_j) \right.$$
$$\left. - \varphi \int_{\max(t, T_{j-1})}^{T_j} d(T_{j-1}, u) \left(\frac{\partial Q_t^i(u)}{\partial u} + r_u \right) du \right) \quad (13.56)$$

For clarity of exposition in this chapter we will generally assume continuous accrual of coupons, but it is straightforward to generalise to cases of practical interest via expressions such as Equation 13.56.

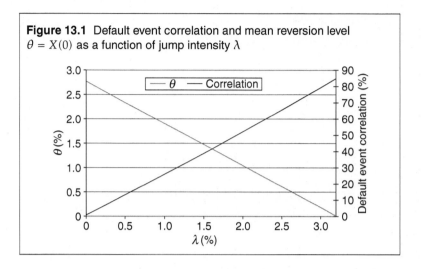

Figure 13.1 Default event correlation and mean reversion level $\theta = X(0)$ as a function of jump intensity λ

Calibration procedure for fully collateralised CDS

The break-even coupon for the CDS contract at time 0 is defined to be the coupon that will set the present value of the contract (Equation 13.53) to 0

$$\hat{c}_i(T) = \frac{1}{A_0^i(0,T)} L_i \left((1 - Q_0^i(T)) - \int_0^T r_v Q_0^i(v) \, dv \right) \quad (13.57)$$

Alternatively, if the contract is quoted on an up-front basis with a fixed contractual coupon c_i, we can express the up-front quote as $\hat{u}_i(T) = U^{\{i\}}(0, X, T)$. Having selected time-independent model parameters for the process (Equation 13.34) for X, we can calibrate $\alpha_i(t)$ piecewise to a chosen term structure of spreads $c_i(T)$ or up-fronts $u_i(T)$ for each of the credits.

DEFAULT EVENT CORRELATION

For a given maturity T, the time-t default event correlation between reference entities 1 and 2 is defined as follows

$$\rho_t^{12}(T) = \frac{q_t^{12}(T) - q_t^1(T) q_t^2(T)}{\sqrt{(1 - q_t^1(T)) q_t^1(T)(1 - q_t^2(T)) q_t^2(T)}} \quad (13.58)$$

PRICING OF CREDIT DERIVATIVES

where $q_t^i(T)$ is as defined in Equation 13.36 and, for $i \neq j$

$$q_t^{ij}(T) = \mathbb{E}_t[\mathbf{1}_{T_i>T}\mathbf{1}_{T_j>T}]$$

$$= \exp\left\{-\int_t^T (\alpha_i(v) + \alpha_j(v))\,dv\right.$$
$$\left. + a(T-t;\beta_i+\beta_j) + b(T-t;\beta_i+\beta_j)X(t)\right\}$$

In the absence of jumps, the corresponding event correlation is very low. If large positive jumps are added (while overall survival probability is preserved), then correlation can increase all the way to 1. We illustrate this observation in Figure 13.1. We set $T - t = 5$ years, $\kappa = 0.5$, $\sigma = 7\%$ and $\phi = 0.15$ (corresponding to an expected jump size $\mathbb{E}[J] = 1/\phi = 6.67$). We then calibrate to two identical credits with a fixed flat spread term structure of 3%, a recovery of 0% and $\beta_i = 1$. Decomposing the survival probability $q_t^i(T)$ gives

$$q_t^i(T) = \exp\left(-\int_t^T \alpha_i(v)\,dv\right)\mathbb{E}\left[\exp\left(-\beta_i \int_t^T X(v)\,dv\right)\right] \quad (13.59)$$

We vary λ and then choose $\theta = X(0)$ in such a way that the component of the survival probability from time t to maturity T deriving from the common factor

$$\mathbb{E}\left[\exp\left(-\beta_i \int_t^T X(v)\,dv\right)\right]$$

is held fixed and the purely idiosyncratic part

$$\exp\left(-\int_t^T \alpha_i(v)\,dv\right)$$

is a small fixed adjustment, calibrated to ensure the survival probability, and hence the CDS is perfectly repriced and $\alpha_i(v) \geq 0$ for all maturities $t \leq v \leq T$.

CVA FOR A CDS CONTRACT
Fully collateralised single CDS

As we have outlined in Equation 13.51, the value of a fully collateralised CDS referencing credit i with notional η_i (a positive sign denotes long protection) can be expressed as the solution of the following pricing problem

$$(\partial_t + \mathcal{L})U^{\{i\}}(t,X,T) - (r+X_i)U^{\{i\}}(t,X,T) = c_i\eta_i - L_i\eta_iX_i \quad (13.60)$$
$$U^{\{i\}}(T,X,T) = 0 \quad (13.61)$$

The solution can be written explicitly in closed form as in Equation 13.53.

Unilateral CVA for a single CDS

Consider the value of a CDS referencing credit 3, executed with a risky counterparty 2. Ignoring the credit risk of reference entity 1, from Equation 13.11 we can express the value of the partially collateralised CDS as the solution to the following pricing problem

$$(\partial_t + \mathcal{L})V^{\{2,3\}}(t, X, T) - (r + X_2 + X_3)V^{\{2,3\}}(t, X, T)$$
$$= c_3\eta_3 - X_2(R_2 U_+^{\{3\}} + U_-^{\{3\}}) - L_3\eta_3 X_3 \quad (13.62)$$
$$V^{\{2,3\}}(T, X, T) = 0 \quad (13.63)$$

Defining the unilateral CVA $W^{\{2,3\}} = V^{\{2,3\}} - U^{\{3\}}$ and subtracting Equation 13.60 from Equation 13.62 we arrive at

$$(\partial_t + \mathcal{L})W^{\{2,3\}}(t, X, T) - (r + X_2 + X_3)W^{\{2,3\}}(t, X, T)$$
$$= X_2 L_2 U_+^{\{3\}} \quad (13.64)$$
$$W^{\{2,3\}}(T, X, T) = 0 \quad (13.65)$$

The solution to this problem is no longer solvable analytically in the general case (although it can be solved for the special case of either the pure jump or the pure diffusion process). However, it can be solved numerically via an appropriate modification of the classical Crank–Nicolson method as we will describe later (see page 365 onwards).

Bilateral CVA for a single CDS

Considering now the case where we incorporate the credit risk of counterparty 1, from Equations 13.12 and 13.13 the pricing problem can be expressed as

$$(\partial_t + \mathcal{L})V^{\{1,2,3\}} - (r + X_1 + X_2 + X_3)V^{\{1,2,3\}}$$
$$= c_3\eta_3 - X_1(U_+^{\{3\}} + R_1 U_-^{\{3\}}) - X_2(R_2 U_+^{\{3\}} + U_-^{\{3\}}) - L_3\eta_3 X_3$$
$$(13.66)$$
$$V^{\{1,2,3\}}(T, X, T) = 0 \quad (13.67)$$

Subtracting Equation 13.60 from Equation 13.66, we arrive at

$$(\partial_t + \mathcal{L})W^{\{1,2,3\}} - (r + X_1 + X_2 + X_3)W^{\{1,2,3\}}$$
$$= X_1 L_1 U_-^{\{3\}} + X_2 L_2 U_+^{\{3\}} \quad (13.68)$$
$$W^{\{1,2,3\}}(T, X, T) = 0 \quad (13.69)$$

Once again, although the solution cannot be expressed in closed form, this can be solved using the numerical scheme described in the next section.

Numerical solution of the PIDE

We decompose the generator $\mathcal{L} = \hat{L} + \lambda \hat{J}$ of the process for X (Equation 13.40) into a diffusion operator $\hat{L}$ and a jump operator $\hat{J}$ which are defined as follows

$$\hat{L}V(t,X) = \kappa(\theta(t) - X)V_X + \tfrac{1}{2}\sigma^2 X V_{XX} \tag{13.70}$$

$$\hat{J}V(t,X) = \phi \int_0^\infty (V(t, X+J) - V(t,X))e^{-\phi J}\, dJ \tag{13.71}$$

We first consider the treatment of the diffusion operator $\hat{L}$. Traditionally, the square root process causes a lot of confusion where boundary conditions are concerned. However, the situation was clarified in Ekström et al (2009). No boundary condition is needed when the so-called Fichera function satisfies

$$\lim_{X \to 0} \left(\mathrm{drift}(X) - \frac{1}{2}\frac{d}{dX}\mathrm{var}(X) \right) \geq 0 \tag{13.72}$$

For square root processes this is equivalent to the Feller Condition. Nonetheless, modern practice suggests that using the PDE as boundary condition always works

$$V_t(t,0) + \kappa\theta(t)V_X(t,0) = 0 \tag{13.73}$$

We use the diffusion equation itself as a far-field condition.

Accordingly, we derive the usual Crank–Nicolson finite difference discretisation for the operator $\hat{L}$, which is almost tridiagonal, except for the left and right blocks, which are 3×3 and 4×4 matrices, respectively: this can handled straightforwardly. We treat the jump term fully explicitly as originally presented in Lipton (2003) (and in more detail in Lipton and Sepp (2010)). In order to do this we introduce the auxiliary function $\varphi(t, X) \equiv \hat{J}V(t,X)$. To second-order accuracy in the small step h we can then derive the following recursion relationship

$$\varphi(t,X) = e^{-\phi h}\varphi(t, X+h) + \frac{1 - e^{-\phi h}}{h\phi}(V(t,X+h) - V(t,X)) + O(h^3) \tag{13.74}$$

The corresponding numerical scheme is very fast and robust.

CVA FOR A CLN

Assuming that the issuer-2 bond $B^{\{2\}}$ has contractual cashflows $\{C_j\}$ at times $\{T_j\}, j = 1, \ldots, M$, in the affine framework, its value at time t can be expressed as

$$B^{\{2\}}(t) = \sum_{j=1}^{M} C_j Q_t^2(T_j) \mathbf{1}_{t \leqslant T_j} + R_2 \left((1 - Q_t^2(T_M)) - \int_t^{T_M} r_v Q_t^2(v) \, dv \right)$$

(13.75)

This expression is based on standard reduced-form assumptions consistent with those used to value CDSs. We do not discuss in detail how to handle the cash-CDS basis, which can nonetheless be incorporated in various ways via adjustments to discount rates. The cashflows $\{C_j\}$ represent both principal and coupon payments, which may in general be either fixed or floating.

Unilateral CVA for a CLN

From Equation 13.25 we find

$$(\partial_t + \mathcal{L}) W^{\{2,3\}}(t, X, T) - (r + X_2 + X_3) W^{\{2,3\}}(t, X, T)$$
$$= X_2 (U^{\{3\}} - R_2)_+ + X_3 ((1 - R_3) - B^{\{2\}})_+ \quad (13.76)$$

$$W^{\{2,3\}}(T, X, T) = 0 \quad (13.77)$$

Bilateral CVA for a CLN

As we highlighted in an earlier section, there are a number of possible treatments of default of the dealer, depending upon contractual terms. We first consider Equation 13.31a as the simplest example of the flip clause. From Equations 13.25 and 13.31 we find

$$(\partial_t + \mathcal{L}) W^{\{1,2,3\}} - (r + X_1 + X_2 + X_3) W^{\{1,2,3\}}$$
$$= X_1 U^{\{3\}} + X_2 (U^{\{3\}} - R_2)_+ + X_3 ((1 - R_3) - B^{\{2\}})_+ \quad (13.78)$$

$$W^{\{1,2,3\}}(T, X, T) = 0 \quad (13.79)$$

In contrast, if we consider case 4, in which there is no flip clause, we arrive at

$$(\partial_t + \mathcal{L}) W^{\{1,2,3\}} - (r + X_1 + X_2 + X_3) W^{\{1,2,3\}}$$
$$= X_1 (L_1 U_-^{\{3\}} + (U^{\{3\}} - B^{\{2\}})_+)$$
$$+ X_2 (U^{\{3\}} - R_2)_+ + X_3 ((1 - R_3) - B^{\{2\}})_+ \quad (13.80)$$

$$W^{\{1,2,3\}}(T, X, T) = 0 \quad (13.81)$$

In both cases the default of the dealer can have a negative as well as a positive effect on the CVA. Usually the presence of the flip clause is worse for the dealer, for obvious reasons. The only exception to this would be where $U^{\{3\}} < 0$, when the dealer may benefit from the termination of the contract, but this is a relatively unimportant "right way" risk.

NUMERICAL RESULTS

We now graphically illustrate numerical results for some of the pricing problems described in the previous section. We consider the case where all three credits have flat spreads of 3%, recoveries of 40%, $\beta_1 = \beta_2 = \beta_3 = 1.40$ and the parameters of the process for X are $X(0) = 3.0\%$, $\kappa = 0.5$, $\theta = 2\%$, $\sigma = 10\%$, $\lambda = 2\%$, $\phi = 1$. This leads to a significant default event correlation of 18.51% at 5Y. We now evaluate the contributions to the bilateral CVA for a five-year par CDS on reference entity 3 for three different cases: uncollateralised CDS, CLN case 1 and CLN case 4. To facilitate comparison, for the CLN we assume that $B^{\{2\}}(t) > 1$ at all times other than the default of reference entity 2, when it is equal to R_2: this eliminates the shortfall term proportional to X_3. Under this assumption, from Equations 13.68, 13.78, 13.80, the right-hand sides of the relevant pricing problems for $W^{\{123\}}$ become

$$\text{Uncollateralised CDS:} \quad X_1 L_1 U_-^{\{3\}} + X_2 L_2 U_+^{\{3\}} \qquad (13.82)$$

$$\text{CLN: Case 1:} \quad X_1 U^{\{3\}} + X_2 (U^{\{3\}} - R_2)_+ \qquad (13.83)$$

$$\text{CLN: Case 4:} \quad X_1 L_1 U_-^{\{3\}} + X_2 (U^{\{3\}} - R_2)_+ \qquad (13.84)$$

Figure 13.2 exhibits the CVAs for an uncollateralised CDS from the point of view of the protection buyer (credit 1). The negative contribution $W_2^{\{123\}}$ from the default of counterparty 2 is reasonably large, while the "own default" contribution $W_1^{\{123\}}$ is positive but very small. This reflects the "wrong way risk" and asymmetry of the CDS payout (Equation 13.82).

It is interesting to contrast this behaviour to Figure 13.3, where the CDS has instead been executed in CLN format with the flip clause. In this case, because the CLN is collateralised, $W_2^{\{123\}}$ is relatively small, although it is still negative: this is because even if reference entity 2 defaults there is still collateral worth R_2, which is better for credit 1 than the case where the CDS is totally uncollateralised.

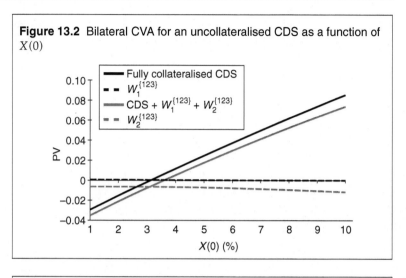

Figure 13.2 Bilateral CVA for an uncollateralised CDS as a function of $X(0)$

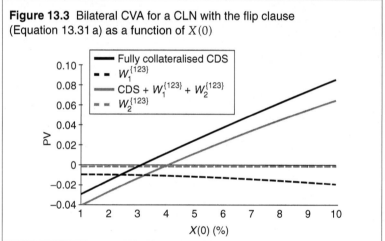

Figure 13.3 Bilateral CVA for a CLN with the flip clause (Equation 13.31 a) as a function of $X(0)$

However, the own default contribution $W_1^{\{123\}}$ is now both negative and large. This is the result of the fact that on default of the dealer the seniority "flips" to the noteholders and derives from the first term in Equation 13.83. Hence, even though the CLN is collateralised, there is still significant counterparty risk with respect to the dealer, but in this case it benefits the noteholders.

We also compare a CLN without the flip clause in Figure 13.4. Here, as a result of the absence of the flip clause, $W_1^{\{123\}}$ is small and positive as in the case of the uncollateralised CDS. The term $W_2^{\{123\}}$ is still negative, but it is small for the same reason as before.

PRICING OF CREDIT DERIVATIVES

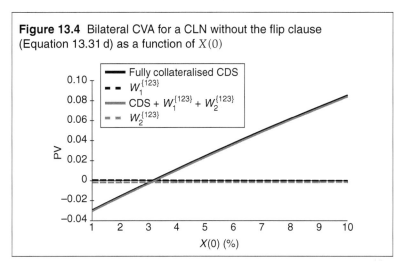

Figure 13.4 Bilateral CVA for a CLN without the flip clause (Equation 13.31 d) as a function of $X(0)$

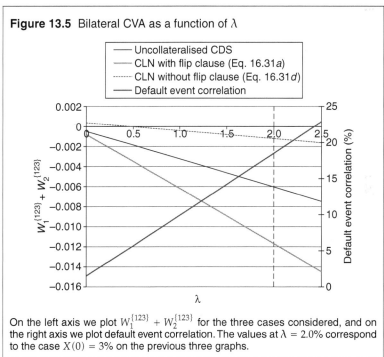

Figure 13.5 Bilateral CVA as a function of λ

On the left axis we plot $W_1^{\{123\}} + W_2^{\{123\}}$ for the three cases considered, and on the right axis we plot default event correlation. The values at $\lambda = 2.0\%$ correspond to the case $X(0) = 3\%$ on the previous three graphs.

In this case at least, the collateralisation acts to significantly reduce counterparty risk.

Finally, in Figure 13.5 we vary λ, keeping all the other parameters of the process for X fixed. We plot the CVA $W_1^{\{123\}} + W_2^{\{123\}}$ for

369

the three cases considered on the left axis and the default event correlation on the right axis. The figure shows clearly that the CVA is small unless there is a significant event correlation, and that jumps are necessary in order to generate this.

Incorporating the fact that $B^{\{2\}}(t)$ may be less than 1 if credit 2 becomes distressed will, from Equations 13.78 and 13.80, introduce additional short-fall terms in Equations 13.83 and 13.84, which would act to increase the negative CVA. Generally, these terms will become significant if reference entity 2 becomes highly distressed.

BILATERAL CVA FOR A PORTFOLIO OF CREDIT DEFAULT SWAPS

Thus far we have considered the case of a single name CDS traded between two risky counterparties. We now consider the N credit portfolio problem for $N > 3$. As before, reference entity 1 denotes us, credit 2 denotes our risky counterparty and $3, \ldots, N$ denotes the reference entities underlying the portfolio of CDS. The notionals of the CDS on credits $i = 3, \ldots, N$, which can be both positive and negative, are denoted by η_i. We focus on the bilateral CVA although it is straightforward to generalise the analysis to the unilateral case if desired.

The difficulty here is a combinatoric one, in that to evaluate the portfolio and hence the contribution to the CVA deriving from a given time horizon, we need to track which credits have survived and which defaulted by the specified time (an analogous problem occurs in computing the CVA on a portfolio of path-dependent barrier options). We then need to evaluate probability weighted contributions to the CVA deriving from every possible future portfolio composition, of which there are $2^{N-2} - 1$. In order to gain insight, before considering the case of general N, we first consider the cases $N = 4, 5$. We will show that, as a result of combinatoric effects, we end up with a coupled system of $2^{N-2} - 1$ PIDEs. For brevity in the pricing problems presented below we do not explicitly state the terminal time-T boundary condition, since it invariably equals 0 as in the cases considered previously.

The case when $N = 4$

The first generalisation of the $N = 3$ case considered in Equations 13.66 and 13.68 is to consider a portfolio of two CDSs referencing credits 3 and 4

$$(\partial_t + \mathcal{L})U^{\{3,4\}} - (r + X_3 + X_4)U^{\{3,4\}}$$
$$= c_3\eta_3 + c_4\eta_4 - X_3(L_3\eta_3 + U^{\{4\}}) - X_4(L_4\eta_4 + U^{\{3\}}) \quad (13.85)$$

which is derived from Equation 13.60 and the fact that

$$U^{\{3,4\}} = U^{\{3\}} + U^{\{4\}} \quad (13.86)$$

Now

$$(\partial_t + \mathcal{L})V^{\{1,2,3,4\}} - (r + X_1 + X_2 + X_3 + X_4)V^{\{1,2,3,4\}}$$
$$= c_3\eta_3 + c_4\eta_4 - (R_1 U_-^{\{3,4\}} + U_+^{\{3,4\}})X_1 - (R_2 U_+^{\{3,4\}} + U_-^{\{3,4\}})X_2$$
$$- (L_3\eta_3 + V^{\{1,2,4\}})X_3 - (L_4\eta_4 + V^{\{1,2,3\}})X_4 \quad (13.87)$$

Once again subtracting Equation 13.85 from Equation 13.87, we arrive at

$$(\partial_t + \mathcal{L})W^{\{1,2,3,4\}} - (r + X_1 + X_2 + X_3 + X_4)W^{\{1,2,3,4\}}$$
$$= X_1 L_1 U_-^{\{3,4\}} + X_2 L_2 U_+^{\{3,4\}} - X_3 W^{\{1,2,4\}} - X_4 W^{\{1,2,3\}} \quad (13.88)$$

Thus, in order to compute $W^{\{1,2,3,4\}}$ we need to have computed $W^{\{1,2,3\}}$ and $W^{\{1,2,4\}}$ via Equation 13.68. By defining the combinations

$$\left. \begin{array}{l} R_\pm^{\{3,4\}} = U_\pm^{\{3,4\}} - U_\pm^{\{3\}} - U_\pm^{\{4\}} \\ S^{\{1,2,3,4\}} = W^{\{1,2,3,4\}} - W^{\{1,2,3\}} - W^{\{1,2,4\}} \end{array} \right\} \quad (13.89)$$

we have the following "simple" equation

$$(\partial_t + \mathcal{L} - (r + X_1 + X_2 + X_3 + X_4))S^{\{1,2,3,4\}} = X_1 L_1 R_-^{\{3,4\}} + X_2 L_2 R_+^{\{3,4\}} \quad (13.90)$$

which neatly summarises portfolio effects. Finally

$$W^{\{1,2,3,4\}} = S^{\{1,2,3,4\}} + S^{\{1,2,3\}} + S^{\{1,2,4\}} \quad (13.91)$$

where $S^{\{1,2,i\}} \equiv W^{\{1,2,i\}}$.

The case when N = 5
Similar arguments lead to

$$(\partial_t + \mathcal{L} - (r + X_1 + X_2 + X_3 + X_4 + X_5))W^{\{1,2,3,4,5\}}$$
$$= X_1 L_1 U_-^{\{3,4,5\}} + X_2 L_2 U_+^{\{3,4,5\}}$$
$$- X_3 W^{\{1,2,4,5\}} - X_4 W^{\{1,2,3,5\}} - X_5 W^{\{1,2,3,4\}} \quad (13.92)$$

As before, rearrangement leads to

$$(\partial_t + \mathcal{L} - (r + X_1 + X_2 + X_3 + X_4 + X_5))S^{\{1,2,3,4,5\}}$$
$$= X_1 L_1 R_-^{\{3,4,5\}} + X_2 L_2 R_+^{\{3,4,5\}} \quad (13.93)$$

where

$$R_\pm^{\{3,4,5\}} = U_\pm^{\{3,4,5\}} - U_\pm^{\{4,5\}} - U_\pm^{\{3,5\}} - U_\pm^{\{3,4\}} + U_\pm^{\{3\}} + U_\pm^{\{4\}} + U_\pm^{\{5\}} \quad (13.94)$$

$$S^{\{1,2,3,4,5\}} = W^{\{1,2,3,4,5\}} - W^{\{1,2,4,5\}} - W^{\{1,2,3,5\}}$$
$$- W^{\{1,2,3,4\}} + W^{\{1,2,3\}} + W^{\{1,2,4\}} + W^{\{1,2,5\}} \quad (13.95)$$

so that

$$W^{\{1,2,3,4,5\}} = S^{\{1,2,3,4,5\}} + S^{\{1,2,4,5\}} + S^{\{1,2,3,5\}}$$
$$+ S^{\{1,2,3,4\}} + S^{\{1,2,3\}} + S^{\{1,2,4\}} + S^{\{1,2,5\}} \quad (13.96)$$

Transforming the problem to the form in Equations 13.90 and 13.93 has the effect of reducing the number of terms on the right-hand side from N to two and transforms the problem so that once the R terms are computed (in closed form), the equations for S are not recursively dependent upon one another. This could be a more efficient representation if we wished to parallelise the computation. Alternatively, it is of course possible to solve Equations 13.68, 13.88 and 13.92 directly and recursively.

The case of *N* credits

If we consider the general case of a universe of N credits $i = 1, \ldots, N$ we arrive at a system of $2^{N-2} - 1$ coupled equations

$$(\partial_t + \mathcal{L})W^{\{1,2\} \cup \Omega} - \left(r + X_1 + X_2 + \sum_{i \in \Omega} X_i\right)W^{\{1,2\} \cup \Omega}$$
$$= X_1 L_1 U_-^\Omega + X_2 L_2 U_+^\Omega - \sum_{i \in \Omega} X_i W^{\{1,2\} \cup \Omega \setminus \{i\}} \quad (13.97)$$

where Ω ranges over all distinct subsets $\Omega \subseteq \{3, \ldots, N\}$ and $\Omega \setminus \{i\}$ denotes the relative complement of $\{i\}$ in Ω. We can re-express these equations as before, by defining

$$R_\pm^\Omega = \sum_{\tilde{\Omega} \subseteq \Omega} (-1)^{n(\tilde{\Omega}) - n(\Omega)} U_\pm^{\tilde{\Omega}} \quad (13.98)$$

$$S^{\{1,2\} \cup \Omega} = \sum_{\tilde{\Omega} \subseteq \Omega} (-1)^{n(\tilde{\Omega}) - n(\Omega)} W^{\{1,2\} \cup \tilde{\Omega}} \quad (13.99)$$

where the sum is over all distinct subsets $\bar{\Omega} \subseteq \Omega$ and $n(\Omega)$ denotes the number of elements in Ω. We arrive at

$$(\partial_t + \mathcal{L})S^{\{1,2\}\cup\Omega} - \left(r + X_1 + X_2 + \sum_{i\in\Omega} X_i\right)S^{\{1,2\}\cup\Omega} = X_1 L_1 R_-^{\Omega} + X_2 L_2 R_+^{\Omega} \tag{13.100}$$

We can recover $W^{\{1,2\}\cup\Omega}$ from

$$W^{\{1,2\}\cup\Omega} = \sum_{\bar{\Omega}\subseteq\Omega} S^{\{1,2\}\cup\bar{\Omega}} \tag{13.101}$$

where once again the sum is over all distinct subsets $\bar{\Omega} \subseteq \Omega$.

Monte Carlo algorithm

In general, solving this problem can be computationally prohibitive in a PIDE framework even for moderate N, because, even though the individual pricing problems are one-dimensional, $2^{N-2} - 1$ evaluations are needed whether we solve Equations 13.97 directly or via the transformed equations (Equations 13.100). Up to $N = 22$, which corresponds to around 10^6 evaluations, the PIDE approach may be viable. However, Monte Carlo (MC) simulation remains feasible even for larger N.

A convenient Monte Carlo algorithm can be formulated by simulating the diffusion process in Equation 13.34 conditional on the number of jumps. Suppose that the simulation is performed over a time interval $[0,T]$. The probability of n jumps in the interval is given by the usual Poisson expression

$$p(n, \lambda T) = \frac{(\lambda T)^n e^{-\lambda T}}{n!}$$

We choose a threshold maximum number of jumps n_J such that

$$1 - \sum_{n=1}^{n_J} p(n, \lambda T) < \varepsilon$$

where ε is a chosen probability threshold. A given expectation can then be decomposed as

$$f = \mathbb{E}_0[F(\{X\})] = \sum_{n=0}^{n_J} p(n, \lambda T) \times f_n + O(\varepsilon) \tag{13.102}$$

$$f_n = \mathbb{E}_0[F(\{X\}) \mid N_T - N_0 = n] \tag{13.103}$$

Here $F(\{X\})$ denotes an arbitrary functional of $\{X(t): t \in [0,T]\}$ and any supplementary random variables such as default times, f

denotes its unconditional expectation and f_n denotes its expectation conditional on n jumps. In order to estimate each of the n_J terms of the form in Equation 13.103 we need to generate sequences of n jump times conditional on the total number of jumps in the interval $[0, T]$ being equal to n. If we denote the time of the nth jump by ω_n, it can be shown by application of Bayes's Rule that for $t \in [0, T]$

$$\Pr(\omega_1 \geq t \mid N_T - N_0 = n) = \left(\frac{T-t}{T}\right)^n \qquad (13.104)$$

By generating a sequence of $U(0,1)$ random variables $\{u_i : i = 1,\ldots,n\}$ and additionally defining $\omega_0 = 0$ we can therefore recursively simulate a sequence of $\{\omega_i\}$ conditional on $N_T - N_0 = n$ as follows

$$\omega_i = \omega_{i-1} + (T - \omega_{i-1})(1 - u_i^{1/(n-i+1)}), \quad i = 1,\ldots,n \qquad (13.105)$$

Assuming that the jumps are exponentially distributed according to Equation 13.35, we can simulate the jump sizes $\{z_i : i = 1,\ldots,n\}$ by generating another sequence of $U(0,1)$ random variables $\{v_i : i = 1,\ldots,n\}$ and setting

$$z_i = -\frac{1}{\phi} \ln v_i, \quad i = 1,\ldots,n \qquad (13.106)$$

In order to simulate the diffusion part of Equation 13.34, we discretise the time-axis into m time steps $\{t_i = i \times T/m : i = 0,\ldots,m\}$. For each simulation we form the ordered set $\{s_i : i = 0,\ldots,m+n\} = \{t_i\} \cup \{\omega_i\}$. We now make use of the fact that in the absence of jumps the cumulative distribution of X is known explicitly (Cox et al 1985)

$$\Pr(X(s_i) < X' \mid X(s_{i-1}) = X) = P^{(\chi^2)}\left(\frac{X'}{\chi_i}; 2(1+\alpha), \frac{\zeta_i X}{\chi_i}\right) \qquad (13.107)$$

where

$$\chi_i = \frac{\sigma^2(1 - e^{-\kappa(s_i - s_{i-1})})}{4\kappa}, \quad \zeta_i = e^{-\kappa(s_i - s_{i-1})}, \quad \alpha = \frac{2\kappa\theta}{\sigma^2} - 1$$

Here $P^{(\chi^2)}(x; \nu, \lambda)$ denotes the non-central chi-squared cumulative distribution function with ν degrees of freedom and non-centrality parameter λ. Efficient implementations are widely available in C++ libraries. In order to simulate a sequence of $\{X(s_i)\}$ incorporating both jumps and diffusion components we generate a set of $U(0,1)$

variables $\{w_i : i = 1, \ldots, m+n\}$. We then set $X(s_0) = X(0)$ and generate, for $i = 1, \ldots, m+n$

$$X(s_i) = \chi_i(P^{(X^2)})^{-1}\left(w_i; 2(1+\alpha), \frac{\zeta_i X(s_{i-1})}{\chi_i}\right) + \sum_{j=1}^{n} z_j \mathbf{1}_{s_i = \omega_j} \quad (13.108)$$

Having simulated the jump-diffusion process in Equation 13.34 we can now simulate default times conditional on the numerical integral of X. We generate the $U(0,1)$ variables $\{x_j : j = 1, \ldots, N\}$. For the jth credit, default is deemed to have occurred in the interval $[0, T]$ if

$$\ln(x_j) \geqslant -\int_0^T X_j(s)\, ds$$

in which case the default time τ_j is given by the solution to

$$\ln(x_j) = -\int_0^{\tau_j} X_j(s)\, ds \quad (13.109)$$

In order to estimate CVA on a portfolio of CDS in the Monte Carlo framework, we return to the formulation in terms of expectations similar to Equations 13.10–13.13. Considering the bilateral case, the expectation (Equation 13.102) takes the form

$$W_1^{\{1,2,3,\ldots,N\}}(0)$$

$$= -\mathbb{E}_0\left[\mathbf{1}_{0 < (\tau_1 \wedge \tau_2) = \tau_1 \leqslant T} L_1 D_{\tau_1}\left(\sum_{j=3}^{N} \mathbf{1}_{\tau_j > \tau_1} U^{\{j\}}(\tau_1)\right)_{-}\right] \quad (13.110)$$

$$W_2^{\{1,2,3,\ldots,N\}}(0)$$

$$= -\mathbb{E}_0\left[\mathbf{1}_{0 < (\tau_1 \wedge \tau_2) = \tau_2 \leqslant T} L_2 D_{\tau_2}\left(\sum_{j=3}^{N} \mathbf{1}_{\tau_j > \tau_2} U^{\{j\}}(\tau_2)\right)_{+}\right] \quad (13.111)$$

Since only scenarios where either credit 1 or credit 2 default in $[0, T]$ contribute to Equations 13.110, 13.111, significant savings can be obtained by only simulating the default times of credits $j = 3, \ldots, N$ in such cases. For the scenarios that contribute, the theoretical values $U^{\{j\}}$ appearing on the right-hand side in the expectations may be efficiently computed using Equation 13.53.

The algorithm presented here is predicated on the fact that jumps are crucial in order to capture the "wrong way" risk. Typically, the jump intensity is relatively low; hence, if we did not introduce a natural form of importance sampling by conditioning on the number of jumps occurring in $[0, T]$, the estimators of Equations 13.110, 13.111 would exhibit high sample standard deviation. Generally, as a result of the low jump intensity, n_J is relatively small and the cost of performing n_J simulations is more than outweighed by the reduction in variance obtained.

CONCLUSIONS

One of the most challenging problems in counterparty risk modelling is evaluating the CVA for a portfolio of credit derivatives. In such cases, the MTM of the portfolio is generally highly correlated with the default risk of the counterparties.

We have presented an overview of the modelling of counterparty risk and CVA for portfolios of CDSs and CLNs. Having determined the payouts involved, we adopted a specific reduced-form affine Cox-process framework in order to evaluate their expectations. To achieve significant default event correlation and capture the effect of "wrong way risk", we needed to incorporate large jumps in the common intensity process underlying the credits.

The problem of handling a large portfolio of CDS contracts quickly becomes computationally challenging in the PIDE framework, as a result of the exponentially large number of possible default scenarios. We have presented a Monte Carlo algorithm that can be efficiently applied in such cases.

In the case of the CLN, the presence or absence of a flip clause has a significant impact on bilateral CVA and can result in situations where the swap counterparty no longer "benefits" and instead "suffers" from their own default. The potential for shortfalls and hence the CVA is also very dependent on the underlying recovery assumptions.

REFERENCES

Brigo, D., and A. Capponi, 2010, "Bilateral Counterparty Risk with Application to CDSs", *Risk Magazine* 23(3), pp. 85–90.

Chen, L., and D. Filipovic, 2007, "Credit Derivatives in an Affine Framework", *Asia-Pacific Financial Markets* 14, pp. 123–40.

Cox, J., J. Ingersoll and S. Ross, 1985, "A Theory of the Term Structure of Interest Rates", *Econometrica* 53, pp. 385–407.

Duffie, D., 2001, "Expert Report of Darrell Duffie", United States Tax Court, Bank One Corporation, Petitioner, versus Commisioner of Internal Revenue, Respondent, Docket Numbers 5759-95 and 5956-97, URL: http://www.stanford.edu/~duffie/bankone.pdf.

Duffie, D., and M. Huang, 1996, "Swap Rates and Credit Quality", *The Journal of Finance* 51(3), pp. 921–49.

Duffie, D., and H. Zhu, 2009, "Does a Central Clearing Counterparty Reduce Counterparty Risk?", Working Paper.

Ekström, E., P. Lötstedt and J. Tysk, 2009, "Boundary Values and Finite Difference Methods for the Single Factor Term Structure Equation", *Applied Mathematical Finance* 16(3), pp. 253–9.

Gregory, J., 2009, "Being Two-Faced over Counterparty Credit Risk", *Risk* 22(2), pp. 86–90.

IASB, 2009, "Credit Risk in Liability Measurement", International Accounting Standards Board Discussion Paper DP/2009/2.

Lipton, A., 2003, "Evaluating the Latest Structural and Hybrid Models for Credit Risk", Presentation, Global Derivatives, Barcelona.

Lipton, A., 2010, "Multiname Random Intensity Models", in R. Cont (ed), *Encyclopedia of Quantitative Finance* (Chichester: John Wiley & Sons).

Lipton, A., and A. Sepp, 2009, "Credit Value Adjustment for Credit Default Swaps via the Structural Default Model", *Journal of Credit Risk* 5(2), pp. 123–46.

Lipton, A. and Sepp, A. 2010, "Credit Value Adjustment in the Extended Structural Default Model", in A. Lipton and A. Rennie (eds), *The Oxford Handbook of Credit Derivatives* (Oxford University Press).

Neuberger, Lord (of Abbotsbury) 2009, "Perpetual Trustee Co Ltd versus BNY Corporate Trustee Services Ltd", [2009] EWCA (Civ) 1160 (Eng), Judgement, November 6, 2009.

Peck, J. M. (Judge), 2010, "Lehman Brothers Special Financing Inc versus BNY Corporate Trustee Services Ltd", Memorandum Decision: Case No. 08-13555 (JMP), Adversary Proceeding No. 09-01242 (January 25, 2010), US Bankruptcy Court, Southern District (Manhattan), URL: http://www.nysb.uscourts.gov/opinions/jmp/180787_86_opinion.pdf.

Pykhtin, M., and S. Zhu, 2006, "Measuring Counterparty Credit Risk for Trading Products under Basel II", in M. Ong (ed), *Basel II Handbook* (London: Risk Books).

Redon, C., 2006, "Wrong Way Risk Modelling", *Risk Magazine* 19(4), pp. 90–5.

Sorensen, E., and T. Bollier, 1994, "Pricing Swap Default Risk", *Financial Analysts Journal* 50(3), pp. 23–33.

Upton, W., 2009, "Credit Risk in Liability Measurement", Staff Paper accompanying Discussion Paper DP/2009/2, URL: http://www.iasb.org/.

Zhu, S., and M. Pykhtin, 2007, "A Guide to Modeling Counterparty Credit Risk", *GARP Risk Review* July/August, pp. 16–22.

14

A Practical Guide to Monte Carlo CVA

Alexander Sokol
CompatibL

The regulatory and internal requirement to measure counterparty risk pre-dates the financial crisis by many years. Most firms carrying derivatives books had the ability to compute counterparty exposures for their trades, and many had built sophisticated Monte Carlo systems to do so. The only thing that was missing was taking the possibility of default seriously. Because of the perceived low probability of default, enormous exposures were allowed to build up at some firms without raising any alarms. For the same reason, the information on exposures available to market participants prior to the crisis was often not used to mitigate counterparty risk despite the low cost of credit insurance in pre-crisis years.

The financial crisis brought new urgency to the efforts in implementing calculation of potential future exposure (PFE) and credit value adjustment (CVA). Having seen the default of Lehman Brothers, and near default of other firms, the market participants were for the first time taking seriously the risk of default and assigning a more realistic probability to it, as evidenced by the dramatic widening of credit spreads during and immediately after the crisis. The increased spreads will probably continue in the years to come, as the euphoria of pre-crisis years is not likely to recur as long as the crisis remains in the collective memory of the trader and risk manager community.

The effect of counterparty risk on portfolio value (CVA) increased dramatically during the crisis, and will continue at higher levels commensurate with the increased credit spreads after the crisis. Historically, credit risk calculations relied on simple approximations which did not fully model the instrument. The overall increase in the levels of CVA proportionally amplified the errors due to crude approximations in calculating it. With CVA taking increased role in profit and loss (P&L) reporting, continued use of these crude approximations has become unsustainable.

Another factor necessitating more rigorous PFE/CVA modelling is the increasing use of credit derivatives to hedge counterparty risk exposure and reduce P&L volatility due to CVA. In order to capture the effect of credit hedging in reducing PFE and CVA, the counterparty risk analytics must model portfolio value accurately to offset it against credit derivative payouts that occur simultaneously with counterparty default. Only modelling instruments rigorously will show the correct amount of reduction in counterparty risk as a result of credit hedging.

A caveat on regulatory and accounting treatment

Having given a preview in this introductory section of what is covered in this chapter, the author would like to make a very important point of what this chapter expressly does not attempt to cover, and that is the regulatory and accounting treatment of the techniques described here.

The shifting nature of regulatory and accounting treatment of PFE/CVA as well as significant country-by-country differences makes it impossible to cover its regulatory and accounting treatment within the scope of this chapter without subjecting the material to the risk of becoming outdated, or applicable to some jurisdictions but not others. The reader is encouraged to supplement this practical guide with materials which cover the accounting and regulatory aspects of PFE/CVA, as well as policy papers and methodology guidelines issued by the country's regulators and accounting standards bodies. For the same reason, the author will refrain from discussing the role of implicit government guarantees in measuring counterparty risk of systemically important institutions and sovereign jurisdictions.

In conclusion of this introductory section, a short note about terminology. Most of the material in this chapter applies equally to PFE and CVA. In what follows, the term CVA will be used generically to describe the calculation process which produces both PFE and CVA as its output except in those cases where the context requires making a distinction between the two.

METHODOLOGY FUNDAMENTALS

This brief section introduces the key concepts involved in modelling of PFE and CVA. The readers who are familiar with the subject are encouraged to skip directly to the sections on the exposure sampling method (see page 384) and the implementation guide to Monte Carlo calculation of PFE and CVA (see page 395). A comprehensive overview of PFE and CVA methodologies can be found in Arvanitis and Gregory (2001), Canabarro and Duffie (2003), De Prisco and Rosen (2005), Picault (2005), Redon (2006), Pykhtin and Zhu (2007) and Pykhtin and Rosen (2009).

Potential future exposure

The PFE profile is the amount of loss due to counterparty default at a given confidence level as a function of time, and maximum PFE (MPFE) is the maximum value of PFE profile: the amount of exposure if the counterparty defaults at the worst possible time. The importance of using the exposure measured at the worst possible time rather than today (current exposure; CE) follows from the typical shape of PFE profile, which increases initially and then decreases to zero when the last instrument in today's portfolio expires. For this typical profile, maximum PFE is significantly higher than CE and is the appropriate measure for evaluating the worst-case counterparty risk scenario.

Additional measures of exposure such as the expected positive or negative exposure (EPE/ENE), and effective expected positive or negative exposure (EEPE/EENE), are calculated from the exposure surface using simple formulas and do not require any complex numerical calculations.

When the model includes additional rating transitions, taking the definition of PFE literally would lead us to conclude that PFE may depend on the probability of rating transitions (other than transition to the in-default rating), if such probability over the life of the portfolio is higher than the confidence level for which PFE is reported. A change in rating will change counterparty's credit and bond spreads, and may also cause a change in the terms of collateral agreement, for example, requiring the counterparty to post more collateral and affecting its exposure.

Despite this argument, the use of rating transitions in calculating PFE has not been embraced by the regulators or the risk management community. The risk managers see the advantages of continuing to treat PFE as the measure independent of any credit event assumptions, a way to separate the data on what happens "if and when" the credit event occurs from the data which embeds the probability of a credit event. As we have seen recently, both fundamental and market implied models of credit event probabilities can go spectacularly wrong during a financial crisis. When computed without use of rating transition probabilities, PFE can continue to provide valuable information about exposures in the absence of reliable credit event probability information. Accordingly, in this chapter we will use the standard PFE methodology, which ignores rating transitions in PFE calculation and only includes them in CVA and issuer risk measures.

Credit value adjustment

CVA is the change in portfolio value due to the possibility of counterparty default. Unilateral CVA takes into account the risk of counterparty default but not the risk of default of the firm itself. Bilateral CVA takes into account the risk of default for both parties. Both measures are equally important for understanding credit value adjustment.

Unilateral CVA quantifies expected value of the credit loss without offsetting it with the gain from the reduced value of the firm's own obligations on the other side of the derivative contract. (The value of the firm's obligations is reduced because the firm also carries a risk of default, which makes these obligations less valuable to the counterparty.) By being independent from the firm's own risk of default, it allows the risk manager to focus on the credit risk caused by the counterparty alone.

Bilateral CVA is the adjustment to fair value of the portfolio of derivative contracts between two parties. Unlike unilateral CVA, bilateral CVA is symmetrical: if two parties use the same models and assumptions, they will arrive to the same CVA-adjusted value of the trades between them. Bilateral CVA takes into account the expected loss to the firm due to the risk of counterparty default, and the expected reduction in value of the firm's obligations (resulting in gain to the firm) due to the risk of the firm's own default.

Bilateral CVA may be somewhat counterintuitive because it rewards the firm for deterioration of its own credit quality. Such deterioration makes the firm's obligations under derivative contracts (pay legs) worth less, while the value of its assets (receive legs) remains the same, causing a net P&L gain. The way this correction works can be seen from the following thought experiment. Let us assume that a firm on the verge of default would like to unwind its portfolio of swaps, which have negative net value to the firm at this time, by paying to the counterparty a small fraction of their par (counterparty risk-free) value. Let us also assume for the sake of this thought experiment that the recovery value is zero and there is no collateral posted. The counterparty will agree to the transaction if they are certain of the imminent default, because after the default they will get nothing. The firm can therefore correctly record the reduced negative value of this swap portfolio on their books because the portfolio can be unwound at a significantly lower cost to the firm than its par value. This reduced negative value is the P&L gain resulting from the firm's deterioration in credit.

Despite the somewhat counterintuitive effect of credit spread change on the firm's P&L and recent debate about the wisdom of allowing firms to post P&L gains resulting from deterioration of market perception of their creditworthiness, the use of CVA in financial reporting is a tremendous step forward compared with the previous practice of ignoring credit risk, which transformed the way credit risk is valued on the books and actively managed as part of derivatives trading.

Measure choice

As the market price of credit risk, CVA is subject to the standard line of reasoning for applying risk neutral valuation. Because risk neutral measure relies on observable, market implied inputs, the standard industry practice is to compute CVA under the risk neutral measure.

The choice of measure is not as straightforward for PFE. Because PFE is a confidence level (quantile) measure and not an expectation, the risk neutral valuation does not apply in the literal sense. In practice, risk neutral PFE and real PFE can strongly deviate from each other at high confidence levels because risk neutral probabilities are very different from real probabilities.

The author believes that both risk neutral PFE and real PFE have their place in counterparty risk analysis. The real measure PFE measures potential future exposure under real world probabilities, while PFE computed under risk neutral probabilities provides better insight into the sources of CVA for the counterparty.

Most of the techniques described in this chapter apply to both risk neutral and real measure calculation equally; the reader should assume that the presentation applies equally to both measure choices except were expressly noted.

EXPOSURE SAMPLING METHOD
Overcoming the challenge of pricing with rare events

We use the term "market evolution simulation" to describe the simulation of continuously observed market variables (including credit spread and other credit-related variables) and the term "credit event simulation" to describe the simulation of rare credit events (rating changes and defaults). A CVA simulation performed from first principles involves pricing the trades and modelling rare credit events simultaneously along the same set of paths, performing both types of simulation at the same time.

While conceptually straightforward, this approach has high degree of computational complexity because credit default events have low probabilities. In order to obtain sufficient number of paths with default events and get a good Monte Carlo estimate of CVA, the simulation must have millions of paths. Not only is calculating market variables and deal cashflows for such a high number of paths computationally expensive, but the resulting CVA estimator is subject to poor convergence because the cashflows being averaged to compute CVA are discontinuous due to credit default events. (This is similar to poor convergence of a barrier option under Monte Carlo simulation due to discontinuous option payout.)

Significant amount of research has been done into improving the credit simulation to overcome the challenge of rare events, resulting in two categories of optimisation methods.

- Importance sampling methods perform credit and market simulation together, but make credit simulation more effective by increasing the likelihood of rare events for a given path through a measure change, or by eliminating the paths where default did not occur (Glasserman and Li 2003; De Prisco and Rosen 2005).
- Methods separating market evolution simulation from credit event simulation perform market evolution simulation first, without modelling credit events, and then use the results of

this simulation to evaluate CVA using an analytical method (Canabarro and Duffie 2003; Redon 2006) or through a separate credit event simulation (see the section on exposure sampling method on page 387).

This chapter focuses on the second category, and specifically on the exposure sampling method, which accelerates credit simulation by drawing samples from the exposure distribution computed during the market simulation. The techniques described in this chapter are applicable to most credit event model types.

Importance sampling methods

A key disadvantage to changing the simulation measure in order to increase the fraction of paths for which default occurs is the effect of such measure change on the ability to use American Monte Carlo for pricing.

In the context of CVA, American Monte Carlo refers to a family of methods which perform pricing of deals with early exercise by using the same Monte Carlo paths as those used in CVA simulation (De Prisco and Rosen 2005). By reusing the same paths, American Monte Carlo methods eliminate the performance bottleneck due to "Monte Carlo within Monte Carlo", namely having to generate a new set of paths for Monte Carlo trade pricing starting from each path and time step of the credit risk simulation. Here we use the term American Monte Carlo broadly to include both the methods based on locating the early exercise boundary (Longstaff and Schwartz 2001; Glasserman and Yu 2004) as well as methods based on computing transition probabilities between paths, such as the stochastic mesh method (Broadie and Glasserman 1997).

Under the importance sampling method, we must perform measure change to make paths where credit events occur more likely to appear in simulation, which requires an offsetting correction for American Monte Carlo. Such a correction is difficult to compute; it also reduces the accuracy of American Monte Carlo pricing because of uneven path distribution. The variant of the importance sampling method, which completely eliminates the paths where default did not occur, is not compatible with American Monte Carlo pricing because the effect of discarded paths cannot be included in pricing.

By not being able to use American Monte Carlo, the methods based on importance sampling are giving up the best available technique for fast and accurate calculation of exposures for complex derivatives.

Analytical calculation of CVA

The analytical calculation of CVA belongs to the second of the two categories described above, namely the methods which separate the simulation of market evolution and credit events. This method does away with the credit event simulation completely, replacing it with numerical integration based on the exposures computed during market simulation and the forward probability of default. Because simulating market evolution does not involve rare credit events, it converges after a much smaller number of paths, which results in significantly reduced computational effort (for example, having to calculate only 10,000 paths instead of millions of paths required with rare events).

The standard formula for CVA is derived by postulating that the probability of counterparty default is uncorrelated with the exposure to the counterparty. Once this assumption is made, the unilateral CVA can be calculated as an integral over time of the expected positive exposure multiplied by the forward probability of default (Canabarro and Duffie 2003; Picault 2005)

$$\text{CVA} = (1 - R) \int_0^\infty \text{EPE}(t) \, \text{PD}(t, t + dt) \, dt \qquad (14.1)$$

where $\text{EPE}(t)$ is the expected positive exposure at time t, $\text{PD}(t, t + dt) \, dt$ is the forward probability of default between times t and $t + dt$ and R is the recovery rate. Even though numerical integration is involved, this method is analytical (or more precisely, semi-analytical), in the sense that it avoids the need to perform Monte Carlo simulation of rare credit events.

By replacing the expected exposure in Equation 14.1 by conditional expected exposure, this method can capture the effect of "wrong way" (or "right way") risk: the correlation between the exposures and the counterparty credit quality (De Prisco and Rosen 2005; Redon 2006). Nevertheless, there are several common situations where, even with the correlation included, the use of conditional or unconditional expected exposures instead of full path-dependent simulation prevents accurate modelling of CVA:

- modelling credit events using a structural default model instead of a reduced form model based on the Poisson process;
- when the cost of credit insurance is correlated with credit event model parameters;
- collateral agreement dependent on credit rating.

In the following section we will show how these limitations can be avoided by using the exposure sampling method.

Introducing the exposure sampling method

The exposure sampling method is a generalisation of the analytical CVA calculation described in the preceding section which follows the approach by De Prisco and Rosen (2005) and Redon (2006) to capture the effect of wrong way risk. However, instead of using conditional expectations in Equation 14.1 directly, it performs the simulation of market evolution first, tabulates the simulated distribution of exposures and then draws samples from this distribution during credit event simulation using one or more additional random shocks for the exposure process.

By not eliminating the credit event Monte Carlo step, the exposure sampling method remains capable of modelling complex collateral rules, credit transitions and other aspects of the first-principles model which the analytical method is not able to capture. The method remains fast because the credit event Monte Carlo is performed not simultaneously with portfolio valuation but separately and with a much faster model, drawing samples from the pre-computed distribution of exposures.

Figure 14.1 shows comparison of data flows using joint simulation of market evolution and credit events (Figure 14.1(a)) versus the exposure sampling method (Figure 14.1(b)), highlighting the difference between performing simultaneous simulation of market evolution and credit events, and performing these simulations separately using the exposure sampling method.

Markovian one-factor exposure sampling

The simplest Markovian one-factor version of the exposure sampling method is implemented as follows. We begin from performing the simulation of market evolution, which produces a distribution of portfolio prices for a given time step as shown in Figure 14.2.

LESSONS FROM THE CREDIT CRISIS

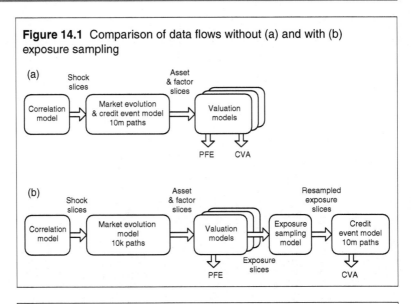

Figure 14.1 Comparison of data flows without (a) and with (b) exposure sampling

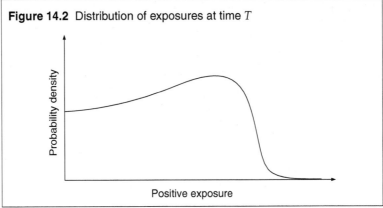

Figure 14.2 Distribution of exposures at time T

At this point, instead of using Equation 14.1, we tabulate an inverse cumulative distribution function from the distribution of exposures computed by Monte Carlo simulation of market evolution, and then perform credit event simulation by using a separate factor correlated with credit event model factors for drawing samples from this tabulated endpoint distribution of exposures, as shown in Figure 14.3. For bilateral CVA, the credit event simulation is done twice: first for the positive exposure using counterparty's credit model, and then for the negative exposure using the firm's credit model. Note that the two credit models need not be the same and may even have different types.

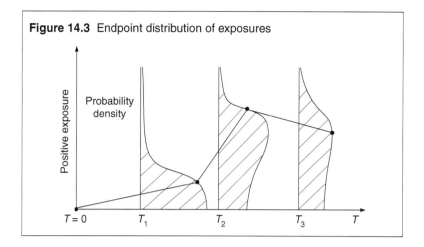

Figure 14.3 Endpoint distribution of exposures

Because evaluating a tabulated inverse cumulative distribution function is nearly instantaneous (microseconds), this calculation method is dramatically faster than performing portfolio valuation for each path, and is as fast as the analytical CVA calculation described above (see page 384) because the bottleneck is the market evolution simulation which takes the same amount of time for both methods.

We emphasise that the exposure sampling method is not limited to this simple one-factor Markovian variant and can also be used to calibrate significantly more sophisticated models of the exposure process, albeit with greater computational effort.

As an example of applying this method, consider unilateral CVA calculation under a simple structural default model, which is driven by a single "distance to default" variable with a threshold at which the default occurs. In this case the credit simulation under the exposure sampling method is two factor, where the first factor is the distance to default variable and second factor is the variable used to draw samples from the pre-computed distribution of exposures. Running such two-factor simulation with no pricing involved takes a small fraction of the time compared with the rest of the calculation.

When bilateral CVA is calculated, without the correlation between credit events of the two counterparties, two separate credit event simulations are sufficient. In the presence of such correlation, both counterparties' credit models must be simulated at the same time together with a single set of factors for exposure sampling.

In using the exposure sampling method, we make two key assumptions.

- This method requires that the correlation between the credit model factors and market evolution factors is expressed only through the shocks driving the parameterised exposure process. The author believes that, far from being a limitation, this approach actually has significant advantages over correlating the marker factors directly, especially in measuring this correlation from the historical and observed market data.

- The method relies on a parametric model of the stochastic process driving the evolution of exposures, which is calibrated to the market evolution simulation. In the simplest variant of the exposure sampling method, the model makes an additional assumption that this process is Markovian and driven by a single factor. The effect of making such an approximation is strongly reduced by the fact that it is revealed only as a second-order effect, through interaction with non-Markovian nature of the credit event model and/or margin model. For credit default models which have no path dependence (eg, a simple reduced-form model with Poisson random arrival rate for credit default), each time interval is independent and the exposure sampling method produces exactly the same result as the first-principles simulation.

In evaluating the acceptability of the assumptions made by the exposure sampling method, it is important to note that they are a subset of the assumptions made in the widely accepted analytical calculation of CVA described above (see page 386) or its extension to wrong way risk. By permitting more sophisticated modelling of credit events and margin calls, as well as including the correlation between exposure and credit event model parameters, the exposure sampling method significantly enhances the accuracy and flexibility of CVA calculation compared with the analytical method, without making any additional assumptions and without changing the computational effort compared with the analytical method.

In the following sections, we describe several practical examples where the exposure sampling method is used for calculations which are impossible with the analytical CVA methods, and prohibitively slow with full Monte Carlo of market evolution and credit events.

Using non-Gaussian shocks

The two fundamental types of credit event models used for CVA are reduced-form models, which assume a random arrival rate process for credit events with intensity which depends on the probability of default (Chapter 13), and structural default models (SDMs) which are based on one or multiple distance to default parameters (Merton 1974; Lipton and Sepp 2009). By using jump diffusion in SDMs, the boundary between the two disappears, as such combined models exhibit features of both model types (Lipton and Sepp 2010).

The exposure sampling method is neutral with respect to the type of shocks used to drive the market evolution and credit event model in CVA calculation. Because the integration is performed numerically, and nowhere in the calculation are we making any assumptions regarding the distribution or correlation of model shocks, this method is well suited for use with highly sophisticated structural default models, including the models with jumps and other non-Gaussian distribution types.

Following a series of financial crises culminating with the global financial crisis of 2008, the use of Gaussian assumptions for valuation or risk measurement have been questioned by risk practitioners, and the alternatives which accommodate rare events have become the subject not only of active research but also of considerable practical interest. One of the impediments of using improved models in practice has been the increased computational effort that more sophisticated models typically require, as they rely less on closed-form formulas and more on simulation methods compared with the preceding generation of models. It is our hope that the exposure sampling method will permit a wider acceptance of the new generation of non-Gaussian credit default models, contributing to the improvement of risk measurement practices in the financial industry.

Capturing wrong way risk

One of the challenges of capturing wrong way risk is the large number of market factors affecting exposures, which have to be correlated with credit default model factors. In order to calibrate their correlation with credit default model parameters to the historical data and to reduce correlation matrix size, this large number of market factors must be condensed into a smaller number of principal components, or ideally into a single factor.

What is this single market factor which best captures the correlation for the purposes of exposure modelling? Because our objective is to model the amount of exposure at the time of default, this factor is the exposure itself. This happens to be exactly the variable which the simplest one-factor Markovian exposure sampling method requires us to use in order to remain applicable (other variants of exposure sampling method are more flexible). This makes it possible to compute CVA with wrong way risk significantly faster than the first-principles simulation of both market evolution and credit events.

In order to measure the correlation of exposure with credit default model parameters from the historical data, for each day in the time series, all trades with the counterparty which are live today are valued based only on cashflows which are not yet paid as of today. This means that all such trades will not have cashflows between the historical date for which valuation is performed and today, and that the portfolio will not include the trades which were terminated between the historical date and today. Any trades or cashflows which have already occurred or were terminated are not relevant for estimating the correlation for the purposes of forward-looking simulation. Once the time series of exposures is calculated, its correlation to the credit model factors can be calculated using standard techniques.

When more complex processes are used for exposure sampling, the correlation of these factors with credit model factors is used instead, and a more complex calibration process is required.

Modelling CVA with rating transitions

When a counterparty is upgraded or downgraded, its credit spread changes, which affects market prices of transactions with the counterparty. The simplest way to model this is to associate each rating transition with excess credit spread, based on the increased cumulative probability of default for the lower rating. Modelling the effect of this in credit simulation is very important if the firm has purchased credit insurance on the counterparty, because a ratings change will change the value of this credit insurance.

In order to model the credit spread change due to the downgrade using the exposure sampling method, we must calculate portfolio prices not only for today's value of the counterparty credit rating, but for all other ratings as well. This does not lead to a significant increase in calculation time because only a small fraction of transactions depend on the credit rating of this specific counterparty. During the simulation of credit events, once a credit rating change occurs along a simulation path, subsequent steps in the calculation switch to sampling from the distribution of exposures for the new rating rather than the old rating. This calculation method does not make any additional assumptions other than those already made in calculating the change in credit spread after a ratings change, and exhibits good convergence in realistic scenarios.

Modelling ratings-dependent collateral agreements

One of the advantages of using the exposure sampling method compared with the analytical calculation of CVA is the possibility of full simulation of collateral position and margin calls. The collateral agreement determines the rules according to which the amount of posted or received collateral is monitored and adjusted. As a minimum, this includes margin threshold, margin call frequency (how often the positions are evaluated for the purpose of issuing a margin call) and minimal margin call amount (the minimal amount which can trigger a margin call). Real-life collateral agreement may be significantly more complex and may include such additional features as time-dependent thresholds.

An important feature of the collateral agreement is the explicit dependence of its parameters on credit ratings of the counterparties. This type of collateral agreement permits higher-rated companies to post less or no collateral, or adjust their collateral less frequently, as long as they maintain their high credit rating. The thinking behind this provision is that in most cases a default is preceded by ratings downgrade, which would permit the other party to request more collateral prior to default: an assumption which has held in several well-publicised cases during the financial crisis, albeit with government intervention to assist the downgraded companies to post additional collateral.

This provision of the collateral agreement is fully compatible with the exposure sampling method. Its modelling can be demonstrated by the following example. Let us assume that the firm has a portfolio of financial industry credit-default swap (CDS) contracts done with a counterparty which is a member of the same financials sector as the reference names on which credit insurance is purchased.

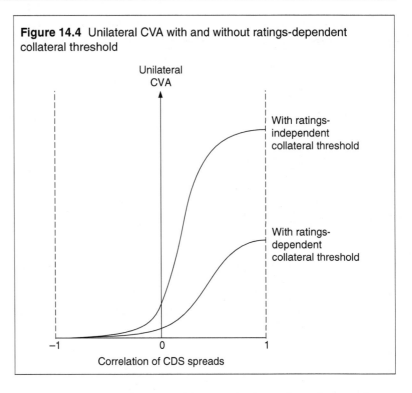

Figure 14.4 Unilateral CVA with and without ratings-dependent collateral threshold

CVA for such a portfolio would strongly depend on the correlation between CDS spreads of instruments in the portfolio and the CDS spread of the dealer itself. Because the dealer is part of the large financials sector, its spread will be positively correlated with the spreads of instruments in the portfolio. This situation exhibits classic wrong way risk and has been covered by multiple publications (see Chapter 13).

The firm may attempt to mitigate this wrong way risk by making collateral terms with the counterparty dependent on the counterparty's rating. Because a highly rated firm is unlikely to default without first going through a series of downgrades, the intuitive conclusion is that its CVA will be significantly reduced, and even further reduced when the correlation is high.

The exposure sampling method fully captures this effect and confirms our intuition. More importantly, it produces a new CVA number capturing the effect of ratings-dependent collateral limits in a simulation that can be calibrated to the historical and observable data and included in CVA reporting. The result of this calculation is shown in the graph of CVA with and without the ratings based threshold versus the correlation between the dealer's CDS spread and the CDS spread of the reference names within the portfolio (Figure 14.4).

IMPLEMENTATION GUIDE

This implementation guide is intended to serve as a blueprint and practical advice for implementing a Monte Carlo CVA process. It specifically focuses on organising the data in a way that lends itself to pricing a large number of different instruments and asset classes together under a single set of paths, an essential CVA requirement. It is this requirement that makes a Monte Carlo CVA implementation significantly more complex than Monte Carlo pricing of one instrument or a group of similar instruments.

In this guide, we describe a generic framework for dealing with large numbers of curves, prices and other observables. This framework allows the addition of new instrument types or even entire asset classes without making fundamental changes to the way the data is organised.

The objective of this framework is to create a set of barriers preventing different types of code from interacting other than through the generic assets, factors and shocks provided by the framework. For example, it prevents market model code from becoming intertwined with the correlation model code, or the instrument pricing code with the market model code. Enforcing these component interaction standards through the CVA framework (in software engineering parlance, the "contract" between components) is vital to the long-term ability to evolve credit models or pricing code and to make other modifications without requiring massive changes throughout the code.

The framework relies heavily on time slices as units of storage through which models involved in different stages of the calculation exchange data with each other. A time slice is an array of values for a given date, where each element of the array corresponds to a single Monte Carlo path. Slices can be used to store values related to assets, factors and shocks, as well as to trades and aggregated data, and can store double, integer or Boolean values.

Generic assets

The first building block of the CVA framework is a generic asset, defined as a real or synthetic underlying of a discount curve and given a globally unique identifier. Some assets are real (currencies, stock prices, commodity prices and anything else that has a price expressed in terms of another asset or currency). Other assets are hypothetical: for example, an underlying to the interest rate index can be considered an asset, for which the index forward curve is the discount curve.

By modelling both real and hypothetical assets in a similar way, and by not making a distinction between different asset types as far as the data framework is concerned, we avoid being bogged down in complexity caused by working with many distinct types of discount or forward curves. An additional bonus is that in most cases the Monte Carlo simulation code does not depend on the asset type either. For example, a cross-currency model for two currencies is similar to a model with one currency and one stock, which might be used to value an equity-linked note. The only difference between them is that the dividend yield on the stock has volatility derived in a different way from the volatility for the currency. Once these curves are expressed as discount factors and entered into the model, most cross-currency/cross-asset models will treat them as equivalent as far as stochastic evolution equations are concerned.

Generic factors

The second building block of the CVA framework is a generic factor. A factor is any observable or derived quantity expressed as single numerical value and given a globally unique identifier (mnemonic). For the CVA calculation, both current and historical values of factors are needed. Daily observation frequency is in most cases sufficient for historical calibration purposes, rate fixings or historical Monte Carlo. For those factors that have closing quotes in different time zones, several identifiers are used, one per time zone.

Some factors are observable and refer to readily available data (FX spot rates, swap rates, stock prices, etc). Other factors are derived from observable data but in a standard and unambiguous way. For example, implied volatility derived from an observable option price is effectively a quoting convention for an observable factor (option price). Other factors are non-observable and known through model-dependent calibration only (eg, vol-of-vol in a stochastic volatility model).

In addition to capturing observed and derived market data, factors are used to represent other data used in calculating exposures and CVA, such as the credit rating, default/no-default state, loss given default (LGD) ratios and other data.

In addition to market data and model factors, another factor type we will need is a trade-specific factor. This type of factor is linked to a specific trade and may represent a state variable indicating whether a deal event had occurred, a dynamic hedge ratio and other state variables which are needed to implement deal ageing.

Because factors can be defined as individual points on a curve, we could argue that we do not need the generic assets introduced in the previous section and that factors alone are sufficient for representing all of the CVA data. While factors are indeed able to replace some features covered by generic assets in the framework, forward bond prices linked to assets play the key role in fast valuation of linear instruments in CVA simulation. This functionality cannot be reproduced by factors alone.

Generic shocks

Shocks are random numbers which drive the multifactor Monte Carlo simulation. Unlike factors and assets (or, to be more precise, curves associated with assets), shocks are not directly accessed by the instrument code; they are used to drive the model evolution and are not accessible to the pricing code directly.

In order to calibrate to the historical data, each shock is assigned a single market factor which is driven solely by this shock and can be used to measure its correlation to other shocks or historical volatility. Sometimes this factor is real (eg, FX spot rate is the factor linked to the driving shock of the FX model). In other cases it is not directly observable and must to be derived from observable data (eg, the short rate, the vol of vol, etc).

Calculation flow with and without exposure sampling

The framework organises the data flows around the three fundamental concepts: generic assets, factors and shocks.

The calculation starts from running the correlation model which generates random shocks which in turn drive the market evolution model. The correlation model generates the following data.

- Slices which store simulated values for each shock S_n and simulation time step T_i.
- Slices which store "historical values" of shocks, backed out from the historical time series of observables linked to each of the shocks. These historical values are used to calibrate the correlation.

Irrespectively of the type of correlation model used to generate them, or the type of stochastic process they will simulate, the shocks are always stored as uniformly distributed values. The uniform representation format is just a storage convention and is unrelated to the process these shocks are modelling.

The next steps in the simulation are the market and credit event models. For the purposes of this guide, we will assume that the exposure sampling method is used (Figure 14.1(b)) so the modelling of market evolution is done first, followed by pricing and aggregation and then followed by credit event modelling.

The market evolution model simulates only continuous market variables, which include credit-related continuous variables such as bond and CDS spreads, but not credit events. The credit event model then uses sampling from the distribution of netted values computed at the preceding step to run simulation with significantly higher number of paths. By separating the models, it becomes possible to run the credit event model, which does not have to value trades and instead relies on resampled distribution from the market evolution model, for tens of millions of paths in order to get better statistics for rare credit events.

The market evolution model generates the following types of slices.

- For each asset A_n, the inverse of the asset value for each simulation time step T_i compounded along a single Monte Carlo path. When applied to currencies, these are Arrow–Debreu prices; here we apply them to any generic asset.
- Zero-coupon bond prices $P(T_i, T_j)$ for each asset A_n observed at time step T_i with maturity at time step T_j.

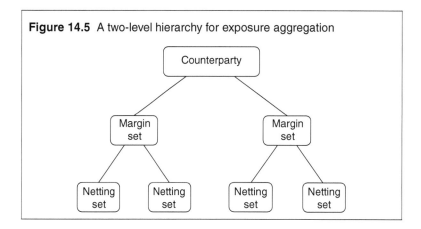

Figure 14.5 A two-level hierarchy for exposure aggregation

- Values of each asset A_n expressed in units of the models' base currency A_0 for simulation time step T_i.

- Values of each factor F_n for simulation time step T_i.

If the pricing code uses only these slices and no other data, the model which is used to generate the slices can be modified without requiring changes in the thousands of pricing functions necessary to perform valuation of a large derivatives portfolio.

The pricing model generates the following types of slices:

- For each netting set N_n and simulation time step T_i', the sum of all trade values within the netting set before netting is applied (pre-netting slice).

- For each trade Tr_n and simulation time step T_i, the values of all deal state variables which are necessary for properly keeping track of deal events in a simulation. These may include information of whether an exercise had occurred, running averages for averaging options or hedge ratios for instruments modelled jointly with their dynamic hedges.

Note that for the purposes of computing CVA it is not necessary to know prices of trades within the netting set individually, except for the purposes of drilling down into pricing data, which can be done on demand. This makes it possible to optimise pricing of linear instruments by consolidating all of the linear cashflows within a given netting set.

The aggregation and margin model generates post-margin slices from which the PFE and CVA can be computed. We assume a two-level hierarchy for exposure aggregation (Figure 14.5).

The netting set is where netting is applied, and the margin set is where margin rules are applied. This hierarchy provides maximum flexibility in implementing margin rules for a combination of multiple legal entities and the presence of both netted and not-netted trades with the same counterparty.

The aggregation code generates the following sequence of slices.

1. For each netting set N_n and simulation time step T_i, positive and negative exposure slices (calculated by setting either negative or positive part of the pre-netting slice to zero).

2. For each margin set M_n and simulation time step T_i, positive and negative pre-margin exposure slices calculated by aggregating post-netting exposure slices from each netting set N_n for the margin set M_n.

3. For each margin set M_n and simulation time step T_i, positive and negative post-margin exposure slices calculated by applying margin rules. This is the step is where the margin model is used to simulate margin calls.

4. For each counterparty C_n and simulation time step T_i, the value of exposure slice obtained by aggregating the values from each of the margin sets M_n for the counterparty C_n.

Under the exposure sampling method, the credit event model comes after the aggregation and margin model (except for ratings-dependent collateral terms) and must generate the following data:

1. for each counterparty C_n and simulation time step T_i, the default/no-default state or the credit rating with the lowest rating being the state of default;

2. for each counterparty C_n and simulation time step T_i, the LGD amount which is obtained from the LGD ratio and may also include any credit insurance payout contingent on counterparty default;

3. using the exposure sampling method, the counterparty exposure resampled on the complete set of paths for the credit simulation;

4. any additional "distance to default" variables required by the credit event model.

From this data, the unilateral and bilateral CVA numbers are produced by standard means completing the calculation process.

Dealing with large number of factors

Unlike an enterprise VaR calculation, which requires modelling the entire firm's portfolio under a single set of Monte Carlo paths, the PFE and CVA can be calculated separately for each counterparty (except when specifically modelling the counterparty correlation). Because a typical counterparty will have trades which involve a small fraction of the entire number of simulation factors, the task of calibrating and running a correlation model for only the factors included in trades with a single counterparty is significantly easier than generating the paths for the entire set of market factors. Nevertheless, this number is still typically much higher than the number (typically 30–50) that can be modelled with a single correlation matrix without running into the calibration or ill-defined matrix issues.

A correlated stochastic process which generates the shocks that the model requires must be calibrated, typically to the historical data. Modelling all of the shocks at once under a single correlation matrix would cause it to become ill conditioned, and would also cause difficulties in calibration due to a limited number of historical observations.

In order to address this, shocks have to be broken down into two groups: the principal components generated using a real correlation matrix, and all other shocks which are modelled by simpler means, either as a linear combination of other shocks (PCA or "beta" approach), or with an additional idiosyncratic volatility on top of a linear combination of other factors (Arvanitis and Gregory 2001).

Pricing by zero-bond slice caching (linear deals)

A typical Monte Carlo simulation of firmwide CVA has two performance bottlenecks. The first bottleneck is a large number of linear or nearly linear instruments, which are simple enough to be traded in large volumes but are still over-the-counter and therefore carry counterparty risk. Examples of such instruments include swaps and FX forwards. While pricing a single instrument is very fast, their large volume presents a formidable performance challenge for Monte Carlo CVA, where pricing function must be called millions of times per trade (eg, for 10,000 paths and 500 time steps, the number of calls is 5 million). This is in contrast to portfolio valuation and P&L analytics, where vanilla instruments rarely become the bottleneck, because they need to be priced only at origin.

The most effective method for linear instrument pricing in CVA is based on caching forward zero-bond prices, and combining them with pre-computed contingent cashflows at each time step. With our CVA framework, a generic zero-bond price is a slice of values at time T of an instrument which pays a unit of the same asset at a future time T' for any simulation path. If the generic asset is a currency, this instrument is a zero-coupon bond with maturity at time T'.

A linear instrument is an instrument whose price does not depend on volatility. This includes any instruments which are based on fixed cashflows, as well as interest rate payments where interest is based on par rate with spread. This may seem like a restrictive list, but it includes two of the leading sources of trade volume in CVA calculations: vanilla swaps and FX forwards. Therefore, any optimisation for this instrument type has a significant effect on the overall performance of CVA simulation.

We will also include in this category the instruments which have a slight quadratic dependence on volatility due to convexity, for example, the mismatch between the interest rate tenor and the payment frequency. For the purposes of pricing under CVA simulation, it is in most cases acceptable to replace the volatility-dependent part by its expected value computed from the market data at origin, and treat the instrument as a linear one with additional spread. This technique is highly accurate for stubs and other situations when the tenor does not exactly match the frequency; it is less accurate when the underlying instrument is very different from the par rate, eg, in case of CMS swaps.

In order to perform fast pricing of linear instruments in CVA calculation, the instruments are first represented as a set of cashflows $C(T_i, T_j)$ as seen on date T_i for payment on date T_j. For instruments with fixed cashflows only, this representation will be the same for each time step. For instruments with floating cashflows, a cashflow which is already fixed for a given observation date will have different representation than for the date where it is not yet fixed.

The value of linear deals is then expressed as the linear combination of cashflows as seen from time T_i and zero-bond prices as seen from the same time T_i, both of which can be pre-computed

$$PV(T_i) = \sum_j C(T_i, T_j) \times P(T_i, T_j)$$

The key advantage of this method is that it does not depend on the number of instruments within the netting set, and therefore is most effective (compared with traditional methods) when the number of instruments is large.

Pricing by American Monte Carlo

For the purposes of this chapter, the generic term "American Monte Carlo" is applied to a variety of techniques for performing backward induction through a set of Monte Carlo paths. This definition includes multiple methods (Broadie and Glasserman 1997; Longstaff and Schwartz 2001; Glasserman and Yu 2004).

The American Monte Carlo methods hold special importance for the calculation of CVA because of their ability to avoid "Monte Carlo within Monte Carlo" by using the same set of paths for pricing and for market simulation (De Prisco and Rosen 2005). Trade values for all paths at time T are computed from the Monte Carlo paths at times $t > T$, using backwards induction back to T. The process is repeated for each time step of the simulation, resulting in trade values for all paths and all time steps computed with the same computational effort as pricing the deal once.

Pricing by control variate interpolation

Using American Monte Carlo for CVA calculations is not always possible for every non-linear deal in the portfolio. Some deals cannot easily be represented in a form which lends itself to American Monte Carlo calculation. For other deals, the time and effort required for such conversion does not justify the benefit if the deal population is small relative to the rest of the portfolio. Sometimes, the firm simply lacks the resources to re-implement pricing for every deal using the American Monte Carlo method.

An alternative to the American Monte Carlo is invoking the pricing function for each path and time step. This is prohibitively expensive in terms of CPU time for any deal which is not priced using a simple closed-form solution. For example, a pricing function using a finite-difference lattice which takes one second for each pricing call will take approximately 270 hours of a single CPU core to compute for 500 time steps and 2,000 paths. And this is only for one deal! Even a massive parallel cluster will not be able to handle this type of a calculation without additional optimisations.

We may be tempted to use interpolation to reduce the number of calls to the pricing function, but there are significant difficulties in such an approach. It is well known that geometry of high-dimensional space makes interpolation between Monte Carlo paths impossible. In order to interpolate, the dimension needs to be reduced first and the only reduction that will carry practical benefit in terms of improving the calculation times is reduction to one dimension; the greater number of points needed to interpolate in two or more dimensions will not bring sufficient benefit.

The best variable to use for interpolation is provided by a control variate: the value of a fast but less accurate pricing function. The instrument is first priced using the fast, less accurate pricing function. Such a function may be obtained by replacing a Bermudan or American exercise with a European exercise, or by approximating an exotic interest rate instrument with a linear one. After the exposures are computed using the fast pricing function, the slow and more accurate function is used at equal intervals in terms of the price distribution quantile, and the difference between the accurate function and the fast function is interpolated using a spline or parametric interpolation function. This method achieves most of the accuracy using a small fraction of pricing calls compared with calling the pricing function for every path and time step.

CONCLUSION

In the first part of this chapter, we reviewed the methodology and industry practice of Monte Carlo PFE and CVA modelling and introduced the exposure sampling method for computing CVA. The exposure sampling method belongs to the family of methods which separate simulation of market evolution and credit events.

The key advantages of the exposure sampling method are as follows.

- It provides nearly the same speed as the analytical CVA calculation.

- Unlike the analytical method, exposure sampling does not require exposure distribution functions to be dealt with for each time step individually, and therefore permits path dependence to be captured in a way that the analytical method can not.

- It is compatible with a wide variety of sophisticated credit event models, including both reduced-form and structural default model types.

- It is compatible with non-Gaussian shocks for both market evolution and credit event models, an important advantage in light of the breakdown of Gaussian models during the financial crisis.

- It permits significantly greater flexibility in modelling credit events and collateral agreements than the analytical method, including the ability to model

    - the correlation between credit event model factors and counterparty exposures for both structural default and reduced form model types,
    - counterparty rating transitions,
    - ratings-dependent collateral agreement terms.

This chapter contains several examples of using the exposure sampling method in situations where the analytical CVA calculation method is inapplicable, and where jointly simulating market evolution and credit events is prohibitively expensive in terms of computing effort for all but the smallest portfolio sizes.

The second part of this chapter is a practical implementation guide for Monte Carlo CVA. The guide introduces a CVA simulation approach which treats uniformly a wide range of different types of curves, market observables and simulation model types. Given the large number of market factors involved in large-scale CVA calculation, using a generic approach to curves and market factor modelling is essential in order to be able to use the same pricing models with multiple CVA models and vice versa. The implementation guide also gives step-by-step instructions on implementing the exposure sampling method introduced on page 387.

REFERENCES

Arvanitis, A., and J. Gregory, 2001, *Credit: The Complete Guide to Pricing, Hedging and Risk Management* (London: Risk Books).

Broadie, M., and P. Glasserman, 1997, "A Stochastic Mesh Method for Pricing High Dimensional American Options". Paine Webber Papers in Money, Economics and Finance, PW9804, Columbia Business School, New York.

Canabarro, E., and D. Duffie, 2003, "Measuring and Marking Counterparty Risk", in *Asset/Liability Management for Financial Institutions* (New York: Institutional Investor Books).

De Prisco, B., and D. Rosen, 2005, "Modelling Stochastic Counterparty Credit Exposures for Derivatives Portfolios" in M. Pykhtin (ed), *Counterparty Credit Risk Modeling* (London: Risk Books).

Glasserman, P., and J. Li, 2003, "Importance Sampling for Portfolio Credit Risk", Research Paper, Columbia University.

Glasserman, P., and B. Yu, 2002, "Pricing American Options by Simulation: Regression Now or Regression Later?", in H. Niederreiter (ed), *Monte Carlo and Quasi-Monte Carlo Methods* (Berlin: Springer).

Lipton, A., and A. Sepp, 2009, "Credit Value Adjustment for Credit Default Swaps via the Structural Default Model", *Journal of Credit Risk* 5(2), pp. 123–46.

Lipton, A., and A. Sepp, 2010, "Credit Value Adjustment in the Extended Structural Default Model", in A. Lipton and A. Rennie (eds), *The Oxford Handbook of Credit Derivatives* (Oxford University Press).

Longstaff, F., and E. Schwartz, 2001, "Valuing American Options by Simulation: A Simple Least-Squares Approach", *Review of Financial Studies* 14(1), pp. 113–47.

Merton, R., 1974, "On the Pricing of Corporate Debt: The Risk Structure of Interest Rates", *The Journal of Finance* 29, pp. 449–70.

Picoult, E., 2005, *Calculating and Hedging Exposure, CVA and Economic Capital for Counterparty Credit Risk*, M. Pykhtin (ed) (London: Risk Books).

Pykhtin, M., and D. Rosen, 2009, *Pricing Counterparty Risk at the Trade Level and CVA Allocations*, FRB Finance and Economics Discussion Series (Washington, DC: The Federal Reserve Board).

Pykhtin, M., and S. Zhu, 2007, "A Guide to Modelling Counterparty Credit Risk", *GARP Risk Review*, July/August, pp. 16–22.

Redon, C., 2006, "Wrong Way Risk Modelling", *Risk Magazine*, May, pp. 38–44.

Part V

Market Efficiency and (In)stability

15

The Endogenous Dynamics of Markets: Price Impact, Feedback Loops and Instabilities

Jean-Philippe Bouchaud
Capital Fund Management

Why do asset prices move so frequently and why is the volatility so high? Why do prices move at all? These are obviously fundamental questions in theoretical economics and quantitative finance, which encompass other, related issues: what is the information reflected by prices, and to what extent market prices reflect the underlying economic reality? Do we understand the origin of crises and crashes?

In this chapter, we review the evidence that the erratic dynamics of markets is to a large extent of endogenous origin, ie, determined by the trading activity itself and not due to the rational processing of exogenous news. In order to understand why and how prices move, the joint fluctuations of order flow and liquidity, and the way in which these impact on prices, become the key ingredients. Impact is necessary for private information to be reflected in prices but, by the same token, random fluctuations in order flow necessarily contribute to the volatility of markets. Our thesis is that the latter contribution is in fact dominant, resulting in a decoupling between prices and fundamental values, at least on short-to-medium timescales. We argue that markets operate in a regime of vanishing revealed liquidity but large latent liquidity, which would explain their hypersensitivity to fluctuations. We discuss several unstable feedback loops that should be relevant to account for market crises.

Efficient markets

The neoclassical paradigm answers our fundamental questions as follows: prices change because new information about the fundamental value of the asset becomes available. If the information is instantly and perfectly digested by markets, then prices should reflect faithfully these fundamental values and only move because of exogenous unpredictable news. This is the efficient-market story, which assumes that informed rational agents would arbitrage away any error or small mispricing and nudge the price back to its "true" value. This is very much a Platonian view of the world, where markets merely reveal fundamental values without influencing them: the volatility is an unbiased measure of the flow of news, and is not related to the trading activity *per se*. Crashes, in particular, can be only exogenous, but not induced by market dynamics itself.[1]

Is this picture fundamentally correct in explaining why prices move and to account for the observed value of the volatility? Judging from the literature, it looks as if the majority of academics still believe that this story is at least a reasonable starting point. The idea of rational agents and efficient markets has shaped the mindset of decision makers and regulators for decades and has permeated a variety of spheres, from international monetary policy to derivative markets and sociology. Scores of financial mathematics papers are deeply rooted in the idea that option markets are efficient. It is standard practice in banks to calibrate unwarranted models using market prices of so-called liquid derivatives, and use these models to price and hedge other (more exotic) derivative instruments: a practice very much prone to non-linear amplification of errors and self-fulfilling feedback loops. In the aftermath of the 2007–9 crisis, a number of scholars and pundits have expressed concern about this whole intellectual construct, in particular about the intrinsic stability of markets,[2] bearing in mind that Keynes had anticipated a lot of these "new" ideas (Keynes 1936). Alan Greenspan himself appears to have been fooled by the "efficient-market" whim. As he admitted:[3]

> those of us who have looked to the self-interest of lending institutions,... myself included, are in a state of shocked disbelief [...] yes, I've found a flaw [in the theory]. I don't know how significant or permanent it is, but I have been very distressed by that fact.

Paul Krugman tried to explain "how economists got it so wrong" (Krugman 2009) as follows:

> As I see it, the economics profession went astray because economists, as a group, mistook beauty, clad in impressive-looking mathematics, for truth.

But in many quarters it is still business as usual. For example, David Altig, from the Atlanta Fed, declared in September 2009:[4]

> I'm less convinced that we require a major paradigm shift. Despite suggestions to the contrary, I've yet to see the evidence that progress requires moving beyond the intellectual boundaries in which most economists already live.

At the time of writing, it is still common practice in the world of quantitative finance and in the derivative industry to use blatantly irrelevant models (such as the local volatility fallacy (Gatheral 2006; Hagan et al 2002),[5] or the use of Gaussian or Archimedean copulas[6]) that can always be brute-force calibrated on market data to spit out meaningless numbers. In the author's view, financial engineering is at the stage of Ptolemy's epicycles before Kepler's ellipses. After so much twisting and tweaking (calibration is the politically correct word for it), epicycles gave more precise predictions than ellipses... but of course, this was no theory.

There are many reasons to believe that markets are very far from efficient in the above traditional sense. To start with, the very concept of a "fundamental value" that can be computed, at least as a matter of principle, with arbitrary accuracy with all information known at time t, appears to be deeply flawed. The number of factors affecting the fundamental value of a company (or of a currency, etc) is so large, and the influence of "unknown unknowns" so predominant, that there should be, at the very least, an irreducible error margin. All valuation models or predictive tools used by traders and market participants (using economic ratios, earning forecasts, etc) or based on statistical analysis that detects trends or mean-reversion are extremely noisy (statistical methods can only rely on a rather short history) and often even biased. For example, financial experts are known on the whole to be over-optimistic and rather imprecise at forecasting the next earnings of a company.[7] News releases are often ambiguous and not easy to interpret, and real information can be buried underneath terabytes of irrelevant data.

If we accept the idea of an intrinsically noisy fundamental value with some band within which the price can almost freely wander (because nobody can know better), the immediate question is: how large is this irreducible uncertainty? Is it very small (say 10^{-4} in relative terms) or quite a bit larger (say 50%, as suggested by Black

(1986), who defined an efficient market as a market giving the correct price to within a factor 2)? If Black is right (which we tend to believe) and the uncertainty in the fundamental value is large, then Keynes's famous beauty contest is a better narrative of what is going on in financial markets, at least in the short term. It is less the exogenous dynamics (news driven) of the fundamental value than the endogenous dynamics of supply and demand that should be the main focus of research.

Another reason why markets cannot be efficient is the limited intelligence of us humans (even if, quite strangely, many academics have a hard time coming to terms with this.[8]) We do make mistakes and have regrets, and we do make sub-optimal decisions. In fact, even perfectly rational agents that have to process information in a finite amount of time are likely to make errors or go for sub-optimal solutions. A good illustration of this is provided by chess: pressed by time, even chess masters do make errors and lose against Deep Blue. Many optimisation problems are indeed very complex, in the sense that the best algorithm to solve them requires a time that grows exponentially as a function of the size of the problem (for example, the size of a portfolio that we wish to optimise (Galluccio *et al* 1998)). Humans just cannot be expected to be any good at such tasks without developing intuitive or heuristic rules, the most common one being: "just do what your neighbour is doing; they might know better". Another one is: "look for patterns, they might repeat" (Arthur 1995; Wyart and Bouchaud 2007).

Market impact

This in fact leads us to a crucial issue, that of market impact, which is the main theme of this chapter. It is both rather intuitive and empirically demonstrated that buy trades are followed by a rise in the price, and sell trades are followed by a price decline. A simple way to try to guess what others are doing is to observe price variations that may reflect the impact of their trades, and therefore their intentions (Kyle 1985). The interpretation of the price impact phenomenon is, however, potentially controversial. In the efficient-market picture, impact is nearly tautological, since informed agents successfully forecast short-term price movements and trade to remove arbitrage opportunities. This results in trivial correlations between trades and price changes, but these correlations cannot be exploited by copycats. In this story, however, uninformed trades should have no price impact (except maybe on short timescales); otherwise, silly trades would, in the long run, drive prices arbitrarily far from fundamental values.

A more plausible story is the following: if Black's idea is correct and the uncertainty in the fundamental value is large, then the amount of information contained in any given trade is necessarily small.[9] Furthermore, modern electronic markets are anonymous, which makes it impossible to distinguish potentially informed trades from non-informed trades. Hence, all trades are equivalent and they must (statistically) equally impact on prices.

The mechanism by which the market reacts to trade by shifting the price is precisely the above copycat heuristic rule, applied at a tick-by-tick level. Since all agents are pretty much in the dark but believe (or fear) that some trades might contain useful information, prices must statistically move in the direction of the trades. As reviewed below, high-frequency data allows much more precise statements to be made about the amplitude and time-dependence of this impact. But the consequence of such a scenario is that even silly trades do impact on prices and contribute to volatility: a mechanism for instabilities, bubbles and crashes, even without any "news" or other fundamental cause for such events.

We therefore have to decide between two opposite pictures for the dynamics of price: exogenous (news driven) or endogenous (impact driven). Of course, reality should lie somewhere in the middle. In the following sections, we will review several empirical findings that suggest that endogenous dynamics is in fact dominant in financial markets.

EXOGENOUS OR ENDOGENOUS DYNAMICS?

Are news releases the main determinant of volatility? Were this true, and in the absence of "noise traders", the price should essentially be constant between news, and move suddenly around the release time of the news. Noise traders should merely add high-frequency, mean-reverting price changes between news, which do not contribute to the long-term volatility of the price.

There are, however, various pieces of evidence suggesting that this picture is fundamentally incorrect. First, high-frequency time series do not look at all like long plateaus dressed by high-frequency noise. On liquid assets, there is very little sign of high-frequency mean

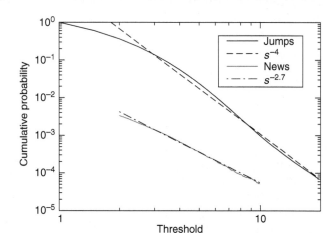

Figure 15.1 Cumulative distribution of s-jumps as a function of s

The scale is log–log. The distribution decays as $\sim s^{-4}$. We also show the number of s-jumps associated with news. Interestingly, this distribution also decays as a power law but with a smaller exponent, $\approx s^{-2.7}$.

Source: Joulin et al (2008).

reversion that could be attributed to noise traders; in other words, the high-frequency volatility is very close to its long-term asymptotic value (see, for example, Bouchaud et al 2004, 2006).[10] Furthermore, volatility is well known to be much too high to be explained by changes in fundamentals (Shiller 1981, 2000), and most large price swings seem to be unrelated to relevant news releases. This was the conclusion reached by Cutler et al (1989) in a seminal study of large daily price changes.[11]

News and no-news jumps

We have recently confirmed in detail this conclusion, now with high-frequency data, using different news feeds synchronised with price time series. We looked for simultaneous occurrences of price "jumps" and intra-day news releases about a given company (Joulin et al 2008).[12] This requires jumps to be defined in a consistent, albeit slightly arbitrary fashion. We chose to compare the absolute size $|r(t)|$ of a one-minute bin return with a short-term (120 minute) flat moving average of the same quantity, $\sigma(t)$, in order to factor in local modulations of the average volatility. An s-jump is then defined such that $|r(t)| > s\sigma(t)$. The number of s-jumps as a function of s is shown in Figure 15.1; it is seen to decay approximately as s^{-4}, consistent with previous work on the distribution of high-frequency returns (Gabaix *et al* 2006; Gopikrishnan 1999; Plerou *et al* 1999). We note once again that this distribution is very broad, meaning that the number of extreme events is in fact quite large. For example, for the already rather high value $s = 4$ we find seven to eight jumps per stock per day! A threshold of $s = 8$ decreases this number by a factor of approximately 10, amounting to one jump every one-and-a-half days per stock. In the same period, we find on average one news item every three days for each stock. These numbers already suggest that a very large proportion of shocks cannot be attributed to idiosyncratic news (ie, a news item containing the ticker of a given stock). This conclusion still holds when we include (possibly also endogenous) collective market or sector jumps in the definition of news. The number of jumps explained by these "macro" events only increases by 20%, but leaves most jumps unexplained.[13] We may also argue that these jumps are due to the arrival of private information. But this cannot be, since an investor really possessing superior information will avoid disturbing the market by trading too quickly, in order not to give away their advantage. As illustrated by Kyle's (1985) model, an insider should do better trading incrementally and discretely. We will discuss below strong empirical evidence that trading indeed occurs incrementally.

More quantitatively, there are striking statistical differences between jumps induced by news and jumps with no news that clearly demonstrate that the two types of events result from genuinely distinct mechanisms. One difference resides in the distribution of jump sizes: as shown in Figure 15.1, the cumulative distribution of jumps with news again has a power-law tail $s^{-\mu}$, but with an exponent $\mu \approx 2.7$, different from the value $\mu = 4$ mentioned above for jumps without news. Interestingly, if we extrapolate these distributions deep into the tail (and far beyond the observable regime), the news-induced jumps eventually become more probable than the no-news jumps, but only for $s \approx 60$!

A second difference is the way the volatility relaxes after a jump. In both cases, we find (Figure 15.2) that the relaxation of the excess volatility follows a power law in time

$$\sigma(t) - \sigma(\infty) \propto t^{-\zeta}$$

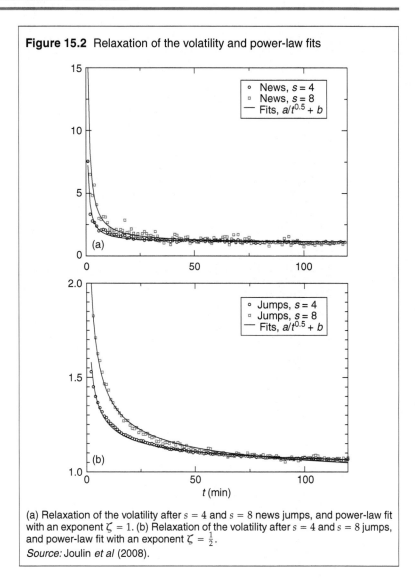

Figure 15.2 Relaxation of the volatility and power-law fits

(a) Relaxation of the volatility after $s = 4$ and $s = 8$ news jumps, and power-law fit with an exponent $\zeta = 1$. (b) Relaxation of the volatility after $s = 4$ and $s = 8$ jumps, and power-law fit with an exponent $\zeta = \frac{1}{2}$.
Source: Joulin et al (2008).

(as also reported in Zawadowski et al (2006) and Lillo and Mantegna (2003)). The exponent of the decay is, however, markedly different in the two cases: for news jumps, we find $\zeta \approx 1$, whereas for no-news jumps we have $\zeta \approx \frac{1}{2}$, with, in both cases, little dependence on the value of the threshold, s. The difference between endogenous and exogenous volatility relaxation has also been noted in Sornette et al (2003), but on a very restricted set of news events. Although counter-intuitive at first, the volatility after a no-news jump relaxes more slowly than after a news jump. This could be due to the fact that a jump without any clear explanation makes traders anxious for a longer time than if a well-identified event caused the jump. The slow, non-exponential relaxation after a no-news jump is very interesting *per se*, and already suggests that the market is in some sense critical.

So, yes, some news does make prices jump (sometimes by a lot), but the jump frequency is much larger than the news frequency, meaning that most intra-day jumps appear to be endogenous, induced by the speculative dynamics that may itself spontaneously cause liquidity micro-crises. In fact, a decomposition of the volatility (made more precise on page 423) into an impact component and a news component confirms this conclusion: most of the volatility seems to arise from trading itself, through the very impact of trades on prices.

Universally intermittent dynamics

Another striking observation, which could be naturally accounted for if price movements do result from the endogenous dynamics of a complex system, is the universality of many empirical stylised facts, such as the Pareto tail of the distribution of returns, or the intermittent, long-memory nature of the volatility. These features are observed across the board, on all traded liquid assets, and are quantitatively very similar. For example, we show in Figure 15.3 the distribution of the relative daily changes of the 60-day implied volatility corresponding to the S&P 100 stocks from January 1, 2001 to January 1, 2006 (Biely 2006). There is no reason whatsoever to expect that the statistics of implied volatility returns should resemble those of price returns. The implied volatility represents the market consensus on the expected volatility of the stocks for the 60 days to come. But as Figure 15.3 illustrates, the distribution of implied volatility returns has the same shape as that of any other traded asset, whatever its nature. In particular, the positive and negative tails of the distribution decay here as $|r|^{-4}$, very much like the tails of the daily price returns of stocks. The Pareto exponent is always found to be in the same ballpark for any liquid asset (stocks, currencies, commodities, volatilities, etc). This suggests that these tails are generated not by strong exogenous shocks, but rather by the trading activity itself, more or less independently of the nature of the traded asset.

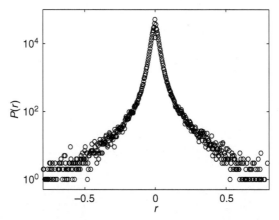

Figure 15.3 Semi-log plot of the probability distribution of the daily returns

Data are given for probability distribution of the daily returns r of the 60-day implied volatility corresponding to the S&P 100 stocks from January 1, 2001 to January 1, 2006. The positive and negative tails of the distribution decay as $|r|^{-4}$, much like the distribution of the underlying stock returns.

The activity and volatility of markets have a power-law correlation in time, reflecting their intermittent nature (Figure 15.3): quiescent periods are intertwined with bursts of activity, on all timescales (Figure 15.4). Interestingly, many "complex" physical systems display very similar intermittent dynamics (Bouchaud 2009): for example, velocity fluctuations in turbulent flows (Frisch 1997); avalanche dynamics in random magnets under a slowly varying external field (Sethna et al 2001); teetering progression of cracks in a slowly strained disordered material (Le Doussal et al 2010).[14] The crucial point about all these examples is that, while the exogenous driving force is regular and steady, the resulting endogenous dynamics is complex and jittery. These systems find a temporary equilibrium around which activity is low, before reaching a tipping point, when avalanches develop, until a new quasi-equilibrium is found (sometimes close to the previous one, sometimes very far from it). In financial markets, the flow of "real" news is of course needed to stir the activity, but the scenario we favour is similar: it is the response of the market that creates turbulence, and not necessarily the external events, barring of course exceptional events that do sometimes severely disrupt markets (for example, Lehman's bankruptcy). As explained above,

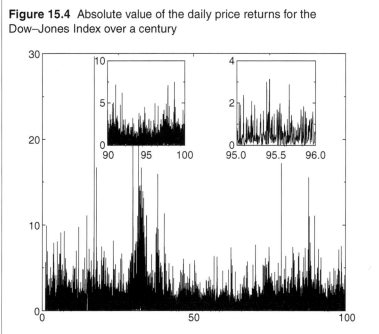

Figure 15.4 Absolute value of the daily price returns for the Dow–Jones Index over a century

Absolute values of the daily price returns for the Dow–Jones Index are given for the 100-year period 1900–2000, with the two insets showing (different scales) 1990–2000 and 1995–6. Note that the volatility can remain high for a few years (like in the early 1930s) or for a few days. This volatility clustering can also be observed on high-frequency (intra-day) data.

these events are, however, much too rare to explain why prices jump so frequently.

In all the above physical examples, the non-trivial nature of the dynamics comes from collective effects: individual components have a relatively simple behaviour, but interactions lead to new, emergent phenomena. Since this intermittent behaviour appears to be generic for physical systems with both heterogeneities and interaction, it is tempting to think that the dynamics of financial markets, and more generally of economic systems, do reflect the same underlying mechanisms. We will come back to these ideas in the conclusion.

ARE MARKETS IN "EQUILIBRIUM"?

Recent access to ultra-high-frequency, tick-by-tick data allows investigation of the microscopics of order flow and price formation. As we will explain below, the analysis of these data sets calls for a substantial revision of the traditional view of the Walrasian "tâtonnement" process, which in theory should allow prices to quickly settle to their equilibrium values.

Trades are long-range correlated!

Each transaction can be given a sign $\varepsilon = \pm 1$ according to whether the trade took place at the ask, and was triggered by a buy market order, or at the bid, corresponding to a sell market order. Market orders cross the half-spread and are usually interpreted as resulting from agents possessing superior information that urges them to trade rapidly, at the expense of less informed traders, who place limit orders. Whether or not this interpretation is correct, it is an empirical fact that such market orders impact on prices, in the sense that there is some clear correlation between the sign of a trade and the following price change. The impact function is a quantitative measure of this, and is defined as

$$\mathcal{R}(\ell) = \langle (p_{n+\ell} - p_n) \cdot \varepsilon_n \rangle_n \qquad (15.1)$$

where p_n is the mid-point price immediately preceding the nth trade, and the average is taken over all trades, independently of their volume.

The efficient-market story posits that each trade is motivated by a new piece of information, which quickly moves the price towards its new value. Since by definition the direction of the news is unpredictable, the resulting string of signs ε_n should have very short-range correlations in time. The surprising empirical result discovered by Bouchaud et al (2004, 2006) and Lillo and Farmer (2004)[15] is that the autocorrelation of the sign of trades is in fact very long ranged, over several days or maybe even months. The sign correlation function decays extremely slowly, as a power law

$$C(\ell) \equiv \langle \varepsilon_{n+\ell} \cdot \varepsilon_n \rangle_n \propto \ell^{-\gamma} \qquad (15.2)$$

where the exponent γ is found to be around 0.5 for stocks and around 0.8 for futures. The fact that these binary strings have long memory (in the sense that $\gamma < 1$) turns out to have important technical consequences, which are discussed below. The long-memory nature of the sign process means that the order flow is highly predictable. Conditional on observing a buy trade now, we can predict with a rate of success a few percent above 50% that the sign of the 10,000th trade from now (corresponding to a few days of trading) will again be positive!

Scant liquidity and trade fragmentation

Where does such a persistent correlation come from? A crucial point is that even "highly liquid" markets are in fact not that liquid. Take, for example, a US large cap stock. Trading is extremely frequent: tens of thousands of trades per day, adding up to a daily volume of roughly 0.1% of total market capitalisation. However, the volume of buy or sell limit orders typically available in the order book at a given instant of time is quite small: only of the order of 1% of the traded daily volume, ie, 10^{-5} of the market cap for stocks. Of course, this number has an intra-day pattern and fluctuates in time, and it can reach much smaller values during liquidity crises.

The fact that the outstanding liquidity is so small has an immediate consequence: trades must be fragmented. It is not uncommon that investment funds want to buy large fractions of a company, often several percent. If trading occurs through the continuous double auction market, the numbers above suggest that to buy 1% of a company requires at least the order of 1,000 individual trades. It is clear that these trades have to be diluted over several days, since otherwise the market would be completely destabilised, leading to unacceptable costs for an aggressive buyer. Thus, if an investment fund has some information about the future price of a stock, it cannot use it immediately, and has to trade into the market incrementally in order to avoid paying its own impact (Kyle 1985). This fragmentation of orders clearly leads to long-range correlations in the sign of trades.[16] Trade fragmentation is direct evidence that most investors are, to some degree, insensitive to price changes. Once the decision to buy has been made, the trade is completed even if the price moves up and down, at least within some bounds on the order of a few days or a few weeks of volatility. This is in line with the idea that the inherent uncertainty on the price is rather large.

Markets slowly digest new information

From a conceptual point of view, the most important conclusion of this qualitative discussion is that prices are typically not in equilibrium, in the traditional Marshall sense. That is, the true price is very different from what it would be if supply and demand were equal, as measured by the honest intent of the participants, as opposed to what they actually expose. As emphasised above, because of "stealth trading", the volume of individual trades is much smaller than the total demand or supply at the origin of the trades. This means that most of the putative information is necessarily latent, withheld by participants because of the small liquidity of the market. Information can only slowly be incorporated into prices.[17] Markets are hide-and-seek games between "icebergs" of unobservable buyers and sellers that have to funnel through a very small liquidity drain. Prices cannot instantaneously be in equilibrium. At best, the notion of equilibrium prices can only make sense when coarse grained over a long timescale, but then the flow of news, and the change of prices themselves, may alter the intention of buyers and sellers.

But why is liquidity, as measured by the number of standing limit orders, so meagre? Because "informed" traders that would use limit orders are reluctant to place large orders that would reveal their information. Liquidity providers who eke out a profit from the spread are also reluctant to place large limit orders that put them at risk of being "picked-off" by an informed trader. Buyers and sellers face a paradoxical situation: both want to have their trading done as quickly as possible, but both try not to show their hands and reveal their intentions. As a result, markets operate in a regime of vanishing revealed liquidity but large latent liquidity.

The long-range nature of the sign correlation, however, leads to a beautiful paradox. As we emphasised above, the sign of the order flow is highly predictable. Furthermore, each trade impacts on the price in the direction of the trade. Why is it, then, that prices can remain statistically efficient in the sense that there is hardly any predictability in the sign of price changes? The resolution of this paradox requires a more detailed description of the impact of each trade, and in particular the time dependence of this impact. This is what we address in the next section.

IMPACT AND RESILIENCE

We discussed the origin of price impact qualitatively in the introduction to this chapter. Even at this microlevel, we are faced with the exogenous versus endogenous debate about the origin of price changes. In the efficient-market picture, as emphasised by Hasbrouck (2007), "orders do not impact prices. It is more accurate to say that orders forecast prices." However, if the market collectively believes that even a small fraction of trades contain true information, the price will on average be revised upwards after a buy and downwards after a sell. But while impact is a necessary mechanism for information to be reflected by prices, its very existence means that "information revelation" could merely be a self-fulfilling prophecy, which would occur even if the fraction of informed trades is in fact zero.

Some empirical facts about impact

In any case, using high-frequency data, we can measure impact accurately. The average change of mid-point between two successive transactions, conditioned to a buy trade or after a sell trade, are found to be equal to within error bars

$$E[p_{n+1}-p_n \mid \varepsilon_n = +1] \approx -E[p_{n+1}-p_n \mid \varepsilon_n = -1] = \mathcal{R}(\ell = 1) \quad (15.3)$$

where we have used Equation 15.1 for the definition of the instantaneous impact. Note that in the definition above we average over all trades, independently of their volume. It is well known that the dependence of impact on volume is very weak: it is more the trade itself, rather than its volume, that affects the price (Bouchaud *et al* 2009; Jones *et al* 1994). This is often interpreted in terms of discretionary trading: large market orders are only submitted when there is a large prevailing volume at the best quote: a conditioning that mitigates the impact of these large orders.

One important empirical result is that the impact $\mathcal{R}(\ell = 1)$ is proportional to the bid–ask spread S: $\mathcal{R}(\ell = 1) \approx 0.3S$. This proportionality holds both for a given stock over time, as the spread fluctuates, and across an ensemble of stocks with different average spreads. This law means that the market instantaneously updates the valuation of the asset almost to the last traded price (in which case we would find $\mathcal{R}(\ell = 1) \approx \frac{1}{2}S$).

What happens on longer timescales? A plot of $\mathcal{R}(\ell)$ versus ℓ reveals that the impact first grows with time by a factor of two or so in the first 100–1,000 trades, before saturating or maybe even reverting back (Bouchaud *et al* 2004, 2006). However, the interpretation of this increase is not immediate since we know that the signs of trades are correlated: many trades in the same direction as the first trade will occur. From this point of view, it is even surprising that $\mathcal{R}(\ell)$ does not grow by more than a factor of two. This is related to the paradox mentioned above.

Another remarkable empirical finding is that the volatility per trade σ_1 is found to be proportional to the instantaneous impact, and therefore to the spread. In fact, we can regress the volatility per trade as a function of the impact, as follows

$$\sigma_1^2 = A\mathcal{R}_1^2 + \mathcal{J}^2 \tag{15.4}$$

where $\mathcal{R}_1 = \mathcal{R}(\ell = 1)$ and $\mathcal{J}^2$ is the contribution of news-induced jumps that should happen with very little trading. We then find that the second contribution is very small compared with the first (Wyart et al 2008). The relation between σ_1 and S again holds both for a single stock over time and across different stocks. A very simplified picture accounting for this finding is that the spread defines a "grid" over which the price moves with a random direction at every trade. Of course, the problem with this interpretation is that the long-ranged nature of the sign correlations should lead to super-diffusion, ie, persistent trends in the price: we are back to the same paradox.

A subtle dynamical equilibrium

Let us assume that the price at trade time t can be decomposed as a sum over past impacts, in the following way

$$p_t = p_{-\infty} + \sum_{t'=-\infty}^{t-1} G(t-t')\varepsilon_{t'} S_{t'} V_{t'}^{\psi} \tag{15.5}$$

where S_t is the spread at time t and V_t is the volume of the trade at that instant. The exponent ψ is found to be quite small:[18] as noted above, it is well documented that the response to the volume of a single trade is strongly concave. The most important quantity in the above equation is the function $G(\ell)$ that "propagates" the impact of the trade executed at time t' up to time t. In other words, G can be interpreted as the impact of a single trade, in contrast to $\mathcal{R}$, which sums up the impact of correlated trades. Within the above model, the relation between the two quantities reads

$$\mathcal{R}(\ell) = K\left[G(\ell) + \sum_{0<n<\ell} G(\ell-n)C(n) + \sum_{n>0}[G(\ell+n) - G(n)]C(n)\right] \tag{15.6}$$

where K is a certain constant and C is the correlation of the signs of the trades (Bouchaud et al 2004, 2006). If impact was permanent, ie, $G(\ell) = G_0$, the long-range nature of the correlation of trades would lead to an ever growing $\mathcal{R}(\ell)$, as $\ell^{1-\gamma}$ for $\gamma < 1$, ie, for a long memory process. Whenever $\gamma > 1$, $\mathcal{R}(\ell \gg 1)$ saturates to a constant. This underlies the significance of the fact that empirically γ is found to be less than unity.

If, on the other hand, $G(\ell)$ decays as $\ell^{-\beta}$ with β exactly tuned to $(1 - \gamma)/2$, then the transient nature of the impact of single trades precisely offsets the long range correlation of the sign of trades. This choice of β leads to both a saturating $\mathcal{R}(\ell)$ and a diffusive price, for which returns are uncorrelated (Bouchaud et al 2004, 2006). The solution of our paradox is therefore that the market is resilient: after the immediate reaction to a trade, the impact slowly mean-reverts back to zero (but in the mean time, of course, new trades occur). Equation 15.6 in fact allows us to determine the unknown function $G(\ell)$ from the empirical determination of $\mathcal{R}(\ell)$ and $C(\ell)$, through matrix inversion (Bouchaud et al 2004, 2006; Eisler et al 2009). The result is plotted in Figure 15.5 for several stocks of the Paris Bourse. We indeed see that $G(\ell)$ decays as $\ell^{-\beta}$ for large ℓ.

The above model can be reformulated in terms of surprise in order flow. Since the order flow is highly correlated, the past history of trades allows us to make a prediction of the sign of the next trade, which we call $\hat{\varepsilon}_t$. Within a linear filter framework, this prediction can be expressed in terms of past realised signs

$$\hat{\varepsilon}_t = \sum_{t'=-\infty}^{t-1} B(t-t')\varepsilon_{t'} \qquad (15.7)$$

where $B(\ell)$ are coefficients. If we forget the fluctuations of the product SV^ψ,[19] it is easy to show that the above transient impact model can be exactly rewritten in terms of a permanent response to the surprise in the order flow, defined as $\varepsilon_t - \hat{\varepsilon}_t$

$$p_t = p_{-\infty} + G(1) \sum_{t'=-\infty}^{t-1} [\varepsilon_{t'} - \hat{\varepsilon}_{t'}] \qquad (15.8)$$

provided the following identification is made

$$G(1)B(\ell) = G(\ell+1) - G(\ell)$$

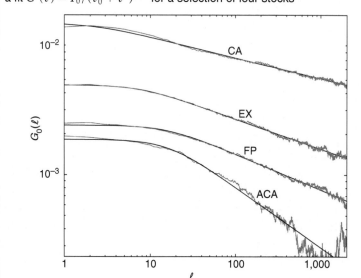

Figure 15.5 Comparison between the empirically determined $G(\ell)$ and a fit $G^f(\ell) = \Gamma_0/(\ell_0^2 + \ell^2)^{\beta/2}$ for a selection of four stocks

The empirically determined $G(\ell)$ (grey lines) are extracted from $\mathcal{R}$ and $\mathcal{C}$ using Equation 15.6, and compared with a fit $G^f(\ell) = \Gamma_0/(\ell_0^2 + \ell^2)^{\beta/2}$ (black lines), for a selection of four stocks: ACA (Crédit Agricole), CA (Carrefour), EX (Vivendi), FP (Total) using data from 2002 (see Bouchaud et al (2004, 2006) for details).

(Bouchaud et al 2009; Gerig 2007). If $B(\ell)$ corresponds to the best linear filter adapted to the long-ranged correlation in the ε values, we easily recover that $G(\ell)$ indeed decays as $\ell^{-\beta}$ with $\beta = (1-\gamma)/2$.

The above interpretation in terms of surprise is interesting because it provides a microscopic mechanism for the decay of the impact of single trades. Let us rephrase the above result in more intuitive terms. Call $p_+ > \frac{1}{2}$ the probability that a buy follows a buy. The unconditional impact of a buy is $G(1)$ (see Equation 15.8). From the same equation, a second buy immediately following the first has a reduced impact, $G^+(1) < G(1)$, since now $\hat{\varepsilon} = 2p_+ - 1 > 0$. A sell immediately following a buy, on the other hand, has an enhanced impact equal to $G^-(1) > G(1)$. If we want the next trade to lead to an unpredictable price change, its conditional average impact must be zero: $p_+ G^+(1) - (1 - p_+) G^-(1) \equiv 0$, which indeed leads to

$$G^-(1) = \frac{p_+}{1 - p_+} G^+(1) > G^+(1)$$

when $p_+ > \frac{1}{2}$ (Gerig 2007). This is the "asymmetric liquidity" effect explained in Lillo and Farmer (2004), Farmer *et al* (2006) and Gerig (2007). This mechanism is expected to be present in general: because of the positive correlation in order flow, the impact of a buy following a buy should be less than the impact of a sell following a sell; otherwise, trends would build up.

Now, what are the mechanisms responsible for this asymmetric liquidity, and how can they fail (in which case markets cease to be efficient, and jumps appear)? One scenario is "stimulated refill": buy market orders trigger an opposing flow of sell limit orders, and vice versa (Bouchaud *et al* 2004, 2006). This rising wall of limit orders decreases the probability of further upward moves of the price, which is equivalent to saying that $G^+(1) < G^-(1)$. This dynamical feedback between market orders and limit orders is therefore fundamental for the stability of markets and for enforcing efficiency. It can be tested directly on empirical data; for example, Weber and Rosenow (2006) have found strong evidence for an increased limit order flow compensating market orders.[20]

This stabilisation mechanism can be thought of as a dynamical version of the supply–demand equilibrium, in the following sense: incipient up-trends quickly dwindle because, as the ask moves up, market order buy pressure goes down, while the limit order sell pressure increases (Handa *et al* 1998). Conversely, liquidity-induced mean reversion, which keeps the price low, attracts more buyers, which is in turn an incentive for liquidity providers to raise their price. Such a balance between liquidity taking and liquidity providing is at the origin of the subtle compensation between correlation and impact explained above. In fact, the relation between volatility and spread noted above is a direct manifestation of the very same competition between market orders and limit orders (Wyart *et al* 2008). Limit orders are only profitable if the spread is larger than the volatility, whereas market orders are profitable in the opposite case. A small spread attracts market orders, whereas a large spread attracts limit orders. In orderly market conditions, an equilibrium is reached, enforcing $\sigma_1 = cS$, where c is a numerical constant (Wyart *et al* 2008). But this constraint can also lead to an instability: a local increase of volatility leads to an opening of the spread, itself feeding back on volatility. This mechanism might be at the heart of the frequent liquidity micro-crises observed in markets, and the associated no-news jumps reported above. The relation between volatility and spread means that there is a kind of "soft-mode": the market can operate at any value of the volatility, provided the spread is adapted (and vice versa). The absence of a restoring force pinning the volatility to a well-defined value is probably responsible for the observed long-memory property, and the slow relaxation of the volatility after a jump (see Figure 15.2).

The problem with impact

In conclusion, although "price impact" seems to convey the idea of a forceful and intuitive mechanism, the story behind it might not be that simple. Empirical studies show that the correlation between signed order flow and price changes is indeed strong, but the impact of trades is neither linear in volume nor permanent, as assumed in several models. Impact is rather found to be strongly concave in volume and transient (or history dependent), the latter property being a necessary consequence of the long-memory nature of the order flow.

Coming back to Hasbrouck's comment, do trades impact on prices or do they forecast future price changes? Since trading on modern electronic markets is anonymous, there cannot be any obvious difference between "informed" trades and "uninformed" trades. Hence, the impact of any trade must statistically be the same, whether informed or not. Impact is necessary for private information to be reflected in prices, but, by the same token, random fluctuations in order flow must necessarily contribute to the volatility of markets. As argued throughout this chapter, our belief is that the latter contribution is significant, if not dominant.

SUMMARY AND PERSPECTIVES

Let us reiterate the main points of this chapter, which were aimed at describing why and how asset prices move and identifying the building blocks of any quantitative model that claims to reproduce the dynamics of markets.

Markets are close to a critical point

We first made a strong case that the dynamics of markets is mostly endogenous and determined by the trading activity itself. The arguments for this are as follows.

- News plays a minor role in market volatility; most jumps appear to be unrelated to news, but seem to appear spontaneously as a result of the market activity itself.
- The stylised facts of price statistics (fat tails in the distribution of returns, long-memory of the volatility) are to a large extent universal, independent of the particular nature of the traded asset, and very reminiscent of endogenous noise in other complex systems (turbulence, Barkhausen noise, earthquakes, fractures, etc). In all these examples, the intermittent, avalanche nature of the dynamics is an emergent property, unrelated to the exogenous drive, which is slow and regular.

In search of a purely endogenous interpretation of these effects, it is natural to investigate to high-frequency, micro-structure ingredients that generate price changes. We have discussed the remarkable long-range correlations in order flow that have far-reaching consequences and force us to revise many preconceived ideas about equilibrium. First of all, these correlations reflect the fact that even "liquid" markets are in fact very illiquid, in the sense that the total volume in the order book available for an immediate transaction is extremely small (10^{-5} of the market capitalisation for stocks). The immediate consequence is that the trades of medium to large institutions can only be executed incrementally, explaining the observed correlation in the order flow. By the same token, the information motivating these trades (if any) cannot be instantaneously reflected by prices. Prices cannot be in equilibrium, but randomly evolve as the icebergs of latent supply and demand progressively reveal themselves (and possibly evolve with time). This feature is an unavoidable consequence of the fact that sellers and buyers must hide their intentions, while liquidity providers only post small volumes in fear of adverse selection.

The observation that markets operate in a regime of vanishing revealed liquidity but large latent liquidity is crucial to understand their hypersensitivity to fluctuations, potentially leading to instabilities. Liquidity is necessarily a dynamical phenomenon that reacts to order flow such as to dampen the trending effects and keep price returns unpredictable, through the subtle "tug-of-war" equilibrium mentioned above. Such a dynamical equilibrium can, however, easily break down. For example, an upward fluctuation in buy order flow might trigger a momentary panic, with the opposing side failing to respond immediately. Similarly, the strong structural link between spread and volatility can ignite a positive feedback loop whereby increased spreads generate increased volatility, which itself causes liquidity providers to cancel their orders and widen the spread. Natural fluctuations in the order flow therefore lead, in some cases, to a momentary lapse of liquidity, explaining the frequent occurrence of price jumps without news. An extreme realisation of this feedback loop probably took place during the "flash crash" of May 6, 2010. We believe that the formal limit of zero liquidity is a critical point (Bak 1996), which would naturally explain the analogy between the dynamics of markets and that of other complex systems, in particular the universal tails and the intermittent bursts of activity. We are, however, lacking a precise model that would allow these ideas to be formalised.[21]

In summary, the picture of markets we advocate is such that the lion's share of high-frequency dynamics is due to fluctuations in order flow. News and information about fundamental values only play the role of "stirring" the system, ie, slowly changing the large latent supply and demand, except on relatively rare occasions where these events do indeed lead to violent shocks. Most of the market activity comes from the slow execution of these large latent orders that cascades into high-frequency fluctuations under the action of the use of liquidity providers and liquidity takers, who compete to exploit all statistical regularities.

The end product of this activity is a white-noise signal. Prices are, in a first approximation, statistically efficient in the sense that there is little predictability left in the time series. But this does not necessarily mean that these prices reflect in any way some true underlying information about assets. We believe, as Keynes and Black did, that the uncertainty in fundamental values is so large that there is no force to anchor the price against random high-frequency perturbations. It is quite remarkable indeed that the high-frequency value of the volatility approximately coincides with the volatility on the scale of weeks, showing that there are very few mean-reverting effects to rein the high-frequency tremor of markets. Only when prices reach values that are, say, a factor of two away from their "fundamental value" will mean-reverting effects progressively come into play. In the context of stocks, this only happens on the scale of months to years.[22] From this point of view, as emphasised by Lyons (2001), "micro-structure implications may be long-lived" and "are relevant to macroeconomics".

Looking forward

Having said all this, the theoretical situation is still rather disappointing. There is at this stage no convincing framework to account for these effects, in the sense of converting the above qualitative ideas into a quantitative model that would, for example, predict the shape of the tails of the return distribution, or the long-range memory of volatility after a suitable coarse-graining in time. In the author's view, this is the most interesting research programme in quantitative finance: to build models from the bottom up such that the value and the dynamics of the parameters (volatility, correlations, etc) can be estimated, or at least understood. Most of the available models to date[23] postulate a linear (in volume) and permanent impact as in the Kyle (1985) model, whereas, as we have shown, impact is both non-linear and transient. It may well be that the assumption of a linear, permanent impact is justified after some coarse-graining in time, say on a daily scale, but this is actually part of the programme that needs to be achieved.

In the meantime, the following strong messages emerge from the above remarks, which are particularly topical after the 2008 crisis.[24]

Even liquid markets are not really liquid, and therefore have no reason to be efficient. We should stop taking market prices at face value, especially in many over-the-counter markets where "liquidity" is deceptive. Quants should quit the obsession of exact calibration on market prices, in particular when the models are absurdly remote from reality. One of the worst examples, in the author's opinion, is the use of local volatility models, which are by construction able to fit any volatility surface, so calibration will always work, and this is unfortunately why the approach is so popular. But using this framework to price more exotic derivatives using plain vanilla instruments can lead to disaster, even if plain vanilla markets were efficient, because the underlying reality has nothing to do with a local volatility process. The situation is obviously even worse if markets are not efficient. Errors are propagated and amplified in a non-linear way, and the price and hedge of illiquid instruments can be totally nonsensical. There are many examples in the quantitative finance literature of erroneous models that can be easily calibrated, and that are therefore used and abused by financial engineers. The use of such models contributes to the propagation of systemic risk, particularly as they increasingly become standard practice.

Collective effects mediated by imitation or contagion pervade markets and lead to instabilities. Prosperity relies heavily on trust, which is an immaterial common good that has no inertia and can dissipate overnight.[25] The mechanisms that foster or destroy trust are intrinsically collective. The most efficient mechanism for contagion is through the dynamics of the price and of the order flow, which is public, common information. Since it is impossible to immediately be sure that a silly trade is indeed silly, its impact on the price can trigger an instability, as was likely to be the case during the flash crash of May 6, 2010. Being influenced by the behaviour of others seems to be one of the most common human traits that persists across history. We are always worried that others may be smarter than we are or may have more information than we do. This imitation propensity is well known to lead to dramatic effects,[26] and must be one of the ingredients leading to crises and crashes (Akerlof and Shiller 2009). The importance of hysteresis, in that respect, cannot be overemphasised (Borghesi and Bouchaud 2007; Bouchaud 2009; Cross 2009; Gordon et al 2009; Michard and Bouchaud 2005).

There are many other contagion mechanisms; we just mention here the use of similar pricing and risk models. More generally, common strategies lead to common positions,[27] and so does the widespread diffusion of similar "toxic" products (eg, collateralised debt obligations). Benchmarking performance to the average of a peer group promotes copycat behaviour. The cross-liability network between financial institutions or between companies can also be instrumental in wreaking havoc.[28]

Another important idea is that agents in financial markets are strongly heterogeneous. Physical systems where individual elements are both heterogeneous and strongly interacting are well known to be inherently fragile to small perturbations. These systems generically evolve in an intermittent way, with a succession of rather stable epochs punctuated by rapid, unpredictable changes, again, even when the exogenous drive is smooth and steady. Within this metaphor of how markets function, competition and complexity could be the essential cause of their endogenous instability.

The main problem with the current theories is that they are based on the idea that we can replace an ensemble of heterogeneous and interacting agents by a unique representative one; in other words, that the micro- and macro-behaviour should coincide (Kirman 1992). Within this framework, crises are expected to require a major external shock, whereas in reality small local disturbances can trigger large systemic effects (the US subprime market represented in itself only a minor fraction of the global credit market but still stoked a global crisis).

Finally, there are a number of explicit destabilising feedback loops that regulators should investigate and abate. Some are a direct consequence of the faith in the efficiency of markets, such as the "mark-to-market" accounting rule, which relies on the idea that market prices are fair and unbiased. Such a pro-cyclical practice applied on credit derivatives contributed to impairing the balance sheet of many financial institutions in 2008, and amplified the mayhem. In the author's opinion, again, the "fair price" idea does not make sense without at least the notion of an intrinsic uncertainty and a liquidity discount based on a pessimistic estimate of the impact cost during a fire sale. Other feedback loops are created by the use of financial derivatives (Brock *et al* 2009; Caccioli *et al* 2008) and/or, as alluded to above, by quantitative models themselves: a vivid example is the crash of 1987, which was a direct consequence of the unwarranted trust in Black and Scholes's perfect replication theory.

There are also nasty feedback loops lurking in the high-frequency, micro-structure side. We have mentioned several times in this chapter the "spread ⇒ volatility ⇒ spread" loop that is probably at the origin of most "spontaneous" liquidity crises (such as the one of May 6, 2010, but also all the daily jumps that we have discussed but that rarely make the news). It would be interesting to investigate mechanisms that help to avert those. For example, dynamic make/take fees that depend on market conditions and on the distance between the placed order and the last traded price could endogenise stabilising feedback loops. This is clearly an issue around which academic research and regulation merge, which makes modelling high frequencies so exciting.

Whether or not the above ingredients can be mixed and tuned to provide a truly quantitative theory of economic and financial crises remains of course, at this stage, a fascinating open problem.

The author thanks Arthur Berd for inviting him to assemble his thoughts and review his own work on these topics (this explains why the reference list is shamefully self-serving). The author also thanks all his collaborators on these subjects, who have helped him shape his understanding of markets: in particular C. Borghesi, L. Borland, Z. Eisler, J. D. Farmer, J. Kockelkoren, Y. Lempérière, F. Lillo, M. Potters and M. Wyart. The author has also enjoyed discussions, over the years, with X. Gabaix, J. Gatheral and M. Marsili.

1 Followers of strict obedience actually believe that the 2008 crisis was indeed induced by a major exogenous cause: maybe China's insatiable appetite for high quality paper, or even the anticipation of Barack Obama's election!

2 See, among the most provocative ones, Soros (2008), Akerlof and Shiller (2009), Farmer and Geanakoplos (2008), Caccioli et al (2008), and, in the context of financial markets, Taleb (2007) or Derman and Wilmott (2009).

3 See Greenspan's testimony before the House Committee on Oversight & Government Reform, October 23, 2008, "The Financial Crisis and the Role of Federal Regulators", Serial No. 110-209.

4 See the blog article "Economists Got It Wrong, But Why?" at http://macroblog.typepad.com/macroblog/2009/09/economists-got-it-wrong-but-why.html.

5 This, by the way, probably explains why Dupire's seminal paper on local volatility models (Dupire 1994) is among the most cited papers in mathematical finance. This is particularly symptomatic of the diseases of financial engineering.

6 See, for example, Mikosch (2006).

7 See, for example, Guedj and Bouchaud (2005) and the references therein.

8 A lot could be said (and some has been said) about the religious roots and the political implications of the rational agent concept.

9 Empirically, the standard deviation of market impact is found to be very large compared with its mean, confirming that the quantity of information per trade must indeed be small.

10 Here we talk about the volatility of the mid-point, not of the traded price, which shows a large, trivial bid–ask bounce.

11 See also Fair (2002) for a more recent discussion with identical conclusions.

12 Overnight news and overnight jumps are not included in the study. "Big" company news releases are usually issued overnight. But this makes the existence of intra-day jumps all the more puzzling!

13 See Joulin et al (2008) for more details.

14 See also Cabrera and Milton (2002); Krawiecki et al (2002) and the references therein.

15 See Bouchaud et al (2009) for a review; parts of the present chapter heavily rely on this reference.

16 See Bouchaud et al (2009) or Wyart et al (2008) for a more thorough discussion of the empirical evidence for this fragmentation interpretation, rather than a copycat mechanism, at least on long timescales.

17 See Lyons (2001) for similar ideas.

18 See Bouchaud et al (2009) for a detailed discussion.

19 It would not be difficult to include them in a model where the whole product εSV^Ψ follows a similar linear regression model on its past values.

20 See also Eisler et al (2009) for similar results.

21 See Challet *et al* (2005) and Mike and Farmer (2008) for a review.

22 See De Bondt and Thaler (1985) and the discussion in Wyart and Bouchaud (2007).

23 That is, agent-based models (Giardina and Bouchaud 2003; Goldstone and Janssen 2005; Hommes 2006; Lux and Marchesi 2000; Samanidou *et al* 2002), minority games (Challet *et al* 2005), herding models (Cont and Bouchaud 2000), Langevin approaches (Bouchaud and Cont 1998), etc.

24 There are obviously many other aspects that we leave aside. The destabilising use of leverage is one of them; see Thurner *et al* (2009) for a recent interesting paper.

25 For a recent model of trust dissipation see Anand *et al* (2009).

26 See, for example, Keynes (1936), Granovetter (1978), Granovetter and Soong (1983), Galam (2008), Brock and Durlauf (2001), Curty and Marsili (2006), Michard and Bouchaud (2005), Borghesi and Bouchaud (2007), Gordon *et al* (2009) and the references therein.

27 See, for example, the Quant Crunch of August 2007 (Khandani and Lo 2010).

28 See, for example, Battiston *et al* (2009), Neu and Kühn (2004), Choi and Douady (2009) and references therein.

REFERENCES

Akerlof, G., and R. Shiller, 2009, *Animal Spirits* (Princeton University Press).

Anand, K., P. Gai and M. Marsili, 2009, "Financial Crises and the Evaporation of Trust", e-print, arXiv:0911.3099.

Arthur, W. B., 1995, "Complexity in Economic and Financial Markets", *Complexity* 1, pp. 20–5.

Bak, P., 1996, *How Nature Works: The Science of Self-Organized Criticality* (New York: Copernicus).

Battiston, S., D. Delli Gatti, M. Gallegati, B. C. Greenwald and J. E. Stiglitz, 2009, "Liaisons Dangereuses: Increasing Connectivity, Risk Sharing, and Systemic Risk", NBER Working Paper 15611.

Biely, C., 2006, CFM Report, Unpublished.

Black, F., 1986, "Noise", *Journal of Finance* 41, pp. 529–43.

Borghesi, Ch., and J.-P. Bouchaud, 2007, "Of Songs and Men: A Model for Multiple Choice with Herding", *Quality & Quantity* 41, pp. 557–68.

Bouchaud, J.-P., 2009, "The (Unfortunate) Complexity of Economic Systems", *Physics World*, April, p. 28.

Bouchaud, J.-P., and R. Cont, 1998, "A Langevin Approach to Stock Market Fluctuations and Crashes", *European Journal of Physics* B 6, pp. 543–50.

Bouchaud, J.-P., Y. Gefen, M. Potters and M. Wyart, 2004, "Fluctuations and Response in Financial Markets: The Subtle Nature of 'Random' Price Changes", *Quantitative Finance* 4, pp. 176–90.

Bouchaud, J.-P., J. Kockelkoren and M. Potters, 2006, "Random Walks, Liquidity Molasses and Critical Response in Financial Markets", *Quantitative Finance* 6, pp. 115–23.

Bouchaud, J.-P., J. D. Farmer and F. Lillo, 2009, "How Markets Slowly Digest Changes in Supply and Demand", in *Handbook of Financial Markets: Dynamics and Evolution*, Handbooks in Finance (Amsterdam: North-Holland).

Brock, W., and S. Durlauf, 2001, "Discrete Choices with Social Interactions", *Review of Economic Studies* 68(2), pp. 235–60.

Brock, W. A., C. H. Hommes and F. O. O. Wagener, 2009, "More Hedging Instruments May Destabilize Markets", *Journal of Economic Dynamics and Control* 33, pp. 1912–28.

Cabrera, J. L., and J. G. Milton, 2002, "On–Off Intermittency in a Human Balancing Task", *Physical Review Letters* 89, Paper 158702.

Caccioli, F., P. Vivo and M. Marsili, 2008, "Eroding Market Stability by Proliferation of Financial Instruments", Working Paper, URL: http://ssrn.com/abstract=1305174.

Challet, D., M. Marsili and Y. C. Zhang, 2005, *Minority Games* (Oxford University Press).

Choi, Y., and R. Douady, 2009, "Chaos and Bifurcation in 2007–08 Financial Crisis", Working Paper, URL: http://ssrn.com/abstract=1522544.

Cont, R., and J.-P. Bouchaud, 2000, "Herd Behaviour and Aggregate Fluctuations in Financial Markets", *Macroeconomic Dynamics* 4, pp. 170–95.

Cross, R., M. Grinfeld and H. Lamba, 2009, "Hysteresis and Economics", *IEEE Control Systems Magazine* 29, pp. 30–43.

Curty, P., and M. Marsili, 2006, "Phase Coexistence in a Forecasting Game", *Journal of Statistical Mechanics*, P03013.

Cutler, D. M., J. M. Poterba and L. H. Summers, 1989, "What Moves Stock Prices?", *The Journal of Portfolio Management* 15, pp. 4–12.

De Bondt, W., and R. Thaler, 1985, "Does the Market Overreact?", *Journal of Finance* 40, pp. 793–805.

Derman, E., and P. Wilmott, 2009, "A Financial Modeler Manifesto", URL: http://www.wilmott.com/blogs/paul/index.cfm/2009/1/8/Financial-Modelers-Manifesto.

Dupire, B., 1994, "Pricing with a Smile", *Risk Magazine* 7, pp. 18–20.

Eisler, Z., J.-P. Bouchaud and J. Kockelkoren, 2009, "The Price Impact of Order Book Events: Market Orders, Limit Orders and Cancellations", e-print, arXiv:0904.0900.

Fair, R. C., 2002, "Events That Shook the Market", *The Journal of Business* 75(4), pp. 713–32.

Farmer, J. D., and J. Geanakoplos, 2008, *The Virtues and Vices of Equilibrium and the Future of Financial Economics*, e-print, arXiv:0803.2996.

Farmer, J. D., A. Gerig, F. Lillo and S. Mike, 2006, "Market Efficiency and the Long-Memory of Supply and Demand: Is Price Impact Variable and Permanent or Fixed and Temporary?", *Quantitative Finance* 6, pp. 107–12.

Frisch, U., 1997, *Turbulence: The Kolmogorov Legacy* (Cambridge University Press).

Gabaix, X., P. Gopikrishnan, V. Plerou and H. Stanley, 2006, "Institutional Investors and Stock Market Volatility", *Quarterly Journal of Economics* 121, pp. 461–504.

Galam, S., 2008, "Sociophysics: A Review of Galam Models", *International Journal of Modern Physics* C 19, pp. 409–40.

Galluccio, S., J.-P. Bouchaud and M. Potters, 1998, "Rational Decisions, Random Matrices and Spin Glasses", *Physica* A 259, pp. 449–56.

Gatheral, J., 2006, *The Volatility Surface: A Practitioner's Guide* (Chichester: John Wiley & Sons).

Gerig, A., 2007, "A Theory for Market Impact: How Order Flow Affects Stock Price", PhD Thesis, University of Illinois, e-print, arXiv:0804.3818.

Giardina, I., and J.-P. Bouchaud, 2003, "Bubbles, Crashes and Intermittency in Agent Based Market Models", *The European Physics Journal* B 31, pp. 421–37.

Goldstone, R., and M. Janssen, 2005, "Computational Models of Collective Behavior", *Trends in Cognitive Science* 9, pp. 424–30.

Gopikrishnan, P., V. Plerou, L. A. Amaral, M. Meyer and H. E. Stanley, 1999, "Scaling of the Distribution of Fluctuations of Financial Market Indices", *Physical Review* E 60, pp. 5305–16.

Gordon, M. B., J.-P. Nadal, D. Phan and V. Semeshenko, 2009, "Discrete Choices under Social Influence: Generic Properties", *Mathematical Models and Methods in Applied Sciences* 19, Supplementary Issue 1, pp. 1441–81.

Granovetter, M., 1978, "Threshold Models of Collective Behavior", *The American Journal of Sociology* 83(6), pp. 1420–43.

Granovetter, M., and R. Soong, 1983, "Threshold Models of Diffusion and Collective Behaviour", *Journal of Mathematical Sociology* 9, pp. 165–79.

Guedj, O., and J.-P. Bouchaud, 2005, "Experts' Earning Forecasts: Bias, Herding and Gossamer Information", *International Journal of Theoretical and Applied Finance* 8, pp. 933–46.

Hagan, P. S., D. Kumar, A. S. Lesniewski and D. E. Woodward, 2002, "Managing Smile Risk", *Wilmott Magazine*, September, pp. 84–108.

Handa, P., R. A. Schwartz and A. Tiwari, 1998, "The Ecology of an Order-Driven Market", *Journal of Portfolio Management*, Winter, pp. 47–56.

Hasbrouck, J., 2007, *Empirical Market Microstructure* (Oxford University Press).

Hommes, C., 2006, "Heterogeneous Agent Models in Economics and Finance", *Handbook of Computational Economics*, Volume 2 (Elsevier).

Jones, C., G. Kaul and M. L. Lipson, 1994, "Transactions, Volume, and Volatility", *Review of Financial Studies* 7, pp. 631–51.

Joulin, A., A. Lefevre, D. Grunberg and J.-P. Bouchaud, 2008, "Stock Price Jumps: News and Volume Play a Minor Role", *Wilmott Magazine*, September/October.

Keynes, J. M., 1936, *The General Theory of Employment, Interest and Money* (London: Macmillan).

Khandani, A., and A. Lo, 2010, "What Happened to the Quants in August 2007? Evidence from Factors and Transactions Data", *Journal of Financial Markets*, DOI: 10.1016/j.finmar.2010.07.005.

Kirman, A. P., 1992, "Whom or What Does the Representative Individual Represent?", *The Journal of Economic Perspectives* 6, pp. 117–36.

Krawiecki, A., J. A. Hoyst and D. Helbing, 2002, "Volatility Clustering and Scaling for Financial Time Series Due to Attractor Bubbling", *Physical Review Letters* 89, Paper 158701.

Krugman, P., 2009, "Why Did Economists Get It So Wrong?", *The New York Times* Magazine, URL: http://www.nytimes.com/2009/09/06/magazine/06Economic-t.html.

Kyle, A. S., 1985, "Continuous Auctions and Insider Trading", *Econometrica* 53, p. 1315–35.

Le Doussal, P., M. Müller, K. J. Wiese, 2010, "Avalanches in Mean-Field Models and the Barkhausen Noise in Spin-Glasses", e-print, arXiv:1007.2069.

Lillo, F., and J. D. Farmer, 2004, "The Long Memory of the Efficient Market", *Studies in Nonlinear Dynamics & Econometrics* 8, Article 1.

Lillo, F. and R. N. Mantegna, 2003, "Power Law Relaxation in a Complex System: Omori Law After a Financial Market Crash", *Physical Review* E 68, 016119.

Lux, T., and M. Marchesi, 2000, "Volatility Clustering in Financial Markets: A Microsimulation of Interacting Agents", *International Journal of Theoretical and Applied Finance* 3, pp. 675–702.

Lyons, R., 2001, *The Microstructure Approach to Foreign Exchange Rates* (Cambridge, MA: MIT Press).

Michard, Q., and J.-P. Bouchaud, 2005, "Theory of Collective Opinion Shifts: From Smooth Trends to Abrupt Swings", *European Physics Journal* B 47, pp. 151–9.

Mike, S., and J. Farmer, 2008, "An Empirical Behavioral Model of Liquidity and Volatility", *Journal of Economic Dynamics and Control* 32, p. 200–34.

Mikosch, T., 2006, "Copulas: Tales and Facts", *Extremes* 9(1), pp. 3–20.

Neu, P., and R. Kühn, 2004, "Credit Risk Enhancement in a Network of Interdependent Firms", *Physica* A 342, pp. 639–55.

Plerou, V., P. Gopikrishnan, L. A. Amaral, M. Meyer and H. E. Stanley, 1999, "Scaling of the Distribution of Price Fluctuations of Individual Companies", *Physical Review* E 60, pp. 6519–29.

Samanidou, E., E. Zschischang, D. Stauffer and T. Lux, 2002, "Microscopic Models of Financial Markets", in F. Schweitzer (ed), *Microscopic Models for Economic Dynamics*, Lecture Notes in Physics (Berlin: Springer).

Sethna, J., K. Dahmen and C. Myers, 2001, "Crackling Noise", *Nature* 410, p. 242–50.

Shiller, R. J., 1981, "Do Stock Prices Move Too Much to Be Justified by Subsequent Changes in Dividends?", *American Economic Review* 71, pp. 421–36.

Shiller, R. J., 2000, *Irrational Exuberance* (Princeton University Press).

Sornette, D., Y. Malevergne and J. F. Muzy, 2003, "What Causes Crashes", *Risk Magazine* 67, February.

Soros, G., 2008, *The New Paradigm for Financial Markets: The Credit Crisis of 2008 and What It Means* (New York: PublicAffairs).

Taleb, N., 2007, *The Black Swan* (London: Random House).

Thurner, S., J. Doyne Farmer and J. Geanakoplos, 2009, "Leverage Causes Fat Tails and Clustered Volatility", e-print, arXiv:0908.1555.

Weber, P., and B. Rosenow, 2006, "Large Stock Price Changes: Volume or Liquidity?", *Quantitative Finance* 6, p. 7–14.

Wyart, M., and J.-P. Bouchaud, 2007, "Self-Referential Behaviour, Overreaction and Conventions in Financial Markets", *Journal of Economic Behavior and Organization* 63, pp. 1–24.

Wyart, M., J.-P. Bouchaud, J. Kockelkoren, M. Potters and M. Vettorazzo, 2008, "Relation Between Bid–Ask Spread, Impact and Volatility in Order Driven Markets", *Quantitative Finance* 8, pp. 41–57.

Zawadowski, A. G., J. Kertesz and G. Andor, 2006, "Short-Term Market Reaction after Extreme Price Changes of Liquid Stocks", *Quantitative Finance* 6, pp. 283–95.

16

Market Panics: Correlation Dynamics, Dispersion and Tails

Lisa Borland
Evnine and Associates Inc

The financial crisis of 2008 prompted us to explore statistical signatures of market panic. In particular, we focus on the properties of the cross-sectional distribution of returns and propose a model for the cross-sectional dynamics. On daily timescales, we find a significant anti-correlation between dispersion and cross-sectional kurtosis such that dispersion is high but kurtosis is low in times of panic, and vice versa in normal times. This appears counter-intuitive at first, because times of panic have wild returns, so-called "black swans" (Taleb 2007) and rare events, which are typically associated with fat-tailed distributions (high kurtosis). We also find that the co-movement of stock returns increases in times of panic. In order to model these dynamics, we have proposed (Borland 2009) a joint stochastic process to describe the behaviour of stocks across time as well as their interactions at each point in time. The basic idea is a simple model of self-organisation, such that there occurs a spontaneous phase transition to a highly correlated state at the onset of panic. We quantify this with a simple statistic, s, the normalised sum of signs of returns on a given day, which captures the degree of correlation in the system. We hypothesise that financial markets undergo self-organisation when the external volatility perception rises above some critical value, and that this is reflected in the behaviour of s, which can be seen as the order parameter of the system. A phenomenological model is proposed which shows good qualitative agreement with real data.

This chapter begins with a review of the known stylised facts observed in time series of returns, as well as a discussion of various plausible models of that temporal behaviour. We then look at some empirical observations of the cross-sectional behaviour of markets,

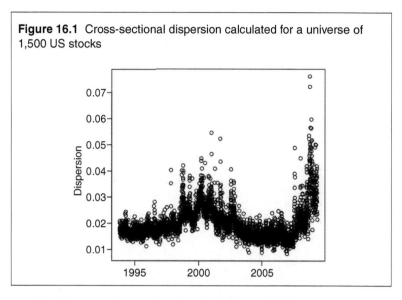

Figure 16.1 Cross-sectional dispersion calculated for a universe of 1,500 US stocks

which is followed by a theoretical section that discusses the interaction of stocks across time. At that point we introduce the notion of a particular macroscopic observable intimately related to the correlations in the system as an order parameter, borrowing concepts from physics to describe what we believe to be evidence of self-organisation from a disordered to ordered state in market dynamics. Finally, we show some numerical simulations and conclude with a discussion of the results.

STYLISED FACTS OF MARKETS ACROSS TIME AND ACROSS STOCKS

The stylised facts of financial instruments across time are quite well known, and in particular it is seen that returns calculated over timescales ranging from minutes to weeks are fitted well by a power-law distribution with the tail index 3 (Bouchaud and Potters 2004; Gopikrishnan 1999; Plerou et al 1999). Several classes of distributions can be fitted to these densities of returns, but, for example, a Student-t with about five degrees of freedom is quite a good choice for daily returns (Borland 2002, 2007; Gell-Mann and Tsallis 2004). A plot of such a fit for the distribution of daily returns of the Dow Jones Index is shown in Figure 16.1. As the timescale increases, the power-law property persists, eventually decaying to a Gaussian (Gopikrishnan 1999; Plerou et al 1999). Another interesting property is that there are periods of high volatility followed by quieter periods. This volatility clustering indicates that there is memory in the volatility process. Furthermore, a multi-fractal analysis of the volatility shows that it is self-similar (Bouchaud and Potters 2004). This means that the volatility clustering occurs on all timescales (intra-day and daily, for example). In addition, the distribution of volatility is modelled well by a lognormal or inverse gamma distribution (Bouchaud and Potters 2004). There is causality in financial time series. For example, the future volatility depends on the past (Borland *et al* 2005; Zumbach and Lynch 2003). Another asymmetric feature is the so-called leverage effect: large negative returns tend to precede higher volatility (Bouchaud *et al* 2001). These statistical features all appear to be rather universal in the sense that they can be found for a variety of financial instruments (stocks and currencies, for example) as well as in different geographic regions and at different periods in time.

Over the years, many models have been proposed to model the dynamics of returns, but not many capture all of the stylised facts. The simplest model is that of Bachelier, later made famous in a slight modification by Black and Scholes (Black and Scholes 1973; Merton 1973). That model assumes that log returns are driven by a Brownian motion with constant drift and constant volatility. The basic price dynamics are captured with this model, but a drawback is that the distribution of log returns is assumed to be Gaussian, and there is no mechanism for volatility clustering or memory. Nevertheless, the Black–Scholes model has gained wide recognition because of its analytic tractability especially when used as a basis to price derivative instruments such as options. Modifications to the Black–Scholes model include stochastic volatility models (Carr *et al* 2003; Heston 1993), for example, the Heston model (Heston 1993), where the volatility itself is assumed to follow a mean-reverting stochastic process. Such models introduce an additional source of randomness, and do not always capture the correct statistical properties of real returns, but lend some analytic tractability to certain problems. Another class of models that seem quite promising is constituted by what we shall refer to as statistical feedback processes. In the early 2000s we proposed a non-Gaussian statistical feedback process where the volatility depends on the probability of the returns themselves (Borland 2002, 2007, 2008; Borland and Bouchaud 2004, 2007). That model captured many of the stylised facts, including

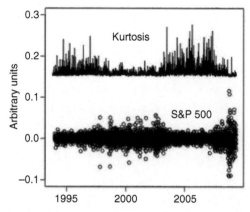

Figure 16.2 In the years that we study, there are two instances of market panic

One is 2002 (the burst of the dotcom bubble), and late 2008 to April 2009. Market volatility spikes, cross-sectional dispersion rises and cross-sectional kurtosis drops during these times.

the persistent power-law distribution of returns, and was used successfully to derive option pricing formulas. However, the model is non-stationary in the sense that returns are always calculated with respect to a particular initial time and initial price. A generalisation of that model to include feedback over multiple timescales was then developed, and we found that this model captured all the known stylised facts (Borland and Bouchaud 2005; Borland et al 2005). In fact, that model is a variation of the Nobel prizewinning Garch family (Bollerslev et al), very similar to a process known as FIGarch (Baillie et al 1996; Zumbach and Lynch 2003).

The cross-sectional behaviour of stocks over time also shows interesting dynamics (Challet et al 2001; Kaizoji 2006; Lillo and Mantegna 2000; Raffaelli and Marsili 2006; Sornette 2002), and in Borland (2009) we discuss in particular the statistical signatures in periods of market panic. The definition that we use for market panic will become clearer later on, but we expect the period 2008–9 to be one of panic, as well as perhaps the years leading up to 2002, which correspond to the bursting of the dotcom bubble, as well as the crash of 1929. The results discussed here are based on the period 1993–2009. Since we are interested in the cross-sectional distribution of stock returns at a given point in time, we look at moments such as the mean, standard deviation, skew and kurtosis. We then look at these as a function of time. The standard deviation of returns is widely referred to as dispersion. Calculated across a universe of 1,500 US stocks and plotted for the time period 1993–2009 (Figure 16.1), it is interesting to see that the level of dispersion becomes relatively high during the time periods defined as panic according to the discussion above. If you then also look at the cross-sectional kurtosis alongside the dispersion, or together with market returns (Figure 16.2), it is quite clear that there is a strong negative correlation between the two quantities, which is in fact about −25%. In times of panic, dispersion is high, yet excess kurtosis practically vanishes. In more normal times, the dispersion is lower but the cross-sectional excess kurtosis is typically very high. The skew and the mean are also correlated with the kurtosis, but we do not focus on these moments in this chapter.

The other cross-sectional quantity that we look at is the correlation across stocks. In Borland (2009), we performed a rolling principal components analysis across the universe of stocks. We saw that the percentage of variance captured by the first principal component varied over time. The larger the percentage of variance captured by this factor, the more we believe that a "market" model exists, or, in other words, the larger the co-movement of stocks. A similar behaviour was seen for cross-sectional volatilities, as well as changes in volatility across all stocks.

A JOINT STOCHASTIC MODEL: SELF-ORGANISATION OF CORRELATION

We would like a model that can explain all of these findings, such that the fat-tailed time series properties of stocks is preserved, while replicating the cross-sectional dynamics. In particular, we want to capture the remarkable reduction in kurtosis and increase in correlations, cross-sectionally, that are characteristic of market panic. In such times, the data is clearly more Gaussian (which can appear counter-intuitive at first). This can be explained partially by the fact that the volatilities of the individual stocks are higher yet more alike in times of panic, a statement that is borne out by the data (Borland 2009). While this might be one effect contributing to our findings, we believe that the behaviour of cross-sectional correlations is what drives the statistical signatures that we found. As a proxy for the collective behaviour of all stocks in the market, we follow Borland

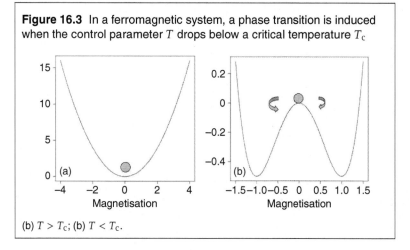

Figure 16.3 In a ferromagnetic system, a phase transition is induced when the control parameter T drops below a critical temperature T_c
(b) $T > T_c$; (b) $T < T_c$.

(2009) and define the following quantity

$$s = \frac{s_{up} - s_{down}}{s_{up} + s_{down}} \quad (16.1)$$

where s_{up} is the number of stocks that have positive returns over a given interval, and s_{down} is the number of stocks that have negative moves on that same interval (for example, a day). If $s = 0$, then roughly the same number of stocks moved up as down, and the assumption is that the stocks had little co-movement and so were uncorrelated. If all stocks move together either up or down, however, the s will be $+1$ or -1 and the stocks will have high correlation. More generally, if $s = 0$ there is no correlation, and we are in a disordered state. However, if $s \neq 0$, then there is correlation and we are in an ordered state. Borrowing some terminology from physics, we call s the order parameter. It is a macroscopic parameter that tells us whether or not there is order and correlation in the system. In physics, particularly in the field of non-equilibrium thermodynamics and synergetics (Haken 1977), the concept of the order parameter is often used to describe systems that exhibit spontaneous self-organisation. Here we review these concepts with the simple example of magnetism, although examples range from chemical kinetics to cloud formation and collective behaviour in both the human and animal worlds.

In a ferromagnetic system, the total magnetic moment depends on the orientation of the individual magnetic spins comprising the system. It is proportional to the quantity

$$m = \frac{m_{\text{up}} - m_{\text{down}}}{m_{\text{up}} + m_{\text{down}}} \quad (16.2)$$

where m_{up} and m_{down} denote the number of spins lined up and down, respectively. The distribution of possible outcomes of this macroscopic quantity is given by

$$P(m) = N \exp(F(m, T)) \quad (16.3)$$

where T is the temperature, N is a normalisation factor and F is the free energy of the system that (due to symmetry arguments) can be written as

$$F = am^2 + bm^4 \quad (16.4)$$

where a and b are parameters. The temperature T is the control parameter in this system, since the magnetic system will be in either an ordered or a disordered state depending on whether T is above or below some critical level. The dynamics of m itself thus follow a Langevin equation

$$\begin{aligned}\frac{dm}{dt} &= -\frac{\partial F}{\partial m} + F_t \\ &= -\tfrac{1}{2}am - \tfrac{1}{4}bm^3 + F_t\end{aligned} \quad (16.5)$$

where F_t is thermal noise. We write

$$a = \alpha(T - T_c) \quad (16.6)$$

where T_c is the critical temperature. These dynamics are nicely illustrated as motion in a potential well V given by $V(m) = -F(m)$, as shown in Figure 16.3. For $T > T_c$, the only minimum is the trivial one at $m = 0$, whereas for $T < T_c$ there are two real roots appearing, yielding non-zero values of m. The sign of m can be positive or negative, depending on which minimum is reached by the system. Due to the noise, the dynamics can also drive m from one minimum to the other. The probability distribution of the system in the disordered state will be a unimodal one, while the probability distribution of m in the ordered state will be bimodal. As T passes from above T_c to below T_c, or vice versa, there is a phase transition from one state to the other.

In the current setting, we treat the variable s much as the magnetic moment m. Indeed, if we look at histograms of s in both panic and

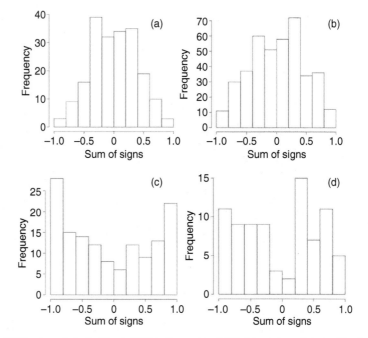

Figure 16.4 In the US financial market, s (the normalised sum of the signs of returns) has a unimodal distribution in normal times and a bimodal distribution in times of panic

(a) Number of stocks March 1996 to December 1996; (b) number of stocks March 2005 to November 2006; (c) number of stocks September 2008 to April 2009; (d) number of stocks July 2002 to November 2002.

normal periods (Figure 16.4) it is seen that, in normal times, s is unimodal, and in times of panic we obtain a bimodal distribution. These results are not simply artefacts of conditioning (Bouchaud and Potters 2003), but are consistent with the framework of a phase transition leading to self-organisation in times of panic.

Following the analogy with magnetism, the dynamics of s are

$$\frac{ds}{dt} = -\frac{a}{2}s - \frac{b}{4}s^3 + F_t \qquad (16.7)$$

with

$$a = \sigma_c - \sigma_0 \qquad (16.8)$$

where F_t is a Gaussian noise term and σ_0 corresponds to the baseline volatility level (and will take on the role of the control parameter). This volatility is assumed to be the same across all instruments, and basically measures the general uncertainty in the environment. Note that it is the feedback effects in the system which induce stock-specific variations in volatility over time, and which can largely explain most of the excess volatility observed in stock time series, whereas the parameter σ_0 is not driving the stock-specific dynamics but simply describes a "global" level of risk. The quantity σ_c would correspond to a critical level of uncertainty, below which the market is in a normal phase, and above which we have the onset of panic. This is consistent with the ideas presented in Donangelo et al (2006), where a market-wide "fear factor" is discussed. In general, collective behaviour in markets has also been discussed, for example, in Bouchaud and Cont (1998) and Zhou and Sornette (2007).

Combining all the dynamics, we have the multi-timescale feedback process for each stock (Borland and Bouchaud 2005)

$$dy_{i+1}^k = \sigma_i^k \, d\omega_i^k \tag{16.9}$$

with

$$\sigma_i^k = \sigma_0 \sqrt{1 + g \sum_{j=1}^{\infty} \frac{1}{(i-j)^y} (y_i^k - y_j^k)^2} \tag{16.10}$$

where k runs over all N stocks and i corresponds to time. The parameter g is a coupling constant that controls the strength of the feedback and y is a factor that determines the decay rate of memory in the system. Across time, this process is stable if

$$\sum_{j=0}^{\infty} \frac{g}{i-j}^y < 1$$

or, approximately, if

$$\frac{g}{1-y} < 1 \quad \text{and} \quad y > 1$$

(Borland and Bouchaud 2005). It captures the known stylised facts if $y = 1.15$ and $g = 0.12$, as is discussed in detail in Borland and Bouchaud (2005).

The random variables ω_i^k are drawn from a Gaussian distribution, uncorrelated in time such that $\langle \omega_i^k \omega_j^k \rangle = \delta_{ij}$, yet amongst themselves at a given point in time i across stocks k they are correlated with a correlation $|s|$. The macroscopic order parameter s is therefore just a signature of the cross-stock correlations, whose dynamic behaviour manifests itself in the order parameter equation

$$\frac{ds}{dt} = -\tfrac{1}{2}as - \tfrac{1}{4}bs^3 + F_t \quad (16.11)$$

For numerical simulations, we cannot really run the dynamics of the normalised sum of signs s directly since it is in fact the dynamics of the underlying correlation $|s|$ of the Gaussian random variables that we need to simulate. In addition, since we have the constraint $|s| \leqslant 1$, we actually obtain $|s|$ from an equation of the same form as Equation 16.11 such that $|s| = |\tanh(\hat{s})|$.

SIMULATIONS OF THE MODEL

In this section we quote results from Borland (2009), where we presented simulations of this model for the joint stochastic process of stocks performed using the multi-timescale model with memory over 30 past time steps. This constitutes a toy model that reproduces some main features of volatility clustering and a fat-tailed distribution of the resulting time series. The baseline volatility σ_0 was set at $\sigma_b = 0.20$, which is a realistic assumption. The correlation was assumed to follow

$$\frac{d\hat{s}}{dt} = -(\sigma_c - \sigma_0)\hat{s} - b\hat{s}^3 + \hat{F}_t \quad (16.12)$$

where $b = 0.01$ and σ_c was chosen to be $\sigma_c = 0.4$ or twice the usual base volatility. The noise term $\hat{F}_t$ was drawn from a zero mean Gaussian distribution with a standard deviation of 0.1. Based on the value of $\hat{s}$, a random Gaussian correlated noise for each stock was calculated using the Cholesky decomposition with a correlation equal to $|\hat{s}|$. At $t = 250$ in our simulation, a large volatility shock was applied to the system such that

$$\sigma_0 = \sigma_b + \sigma_{\text{shock}} \quad (16.13)$$

with $\sigma_{\text{shock}} = 0.6$, which was based on the level of the VIX in late 2008. This induced the phase transition from the disordered state, where correlation among stocks are relatively low, centred around zero, to a highly ordered state, where the correlations are non-zero.

Results show that the main features of financial markets are captured within this framework. The correlation $|s|$ went from 0 (the disordered state) to $|s| \approx 0.8$ (the ordered state) at the time of the volatility shock. After the shock subsided, the system returned to the

Figure 16.5 Market volatility rises in the panic time, induced at time $t = 250$ when $\sigma_0 > \sigma_c$

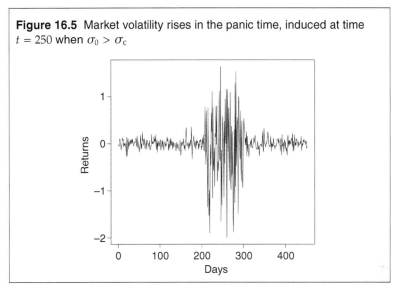

Figure 16.6 At the onset of panic ($t = 250$), cross-sectional dispersion increases markedly as a signature of the phase transition, while kurtosis drops

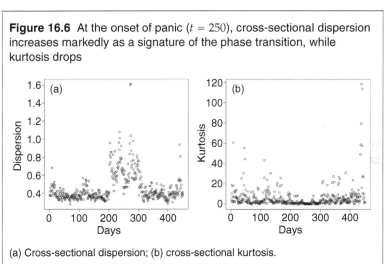

(a) Cross-sectional dispersion; (b) cross-sectional kurtosis.

disordered state again. A plot of the mean superposition of 200 realisations, which represents the market is shown in Figure 16.5. As expected, the market volatility rises when s is in the ordered state, which corresponds to the panic phase. In addition, Figure 16.6 shows that the cross-sectional dispersion rises during the market panic, while the cross-sectional kurtosis drops close to zero. The correlation between the two quantities in this example is −0.17, consistent with

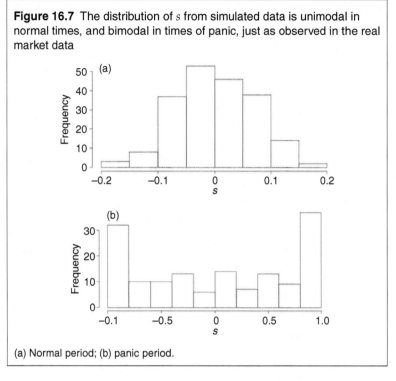

Figure 16.7 The distribution of s from simulated data is unimodal in normal times, and bimodal in times of panic, just as observed in the real market data

(a) Normal period; (b) panic period.

empirical observations that also showed a strong negative correlation. We also plotted histograms corresponding to the distribution of the order parameter s in the normal market phase as well as in the panic phase (Figure 16.7). These distributions are in excellent agreement with the empirical observations of the real market data, namely unimodal in the normal phase and bimodal during the panic time.

When the volatility shock that was applied to the system at some point dies away (in our example this happens around $t = 350$), the market returns to the disordered state. In Borland (2009) the possible dynamics of how the shock subsides are briefly discussed, with the conclusion that the results were qualitatively robust to the actual mechanism of the shock decay.

In this model, the phase transition is triggered by an exogenous volatility shock, which reproduced the observed statistical signatures of real data, in particular increasing market volatility and cross-sectional dispersion while reducing cross-sectional kurtosis. In some ongoing work we have also found some interesting asymmetries in the data and have extended the model discussed here to one where both exogenous and endogenous shocks (such as anomalously large negative returns) can trigger panic. We have also studied the cross-sectional dynamics of stocks on different timescales. This work will be the topic of a future paper.

CONCLUSIONS

In this chapter we have discussed some properties of the cross-sectional distribution of returns over different time periods. In particular, we presented the result found in Borland (2009): there is a significant anti-correlation between cross-sectional dispersion and cross-sectional kurtosis. This is such that in normal times, dispersion is low but kurtosis is high, whereas in times of panic dispersion is high and kurtosis is low. This appears counter-intuitive at first, because times of panic have rare events and "black swans" (Taleb 2007), which would typically lead to fat-tailed distributions and high kurtosis. Instead, what happens is that the general shape of the distribution in times of panic is more Gaussian, but with a higher standard deviation. In other words, in times of panic, black swans are simply everywhere, making them, in a distributional sense, much less rare. We also discuss the increased co-movement of stock returns in times of panic. The normalised sum of signs of returns on a given day captures in a simple way the degree of correlation in the system. This parameter, s, can be seen as the order parameter of the system because if $s = 0$, there is little correlation, whereas for $s \neq 0$ there is high correlation among stocks.

An analogy is made to the theory of self-organisation and non-equilibrium phase transitions and we find within this framework that financial markets undergo spontaneous self-organisation when the external volatility perception rises above some critical value. Indeed, it is seen from historical market data that s follows a unimodal distribution in normal times, shifting to a bimodal distribution in times of panic. This is consistent with a phase transition between the disordered (normal) and ordered (panic) states.

Simulations of a joint stochastic process for the ensemble of stocks across time use a multi-timescale feedback process in the temporal direction and an equation for the order parameter s to describe the dynamics of the cross-sectional correlations $|s|$ across stocks. Numerical results of such simulations show good qualitative agreement with what is observed in market data.

We are pursuing more research along the lines of this model. We have looked at similar dynamics on different timescales and find an interesting interplay between exogenous and endogenous shocks to the volatility. We are also working on calibrating the model to market data. Most importantly, we want to see if there are any early warning signals of the onset of panic which would have obvious applications for trading strategies and risk control.

REFERENCES

Baillie, R. T., T. Bollerslev and H. O. Mikkelsen, 1996, "Fractionally Integrated Garch", *Journal of Econometrics* 31, p. 3.

Black, F., and M. Scholes, 1973, "The Pricing of Options and Corporate Liabilities", *Journal of Political Economy* 81, pp. 637–59.

Bollerslev, T., R. F. Engle and D. B. Nelson, 1994, "Arch Models", in R. F. Engle and D. McFadden (eds), *Handbook of Econometrics*, Volume 4 (Amsterdam: Elsevier Science).

Borland, L., 2002, "A Theory of Non-Gaussian Option Pricing", *Quantitative Finance* 2, pp. 415–31.

Borland, L. 2007, "Erratum: A Theory of Non-Gaussian Option Pricing", *Quantitative Finance* 7, p. 701.

Borland, L., 2008, "Non-Gaussian Option Pricing: Successes, Limitations and Perspectives", in C. Riccardi and E. Roman (eds), *Anomalous Fluctuation Phenomena in Complex Systems: Plasmas Fluids and Financial Markets* (Kerala: Research Signpost).

Borland, L., 2009 "Statistical Signatures in Times of Panic: Markets as a Self-Organizing System", eprint, http://arxiv.org/abs/0908.0111v2.

Borland, L., and J.-P. Bouchaud, 2004, "A Non-Gaussian Option Pricing Model with Skew", *Quantitative Finance* 4, pp. 499–514.

Borland, L., and J.-P. Bouchaud, 2005, "On a Multi-Time Scale Statistical Feedback Model for Volatility Fluctuations", Working Paper.

Borland, L., and J.-P. Bouchaud, 2007, "Erratum: A Non-Gaussian Option Pricing Model with Skew", *Quantitative Finance* 7, p. 703.

Borland, L., J.-P. Bouchaud, J.-F. Muzy and G. Zumbach, 2005, "The Dynamics of Financial Markets: Mandelbrot's Multifractal Cascades, and Beyond", *Wilmott Magazine*, March.

Borland, L., and Y. Hassid, 2010, "Market panic on different time-scales", eprint, arXiv: 1010.4917v1 [q-fin.ST].

Bouchaud, J.-P., and R. Cont, 1998, "A Langevin Approach to Stock Market Fluctuations and Crashes", *The European Physics Journal* B 6, pp. 543–50.

Bouchaud, J. P., and M. Potters, "Comment on: 'Two-Phase Behavior of Financial Markets'", Preprint, URL: http://arxiv.org/abs/cond-mat/0304514.

Bouchaud, J.-P., and M. Potters, 2004, *Theory of Financial Risks and Derivative Pricing*, Second Edition (Cambridge University Press).

Bouchaud, J.-P., A. Matacz and M. Potters, 2001, "The Leverage Effect in Financial Markets: Retarded Volatility and Market Panic", *Phyiscal Review Letters* 87, 228701.

Carr, P., H. Geman, D. Madan and M. Yor, 2003, "Stochastic Volatility for Lévy Processes", *Mathematical Finance* 13, p. 345.

Challet, D., M. Aarsili and Y. C. Zhang, 2001, "Stylized Facts of Financial Markets and Market Crashes in Minority Games", *Physica* A 294, pp. 514–24

Donangelo, R., M. H. Jensen, I. Simonsen and K. Sneppen, "Synchronization Model for Stock Market Asymmetry", *Journal of Statistical Mechanics: Theory and Experiment*, 2006, L11001.

Gell-Mann, M., and C. Tsallis, 2004, *Non Extensive Entropies: Interdisciplinary Applications* (New York: Oxford University Press).

Gopikrishnan, P., V. Plerou, L. A. Amaral, M. Meyer and H. E. Stanley, 1999, "Scaling of the Distribution of Fluctuations of Financial Market Indices", *Physical Review* E 60, p. 5305.

Haken, H., 1977, *Synergetics: An Introduction* (Berlin: Springer).

Heston, S. L., 1993, "A Closed-Form Solution for Options with Stochastic Volatility with Applications to Bond and Currency Options", *Review of Financial Studies* 6, pp. 327–43.

Kaizoji, T., 2006, "Power Laws and Market Crashes", *Progress in Theoretical Physics Supplement* 162, pp. 165–72.

Lillo, F., and R. Mantegna, 2000, "Variety and Volatility In Financial Markets", *Physical Review* E 62, pp. 6126–34.

Merton, R. C., 1973, "Theory of Rational Option Pricing", *Bell Journal of Economics and Management Science* 4, pp. 143–82.

Plerou, V., P. Gopikrishnan, L. A. Amaral, M. Meyer and H. E. Stanley, 1999, "Scaling of the Distribution of Price Fluctuations of Individual Companies", *Physical Review* E 60, p. 6519.

Raffaelli, G., and M. Marsili, 2006, "Dynamic Instability in a Phenomenological Mode of Correlated Assets", *Journal of Statistical Mechanics: Theory and Experiment* 2006, L08001.

Sornette, D., 2002, *Why Stock Markets Crash: Critical Events in Complex Financial Systems* (Princeton University Press).

Taleb, N. N., 2007, *The Black Swan: The Impact of the Highly Improbable* (London: Random House).

Zhou, W.-X., and D. Sornette, 2007, "Self-Organizing Ising Model of Financial Markets", *The European Physical Journal* B 55, pp. 175–81.

Zumbach, G., and P. Lynch, 2003, "Market Heterogeneity and the Causal Structure of Volatility", *Quantitative Finance* 3, p. 320.

17

Financial Complexity and Systemic Stability in Trading Markets

Matteo Marsili; Kartik Anand

Abdus Salam International Centre for Theoretical Physics;
Technische Universität Berlin

In this chapter we address the systemic consequences of the increased complexity in financial markets. This trend may be thought of as a response to a demand by investors for access to new assets and markets, better transferring and trading of risks and ever higher yields. There are several dimensions in which complexity has increased over past decades. Foremost of these has been the information technology (IT) revolution, which, with the rise of electronic markets, has allowed unfettered trading at ever increasing frequencies. We have witnessed an evolution that has lead to greater diversity in the population of traders in financial markets. This diversity includes, amongst others, hedge funds and investment banks specialising in niche markets and deploying more and more aggressive speculative strategies.[1]

Concurrent with developments on the IT side, the repertoire of trading instruments has expanded considerably, in both scope and volume. Innovations in financial engineering and computational methods have increased the sophistication of derivative products. The process of securitisation is one such example of structured finance wherein the financial institution pools together its illiquid assets (such as mortgages and credit card debt) and issues seemingly liquid and tradeable securities. Owing to the practice of tranching of liabilities according to a priority ordering of payments and losses, these asset-backed securities (ABSs) enable enhanced risk diversification and credit quality control. The ABS market has grown tremendously since 2000, leading to a credit boom in both industrialised and developing economies the world over. In the US, as noted by Adrian and Shin (2009), by the second quarter of 2007, the total assets held by institutions issuing securities was substantially larger than the assets held by more traditional banks.

On the evidence of such developments, it is widely believed that increased diversity and complexity of financial markets enhances efficiency. Such considerations are routinely employed to explain the growth of hedge funds. In this regard, Danielsson and Zigrand (2007) have suggested that

> Hedge funds provide considerable benefits [...] to the economy at large by facilitating price discovery, market efficiency [and] diversification.

Citing the expansion of the repertoire of financial instruments, Merton and Bodie (2005) observe that innovations in financial engineering can make markets "spiral toward the theoretically limiting case of zero marginal transactions costs and dynamically complete markets."

This concept of complete markets is a cornerstone in the edifice of General Equilibrium Theory (GET). A market is said to be complete[2] when every contingent claim can be replicated by a portfolio of traded assets. Many asset-pricing models assume market completeness, as this facilitates computation of a price for any contingent claim. Another attractive feature, as argued by Allen and Carletti (2007), is that in complete markets there can be no market failures and, moreover, the adverse effects of a financial crisis will not materialise. The International Monetary Fund (IMF) also shared similar views in their Global Financial Stability Report in April 2006 (IMF 2006), which stated that the growing diversity of investors and dispersion of credit risks has made the financial system more resilient.

Thus, the dominant sentiment amongst financial regulators (Gopinath 2010; Turner 2010), especially during the first decade of the 21st Century, has been one where complete markets were the "Holy Grail of market regulation". As a consequence, regulatory frameworks in several economies were structured towards the pursuance of the completion of markets.

The benefits from this expansion of financial markets are readily evident, especially in terms of the increased liquidity. This has helped drive technological innovation, economic development and poverty alleviation schemes. Nevertheless, concerns have been raised from within the financial industry as to the unintended adverse consequences[3] of increased complexity[4].

Concerns were also raised by Rajan (2005) as to the increased information asymmetries introduced into markets by newly engineered financial instruments, with credit derivatives such as collateralised debt obligations (CDOs) and CDO-squared receiving singular criticism (IMF 2008). For example, investors dealing with these complex instruments are often forced to rely on reports by ratings agencies to inform their investment decisions[5] (Financial Stability Forum 2008). In the securitisation process itself, the pool of assets is typically moved off the balance sheet of the issuer of loans, thereby delinking the pool from the credit risks faced by the issuer. This introduces an element of moral hazard (Ashcraft and Schuermann 2008) whereby the issuer operates with lax standards by providing loans to less creditworthy individuals and households.

In the aftermath of the credit crisis of 2007, there is a general agreement[6] that these market imperfections and informational asymmetries exacerbated the situation. Within the neoclassical view, this situation calls for the development of new regulatory institutions to restore the ideal conditions of frictionless and efficient markets. Again quoting Merton and Bodie (2005):[7]

> In the longer run, after [such] institutional structures have had time to fully develop, the predictions of the neoclassical model will be approximately valid for asset prices and resource allocations.

This chapter challenges the view articulated in Merton and Bodie (2005) and addresses whether increased complexity promotes or erodes systemic financial stability, even under ideal market conditions. We shall proceed using examples, discussing stylised models of economies or financial markets, which allow for a full and detailed understanding of the systemic properties. This approach highlights particular feedback effects which can only be fully appreciated at the collective level, within such a detailed description, and would escape from a microeconomic analysis.

The study of these stylised representations of real financial markets draws heavily on the concepts and tools of statistical mechanics, a branch of physics which aims at understanding macroscopic phenomena in a bottom-up approach, from the interaction of microscopic constituents. At a generic level, the questions we are interested in addressing involve situations where a number of different processes or individuals interact with each other and evolve simultaneously. Examples include the molecules in a gas, the servers making up the Internet and traders in the stock market. Aggregating the influence of each and every agent in the system is an insurmountable task. Nevertheless, statistical regularities often emerge while describing the behaviour of large populations. So, for example, the complex motion of molecules in a fluid can be summarised, at the macroscopic level, by simple laws which apply to most gases. The study of substances ranging from alloys to glasses, which falls under the field of condensed matter physics, is no different. Similarly, inasmuch as the collective behaviour in the simplified world reproduces key aspects of the real world, the simplified models of financial markets we will discuss can be thought of as providing insights for promoting systemic financial stability. Such a bold extrapolation is supported by the aforementioned statistical nature of the collective behaviour, which makes it robust to different specifications at the micro-level. This robustness is what allows us to choose, within all possible models which reproduce a given macro-behaviour, the simplest ones, which can hopefully be understood in detail.

Hence, the focus will be on interactions, fluctuation phenomena and heterogeneity and we shall aim at classifying statistical laws governing the collective behaviour, (akin to phases (eg, solid, liquid or gas) of matter in physics, depending on the model's parameters. A central issue, in this perspective, is understanding when the collective behaviour undergoes sharp changes or acquires qualitatively different properties. Such changes go under the name of phase transitions in physics (eg, liquid–gas). So, for example, we shall focus on locating the transition from a stable to an unstable equilibrium, or from an informationally efficient market to an inefficient market, or in understanding when and why trust, and the underlying credit network which sustains it, "evaporates", leading to a freeze in the interbank market. Simple models allow us to shed light on the phenomena which accompany the transitions and on their nature. For example, the statistical behaviour can change in a continuous manner or sharply and abruptly, as key parameters vary.[8] This approach allows us to address, for example, the issue of understanding what aspect of a systems makes the transition sharp and what measure can be taken to mitigate the discontinuity.

The statistical mechanics approach is particularly suited to addressing systems of high complexity, owing to spectacular advances in the theory of disordered systems in physics (Mezard *et al* 1986). One particular insight we shall exploit from these approaches is that of describing a complicated system of heterogeneous interacting units as a system with random interactions, whose typical behaviour in the limit of large system's size can be characterised analytically. While this description can be extended to deal with heterogeneous agents with different "sizes", we focus on cases where the collective behaviour of the system is not governed by the behaviour of few "large" players.

Similar ideas have previously been used to investigate how increased complexity affects the stability of ecosystems. In these studies complexity was synonymous with diversity in types of species. Using a simple random ecosystem model, May (1972) demonstrated that as the number of species in the ecosystem crosses a critical value the system switches sharply from displaying stable to displaying unstable behaviour. May *et al* (2008) argue further that there is common ground in analysing the stability of ecosystems and financial systems. Similar considerations were voiced by Haldane (2009), who suggested that the

> [d]egradation of ecosystems [...] and the disintegration of the financial system [are] essentially a different branch of the same network family tree.

With these tools, we shall proceed in addressing the issue of increasing complexity in financial markets along several different directions. First, we shall focus on the expansion in the diversity of trading strategies, in order to address the systemic consequences of the expansions of hedge funds. Within the cartoonish picture of the financial market which we discuss, such an expansion indeed improves information and allocation efficiency. But when markets approach the ideal limit of information efficiency, instabilities and strong fluctuations typically arise. This suggests that excess volatility and fat-tailed return distributions arise as a consequence of pursuance of information efficiency in competitive markets.

A striking non-trivial finding is that the nature of the stationary state changes dramatically, with a drastic reduction in volatility, as soon as traders start to account, even approximately, for their impact on the market. This suggests that developments in financial engineering, which include effects of illiquidity in pricing and risk management, might have unexpected stabilising consequences at the systemic level (Caccioli *et al* 2010).

The second issue we address is that of increasing complexity and diversity in the repertoire of available financial instruments. We first discuss an equilibrium approach, which confirms that the introduction of more financial instruments indeed brings the market closer to the ideal limit of complete markets. However, this limit is a singular one, with the locus where markets achieve completeness coinciding with the boundary of an unstable phase. Close to this limit, allocations are extremely unstable and susceptible to perturbations in the parameters. The ideal limit of complete markets is only achieved if financial institutions hedge the risk of new instruments with portfolios of existing ones. On the one hand this reduces the residual risk, and hence the risk premium which banks charge and, on the other hand, it generates a volume of trading for hedging new instruments which diverges as the market approaches completeness. The combined effects of financial innovation and hedging provide an upper bound for the size of the financial sector for a given price indeterminacy. Such insights carry through to simple models of derivative markets, where the impact of derivative trading on the underlying can be included. Such theoretical predictions may serve as a benchmark for regulators to judge the stability of the real financial system.

Finally, we investigate the behavioural implications, at the individual level, of increasing financial complexity and systemic stability. As modern IT infrastructure, at times, struggles to cope with the structural complexity of financial activity, it is reasonable to suppose that decision making by individual traders must increasingly rely on trust in the efficient functioning of the system. Trust, either about solvency of counterparties or in the soundness of securities we are buying, is a prerequisite for the smooth functioning of markets, as previously highlighted by Sen (2009). Moreover, trust obeys a self-reinforcing dynamic: the financial system works because traders trust that it works, but, by the same token, financial markets collapse as the trust evaporates.

We will discuss two simple models that demonstrate how the transitions between these two states can occur. The first model describes the evaporation of trust in a credit network, which provides a stylised description of the freeze of the interbank credit market in the 2007–8 crisis. Our second model describes the breakdown in trading between a network of investors or banks, such as that observed in the ABS market during the 2007–8 crisis. In both cases, the crisis has its roots in the seemingly naive trustworthiness of financial agents in either their counterparties or credit ratings of securities by ratings agencies. Agents lent to counterparties unconditional on the financial position of the borrower, or they bought into securities without undertaking an independent credit quality assessment. Such behaviour was encouraged by both the increased complexity of securities, making it prohibitively expensive for many agents to perform their own due-diligence, and the lack of transparency of the financial systems.

In both cases, under deteriorating conditions, the crisis manifests as a sharp transition characterised by hysteresis. In other words, agents collectively respond in a sudden and sharp manner to a gradual change in the prevailing conditions and, to restore the pre-collapse equilibrium, conditions have to improve well beyond the tipping point.

These models are far from providing a realistic description of financial crises. They do, however, provide a comprehensive picture of a simplified world that highlights the non-trivial role of particular factors and feedbacks at the systemic level. In this view, issues of financial stability are traced back to the equilibrium or dynamical properties of random structures underlying the specific models.[9] Though stylised, we believe that these approaches provide a credible avenue for addressing systemic risk issues in financial markets in particular, and in socioeconomic systems in general: an avenue which, as far as we know, has no alternative besides agent-based computational approaches.

INFORMATION EFFICIENCY AND INCREASING DIVERSITY IN TRADING STRATEGIES

A market is said to be efficient with respect to an information set if the public revelation of that information would not change the prices of the securities. We define "strong efficiency" as the case where this set includes information available to all market participants, including their private information.

The argument in support of the Efficient Market Hypothesis, as proposed by Fama (1970), is that traders who have private information on the performance of an asset will buy or sell shares of the corresponding stock in order to make a profit. As a result, prices will move in order to incorporate this information, thus reducing the profitability of that piece of information. In equilibrium, when all informed traders are allowed to invest, prices must be such that no profit can be extracted from the market on the basis of their information. Hence, markets behave as information aggregating devices and, in the ideal limit, market prices are expected to reflect all possible information.

This intuition has been formalised in simple models with few traders. The classic work of Kyle (1985) shows that, in a market where a single informed agent trades with a market maker in the presence of noise traders, the information held by the informed trader will ultimately be transmitted into prices. The extension to the case of many traders, each with a different piece of information, has been discussed by Berg *et al* (2001), who consider a market with a large number of traders, each of whom receives a signal for the expected dividends and invest accordingly in an optimal manner. They go on to demonstrate that when the number of different types of informed agents increases beyond a threshold (which is proportional to the number of states of the world), the market becomes informationally efficient in the strong sense.

However, as previously argued by Grossman and Stiglitz (1980), when markets are truly informationally efficient, traders have no incentive to gather private information, because prices already convey all possible information. Hence, the more informed traders there are in a market, the smaller their incentives to seek information. This suggests that when markets are close to being efficient the convergence to equilibrium relies on agents responding to weaker and weaker signals. Or, conversely, that the equilibrium becomes more and more sensitive to perturbations (eg, mis-specification in prices or dividends). Moreover, in the presence of costs for gathering information, non-informed traders should dominate the market when markets become informationally efficient.

These conjectures by Grossman and Stiglitz (1980) were also confirmed in the contributions of Berg *et al* (2001). The sensitivity of the equilibrium to perturbations can indeed be quantified explicitly in terms of a susceptibility, which measures how much investment

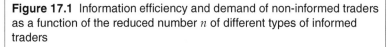

Figure 17.1 Information efficiency and demand of non-informed traders as a function of the reduced number n of different types of informed traders

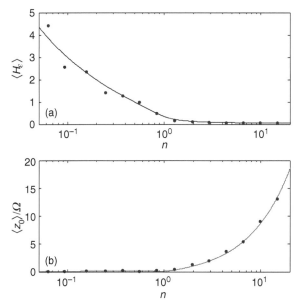

Here $n = N/\Omega$, where Ω is the number of states and N is the number of different types of informed traders. Solid lines refer to the analytic results for $N, \Omega \to \infty$, whereas points refer to numerical simulations with $\Omega = 32$. Information efficiency $\langle H_\varepsilon \rangle$ (see part (a)) is defined as the distance of realised returns from dividends. As the number n of traders who have partial information on the dividends increases, realised returns approach dividends and the market approaches the ideal case of information efficiency ($\langle H_\varepsilon \rangle = 0$). When this happens (see part (b)), the demand z_0 of non-informed traders raises and dominates the demand of informed agents (see Caccioli and Marsili (2010) for details).

of individual agents changes when prices are perturbed. This susceptibility diverges when the market approaches efficiency and is infinite in the efficient market phase, which is obtained when the number of differently informed traders exceeds the critical value. We note in passing that this pronounced susceptibility also implies that the market impact of individual traders becomes relevant. In other words, the equilibrium obtained when agents behave as price-takers is different from that for markets that are not perfectly liquid. In particular, the latter equilibrium is more stable, suggesting that the proliferation of trading algorithms that account for market illiquidity will ultimately have a stabilising effect on markets.[10]

Caccioli and Marsili (2010) extended the contributions of Berg *et al* (2001) to include a cost for information and non-informed traders. As previously conjectured, we find that, as the market becomes informationally efficient, non-informed traders start to dominate, as shown in Figure 17.1. The interplay between informed and non-informed traders is one of the key elements in explaining market dynamics, as substantiated by the literature on heterogeneous agent models (Hommes 2006; Lux and Marches 1999). Informed traders, so-called fundamentalists, typically have a stabilising effect, whereas non-informed traders, eg, trend followers or chartists in general, can destabilise the market and induce bubble phenomena. Still, the link between information efficiency and the occurrence of bubbles has not been investigated in these models and it represents an interesting avenue of future research.

In order to address the effects of the expansion of hedge fund activity on information efficiency and financial stability, a different type of approach is needed. Statistical arbitrage, which is a prevalent trading strategy[11] used by hedge funds does not depend on information on fundamentals, but rather exploits the misalignment in prices created by others in order to make a profit. This calls for a description of financial markets as an "information ecology", where different species of agents interact along an "information food chain". Speculators (eg, hedge funds) "predate" on market inefficiencies (statistical) arbitrage opportunities created by other investors. The relevance of these two different types of agents has been discussed at length in the empirical literature: Frankel (1996) and Osler (2006) distinguish between commercial traders (or hedgers) and financial speculators; Lillo *et al* (2008) find evidence for the presence of two species of investors in the Spanish stock market: liquidity providers, mostly engaged in market making activity, and liquidity takers, who need to execute large orders. The latter, in order not to suffer excessively from market impact, chop their orders into small transactions, spreading them over a long time interval. The persistence of this behaviour produces predictable trading patterns, effectively injecting information into the system.

The interplay between these two types of agent and their effect on market efficiency is described concisely by the minority game (MG) as introduced by Challet *et al* (2005). Here, commercial traders or liquidity takers have a predictable behaviour and hence they inject information (or statistical arbitrages) into the market. Speculators, instead, are adaptive: not unlike hedge funds, they have a narrow set of trading strategies based on public information[12] (eg, the price time series itself) and adopt those strategies which have the highest performance in terms of expected return. In brief, the difference between the two species of agents lies uniquely in the fact that while the former have a single trading strategy, and their behaviour is predictable on the basis of public information, speculators have more than one trading strategy and they adopt the one with the highest performance. The trading strategies are assigned to the pool of each agent by drawing them independently from the set of all such strategies. In this respect, the MG describes a situation of full heterogeneity, where each agent is different from any other agent.

Traders in the MG are agents pitted against each other in a simplified market environment provided by the minority rule; without entering into details, which may be found in Challet *et al* (2001, 2005), this rule states that the optimal choice is that placing the agent in the minority group, and consequently the best strategy is the one predicting the minority side most frequently. This environment is adequate for describing a financial market as a soup of interacting trading strategies (Farmer and Joshi 2002), subject to evolutionary selection, where the profitability of a strategy is not defined *a priori*, but rather depends on the composition of the soup.

The typical behaviour of the market described by the MG can be discussed in terms of a few parameters. It is a remarkable fact that these quantities and the relation between them can be computed analytically in the limit of infinitely many agents ($N \to \infty$) and infinitely many values of the public information ($P \to \infty$). Non-trivial results arise when the ratio $n = N/P$ between these two numbers (the reduced number of agents) is kept finite.

Here we will restrict our discussion to the dependence on the (reduced) number of traders of different types. The key quantities that characterise the collective behaviour are as follows:

- the volume V of trading activity, which is the number of agents actively trading;
- the predictability H of the market, which is a quantitative measure of the market's information efficiency; when $H > 0$ the returns are statistically predictable on the basis of the information given to agents, whereas when $H = 0$ it is not;

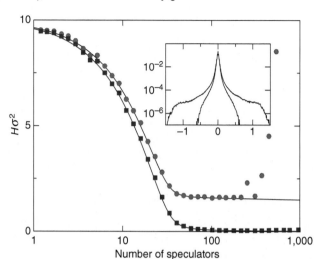

Figure 17.2 Predictability H and volatility σ^2 as a function of the number of speculators in the minority game

Here speculators specialise in a single trading strategy: they trade accordingly if its performance exceeds a threshold (taken to be $\varepsilon = 0.1$ here), otherwise they do not trade (Challet et al 2001, 2005). Solid lines refer to the analytic results for $N, P \to \infty$, whereas points refer to numerical simulations with $P = 10$. The inset shows the distribution of returns for 200 and 500 speculators in numerical simulations ($P = 10$).

- the volatility σ^2, which measures the strength of fluctuations of stock prices.[13]

The behaviour of H as a function of the number of speculators (see Figure 17.2) captures the main insight on information efficiency: a market with few speculators offers profitable gain opportunities ($H > 0$) to further speculators. However, as more speculators join the game, the market becomes more information efficient (ie, H decreases). The number of speculators will stabilise when the market is nearly unpredictable ($H \approx 0$).

The inset shows that, precisely in the region where the market is nearly information efficient, the distributions of returns acquire anomalous properties, such as fat tails, which are reminiscent of those observed in real markets. Far from this region, ie, when $H > 0$, returns are normally distributed. This implies that (marginal) information efficiency and anomalous fluctuations are two sides of the same coin, as they occur in the same region.

The MG also sheds light on the nature of the interactions between different types of traders in market ecologies. It confirms that the presence of speculators improves information and allocation efficiency in the region $H > 0$, even for commercial customers. Indeed, the profits of non-adaptive traders (commercial traders or liquidity takers) improve when the number n of speculators increases, as long as $H > 0$.

There are several non-trivial hints on market behaviour that the MG offers.[14] But probably the most remarkable lesson of the MG is that concerning the role of the apparently innocent price-taking approximation on which agents' behaviour, as well as most of financial engineering, relies. In brief, market prices clearly depend on the actions of traders. However, each single trader might regard themselves as negligible with respect to "the market". This leads traders to take prices as fixed, neglecting their impact on them (the price-taking approximation). The MG reveals that this seemingly innocuous approximation leads agents to overestimate the worth of strategies they are not currently playing, and it accumulates over time, causing agents to abandon optimal strategies for suboptimal ones. This strategy switching is what causes market volatility. Conversely, by accounting for the market impact of their strategies, even approximately, agents can collectively reduce significantly market's volatility.

In summary, heterogeneous agents models show that the regime where markets attain information efficiency is a very peculiar one. The equilibrium of these models when the market is efficient is rather fragile, as it is plagued by high volatility and the dominance of non-informed traders.

The very fact that non-informed traders start trading massively when market efficiency is approached in fact suggests that information efficiency can trigger the occurrence of bubbles and instabilities.

Ultimately, our results suggest that excessive insistence on information efficiency in market regulation policies, as, for example, in the debate on the Tobin tax (Bianconi *et al* 2009), could have the unintended consequence of propelling financial bubbles, such as those which have plagued international financial markets in recent decades.

PROLIFERATION OF FINANCIAL INSTRUMENTS: SPIRALLING TOWARDS COMPLETE MARKETS

A key function of financial markets is that of allowing inter-temporal exchanges of wealth, in a state contingent manner. Taking this view, Asset Pricing Theory (APT) makes it possible to give a present monetary value to future risks, and hence to price complex derivative contracts.

APT neglects the feedback of trading on market's dynamics, describing markets as being perfectly liquid, in a regime of perfect competition where no-arbitrages exist: assumptions which are approximately verified in stable market conditions. In addition, the proliferation of financial instruments provides even more instruments for hedging and pricing other derivatives. In theory, with the expansion of the repertoire of available trading instruments, markets approach the limit of complete markets, where every contingent claim can be replicated by a portfolio of existing instruments, thus eliminating risk altogether.

In this section we challenge this view by studying the effects of the proliferation of financial instruments in stylised models of financial markets. Within a simple framework, these models reproduce full-blown financial complexity by describing a market where financial instruments are vectors in a high-dimensional probability space, drawn at random from a given distribution. In the limit of a large number of financial instruments, when the size of the probability space also diverges, the properties of the equilibria of these models can be characterised in detail.

Systemic stability can be addressed by investigating two related issues: first, assuming that markets are perfectly liquid (ie, that prices are exogenous random processes), it is interesting to address the stability properties of the equilibria in allocations as more and more financial instruments are introduced; a second important issue is to understand the effect of trading in derivative markets on underlying markets, when the latter are not perfectly liquid. In both cases, we will see that, within the simple set-up considered, the proliferation of financial instruments erodes financial instability. Interestingly, the same conclusion was reached in a model with heterogeneous agents (Hommes 2006), upon adding more and more Arrow securities. It is worth stressing that such market instability arises within models that assume perfect competition and do not assume information asymmetries. Market imperfections clearly played a major role in the 2007–8 crisis (Ashcraft and Schuermann 2008; Rajan *et al* 2008; Turnbull *et al* 2008). The point we make here is that, even if it were possible to get rid of market imperfections by appropriately designed institutions, the free expansion in the complexity of financial markets might still pose problems for systemic stability.

The proliferation of financial instruments in an ideal world

The consequences of financial innovations in an ideal setting where markets are perfectly liquid has been addressed by Marsili (2009). Here, financial engineers create and offer trading instruments to consumers (modelled for simplicity by a single representative consumer) who themselves seek to optimally allocate their wealth for an uncertain future. In particular, financial innovation is driven by consumer demand. The equilibrium set-up is a simple one-period economy where asset prices at the initial date $t = 0$ are fixed by market clearing and prices at the final date depend on the realisation $\omega = 1, \ldots, \Omega$ of the state of nature at $t = 1$. The assets offered by the financial instruments have returns r^ω at $t = 1$ which depend on ω and are such that the expected return $E[r] = -\varepsilon/\Omega$ is finite. With $\varepsilon > 0$ assets can be thought of as insurance contracts which consumers may be interested in buying. Let N be the number of such assets which are engineered by the financial industry. Marsili (2009) assumes that assets are generated by a random draw from all vectors of returns r^ω with given expected return, ie, with $\sum_\omega r^\omega = -\varepsilon$. Such an assumption, although naive, produces a market with high financial complexity. In the sequence of equilibria which is obtained upon introducing more and more assets, we can think of their random generation as reproducing a process of genuine innovation in the financial industry.

The consumers' problem at $t = 0$ is that of allocating optimally their initial ($t = 0$) wealth w_0 in order to maximise their expected utility $E[u(c)]$, which depends on their consumption c^ω at $t = 1$. Spot markets for consumption goods at $t = 1$ have prices p^ω that depend on the realisation of the state of nature ω. (That of consumers being interested in buying an umbrella if it rains at $t = 1$ is a classic example.) In the absence of contingent commodity markets, consumers can achieve their goal by buying a portfolio z of assets whose return $z \cdot r^\omega$ is such that the market payout yields the optimal consumption bundle $c^\omega = (w_0 + z \cdot r^\omega)/p^\omega$. The solution of the consumers' problem determines the set of assets which are actually traded, ie, those with positive entries in the consumers' portfolio. The assets which are not bought can be thought of as unsuccessful financial innovations which have not been adopted.[15] Hence, the number $N_{z>0}$ of assets traded in the market is less than or equal to the number N of assets engineered by the financial industry. Secondly, the solution of the optimal investment plan of consumers also determines the risk-neutral measure.

The properties of the equilibrium of this economy can be studied analytically in the limit $\Omega, N \to \infty$ with $n = N/\Omega$ finite. The other key parameter is the risk premium, ε, which financial firms charge to consumers. The result of this analysis (Marsili 2009) can be summarised as follows.

- A well-defined solution exists for $\varepsilon > 0$ and for $n < n_c(\varepsilon)$ for $\varepsilon \leq 0$. In the complementary region ($\varepsilon \leq 0$ and $n \geq n_c(\varepsilon)$) the equilibrium is unstable as there are arbitrages (portfolios with a non-negative return in all states).
- Markets are complete on the line $\varepsilon = 0, n \geq n_c(0) = 2$. This line, as stated above, separates the stable region from the unstable region.
- Portfolio allocation becomes more and more susceptible to the precise specification of the problem (ie, returns r^ω and prices p^ω) as the economy approaches the line of complete markets. This means that the susceptibility χ, which measures the change in allocations, $\delta z = \chi \delta p$, for an infinitesimal change δp in prices (or returns), diverges as markets become complete.

In brief, the situation where market completeness is reached by a deregulated process of financial innovation is typically a singular one. "Typically" here means occurring with probability 1, in almost all realisations of a random economy such as the one discussed above. This situation is very different from that discussed in textbook examples when the number of assets is small (two or three). This shows the peculiar nature of statistical laws which emerge in the limit of large complexity, ie, when the number of assets is large and when the state space is also large.

Furthermore, the set-up of Marsili (2009) also allows us to address the consequences of the proliferation of instruments in a competitive financial industry. There we expect the risk premium to be set by perfect competition. When a firm is selling a new financial instrument, it may consider hedging the risk it entails by holding a portfolio w of existing assets. This means that the residual risk which firms need to price decreases as the repertoire of available financial instruments expands. If ε is an increasing function of the residual risk, it is reasonable to expect that ε also decreases as n increases. This realises the prediction of Merton and Bodie (2005), with the economy "spiraling toward the theoretically limiting case of zero marginal transactions costs and dynamically complete markets." However, as we have seen, this limit is a singular one and is plagued by instabilities in allocations. Furthermore, in the limit where markets approach completeness, the size $|w|$ of the portfolio needed to hedge a single contract being sold to consumers diverges. Here $|w|$ can be taken as a measure of the relative size of the financial sector compared with the real economy. Indeed, it is the amount of trading due to hedging which is implied by a unit of transaction towards the real economy. Hence, even within an ideal economy, financial innovation erodes financial stability on the one hand, and promotes boundless expansion of the financial sector on the other.

These twin predictions can be combined to provide a stability diagram which, for a given level of price indeterminacy δp, predicts the maximal size $|w|$ of the financial sector compared with the real economy (see Figure 17.3). The key here is that the quantities δp and $|w|$ are measurable for different economies. Hence, this prediction could shed light on real economies, thereby providing regulators further insight into systemic stability issues. While the theoretical predictions are for ideal economic conditions, instabilities in real economies might be much stronger, due to positive feedback effects such as those we shall discuss in the next section.

The proliferation of financial instruments in an interacting market

Markets are never perfectly liquid. It is, indeed, their illiquidity that facilitates the aggregation of information into prices. Liquidity is, in fact, a function of timescale and volume size (Bouchaud *et al* 2008; Dacorogna *et al* 2001). This calls for a view of financial markets as interacting systems. In this view, trading strategies can affect the market in important ways. Both theoretical models and

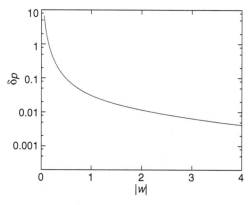

Figure 17.3 Stability diagram for the ideal economy discussed in Marsili (2009)

Stability in the allocations requires that the indeterminacy $\delta z = \chi \delta p$ of consumers' portfolios should be negligible with respect to the size z of portfolios. This implies that price indeterminacy $\delta p \ll \delta p^* \equiv z/\chi$. As financial innovation expands the repertoire of trading instruments, allocations become more and more susceptible to indeterminacies in prices (ie, χ increases), and the size $|w|$ of the portfolio needed to hedge a unit of assets sold to consumers increases. The figure shows the (parametric) plot of $\delta p^* = z/\chi$ versus $|w|$, which are both functions of n, once the dependence of ε on n is fixed, assuming a given risk behaviour of banks (here taken to be mean–variance optimisers). Allocations are unstable in an economy in the upper-right region, ie, with a large financial sector and/or large price indeterminacy.

empirical research show that trading activity implied by derivatives affects underlying markets in non-trivial ways (Avellaneda and Lipkin 2003; Jeannin *et al* 2008). Brock *et al* (2008) show that, in a model of heterogeneous interacting agents, the proliferation of financial instruments (Arrow's securities) leads to market instability.

Caccioli *et al* (2009) contrasts the picture of markets on which APT is based (which assumes that prices are exogenously given and independent of trading activity) with a simple model of the market as an interacting system, where prices are affected by trading on the underlying and on derivatives.

We refer the interested reader to Caccioli *et al* (2009) for details, but suffice to say that the set-up is very similar to the one described above, with the exception that here derivatives are contracts that deliver an amount of the underlying asset which depends on the realisation of the state. Besides selling derivatives, financial firms still need to trade on the underlying markets to meet obligations arising from derivative contracts. This generates a demand on underlying markets which modifies prices. The statistical properties of the equilibrium can again be computed analytically.

In their setting, Caccioli et al (2009) demonstrate that the proliferation of derivatives brings the market to a state which closely resembles the efficient arbitrage-free, complete market described by APT. However, as in the previous model, the region of the phase space when the markets approach completeness is characterised by a phase transition between a supply-limited equilibrium to a demand-limited one. Close to the transition, small perturbations in the risk perception of banks can provoke dramatic changes in the volume of traded derivatives, and large fluctuations are observed in response functions.

The uncontrolled proliferation of financial instruments has two main consequences:

(i) systemic stability is eroded, driving the market to a critical state characterised by large susceptibility, strong fluctuations and enhanced correlations;

(ii) a sharp rise in the traded volume of derivatives is provoked.

Taken together, these results suggest that market completeness may not be compatible with a stable market dynamics. Therefore, financial stability acquires the properties of a common good, which suggests that appropriate measures should be introduced into derivative markets, in order to preserve stability.

As suggested in the conclusion of the previous subsection, here too we may construct a stability diagram, where the level of price indeterminacy δp will predict the maximal size $|w|$ of the financial sector. As before, the theoretical predictions may serve as a benchmark and provide insights for the stability of real economies. Moreover, these predictions may be used to discern the role of cross-border trading (globalisation) towards systemic stability.

SECURITISATION, CREDIT DERIVATIVE MARKETS AND INCREASING COMPLEXITY

As recognised by Dasgupta (1988) and Sen (2009), amongst others, the smooth operation of market-based economies relies on trust. Money, as a vehicle for trust, enables us to derive goods and services from others who we do not know and have no reason to trust.

The explosive growth of credit markets the world over is indicative of trusts' vital role to economic activity. When trust in financial transactions sets in as a self-reinforcing social norm, it promotes market liquidity and the economy approaches the idealised setting described by the General Equilibrium Theory.

However, besides the "good" equilibrium, where trust prevails, there may also be a polar opposite situation where individuals mistrust each other. Consequently, markets are illiquid and credit is hard or very costly to obtain, making it difficult for individuals to cope with risks and market volatility. As a result, defaults are more frequent, thereby reinforcing the general sense of mistrust.

This section discusses recent attempts to model how trust may evaporate in the face of deteriorating conditions, leading to market freezing. The key issue is to understand, even at only the descriptive and qualitative level, why and when the transition between the good equilibrium and the bad equilibrium is a smooth one and when we expect it to be sharp.

The 2007 crisis showed that a quite sharp transition can take place in the relatively short time span of few days. For example, the freeze in interbank credit market was accompanied by a tenfold rise in the short-term Libor rate within the month of August 2007. A similar increase in the spreads of ABSs, and a corresponding drop in their price, was also reported in the same period. Understanding which parameter controls the nature of the transition between the two states might provide useful input for regulation and market design.

In what follows we first discuss an agent-based model, proposed in Anand *et al* (2009, 2010a), of an (interbank) credit network in order to investigate the conditions for the systemic collapse of trust in these systems. The second part of the section focuses on market freezing in a market for assets with a complex structure, such as ABSs or CDOs. In the first case, economic activity in the good state relies on individuals trusting counterparties at the time of loaning; in the second, individuals may opt to trust the quality of assets they are offered by others, relying on public information (eg, credit rating) and on the expectation that secondary markets for such assets are liquid (The Bond Market Association 2002). In both cases, the self-reinforcing nature of trust manifests as a sharp collapse of the system, as conditions deteriorate. The behaviour of the model is also characterised by hysteresis and resilience: once the system falls from the good state to the bad state, the latter remains stable even when conditions improve beyond the tipping point. The good state also exhibits the same resilience.

The evaporation of trust in credit networks

Morris and Shin (2003, 2008) have suggested that financial crises follow a self-fulfilling dynamics, highlighting the importance of strategic uncertainty as opposed to structural uncertainty. For example, in the case of a bank run, a depositor may consider withdrawing their funds because of doubts over the bank's balance-sheet position (structural uncertainty). The other depositors may also have concerns on the soundness of the bank's balance sheet, or they may harbour fears that other depositors will withdraw their funds.

The global games framework of Morris and Shin (2003) formalises such situations in terms of coordination games between multiple lenders involved with a single, risky counterparty. In the Nash equilibrium of such models, some agents reason that someone else may decide to be cautious and withdraw from the lending arrangement, or at least that someone will reason that someone will withdraw, and so forth. Thus, small seeds of doubt reverberate across all lenders, leading to a wholesale withdrawal of lending and the bankruptcy of the counterparty.

In the simplest setting, default occurs if the number of agents withdrawing is larger than a threshold ℓ_c and the key parameter is the cost c which agents incur if lending to a defaulting agents; Morris and Shin (2008) refer to this as the cost of miscoordination.

As the 2007–9 crisis made clear, small seeds of doubt about one counterparty can reverberate across the entire global financial system, affecting credit markets from New York to Sydney. Agents are likely to be involved in a number of different coordination games, such as those described above, against each other. This calls for the extension of the insights from global games, which pertain to a single financial institution, to the system level, in order to understand the widespread contagion of scepticism and the collapse of trust. Anand et al (2009, 2010a) do this by considering a population of agents (or banks) engaged in mutual lending relationships. Formally, the credit network is modelled as a directed graph, with nodes representing agents and where each link stands for a (short-term) loan from a lender to a borrower.

Each bank borrows as a means of raising funds in order to invest in illiquid assets with long-term maturity. Loans are of a short-term nature, and when they are renegotiated the lenders participate in a global game in which each of them has to decide whether to roll over their loans or withdraw. Anand *et al* (2009, 2010a) assume that if the amount of loans to lenders who withdraw exceeds the amount of liquid assets on the bank's balance sheet (which is the sum of short-term loans granted by that bank to other banks plus cash), then that bank defaults: all links (loans) to and from this bank decay, and the bank is replaced by a new bank with no loans. This seems an extreme description of the state of financial distress a bank is subject to when it suffers a run. What typically happens is that a distressed bank needs to perform a fire sale of its illiquid assets; it will not roll over its loans to other banks, and its obligation to other banks will be settled on a longer timescale. Therefore, as long as links represent short-term loans, the situation is as if all links to and from the defaulting bank decay.

In addition to the process by which loans are renegotiated just described, the credit network also evolves by the creation of new links and the decay of existing ones. Both are modelled as Poisson processes. The former mimics the arrival of new investment opportunities to a randomly chosen bank, which prompts that bank to raise capital by borrowing from another (randomly chosen) bank. As a manifestation of trust, the link is established regardless of the financial position of the bank. Each illiquid asset represents a project with a finite lifetime. When the project reaches maturity, the corresponding loan is terminated and settled by the parties and, as a consequence, the corresponding link decays.

A compact description of the dynamics is possible if each bank is represented by a point in the space of assets (loans to other banks or outgoing links) and liabilities (loans from other banks, or incoming links), as shown in Figure 17.4. Then the renegotiation game will have no effect unless the bank happens to have assets worth less than the critical value. For a given cost of miscoordination c, this condition identifies the unstable region (the shaded region in Figure 17.4). The creation or decay of loans corresponds to steps towards the top right of the figure or towards bottom left of the figure, respectively, for the two agents involved.

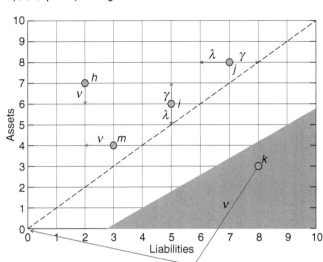

Figure 17.4 Schematic of elementary processes in the liabilities–assets plane ((ℓ, a)-plane) during the evolution of the credit network

The shaded area corresponds to the unstable region where default takes place. γ labels processes in which a credit relationship $i \to j$ is established. Agent i gains an asset ($a \to a + 1$), while j increments the number of liabilities it holds ($\ell \to \ell + 1$). λ labels link decay when the corresponding loan reaches maturity and expires. Finally, ν labels the process where debtor k reveals its balance-sheet position, (ℓ_k, a_k), to their creditors. If k is found to be in the shaded region, foreclosures take place and k defaults, loosing all their links: (ℓ_k, a_k) $\to$ (0, 0). Agent m, who had borrowed from k, loses one liability ($\ell_m \to \ell_m - 1$), while agent h who lent to k loses an asset ($a_h \to a_h - 1$).

This set-up extends the global game approach to the system level using a model of network growth. If we assume that renegotiation is contingent on the arrival of signals about counterparties (ie, on the borrower's financial position) the model describes how the seeds of distrust may spread across a large population of agents engaged in credit relationships with each other.

The results may be summarised as follows: the financial system can converge to a "good" equilibrium in which a dense network of credit relations exists and the risk of a run, and subsequent default, is negligible. Such a state materialises when the cost of miscoordination c is small enough. When the cost of coordination is large, a "bad" equilibrium comes into being, where the credit network is sparse because investors are more skittish and prone to prematurely foreclosing their credit relationships. In the bad state, projects

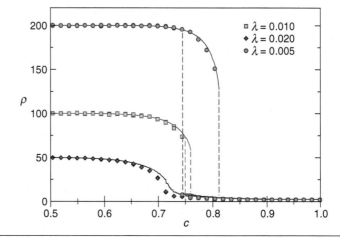

Figure 17.5 Average density in the network (ie, average number of loans) in a population of 1000 banks, as a function of cost of miscoordination c, for large maturity mismatch (in terms of the parameters of Anand et al (2009) $v = 2$ and $b_0 = 2$)

rarely reach maturity, because lenders are not willing to roll-over their loans.

When the maturity mismatch is large, ie, when short-term loans are used to finance long-term projects, we note the following features:

(i) the transition between the two equilibria is sharp;

(ii) the regions of existence of the two equilibria overlap.

This means that there is an intermediate range of c where both equilibria are possible, as shown in Figure 17.5. When the maturity mismatch is reduced, the region where the two equilibria coexist shrinks, and beyond a threshold value the transition turns from discontinuous to continuous. This highlights the role played by the maturity mismatch in determining the severity of liquidity crises. Nevertheless, it is important to realise that, for the generation of wealth, banks need to allow for a certain degree of maturity mismatch, which then serves as a money multiplier. Thus, in efforts to stem future crises, central banks need to take into due consideration the *ex post* impact of caps on leverage ratios, which control the level of maturity mismatch.

The consequence of the overlapping of equilibria is that, when conditions deteriorate (ie, c increases) an economy with a dense credit network may fall abruptly into the bad state. But in order to revert to the "good" equilibrium, conditions may need to improve well beyond the tipping point. This matches with the observation that trust in financial markets was very slow to recover after the 2007–9 crisis, in spite of massive measures taken by central banks. Such measures, in particular, can be translated to the simplified setting of our model and it can be argued that this has the effect of reducing the region of instability, either by reducing the miscoordination cost c (eg, reduction of interest rates or guarantees on toxic assets) or by increasing liquidity (eg, bailout). We refer the reader to Anand *et al* (2009) for a detailed discussion.

This approach represents only a first step in trying to model the breakdown of trust in market economies in general, and financial networks in particular. Specific details and rigorous economic modelling are necessary to properly understand any particular episode of financial crisis. There is nonetheless scope for approaches, such as the present one, which aim at clarifying both the mechanisms by which trust evaporates and the key variables that may be the target of policy intervention in times of crisis or of regulation in order to avoid systemic crises.

Trading complex assets: to trust or not to trust?

The growth in credit derivative markets before the 2007–8 crisis was nothing short of meteoric. As noted in Adrian and Shin (2009), by the second quarter of 2007 the total assets held by issuers of ABSs in the US (which the authors collectively refer to as the "shadow banking system") was approximately US$16 trillion and substantially larger than those held by banks, which totalled approximately US$12 trillion. The growth rate of assets for ABS brokers, especially since the mid-1980s, has far exceeded those of commercial banks to the point that the vast majority of homeowner mortgages are held within the shadow banking system. As more and more prime-rated homeowners took on mortgages, the banks, being awash with liquidity, were more freely willing to underwrite mortgages for homeowners rated subprime. Paradoxically, however, many of the purchasers of the securities turned out to be the banks themselves.

Three factors contributed to this exponential growth.

(i) Investors' decisions were made predominantly on the basis of publicly available signals, without independent credit analysis. Partly this was due to over-reliance on the information provided by rating agencies. In principle, rating agencies were supposed to provide an impartial assessment of the asset. In practice, however, rating agencies are paid for their services not by the investors but by the issuers of these securities, thus generating a conflict of interest.[16]

(ii) The secondary market for ABSs (and mortgage-based securities (MBSs), in particular) was advertised as being liquid and so it was generally perceived (Sabarwal 2006). Hence, buying MBSs became acceptable, under the assumption that others considered MBSs to be liquid (and hence tradeable). This in turn reinforced the assumption that MBSs were liquid. Therefore, as more and more investors adopted this rule, ie, trading in ABSs without conducting independent credit analysis, it became profitable for others to follow suit and adopt the same rule in turn.

(iii) A similar failure in information gathering also characterised the subprime mortgage market (Rajan *et al* 2008). The increased distance between risk origination (the subprime borrowers) and risk bearers (investors holding the ABSs) induced intermediaries to grant subprime loans without proper analysis of the reliability of borrowers. In other words, the network linking lenders and borrowers evolved in such a way to increase the opacity of the system. Despite the increased connectivity and density, information did not flow.

Thus, the spread of such behaviour among investors led to a failure of markets to aggregate signals and reveal information on the fundamental value of assets. As a result, investors, seemingly blindly, bought into the ABS market and unwittingly assumed far greater risks. Again, the individual choices were not irrational but they had major consequences at the aggregate level.

Indeed, the dire consequences of these developments were made painfully apparent when the subprime mortgage bubble burst and the crisis developed. As economic conditions in the US started to cool down in the mid-2000s, in response to contractionary monetary policy, defaults on mortgages in the subprime sector increased.

This, together with the impact of the resultant decline in real-estate prices, meant that it became more difficult to re-sell the property to recoup the original value. This, in turn, meant that the price of all the securities diminished, since it was not clear which were "toxic". As the prices of securities plummeted, investors started losing trust in the future profitability of the issuers of securities and chose instead to horde their liquidity. This resulted in a freeze of the credit and credit derivatives markets, thereby causing a large increase in ABS spreads.

This story of asymmetric information and herding of investors is endemic to all previous asset-pricing and credit bubbles, including the 1920s telecommunication bubble, as recounted by Eichengreen and Mitchener (2003), and the 1990s dotcom bubble and subsequent burst. In the subprime crisis it become clear that the problem was exacerbated by the collective "decision" not to gather information.

Anand *et al* (2010b) model the general mechanism whereby investors, as a rule, trade securities without giving due diligence to fundamental information. The rationale motivating investors is simply that it is profitable to adopt this rule, because other investors have already adopted it.

The system consists of $i = 1, \ldots, N$ agents, which, in the case of the subprime crisis, we can think of as the banks who were both the issuers (via special purpose entities) and the investors in these ABSs. Each agent i is characterised by a variable $z_i \in \{0, 1\}$, which specifies whether they adopt ($z_i = 1$) or do not adopt ($z_i = 0$) the following behaviour (or "rule" for short): purchase an asset-backed security, relying on signals from the rating agencies, without independently evaluating the fundamental value of underlying assets.

The rationale for adopting the rule is based not on the fundamental quality of the asset but rather on the fact that others also follow the rule. If, in fact, enough other participants do so, the agent becomes convinced, not irrationally, that the ABS is highly liquid and hence easy to trade.

The model assumes that the ABS is toxic with probability p, where "toxic" means, for example, that the underlying asset was incorrectly graded and that the original borrower of the loan has already defaulted or has a higher probability of default. The cost of purchasing a security is $c < 1$, whereas the payout from successfully re-selling the security is normalised to unity. Agents are linked together with trading partners in a financial network. This captures the fact that the secondary market for trading ABSs and other credit derivatives is not centralised but instead takes place over-the-counter, as described in Sabarwal (2006), with traders in one firm directly calling up other traders to sell their securities.

When agent i receives an offer to buy new ABSs, they consider whether or not to follow the rule. The line of reasoning the agent pursues is to first determine the probability that, if they adopt the rule and subsequently attempt to re-sell the security, the potential buyer (agent j) will refuse to buy the security. This will be because agent j does not follow the rule and thus may verify that the underlying asset is toxic. In this event, agent i will incur a loss of c with probability $p(1 - z_j)$, where j is the index of the potential buyer. The expected payout to i from following the rule, ie, $z_i = 1$, is

$$u_i(z_i = 1) = 1 - p(1 - \bar{z}_i) - c$$

where $\bar{z}_i = \mathbb{E}[z_j]$ is the expected value of z_j for the neighbours j of agent i. When agent i buys the asset, they do not know *ex ante* to whom they will sell the security or which neighbours follow the rule. In other words, agent i cannot observe the type z_j of their neighbours, but can instead estimate the probability $\bar{z}_i$ that a buyer in their neighbourhood follows the rule, which is the average of z_j in i's neighbourhood. The expected payout to agent i from not following the rule is

$$u_i(z_i = 0) = (1 - p)(1 - c) - \chi_i$$

where $\chi_i > 0$ is the cost of gathering information. The rationale here is that, if agent i determines the asset to be toxic, they will only incur the cost of performing the risk analysis. If the asset turns out not to be toxic, with probability $1 - p$, the agent will be able to re-sell the security easily and hence the payout is $1 - c - \chi_i$.

Hence, the best response of agent i when they get the opportunity of buying a new ABS is $z_i^* = 1$ if $p(\bar{z}_i - c) + \chi_i > 0$ and $z_i^* = 0$ otherwise. Anand *et al* (2010b) look for the fixed point of the dynamics where each agent responds optimally, given the actions of their neighbours or at the stationary state where agents use a probabilistic choice model of the logit type (Weisbuch *et al* 1998). The results are displayed in Figure 17.6 for different values of the intensity of choice parameter B of the logit function. The state where everybody follows the rule ($z_i = 1$, for all i) is a fixed point of the best response

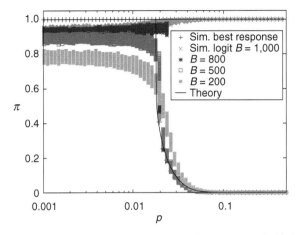

Figure 17.6 Prevalence $\bar{\pi} = E[z]$ of rule followers, as a function of p, for a model with $c = 0.9$, $k = 11$ and an exponential distribution of χ_i with mean 0.01

The results of numerical simulations (best response) are compared with the theory (solid line). Results for noisy best response $P\{z_i = 1\} = e^{Bu_i(1)}/(e^{Bu_i(1)} + e^{Bu_i(0)})$, with $B = 200, 500, 800$ and $1,000$ are also shown.

case ($B \to \infty$) for all values of p. Indeed, when everybody follows the rule, no trade is ever refused, independently of the quality of the assets, precisely because no-one checks the quality of assets. For large values of p, however, this fixed point coexists with one where most of the agents perform their independent credit analysis ($z_i = 0$).

Figure 17.6 also shows, however, that the rule-dominated equilibrium loses stability for high p, if the intensity of choice parameter B is not large enough. For intermediate vales of B, as p increases, we have a sharp transition from the state where the vast majority follows the rule, to a situation where most of the agents do not follow it.

To appreciate how this model leads to herding, imagine starting from a market in which there are only fundamentalists, ie, no-one follows the rule ($z_i = 0$ for all i). Those agents with cost $\chi_i > pc$ will find it profitable to adopt the rule. A large cost may be understood as the securities being very complex, for example, after multiple repackaging. In turn, this will make it appear to be profitable for some of their neighbours to also follow the rule and similarly for the neighbours of these neighbours. If the rule spreads to the extent that $\bar{z} > c$, then all agents, even those for whom information is available for free, will follow the rule, and no-one will look for information.

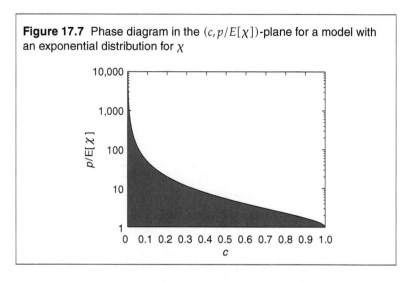

Figure 17.7 Phase diagram in the $(c, p/E[\chi])$-plane for a model with an exponential distribution for χ

This insight can be confirmed by a mean-field analysis of the fixed point if $B \to \infty$ (the solid line in Figure 17.6) and, for a particular choice of the distribution of costs it is possible to derive a phase diagram of the model (see Figure 17.7). This shows that, when assets are safe (small p) or very complex to evaluate (large costs χ_i), the dominant equilibrium is one where no-one performs credit analysis ($z_i = 1$). But when default starts to materialise (increasing p) or economic conditions worsen (increasing c) the economy may enter the region where both equilibria exist. At this point, a sudden transition to the other equilibrium is possible.

This scenario matches qualitatively with accounts of the 2007–8 collapse of credit derivative markets. With the introduction of more and more innovations in financial engineering of securitisation, financial products became increasingly complex. In consequence, the cost of assessing the quality of credit derivatives increased in the first decade of the 21st Century. It has been forcefully argued by Shiller (2008) and others that by 2007 considerable evidence of the bad credit quality of subprime-based ABSs had been steadily accumulating (increasing p).[17] In addition, falling prices in the housing market made it more difficult to recover the investment in defaulted loans (increasing c).

The key point underlined by the model is that the lack of due diligence in credit risk analysis among investors can lead to a failure of markets to aggregate signals and reveal information on the fundamental value of assets. This leads investors to buy assets blindly, unwittingly assuming far greater risks. Again, the individual choices are not irrational but they have major consequences at the aggregate level. The mechanism evokes that of information cascades or rational herding (Chamley 2004), where, in a population of agents with noisy information on some economic observable, it becomes rational to base any decision on the information inferred from the (investment) behaviour of others. This, however, has the consequence that individual behaviour no longer conveys private information, but just amplifies the signal of the crowd. As a result, information aggregation fails and the crowd turns out to consecrate random choices.

The crucial difference, in our case, is that individuals decide to neglect information because, on the assumption that others will also do so, this is the rational thing to do. And because this is the optimal choice, the assumption that others will also do so is justified. So information aggregation fails because agents rationally decide not to gather information, given that others will also do that.[18]

In models of rational herding, such as Curty and Marsili (2006), the conclusion is similar: by following simple and rational rules, traders can drive a market into a fragile state in which the very justification of the rules is undermined. Small changes in the macroeconomic environment coupled with the contagious spread of behavioural rules can gradually but almost imperceptibly undermine the system. Unfortunately, the result of these gradual changes can be catastrophic at the aggregate level.

CONCLUSIONS

There are two elements common to all models discussed in this chapter. The first is the tension between efficiency and systemic stability and the second is related to the role of information.

With respect to the first issue, it appears that systemic financial stability is generally eroded by the expansion of markets in complexity, which usually promotes efficiency. In the case of the first two models, efficiency is related to information aggregation and risk diversification, respectively. In the last section it is related to liquidity.

Instead, stability is measured by the susceptibility of the equilibrium to the variation of underlying parameters. The divergence of the susceptibility is not evident in simple models of microstructure with few types of traders (as, for example, in Kyle (1985)) or in textbook examples of APT (Pliska 1997). Rather, it manifests clearly in the complex case of many heterogeneous investors (eg, hedge funds) or when many different trading instruments are present.

The previous section addresses stability in terms of underlying self-reinforcing mechanisms generically related to trust, which ensure smooth functioning and liquidity of markets. Such self-reinforcing mechanisms may, however, break down and lead to sudden collapses in markets.

The second central issue which this chapter addresses is that of the non-trivial role that information plays in financial markets. First, we have argued that the capacity of markets to properly aggregate information has its limits, in the sense that the closer the markets are to being informationally efficient, the more they are prone to non-informed traders taking a dominant role. Information also plays a non-trivial role in the models discussed in the previous section. First, we may argue that, in a credit network, if news on the financial positions of lenders was disclosed very frequently, this might prompt lenders to renegotiate loans more frequently, thus increasing further the maturity mismatch. Paradoxically, the results in Anand *et al* (2009, 2010a) suggest that increasing transparency (ie, more frequent, accurate financial reporting) aggravates systemic stability by making the systems respond more sharply to deteriorating conditions. Indeed, we would expect transparency to be relatively loose in good times and to get tighter as conditions worsen, ie, when the system approaches the transition to the bad state. Precisely the opposite (ie, looser transparency in bad times than in good ones) is what the simplified model in Anand *et al* (2009, 2010a) suggests would alleviate a systemic crisis and help restore market-wide confidence. A similar message is conveyed by the model in Anand *et al* (2010b), ie, in good times, when assets are very rarely toxic or are correctly rated, traders are encouraged to neglect due diligence on the assets' valuation, whereas in bad times traders become skittish and careful in gathering correct information.

Even though they are very stylised and unrealistic in many respects, these models shed light on complex behaviour at the aggregate level that may provide hints on regulation addressed to curb systemic stability. In particular, what these models highlight in one way or another is that perfect competition and individual rationality alone do not provide incentives for systemic stability. In this respect, as argued by Morris and Shin (2008), systemic stability should be considered as a public good.

1. See the plenary talk of Pliska (2010) at the Sixth World Congress of the Bachelier Finance Society for an overview of the risks and opportunities in electronic market making.

2. See Flood (1991) for a gentle introduction to complete markets.

3. Bookstaber (2007) suggests that "The financial markets that we have constructed are now so complex, and the speed of transactions so fast, that apparently isolated actions and even minor events can have catastrophic consequences [...]. More often than not, crises aren't the result of sudden economic downturns or natural disasters. Virtually all mishaps over the past decades had their roots in the complex structure of the financial markets themselves."

4. Finding a workable definition of complexity is difficult; generically, we use this term to describe a situation of great interdependence and heterogeneity, in a system with many degrees of freedom. This is the sense in which the term has been used by other authors as well: in the context of structured finance, Fender and Mitchell (2005) identify pooling of illiquid assets and the tranching of liabilities as the main factors contributing to the complexity of products generated. On a more theoretical footing, Brunnermeier and Oehmke (2009) discuss the fact that the implications of complexity are typically not addressed by classical asset-pricing theories, which assume all agents to be perfectly rational. As such, all market participants will readily be able to perform complicated calculations. However, when we introduce agents with bounded rationality, who have limited computational ability, increased complexity may lead to an information overload for investors. Following similar considerations, Caballero and Simsek (2009) introduce a model of financial crises where runs of investors occur if the cost of gathering information on the health of counterparties becomes prohibitively high. In the context of the financial network, Haldane (2009) suggests that the proliferation of credit risks across the network of banks has made "knowing your ultimate counterparty's risk [...] like solving a high-dimension Sudoku puzzle."

5. In September 2009, the US Securities and Exchange Commission voted to regulate ratings agencies better. The chairman of the Commission, Mary Schapiro, said, "These proposals are needed because investors often consider ratings when evaluating whether to purchase or sell a particular security. That reliance did not serve them well over the last several years." (US Securities and Exchange Commission 2009).

6. Some of the academic articles on the causes of the crisis include Ashcraft and Schuermann (2008), Turnbull et al (2008), Acharya and Richardson (2009) and Smaghi (2010).

7. Note, however, that even within the general equilibrium framework, increased complexity (eg, the proliferation of financial instruments in incomplete markets) does not always enhance efficiency (Cass and Citanna 1998; Hart 1975).

8. A notable example of a continuous transition is epidemics in a population. There, as the contagion rate increases, prevalence sets in continuously, with the fraction of infected individuals becoming non-zero after a critical threshold. The transition between a liquid and a gas, instead, is discontinuous, with the density changing abruptly as the temperature varies across the transition.

9. In brief, increased sophistication and diversity in trading strategies and financial instruments makes the equilibrium of the economy shallower and hence more prone and susceptible to perturbations. Deteriorating conditions in complex financial markets determine the collapse of underlying trading or credit networks.

10. Caccioli et al (2010) argue that liquidity considerations have a stabilising effect in portfolio management, for similar reasons.

11. See Noyer (2007) for a discussion of different types of strategy used by hedge funds.

12. A trading strategy is a mapping between public information and actions; in the MG public information can take a finite number P of values, whereas actions can be of two types. Hence,

there are 2^P different trading strategies. The number P of possible information patterns is taken to be proportional to N, ie, $P = N/n$ and the limit $N \to \infty$ is considered.

13 Marsili (2001) describes how prices may be defined in terms of a market clearing mechanism.

14 One such hint is that the collective properties are largely independent of the assumption that the information processed by agents either is endogenously generated by the market process itself or has an exogenous origin (depending, for example, on sunspot activity; see Cavagna (1999) for more details). Furthermore, the collective behaviour turns out to be independent of how payouts are defined, as long as they respect the minority rule and are symmetric for inversion of the two actions. Another non-trivial result is that in efficient markets ($H = 0$) the volatility (σ^2) decreases as agents adopt a noisy response rule. This is counter-intuitive, as macroscopic fluctuations usually grow larger when the noise at the microscopic level (the agents' decision rule, here) increases. Equally striking is the fact that macroscopic fluctuations are independent of microscopic noise when $H > 0$ (Challet et al 2005, Sections 3.3.5 and 3.4).

15 In the sequence of equilibria discussed above, this makes the process of innovation in the financial industry a non-trivial one. Indeed, in spite of the creation of a new instrument being an independent and identically distributed (iid) draw, the innovations which are adopted are not iid, but rather depend on the whole set of already adopted innovations.

16 The Financial Stability Forum (2008) observed that "some institutional investors have relied too heavily on ratings in their investment guidelines and choices, in some cases fully substituting ratings for independent risk assessment and due diligence." As a reaction to this document, some organisations (like the European Fund and Asset Management Association) laid out guidelines to avoid the over-reliance on ratings agencies.

17 It can be argued that default probabilities were grossly underestimated by rating agencies. This was partly due to misaligned incentives arising from the fact that rating agencies were paid by the very issuers of the securities they were rating. This would suggest, within the naive picture of the crisis provided by our model, that investors were basing their choice of whether or not to adopt the rule on the basis of a hypothetical value of p which was lower than the real one. Eventually, however, the disclosure of information on defaults of subprimes and revelation of losses in financial institutions percolated through the market, which quickly realigned investors' beliefs (ie, p). This suggests that the increase in p, the perceived probability of toxicity, might have been sharp rather than gradual during the crisis.

18 It may be argued that an over-reliance on ratings agencies was instigated by regulators who stipulated that capital reserves should be based on the ratings of securities owned. Higher-rated securities required lower capital to be set aside, which was appealing to the banks and investors who bought and traded them.

REFERENCES

Acharya, V. V., and M. P. Richardson, 2009, "Causes of the Financial Crisis", *Critical Review* 21, pp. 195–210.

Adrian, T., and H. S. Shin, 2009, "Money, Liquidity and Monetary Policy", *American Economic Review* 99, pp. 600–5.

Allen, F., and E. Carletti, 2007, "What Is the Rationale for Regulating Banks?", *Banking and Finance Monitor* 2, pp. 40–3.

Anand, K., P. Gai and M. Marsili, 2009 "Financial Crises and the Evaporation of Trust", URL: http://ssrn.com/abstract=1507196.

Anand, K., P. Gai and M. Marsili, 2010a, "The Rise and Fall of Trust Networks", in *Artificial Economics*, Lecture Notes in Economics and Mathematical Systems, Volume 645 (Berlin: Springer).

Anand, K., A. Kirman and M. Marsili, 2010b, "Epidemics of Rules, Information Aggregation Failure and Market Crashes", URL: http://ssrn.com/abstract=1624803.

Ashcraft, A. B., and T. Schuermann, 2008, "Understanding the Securitization of Subprime Mortgage Credit", Federal Reserve Bank of New York Staff Report 318.

Avellaneda, M., and M. D. Lipkin, 2003, "A Market-Induced Mechanism for Stock Pinning", *Quantitative Finance* 3, pp. 417–25.

Berg, J., M. Marsili, A. Rustichini and R. Zecchina, 2001, "Statistical Mechanics of Asset Markets with Private Information", *Quantitative Finance* 1, pp. 203–11.

Bianconi, G. T. Galla, M. Marsili and P. Pin, 2009, "Effects of Tobin Taxes in Minority Game Markets", *Journal of Economics Behavior and Organization* 70, pp. 231–40.

The Bond Market Association, 2002, "An Investor's Guide to Pass Through and Collateralized Mortgage Securities", Report.

Bookstaber, R. M., 2007, *A Demon of Our Own Design: Markets, Hedge Funds, and the Perils of Financial Innovation* (Hoboken, NJ: John Wiley & Sons).

Bouchaud, J. P., J. D. Farmer and F. Lillo, 2008, "How Markets Slowly Digest Changes in Supply and Demand", e-print, arXiv:0809.0822.

Brock, W. A., C. H. Hommes and F. O. O. Wagener, 2008 "More Hedging Instruments May Destabilize Markets", University of Amsterdam CeNDEF Working Paper 08-04.

Brunnermeier, M. K., and M. Oehmke, 2009, *Complexity in Financial Markets* (Princeton University Press).

Caballero, R. J., and A. Simsek, 2009, "Complexity and Financial Panics", NBER Working Paper 14997.

Caccioli, F., and M. Marsili, 2010, "On Information Efficiency and Financial Stability", URL: http://arxiv.org/abs/1004.5014.

Caccioli, F., M. Marsili and P. Vivo, 2009, "Eroding Market Stability by Proliferation of Financial Instruments", *European Journal of Physics* B 71, pp. 467–79.

Caccioli, F., S. Still, M. Marsili and I. Kondor, "Optimal Liquidation Strategies Regularize Portfolio Selection", URL: http://arxiv.org/abs/1004.4169.

Cass, D., and A. Citanna, 1998, "Pareto Improving Financial Innovation in Incomplete Markets", *Economic Theory* 11, pp. 467–94.

Cavagna, A., 1999, "Irrelevance of Memory in the Minority Game", *Physical Review* E 59, pp. R3783–6

Challet, D., A. Chessa, M. Marsili and Y. C. Zhang, 2001, "From Minority Games to Real Markets", *Quantitative Finance* 1, pp. 168–76.

Challet, D., M. Marsili and Y. C. Zhang, 2005, *Minority Games: Interacting Agents in Financial Markets* (Oxford University Press).

Chamley, C. P., 2004, *Rational Herds: Economic Models of Social Learning* (Cambridge University Press).

Curty, P., and M. Marsili, 2006, "Phase Coexistence in a Forecasting Game", *Journal of Statistical Mechanics*, P03013.

Dacorogna, M. M., R. Gençay, U. Müller, R.-B. Olsen and O. V. Pictet, 2001, "An Introduction to High-Frequency Finance" (London: Academic Press).

Danielsson, J., and J. P. Zigrand, 2007, "Regulating Hedge Funds", in *Financial Stability Review: Special Issue on Hedge Funds*, C. Noyer (ed), pp. 29–36 (Paris: Banque de France).

Dasgupta, P., 1988, *In Trust: Making and Breaking Cooperative Relations* (London: Basil Blackwell).

Eichengreen, B., and K. Mitchener, 2003, "The Great Depression as a Credit Boom Gone Wrong", BIS Working Paper 137.

Fama, E. F., 1970, "Efficient Capital Markets: A Review of Theory and Empirical Work", *Journal of Finance* 25, pp. 383–417.

Farmer, J. D., and S. Joshi, 2002, "The Price Dynamics of Common Trading Strategies", *Journal of Economics Behavior and Organization* 14, pp. 149–71.

Fender, I., and J. Mitchell, 2005, "Structured Finance: Complexity, Risk and the Use of Ratings", *BIS Quarterly Review*, June, pp. 67–79.

Financial Stability Forum, 2008, "Report of the Financial Stability Forum on Enhancing Market and Institutional Resilience", Report, Financial Stability Board.

Flood, M. D., 1991, "An Introduction to Complete Markets" *The Federal Reserve Bank of St Louis Review* 73, pp. 32–57.

Frankel, J. A., 1996, "How Well Do Markets Work: Might a Tobin Tax Help?", in M. U. Haq, I. Kaul and I. Grunberg (eds), *The Tobin Tax*, pp. 41–82 (Oxford University Press).

Gopinath, S., 2010, "Pursuit of Complete Markets: The Missing Perspectives", URL: http://www.bis.org/review/r100304d.pdf.

Grossman, S. J., and J. E. Stiglitz, 1980, "On the Impossibility of Informationally Efficient Markets", *American Economic Review* 70, pp. 393–408.

Haldane, A., 2009, "Rethinking the Financial Network", Speech, URL: http://www.bank ofengland.co.uk/publications/speeches/2009/speech386.pdf.

Hart, O., 1975, "On the Optimality of Equilibrium When the Market Structure Is Incomplete", *Journal of Economic Theory* 418, pp. 439–42.

Hommes, C. H., 2006, "Heterogeneous Agent Models in Economics and Finance", in L. Tesfatsion and K. L. Judd, *Handbook of Computational Economics 2: Agent-Based Computational Economics*, Handbooks in Economics, Volume 28, pp. 1426–61 (Elsevier).

IMF, 2006, "Global Financial Stability Report", April.

IMF, 2008, "Global Financial Stability Report", October.

Jeannin, M., G. Iori and D. Samuel, 2008, "The Pinning Effect: Theory and a Simulated Microstructure Model", *Quantitative Finance* 8, pp. 823–31.

Kyle, A., 1985, "Continuous Auctions and Insider Trading", *Econometrica* 15, pp. 1315–35.

Lillo, F., E. Moro, G. Vaglica and R. N. Mantegna, 2008, "Specialization of Strategies and Herding Behavior of Trading Firms in a Financial Market", *New Journal of Physics* 10, no. 043019.

Lux, T., and M. Marches, 1999, "Scaling and Criticality in a Stochastic Multi-Agent Model of a Financial Market", *Nature* 397, pp. 498–500.

Marsili, M., 2001, "Market Mechanism and Expectations in Minority and Majority Games", *Physica A* 299, pp. 93–103.

Marsili, M., 2009, "Complexity and Financial Stability in a Large Random Economy", URL: http://ssrn.com/abstract=1415971.

May, R. M., 1972, "Will a Large Complex System Be Stable?", *Nature* 238, pp. 413–4.

May, R. M., G. Sugihara and S. A. Levin, 2008, "Ecology for Bankers", *Nature* 451, pp. 893–5.

Merton, R. C., and Z. Bodie, 2005, "Design of Financial Systems: Towards a Synthesis of Function and Structure", *Journal of Investment Management* 3, pp. 1–23.

Mezard, M., G. Parisi and M. Virasoro, 1986, *Spin Glass Theory and Beyond* (Singapore: World Scientific).

Morris, S., and H. S. Shin, 2003, "Global Games: Theory and Applications", in M. Dewatripont, L. P. Hansen and S. J. Turnovsky (eds), *Advances in Economics and Econometrics: The Eighth World Congress*", pp. 56–114 (Cambridge University Press).

Morris, S., and H. S. Shin, 2008, "Financial Regulation in a System Context", in D. W. Elmendorf and N. G. Mankiw and L. H. Summers (eds), *Brookings Papers on Economic Activity* (Washington, DC: Brookings Institute Press).

Noyer, C. (ed), 2007, *Financial Stability Review: Special Issue on Hedge Funds* (Paris: Banque de France).

Osler, C. L., 2006, "Macro Lessons from Microstructure", *International Journal of Finance and Economics* 11, pp. 55–80.

Pliska, S. R., 1997, *Introduction to Mathematical Finance: Discrete Time Models* (Oxford: Blackwell).

Pliska, S. R., 2010, "Electronic Market Making: Potential Profits and Research Opportunities", *Proceedings of the Sixth World Congress of the Bachelier Finance Society*.

Rajan, R., 2005, "Has Financial Development Made the World Riskier?", NBER Working Paper 11728.

Rajan, U., A. Seru and V. Vig, 2008, "The Failure of Models that Predict Failure: Distance, Incentives and Defaults", Chicago GSB Research Paper 08-19.

Sabarwal, T., 2006, "Common Structures of Asset-Backed Securities and Their Risks", *Corporate Ownership and Control* 4(1), pp. 258–65.

Sen, A., 2009, "Capitalism Beyond the Crisis", *New York Review of Books*, 56(5).

Shiller, R. J., 2008, *The Subprime Solution: How Today's Global Financial Crisis Happened, and What to Do about It* (Princeton University Press).

Smaghi, L. B., 2010, "From Boom to Bust: Towards a New Equilibrium in Bank Credit", URL: http://www.ecb.int/press/key/date/2010/html/sp100129.en.html.

Turnbull, S. M., M. Crouhy and R. A. Jarrow, 2008, "The Subprime Credit Crisis of 07", URL: http://ssrn.com/abstract=1112467.

Turner, A., "The Uses and Abuses of Economic Ideology", URL: http://www.project-syndicate.org/commentary/turner1.

US Securities and Exchange Commission, 2009, "SEC Votes on Measures to Further Strengthen Oversight of Credit Rating Agencies", URL: http://www.sec.gov/news/press/2009/2009-200.htm.

Weisbuch, G., O. Chenevez, J.-P. Nadal and A. Kirman, 1998, "A Formal Approach to Market Organization: Choice Functions, Mean Field Approximation and Maximum Entropy Principle", in A. Orlean and J. Lesourne (eds), *Advances in Self-Organization and Evolutionary Economics*, pp. 149–59 (Economica).

18

The Martingale Theory of Bubbles: Implications for the Valuation of Derivatives and Detecting Bubbles

Robert A. Jarrow; Philip Protter
Cornell University and Kamakura Corporation; Cornell University

After the 2007–9 credit crisis, caused by a crash in housing prices (the bursting of an alleged housing price bubble), asset price bubbles received considerable attention in the financial press and regulatory arena.[1] Before this episode, however, the modelling of asset price bubbles had a long history in economics.

Classical economics studied the existence and characterisation of bubbles in discrete-time, infinite- and finite-horizon, equilibrium models. It has been shown that bubbles cannot exist in finite-horizon rational expectation models (Santos and Woodford 1997; Tirole 1982). They can arise, however, in markets where traders behave myopically (Tirole 1982), where there are irrational traders (De Long *et al* 1990), in infinite-horizon growing economies with rational traders (O'Connell and Zeldes 1988; Tirole 1985; Weil 1990), economies where rational traders have differential beliefs and when arbitrageurs cannot synchronise trades (Abreu and Brunnermeier 2003) or when there are short-sale/borrowing constraints (Santos and Woodford 1997; Scheinkman and Xiong 2003). For reviews of the literature see Camerer (1989) and Scheinkman and Xiong (2004).

Equilibrium models impose substantial structure on the economy: in particular, investor optimality and a market clearing mechanism equating aggregate supply to aggregate demand. Price bubbles have also been studied in less restrictive settings, using the insights and tools of mathematical finance. We call this alternative approach to studying asset price bubbles the "martingale theory of bubbles".

The aforementioned papers are mainly concerned with the characterisation of bubbles and the pricing of derivative securities in finite-horizon economies satisfying the "no free lunch with vanishing risk (NFLVR)" hypothesis (Cox and Hobson 2005; Heston *et al* 2007; Loewenstein and Willard 2000a,b). Therein, bubbles violate many of the classical option pricing theorems and, in particular, put–call parity. In contrast to equilibrium pricing, these violations occur due to the absence of sufficient structure on the economy within the NFLVR framework. NFLVR only imposes a restriction on the economy due to the optimality of individual traders (acting independently).

Since bubbles are a market-wide phenomenon, thought to be generated by the collective actions of all traders, it seems appropriate that, when considering their existence, we need to impose some additional structure on the economy beyond NFLVR. As discussed above, classical economic modelling requires that the asset price process satisfy an economic equilibrium. However, this is too strong a restriction. Consistent with this intent, but less restrictive than imposing an economic equilibrium, Jarrow *et al* (2006, 2010b) added Merton's (1973) no-dominance (ND) condition. ND is a restriction imposed by the collective action of all traders. Adding ND implies that many of the classical option pricing theorems are again satisfied, including put–call parity, and that asset price bubbles can only exist in incomplete markets. We follow this intermediate approach below.

The purpose of this chapter is to review the martingale theory of bubbles under both the NFLVR and ND hypotheses and, in particular, to understand its implications for the valuation of derivatives and detecting asset price bubbles. An outline of this chapter is as follows. The next section presents the basic model structure; we then discuss the existence and characterisation of asset price bubbles, before discussing the implications for valuing derivatives and detecting bubbles. A brief conclusion, related to the impact of price bubbles on risk management decision making, follows.

THE MODEL

This section introduces the model used to study asset price bubbles. The analysis is based on the papers by Jarrow *et al* (2006, 2010a,b) and Jarrow and Protter (2009, 2010a).

Market price process

We consider a continuous-trading finite-horizon economy $[0, T^*]$ with frictionless and competitive markets. By "frictionless" we mean that there are no transaction costs or impediments to trade. By "competitive" we mean that all traders in our economy act as price takers believing that their trades have no quantity impact on the market price. We consider a finite-horizon economy because in an infinite-horizon economy, as shown by Jarrow *et al* (2010b), two additional types of bubbles can exist due specifically to the fact that time is unbounded.

Let $(\Omega, \mathcal{F}, \mathbb{F}, P)$ be a filtered complete probability space characterising the randomness in the economy. We assume that the filtration $\mathbb{F} = (\mathcal{F}_t)_{0 \leq t \leq T^*}$ satisfies the "usual hypotheses" (Protter 2005). Traded in our economy are a risky asset and a money market account. We denote the time-t value of a money market account as

$$B_t = \exp\left(\int_0^t r_u \, du\right) \qquad (18.1)$$

where r is a non-negative adapted process representing the default-free spot rate of interest.

Let $\tau \leq T^*$ be a stopping time which represents the maturity (or life) of the risky asset. Let $D = (D_t)_{0 \leq t < \tau}$ be a càdlàg semimartingale process adapted to $\mathbb{F}$ which represents the cumulative cashflow process from holding the risky asset. Let $X_\tau \in \mathcal{F}_\tau$ be the time-τ terminal payout or liquidation value of the asset. We assume that both $X_\tau, D \geq 0$.

Let the market price of the risky asset be given by the non-negative càdlàg (ie, right continuous with left limits) semimartingale $S = (S_t)_{0 \leq t < \tau}$ representing the price ex-cashflow (since S is càdlàg). Last, we let W be the wealth process associated with the market price of the risky asset plus accumulated cashflows, ie

$$W_t = \mathbf{1}_{\{t < \tau\}} S_t + B_t \int_0^{t \wedge \tau} \frac{1}{B_u} dD_u + \frac{B_t}{B_\tau} X_\tau \mathbf{1}_{\{\tau \leq t\}} \qquad (18.2)$$

Note that all cashflows are invested in the money market account.

We assume that the market is incomplete.[2] The importance of market incompleteness was discussed in the introductory section and it will be revisited later.

Well-functioning economy

We want to consider the existence and characterisation of asset price bubbles in a well-functioning economy. By "well functioning" we mean that the economy must satisfy the following two conditions:

- it should contain no arbitrage opportunities in the sense of NFLVR;
- it should have no dominated assets trading.

NFLVR is a standard restriction imposed in the options pricing literature and it is due to Delbaen and Schachermayer (1994, 1998). We impose this condition because if bubbles were to create an NFLVR, we would expect the actions of arbitrageurs to quickly remove them from the economy. NFLVR is a weak restriction on an economy because it is trader specific and based on individual optimality. As such, it does not impose any restriction on the economy generated by the collective actions of all traders.

Since bubbles are a market-wide phenomenon, thought to be generated by the collective actions of all traders, it seems appropriate that when considering their existence, we need to impose some additional structure on the economy in this regard. Traditional economic modelling would require that the asset price process satisfies an economic equilibrium. However, this is too strong a restriction because it requires a complete specification of every traders' preferences and endowments, and it necessitates fixing a particular market clearing mechanism (eg, Walrasian or Nash equilibrium). Consistent with this intent, but less restrictive, we assume Merton's (1973) no-dominance condition.

An asset A is said to dominate asset B if A's time-0 price is less than or equal to B's, yet A has payouts (dividends and liquidating value) that are always at least as large as B's, and with positive probability strictly larger. Assuming the economy satisfies ND is a restriction imposed by the collective action of all traders. Indeed, no trader would want to hold the dominated asset in their portfolio. Yet, this individual action would not remove the mispricing from the economy. But, if all traders act in this way, there would be no demand for the dominated asset, and its price could not be sustained in any reasonable notion of an economic equilibrium. Without fixing a particular market equilibrium, therefore, ND captures the essence of supply equalling demand.

In summary, therefore, we only study the existence and characterisation of asset price bubbles under both the individual trader-imposed restriction (NFLVR) and the collective trader-imposed restriction (ND).

DEFINITION, EXISTENCE AND CHARACTERISATION

This section defines a price bubble, then studies its existence and characterisation. First, we need to define the asset's fundamental value. Under the NFLVR assumption, by the first fundamental theorem of asset pricing (Delbaen and Schachermayer 1994, 1998), we have the existence of an equivalent probability measure Q such that W_t/B_t is a local martingale. Q is called an equivalent local martingale measure (ELMM). We note in passing that, since $W_t/B_t \geq 0$, this implies that W_t/B_t is a non-negative supermartingale. Simple algebra shows that this implies that the asset price plus accumulated cashflow process

$$\frac{1}{B_t}\left(S_t + \int_0^t \frac{1}{B_u} dD_u\right) \tag{18.3}$$

is also a Q local martingale and a non-negative supermartingale as well. We will use these observation below.

Given that the market is incomplete, by the second fundamental theorem of asset pricing (Jarrow and Protter 2008), we know that the ELMM Q is not unique and that there exists a continuum of possible ELLMs. To define the fundamental value, we need to identify the unique ELMM from the collection of all possible ELMMs reflected in the market price. For example, if sufficient static trading in call options exists, then the ELLM can be uniquely identified via the call option prices.[3] For the remainder of this chapter, we assume that the market-selected ELLM Q has been determined.

Definition

Given the market-selected ELLM Q, we define the fundamental price of the risky asset as

$$S_t^* = E_Q\left(\int_t^{\tau \wedge T^*} \frac{1}{B_u} dD_u + \frac{X_\tau}{B_\tau} \mathbf{1}_{\{\tau \leq T^*\}} \,\bigg|\, \mathcal{F}_t\right) B_t \tag{18.4}$$

The asset's fundamental value represents the present value of the asset's future cashflows, if the asset is held until liquidation. The present value operator is computed as the expected discounted value, where the expectation operator based on the ELLM takes into account the asset's risk. In fact, the ELLM is alternatively called a risk-adjusted probability measure to reflect this characteristic. We note that the ELLM Q makes

$$\frac{1}{B_t}\left(S_t^* + \int_0^t \frac{1}{B_u} dD_u\right) \qquad (18.5)$$

into a (uniformly integrable) martingale.

The asset's price bubble is defined to be the difference between the asset's market and fundamental price, ie,

$$\beta_t = S_t - S_t^* \qquad (18.6)$$

Using the facts that

- Expression 18.3 is a Q local martingale and a non-negative supermartingale with terminal value

$$B_T \int_0^T \frac{1}{B_u} dD_u + X_T$$

and

- Expression 18.5 is a (uniformly integrable) martingale with terminal value

$$B_T \int_0^T \frac{1}{B_u} dD_u + X_T$$

we see that the asset's price bubble is non-zero if and only if Expression 18.3 is a strict Q-local martingale (ie, a local martingale that is not a martingale). This distinction, between a strict local martingale (bubble) and a martingale (no bubble) is why this theory is called the "martingale theory of bubbles". There is an alternative theory of asset price bubbles based on charges (finitely additive linear operators). However, Jarrow et al (2010b) show that these are equivalent theories.

Existence

There exist many market asset price processes that are strict local martingales (and not martingales), thereby exhibiting price bubbles (Hobson 2010; Sin 1998). We provide an example consistent with both NFLVR and ND.

Example 18.1 (stochastic volatility). This example is due to Sin (1998). Assume there are no cashflows on the underlying asset and let (S_t, v_t) satisfy

$$\frac{dS_t}{S_t} = r_t\, dt + v_t^\alpha (\sigma_1\, dZ_{1t} + \sigma_2\, dZ_{2t})$$

$$\frac{dv_t}{v_t} = \rho(b - v_t)\, dt + a_1\, dZ_{1t} + a_2\, dZ_{2t}$$

under the ELMM Q where (Z_{t1}, Z_{t2}) is be a two-dimensional Brownian motion, $S_0 = x$, $v_0 = 1$, $\alpha > 0$, $\rho \geq 0$, $b > 0$, $a_1, \sigma_1, a_2, \sigma_2$ are constants that satisfy $a_1\sigma_1 + a_2\sigma_2 > 0$. Then, S_t/B_t is a strict local martingale under Q if and only if $a_1\sigma_1 + a_2\sigma_2 > 0$.

Characterisation

Jarrow et al (2006) prove the following characterisation theorem, modified for our finite-horizon assumption.

Theorem 18.2. Any non-zero asset price bubble β is a strict Q-local martingale with the following properties:

1. $\beta \geq 0$,
2. $\beta_\tau = 0$,
3. if $\beta_t = 0$, then $\beta_u = 0$ for all $u \geq t$, and
4. if no cash flows, then

$$S_t = E_Q\left(\frac{S_T}{B_T}\,\bigg|\,\mathcal{F}_t\right)B_t + \beta_t - E_Q\left(\frac{\beta_T}{B_T}\,\bigg|\,\mathcal{F}_t\right)B_t$$

for any $t \leq T \leq \tau \leq T^*$.

This theorem states that the asset price bubble β is a strict Q-local martingale. Condition (1) states that bubbles are always non-negative, ie, the market price can never be less than the fundamental value. Condition (2) states that the bubble must burst on or before τ. Condition (3) states that if the bubble ever bursts before the asset's maturity, then it can never start again. In other words, condition (3) states that in the context of our model, bubbles either must exist at the start of the model, or they never will exist. And, if they exist and burst, then they cannot start again. Requiring bubbles to exist since the beginning of the modelling period is clearly a weak spot of the theory; a reasonable theory needs the concept of "bubble birth". This is provided, fortunately, in Jarrow et al (2010b). The problem is that once a non-negative local martingale is 0 then it stays at 0 forever. The idea is that a risky asset price process S which is a *bona fide* martingale under a risk-neutral measure Q can become a strict local martingale under a different risk-neutral measure Q^*. Thus, if the market, which has chosen risk-neutral measure Q as we can tell via an analysis of its option price structure (via the technique provided in Jacod and Protter (2010b)), decides to change to another risk-neutral measure Q^*, then the price process status can change from a fundamental price to a bubble price. Therefore, bubble birth can occur when the market selects a different risk-neutral measure. The change from one risk-neutral measure to another can be thought of as corresponding to a market changing from being conservative to being speculative, at least as far this particular risky asset is concerned. Finally, condition (4) relates the asset price at time t to the conditional expectation of its price at time T plus the asset's price bubble.

VALUING DERIVATIVES

This section considers the valuation of derivative securities written on the risky asset when the risky asset price has a bubble. For simplicity, we focus on the standard derivatives: forward contracts and European and American call and put options. We first need to formalise the definition of the fundamental price of a derivative security. To simplify the notation, we assume that the risky asset S pays no cashflows.

Definition

We define an arbitrary (European-type) derivative security on the risky asset S to be a financial contract that has a random payout at time $T \leqslant T^*$, where T is called the derivative's maturity date. The payout is given by $H_T(S)$, where H_T is a functional on $(S_u)_{u \leqslant T}$. As is true in practice, our definition of a derivative security reflects the fact that the financial contract's payouts are written on the market price of the risky asset, and not its fundamental value. This is a subtle and important observation.

We denote the time-t market price of a derivative security H by $\Lambda_t(H_T(S))$. Then, analogous to the risky asset, the fundamental price of the derivative security is defined as the conditional expectation of the derivative's time-T payout using the market-selected ELLM

THE MARTINGALE THEORY OF BUBBLES

Q, ie

$$E_Q\left(\frac{H_T(S)}{B_T}\ \bigg|\ \mathcal{F}_t\right)B_t$$

Finally, the derivative security's price bubble δ_t is defined as the difference between its market price and fundamental value

$$\delta_t = \Lambda_t(H_T(S)) - E_Q\left(\frac{H_T(S)}{B_T}\ \bigg|\ \mathcal{F}_t\right)B_t \qquad (18.7)$$

Given this definition, we can now explore whether derivative's inherit the underlying asset's price bubble or not.

Bounded payout derivatives

The following lemma, first proven in Jarrow *et al* (2010b), is useful when considering the standard derivative contracts.

Lemma 18.3. Let $H_T(S)$ have bounded payouts. Then the derivative's price has no price bubble, ie

$$\Lambda_t(H_T(S)) = E_Q\left(\frac{H_T(S)}{B_T}\ \bigg|\ \mathcal{F}_t\right)B_t \qquad (18.8)$$

The proof of this lemma follows from the observation that bounded and positive supermartingales are martingales. For derivatives that have bounded payouts, the standard risk-neutral valuation method applies, regardless of the existence of a bubble in the underlying asset's price.

As a simple application of this lemma, we apply it to default-free zero coupon bonds. A default-free zero coupon bond is defined to be a security that pays a certain US dollar amount at time T. We denote its time-t market price as $p(t, T)$. Since a zero-coupon bond's price is bounded, we have that zero-coupon bond prices have no price bubbles; hence

$$p(t, T) = E_Q\left(\frac{1}{B_T}\ \bigg|\ \mathcal{F}_t\right)B_t \qquad (18.9)$$

This risk-neutral valuation formula is consistent with the Heath–Jarrow–Morton term-structure models (Heath *et al* 1992), implying that arbitrage-free term-structure models exhibit no asset price bubbles.

Forwards and European call and put options

In this section we consider three standard derivative securities – a forward contract, a European put option and a European call option

– all on the same risky asset. Each of these derivative securities are defined by their payouts at their maturity dates.

A forward contract on the risky asset with strike price K and maturity date T has a payout $[S_T - K]$. We denote its time-t market price by V_t. This represents a slightly more general definition of a forward contract because it allows the strike price K to be specified arbitrarily. The usual market convention is to determine the strike price such that the market price of the forward contract when written (time t) is zero. In this case, the strike price is called the forward price, which we denote as f_t. We will discuss the forward price later.

A European call option on the risky asset with strike price K and maturity T has a payout $[S_T - K]^+$, with time-t market price denoted by C_t. Finally, a European put option on the risky asset with strike price K and maturity T has a payout $[K - S_T]^+$, with time-t market price denoted by P_t.

Let V_t^*, C_t^* and P_t^* denote the fundamental values of the forward contract, call option and put option, respectively. The following theorems follow immediately.

Theorem 18.4 (put–call parity in fundamental values).

$$C_t^* - P_t^* = V_t^* = S_t^* - p(t,T)K \qquad (18.10)$$

This theorem follows by taking conditional expectations of discounted payouts for the various derivative contracts. Put–call parity for the fundamental prices holds regardless of whether or not there are bubbles in the asset's market price.

Perhaps surprisingly, put–call parity also holds for market prices, regardless of whether or not the underlying asset price has a bubble.

Theorem 18.5 (put–call parity in market prices).

$$C_t - P_t = V_t = S_t - p(t,T)K \qquad (18.11)$$

This theorem and its proof are identical to those originally given in Merton (1973), which depend crucially on the no-dominance assumption. If only NFLVR holds, then put–call parity in market prices need not hold. For an example, see Jarrow et al (2006). For related discussions of the economy without ND see also Cox and Hobson (2005).

Note that this theorem also values the forward contract (the second equality). Given this expression, we can determine the forward price as

$$f_t = \frac{S_t}{p(t,T)} = \frac{S_t^* + \beta_t}{p(t,T)} \qquad (18.12)$$

This is the standard expression for the forward price as the "future value" of the spot price. Note that the forward price inherits the asset's price bubble as indicated by the second equality.

Theorem 18.6 (put prices).

$$P_t = P_t^* \qquad (18.13)$$

The proof of this theorem is trivial. Note that the payout to the put option is bounded by K; hence, the result follows from the lemma. European put options always equal their fundamental values, regardless of whether or not the underlying asset's price has a bubble. We will revisit this observation when we discuss the empirical testing of bubbles later in the chapter.

Theorem 18.7 (call prices).

$$C_t - C_t^* = S_t - E_Q\left(\frac{S_T}{B_T} \mid \mathcal{F}_t\right) B_t = \beta_t - E_Q\left(\frac{\beta_T}{B_T} \mid \mathcal{F}_t\right) B_t \qquad (18.14)$$

The proof follows from combining put–call parity in market prices and Equation 18.13. We see that the call option market price differs from its fundamental value by exactly the underlying asset's price bubble. Furthermore, the magnitude of the call option's bubble is independent of the strike price. This observation can be used to facilitate an empirical test for asset price bubbles (see the relevant section below).

Perhaps surprisingly, in the presence of an asset price bubble, the standard risk-neutral valuation method cannot be used to value the call option. Hence, if we believe an asset exhibits a price bubble, then the standard option pricing methodology for pricing call options (eg, the Black–Scholes model) does not apply.

American call options

This section studies the impact that asset price bubbles have on American call options. We let C_t^A denote the market price of an American call option with strike K and maturity T. The definition of the American call's fundamental value is

$$C_t^{A*} = \sup_{\eta \in [t,T]} E_Q\left(\frac{[S_\eta - K]^+}{B_\eta} \mid \mathcal{F}_t\right) B_t \qquad (18.15)$$

Jarrow et al (2010b) prove the following theorem using standard techniques.

Theorem 18.8 (American call prices). Assume that the jump process of the asset's price, $\Delta S := (\Delta S_t)_{t \geq 0}$, where $\Delta S_t = S_t - S_{t-}$ is such that there exists some function g and a uniformly integrable martingale X such that

$$\Delta S_u \leq g\left(\sup_{t \leq r < u} S_r\right)(1 + X_u)$$

Then,

$$C_t = C_t^A = C_t^{A*} \tag{18.16}$$

This theorem is the generalisation of Merton's (1973) famous No Early Exercise Theorem, ie, given the underlying asset pays no cashflows, otherwise identical American and European call options have equal prices. This is the first equality in Equation 18.16. Just as in the classic theory (using the same ND argument), this implies that American call options on an asset with no cashflows are not exercised early.

The second equality proves the surprising result that American call option prices exhibit no bubbles. This result follows because the stopping time associated with the American call's fundamental value (as distinct from the exercise strategy of the American call's market price) explicitly incorporates the price bubble into the supremum. Indeed, the fundamental value of the American call option is the minimal supermartingale dominating the value function. If there is a price bubble, then the stopping time associated with the American call option's fundamental value is stopped early with strictly positive probability.

This is best understood by examining the difference between the fundamental values of the European and American call. If stopping early had no value, then it must be true that $C_t^{A*} = C_t^*$. However, by Equation 18.14, an asset price bubble creates a difference between American and European calls' fundamental prices, ie

$$C_t^{A*} - C_t^* = C_t - C_t^* = \beta_t - E_Q\left(\frac{\beta_T}{B_T} \mid \mathcal{F}_t\right) B_t > 0$$

The intuition for the possibility of stopping early is obtained by recognising that the market price equals the fundamental value plus a price bubble. The price bubble is a non-negative supermartingale that is expected to decline. Its effect on the market price of the asset is therefore analogous to a continuous dividend payout. And, it is well known that continuous dividend payouts make early exercise of (the fundamental value of) an American call possible.

Futures contracts

This section studies the impact that asset price bubbles have on futures contracts and is based on Jarrow and Protter (2009).

A futures contract is similar to a forward contract. It is a financial contract that requires purchase (the long position) of the risky asset S at time T for a predetermined price, called the futures price. However, the payment procedure for the futures contract is different from that of a forward. The prearranged payment procedure for the futures is called "marking-to-market". Marking-to-market obligates the purchaser to accept a continuous cashflow stream equal to the continuous change in the futures prices for this contract determined so that the market value of the futures contract is always zero.

Notation helps to clarify the futures contract's specification. Let F_t denote the time-t market futures price of a futures contract with maturity T on the risky asset S. The continuous cashflow stream to the futures contract is equal to dF_t. And, at maturity, the last futures price must equal the asset's market price $F_T = S_T$.

Now, consider a portfolio that is long one futures contract. The wealth process of this portfolio at time T is given by

$$B_T \int_0^T \frac{1}{B_u} dF_u \qquad (18.17)$$

Using our general notation for the market price of a derivative with a cashflow as given by Equation 18.17, we define the market futures price $(F_t)_{T \geq t \geq 0}$ as any càdlàg semimartingale process such that the market price of the futures contract is always zero and whose time-T value matches the spot price for the risky asset, ie

$$\Lambda_t \left(B_T \int_t^T \frac{1}{B_u} dF_u \right) = 0 \quad \text{for all } t \in [0, T] \text{ and } F_T = S_T \qquad (18.18)$$

Using the fundamental value of the futures contract as given above (Equation 18.7), Jarrow and Protter (2009) show that the fundamental futures price is equal to

$$F_t^* = E_Q(S_T \mid \mathcal{F}_t) \qquad (18.19)$$

This, of course, is the classical definition of the futures price.[4] Jarrow and Protter (2009) also prove the following theorem relating market and fundamental futures prices.

Theorem 18.9 (futures prices). Let y_t be a local Q martingale with $y_T = 0$. Then

$$F_t = E_Q(S_T \mid \mathcal{F}_t) + y_t = E_Q(S_T^* \mid \mathcal{F}_t) + E_Q(\beta_T \mid \mathcal{F}_t) + y_t \quad (18.20)$$

is a market futures price process.

The importance of this theorem, using the second equality, is that a market futures price can have a price bubble y_t that is independent of, and in addition to, the underlying asset's price bubble β_t. This additional price bubble is due to the continuous marking-to-market of the futures contract. And, unlike the underlying asset's price bubble, which is always non-negative, a futures price bubble can be positive or negative.

This has two important implications. Firstly, as indicated by this theorem, the price discovery role of futures prices is undermined by both the existence of price bubbles in the underlying asset's price and the market futures price itself. Secondly, this extra price bubble adds an additional wedge between forward and futures prices beyond that due to stochastic interest rates.[5]

FOREIGN CURRENCY BUBBLES

This section, based on Jarrow and Protter (2010a), applies the martingale theory of bubbles to understanding foreign currency exchange rate bubbles. For simplicity, we will consider the US dollar versus euro exchange rate.

We continue with the US dollar-denominated money market account introduced in the previous sections, with time-t dollar value B_t. Furthermore, we assume trading in a euro-denominated money market account with time-t value in euros given by $\hat{B}_t$. Let Y_t be the spot exchange rate of US dollars per euro. We assume, of course, that all of these processes are adapted with respect to the filtration $\mathbb{F}$.

The US dollar-denominated risky asset, whose asset price bubble we first investigate, is the US dollar value of the euro money market account (MMA), ie

$$S_t = Y_t \hat{B}_t \quad (18.21)$$

This is the market price. The fundamental value of the US dollar value of the euro MMA is

$$S_t^* = E_Q\left(\frac{Y_{T^*}\hat{B}_{T^*}}{B_{T^*}} \,\bigg|\, \mathcal{F}_t\right) B_t \qquad (18.22)$$

Hence, this risky asset's price bubble (in US dollars) is

$$\beta_t = S_t - S_t^* \qquad (18.23)$$

All the previous theorems can be applied to the triplet $\{S_t, S_t^*, \beta_t\}$; in particular, we know that this asset's price bubble is non-negative. Furthermore, this identification will enable us to eventually understand the valuation of foreign currency derivatives in the presence of foreign currency bubbles. But, before this is accomplished, we first need to construct the mapping from β_t to the exchange rate bubble itself.

To obtain this mapping, we first define the fundamental (US dollar/euro) exchange rate as

$$Y_t^* \equiv \frac{1}{\hat{B}_t} S_t^* = E_Q\left(\frac{Y_{T^*}\hat{B}_{T^*}}{B_{T^*}} \,\bigg|\, \mathcal{F}_t\right) \frac{B_t}{\hat{B}_t} \qquad (18.24)$$

The fundamental exchange rate is the fundamental US dollar value of the euro MMA divided by the euro value of the MMA. Hence, the (US dollar/euro) exchange rate bubble is then

$$\beta_t^Y \equiv Y_t - Y_t^* = \frac{\beta_t}{\hat{B}_t} \geq 0 \qquad (18.25)$$

This is our mapping. We see that an exchange rate bubble is the risky asset's price bubble divided by the market price of the euro MMA in euros. We also note that the (US dollar/euro) exchange rate bubble must be non-negative. This is because we are using the US dollar as the numéraire.

Next, let us consider the (euro/US dollar) exchange rate $1/Y_t$. Defining the fundamental (euro/US dollar) exchange rate to be $1/Y_t^*$, we see that the bubble in the (euro/US dollar) exchange rate is then given by

$$\beta_t^{1/Y} \equiv \left(\frac{1}{Y_t} - \frac{1}{Y_t^*}\right) \leq 0$$

which is negative.

We can extend this formulation to consider the relation between foreign currency exchange rate bubbles and price level inflation in the underlying economies. This formulation, however, is left to the literature (Jarrow and Protter 2010a).

DETECTING BUBBLES

This section discusses three different approaches that can be used to identify asset price bubbles. We are given the historical time series consisting of market prices for the risky asset S_t, the cumulative cashflows D_t, call option prices C_t and put prices P_t.

Joint hypothesis with $\{r_t, D_t, X_t, \tau, Q\}$

The first method is based on Equation 18.6, which we repeat here in modified form

$$\beta_t = S_t - E_Q\left(\int_t^{\tau \wedge T^*} \frac{1}{B_u} dD_u + \frac{X_\tau}{B_\tau} 1_{\{\tau \leq T^*\}} \,\bigg|\, \mathcal{F}_t\right) B_t \qquad (18.26)$$

To identify the bubble β_t in this expression, we need a stochastic model for $\{r_t, D_t, X_t, \tau, Q\}$.

Then, given historical time series data on $\{S_t, D_t\}$, we can estimate the right-hand side of Equation 18.26 and test to see if $\beta_t > 0$. This approach (except for the model structure) characterises the existing literature on testing for the existence of asset price bubbles.[6]

The difficulty with this approach for identifying asset price bubbles is that the empirical validation of their existence depends on the joint hypotheses regarding $\{r_t, D_t, X_t, \tau, Q\}$. Differences in the assumed structure can lead to different conclusions regarding the existence of asset price bubbles.

Joint hypothesis with $\{S_t\}$

The second method is based on specifying a stochastic process for S. We discuss the approach from Jarrow et al (2010a). For this approach, we only impose NFLVR, so that we can identify bubbles in a complete market setting as well as in an incomplete market setting.

Let the asset price process be the standard stochastic differential equation driven by a Brownian motion Z

$$dS_t = \sigma(S_s) dZ_s + \mu(S_s) ds, \quad S_0 = x \qquad (18.27)$$

Here, the asset's price volatility $\sigma(S_t)$ is stochastic and depends on the level of the asset's price. Then, under the ELLM Q, Equation 18.27 simplifies to

$$\frac{S_t}{B_t} = S_0 + \int_0^t \sigma(S_s) dZ_s \qquad (18.28)$$

In this situation, it is known (Ekström and Tysk 2009; Kotani 2006; Mijatović and Urusov 2010) that the process (S/B) is a strict local martingale if and only if

$$\int_0^\infty \frac{x}{\sigma(x)^2} \, dx < \infty \qquad (18.29)$$

We cannot really ascertain from data whether the integral in Equation 18.29 is finite or not, but what we can do is to estimate the coefficient $\sigma(x)$ for the range of values x assumed by the price process S; then we can study the behaviour of σ within this range, and extrapolate, if the behaviour is clear, to determine the likely convergence or divergence of the integral in Equation 18.29. In other words bubbles exist only if the asset's volatility is "large" (as defined by the satisfaction of Equation 18.29). This is an intuitively plausible necessary and sufficient condition for the existence of asset price bubbles.

We can use asset price data $\{S_t\}$ to test Equation 18.29. The advantage of this method is that, although it depends on a joint hypothesis, the form of the stochastic process for S can be independently tested.

Using derivatives $\{C_t, P_t\}$

The third method is based on Equations 18.13 and 18.14, repeated here in modified form

$$P_t = E_Q\left(\frac{[K - S_T]^+}{B_T} \,\Big|\, \mathcal{F}_t\right) B_t \qquad (18.30)$$

$$C_t = E_Q\left(\frac{[S_T - K]^+}{B_T} \,\Big|\, \mathcal{F}_t\right) B_t + \beta_t - E_Q\left(\frac{\beta_T}{B_T} \,\Big|\, \mathcal{F}_t\right) B_t \qquad (18.31)$$

Equation 18.30 is the risk-neutral valuation formula for a put's price and Equation 18.31 is a modified risk-neutral valuation formula for the call's price. Equation 18.31 embeds the asset's price bubble.

We assume that we are given historical market prices for $\{S_t, D_t, C_t, P_t\}$. With these prices, we can build a model for $\{S_t, D_t, Q\}$, use the risk-neutral valuation formulas from these expressions, and test to see if

$$\beta_t - E_Q\left(\frac{\beta_T}{B_T} \,\Big|\, \mathcal{F}_t\right) B_t > 0$$

The advantage of this approach is that any model hypothesised for $\{S_t, D_t, Q\}$ can be first tested on put prices $\{P_t\}$ for its validity, before using the call prices $\{C_t\}$ to test for the existence of price bubbles.

This ability to test the validity of the hypothesised model directly eliminates the "curse of the joint hypothesis" embedded in the first method, and less so in the second method discussed previously.

CONCLUSION

In this chapter we have reviewed the martingale theory of bubbles and discussed its implications for valuing derivatives and detecting bubbles. When price bubbles exist, they distort the economic decisions of investors, financial institutions and regulators. This is true because these economic decisions are based on market prices and not fundamental values. When bubbles exist, market prices and fundamental values differ, leading to errors in decision making.

As financial engineers, the authors are particularly interested in those distortions related to risk management. First, as noted in this chapter, the tools for risk management, financial derivatives, are not priced or hedged in the standard textbook fashion. This can lead organisations who use the standard textbook formulations to mismanage risk. Second, from a regulatory perspective, the determination of economic capital will be too low because, in the presence of bubbles, the drift on the relevant asset price evolutions are too large (too optimistic). Finally, investment decisions of pension funds and institutions will also be distorted because risky asset prices will look more attractive than they should. These distorted economic decisions reduce societal welfare.

These distortions can only be avoided if decision makers can detect bubbles in real time, and manage the risks with the appropriate models. It is our hope that this chapter provides some useful tools in this regard.

The authors were supported in part by NSF Grant DMS-0604020.

1 See William Dudley, "Asset Bubbles and the Implications for Central Bank Policy", speech, April 7, 2010 (available at http://www.ny.frb.org).

2 For a definition, see Jarrow and Protter (2008).

3 See Jacod and Protter (2010b), Schweizer and Wissel (2008) and Carmona and Nadtochiy (2009) in this regard.

4 See Duffie (2001, p. 143) or Shreve (2004, p. 244).

5 See Jarrow and Protter (2009) for more discussion of the relation between forward and futures prices.

6 See Camerer (1989) and Jarrow *et al* (2010b) for more discussion of these tests.

REFERENCES

Abreu, D., and M. Brunnermeier, 2003, "Bubbles and Crashes", *Econometrica* 71(1), pp. 173–204.

Camerer, C., 1989, "Bubbles and Fads In Asset Prices", *Journal of Economic Surveys* 3(1), pp. 3–41.

Carmona, R., and S. Nadtochiy, 2009, "Local Volatility Dynamic Models", *Finance and Stochastics* 13(1), pp. 1–48.

Cox, A. M. G., and D. G. Hobson, 2005, "Local Martingales, Bubbles and Option Prices", *Finance and Stochastics* 9(4), pp. 477–92.

Delbaen, F., and W. Schachermayer, 1994, "A General Version of the Fundamental Theorem of Asset Pricing", *Mathematische Annalen* 300(3), pp. 463–520.

Delbaen, F., and W. Schachermayer, 1998, "The Fundamental Theorem of Asset Pricing for Unbounded Stochastic Processes", *Mathematische Annalen* 312(2), pp. 215–50.

De Long, J. B., A. Shleifer L. Summers and R. Waldmann, 1990, "Noise Trader Risk in Financial Markets", *Journal of Political Economy* 98(4), pp. 703–38.

Duffie, D., 2001, *Dynamic Asset Pricing Theory*, Third Edition (Princeton University Press).

Ekström, E., and J. Tysk, 2009, "Bubbles, Convexity, and the Black–Scholes Equation", *Annals of Applied Probability* 19, pp. 1369–84.

Heath, D., R. Jarrow and A. Morton, 1992, "Bond Pricing and the Term Structure of Interest Rates: A New Methodology", *Econometrica* 60, pp. 77–105.

Heston, S., M. Loewenstein and G. A. Willard, 2007, "Options and Bubbles", *Review of Financial Studies* 20(2), pp. 359–90.

Hobson, D., 2010, "Comparison Results for Stochastic Volatility Models via Coupling", *Finance and Stochastics* 14, pp. 129–52.

Jarrow, R., and P. Protter, 2008, *An Introduction to Financial Asset Pricing*, in J. Birge and V. Linetsky (eds), Handbooks in Operations Research and Management Science, Volume 15 (Elsevier).

Jarrow, R., and P. Protter, 2009, "Forward and Futures Prices with Bubbles", *International Journal of Theoretical and Applied Finance* 12(7), pp. 901–24.

Jarrow, R., and P. Protter, 2010a, "Foreign Currency Bubbles", Working Paper, Cornell University.

Jacod, J., and P. Protter, 2010b, "Risk Neutral Compatibility with Option Prices", *Finance and Stochastics* 14, pp. 285–315.

Jarrow, R., P. Protter and K. Shimbo, 2006, "Asset Price Bubbles in a Complete Market", *Advances in Mathematical Finance*, Special Issue In Honor of Dilip B. Madan, pp. 105–30.

Jarrow, R., Y. Kchia and P. Protter, 2010a, "How to Detect an Asset Bubble", Working Paper, Cornell University.

Jarrow, R., P. Protter and K. Shimbo, 2010b, "Asset Price Bubbles in Incomplete Markets", *Mathematical Finance* 20(2), pp. 145–85.

Kotani, S., 2006"On a Condition that One-Dimensional Diffusion Processes are Martingales", in *In Memoriam Paul-André Meyer: Séminaire de Probabilités XXXIX*, Lecture Notes in Mathematics, Volume 1874, pp. 149–56 (Springer).

Loewenstein, M., and G. A. Willard, 2000a, "Rational Equilibrium Asset-Pricing Bubbles in Continuous Trading Models", *Journal of Economic Theory* 91 (1), pp. 17–58.

Loewenstein, M., and G. A. Willard, 2000b, "Local Martingales, Arbitrage and Viability: Free Snacks and Cheap Thrills", *Economic Theory* 16, pp. 135–61.

Merton, R. C., 1973, "Theory of Rational Option Pricing", *Bell Journal of Economics* 4(1), pp. 141–83.

Mijatović, A., and M. Urusov, 2010, "On the Martingale Property of Certain Local Martingales", *Probability Theory and Related Fields*, DOI:10.1007/s00440-010-0314-7.

O'Connell, S., and S. Zeldes, 1988, "Rational Ponzi Games", *International Economic Review* 29(3), pp. 431–50.

Protter, P., 2005, "Stochastic Integration and Differential Equations", in *Stochastic Integration and Differential Equations*, Version 2.1, Stochastic Modelling and Applied Probability, Volume 21, Second Edition (Springer).

Santos, M., and M. Woodford, 1997, "Rational Asset Pricing Bubbles", *Econometrica* 65(1), pp. 19–57.

Scheinkman, J., and W. Xiong, 2003, "Overconfidence and Speculative Bubbles", *Journal of Political Economy* 111(6), pp. 1183–219.

Scheinkman, J., and W. Xiong, 2004, "Heterogeneous Beliefs, Speculation and Trading in Financial Markets", Working Paper, Princeton University.

Shreve, S., 2004, *Stochastic Calculus for Finance II: Continuous Time Models* (Springer).

Schweizer, M., and J. Wissel, 2008, "Term Structures of Implied Volatilities: Absence of Arbitrage and Existence Results", *Mathematical Finance* 18, pp. 77–114.

Sin, C., 1998, "Complications with Stochastic Volatility Models", *Advances in Applied Probability* 30, pp. 256–68.

Tirole, J., 1982, "On the Possibility of Speculation under Rational Expectations", *Econometrica* 50(5), pp. 1163–82.

Tirole, J., 1985, "Asset Bubbles and Overlapping Generations", *Econometrica* 53(5), pp. 1071–1100.

Weil, P., 1990, "On the Possibility of Price Decreasing Bubbles", *Econometrica* 58(6), pp. 1467–74.

Part VI

Lessons for Investors

19

Managing through a Crisis: Practical Insights and Lessons Learned for Quantitatively Managed Equity Portfolios

Peter J. Zangari
Goldman Sachs

What challenges do investment professionals face when they manage portfolios through a financial crisis? What lessons can be learned from such an experience? In this chapter, we discuss how the 2007–10 credit crisis affected[1] quantitative equity investment management and how this experience will affect this investment style for years to come.[2]

Quantitative equity portfolios invest primarily in stocks and are actively managed against a benchmark. The benchmark may be a well-defined equity portfolio (eg, the S&P 500 Index portfolio) or the risk-free rate (cash). Portfolio weights are derived, in part, from computer-based models and result from a systematic, reproducible[3] investment process. Their underlying investment strategies rely on some combination of mathematical, statistical and economic models, and the testing that goes into assessing their efficacy is scientific and data intensive. In addition to formal models, some quantitative investment styles employ fundamentals-based economic intuition. Following an extended period of strong performance in the early-to-mid-2000s, many quantitatively managed equity portfolios began to face an exceptionally challenging period. This period coincided with the advent of the global credit crisis.

Some early signs of the crisis, particularly as it relates to subprime losses, appeared in early 2007.[4,5] Losses associated with the crisis contributed to the so-called "Quant Crunch" that occurred in August

2007. For quants, this event ushered in, and in some cases perpetuated, a very challenging period in terms of day-to-day portfolio management and investment performance. For example, as a result of the general poor performance in 2006–7, managers faced significant outflows in a number of their strategies. These outflows resulted in periods of de-leveraging and de-risking across the industry as managers were forced to raise cash.

As the broader economy was affected by the crisis and the corresponding response by governments worldwide, the investment environment continued to be challenging. For example, we observed the following shock waves.

- In 2008, the collapse of Lehman Brothers spurred increased operational risks associated with stock lending, collateral and cash management.

- In the third quarter of 2008 and, again, beginning in early March 2009 as stock markets began to rally worldwide, price momentum (a common investment strategy for some quants) suffered significant drawdowns.

- In 2010, the financial stability of sovereigns came into focus as credit default swap (CDS) spreads widened for some countries, (eg, Greece, Portugal) to unprecedented levels.

Each wave presented managers with a set of unique and, in some cases, unprecedented challenges. Managers who worked through these events were forced to evaluate and enhance their investment processes and platforms so as to not only weather the storm but be better prepared to face future disruptions. Looking ahead, successful managers (that is, those who achieve their well-defined investment objectives and uphold their fiduciary responsibilities) will be those who understand, appreciate and proactively respond to the challenges confronted during the crisis.

This chapter is organised as follows. We discuss the effect of the crisis on various aspects of a quantitative equity investment process. Specifically, for a fundamentals-based, low-frequency strategy, we describe the investment process and the impact of the crisis in terms of models and data, day-to-day portfolio management (or what we call "production") and risk management.

THE DIFFERENT FLAVOURS OF QUANTITATIVE EQUITY INVESTING

What do we mean by quantitative equity investing? Quantitative equity investing may refer to various styles of building and managing investment strategies. Broadly, we classify these different styles as fundamentals based and mathematically or statistically based.[6] While both styles may employ statistical or mathematical models, the reader should think about their differences in terms of the portfolio manager's investment thesis. In the case of fundamentals-based quantitative management, the portfolio manager begins with an idea based on economic intuition when developing a strategy, whereas a manager who employs a mathematically based philosophy considers only patterns in data or mathematical relationships. The infrastructure requirements supporting model development, portfolio and risk management and trading can be substantial, depending on the specifics of the strategies involved as well as the number of portfolios managed. For example, strategies with very short holding periods (eg, measured in seconds or minutes) and involving large numbers of stocks require relatively sophisticated technology for both model development and testing, as well as trading. Such relatively "low latency" strategies pay particular attention to the time it takes to incorporate new information into their model and create a new set of trades.[7] These strategies are statistically or mathematically based. On the other hand, strategies which have much lower turnover or longer holding periods (measured in months) would not have such demands on technology. Such strategies are usually associated with the fundamentals-based approach. A clear exception is a strategy which manages a large a number of bespoke equity portfolios,[8] In this case, technological demands can be high given the relatively large number of portfolios that need to be managed across many different models and strategies. In this chapter, we focus on the investment process associated with the fundamentals-based factor-model approach, which incorporates relatively low turnover.[9]

THE WAVES AND THEIR EFFECTS

A good deal has been written and continues to be written about the 2007–10 crisis and its effect on the economy, the financial industry and quantitative investing. Khadani and Lo (2007), Patterson (2010) and Brown (2010) explore the quantitative investment process and how it was affected by the crisis. We characterise the impact of the crisis on quantitative investing and lessons learned in terms of reactions and responses to three waves. In brief, these waves and their impact are as follows.

Quant crunch

During the period August 3 to August 9, 2007, several prominent, quantitatively managed funds produced extraordinarily negative intra-day and daily returns.[10] Based on research and analysis conducted by academics and industry practitioners, this event was the result of widespread unwinding of common or "crowded" positions. The unwinding itself was precipitated by the need to raise capital from relatively liquid securities in reaction to (initially unrelated) losses from the subprime crisis. During this period, levered, market neutral equity portfolios went into what Brunnermeier (2009) calls a "liquidity spiral". Such spirals arise when lower prices induce liquidations, which then lower prices further. In other words, funding requirements for the portfolio increase as collateral value erodes and margins increase.

The reaction by some quantitative managers to such an event was multi-fold. First, the idea that investment strategies were common and crowded led to the pursuit of so-called proprietary strategies (or "factors" in quantitative managers' parlance). Second, intra-day monitoring of performance and risk came into focus. This was the result of realising severe intra-day losses over this period. Since the low-frequency strategy is considered to be a "long-term investment", before the crisis portfolio returns and risk estimates were monitored on a daily, weekly or even monthly basis. In fact, daily monitoring would have been considered an industry best practice. Third, the practical reality of managing levered portfolios in a period when prices were under intense pressure underscored the importance of (funding) liquidity management, ie, the ease with which managers can obtain funding for their strategies (Brunnermeier 2009; Pedersen 2009).

Lehman Brothers' collapse

The collapse of Lehman on September 15, 2008, sent shock waves throughout the global financial community. In particular, its collapse greatly amplified operational risk within the investment process.

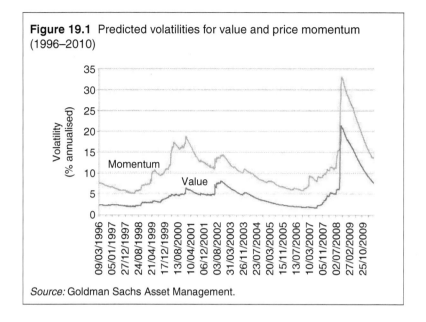

Figure 19.1 Predicted volatilities for value and price momentum (1996–2010)

Source: Goldman Sachs Asset Management.

This is the risk associated with the verification of the existence, location and valuation of securities and cash, ie, positions, held at third parties such as prime brokers and custodians. Such information is critical for day-to-day portfolio management and for calculating and reporting investment performance. Without an accurate and verifiable account of portfolio positions, portfolio management effectively shuts down. Also, during this period, governments imposed various restrictions on short selling.[11] Such restrictions, imposed at short notice, added significant complexities to daily portfolio management.

To get a sense as to the impact of this event on quantitative managers, Figure 19.1 shows time series of predicted volatilities for value (black) and price momentum (grey) strategies from September 1996 to May 2010. The dramatic peak in volatility towards the latter part of the period corresponds to the Lehman event.

The Lehman event and its impact were by no means unique to quantitative managers. However, given that many such managers employed leverage and actively managed thousands of stocks, they were particularly susceptible to this event. A clear lesson is that, to mitigate operation risk, managers should take steps including using multi-prime broker arrangements, periodically reassessing stock

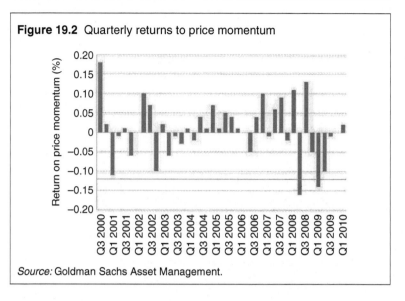

Figure 19.2 Quarterly returns to price momentum

Source: Goldman Sachs Asset Management.

lending programmes and developing the appropriate infrastructure to monitor stock positions on a continuous basis.

The price momentum investment strategy

The price momentum investment strategy (ie, factor) is represented by a portfolio of stocks which has positive (long) exposure to stocks that have had positive performance, say, over the past year, and negative (short) exposure to stocks that have had negative performance over the same period. As we would expect, the price momentum factor generates poor performance when stocks abruptly reverse course, such as at around the peak of a rally or around the bottom of a correction. In the summer of 2008[12] and again in spring of 2009,[13] the price momentum factor realised very large drawdowns. Figure 19.2 shows a time series of returns to the global price momentum factor from Q3 2000 to Q2 2010.

While a quant's investment decisions are driven primarily by a well-researched model, there are clearly circumstances where independent judgement is not only desirable but necessary. In fact, incorporating judgement into quantitative investing should be part of the process and not considered an exception. It is a core part of managing model risk. An example of when judgement is required is when a manager observes returns which are grossly inconsistent[14] with their model's forecasts.

In order to understand an investment process and its functioning, it is important to understand the terminology that describes it. In the next section we describe some key components of a representative fundamentals-based quantitative investment process.[15]

THE INVESTMENT PROCESS
Models and data
This section provides a brief description of the role that models and data play in the investment process.

Models
A quantitative equity portfolio manager's investment decisions start with defining their investment universe. An investment universe is a set of stocks over which a manager will make decisions such as going long or short a stock, or under or over weight relative to what a benchmark portfolio holds. In the case of a long-only manager, that is, a manager who does not short any stocks, the universe is determined largely by the stocks held by the benchmark. Given a universe of names, the manager forms a portfolio using mean–variance optimisation. That is, given a set of inputs defining stock-level expected returns, risk and transaction-cost estimates, the optimal portfolio is the solution to a portfolio optimisation problem which maximises portfolio expected return, net of transaction-costs, while penalising risk. Conventionally, risk is defined in terms of portfolio standard deviation, and portfolio alpha is based on stock-level alphas. The portfolio standard deviation is derived from a risk model (ie, a covariance matrix), which is defined in terms of factor volatilities and correlations, and idiosyncratic volatilities.

In the fundamentals-based approach, the linear cross-sectional factor model is the workhorse for building stock-level alphas and risk estimates. Some of the earliest work on this model can be found in Rosenberg *et al* (1973). Litterman (2003) provides a more recent review of this model. In short, this model attempts to explain the cross-section or dispersion of stock returns (over a day, for example) in terms of a linear combination of predefined variables which, in the quantitative investment literature, are often referred to as "factors". Unfortunately, the term "factor" can often lead to confusion, since its definition depends on how it is used in the investment process. For the purposes of this discussion, the reader should think of a factor as a portfolio of stocks that represents an investment idea which the manager wants to use to capture alpha or manage risk, or both. We refer to a factor whose primary purpose is to capture alpha as a "return factor". Similarly, risk factors are those which have risk (ie, volatility) and which co-vary with other factors, but which generate no alpha (or, at least, no alpha that can be captured in the broader investment process). When we build a portfolio, we do so to gain exposure to return factors and minimise (or, at least control) exposure to risk factors. Since we want to control the amount of exposure we get from risk factors, these are sometimes called control factors.

Mathematically, the linear cross-sectional factor model posits a cross-sectional relationship between security returns and their exposures to factors

$$R(t) = B(t-1)F(t) + e(t) \tag{19.1}$$

where, here, time is measured in days, and one business day is defined from the previous close of business (COB) at date t to the next close COB at date $t + 1$. $R(t)$ is an N-vector (cross-section) of stock returns for a relevant universe computed from $t - 1$ to t.

$B(t-1)$ is an N (stocks) $\times$ K (factors) matrix of factor exposures. There are K factors, each representing a column in B. Note that the nth row of B represents, for the nth stock, its "weight" in each of the K factors. Considering these weights as a measure of a stock's exposure to the various investment ideas, this matrix is often referred to as an exposure matrix.

$F(t)$ is a K-vector of factor payouts or returns to each of the K factors. Note that in this model, these payouts are unobserved and are estimated via regression.[16]

$e(t)$ is an N-vector of idiosyncratic returns. This variable gets quite a bit of attention from both portfolio managers and investors (clients), as it represents, in effect, a component of returns that is not explicitly defined by the investment model, ie, the collection of factors which we believe to describe return and risk.

By estimating Equation 19.1 over consecutive days, we produce a time series of factor and idiosyncratic (ie, specific) returns. Given this time series, we can estimate a covariance matrix of factor returns (S) and variances for the idiosyncratic returns (D). From Equation 19.1, we have what we refer to as the risk model

$$V = BSB^T + D \qquad (19.2)$$

There are many ways to construct stock-level alphas. For example, stock-level alphas can be constructed by first computing time series of factor returns and then averaging them over time.[17] We can represent these alphas by

$$\alpha = Bw \qquad (19.3)$$

where w is a K-vector of factor premia. Managers can construct these weights using historical data, priors or some combination of priors and historical data.

How does a manager select factors that belong to Equation 19.2? The manager may use a combination of economic intuition and statistical testing. In terms of statistics, managers study the t-statistics of the time series of factor returns. Specifically, they compute so-called Fama–MacBeth t-statistics.[18]

Transaction costs inform the optimisation problem about stock-level liquidity and how trading may affect market prices. A typical transaction cost model consists of two components: bid–ask spread and market impact. The bid–ask spread measures a stock's liquidity. That is, the wider (narrower) the spread, the less (more) liquid the stock. An estimate of the stock's total trading cost is defined in terms of the spread between the execution price and some reference or benchmark price. For example, a model for the per-unit transaction cost for the nth stock can be written as

$$\text{Per-unit transaction cost} = \text{per-unit cost}$$
$$= a + b(\text{TradeSize})^c \qquad (19.4)$$

where a represents the bid–ask spread; b captures market impact, c specifies the functional relationship between per-unit transaction cost and trade size and "TradeSize" represents the number of shares traded.

We can estimate parameters a, b and c from a cross-sectional regression of transaction cost on trade size.

Measuring and capturing market impact is of particular interest to quants who are concerned about how their trading affects prices. This is true particularly for those who believe that their strategies may be crowded, or at least have the potential to be crowded. As we discuss in the penultimate section, properly accounting for market impact is a critical part of strategy development and an important lesson from the credit crisis.

Data and data management

While models, model development and deployment are an essential part of quantitative investment management, data is its lifeblood. These models are data intensive and require relatively sophisticated data management tools to source and maintain the various vendor feeds. There are two ways in which data and data management enter into the investment process. One is in terms of the research process. The other is in terms of day-to-day portfolio management.

Fundamentals-based quantitative managers are large consumers of data. Traditionally, managers have tended to think of potential enhancements to one of their models and then seek the requisite data to compute whatever is needed (assuming the data exists). Historically, the data used in the investment process has been sourced from well known providers of market, economic, fundamental and other company-specific data. Once feeds have been established from the vendor, the data is taken in-house and analysed. Researchers spend considerable time checking the data for inaccuracies and normalising it[19] so that it can be processed alongside other data sourced from other vendors.

To be a bit more specific, the data that we are referring to is what is known as "structured data". That is, the data whose content, format and definitions are well defined and known ahead of time (ie, ahead of incorporating them into the investment process). Researchers build models taking these data as given, ie, exogenous to the research effort.

As will become clearer in the next section, quantitative managers have begun to redefine how they think of data and how it is used in the investment process. This is the result of managers pursuing so-called proprietary factors as well as advances in the field of natural language processing (NLP). Data, as we will see, is in some cases endogenous to the research process. That is, a data set that is used to construct return factor exposures is an output of the research process.

In addition to research, data management plays a critical role in the day-to-day portfolio management process.[20] It involves various aspects of cleaning and verifying data used in portfolio construction, which include the following.

- Pre-optimisation position checks: these are the checks performed prior to running optimisations to rebalance portfolios.
- Identifying, storing and representing (to the optimiser) various constraints and guidelines.
- Timely processing of corporate actions.
- Coordinating with custodians and prime brokers to verify, value and reconcile positions, including cash held and, where applicable, stocks on loan.

As we will discuss later on, during the collapse of Lehman Brothers the operational risk associated with custodial and prime broker relationships increased greatly and this event painfully demonstrated the potential costs of not properly managing operational risk.

Backtesting and strategy development

Backtesting is a way to assess a strategy's potential performance. It can be an important tool to help a manager understand how a strategy will perform once it goes into production. In addition to providing a sense for what type of returns the strategy may generate, backtests can provide some guidance in terms of portfolio risk and exposure that the manager can expect.

In a typical backtest, a portfolio is rebalanced sequentially as if it were actually managed for a client and traded. This requires time-series information on stock prices and returns, corporate actions, models, etc. Alternatively, backtests can take the form of running "paper portfolios", where a manager essentially builds a portfolio and assesses its performance through mimicking the exact production process (portfolio construction), except that there is no trading.

Employing backtests to help evaluate a strategy is a not uncommon practice. However, the interpretation and evaluation of backtest results can be difficult, at best, and misleading, at worst. Traditionally, a key challenge with interpreting backtest results is that they are overly optimistic about a strategy's potential. Such biased results emanate from two sources.

(i) Model enhancements are tested and developed over some historical data set, and therefore the fact that a strategy does well over a historical backtest period is a reflection not so much of its future potential as of how it was constructed. For example, a strategy which tilts on (ie, gets exposure to) a particular factor might do well simply because the factor did well historically over the backtest period and not because of any ability to anticipate the future.

(ii) Unless modelled explicitly, backtests ignore the complex interaction between trading and stock prices. For example, in production, when a portfolio is constructed and the resulting trades are executed, these trades affect prices. Depending on market dynamics and portfolio size, this impact can persist over an extended period of time and can materially affect performance.

In light of the Quant Crunch and subsequent de-risking, the second point has received a considerable amount of attention. As we discuss later, the crisis should challenge managers to reassess the way they run backtests so that they produce a more accurate picture of potential performance.

Portfolio management and production

The representative investment management process that we are discussing takes models and builds and trades portfolios on a regular basis.[21] This process, by which models are estimated and portfolios are built and traded to generate client profit and loss, is what we refer to as "production". Next, we describe production in terms of portfolio operations and portfolio construction.

Portfolio operations

Though they may be perceived as mundane, portfolio operations are a critical part of portfolio management. For the purposes of this discussion, we define portfolio operations as the responsibilities associated with ensuring portfolio position integrity, maintaining and managing cash balances and establishing and managing custodial accounts and prime broker relationships.[22] A successful portfolio operations effort is one that

(i) provides complete and timely transparency on portfolio positions,

(ii) minimises operational risk associated with day-to-day portfolio management, and

(iii) successfully performs (i) and (ii) while allowing the portfolio manager to achieve their investment objective.

By "transparency" we mean the ability to value and locate all portfolio positions (ie, where they are held, what counterparties hold them, etc), including any securities on loan.[23]

Portfolio construction

Portfolio construction is the process of creating a set of trades to better align a current portfolio with its investment objectives. It is a critical part of day-to-day production. For managers who build portfolios using mean–variance optimisation, this is the part of the process that employs an optimiser. More specifically, portfolio construction works as follows. Given an initial set of starting positions, a benchmark portfolio, model inputs (risk, alpha and t-costs), an objective(s), client guidelines and other constraints or restrictions, these inputs are fed into an optimiser to generate suggested trades to reach the target portfolio. A timeline for portfolio construction is given in the following example.

(i) Build models (alpha, risk, t-cost) using information as of COB $t-1$. This involves cleaning and processing data on day t.
(ii) Given the model data and inputs from $t-1$, rebalance (ie, optimise) portfolios on t.
(iii) Trade portfolios on day t.

Portfolio rebalance frequency varies with portfolio manager and strategy. For many quantitative managers, particularly those using the models and processes discussed herein, the frequency can vary from daily (ie, a portfolio is rebalanced every day) to monthly. The rebalance cycle frequency is a function of the speed at which the factors turn over. That is to say, the faster the weights comprising a factor change, the higher the rebalance frequency required to maintain a certain level of exposure (all other things being equal).

Finally, and as presented above, model building, portfolio construction and trading are discrete processes. The model gets built, the portfolio and trades are formed and then the resulting trades are sent out for execution. In light of the 2007–10 crisis, there should be an increase in focus on the interaction between these three areas and, in particular, the interaction between portfolio construction and trading. As discussed later, there should be a considerable move, in some regard, towards a world where trading is informing portfolio construction (via updated transaction costs, for example) in a more regular way than simply taking transaction costs as exogenous.

Risk management

While risk management can take on many different meanings, at its core it is about maximising enterprise value. Its about maximising alpha within an environment (people, processes and systems) that is committed to identifying, evaluating and managing risks. This commitment manifests itself through the dedication of resources and a culture that stresses the importance of risk management (Golub and Crum 2010b).

Investment risk management consists of identifying risks; this requires measuring and monitoring risks, properly interpreting and understanding risks and adapting the investment process to manage risks appropriately. Investment managers face various types of risk including market, fiduciary, credit, counterparty, operational and legal risks, among many others. Effective risk management cannot be done independently of the investment process. Rather, it should take place at various stages within the investment process, ie, during model development, backtesting, portfolio construction and trading.

Measuring and assessing risk

Though risk management proper includes the management of various types of risks, in this section we focus on market risks, ie, risks which relate portfolio returns to returns on the market and returns on the underlying positions. Focusing specifically on equity portfolios, market risks have traditionally been assessed by looking at position exposures (eg, whether you are over- or underweight a position relative to benchmark), portfolio volatility or tracking error[24] and contributions (at the position or factor level) to tracking error. Such contributions to tracking error (CTE) have been a staple of quantitative equity risk management for some time. This is because portfolio risk is defined in terms of volatility or standard deviation. CTE is defined as the derivative or change in portfolio volatility given a change in some underlying position. An attractive feature of CTE, unlike simply looking at exposures, is that it is a function of the position in question, the volatility of that position and the correlation of that position with other positions in the portfolio. The volatility and correlations are based on the linear cross-sectional factor model (Equation 19.2). Hence, any correlation among stock positions must come through the factors as defined in the risk model.

In this context, risk measurement depends heavily on the ability of factor volatilities and correlations capturing risk. In an effort to hedge against some of the inherent model risk, it is often supplemented with stress tests and scenario analysis.

Reporting

As stated at the beginning of this section, risk monitoring is a key function of risk management. Therefore, good risk management demands good reporting. Timely, accurate and readily accessible reports which provide information on positions, portfolio risks, sources of risk and return, trade orders and other pertinent information are critical to ensuring the transparency required to help identify risks. A reporting infrastructure which can produce and support hundreds and possibly thousands of reports is particularly important in a process that manages a large number of separate accounts (ie, large-scale management). There are three important aspects of reporting: distribution, analytics, or content, and what we refer to as "content display".

- Distribution relates to making reports available to consumers. This is particularly important for managers who manage a large number of separate accounts, as more traditional methods which rely on spreadsheets, for example, make it difficult if not impossible to distribute reports in a timely manner. Advances in Web-based reporting over the past decade have facilitated such reporting.

- Analytics, or content, defines the substance of the reports which supports the decision making process.

- Content display refers to how the material contained in a report is displayed. In many ways this aspect of reporting is the most critical, particularly when (as is almost always the case), a manager has limited time to read and interpret data and the data is of a high-dimensional nature (ie, the manager's portfolio consists of hundreds of stocks).

As discussed in the next section, good reporting is indispensable in times of crisis, not only for telling management what their present risks and positions are but to help them think through how different scenarios will affect their investment decisions.

FUTURE DIRECTIONS

In this section, we discuss reactions to the crisis, lessons learned and future directions for quantitative equity portfolio management. The crisis affected virtually every aspect of the quantitative investment process. As a result, managers must reassess their current process and methodologies and focus on both short- and longer-term enhancements. The focus on short-term enhancements and adjustments is critical, as it is unknown when the crisis will end. Longer-term enhancements range from improving one or more particular areas to surveying the complete investment process and re-thinking virtually every aspect. The overall impact of some of the effects of the crisis on quantitative equity portfolio management may be summarised as follows.

- **Operational risk.** The 2007–10 crisis drew attention to operational risk. Abruptly, managers came to realise risks associated with simply running their day-to-day investment process. Such risks relate to cash management, managing custodial and prime broker relationships, managing collateral and getting timely and accurate marks on positions. In response, managers should redouble efforts to make sure that the appropriate controls are in place to better manage operational risk. During a crisis it is also important to have the capability (ie, infrastructure) to make changes to the investment process based on qualitative judgement (eg, to bring down risk over and above what a model may be suggesting). This is particularly true for managers responsible for a large number of accounts. Failure to have an infrastructure which can support large, tactical changes to portfolios can leave a manager with very limited options in times of market stress.
- **Liquidity risk.** The Quant Crunch, in particular, demonstrated the potentially damaging effects of unwinding large positions quickly. This can lead to what Litzenberger and Modest (2008) refer to as "trade-driven losses". The crisis put tremendous

stress on levered portfolios, which experienced large negative returns. In situations where there is not enough cash on hand to cover margin calls, managers are required to raise cash. This involves reducing or closing positions which, for relatively large funds, adds to position price pressure and compounds negative performance. As a result of this experience, managers should employ a formal framework for measuring and assessing liquidity risk that includes assessing the price impact of liquidating positions over different time periods.

- **Endogenous data and proprietary research.** Researchers will want to focus on developing and incorporating proprietary factors. In some cases, the search for proprietary factors will change the way researchers use and incorporate data. This involves exploring ways that make the data that they use to build their signals endogenous to their research process. For example, there is technology which "reads" electronic news articles and converts unstructured data into structured data, which can be used to build a new signal. In this situation, the content (extracted data fields) is at the complete discretion of the researcher.

- **Linear factor model.** As researchers develop new ways to estimate factors, it is natural to also rethink a cornerstone of the research process: the linear cross-sectional factor model. An important limitation of this model relates to how factor payouts are estimated via least squares. Relatively recent advances in statistics provide interesting alternatives which can help researchers provide a more systematic and robust way of identifying and including factors in their investment process. So-called least absolute shrinkage and selection operator (Lasso) and least angular regression (LAR) models may prove very useful in this regard (Hastie *et al* 2009).

- **Capacity.** The larger a fund's assets under management (AUM),[25] the more difficult it is for the fund to attain its investment objectives, all other things being equal. The goal of capacity analysis is to quantify the relationship between the size of a portfolio or strategy (eg, the total dollar exposure that it manages) and its ability to generate alpha and manage risk, net of transaction costs. The 2007–10 crisis has affected the way managers think about and manage investment and trading capacity. Specifically, the crisis underscored the significant challenges faced by large funds relative to smaller ones. As a result of the greater focus on capacity and the need to better understand the interaction between fund size and market impact due to trading, managers should enhance the methods and associated infrastructure which are used to assess a strategy's potential performance. For example, if a manager uses backtests to assess potential performance, the backtests should be able to properly account for how the growth in a strategy's assets affects performance.

- **Contagion risk.** The crisis will lead to a greater focus on contagion risk. Equity portfolio managers who traditionally rely almost exclusively on equity risk factor models should pay much closer attention to metrics which measure the risk within non-equity asset classes and across equity and non-equity assets.

  The need to better understand contagion should force managers to develop tools to help them assess and interpret the cross-effects of a large number of factors which span multiple asset classes. Relatively recent developments in business intelligence reporting, also sometimes referred to as data visualisation, will help managers evaluate the interconnectedness of numerous markets and factors. Such reporting is interactive, ie, it allows the manager to interact with the data in real time, so that there is a feedback loop between the questions they want to explore and the report they want to see. Such reporting is an important step in increasing the transparency of the investment process and will help to identify and manage contagion risk.

- **Drawdown control.** Drawdown control has a relatively long history in the hedge fund space. It can be an effective way for managers to manage downside risk when their current risk procedures (which rely on a covariance matrix, for example) do not perform as expected or if a manager simply wants to further reduce the chance of observing a large negative portfolio loss. In addition to common risk controls, which rely on a factor-based covariance matrix, managers should seriously consider employing some form of drawdown control in their investment process. Drawdown control is effectively a constraint on the investment process. As a result, there is a cost associated with it. Therefore, a prudent manager needs to assess such costs and determine how to employ drawdown control in such a way that they understand its impact on the overall investment process and can quantify its costs.

- **Adaptability.** During crisis periods, portfolio management goes through three phases. The first phase is the assessment of your positions and exposures and to understand how they affect performance. Time is of the essence in this phase, so it is imperative to know this information in real time. In the second phase, managers discuss the situation and what actions, if any, need to be taken to adapt to the current environment. The third phase, if necessary, is to take action.

For example, in periods of extraordinarily high market risk, a manager may decide to bring down risk (ie, lower the amount of risk that a set of portfolios is targeting). In order to determine specific next steps, a manager should run a set of tests to calibrate how much to reduce risk and the time period necessary. These decisions are based on considerations of market impact and some assessment of how long current market conditions may persist. In such an environment, it is absolutely critical for the manager to rely on an infrastructure which allows them to quickly and efficiently effect production changes. Maximal efficiency occurs when the research environment used to conduct testing mirrors the production environment. That is to say, the impact of a production change as evaluated in the research environment should be the same as when evaluated in the actual production environment. Such a seamless integration between research and production environments[26] is key to providing the nimbleness required for a dynamic portfolio management process. Inconsistencies between research and production environments result in an error-prone investment process.

Models and data

This section discusses future developments in models and data.

Models

In the realm of modelling, researchers will continue to seek out new sources of alpha as well as better ways to estimate risk and transaction costs. A primary motivation (and one that has been widely written about) is to seek new sources of alpha by moving away from crowded factors and trades, towards so-called proprietary factors. In so doing, researchers should seek the smallest set of factors that generate alpha and capture risk.

In addition to searching for proprietary factors, researchers should think critically about how they assess factor efficacy in the context of the linear cross-sectional factor model (Equation 19.1). Namely, in addition to factor definition, researchers should focus on model selection (ie, determining which factors should be included in the model). Based on published work at least, this line of research seems to have been overlooked by investment management industry practitioners.

Why is this topic important? In response to the 2007–10 crisis, and the Quant Crunch in particular, managers began rethinking their risk and return factors. As a result, there are a potentially large number of candidate factors to be considered for inclusion into their alpha and risk models. Furthermore, when we estimate Equation 19.1 by using the least-squares method, we are imposing certain restrictions, which may be inconsistent with the manager's views, on the investment process. For example, for identification purposes, the ordinary least-squares (OLS) method requires that the number of observations in a cross-section be greater than the number of regressors. It is this structure which can be an important determinant when deciding which factors should be included in the alpha and risk models. Given a large set of factors that are already included in the investment process, it is statistically challenging to add new factors, simply due to the limitations of the estimation process. Similarly, if the set of factors that the researcher would like to add to the model are highly correlated (either with each other or with the current factors), estimation can range from difficult to impossible. This work is ultimately a lesson in dimension reduction.

Such issues should encourage managers to seek methods which allow them to systematically reduce a large-dimensional space of factors. This can be done by letting the data help them select the relevant factors in explaining the cross-section of returns. Such methods, which include statistical shrinkage methods for linear regression, should serve well to supplement a manager's prior as to what factors belong in the model and, therefore, their investment process. Examples of such methods include Lasso, which was proposed by Tibshirani (1996), and LAR, which was proposed by Efron *et al* (2004).

When motivating the Lasso to address some shortcomings with OLS, Tibshirani (1996, p. 267) notes that

> there are two reasons that a data analyst may not be satisfied with OLS estimates. The first is prediction accuracy: the OLS estimates often have low bias but large variance; prediction accuracy can sometimes be improved by shrinking or setting to 0 some coefficients.... The second reason is interpretation. With a large number of predictors, we often would like to determine a smaller subset that exhibits the stronger effects.

Finally, in practice, researchers assess a factor's efficacy by evaluating the time-series Fama–MacBeth *t*-statistics of the factor returns which are generated from sequentially estimating Equation 19.1. One important question that seems to have received little attention is how misspecification in the cross-section affects time-series inference. For example, if a researcher does not include a particular factor in the cross-section, how does this affect the time-series inference of a factor that is included, assuming that these factors do not have non-zero correlation? It is questions such as these that managers should address as part of their model due-diligence process.

Data and data management

As researchers pursue proprietary sources of alpha, one of the potentially significant developments affecting quantitative equity portfolio management will be in the areas of computer science, linguistics and data, and their combined role in the research process. This work involves advances in the field of natural language processing.

Among other things, NLP and its related fields involve the design and implementation of computer programs which create structured data sets from unstructured data. As noted earlier, structured data is data that is stored according to a data model (any well-known database) and that is easily usable by a computer program. Unstructured data, on the other hand, is not easily usable or read by a computer and, rather, a bespoke program needs to be written, sometimes, depending on need, by someone with expertise in linguistics. Examples of unstructured data include text from articles or documents.

Traditionally, as described earlier, data supporting the construction of return and risk factors was viewed mainly as exogenous to the research process. That is to say, a manager would construct an idea for a new signal based on, say, economic intuition, and then find a vendor that could provide the required data. An obvious example is that if a manager thought "value" was a signal to which they wanted to gain exposure, they would seek company book value and price data.

Looking ahead, an increasing amount of data used in research will be endogenous to the research process. That is, the researcher will use computer programs to read articles and construct their own structured data set from some unstructured data set.

Let us consider a simple, hypothetical example to make the discussion above concrete. Suppose a manager is interested in better understanding the relationship between the stock returns of automotive companies and the attributes of the cars that they sell. Examples of attributes include car model, colour, geographical location of sales, etc). Further, suppose that the manager can obtain electronic versions of automotive reviews which are often provided by some third party. Since the reviews are in human-readable form, the manager needs to figure out a way to convert this information into a database which, for each automotive company, would allow him to create time-series data of returns and of the various automotive attributes. The researcher could use a computer program to scan for "key words" and use these as a basis for the newly constructed database. More importantly, however, the researcher could use a computer program to infer additional information about the reviewer's overall assessment of the car or any other "soft" attribute based on parsing phraseology. Given this information, the researcher can then build signals. Clearly, an attractive feature of this approach is that the manager has more control over how to define the attributes rather than having them exogenously defined by a data vendor.

Backtests and strategy development

A very challenging but important aspect of strategy development is to try to quantify how a particular strategy would perform in a crisis and how difficult it would be to change the strategy's risk profile in a crisis environment. For example, a manager should have a reasonable estimate of what it would cost (in terms of transaction costs) to lower a portfolio's risk level.

Stress testing is often used to evaluate a strategy's performance in stress market environments.[27] For example, a portfolio or risk manager might want to know what the expected impact on portfolio performance would be if the stock market falls by 20% over three days. Though traditional stress testing is potentially useful, it does not provide the manager with a complete picture of performance including the scenario at hand as well as the performance pre- and post scenario. Backtests may be helpful in providing a more complete picture of performance.

The crisis demonstrated how quickly portfolio performance can turn, as well as the potential for extreme drawdowns over very short time periods and, when this happens, how performance is driven primarily by liquidity supply and demand. The fact that an investment strategy can affect prices, which, in turn, affect its performance, is a feature that must be adequately captured in backtests. Failure to do to so ignores a very important message. In fact, an important objective of backtests should be to understand how market impact and capacity affects performance over different market cycles.

The key challenge with the way that backtests are usually run is that they use market data which is the result of what has actually occurred in the past, ie, they are a function of actual production trades. In other words, observed returns are used. The market impact from the backtested strategy is not considered when assessing its performance. Looking ahead, researchers should develop backtesting methods which allow them to understand how a backtested strategy affects market impact. Among other things, this requires adjusting observed market prices for historical market impact.

Portfolio management and production

During the crisis, operational risk increased dramatically, particularly in the area of portfolio operations and portfolio construction. This highlights the need for a much greater focus on assessing and managing operational risk.

Portfolio operations

As managers learn from the 2007–10 crisis and seek to minimise operational risk going forward, they should be sure to consider the following.

- Prime broker agreements should be regularly reviewed to make sure terms are consistent with current and anticipated market conditions. This review should include a complete and accurate understanding of contractual terms related to trading positions, collateral and rehypothecation of securities.
- Multi-prime broker arrangements should be entered into in order to diversify operational risk by spreading business among a number of prime brokers. In times of crisis, in particular, this will provide the manager with options for moving cash and securities to safer custody. Managers should be particularly mindful of rehypothecation arrangements.[28] Rehypothecation means that the collateral posted by a prime brokerage client (eg, hedge fund) to their prime broker can also be used as collateral by the prime broker for their own purposes (Singh and Aitken 2009).
- The manager should understand not only where assets are being held, but also the contractual provisions and legal remedies that exist should a prime broker or other counterparty default.
- The manager should seek to avoid unsecured exposure to a prime broker through tri-party arrangements where a prime broker provides financing and short-selling secured by pledged collateral (long securities and cash) which is held by a third party, such as a bank.
- Funding costs should be optimised and unnecessary counterparty exposure should be minimised.
- Regular and rigorous reconciliations should be performed with all counterparties in order to ensure that daily margin requirements are based on the correct set of positions and with agreed-upon terms.

Portfolio construction

As discussed earlier, the Quant Crunch shone a spotlight on crowded positions. As a result, managers should pay much closer attention to their specific positions and try to ascertain which are deemed to be crowded. One way to assess whether a position is crowded is to try to figure out if it is held broadly by competitors. There are a few potential sources of position level information which a manager will find useful. In the case of mutual funds, position level data is available quarterly from the SEC.[29] Given this information, a manager may, for example, impose a penalty or a specific constraint on the how much of a particular stock they want to hold and/or trade given that they know that this stock is held widely among competitors.

Another lesson for portfolio construction relates to risk reduction. In periods of stress, managers may be forced or simply desire to de-risk over a relatively short period of time. De-risking is particularly challenging for managers who manage a large quantity of portfolios and need to take action on all of them. For example, suppose a manager manages 100 global equity portfolios, half of which target 550 basis points (bp) of risk and the others target 80bp. Due to market events and some subsequent analysis, the manager decides that they want to reduce risk by 35% and 15% for the high and (relatively) low risk portfolios, respectively. The analysis shows that the best course of action (eg, maximise the *ex ante* information ratio given current market conditions) would be to de-risk all portfolios as soon as possible. The manager may very well know what to do but sometimes the more important question is whether they can actually do what they need to do. The question of "can" is important because de-risking over short-periods of time requires, among other things,

- the infrastructure necessary to conduct large-scale rebalances,[30]
- estimates of market impact and estimates of so-called spillover effects, and
- updated transaction-cost estimates which are reflective of the current environment.

Regarding this last requirement, as managers seek ways to improve managing liquidity risk, we will see more timely updates of trading data migrate further "upstream" and serve as an input to portfolio construction. This will take the form of real-time or near real-time liquidity estimates for portfolio optimisation.

Risk management

In terms of risk management, there are various lessons to be learned. The first involves contagion. What were previously thought to be unrelated events became highly correlated during the crisis. A second lesson involves the use risk of controls (namely, drawdown control) in addition to more traditional risk measures which rely on a factor risk model. A third relates to capacity, that is, understanding a fund's maximum AUM and managing the fund accordingly. Another clear lesson from the crisis is that even if you knew what to do and when to do it, the size of the fund could be a significant impediment, since trading activity to reduce risk and exposure could result in so-called trade-driven losses.[31]

Measuring and assessing risk

Contagion risk occurs when what were previously thought to be uncorrelated events become highly or even perfectly correlated. As a result, what was thought to be a diversified portfolio (pre-contagion) transforms into an undiversified one.

The Quant Crunch is an example of financial contagion. An event in what was then perceived to be a completely unrelated market (subprime loans) fuelled massive unwinding and de-risking among several quants. As a result, quantitative equity strategies performed poorly. Not surprisingly, managers who relied almost exclusively on equity factor risk models to manage their portfolio risk had an extremely difficult time anticipating and managing risk.

In response to the crunch, some managers began developing metrics which explicitly capture the risk and performance in non-equity markets as a way to alert them to potential market disruptions. Such metrics would, for example, incorporate credit spreads, volatility (implied and realised) and returns on various markets.[32] For example, a widening of CDS spreads in conjunction with an increase in fixed-income implied volatilities could signal heightened contagion risk.

As noted earlier (Khandani and Lo 2007), there was a massive build up in assets in the lead up to the quant crisis. As money flowed into strategies, questions regarding capacity arose, ie, how the size of a fund affects its ability to generate alpha. A related interpretation of this question, which came into focus post crisis, is how much and how fast a fund can take down risk in market disruption. The "how much" and "how fast" are determined by the negative impact on performance caused by trade-driven losses. Measurement and assessment of capacity have a clear place in the overall investment and risk management process and, therefore, it is important to have appropriate tools to measure capacity.

There are various ways to measure capacity.[33] One approach is to run a set of backtests at various AUMs and measure how performance changes at the various levels. As the size of a portfolio grows, so does the likelihood that it will incur trade-driven losses at some point. Therefore, in order to generate sensible capacity estimates, backtest performance must appropriately adapt stock prices and returns to reflect how trading-induced market impact affects returns at various AUM levels. Simply taking observed prices and returns as given will ignore market impact and, therefore, lead to an overestimation of capacity estimates.

Reporting

In times of crisis, timely and accurate reporting is critical. Knowledge of what your positions are, where they are held, who the counterparty is, etc, is crucial information. We should expect to see further development in the infrastructure that supports such reporting.

Looking ahead, managers will continue to pursue tools which help them understand contagion risk, in particular. A natural challenge with quantifying sources of return in a typical quantitative equity portfolio is that the manager must deal with high-dimensional data sets: time series of hundreds (if not thousands) of active stock bets, tens of factors and thousands of stock factor exposures. As a result, we should also expect to see managers employing reporting tools and analytics which allow them to view and interact with high-dimensional data in an efficient way.

While the market offers statistical tools for mining high-dimensional data sets, being able to visualise and interact with (ie, search for relationships in) high-dimensional data, in real time, provides a powerful way of understanding sources of risk and return. The intersection of business intelligence, analytics and data visualisation should be an important and exciting area for quantitative managers for years to come as they work towards ways to better manage the risk in their portfolios.

CONCLUSION

In this chapter we have described a demonstrative quantitative equity investment process and some of the challenges faced during the 2007–10 crisis. The crisis manifested itself in a series of waves which generated unique and unprecedented problems. Managers have not only to work through the tail-end of the crisis but take serious stock of their current investment process and retool, where necessary, to better prepare for future disruptions. Such improvements require a comprehensive review of the investment process, touching on everything from research to infrastructure and operations and risk management and reporting.

1. Throughout this chapter, we refer to the crisis as a past event. We do so simply because we can point to past events or "shock waves" associated with the crisis and explain what they taught us. This is not a statement about whether or not we believe the crisis is over at the time of writing in September 2010.
2. We use the term "quant" as shorthand for "quantitative equity manager".
3. That is, a manager can reproduce their investment results from first principles.
4. Performance of some US equity funds started to turn consistently negative in the spring/summer of 2006.
5. The first real signs of the credit crunch related to subprime losses appeared as an increase in the ABX (home equity) Index (which reflects the cost of insuring a basket of mortgages of a certain rating against default) in February 2007.
6. See Narang (2009) for an in-depth discussion on quantitatively managed methods.
7. There are ultra-low latency strategies that trade at the sub-second range, which are not discussed in this chapter.
8. Customised to client needs in the form of separate accounts.
9. The definition we provide here resembles what Khandani and Lo (2007) refer to as "quantitative equity market neutral", although ours is a more general version.
10. This phenomenon affected global-developed regions (US, UK, Japan and mainland Europe).
11. In the US, the Securities and Exchange Commission imposed a ban on short selling on 799 financial stocks from September 19, 2008, until October 2, 2008.
12. Beginning sometime around July 14, 2008, in the US.
13. Beginning on March 9, 2009, corresponding to the beginning of worldwide equity markets rebound.
14. For example, if we observe multiple standard deviation events or highly serially correlated returns (when the model assumes returns to be serially uncorrelated).
15. The reader should note that there are probably countless variations of the process presented herein and, therefore, the process we present should simply be taken to be demonstrative.
16. This is often a key point of confusion for those who have experience with time series but not cross-sectional factor models.
17. See *Jones et al* (2007), for example.
18. See Fama and MacBeth (1973) for details.

19 Each data source has its own (though not necessarily unique) way of identifying a company. Normalisation is the process of mapping the various identifiers to one unique identifier associated with that stock.

20 See PriceWaterhouseCoopers (2009).

21 For long-only portfolios other critical inputs usually include benchmark portfolios, client guidelines (in the case of separate accounts) and other portfolio constraints.

22 The latter responsibility is closely related to opening and closing accounts.

23 For funds and separate accounts with no leverage, assets are kept at a custodian. For portfolios that are levered, assets are kept at a prime broker.

24 Tracking error is defined here as the volatility of active returns, where active returns are the difference between the portfolio returns and benchmark returns (Litterman 2003).

25 For unlevered portfolios, size refers to AUM, whereas for levered portfolios it refers to total economic exposure.

26 This integration may be thought of in terms of sourcing the same underlying data, models and portfolio construction parameters, and yet the infrastructures supporting research and production are independent, so that changes to one can cannot affect the other.

27 There are various ways to conduct scenario analysis and we will not discuss them here.

28 Hypothecation means the pledge of securities to a lender as collateral for a loan. Rehypothecation means the onward pledge by the lender to a third party.

29 Information contained in the SEC reports are for long-only positions. Managers also must report positions where they hold more than 5% of company ownership.

30 Multi-portfolio optimisation is often employed when multiple portfolios are rebalanced and traded simultaneously. A key objective here is to share information on transaction costs across portfolios when optimising.

31 See Litzenberger and Modest (2008) for a discussion.

32 See, for example, Goldman Sachs Asset Management (2008) and Golub and Crum (2010a).

33 See, for example, Kahn and Shaffer (2005).

REFERENCES

Brown, B. R., 2010, *Chasing the Same Signal: How Black-Box Trading Influences Stock Markets from Wall Street to Shanghai* (Chichester: John Wiley & Sons).

Brunnermeier, M. K., 2009, "Deciphering the 2007–2008 Liquidity and Credit Crunch", *Journal of Economic Perspectives* 23(1), pp. 77–100.

Efron, B., T., Hastie, I. Johnstone and R. Tibshirani, 2004, "Least Angle Regression", *Annals of Statistics* 32(2), pp. 407–99.

Fama, E., and J. MacBeth, 1973, "Risk, Return, and Equilibrium: Empirical Tests", *Journal of Political Economy* 81(3), pp. 607–36.

Fuss, R., K. Reinhard, P. Rindler and M. Tyrell, 2009, "The Anatomy of the Quant Crisis: A Real Investment Cycle Approach", Working Paper, European Business School (EBS) and Zeppelin University, Oestrich-Winkel and Friedrichshafen.

Goldman Sachs Asset Management, 2008, "Quantcentration: Implications for Quantitative Equity Investing", Report, March.

Golub, B. W., and C. C. Crum, 2010a, "Risk Management Lessons Worth Remembering from the Credit Crisis of 2007–2009", *Journal of Portfolio Management*, Spring, pp. 21–44.

Golub, B. W., and C. C. Crum, 2010b, "Reflections on Buy-Side Risk Management after (or Between) the Storms", *Journal of Portfolio Management*, Summer, pp. 1–9.

Hastie, T., R. Tibshirani and J. Friedman, 2009, *The Elements of Statistical Learning: Data Mining, Inference, and Prediction*, Second Edition (Berlin: Springer).

Jones, R., T. Lim and P. J. Zangari, 2007, "The Black–Litterman Model for Structured Equity Portfolios", *Journal of Portfolio Management*, Winter, pp. 24–33.

Kahn, R., and J. S. Shaffer, 2005, "The Surprisingly Small Impact of Asset Growth on Expected Alpha", *Journal of Portfolio Management* 32(1), pp. 49–60.

Khandani, A. E., and A. W. Lo. 2007, "What Happened to the Quants in August 2007?", *Journal of Investment Management* 5(4), pp. 29–78.

Litterman, R., 2003, *Modern Investment Management: An Equilibrium Approach* (Chichester: John Wiley & Sons).

Litzenberger, R., and D. Modest, 2008, "Crisis and Non-Crisis Risk in Financial Markets: A Unified Approach to Risk Management", Working Paper, July 15, URL: http://ssrn.com/abstract=1160273.

Narang, R., 2009, *Inside the Black-Box: The Simple Truth about Quantitative Trading* (Chichester: John Wiley & Sons).

Patterson, S., 2010, *The Quants: How a New Breed of Math Whizzes Conquered Wall Street and Nearly Destroyed It* (New York: Crown Business).

Pedersen, L. H., 2009, "When Everyone Runs for the Exit", *International Journal of Central Banking* 5(4), pp. 177–99.

PriceWaterhouseCoopers, 2009, "Lehman Brothers' Bankruptcy: Lessons Learned for the Survivors", Financial Services Research Institute (FSRI) Publications.

Rosenberg, B., M. Houglet and V. Marathe, 1973, "Extra-Market Components of Covariance among Security Prices", Working Paper RPF-013, Research Program in Finance, University of California, Berkeley.

Serbin, V., P. M. Bull and H. Zhu, 2009, "The Capacity of Liquidity-Demanding Equity Strategies", *Journal of Portfolio Management* 36(1), pp. 78–89.

Singh, M., and J. Aitken, 2009, "Deleveraging after Lehman: Evidence from Reduced Rehypothecation", IMF Working Paper 09/42.

Tibshirani, R., 1996, "Regression Shrinkage and Selection via the Lasso", *Journal of the Royal Statistical Society: Series B* 58, pp. 267–88.

20

Active Risk Management: A Credit Investor's Perspective

Vineer Bhansali
PIMCO

The credit crisis which began in 2007 taught us many lessons about the importance of the "robustness of process" of risk management. As the crisis metamorphosed from a relatively isolated area of mortgages to the financial sector to corporates and ultimately to sovereign credit, we learnt some important principles that will impact on portfolio construction in fundamental ways. This chapter will provide a credit investor's perspective on tail-risk management of credit portfolios.

The most important lesson learnt is that, though the details of this crisis were different, in many ways the recent episode also had striking similarities to past crisis events. Among these similarities is the central role played by de-leveraging, illiquidity and flight to quality. Once again, the central importance of equity and funding markets to other markets was revealed. Asset prices became increasingly correlated, and the ability to anticipate even short-term portfolio returns for risky securities became impossible. The response from aware investors required a delicate balancing act: one that is conscious of the elements that persist through these recurrent crises yet is flexible in its response to their evolution. This ultimately results in actively and constantly searching for both endogenous and exogenous tools for risk management.

This crisis has taught us that well-positioned portfolios are not only those that outperform in periods of normalcy, but are those that can weather the storms. Whether we can anticipate the exact nature of these rare events is doubtful; but just as homes in natural-disaster-prone areas are designed to withstand significant stresses, portfolios in increasingly accident-prone markets are designed with structural risk-control to survive severe market catastrophes. While the nature of these catastrophes changes with time, there are usually sufficient opportunities to fortify portfolios against the most perverse ones at a reasonable and relatively small cost to portfolio performance over the short term (over the long term we believe hedging is actually return enhancing once coupled with the ability to respond aggressively). This offensive risk management approach is increasingly being used by portfolio managers to construct portfolios that are robust under volatile and highly unpredictable financial conditions. Indeed, our recent research shows that a portfolio of active tail hedges would have improved not only the defensive posture of investment portfolios over long horizons, but also their expected performance, since having access to non-linear instruments can generate excess liquidity when it is needed. Tail hedging does this by following a pre-commitment strategy to add to risky assets when they are most attractive. In other words, as the rest of the market delivers, the investor with excess liquidity has the rare opportunity to substantially improve long-term portfolio returns.

At a macro level, we can think of credit portfolios as a collection of options (options to default). Risk management consists of individually valuing the risks and returns to each option in isolation, and also valuing the risks and returns to the portfolio of all the options. When the expected return to an individual short option position is low or negative, active risk management requires the reduction of some of the positions, and the mix of direct and indirect hedges for the portfolio in aggregate. Let us first take a look at the lessons we have learnt since the crisis began.

LOOKING BACK, LOOKING FORWARD

This crisis was different in its details, but very similar in general features to past crises in its symptoms and effects. Again there were a rapid fall in asset values, increased correlations, increased volatility, risk-aversion and bonds behaving badly, ie, tracking equity risks more than we would have thought.

Common risks drove portfolio performance

Assets are more similar than they look. Asset class diversification does not necessarily mean risk reduction. One hallmark of the investment environment prior to the crisis was that there was excessive asset class pollution. One major theme we will keep returning to is that macro risk-factor sensitivity is more important than idiosyncratic risk for a large class of investments. For instance, the exposure to the housing market was key in the 2008 crisis, and the sensitivity to the related risk factor would have kept investors from building large positions in mortgage backed securities. Very few stress tested their portfolios to significant housing market shocks, focusing rather on "arbitrage" opportunities. One key lesson learnt is that when it comes to portfolio construction, getting the big things right is more important than getting the little things wrong.

Liquidity must be liquid

There was a false sense of security in illiquid liquid instruments, such as tranches from collateralised debt obligations (CDOs) that were sold as cash equivalents. Liquidity premiums were mispriced as there was a general desire to boost returns by selling "lottery tickets" (securities with carry from low probability/high-severity) in levered form. Many investors ran an implicit carry trade, with mismatched horizons of assets and liabilities. Having grown up in an equity bull market, systemic risk and its damages were underestimated. For an investing style trained on mean-reversion, it was a surprise to realise that systemic risk distortions can last for a long time and that doubling down by increasing the bet does not always pay.

Leverage was everywhere

There was explicit leverage through outright borrowing made easy as lending standards were relaxed. But there was also hidden leverage in complex, opaque structures. This was a packaged way for those who could not easily lever to get the leverage "built-in" to the assets they were buying. Vendor financing which provided incentives to take more risk enabled dealers to distribute product and purchasers to obtain leverage. The CDO industry came up with new ways to deliver higher yields and, either voluntarily or involuntarily, the rating agencies, who are supposed to be able to limit such abuse, were taken along for the ride.

Risk modelling assumed ideal conditions

The creators of models know that models are idealisations, not reality, and models can and do fail. The outputs are only as good as idealised inputs. However, idealised inputs like normal distributions and low transaction costs and the unquestioning belief in printed matter (eg, financial statements) led to a collective failing to evaluate the proper risks. Investors were using similar modelling frameworks. Most importantly, the role of government and its potential influence on asset prices was ignored.

Fat-left-tail events happen

We can think of the increased volatility in the financial markets as partly a consequence of the increased participation and the "tight-coupling" of markets and participants. Just as the warming of the sea surface temperature has resulted in more frequent and more severe hurricanes, which cause more damage due to the increase in coastal populations, the markets have gone through their own global warming. There are now more low probability events, with higher severity outcomes. There were plenty of opportunities to bring excessive risk under control but investors voluntarily chose not to do so due to a belief in short-term mean reversion.

Systemic shocks exposed heterogeneity

In a period of extreme financial stress, traditionally fungible micro risk factors did not produce similar results (heterogeneous risk) leading to wider range of performance. This heterogeneous risk was exacerbated by government intervention in the financial system, market participants with limited capital and the liquidity needs of investors. The performance of different parts of the capital structure (ie, sub-debt versus senior debt) shows this inhomogeneity. Capital structure positioning has been important, as heterogeneous risk has exposed the dissimilarity between different parts of a firm's debt obligations.

So what can we do about these risks looking forward? How can we learn from the lessons and construct more robust portfolios for the inevitable next crisis that will happen? Here is a short list of things we absolutely need to do.

- **Identify and limit key risk factors and concentrations.** We need to differentiate risk-factor diversification from asset class diversification. As we will discuss, it is easy to take false comfort in asset-based diversification which does not work due to common risks.

- **Evaluate the need for real liquidity.** Manage cash balances aggressively, ie, keep liquidity or defensive instruments available not only to weather rare events, but also to take advantage of the opportunities they provide. Imagine rare events that might not have happened in the past but are possible though improbable. To do this, the best approach is stress testing. One way to simulate the impact of stresses is to construct a combination of the worst of all historical shocks plus imagined super-shocks. Allocate sufficient reserves against the stresses but opportunistically deploy cash where liquidity is being egregiously priced. Pay attention to the severity more than to the ability to forecast probabilities.
- **Back to basics.** Understanding risk comprehensively requires transparency. Structural complexity can be the enemy of transparency. Excessive layering or hedging typically obfuscates hidden risks. An investor needs to ask honestly "do esoteric strategies and structures really help you meet investment objectives?"
- **Build in tail insurance.** It is almost always possible to buy cheap protection against some tail risk in creative ways. Tail insurance reduces "black hole" or loss of principal risk. We should think of tail hedges as a separate asset class, since normal assets behave differently in periods of stress. Every portfolio should allow for some exposure to insurance-like instruments. As we discuss later, while investors usually think of tail hedging as a cost, it should really be considered "offensive risk management", since the opportunities that become available can improve long-term performance of portfolios. Thus, it offers short-term catastrophe mitigation and long-term opportunity. The key idea here is that when correlations rise, basis risk becomes less important than having the right macro hedges. Use forecasting ability to find insurance that others are overlooking. market dislocations and incentives create inefficiencies in the long dated financial catastrophe insurance market as was witnessed in the recent crisis.
- **Manage counterparty risk.** Be aggressive with collateral management and dynamically evaluate counterparty credit. Other than diversification of exposures to counterparties, aggressive collateral standards can mitigate many of the risks in this area.

ACTIVE RISK MANAGEMENT IS A NECESSITY NOT A LUXURY

Any car owner or homeowner will attest that the benefit of having appropriate amounts of disaster insurance is financial survival. When applied to investors, there is a secondary benefit: the survivors are better able to take advantage of reduced liquidity and attractive prospective returns. Thus, tail insurance is an offensive strategy for the long term, even though it may appear to be a cost in the short term. When a homeowner purchases insurance against a catastrophic event that might destroy the roof over their head, they do not regret having paid the premium at the end of the year. If we think of investment portfolios in a similar vein, it seems almost incomprehensible that investors would decide to run portfolios without tail insurance.

The single most important reason investors give for not including tail-risk management strategies in their portfolios is that it reduces returns. While there is no arguing with the fact that spending on tail risk requires sacrificing returns in the short term (via either moving off the optimal frontier of risky assets or spending explicitly on insurance), the reality is that, over long horizons, the same insurance results in a multi-period enhancement of the return characteristics of the portfolio. An investment portfolio with myopia can, in our view, result in an almost certain risk of ruin in the long run.

ACTIVE RISK MANAGEMENT REDUCES "SUNK" COSTS

Proper tail-risk management can obviously reduce the risk of negative outcomes for a portfolio. As we show in two forthcoming papers (Bhansali and Davis 2011a,b), the expected return, *ex ante*, of a portfolio with tail hedges is better than an unhedged portfolio. The reason is straightforward. By purchasing efficient tail hedges, the portfolio can allocate more capital to the investments that offer a higher expected return. In other words, by self-insuring part of the portfolio losses, and insuring against catastrophic losses, some risk budget is freed up to skew the return profile in an asymmetric fashion. We also show that this is not simply theoretical. By creating a simple model of the volatility surface for the equity options market (for backfilling to 1928) we show that a portfolio with hedges can actually outperform a simple buy and hold or even a portfolio with buy and hold (not actively managed) hedges. The important point is that, even with simple mechanical rules for monetisation of these

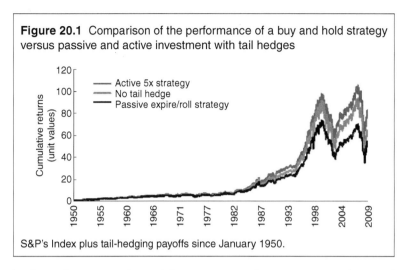

Figure 20.1 Comparison of the performance of a buy and hold strategy versus passive and active investment with tail hedges

S&P's Index plus tail-hedging payoffs since January 1950.

hedges, the expected portfolio returns can be superior to a buy and hold portfolio.

Long-horizon investors have traditionally assumed that they need not purchase tail risk hedges against rare but severe events that can adversely impact their portfolios. Even when tail risk hedges are justified, they are interpreted as a cost that reduces the expected returns of the portfolio. Our conversations with investment officers suggest that their biggest challenge is convincing investment committees to commit to this cost and risk underperformance relative to their peer group. More precisely, in our work we show that the shadow value of a tail hedging program is positive. Figure 20.1 shows the long-term benefits of an active monetisation strategy (following a naive rule), over a simple buy and hold strategy with and without passive tail hedges. As we can see, far from just being sunk costs, active tail hedging can add to the overall performance of the portfolio. This should not be surprising, since a traditional buy and hold portfolio takes all the risks and tries to control for them (from 0% loss to a large loss). If we are willing to take the small losses (volatility) as given and insure against the very large losses, then our overall risk taking ability and hence prospective returns should improve.

PORTFOLIO TAIL-RISK MANAGEMENT MITIGATES SYSTEMIC RISK EXPOSURES

Systemic risk brings under pressure the ability to carry levered holdings, so if leverage is a permanent risk in our economy, the likelihood of tail-risk events increases as the risk of de-leveraging increases. In such episodes everyone desires liquidity and no one is willing to provide it. Financing and liquidity are "macro risks", and hence their proper valuation requires macro models, and proper hedges require macro tools and market instruments.

This observation has far-reaching consequences. The main consequence is that tail risk becomes a macro risk, and to forecast and control against it we need to step outside the world of historical estimates and calibration and forecast structural changes, and imagine improbable, high severity scenarios. The immense benefit of thinking of tail risk in terms of a macro risk is simplification of hedges. Macro markets are the deepest markets, and typically there is some sort of insurance that remains attractively priced for long enough because of the sheer mass of capital re-allocation needed to align all of them. When systemic crises happen, correlations also rise in their absolute value. This provides a "free lunch" in that a completely disconnected macro market of normal times becomes a good hedge against the tails in distressed times. It is more efficient to sacrifice basis risk and close match between hedges in order to obtain efficiency of hedges. For example, due to the "beta" of credit to other markets, credit market tail-risk events are frequently hedged better with equity options and currency options than with customised credit hedge instruments. Indeed, this blurs the distinction between an active position and a hedge, but when the dust settles the classification of a position into *ex post* categories is less important than the economic benefits it confers.

COSTS AND OPPORTUNITIES VARY

Credit market hedges were extremely cheap in 2007, because of the incessant selling of structured products and the demand driven by excess liquidity. Immediately after the crisis these same hedges were not as attractively priced (though there are others that were). Thus, hedging credit with credit market instruments was less attractive than hedging credit with indirect instruments from other markets. The estimation of option prices and sensitivities in general is based on the academic foundations of continuous trading and risk-neutral investors. As we have remarked previously (Bhansali 2007b), these ideal conditions are rarely met in turbulent markets. Hence, use of what are now traditional models of option pricing is flawed by construction when applied to tail hedges. A viable alternative approach is to run scenarios to which investors are averse, and evaluate the expected value of portfolios under those scenarios with and without insurance assets. The difference in these two portfolio values is the proper price for the insurance from the investor's perspective, and might be superior to the market price of the insurance. We all know that catastrophe insurance can trade too cheaply in the natural insurance markets; it is possible for this to also happen in the world of finance, especially in a world of innovative financial engineering that ports risks from one type of market to another type of market.

Why is it that cheap tail hedges can be found in almost all market environments? There are many candidate reasons. For example, speculative demand of particular types and classes of assets may drive the price of these assets very high. In periods of low returns, as observed until the middle of 2007, "yield hoggers" increased options sales as a source of carry. The belief of mean-reversion participants is that out-of-the-money options will never be exercised. This is generally true, except that, as the leverage in the market place increases due to everyone simultaneously doing levered option sales, the notional size has to increase to generate the same carry. At some point this type of system becomes susceptible to small noise-induced instabilities and creates a domino effect of hedgers all trying to cover their deltas at the same time (the other choice is to risk certain ruin).

An example will make this clearer.

- Before the credit crisis, in June 2007, a 7–100% tranche on the IG8 10-year index cost 15.63 basis points (bp) per year. The running cost is the coupon per year of spread duration, which equalled 2bp. Since the tranche rolls down to a shorter maturity, per year the roll-down is 2.67bp for a total of 4.67bp of cost. To buy protection on US$1 billion notional, total lifetime cost was about US$12 million (cost times a PV01 of 7.45).
- The same tranche in February 2008 was trading at 91bp per year. Then, the running cost (coupon) per year of spread duration is 10.1bp, roll-down is 2.2bp, giving a total of 12.3bp per year. The new total lifetime cost is about US$67 million.
- The delta of the tranche before the crisis was approximately 0.53, which when multiplied by the spread duration of the 10-year index of 7.45 gives an approximate sensitivity of 3.95% per

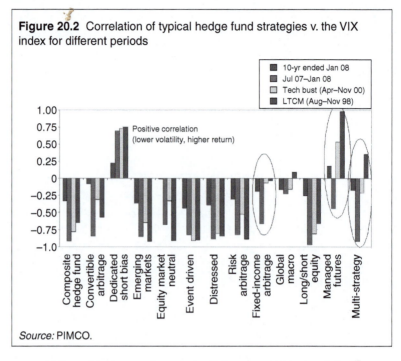

Figure 20.2 Correlation of typical hedge fund strategies v. the VIX index for different periods

Source: PIMCO.

100bp of index widening. In February 2008, the delta rose to 0.77 (since the index widened and was closer to at-the-money), giving almost 5.66% of spread risk.

It can immediately be seen why super-senior levered notes are in severe distress at the time of writing (and why the reverse of selling insurance was so rewarding). First, the mark-to-market loss was huge (five times) since it equals the net present value of premium change. Second, the mark-to-market benefits from convexity (the delta increased) and, third, the collateral that has to be posted to make up for the mark-to-market fluctuations is much more expensive (lower T-bill rates, and higher Libor rates). The fact that all these happened simultaneously is typical of systemic tail events.

THERE ARE MANY WAYS TO IMPLEMENT TAIL-RISK HEDGING AND THE TRADE-OFFS ARE ALWAYS CHANGING

The simplest way is to buy insurance securities. For instance, credit market crises almost always occur with de-leveraging and a grab for liquidity which usually results in treasuries rallying in price terms, especially those at the shortest maturities. So short-term cash and treasuries are a natural asset-based hedge for tail risk. But these securities can become overpriced due to other technical reasons. The second option is to buy contingent claims, or "option-like" securities. At the beginning of the crisis, out-of-the-money tranches on CDX and iTraxx indexes were literally being given away due to the demand for default remote structured transactions such as CPDOs, levered super-seniors, etc. These option-like payouts were priced below their expected value under a significant systemic risk outcome. The third alternative is to invest in strategies that are negatively correlated to tail risks. Essentially, this approach balances risks in portfolios with risk-factor exposures that are likely to negate some of the adverse returns embedded inside the portfolio. Amongst the traditional established strategies, Figure 20.2 demonstrates that only the systematic, trend-following managed-futures strategy provides positive correlation with tail-risk indicators such as the VIX, while also being largely uncorrelated to the stock market. Copious amounts of research has been done to demonstrate that trend-following strategies behave like a long position in lookback straddles, and hence have naturally long-tail risk (Fung and Hsieh 2001). The fourth approach is to move the portfolio off the optimal frontier, ie, accept less return for the same amount of risk. This approach explicitly recognises that the simplest mean–variance optimal frontier falsely assumes that risk can be measured by volatility alone, and that the investor has perfect forecasting ability. One example of this approach is to reduce the exposure to spread products, such as corporate bonds, or low quality mortgages. Such spread products have higher yield because of embedded default and illiquidity options and hence more vulnerable to systemic shocks. Unfortunately, such dynamic hedging has limitations.

MORE THAN JUST DYNAMIC REPLICATION

The problem with these types of zero-cost tail solutions is that they assume liquidity will be present in crises, and usually liquidity evaporates during systemic shocks. When everyone else is trying to put on the same hedges, there is no assurance that an investor will be able to do so before others. In the approach we are describing, the portfolio is subjected to reasonable but rare super-shocks, and insurance is purchased using one of the four techniques above. So there is an explicit price to be paid for the hedge. The role of the portfolio manager is to reduce the cost of these hedges over the hedge horizon. Particularly with a long enough horizon, hedges can be usually bought very cheaply. For instance, even during the height of the crisis, long-dated options on forex such as the US dollar–yen exchange rate had negligible cost over a one-year horizon, due to the roll-up of forward rates from the interest rate differential between US dollar rates and yen rates (Bhansali 2007c). In periods of stress, one common outcome is de-leveraging and flight to low-yielding currencies such as the yen. This directionality of the forex movement and the associated increase in volatility makes the real-world expected value of the hedging package much higher than the theoretical, risk-neutral value. So it is the possibility of asymmetric payouts in particular states of the world that make the hedges worth more to the investor than their stand-alone theoretical value.

TRADITIONAL VALUATION MODELS BECOME LARGELY IRRELEVANT

To ascertain the value of a particular tail hedge, it is critical that the scenario analysis be performed with many variations of the inputs for the parameters. The inputs are more important than the level of refinement of the models. In the simple language of Black–Scholes options, this boils down to running the performance of option positions under various maturity, rate, volatility and spot rate environments, using the option model simply as a crude non-linear transformation machine between inputs and outputs. Special attention has to be paid to consistently taking the volatilities and correlations to extreme values, because the underlying assumption of joint lognormality undervalues the tails of the distribution (Bhansali and Wise 2001). It is also possible to approach the problem by specifying other distributions with naturally fat tails, such as the Lévy distribution, and today's computational power makes it easy to substitute theoretical, closed-form solvable models with empirical distributions that can be evaluated numerically, especially on the tails.

The extension of Black–Scholes to credit is the Gaussian copula model. While lacking detail, it still has the ability to give good intuition about the performance of tranches in periods of stress. In Table 20.1, we display the performance of a 7–100% tranche on the IG8 index for instantaneous shocks and one-year delayed shocks.

ACTIVE RISK MANAGEMENT

Table 20.1 Tranche shock scenario analysis

Price date	Index	Tenor	Funded	Att. point (%)	Det. point (%)	Coupon (bp)
26/3/2008	IG8	10	0	7.00	100.00	76.7

Spread boost (bp)	Correlation unchanged	Low correlation	High correlation
−25	−1.36	−0.39	−2.49
−10	−0.55	0.45	−1.68
0	0.00	1.00	−1.13
10	0.55	1.56	−0.57
25	1.39	2.39	0.29
50	2.77	3.76	1.74
100	5.54	6.46	4.66
200	10.84	11.58	10.25
Attachment (%)	63.38	95.08	31.69
Detachment (%)	0.00	0.00	0.00

Spread boost (bp)	Correlation unchanged	Low correlation	High correlation
−25	−1.99	−1.07	−3.08
−10	−1.28	−0.34	−2.38
0	−0.80	0.16	−1.91
10	−0.32	0.65	−1.42
25	0.41	1.38	−0.67
50	1.65	2.60	0.61
100	4.10	5.01	3.20
200	8.89	9.64	8.26
Attachment (%)	63.38	95.08	31.69
Detachment (%)	0.00	0.00	0.00

This table shows the shock to the 7–100% tranche of the IG8 CDX index. In the second table we shock the spreads of the index (displayed in the first column). The second, third and fourth columns show the performance of the hedge under different base correlation assumptions using a Gaussian copula model. The third table repeats the exercise for a one-year horizon shock, so it incorporates time decay in the hedge.

The particular data used is not as relevant as the fact that the scenario analysis illustrates the profile of the hedges with changing correlation assumptions. The point here is that the tranche returns

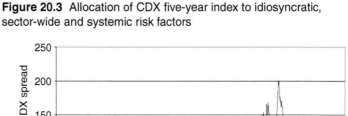

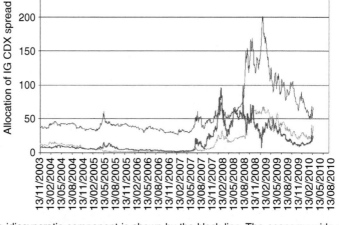

Figure 20.3 Allocation of CDX five-year index to idiosyncratic, sector-wide and systemic risk factors

The idiosyncratic component is shown by the black line. The economy-wide risk is shown by the dark-grey line and is at highly elevated levels. The sectoral risk shown by the light-grey line.
Source: Bhansali *et al* (2008).

can be different as the implied base correlation moves around. In periods of systemic stress, correlations between credit entities rise as we go from first to second column, so there is additional convexity from the correlation variable. This prospectively makes the hedge perform better for increased correlation in periods of stress. The one-year horizon shock accurately captures the cost or time decay as the tranche (which is merely an option on losses) shortens in maturity.

PARTICIPANT ACTIONS BECOME MORE RELEVANT

In Bhansali *et al* (2008) we break down the index spreads for various indexes using a three-jump approach first used by Longstaff and Rajan (2008). The third component of the spread, which corresponds to systemic risks, has clearly become elevated in the recent crisis, and may only revert to "normal" levels with a long lag and after substantial liquidity is provided to alleviate solvency fears. Regression of other markets, such as municipals, asset backeds, etc, on the systemic component of the spread shows significant dependence of prospective returns on how the systemic risk factor changes. In other words, many asset classes carry large amounts of systemic illiquidity risk. No wonder that, at the time of writing, municipal bonds, especially general obligation bonds of natural AAA-rated states, are trading at higher yield levels than even treasuries, despite the fact that they are tax exempt. The impact of government action on systemic risks is obvious when we compare the systemic and idiosyncratic components in Figure 20.3. Prior to the Bear Stearns collapse in spring 2008, the systemic component had already started to rise and became the same order of magnitude as the idiosyncratic spread component. When the US government provided unprecedented liquidity, this component of spreads started to narrow. With the mid-September failure of Lehman Brothers, the authorities had to make a choice in which they sacrificed the interest of common equity holders relative to senior debt holders. We see that the tranche markets immediately responded to this choice with the idiosyncratic component blowing out. This, as further discussed next, coincided with the meltdown of the equity market that saw a decline of almost half of its capitalisation.

We can think of modelling asset prices as a product of payouts, probability distributions and discounting. A government with unlimited legal and monetary powers can quickly change any or all of these elements of pricing, altering asset values and risk in a fundamental way. Thus, incorporating the effect of participants starts to play a critical role in risk management, which unfortunately has been swept under the carpet in traditional pricing models. We discuss this in detail in a recent paper on the impact of government actions on the markets (Bhansali 2010a).

Private participants' actions can also influence the actions of governments. The sharp depreciation of the Eurozone currencies in the middle of 2010 showed that stresses generated in markets can influence sovereign unions, as rumblings of an EU breakup started to appear in the press. The situation morphed into one akin to the proverbial "game of chicken". Governments, due to mutual lack of cooperation among themselves, with their banks and individuals, and even with extra-governmental organisations such as the IMF (International Monetary Fund), engaged in multiple non-cooperative games. The outcome of these games of strategy can be sub-optimal and regime changing, creating increased risk in markets.

ASSET CLASS DIVERSIFICATION IS A WEAK RISK MANAGEMENT TOOL

The construction of a tail portfolio hedge depends on three inter-related inputs. First, what is the scenario behaviour, or "beta" of the portfolio. Second, what is the "deductible" or the amount of loss that the investor is willing to self-insure. Third, what is the cost that the investor is willing to spend on the hedge. The best combination of hedges is the one that balances return and risk. It performs by reducing the negative return to the portfolio in the stress scenario, and in addition controls the risk at the horizon to the dangerous factors in the stress scenario. This evaluation of tail hedges with a holistic perspective of the portfolio is critical, as our experience with bond markets in the two years since 2008 has demonstrated.

Bond people like to think of bonds as a separate asset class from equities. Alas, the performance of fixed income markets in 2008 showed us that bonds have a lot of equity risk in them. Until the Lehman bankruptcy, the equity market was living in its own world: the default brought home in a hurry the truth that equity holders are ultimately taking the bulk of the enterprise risk. Since then every bond class other than treasuries has tracked the gyrations of the equity markets. Conceptually, this makes sense, since equity markets the domain of "animal spirits", and increasing risk-aversion is experienced first hand when we meet equity markets in a free fall. The well-known Merton model that links credit spreads to equities is indeed based on the relationship of both equities and bonds issued by a corporation to the underlying assets, and so the observation that a fall in the asset value of companies impacts on both corporate stocks and bonds is hardly surprising. What is shocking is that so many asset classes that have nothing to do with corporations and their assets have become so correlated to equities. Pure alpha strategies have shown little alpha and much equity market beta. Since the crisis, a watchful investor could generally guess the daily direction of bond levels and yield curve shape, currencies, commodities and credit by just observing the changes in the equity market. This correlation of assets at the macro level has brought home the fact that much of the real risk of investments resides in the equity markets, and when the cuts from de-leveraging get as close to the backbone of finance as they did in 2009, the equity market becomes the final risk shock absorber. Even though the stock market itself remained fairly liquid through the crisis (at the time of writing), falling equity prices are more likely than rising equity prices to result in falling liquidity of other asset classes. At the end of the day, in a levered economy in which assets are supported by a diminishing equity base, each unit of falling equity prices magnifies very drastically the economy-wide leverage. If we are on a path of de-leveraging that is not at its final resting place, then this "denominator effect" (where equity is the denominator and the net assets are the numerator) will require a further downwards adjustment of the numerator, ie, of asset valuation broadly.

To see the impact of this simple approach in more detail, let us return to asset pricing done the Arbitrage Pricing Theory way. By definition, the beta of the stock market to itself is 1. The beta of any other security is the correlation of its returns multiplied by the ratio of the volatility of the asset to the volatility of the stock market. So if a security such as a Treasury Bond shows a beta of -0.10, this means that its returns are negatively correlated to the stock market. On the other hand, high yield bonds show an equity beta of almost 1, ie, not only are they positively correlated to the stock market, but they have volatility in the same order of magnitude as the equity market. We would only want to buy such a security if the compensation for holding the default risk exceeded the risk from the market volatility of the equity market by a wide margin. Many hedge funds and other absolute return strategies turned out to be absolute negative strategies in 2008 for similar reasons: they were short hidden equity, or equivalently, liquidity risk. Higher equity beta should, in efficient markets, compensate with higher return, or so goes the capital asset pricing model (CAPM), but higher beta also means higher drawdown and tail risk.

If asset class diversification does not help in reducing catastrophic portfolio risk, then maintaining substantial amounts of liquidity, or explicit hedging instruments are probably the only practical alternatives for a participant. Certainly algorithms such as mean–variance optimal portfolios can provide only a fake sense of comfort.

One issue that comes up is that if everyone buys tail insurance, would it not make the insurance extremely expensive. While this is true, and has driven put–call skews after crises to new highs, there are still pockets of opportunity that arise due to dislocation. For example, as credit tail hedges become expensive, and interest rates in developed nations fall in sympathy, the price of protecting against rate rises falls drastically. In addition, an investor can also take advantage of dislocated volatility and spread curves to construct long-short positions that provide a more cost effective and potent tail hedge.

SEVERITY IS MORE IMPORTANT THAN PROBABILITY

The probability question for tail events is typically not answerable by looking at traded option prices, since they are based on assumptions that typically fail for very rare events. The reason is that the pricing of tail options in particular carries a significant amount of risk premium compensation to the seller (lottery ticket risk), which alters the probability distribution. Simulation that is based on past observations is also not a totally satisfactory approach, since each crisis is different in severity and magnitude. The practical approach to coming up with probabilities can take a number of parallel approaches. One approach is to sample from historical events with replacement, and magnify the rare event likelihood by some scale factor (this effectively reshapes the tails). Simultaneously, changes in a tail-risk indicator such as the VIX can be measured to indicate the likelihood of being in a crisis versus a normal environment in which correlations and volatilities from a distressed regime are used.

We have already demonstrated that, in events of systemic importance, many asset classes suffer substantial losses. Since these losses happen due to the sharp removal of liquidity and leverage, focusing on the probability alone ignores the fact that the damage happens due to the size of the shock. The lesson is that, regardless of how these probabilities are estimated, investors should look to accumulate cheap tail hedges that benefit the portfolio. The probability calculation is less important than knowing that hedges exist, which can make the difference between survival and almost certain ruin.

CONCLUSION

Active management of tail hedges might seem to be a contradiction since it transfers some responsibility of long-term portfolio performance to the risk management function. But this is necessary. First, as we have highlighted above, costs are highly variable. Second, counterparty risk is a real risk and its management is critical to a hedge portfolio since the counterparty has to be around to make good on the contract. The risks to such contracts are many, and not controlling portfolios against failure to pay is a recipe for disaster. For instance, many investors found that insurance written by monoline insurers was not as solid as they had thought. Third, transactions costs are asymmetric: when there is a crisis more participants are willing to incur these costs. In our experience, when there is demand surge, the seller of reinsurance is the price setter for liquidity. This knowledge helps reduce the frictions on a hedge portfolio when implemented in a disciplined manner over time.

In addition, active management opens up opportunities to add pseudo-alpha (value that reduces the cost of the hedge) as markets become segmented and create short-term dislocations. Since hedges are usually implemented through derivatives, another key issue is one of financing: for out-of-the-money equity options and forex options, the payment is usually made up front; on the other hand, for credit derivatives, the payment is "pay as you go", and it is possible to build in a substantial degree of notional leverage. Staying on top of these micro elements of the hedging market can make all the difference between a tail hedge approach that works and one that does not.

In this chapter, we have offered some perspectives on tail-risk hedging from an investor's perspective. The essential insight is that tail risks for typical diversified portfolios occur from systemic risks and rising correlations. Thus, a proper tail-risk hedging approach takes into account the relative pricing of broad macro markets and strategies, and evaluates the best alternatives from combinations of these alternatives to immunise the portfolio against improbable but not impossible shocks. This process benefits immensely from an active approach to hedging.

REFERENCES

Bhansali, V., 2007a, "Markowitz Bites Back: The Failure of CAPM, Compression of Risky Asset Spreads and the Path Back to Normalcy", PIMCO Viewpoints, Spring, URL: http://www.pimco.com/.

Bhansali, V., 2007b, "Putting Economics (Back) into Quantitative Models", *Journal of Portfolio Management* 33(3), pp. 63–76.

Bhansali, V., 2007c, "Volatility and the Carry Trade", *Journal of Fixed Income* 17(3), pp. 72–84.

Bhansali, V., 2008, "Correlation Risk: What the Market Is Telling Us and Does It Make Sense?", in N. Wagner (ed), *Credit Risk: Models, Development and Management* (London: Chapman and Hall).

Bhansali, V., 2010 "The Ps of Pricing and Risk Management, Revisited", *Journal of Portfolio Management* 36(2), pp. 106–12.

Bhansali, V., and J. M. Davis, 2011a, "Offensive Risk Management: Can Tail Risk Hedging Be Profitable?", *Journal of Portfolio Management*, in press, URL: http://ssrn.com/abstract =1573760.

Bhansali, V., and J. M. Davis, 2011b, "Offensive Risk Management II: The Case for Active Tail Risk Hedging", *Journal of Portfolio Management*, in press, URL: http://ssrn.com/abstract=1601573.

Bhansali, V., and M. B. Wise, 2001, "Forecasting Portfolio Risk in Normal and Stressed Markets", *Journal of Risk* 4(1), p. 977.

Bhansali, V., R. Gingrich and F. A. Longstaff, 2008, "Systemic Risk: What Is the Market Telling Us?", *Financial Analysts Journal* 64(4), pp. 16–24.

Fung, W., and D. A. Hsieh, 2001, "The Risk of Hedge Fund Strategies: Theory and Evidence from Trend Followers", *The Review of Financial Studies* 14(2), pp. 313–41.

21

Investment Strategy Returns: Volatility, Asymmetry, Fat Tails and the Nature of Alpha

Arthur M. Berd
Capital Fund Management

The key question in investment management is to understand the sources of investment returns. Without such understanding, it is virtually impossible to succeed in managing money. Even risk management, usually a more scientific endeavour compared with the murky craft of predicting directional or relative movements of asset prices, becomes difficult if we have no proper framework within which to think about the future return distributions.

In this chapter, we explore the importance of non-Gaussian features of returns, such as time-varying volatility, asymmetry and fat tails. We demonstrate, using an empirical model of hedge fund strategy returns, that these non-Gaussian features significantly affect the expected returns. Moreover, we demonstrate that the volatility compensation is often a significant component of the expected returns of the investment strategies, suggesting that many of these strategies should be thought of as being "short vol". The notable exceptions are the CTA strategies[1] and certain fixed income and FX strategies. We suggest a fundamental explanation for this phenomenon and argue that it leads to important adjustments in capital allocation.

This review is based on a series of conference presentations (Berd 2008, 2009) and privately communicated strategy calls (Berd 2007; Berd and Tetyevsky 2002) made by the author both before and after the financial crisis, which until now have not been assembled in a coherent manner. The crisis experience has largely confirmed our intuition. In particular, we believe that the "Quant Crunch" experience in August 2007, and the widespread large losses in the period from September 2008 to March 2009, followed by large gains between

March 2009 and early 2010, are in line with the volatility dependence of strategy returns.

There are many theories and plausible hypotheses about the driving factors explaining the returns. The Capital Asset Pricing Model (Sharpe 1964; Lintner 1965; Mossin 1966), which postulates a specific relationship between the expected excess returns of assets and their co-variation with market returns, is among the pillars of modern financial theory. A more elaborate and pragmatically more satisfying Arbitrage Pricing Theory (Ross 1976) expands on CAPM insights by adding more explanatory variables and allowing more flexibility in defining the common driving factors. The popular Fama–French framework (Fama and French 1993) can be seen as a particularly successful example of APT in application to stock returns.

The majority of these theories are focused on explaining the returns of tradeable assets, such as stocks, bonds or futures. While this is clearly the most granular level which is of interest to the researchers, we believe there is much to be gained by focusing instead on returns of typical investment strategies. Indeed, over the past decades, many such strategies, from quantitative long–short equity investing to CTA and to convertible arbitrage, have become well-established and boasting must-have allocations in most alternative investment portfolios.

We can take this argument even further, stating that not only it is possible to model the strategy's returns without knowing its composition, but it is actually important to do that. Suppose we had the benefit of knowledge of some particular hedge fund's portfolio composition at a given point in time. Would that give us a better understanding of the nature of its returns over time? The answer, of course, is "it depends". If the strategy is slow and with low turnover, then, yes, the current composition does provide important clues for the future returns. However, if the strategy has either high turnover or potentially large trading activity driven by market events, then the current composition can actually be quite misleading for predicting the future returns.

Let us consider two simple cases. In the first, the strategy at hand is what used to be called "portfolio insurance", which in essence was trying to replicate the downside S&P 500 put-option position by dynamically trading in the S&P 500 futures. Clearly, this strategy has a pretty high turnover, driven by the daily fluctuations of the S&P 500

Index. Moreover, its return pattern, by design, matches not that of a linear futures position, but that of a non-linear option position. In particular, the strategy is supposed to make money if the market fluctuates strongly but returns roughly to the same level over time, while the linear futures position, of course, would have close to zero return in this case.

In the second example, consider a simplified macro strategy, where the portfolio manager switches between the long and short positions in some macro index, such as the very same S&P 500 futures, depending on a bullish/bearish signal for the economy, eg, based on some macroeconomic model. These signals, by construction, would not change very frequently, sometimes staying in one state for many months or even years. But when they do, the impact on the strategy will be dramatic: it will reverse the sign of the returns. So, if we are interested in the distribution of the returns of such a strategy over the long period of time encompassing the business cycle, they will be quite different from the distribution of the underlying S&P 500 returns, even if for a typical month the returns might actually be identical.

So, it appears that in order to estimate the returns characteristics of the strategy, it is less important to know what the strategy trades, and more important to know how it trades. Moreover, the majority of professional investors who actually produce these returns exhibit a good level of discipline in what they do. Depending on their style and competitive advantage, they typically stick to certain patterns of behaviour and are driven by relatively stable methodologies which they use for estimating risks and returns within their universe of tradeable securities, and for allocating capital across particular investments. It is these behaviour patterns and stable methodologies that leave their imprint on the corresponding strategy returns. And while this statement is obviously true with respect to so called "quantitative" or "systematic" investment managers, we think it largely applies even to investors following the discretionary style, such as value-driven investors like Warren Buffett or Peter Lynch, or macro investors like George Soros or Bill Gross.

We could go a step further and say that each of the investment funds can be considered an independent company, whose stock (NAV) performance reflects the business model and the management style of that company. Unlike bricks-and-mortar businesses, such "virtual" companies do not have assets in which their business model is engrained. And looking at their balance sheet produces little more than the knowledge of their leverage and other basic facts. Unlike Gillette or Starbucks, you cannot really judge these companies by what products or services they produce, or what factories and stores they have. And while in real companies the management style also matters quite a lot (think Apple and Steve Jobs, or GE and Jack Welch), in the virtual financial holding companies that the investment funds really are, the management style and methodology is really the only thing that matters.

So, how can we discern meaningful patterns in such nebulous things as management style and methodology? How can we model investment strategy returns? There are three basic ways to model them, in order of decreasing granularity.

Micro-replication: in this approach, we actually try to figure out what each particular strategy does, build a systematic process similar to it in complete detail including specific trading signals in variety of chosen instruments, and then fine tune a few parameters to match the observed returns of the investment strategy benchmark, such as a particular hedge fund index.

Macro-replication: in this approach, we try to figure out which macro variables influence the strategy's returns, and try to build a time-series forecasting model with these variables.

Parametric: in this approach, the strategy return time series is modelled endogenously, in a manner similar to modelling "elementary" asset returns, eg, by well-known econometric methods.

The parametric approach, following the pioneering work of Fung and Hsieh (1997), attempts simply to understand the properties of hedge fund returns, while the replication approaches (see Takahashi and Yamamoto (2010) for a recent review) attempt to model the hedge fund strategies themselves in their full dynamics, in either a bottom-up or top-down manner. Each of the approaches has its pros and cons.

Micro-replication (Agarwal and Naik 2000; Wallerstein *et al* 2010) has been successful in mimicking some mainstream hedge fund strategies, such as CTA, equity stat arb or merger arb, so much so that there exist ETFs and ETNs making such strategies available for broad investor audience, eg, IndexIQ's IQ Hedge Multi-Strategy Tracker

(QAI). But for many other types of strategies, such an approach is hopelessly difficult and ambiguous.

The macro-replication is somewhat more universally applicable, especially in strategies which are known as "alternative beta", ie, where the performance of the strategy is driven by its exposure to well-identified market risk factors (Fung and Hsieh 2002, 2004; Hasanhodzic and Lo 2007), albeit ones that are not identical to an overall market index (such as value-versus-growth factor, carry trade, etc). Here too, certain alternative beta strategies have been sufficiently popular to launch a widely marketed ETF or ETN, for example, iPath Optimized Currency Carry ETN (ICI) and iPath S&P 500 VIX Short-Term Futures ETN (VXX). Such an approach, by design, does not explicitly model the strategy's pure alpha, treating it as a residual constant return. It also assumes that the strategy maintains a constant exposure to the chosen set of macro factors, which is also not necessarily a universally valid assumption.

On the other hand, the parametric approach, which we advocate in this chapter, does not concern itself with the detailed composition of returns or indeed with their attribution to other observable market factors. Instead, it treats the investment strategies in a holistic manner, as opaque financial assets with little more than their net asset values (NAVs) and returns visible to outside observers. It is universally applicable to any strategy that we may consider modelling, without contaminating the analysis with additional assumption on what goes on inside the portfolio manager's mind.

The main question here is the stability and interpretability of the results. The way to attain a positive answer to this question is not to modify the econometric model or make it more complex, but to choose a well-designed set of benchmark indexes or fund peer groups for estimation. This is akin to the old approach of modelling all stocks on the basis of their price/earnings (PE) ratios, but recognising that companies from different industry sectors or with widely different market caps may have substantial differences in the manner in which their PE impacts their future returns. There, too, the simple solution is to divide the universe of all stocks into relatively uniform peer groups, and to only compare the PE ratios within the same group.

Thus, to get sensible results from our chosen parametric approach, we must apply it to a set of investment strategy indexes which we believe have been constructed in a sufficiently uniform manner and with the appropriate amount of granularity. This requirement has led us to select the Lehman Brothers Hedge Fund Index, which was a part of the overall suite of global indexes built and maintained by Lehman's index group, and benefited from the thorough and disciplined rules-based methodology applied there in the same manner as their better known US Aggregate Bond Index. In our opinion, this set of indexes was much more complete and much better designed than the more widely disseminated CS Tremont, Hennessee or HFRI Indexes. While the latter have been around for longer and have possibly more hedge funds in their coverage, they use classification schemes which are outmoded and do not correspond to actual segmentation of the hedge fund universe by investment style or product focus. The Lehman Brothers Hedge Fund Index had, in contrast, a full set of available sub-indexes classified by style, product or region, all constructed in their typical consistent fashion. Unfortunately for the analysts, this index product did not survive the demise of the parent company and was discontinued by Barclays Capital in early 2009. Still, it offered a consistent set of data from early 2000 until the end of 2008, a period that saw two recessions, two market crashes and a multi-year boom, and so it appeared to still be the best choice for our research purposes, despite not being available after 2009.

AN ECONOMETRIC MODEL OF STRATEGY RETURNS

In this section, we specify the econometric model of investment strategy returns. Our model is a straightforward generalisation of the celebrated Garch family of models (Engle 1982; Bollerslev 1986; Bollerslev et al 1994), which is designed to capture the well-known stylised facts regarding the dynamics of financial time series, such as the clustering and mean reversion of time-varying volatility, fat-tailed distribution of periodic returns and asymmetric volatility responses which serve as a dynamic mechanism of generation of non-Gaussian features of long-run aggregate returns. Given that some investment strategies exhibit not only long-term asymmetries but also quite visible short-term asymmetries, we expand the definition to also include asymmetric fat tails of periodic returns. Finally, as it is the primary objective of our study, we allow non-zero conditionally time-varying means of the periodic returns.

We shall call this setup a generalized asymmetric autoregressive conditional heteroscedasticity (Gaarch) model (Berd 2008, 2009). The Gaarch(1, 1) model includes a single lag for both past returns and past conditional volatilities (excess variances)

$$r_t = \mu_t + \sigma_t \varepsilon_t \tag{21.1}$$

$$\mu_{t+1} = \alpha + y \sigma_{t+1}^2 \tag{21.2}$$

$$\sigma_{t+1} = \sigma_0 \sqrt{1 + \chi_{t+1}} \tag{21.3}$$

$$\chi_{t+1} = [m_2^- \eta^- + m_2^+ \eta^+ + \beta] \chi_t$$
$$+ \eta^- (1 + \chi_t)(\varepsilon_t^2 \cdot 1_{\varepsilon_t < 0} - m_2^-)$$
$$+ \eta^+ (1 + \chi_t)(\varepsilon_t^2 \cdot 1_{\varepsilon_t \geqslant 0} - m_2^+) \tag{21.4}$$

$$m_2^- = E\{\varepsilon^2 \cdot 1_{\varepsilon < 0}\} \tag{21.5}$$

$$m_2^+ = E\{\varepsilon^2 \cdot 1_{\varepsilon \geqslant 0}\} \tag{21.6}$$

Here we used the following notation.

- r_t is the single-period (in our case, monthly) return of the asset.
- ε_t are the residual returns for the period ending at t, which are independent and identically distributed variables with zero mean and unit variance.
- μ_t is the conditional mean of asset returns for the period ending at t.
- σ_0 is the unconditional volatility of asset returns.
- σ_t is the conditional volatility of asset returns for the period ending at t.
- χ_t is the conditional excess variance, equal to the percentage difference between the conditional and unconditional variance $\chi_t = \sigma_t^2 / \sigma_0^2 - 1$.
- $m_2^\pm$ are the truncated upside and downside second moments of single-period residual returns.

The specification of the Gaarch model incorporates a scale-invariant reparameterisation of the standard stationary Garch model (Engle 1982; Bollerslev 1986), separating the level of the unconditional volatility σ_0 and the conditional excess variance χ_t process. The dynamic asymmetry of volatility is specified in a manner similar to threshold-Garch (Tarch) (Zakoïan 1994) (see also GJR-Garch

(Glosten et al 1993)), but we redefined the Arch terms in a more symmetric fashion, without specifying which of the signs (positive or negative) is more influential. This is because in some asset classes, notably credit and volatility, the upside shocks are more influential, while in others, like equities or commodities, the downside shocks are more influential. The symmetric specification is obviously equivalent to Tarch but allows us to have a more natural positivity restriction on Arch coefficients, if so desired.

The conditional mean specification in Equation 21.2 is more or less in line with the conventional APT assumptions, if we assume that the strategy is uncorrelated with the overall market and that variability of returns is priced as an alternative beta. The unconditional mean α can be considered the "true alpha" of the strategy, ie, its excess return above the compensation for systematic risks that the strategy takes.

The conditional mean process can also be rewritten in a form that allows a more subtle attribution of expected returns. Introducing the parameter $\Gamma = \gamma \sigma_0^2$, which we will call "convexity compensation" because it resembles the additional return that any convex investment acquires under fair pricing rules, and using the definition of the excess variance process χ_t, we get

$$\mu_t = \alpha + \gamma \sigma_0^2 + \gamma \sigma_0^2 \left(\frac{\sigma_t^2}{\sigma_0^2} - 1 \right) = \alpha + \Gamma + \Gamma \chi_t \qquad (21.7)$$

This equation can be interpreted as a three-way attribution of conditional expected returns to the true alpha α, the convexity compensation Γ and time-varying excess variance compensation (the latter has an unconditional expected value of zero). We can also add the first two constants to get the risk-adjusted alpha of the strategy

$$\hat{\alpha} = \alpha + \Gamma \qquad (21.8)$$

Finally, let us specify the distribution of the return residuals ε_t. Our main criteria are that it must be parsimonious (ie, have no more than two free parameters to describe the asymmetric fat tails of a standardised distribution with zero mean and unit variance) and that the estimation of these parameters should be robust with respect to the deviation of sample returns from the zero mean assumption. The latter criterion is necessary because we would like as much separation as possible between the estimation of the Gaarch conditional mean and the estimation of the distribution of residuals.

The requirement of robustness with respect to sample mean suggests that we should consider distributions whose asymmetry is defined by their tail dependence, rather than by introducing a third-order skewness term which could be influenced by the estimate of the mean. From a variety of well-known skewed fat-tailed distributions, Jones–Faddy skewed t-distribution (Jones and Faddy 2003) fits our criteria best. The probability density and cumulative density functions of this distribution are

$$f(x \mid v^-, v^+) = \frac{1}{2^{v-1}\sqrt{v}B(\frac{1}{2}v^-, \frac{1}{2}v^+)}$$
$$\times \left(1 + \frac{x}{\sqrt{v+x^2}}\right)^{(v^-+1)/2} \left(1 - \frac{x}{\sqrt{v+x^2}}\right)^{(v^++1)/2}$$
(21.9)

$$F(t \mid v^-, v^+) = I\left(\frac{1}{2}\left(1 + \frac{t}{\sqrt{v+t^2}}\right), \frac{v^-}{2}, \frac{v^+}{2}\right) \quad (21.10)$$

where $v = (v^- + v^+)/2$, $B(a,b)$ is the beta function and $I(z,a,b)$ is the incomplete beta function.

The parameters v^- and v^+ have the meaning of the left and right tail parameters, as can be seen from the asymptotics of this distribution

$$f(x \mid v^-, v^+) \to \begin{cases} |x|^{-v^- -1} & \text{for } x \to -\infty \\ |x|^{-v^+ -1} & \text{for } x \to +\infty \end{cases} \quad (21.11)$$

The distribution (Equation 21.9) becomes equivalent to the conventional Student t-distribution when $v^- = v^+$, which in turn nests the Gaussian one when $v \to +\infty$, and therefore our entire model specification allows for the goodness-of-fit comparisons between different models and for the likelihood ratio tests of statistical significance of the estimated parameters.

THE TAXONOMY OF PATTERNS IN HEDGE FUND STRATEGY RETURNS

In this section, we attempt to classify the dependence of the quantitative characteristics of hedge fund strategy returns, seen through the empirical fit of the Gaarch model, on the type of peer group and other qualitative characteristics. We specifically highlight the non-Gaussian features of the returns, including the presence of fat tails, the asymmetry between the upside and downside tails, the volatility level and its dynamics and, in particular, the asymmetry of volatility response to return shocks (asymmetric leverage effect).

From Drost and Nijman (1993) and Berd *et al* (2007) we know that the relative order of importance of these characteristics from the perspective of description of intermediate/long-term distribution of returns in financial time series is as follows.

1. Persistence and mean reversion of vol (Garch terms): this governs the behaviour of conditional volatility and the vol of vol at intermediate timescales.
2. Asymmetric volatility response (Tarch terms): this is the leading contributor to the non-Gaussian features (tails and asymmetry) of long-run aggregated returns.
3. Fat-tailedness and asymmetry of periodic returns (non-Gaussian shocks): this is important for the short term (up to several periods).

We will confine the discussion in this section to the dynamic properties of the returns, and will postpone the discussion of the conditional means (expected returns) till the next section.

We apply the Gaarch model specified above (see the section on page 570) to the Lehman Brothers Hedge Fund Index (LBHF) and its sub-indexes. Given the limited historical monthly data for these indexes, available only from January 2000 until January 2009, and given the extreme realisations of the returns and volatilities in the second part of 2008, which would have dominated the small dataset and skewed the estimation of parameters significantly, we have chosen a somewhat shorter period of January 2000 until April 2008 as our sample period for estimation.

To ensure a better diversification of the sub-index returns, we used the equal-weighted version of the LBHF Index. While this may limit the applicability of our results from the perspective of investability of the corresponding representative indexes, using the assets-under-management-weighted (AUM-weighted) version would have subjected our data sample to the dominance of a small number of very large funds, making the corresponding index returns much more idiosyncratic. The equal-weighted version returns, on the other hand, appear quite systematic, and therefore we are able to obtain reasonable model fits despite the limited length of time series.

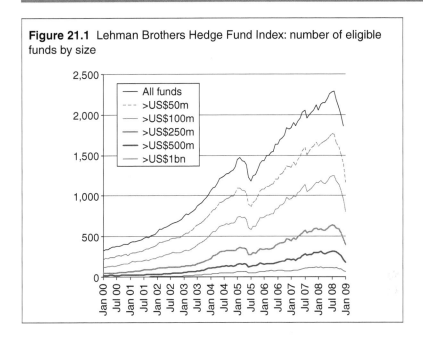

Figure 21.1 Lehman Brothers Hedge Fund Index: number of eligible funds by size

Table 21.1 Estimation of Gaarch model for LBHF size sub-indexes

Index (fund size US$)	Expected returns			Volatility dynamics				Tails	
	$\hat{\alpha}$	α	Γ	σ_0	η^-	η^+	β	v^-	v^+
All funds	8.25	16.05	−7.80	5.30	0.26	0.03	0.70	15.24	16.95
> 50m	7.86	15.20	−7.34	5.23	0.31	0.07	0.65	15.50	15.82
> 100m	7.32	15.23	−7.91	5.05	0.29	0.11	0.69	19.40	19.70
> 250m	7.19	14.21	−7.01	4.70	0.30	0.15	0.69	25.41	29.75
> 500m	6.98	13.59	−6.61	4.83	0.29	0.19	0.56	34.89	200.00
> 1bn	6.68	12.28	−5.60	4.31	0.39	0.47	0.44	48.78	200.00

The growth of the number of hedge funds eligible for inclusion in the LBHF Index is shown in Figure 21.1. The universe of funds in the index has grown from 325 in the beginning of 2000 to the peak number of 2,288 by August 2008, before dropping back to 1,583 by early 2009.

The results of the model fit for different size buckets of the LBHF Index are shown in Table 21.1. We also report the results of the model fit for style and asset class sub-indexes of the LBHF Index in Tables 21.2 and 21.3, respectively. In each table, we indicate the

Table 21.2 Estimation of Gaarch model for LBHF style sub-indexes

Index	Expected returns			Volatility dynamics				Tails	
	$\hat{\alpha}$	α	Γ	σ_0	η^-	η^+	β	ν^-	ν^+
Macro/directional	8.17	19.54	−11.37	6.85	0.19	0.02	0.73	11.74	11.52
Macro	7.77	12.95	−5.18	7.34	0.18	0.14	0.74	6.89	6.07
Long–short	9.26	22.27	−13.01	7.70	0.21	0.04	0.76	7.14	9.90
LS long only	16.51	23.67	−7.16	12.69	0.18	0.15	0.77	19.67	200.00
LS long bias	9.00	20.81	−11.81	9.56	0.26	0.00	0.75	7.81	9.05
LS variable bias	8.50	20.44	−11.94	5.84	0.20	0.10	0.74	12.72	18.02
LS short bias	0.37	6.03	6.40	8.57	0.12	0.11	0.81	11.77	10.50
CTA	7.44	2.95	10.39	10.34	0.12	0.09	0.65	200.00	52.06
CTA fundamental	7.58	5.49	2.09	7.14	0.16	0.06	0.80	166.36	100.45
CTA trend-following	8.40	−6.60	15.01	13.52	0.11	0.09	0.63	200.00	47.46
Relative value	7.87	12.68	−4.80	3.22	0.32	0.00	0.75	53.27	200.00
RV statistical arbitrage	8.65	15.03	−6.38	4.17	0.21	0.00	0.64	11.41	14.74
RV special situations/event driven	9.09	17.69	−8.60	4.46	0.16	0.00	0.88	36.77	200.00
RV distressed	9.32	16.18	−6.85	5.20	0.15	0.00	0.85	91.89	200.00
RV Reg D	9.48	13.20	−3.72	4.39	0.18	0.00	0.80	15.90	8.63
RV merger arbitrage	7.71	12.97	−5.26	3.99	0.20	0.22	0.71	21.45	125.73
RV market neutral-equity only	5.33	7.37	−2.04	3.23	0.18	0.20	0.73	4.85	5.99
RV broad relative value	8.30	13.09	−4.79	2.67	0.37	0.00	0.74	39.96	153.00

hierarchy of the sub-indexes by tabbing, eg, the CTA trend-following sub-index within the CTA Index is indicated by an extra tab level.

For the ease of comparison with well-known industry metrics, we report the values of risk-adjusted alpha $\hat{\alpha}$, true alpha α, convexity compensation Γ and unconditional volatility σ_0 in annualised percentage points terms. The coefficients which drive the volatility dynamics of the model are reported in Gaarch convention, including the downside η^- and upside η^+ Arch coefficients and the Garch coefficient β. Finally, we report the left ν^- and right ν^+ tail degrees of freedom of the Jones–Faddy skewed Student t-distribution of the residual returns.

Size dependence

As we can see from Table 21.1, the model fit is fairly uniform across all the size sub-indexes, with the unconditional volatility gradually decreasing from 5.30% across all funds, to 4.31% across funds with AUM greater than US$1 billion. Note that the distribution of fund sizes is heavily dominated by smaller funds, and therefore the equal-weighted indexes with low size cut-off are actually representative of small fund performance.

The most notable size dependence is the gradual convergence of the returns to more symmetric and normal distribution as the cut-off fund size grows. This is evidenced both by the diminishing difference between the downside (η^-) and upside (η^+) Arch coefficients and by the growing degrees of freedom both in the left (ν^-) and the right (ν^+) tails. Moreover, for the funds greater than US$500 million the right tail of the distribution actually becomes normal ($\nu = 200$ is a limiting value in our numerical estimation procedure, indicating a convergence to normal case which formally corresponds to $\nu \to +\infty$).

This could be explained by the hypothesis that the larger funds tend to be more internally diversified, following multi-strategy investment process, and are therefore, on average, less subject to tail risk and asymmetric leverage. Of course, this could also be a sign of a more stringent risk management and especially more careful operational risk management in larger funds, which minimises the likelihood of margin-call-induced forced selling and subsequent drawdowns (notwithstanding the negative examples of Amaranth, Sowood and a few other funds).

Table 21.3 Estimation of Gaarch model for LBHF asset class sub-indexes

Index	Expected returns			Volatility dynamics				Tails	
	$\hat{\alpha}$	α	Γ	σ_0	η^-	η^+	β	ν^-	ν^+
Multi-market	8.29	16.94	−8.65	5.28	0.18	0.00	0.72	129.44	200.00
MM macro/directional	8.69	16.14	−7.45	7.15	0.19	0.02	0.73	100.00	83.86
MM relative value	8.11	17.64	−9.54	4.01	0.19	0.00	0.86	67.51	200.00
MM multi-style	8.58	16.84	−8.27	4.97	0.23	0.00	0.79	132.04	200.00
Fixed income	9.46	12.61	−3.15	2.57	0.30	0.19	0.60	183.83	183.23
FI macro/directional	11.01	7.63	3.38	5.67	0.24	0.20	0.69	127.6	88.35
FI relative value	9.17	11.87	−2.70	2.33	0.20	0.08	0.66	19.78	27.07
FI multi-sector	9.64	8.36	1.29	3.41	0.21	0.12	0.73	7.30	9.21
FI government	8.96	7.27	1.69	3.69	0.22	0.20	0.71	4.71	4.42
FI corporate	10.61	13.29	−2.67	4.30	0.49	0.32	0.44	8.57	9.24
FI mortgages/securitised	9.02	9.10	−0.08	2.82	0.21	0.27	0.66	3.02	3.92
Equity	8.33	19.67	−11.34	7.19	0.22	0.03	0.77	6.30	8.40
EQ macro/directional	8.43	24.25	−15.83	8.06	0.15	0.02	0.82	5.87	7.43
EQ long–short	9.10	23.22	−14.12	7.91	0.22	0.05	0.75	7.24	9.71
EQ long only	16.49	28.49	−12.00	15.65	0.22	0.15	0.71	14.36	200.00
EQ long bias	8.76	21.49	−12.74	9.49	0.17	0.00	0.84	7.30	8.37

Table 21.3 Continued

Index	Expected returns		Volatility dynamics				Tails	
	$\tilde{\alpha}$	α	Γ	σ_0	η^-	η^+	β	ν^-	ν^+
EQ variable bias	8.67	20.81	−12.14	6.07	0.21	0.11	0.74	11.65	17.54
EQ short bias	−0.88	−12.03	11.14	9.80	0.06	0.06	0.90	164.82	90.8
EQ relative value	6.57	12.04	−5.47	4.22	0.31	0.00	0.79	46.79	200.00
EQ market neutral	5.33	7.37	−2.04	3.23	0.18	0.20	0.73	4.85	5.99
EQ other relative value	7.88	14.67	−6.79	5.47	0.25	0.00	0.83	15.31	38.23
EQ multi-sector:	8.72	20.08	−11.36	6.67	0.30	0.08	0.65	9.70	15.61
EQ energy	10.43	23.90	−13.47	10.95	0.21	0.09	0.82	7.57	10.88
EQ finance	11.01	3.18	7.83	7.60	0.12	0.05	0.84	46.04	200.00
EQ health care	9.88	9.60	0.29	16.09	0.20	0.25	0.67	5.67	7.01
EQ technology	4.38	18.17	−13.79	11.55	0.10	0.12	0.87	5.32	6.28
EQ real estate	7.20	12.61	−5.41	8.27	0.42	0.16	0.55	3.87	4.26
FX	5.62	2.81	2.81	7.35	0.10	0.08	0.85	200.00	28.51
Commodities	8.20	−3.58	11.78	11.92	0.17	0.08	0.60	191.59	60.7
Convertibles	7.88	12.13	−4.25	4.35	0.28	0.07	0.75	5.02	7.01
Broad market	8.28	16.56	−8.28	5.75	0.24	0.01	0.61	200.00	122.73
BR developed only	7.25	13.13	−5.87	4.88	0.25	0.00	0.80	8.54	10.26
BR emerging only	18.18	35.33	−17.14	10.9	0.22	0.31	0.58	11.31	29.12

Another visible dependence is the growing importance of the time-variability of volatility for bigger funds, evidenced by the relatively larger values of the Arch coefficients and smaller values of the Garch coefficient. This could simply be due to the fact that we have many fewer funds in the large fund category, and therefore the sub-index itself is much less diversified, leading to greater importance of idiosyncratic return shocks month to month.

An important caveat is that the number of funds drops significantly as the cut-off size grows, as seen from Figure 21.1. Therefore, our results for the larger size funds are subject to greater statistical errors than for the smaller ones.

Style dependence

The results of the model fit for different style sub-indexes of the LBHF Index are shown in Table 21.2. Here, there is a far bigger diversity of results, stemming from significant differences in the investment processes followed by the managers in each of these peer groups. The sub-indexes are grouped in three major sectors: macro/directional, CTA and relative value (RV), with finer subdivisions within each sector. We see dramatic contrast between the groups with respect to asymmetry and fat-tailedness of returns.

For example, some strategies, such as event driven, distressed and broad relative value, and all of the CTA strategies, have tails approaching the normality, as evidenced by large values of tail degrees-of-freedom parameters. On the other hand, certain strategies, such as the macro, long–short with variable bias, and many of the relative value strategies, exhibit strong fat tails in their periodic returns distribution.

The static asymmetry of periodic returns is captured by the difference in the left and right tail parameter. We see some cases where this asymmetry is very large, for example: LS long-only strategies, which has fat left tail and normal right tail; CTA composite, which has a normal left tail and a mildly fat right tail; the relative value composite, which has a mildly fat left tail and a normal right tail.

The dynamic asymmetry of returns, captured by the difference between the downside and upside Arch coefficients, is also markedly different across the strategy styles. For some, such as macro composite, CTA composite and CTA trend-following, LS long only, LS short bias, RV merger arbitrage and RV market-neutral equity, the difference is minimal and the dynamic asymmetry is insignificant. For others, such as fundamental CTA, and the vast majority of the relative value strategies, the downside Arch coefficient is much greater than the upside one, signifying that there is a strong dynamic asymmetry, which is known to generate strong downside asymmetry of aggregate returns over long horizons (see Berd *et al* (2007) and references therein). There are no strategies where the upside Arch coefficients would be much greater than the downside, ie, there are no strategies which would exhibit strong upside asymmetry of the aggregated returns over long horizons.

In each of these cases, we can see the vestiges of the corresponding strategy process in the distribution of its returns. Let us list some of the more obvious ones.

The CTA strategies trade futures, which have a linear risk profile. Moreover, in the vast majority of cases, they tend to have a reasonably low turnover, such that the biggest positions are held for a month or more. This makes the strategy returns over a month horizon (which is the periodicity of the returns in our sample) close to normal, because the daily fluctuations of the asset returns are allowed to aggregate over a month without strongly correlated position changes. This explanation is especially true for fundamental CTA strategies, and less so for trend-following ones, which occasionally dabble in the higher frequency trading that can scramble returns away from normal. Moreover, the fundamental CTA, being more prone to holding large futures positions over long periods of time, exhibits a stronger dynamic asymmetry of returns which is more in line with general market behaviour, whereas the trend-following CTA has less dynamic asymmetry because its typical holdings are less biased towards being long the market.

On the other hand, most relative value strategies actually behave like a carry trade, selling something that is rich (lower yielding in expected return) and buying something that is cheap (higher yielding in expected return). For any such strategy, the typical return profile is highly asymmetric, because it can get caught in a forced unwind of this "carry trade", which usually happens violently. The proverbial "collecting nickels in front of a steamroller" strategy, which the relative value is in large part, is indeed subject to an occasional run-down by the steamroller! Hence, we see it manifested in both static and dynamic asymmetry of returns on the downside.

The few exceptions from this rule also are telling. Both the event driven and (especially) distressed relative value strategies are quite different, in that they typically have much more balanced upside-versus-downside trade profiles. For example, a distressed bond, which trades at 40 cents on a US dollar, has an upside of 60 cents versus a downside of 40 cents, which is a dramatically different profile than a typical yield-based relative value bond trade, where we hope to collect a few tens of basis points but take a full principal risk (albeit with low probability).

Finally, we can make sense of the patterns observed in various flavours of long–short strategies, by noting that the long bias and variable bias strategies are similar to more imprecise and loosely built relative value strategies, and correspondingly they exhibit similar features, namely fat tails and dynamic asymmetry of volatility. On the other hand, the long only and short bias strategies are quite different in their process. They are often run by fundamental managers who put on large conviction trades and do not rely on formal hedging for risk management. Most importantly, because they do not hedge, they also cannot employ a lot of leverage, which is usually the main cause of the asymmetric volatility response. This is indeed reflected in the much more symmetric pattern across the downside and upside fitted Arch coefficients for these strategies.

Asset class dependence

The results of the model fit for different asset class sub-indexes of the LBHF Index are shown in Table 21.3. The segmentation by traded asset class appears to have less discriminatory power over the return characteristics, in part because, within each asset class, different hedge funds pursue different investment styles. In fact, the subsectors classified by the investment style exhibit a stronger dispersion of model characteristics, then the top level of this classification.

The most notable fact is that, for those asset classes which admit a large variety of investment styles, encompassing both the macro or CTA styles and the relative value styles, the corresponding top-level composite index exhibits almost normal distribution of periodic returns. This is most likely to be due to the mutually diversifying effects of those sub-styles in each asset class composite. The

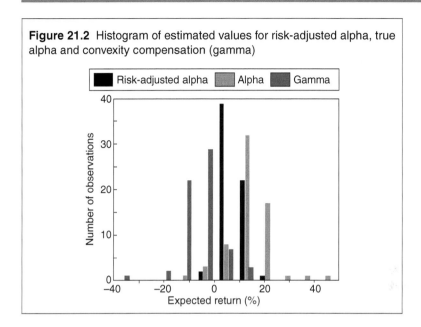

Figure 21.2 Histogram of estimated values for risk-adjusted alpha, true alpha and convexity compensation (gamma)

exceptions (convertibles and equity composites) are most likely to be overly dominated by thematic and sectoral funds and the corresponding composite is simply not diverse enough in style to achieve the normality of returns.

In this classification, we see for the first time the difference between the funds focused on the emerging markets (EMs) versus those trading in developed markets only. It is telling that the emerging market funds exhibit larger variability of volatility, but with less asymmetry: a feature generally present in strategies which are exposed to a lot of idiosyncratic return sources, as opposed to the ones whose returns are more systematic in nature. The lower typical leverage levels could also be an explanatory factor for this difference.

THE NATURE OF ALPHA

Let us now turn our attention away from the volatility dynamics and distribution of return shocks and towards the expected returns and their dependence on the conditional volatility. In all three results Tables 21.1–21.3 we show the estimates of the true alpha α, convexity compensation $\Gamma = \gamma \sigma_0^2$ and the risk-adjusted alpha $\hat{\alpha} = \alpha + \Gamma$.

The first thing that strikes the eye is the remarkable uniformity of the risk-adjusted alpha estimates across all LBHF sub-indexes, despite a substantially varied levels of true alpha and convexity compensation. The histograms of distributions of these model parameters are shown in Figure 21.2.

The few notable outliers are: LS long only (in style sub-indexes) and EQ long only (in asset class sub-indexes), which benefited from the "bubble-esque" run-up in asset prices from 2000 until first half of 2008 (our sample period), and LS short bias and EQ short bias, which suffered from the same historical fact. We also note the outsized risk-adjusted returns in the broad emerging markets sub-index, which is explained by a secular rise in the emerging markets integration in the global capital markets and also to some extent by the super-fast economic growth and the bubble-like run-up in the key commodity prices, affecting EM investments.

Save these few exceptions, the rest of the sectors exhibit risk-adjusted alpha between 5% and 10%, with most clustered around the magic "8%" number that must warm the hearts of pension fund managers everywhere, because it is precisely what they often assume for the long-term expected returns in their portfolios. We will reserve judgement on whether this number is reliable going forward; this is the subject of much discussion these days between the "old normal" and "new normal" paradigm proponents.

What is even more remarkable than the uniformity of the risk-adjusted alphas is that the vast majority of hedge fund sectors exhibit positive true alpha but negative convexity compensation Γ. Remembering that the same value of Γ also enters the time-varying component of the conditional mean $\Gamma \chi_t$ (see Equation 21.7), we are led to conclusion that when the volatility of the strategy returns increases ($\chi > 0$), these strategies tend to lose money and, vice versa, their returns get a positive boost whenever their return volatility is lower than the unconditional forecast ($\chi < 0$).

It is important to note that in our Gaarch model's conditional mean specification (Equation 21.2) the relationship is between the "forecast" of the conditional variance for the next time period σ_{t+1}^2 and the conditional expected (mean) return for that future period μ_{t+1}. In other words, this is not the usual leverage effect in financial time series, which runs in the opposite direction: large realised returns precede increasing volatility. The effect we are describing might be consistent with the notion that somehow the relationship between the mean return and the scale of the return distribution in

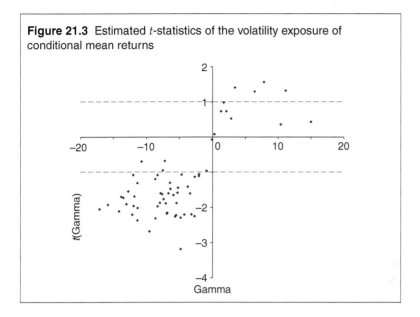

Figure 21.3 Estimated t-statistics of the volatility exposure of conditional mean returns

a given period is fixed, and then the predictive power of the volatility forecast over the mean return is simply by translation, due to clustered volatility. That would be an easy answer, except it would require that the mean return be always "positively" proportional to the forecasted volatility, which is actually the opposite of what we observe in the vast majority of cases.

In fact, we have discovered empirically that most hedge fund strategies have expected returns which are negatively proportional to the forecasted variance, and so are essentially "short vol". Of course, this is not the same meaning of this phrase as usually used by traders, ie, the vast majority of these strategies do not actually have a negative exposure to some option-like instruments. Rather, what they have is a systematic pattern of investment which produces returns similar to those that would be produced by a short option position. Figure 21.3 demonstrates that in most cases the volatility exposure coefficients are statistically significant. In fact, for most of the negative values observed we have t-statistics greater than 1 in absolute value, and for some even greater than 2.

The statement about being short vol applies to all of the broad-based LBHF sub-indexes, all Relative Value sub-indexes, and to most long–short strategies, but it does not apply to LS short bias, CTA, CTA Trend-following style sub-indexes, and to FI macro/directional, FI multi-sector, FI government, EQ short bias, FX and commodities asset class sub-indexes.

We believe that both the positive and the negative examples of this statement are very relevant for understanding of the nature of investment strategy alpha. In the remainder of this section we will present a laundry list of both fundamental and technical reasons explaining why are most investment strategies short volatility, and what drives the exceptions.

Fundamental reasons

- Volatility is a synonym for "risk". It is tough to have both a positive expected return and benefit from risk. If it was easily done, everyone would do it, and would thus change the properties of those strategies. So, the strategies appear to be short vol partly for Darwinian reasons, because they are successful.

- Any well-defined investment strategy is intrinsically short an opportunity to reallocate to other strategies, which is usually triggered by either large loss or a large gain over some medium-term horizon. This can be interpreted as if the strategy contained a short straddle option on its own medium-term trailing returns, which naturally leads to a negative relationship between past volatility and future expected returns.

- As a corollary to the previous point, we should mention that the cash asset can be considered a long opportunity option. The dry powder in your wallet gives you the opportunity to deploy it whenever you wish. Again, if the cash is long vol, then having spent the cash and invested in a strategy, the investors get shorter vol.

- The ultimate demand to be long risk comes from the real economy, where the main risk takers, the entrepreneurs, would like to share these risk exposures with outside investors. Therefore, investors in aggregate must be short the risk level (ie, lose money when the risk goes up), otherwise they would serve no useful purpose for the real economy.

Technical reasons
- Liquidity reasons: it is difficult to maintain a positive vol/convexity strategy with large capacity, unless we take large directional risks "and" are willing to sacrifice potentially sizeable carry costs. Providing liquidity is the only way to handle large capacity, and it leads to being short vol.
- Leverage and financing: most relative value strategies are designed to capture small pricing differences, and therefore must be leveraged to achieve reasonable nominal returns. This leverage and financing requirement, which is naturally short-term and subject to refinincing risk, exposes all relative value strategies to volatility risk (ie, risk of uncertain volatility), when an increase in perceived vol will lead to higher margin requirement and trigger more trading and increased losses. This mechanism, in particular, was in abundant display during the recent crisis.
- Any convergence, contrarian or relative value strategy that is betting on some sort of mean reversion or a convergence of some risk/return metrics is naturally short vol, because it explicitly bets against the wings of the returns distribution. We shall illustrate this point below in greater detail.
- Many relative value strategies are really "carry trades", buying the higher yielding (cheap) asset and selling short the lower yielding (rich) one. And, like all carry trades, they are also naturally short vol because they are exposed to decompression risk, which is in turn directional with vol.

Reasons behind the exceptions
- As a corollary to our statement about convergence strategies, we can deduce that the momentum, trend-following strategies (which are essentially the opposites of the convergence) are naturally long vol. The CTA, CTA trend-following, and commodities strategies fall under this rule.
- The niche for opportunistic/directional players always exists, but will always be limited in capacity. Notable exceptions from this are the directional fixed income (particularly in the government sector) and FX strategies, where the "other side" of the trade is the global economy and central banks, which

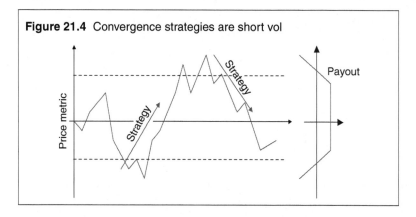

Figure 21.4 Convergence strategies are short vol

are acting as risk absorbers rather than risk demanders. The FI macro/directional, FI multi-sector, FI government and FX strategies fall under this rule.

- The short bias strategy's long-vol exposure is somewhat coincidental: the higher volatility is generally associated with downside markets, which in turn benefit the short bias strategy, so it is the market asymmetry that plays the role here.

Why are convergence strategies short vol, while momentum strategies are long vol?

Any convergence strategy, when implemented in a disciplined way, will ultimately buy some assets when their price is "too low" and will sell them when their price is "too high", whatever the metrics they use to determine these thresholds. As a result, such strategies are betting that the prices will stay closer to the middle of the distribution and therefore betting against the wings of distribution. This is essentially a short strangle position on the assets, and is therefore naturally short volatility, but it benefits from a positive carry (collecting option premiums).

The propensity of convergence strategies to be short vol is even clearer at the times of sudden change in volatility regime. Even if the strategy was correct in both regimes, meaning that it has set the appropriate thresholds and will on average make money by buying low and selling high in each of these regimes, it will inevitably lose money when the low vol regime is transitioning to a high-vol regime, and correspondingly the thresholds are being widened out. This logic is illustrated in Figures 21.4 and 21.5.

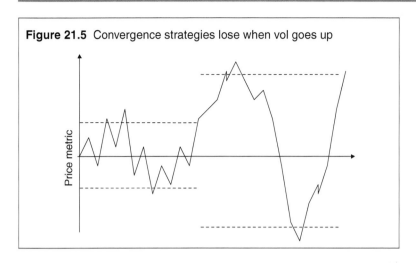

Figure 21.5 Convergence strategies lose when vol goes up

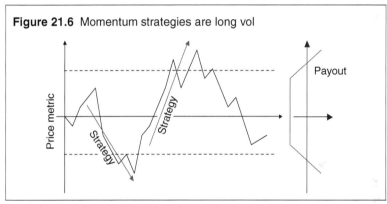

Figure 21.6 Momentum strategies are long vol

On the other hand, any momentum strategy, when implemented in a disciplined way, will buy some assets when their price is going up and sell them when their price is going down, using some sort of metrics to establish a proper timescale and thresholds. As a result, contrary to convergence strategies, these are betting that the prices will move further away from the middle of the distribution. This is essentially a long strangle position on the assets, and is therefore naturally long vol, but suffers from a short carry. This logic is illustrated in Figure 21.6.

The observation that the trend-following strategies have option-like behaviour has been made in a much more detailed manner in a notable paper by Fung and Hsieh (2001), building on an earlier work by Glosten and Jagannathan (1994). What we argue here is that this insight applies almost uniformly across all hedge fund styles, once we recognise the differences in their volatility dynamics.

Note that when we talk about the disciplined investment process we do not necessarily mean a black-box, quantitative approach to investing. Certainly, it fits the bill. But so does a process followed by most traditional, discretionary portfolio managers who have their own step-by-step approach to determining the good investment opportunities. Warren Buffett is certainly not a quant, but his value style of investment is eminently disciplined and perhaps even repeatable (or so he hoped in hiring a replacement for himself recently), and is therefore very much subject to the same patterns that we have identified. In fact, we could probably explain a good deal of Buffett's investment returns by noting that he runs a distressed contrarian strategy (therefore somewhat short vol, but not as much as other relative value strategies, and less subject to asymmetric drawdowns), and he also keeps around a great deal of cash which, as we mentioned above, has some long-vol characteristics, especially when coming out of recessions when the opportunity value of cash is greatest.

PRACTICAL LESSONS

The most important result which we obtained here is that the vast majority of mainstream investment strategies have negative volatility exposure, whether or not they actually know it. We call this an "implicit volatility exposure", to distinguish it from implied volatility exposure, which we obtain when trading options.

It is very difficult to manage such an exposure if we do not recognise it explicitly. The false sense of being hedged or being market neutral lulls many portfolio managers into the trap of high leverage and leaves them exposed to the risk of sudden margin calls when the vol goes up, which is the most painful way to discover your dependence on a risk factor.

We believe that this was in some way a contributing factor towards the "Quant Crunch" of 2007, as well as towards the more benign but equally befuddling behaviour of quant strategies in 2009 after the beginning of The Federal Reserve's quantitative easing programme. Just a month before the Quant Crunch, two Bear Stearns hedge funds focused on structured credit blew up, followed by Sowood, another credit hedge fund focused on leveraged loan investing. That marked the turning point for the market volatility, which went up from the multi-year lows. As noted elsewhere in this book (Chapter 5), the Quant Crunch was caused by a liquidity squeeze in the crowded quantitative long–short equity space. But what precipitated this squeeze was the notch up in the volatility.

As for the 2009 "great recovery", which left behind many traditional quant managers, it also seems to fit our description. What The Fed has done from March 2009 (and is doing at the time of writing again with QE2), is acting as a risk absorber, and actively damping the level of all risks in the market. This leads to a fast drop in vol and a correspondingly large outperformance of convergence strategies. However, the outperformance was even greater for the extreme mean-reversion strategy pushing up the prices of every stock that went particularly far down in the preceding crisis period (what the CNBC pundits were calling a "melt-up" of the markets). This left the more mainstream slow-turnover quant strategies, which often identify risky stocks to short in order to maintain market neutrality, dangerously squeezed by this run-up in the "crappy" stocks. Simultaneously, it meant a significant headwind for trend-following strategies, which not surprisingly did not do very well in 2009.

So, what should the investors do with all these insights? There are several ways the implicit volatility risks can be managed once they have been identified. First and foremost, we can employ style and strategy diversification. Combining the strategies which are naturally short vol with those that are long will lead to a better overall portfolio. This is why all funds of funds must have a healthy allocation to CTAs and other trend-following strategies, and to macro fixed income and FX strategies, since those are the ones that have positive vol exposure yet still can offer a reasonable capacity.

An even better approach is to add explicit (or implied) volatility exposure to the portfolio, by investing in volatility strategies. Volatility as an asset class has been on the rise in recent years, although it still suffers from the lack of respect resulting in the absence of appropriate silo in which to put an allocation to this strategy (that is to say, it has not yet achieved a mainstream status) and many institutional investors do not think it can handle the size issues very well. Also, a lot of investors associate volatility strategies with just protective put option buying ("black swan" insurance), the cost of which is often prohibitive. We actually prefer dynamic volatility strategies mixing both directional, relative value and tail risk protection styles, which can provide the right amount of protection while also earning some alpha along the way, rather than costing an arm and a leg as pure insurance strategies do. We believe that the ideal volatility strategy mix must achieve return characteristics somewhat similar to fixed income macro strategies (Table 21.3), combining small but positive true alpha with positive (and large) convexity compensation, with the fatter upside tail of the return shocks and no dynamic asymmetry. This cannot be achieved by trading volatility in any single asset class, but it might be possible if we build a comprehensive volatility strategy encompassing different asset classes and investment styles (Berd 2007, 2009).

Moreover, we can draw even further parallels between the current market conditions and the lessons learned from the past. As we mentioned in the previous section, the FX and fixed income macro and government strategies are among the few exceptions which exhibit both positive true alpha and positive convexity compensation. This is due to the fact that they actually trade not so much against other market participants but against the macro-economic forces of global governments and central banks, which are intentionally absorbing risks or, as we might interpret it, are selling vol so cheaply that it is possible to maintain a positive convexity while still earning small but positive carry costs.

Given that the global economy currently appears to be on "life support" from various governments, we think that not only the FX and FI macro and government strategies but also many other strategies such as those investing in equities or distressed debt will naturally acquire the same characteristics stemming from the governments' supply of cheap vol. This is a fascinating, even if highly speculative, thought. Testing it and implementing its consequences for investment strategies going forward will be a very worthy challenge.

> The author thanks the many colleagues with whom he has discussed these topics over the years, including Robert Engle and Artem Voronov, Arthur Tetyevsky, Mark Howard, Eric Rosenfeld, Bob Litterman, Marc Potters and Jean-Philippe Bouchaud.

1 CTA funds are commonly known as "commodity trading advisors", though the modern CTA investors often trade in futures of all asset classes, not just commodities.

REFERENCES

Agarwal, V., and N. Y. Naik, 2000, "Performance Evaluation of Hedge Funds with Option-Based and Buy-and-Hold Strategies", Hedge Fund Centre Working Paper HF-003, London Business School.

Berd, A. M., 2007, "Investing through Volatility Cycles", QA Capital, Presentation, October.

Berd, A. M., 2008, "Empirical Models of Investment Strategy Returns: Asymmetry, Fat Tails and the Nature of Alpha", Presented at Quant Congress Europe, London, November.

Berd, A. M., 2009, "Volatility of Investment Strategies vs Volatility as an Investment Strategy", presented at ICBI Global Derivatives Trading and Risk Management Conference, Rome, April.

Berd, A. M., and A. Tetyevsky, 2002, "Wag the Dog: the Impact of Volatility on Credit Strategies", Lehman Brothers Credit Strategies, Working Paper, November.

Berd, A. M., R. F. Engle and A. Voronov, 2007, "The Underlying Dynamics of Credit Correlations", *Journal of Credit Risk* 3(2), pp. 27–62.

Bollerslev, T., 1986, "Generalized Autoregressive Conditional Heteroskedasticity", *Journal of Econometrics* 31, pp. 307–27.

Bollerslev, T., R. F. Engle, and D. Nelson, 1994, "Arch Models", in D. F. McFadden and R. F. Engle (eds), *The Handbook of Econometrics*, Volume IV (Amsterdam: North-Holland).

Drost, F. C., and T. E. Nijman, 1993, "Temporal Aggregation of Garch Processes", *Econometrica* 61, pp. 909–27.

Engle, R. F., 1982, "Autoregressive Conditional Heteroscedasticity with Estimates of the Variance of United Kingdom Inflation", *Econometrica* 50, pp. 987–1006.

Fama, E. F., and K. R. French, 1993, "Common Risk Factors in the Returns on Bonds and Stocks", *Journal of Financial Economics* 33, p. 3.

Fung, W., and D. A. Hsieh, 1997, "Empirical Characteristics of Dynamic Trading Strategies: The Case of Hedge Funds", *The Review of Financial Studies* 10(2), pp. 275–302.

Fung, W., and D. A. Hsieh, 2001, "The Risk in Hedge Fund Strategies: Theory and Evidence from Trend Followers", *The Review of Financial Studies* 14(2), pp. 313–41.

Fung, W., and D. A. Hsieh, 2002, "Asset-Based Style Factors for Hedge Funds", *Financial Analysts Journal* 58(5), pp. 16–27.

Fung, W., and D. A. Hsieh, 2004, "Hedge Fund Benchmarks: A Risk-Based Approach", *Financial Analysts Journal* 60(5), pp. 65–80.

Glosten L. R., and R. Jagannathan, 1994, "A Contingent Claim Approach to Performance Evaluation", *Journal of Empirical Finance* 1, pp. 133–60.

Glosten, L. R., R. Jagannathan and D. Runkle, 1993, "On the Relation between the Expected Value and the Volatility of the Nominal Excess Return on Stocks", *Journal of Finance* 48, pp. 1779–801.

Hasanhodzic, J., and A. W. Lo, 2007, "Can Hedge-Fund Returns Be Replicated?: The Linear Case", *Journal of Investment Management* 5(2).

Jones, M. C., and M. J. Faddy, 2003, "A Skew Extension of the t-Distribution, with Applications", *Journal of Royal Statistical Society* B 65(1), pp. 159–74.

Lintner, J., 1965, "The Valuation of Risk Assets and the Selection of Risky Investments in Stock Portfolios and Capital Budgets", *Review of Economics and Statistics* 47, p. 13.

Mossin, J., 1966, "Equilibrium in a Capital Asset Market", *Econometrica* 34, p. 768.

Ross, S. A., 1976, "The Arbitrage Theory of Capital Asset Prices", *Journal of Economic Theory* 13, p. 341.

Sharpe, W. F., 1964, "Capital Asset Prices: A Theory of Market Equilibrium under Conditions of Risk", *Journal of Finance* 19, p. 425.

Takahashi, A., and K. Yamamoto, 2010, "Hedge Fund Replication", in Y. Watanabe (ed), *The Recent Trend of Hedge Fund Strategies*, Chapter 2, pp. 57–95 (Hauppauge, NY: Nova Publishers).

Wallerstein, E., N. S. Tuchschmid and S. Zaker, 2010, "How Do Hedge Fund Clones Manage the Real World?", *Journal of Alternative Investments* 12(3), pp. 37–50.

Zakoïan, J.-M., 1994, "Threshold Heteroskedastic Models", *Journal of Economic Dynamics and Control* 18, pp. 931–55.

Index

(page numbers in italic type relate to tables or figures)

A

adjustable-rate mortgages (ARMs) 4, 59, 189
AIG, xxvii, 129, 135, 147–50
   before crisis, 143–4
   collateral dynamics of, *150*
Ambac, xxvii
American Monte Carlo, 385–6, 403–4
Arbitrage Pricing Theory (APT), 566

B

Barclays Capital, 570
Bear Stearns, xxv, 51, 129, 134, 204–5, 559, 590
Black, Fischer, xvii, 412–3, 430
Black–Scholes model, 195, 198, 433, 441, 503, 556
Black swan, xli, 270, 439, 451, 591
bubbles, Martingale theory of, 493–510
   characterisation, 499
   definition, 497–8
   detecting, 508–10
   existence, 498–9
   foreign-currency, 506–7
   model, 494–7
      and market price process, 495
      and well-functioning economy, 496–7
   valuing derivatives, 500–6
      and American call options, 503–5
      bounded-payout, 501
      and forwards and European call and put options, 501–3
      and futures contracts, 505–6
Buffett, Warren, xxvii, 567, 590

C

Capital Asset Pricing Model (CAPM), 561, 566
central counterparties (CCPs), xxix–xxxi
Citibank, xxv
clearinghouses:
   centralised, 154–5
   limitations of, 156–7
Cohn, Gary, 124
combined loan-to-value (CLTV) 24–5, 27–8, 30, 46
contingent claims analysis (CCA) 187, 195–8, 211–14
   systemic methodology of, 200–1
counterparty clearing, 145–7
credit derivatives, *362*, *368*, *369*
   and affine model, with common and idiosyncratic factors, 358–62
   and calibration procedure for fully collateralised CDS, 362
   coordinate transformation, 360
   framework, 358–60
   and fully collateralised CDS pricing, 361
   and CDS contract, CVA for, 363–5
   and bilateral CVA for single CDS, 364–5
   and fully collateralised single CDS, 363–4
   and unilateral CVA for single CDS, 364
   and CDSs, bilateral CVA for, 370–6
   and Monte Carlo algorithm, 373–6

and N credits, 372–3
  when $N = 4$, 370–1
  when $N = 5$, 371–2
and CDSs, CVA for, 348–59
and credit-linked notes, 352–4
  bilateral CVA for, 366–7
  bilateral value adjustment, 354–6
  CVAs for, 366–7
  unilateral CVA for, 366
  unilateral value adjustment, 352–4
and default event correlation, 362–3
fully collateralised CDS, 349–50, 363–4
  calibration procedure for, 362
  pricing, 361
  single, 363–4
and numerical results, illustrated, 367–70
and partial integro-differential equation (PIDE), numerical solution for, 365
partially collateralised CDS: unilateral and bilateral value adjustments, 351–2
and practical issues and controversies, 357–8
pricing of, with and without counterparty and collateral adjustments, 347–76
role of, in credit crisis, 130–6
and shortfall for credit-linked notes, 348–58
and single CDS, bilateral CVA for, 364–5
and single CDS, unilateral CVA for, 364
uncollateralised CDS: bilateral CVA, 351
uncollateralised CDS: unilateral CVA, 350–1
valuation of portfolio of CDS positions, 348–9

credit networks, evaporation of trust in, 475–9
credit-linked notes, 352–4
  bilateral CVA for, 366–7, *368, 369*
  bilateral value adjustment, 354–6
  CVAs for, 366–7
  unilateral CVA for, 366
  unilateral value adjustment, 352–4

D

default event correlation, 362–3
derivative markets, post-crisis structural reform of, 151–5
  centralised clearinghouses, 154–5, *155*
  clearing, 153
  participants, 153
  regulators, 152–3
  segregation of collateral, 154
  trading on an exchange or alternate swap execution facility, 153
derivatives markets, *130, 131, 132, 133, 135, 139, 140, 143, 148, 152, 158*
  and clearing among clearinghouse members, 158
  and clearinghouses, centralised, 154–5
  and clearinghouses, limitations of, 156–7
  and corporate credit-default swap growth, single-trance CDO contribution to, 132
  and counterparty clearing, 145–7
  crisis role of, 130–6
  and pre-crisis, 136
  impact of crisis on, 129–64
  and infrastructure developments, *137–8*
  and initial margin and leverage, 142

and initial margin,
    determinants of, 140–1,
    141
and initial margin,
    framework for setting,
    141–2
and innovation, regulation
    outpaced by, 134–6
and innovation,
    understanding outpaced
    by, 134
and leverage, 139
limiting systemic risk of,
    initial and variation
    margin's role in, 139–40
and mortgage market, 129–30
and OTC, pre-crisis changes
    to, 136
and post-crisis reform,
    central counterparty
    clearing, 145–7
post-crisis, legacy of
    asymmetric collateral
    posting in, 145
post-crisis structural reform
    of, 151–5
pre-crisis, systemic risk issues
    concerning, 136–45
regulatory framework for, *152*
US regulation of, condensed
    history of, 146–7
distressed exchanges (DEs)
    167–83, *172–3, 174, 175*
in corporate restructurings,
    167–83
defaults of, in CDS swap
    market, 169–70
implications of, 168–9
in 2008, 170–1
recovery rates on, 174–5
subsequent development of,
    181, 182
subsequent performance of,
    175–8, *176–9, 180*
trend of, 178–80
Dodd–Frank Wall Street Reform
    and Consumer Protection
    Act, 129, 146, 152, 157

E

Efficient Market Hypothesis, 462
equity portfolios with
    fundamental factors, *266,
    267, 269, 272, 273, 274, 275,
    276, 277*
    Barra extreme risk model,
        267–9
    and forecast accuracy,
        measuring, 278–9
    and forecast accuracy,
        statistical tests of, 270–2,
        272
    models, 270
    test portfolios, 271
    test statistics, 271–2
    forecasting, 265–79
    and pair portfolios, 276
    results, 272
        and tilt portfolios, total
            and active risk of, 272
        and tilt portfolios, risk by
            regime, 274–6
evaporation of trust in credit
    networks, 475–9

F

Fama, Eugene, 566
financial crisis:
    avoiding, 14–19
        agency costs, 14–16
        and models, need for, 18
        and models, use of, 18–19
        transparency, 16
    and credit investor's
        perspective into active risk
        management, 545–63, *551,
        554, 557, 448*
    and asset-class
        diversification as a weak
        risk-management tool,
        560–2
    looking back and forward,
        546–9
    necessity, not luxury, 550
    and participant actions,
        relevancy of, 558–9

597

and portfolio tail-risk management, systemic risk exposures mitigated by, 551–2
and reduction of "sunk" costs, 550–1
and dynamic replication, more than, 555–6
and severity as more important than probability, 562
and tail-risk hedging, 554–5
and traditional valuation models, irrelevancy of, 556–8
and varying costs and opportunities, 552–4
and derivatives markets, *130, 131, 132, 133, 135, 139, 140, 143, 148, 152, 158*
and clearing among clearinghouse members, 158
and clearinghouses, centralised, 154–5
and clearinghouses, limitations of, 156–7
and corporate credit-default swap growth, single-trance CDO contribution to, 132
and counterparty clearing, 145–7
crisis role of, 130–6
impact of crisis on, 129–64
and infrastructure developments, *137–8*
and initial margin and leverage, 142
and initial margin, determinants of, 140–1, *141*
and initial margin, framework for setting, 141–2
and innovation, regulation outpaced by, 134–6
and innovation, understanding outpaced by, 134
and leverage, 139
limiting systemic risk of, initial and variation margin's role in, 139–40
and mortgage market, 129–30
and OTC, pre-crisis changes to, 136
post-crisis, legacy of asymmetric collateral posting in, 145
and post-crisis reform, central counterparty clearing, 145–7
post-crisis structural reform of, 151–5
pre-crisis, systemic risk issues concerning, 136–45
regulatory framework for, *152*
US regulation of, condensed history of, 146–7
and impetus for regulatory change, 147–51
implied credit correlation metrics before and during, 283–316, *293, 294, 297, 298, 303, 308, 309, 310, 311, 314*
expected tranche loss surface, 312–14
Gaussian copula model, 288–98
implied copula, 299–307, 311–12
market quotes, 286–8
more recent data, application to, 307–8
key features of, 188–93
lessons from, 3–21
ABS CDOs, 9–12, *10, 11, 12* 13, 16–18
asset-backed securities (ABSs) 8–12, *8, 10, 11, 12,* 13, 16

collateralised debt
obligations (CDOs) 9–10,
10
and ratings, 13–14
and regulatory changes, 19
securitisation, 7–12
US housing market, 3–7, *4*
lessons and practical insights
concerning, 515–43
future directions, 530–41
and investment process,
521–30
OTC derivatives and,
xxv–xxvii
origins, outcomes, lessons
from, debating, xxii
and quantitatively managed
equity portfolios, 515–43,
519
crisis's effects on, detailed,
530–3
different flavours of, 517
future directions, 530–41
and investment process,
521–30
and portfolio management
and production, 537–9
and risk management,
539–40
and waves, effects of,
517–18
and regulatory change, 19
impetus for, 147–51
structural reform of
derivatives markets after,
151–5
centralised
clearinghouses, 154–5, *155*
clearing, 153
participants, 153
regulators, 152–3
segregation of collateral,
154
trading on an exchange or
alternate swap execution
facility, 153
systemic risk during,
contribution of

asymmetric collateral
posting to, 144–5
financial instruments,
proliferation of: spiralling
towards complete
markets, 468–73
ideal in ideal world, 469–71
interacting in interacting
market, 471–3
financial-instability hypothesis,
53
French, Kenneth, 566
forecast accuracy, statistical tests
of, 270–2, *272*
models, 270
test portfolios, 271
test statistics, 271–2

G

Garch model, xliv, *220*, 225, 269,
285, 442, 570–1
Glass–Steagall Act, xxiv
Goldman Sachs, 124, *519, 520*,
543
Greenspan, Alan, 21, 410
Gross, Bill, xxxii, 567

I

Iceland:
banking system of, *see*
Icelandic banking system
consumption spree in, 76
house and stock prices of, rise
in, 73–5, *74*
private-sector credit boom in,
71–3, *73*
Icelandic banking system,
65–116, *66, 67, 68, 69, 71,
72, 73, 74, 75, 76, 77, 78, 79,
82, 83, 84, 85, 86, 87, 89, 91,
93, 94, 99, 103, 105, 109,
111, 114, 115*
asset quality of, 97–104
and loans to household
sector, 99–101, *100, 101*
and poor corporate
governance and leveraged
bank owners, 102–4

599

and sharp rise in loans to corporate sector, 95–9, *96*, *97*
and trading assets, size of, versus peers' 101–2, *102*
collapse of, 65–116
early-warning indicators of crisis in, 69–70
and large bank balance sheets, 70–1
and HF Fund, *72*, 72–3, 99–100
liabilities of, *104*
and mini crisis of, 2006 79–81
Nordic peers of, qualitative fundamentals below, 90
and persistent current-account deficit, 76–8
post-2006 funding of, 104–15
deposit finance outside country, 106–7, *107*, *110*
and exchange-rate collapse, 110–13, *113*
and short-term collateralised loan, 110–13, *112*
unsecured securities, 105–6
and private-sector credit boom, 71–3
and rapid stock- and house-price rise, 73–5, *74*
and real exchange-rate appreciation, 75
and short-term external debt, high amount of, 78–9
gross, *79*
soundness of, despite problems, 81–94
and Aaa league, 90–2
and capital ratios and leverage, 85–8, *87*
and high returns on equity, 84
and low market-implied credit rating, 92–3, *93*
and modest problem loans, 83–4
and quantitative financial fundamentals, 82–9
and satisfactory liquidity positions, 88–0
sovereign's inability to help, 113
spot and forward positions of, *98*
triple crisis in, 67–9
implied credit correlation metrics before and during financial crisis, 283–316, *293*, *294*, *297*, *298*, *303*, *308*, *309*, *310*, *311*, *314*
expected tranche loss surface, 312–14
Gaussian copula model, 288–98
base correlation, 294–6, *296*
compound correlation, 291–5, *295*
implied correlation, 297–8
one-factor, 290–1
implied copula, 299–307, 311–12
calibration of, 301–3
in-crisis, 311–12, *312*
index and tranche NVP, 304–6, *305*
numerical results, 306–7
market quotes, 286–8
more recent data, application to, 307–8
implied in-crisis correlation, 307–11
innovation, regulation outpaced by, 134–6
innovation, understanding outpaced by, 134
innovative financial instruments:
and counterparty risk, 248–50
exposure, 248–9
and credit-rating agencies, 257–60

implications, 258–9
and rating,
understanding, 257–8
and rating, use of, 259–60
design characteristics of,
241–3
factor sensitivity, 241–3
market disruptions, 243
hedging of, 246–7
implications for, 239–40,
249–50
liquidity, 243–8
education, 244–5
and hedging, 246–7
and new-product pricing, 245
and transparency, 247
managing and measuring
risk in, 231–62
pricing, 234–41
basic setup, 235–6
bottom-up approach,
236–8
modelling assumptions, 236
new product, ease of,
245–6
top-down approach, 238–9
and risk management, 250–7
and accounting incentives,
255
mark-to-model, 256
and model parameters,
252–3
and senior management,
255–6
testing, 253–4
and unintended
consequences, 254–5
investment strategy returns,
565–92, 575, 576, 578–9,
583, 585, 588, 589
economic model of, 570–3
practical lessons, 590–2
taxonomy of patterns in,
573–83
and alpha, nature of,
583–90
and asset class
dependence, 582–3
and size dependence, 577,
580
and style dependence,
580–2

J

Jobs, Steve, 568

K

Keynes, John Maynard, 51–3,
410, 412, 435
Krugman, Paul, xxxii, 410

L

Lehman Brothers, 51, 129, 134,
141, 144, 149, 151, 161, 190,
202, 205, 357, 370, 418, 516,
518–20, 559, 560
Hedge Fund index of, 570,
574–5, 575
Lynch, Peter, 467

M

market-implied expected losses
and contingent liabilities,
215–19
markets, *414, 416, 418, 419, 426*
efficient, 409–12
endogenous dynamics of,
409–35
or exogenous? 413–19
equilibrium of, 419–22
and long-range-correlated
trades, 420–1
and scant liquidity and
trade fragmentation, 421
and slow digest of new
information, 422
subtle and dynamic, 424–8
financial complexity and
systemic stability in,
455–87, *463, 466, 472, 477,
478, 483, 484*
and information efficiency
and increasing diversity in
trading strategies, 461–7

and proliferation of
financial instruments:
spiralling towards
complete markets, 468–73
impact of, 412–13
problem with, 428
and resilience, 422–8
new information slowly
digested by, 421–2
and news and no-news
jumps, 414
panics within, 439–52, *440*,
442, 444, 446, 442, 449, 450
joint stochastic model,
443–51
joint stochastic model,
simulations of, 448–51
perspectives, 428–9
looking forward, 431–4
markets that are close to
critical, 428–31
resilience and impact of,
422–8
empirical facts about,
423–4
and subtle, dynamic
equilibrium, 424–8
securitisation,
credit-derivative markets
and increasing complexity,
473–85
and complex assets, 479
and evaporation of trust,
475–9
stylised facts of, across time
and across stocks, 440–3
and universally intermittent
dynamics, 417–19
MBIA, xxvii
MBSs, CMOs and CDOs of ABS,
pricing of, 319–43
ABS-type products and
stochastic intensities,
325–8
discussion and practical
issues, 337–40
and "perfect" world, 340–2
top-down approach, 328–37

Merrill Lynch, xxv, 12, 21, 80,
106, *130, 131, 132, 133, 141,
148, 150, 152, 155, 158, 159,
160, 161, 162, 163*
Merton model, 195, 198, 202, 225,
322–6, 560
Minsky, Hyman P. 49–63
economic journey of, 55–63
policy reactions to, 61–3
financial-instability
hypothesis summarised
by, 53–4
and US housing market,
56–61
see also shadow banking
system
Monte Carlo CVA practical
guide to, 379–405
exposure sampling method,
384–95, *388, 389*
and CVA analytical
calculation of, 386–7
and CVA with weighting
transitions, 392–3
importance sampling
methods, 385–6
Markovian one-factor
exposure sampling, 387–90
non-Gaussian shocks, use
of, 391
pricing with rare events,
challenge of, 384–5
and ratings-dependent
collateral agreements,
393–5, *394*
and wrong-way risk,
capturing, 391–2
implementation guide,
395–404, *399*
calculation flow with and
without exposure
sampling, 397–401
generic assets, 396
generic factors, 396–7
generic shocks, 397
and large numbers of
factors, 401

pricing by American
  Monte Carlo, 403–4
 pricing by zero-bond slice
  catching, 401–3
 methodology fundamentals,
  381–4
  credit value adjustment,
   382–3
  measure choice, 383–4
  potential future exposure,
   381–2
Morgan Stanley, 81
mortgage losses, a new approach
  to decomposing, 23–47, 42
 cumulative, by vintage, 33
 data:
  and experiments, 39–42
  and model, 29–33
 experiments and data, 39–42
 model and data, 29–33
  data, 31–2
  economic, 30
  loan-level, 30–1
  overview, 29–33
  simulation algorithm
   concerning, 31
 and subprime losses, impact
  of underwriting on, 42–5, 44
 and underwriting quality,
  33–9, 34, 36–7
  and average loss
   estimates, 36–8, 38

P

partial integro-differential
  equation (PIDE),
  numerical solution of, 365
proliferation of financial
  instruments: spiralling
  towards complete
  markets, 468–73
 in ideal world, 469–71
 in interacting market, 471–3
Prudent Investor Act, xxxii
Prudent Man Rule, xxxii

Q

Quant Crunch, xxix, 518

and future quantitative
  investing, 121–6
quantitative investing, 121–6
 and quant crunch, 121–6
quantitatively managed equity
  portfolios, 515–43, *519*
 crisis's effects on, detailed,
  530–3
  adaptability, 533
  capacity, 531–2
  contagion risk, 532
  data and models, 533–7
  drawdown control, 532–3
  endogenous data and
   proprietary research, 531
  linear factor model, 531
  liquidity risk, 530–1
  operational risk, 530
 different flavours of, 517
 future directions, 530–41
 and investment process,
  521–30
  models and data, 521–6
  portfolio management and
   production, 526–8
  risk management, 528–30
  models and data, 533–7
 and portfolio management
  and production, 537–9
  operations, 537
 and risk management, 539–40
  measuring and assessing,
   540–1
  reporting, 541
 and waves, effects of, 517–18
  and Lehman collapse,
   518–20
  and price-momentum
   investment strategy, 520–1
  and quant crunch, 518

R

regulatory change, impetus for,
  147–51
residential mortgage-backed
  securities (RMBSs) 23,
  31–2

risk management, investor's perspective into, 545–63, *551, 554, 557, 448*
   and asset-class diversification as a weak risk-management tool, 560–2
   looking back and forward, 546–9
     and fat-left-tail events, 548
     leverage and leverage, 547–8
     liquidity and liquidity, 547
     portfolio performance, and common risks, 546–7
     and systemic shocks and heterogeneity, 458–9
   necessity, not luxury, 550
   and participant actions, relevancy of, 558–9
   and portfolio tail-risk management, systemic risk exposures mitigated by, 551–2
   and dynamic replication, more than, 555–6
   and reduction of "sunk" costs, 550–1
   and severity as more important than probability, 562
   and tail-risk hedging, 554–5
   and traditional valuation models, irrelevancy of, 556–8
   and varying costs and opportunities, 552–4

S

securitisation market, interlinkages in, *191*
securitisation, credit-derivative markets and increasing complexity, 473–85
   and complex assets, 479
   and evaporation of trust, 475–9
shadow banking system, 49–63
   conventional banking versus, 51–2
   and financial-instability hypothesis, 53
   nature and origin of, 49–50
   and regulators and rating agencies, 50–1
   and US housing market, 56–61
   see also Minsky, Hyman P.
Soros, George, xxxii, 434, 567
subprime losses, impact of underwriting on, 42–5, *44*
"sunk" costs, active risk management reduces, 550–1
systemic and sovereign risk, *203, 204, 205, 206, 208, 218, 222–3*
   case study concerning, 201–6
   and contingent claims analysis (CCA) 187, 195–8, 211–14
   systemic methodology of, 200–1
   and interconnections, contagion and destructive-feedback loops, 193–5
   and key features of credit crisis, 188–93
   macro risk analysis of financial crises and interactions with, 206–11
   and market-implied expected losses and contingent liabilities, 215–19
   measurement and analysis of, missing elements in, 192–3
   and measuring expected losses and contingent liabilities from the financial sector, 198–9
   modelling, 187–226
   and new measure of risk-adjusted economic output value, 211–14

and risk exposures and
  risk-adjusted balance
  sheets, 193
and securitisation market,
  interlinkages in, *191*
and sovereign CCA balance
  sheet and the financial
  sector, interaction and
  feedback between,
  209–11
and systemic CCA compared
  with other systemic
  risk measures,
  219–24, *220*

U

underwriting quality, 33–9, *34*,
  36–7
  and average loss estimates,
    36–8, *38*
US housing market, 3–7, *4*; *see
  also* financial crisis: lessons
  from
  and Minsky, 56; *see also*
    Minsky, Hyman P.

W

Welch, Jack, 568